CW00406874

MOTOCOURSE™

THE WORLD'S LEADING GRAND PRIX & SUPERBIKE ANNUAL

Hazleton Publishing

CONTENTS

MOTOCOURSE
2004–2005
is published by:
Hazleton Publishing Ltd,
5th Floor, Mermaid House,
2 Puddle Dock, London,
EC4V 3DS.

Colour reproduction by
Radstock Repro,
Frome, Somerset

Printed in England by
Butler and Tanner Ltd,
Frome, Somerset

Hazleton Publishing Ltd is a member of Profile Media Group Plc.

ISBN: 1 903135 36 2

DISTRIBUTORS

UNITED KINGDOM
Vine House
Waldenbury
Chailey
East Sussex
BN8 4DR

Telephone: 01825 723398
email: sales@vinehouseuk.co.uk

REST OF THE WORLD
Menoshire Ltd
Unit 13
21 Wadsworth Road
Perivale
Middlesex UB6 7LQ
Telephone: 020 8566 7344
Fax: 020 8991 2439

FOREWORD by Randy Mamola 5

EDITOR'S INTRODUCTION 6

THE TOP TEN RIDERS OF 2004 Ranked by the Editor 8

IRTA
The best-run Grand Prix meeting of 2004 14

THE STATE OF RACING by Michael Scott 16

A NEW GOLDEN AGE?
MotoGP technical review by Neil Spalding 20

RE-TURNING JAPANESE
Mark Graham on the new breed of MotoGP contenders from Japan 30

BIG BANG REDUX
Kevin Cameron considers engine and tyre matters 34

VAL THE IMPALER
Michael Scott profiles the 'new' Valentino Rossi 38

2004 TEAMS AND RIDERS by Michael Scott 42

2004 GRANDS PRIX 50

WORLD CHAMPIONSHIP RESULTS by Kay Edge 148

SUPERBIKE WORLD CHAMPIONSHIP REVIEW by Gordon Ritchie 150

SIDECAR WORLD CHAMPIONSHIP REVIEW by John Mackenzie 174

ISLE OF MAN TT REVIEW by Mac McDiarmid 176

UNITED STATES REVIEW by Paul Carruthers 180

BRITISH SUPERBIKE REVIEW by Gary Pinchin 184

OTHER MAJOR RESULTS compiled by Kay Edge 188

editor
MICHAEL SCOTT

publisher
EDDIE TAYLOR

art editor
STEVE SMALL

sales promotion
LAURA FELL

results and statistics
KAY EDGE

chief photographers
GOLD & GOOSE
Peter Fox
David Goldman
Mirco Lazzari
Patrik Lundin
Chippy Wood

Telephone: (0)20 8444 2448
E-mail: office@goldandgoose.com

Acknowledgements

The Editor and staff of MOTOCOURSE wish to thank the following for their assistance in compiling the 2004-2005 edition: Marc Petrier *(FIM)*, Paul Butler and Mike Trimby *(IRTA)*, Eva Jirsenska *(Dorna)*, Chuck Aksland, Gerry Biasi, Jerry Burgess, Peter Clifford, Carlo Fiorani, Ali Forth, Iain Mackay, Randy Mamola, Gary McLaren, Dean Miller, Tom O'Kane, Steve Parrish, Shinichi Sahara, Stuart Shenton, Garry Taylor, Debbie van Zon, Ian Wheeler, Rupert Williamson, Warren Willing, Jan Witteveen, as well as numerous colleagues and friends.

Photographs published in MOTOCOURSE 2004-2005 have been contributed by: Gold & Goose, Malcolm Bryan/BPC, Clive Challinor, Dave Collister, John Mackenzie, Dave Purves, Tom Riles.

Dust-jacket photograph: MotoGP World Champion Valentino Rossi on the Yamaha.

Title page photograph: World Superbike Champion James Toseland on the works Ducati.
Photographs: Gold & Goose

www.motocourse.co.uk

FOREWORD
by RANDY MAMOLA

WHEN I started racing at the age of 12 I couldn't have imagined where it would take me - or what it would be like more than 30 years later. I was just a kid from Santa Clara, California.

It's been an incredible journey –it would take book after book. But just to take the great world champions I raced with: Barry Sheene, Wayne Rainey, Eddie Lawson, Kenny Roberts, Kevin Schwantz, Freddie Spencer, Mick Doohan, Wayne Gardner – imagine that.

All these guys brought something new and something special. You could see it at the time, and we can still see it, looking back.

And now we are looking at someone else bringing that magic. You know who I am talking about. And maybe that kid knows something that none of the others knew. Not just that he has magic, but how to work it, how to take full advantage of it.

Valentino isn't the only one, even today. You look at what Dani Pedrosa has already achieved and you look at the baby riders coming through, and you just have to wonder where it is going to take us. I can't imagine. Can you?

I am very proud to be writing a foreword to Motocourse. This is our book - the Bible of MotoGP - our record not just of what happened this year, but what happened, and how it happened and what it meant going all the way back to 1976. Barry, God bless him, was our champion then. What a journey.

And it's not just the racing. MotoGP has brought to the world something apart from excitement and breathtaking entertainment. It has brought life and hope to hundreds of thousands of people through its own charity. Riders for Health operates throughout Africa, working with everyone from village communities to the United Nations. It is recognised throughout the diplomatic community as bringing something that simply wasn't there before.

Which now I think about it is just like the magic racers I was talking about. What a journey. It's taking us all to new and exciting places and it even took me to Buckingham Palace.

But that's another story, for another time. Meanwhile, have another great racing year. And above all enjoy the ride. Who knows where we are going?

Photograph: Gold & Goose

EDITOR'S INTRODUCTION

SUNDAY AFTERNOON

Above: Race time, and the hype comes true, for 45 minutes. Gibernau, Rossi, Biaggi, Barros and Hayden play their game.

Photograph: Gold & Goose

AS a gruelling and epic grand prix season drew to its close, I found a phrase running though my mind with increasing frequency.

"At least they still have a motorbike race on Sunday."

Thus the eternal truth, the madness and the logic, the aggression and the science, the courage and the control. A motorbike race. The best motorbike race in the world.

Thus did grand prix racing survive the loss of innocence in 2004.

Actually, this is an ever-repeated process. Innocence serially lost is also serially regained. Each recovery, however, requires more than the previous; each new generation's star must burn brighter.

This time round it was the exception among the exceptional, Valentino Rossi. The loss of innocence came as he revealed that behind the elfin charm there is a ferocious competitor with as much mercy on his rivals as a dum-dum bullet. It was something to see.

Rossi's victory on the underdog Yamaha proved once again that the rider is more important than the motorcycle. With only one such rider, however, this was little comfort to the defeated manufacturers. The third year of the four-strokes saw two things: firstly all the machines made some sort of a step forwards; secondly, in spite of this, the gap between the winners and the losers grew wider. Worryingly so in the case of Proton and Aprilia. And, rather surprisingly, Ducati.

GP racing has always included precarious elements – it is part of its nature. Overall, the show has grown impressively.

Along the way, a certain raffish charm has been lost. MotoGP is not yet as aloof and exclusive as F1, but in the past two or three years much has changed. Platitudes have replaced plain speaking to an alarming extent. At the same time, professionalism (and good racing) have brought a new prosperity in terms of crowd numbers and overall market penetration.

The appearance of health does not reach down to the lesser GP classes. The 125s are safe enough, the kindergarten role reinforced by a new age limit next year. The 250s are on borrowed time, however, and somehow the racing reflects it. Sooner or later the last of the big-time racing two-strokes will inevitably be replaced by 600 Supersports, or something similar.

The fly in Dorna's ointment is, as ever, the Flammini Group, owners of 600 Supersport rights. But who can predict the eventual outcome, for it was the same Flammini Group who in 2004 proved the impossible possible.

World Superbike racing's self-help programme is one facet of this record of a pivotal year of important changes. The increased stature of British Superbike racing was another. There was realignment also at the TT, changing to mesh more closely with the real world.

And the beleaguered and twice-abandoned Sidecars narrowly survived.

As ever, MOTOCOURSE records and analyses it all, the visual spectacle captured by the year's best photographs.

More important in the long-term was another story, also covered in detail ... the new technical directions of the latest MotoGP machines. Led by the growling re-timed Yamaha, the factory machines are exploring novel ways of rearranging traditional firing intervals, and discovering new levels of grip and performance as a result.

The reasons are abstruse, the science not yet fully understood, and the explanations compelling. After a spell when F1 technology seemed ready to intrude, the strange and complex science of motorcycle engineering has once again thrown up mysteries all on its own.

The importance is the ultimate relevance to street motorcycles. After three years, MotoGP prototypes are already fulfilling a valuable potential to the industry, and to motorcyclists everywhere.

So racing does mean something, after all.

Even better than that ... they still have a motorbike race on Sunday.

MICHAEL SCOTT
Wimbledon, London
December, 2004

Top: **Every year a little bigger... the mushrooming paddock at Jerez.**

Above: **World Superbike racing rediscovered itself, rather unexpectedly.**

Left: **England's James Toseland won a tense SBK contest.**

Photographs: Gold & Goose

TOP TEN RIDERS OF 2004

1	Valentino Rossi
2	Makoto Tamada
3	Sete Gibernau
4	Max Biaggi
5	Shinya Nakano
6	Colin Edwards
7	Loris Capirossi
8	John Hopkins
9	Dani Pedrosa
10	Ruben Xaus

Photographs by Gold & Goose

1 VALENTINO ROSSI

VALENTINO'S title win in his first year with Yamaha was the proof, as if anyone needed it – in every aspect of racing ability, the 25-year-old Italian is among the giants of the sport. Right up there with Mike Hailwood, even.

His elfin charm diminished both by the years and by the vast pressure of simply being himself, the Rossi of 2004 was a formidable presence wherever he went. Nobody can now believe that he takes racing as lightly as he once might have liked to pretend.

His gesture of leaving dominant Honda to join underdogs Yamaha was sporting, defiant and well-timed. It coincided with a technical spurt from Honda's long-standing and most successful rival.

His response to the ever-present threat of Gibernau, chief warrior for his previous employer, underlined the point. When things got tough towards the end of the year, Rossi seized on the chance to make it personal. He blamed Sete fair and square for his penalisation and general misfortunes at Qatar. Who can say how much this public enmity contributed to the dismantling of Sete's challenge over the closing races.

And things did get tough. They were tough all along. Rossi's Yamaha was only sometimes as nimble as its reputation suggested. In fact it was a handful in the wet. And, compared with the Hondas (and the Ducatis), it was both sluggish in acceleration and lacking in top speed.

Rossi's great gifts transcended these weaknesses. More even than race-craft, psychology or aggression, in all of which he excelled, it was riding talent that won him the first race in South Africa, three in a row in Italy, Catalunya and Assen, and carried him on – through brinkmanship and even crashes – to a state of dominance by the end of the season.

Rossi had a vital partner in Jeremy Burgess. The two work hand in glove, a perfect fit. For next year, once again, the combination looks unbeatable.

Gauloises Fortuna Yamaha Team

2004 World Championship – 1st (MotoGP)

Race wins – 9 • Pole positions – 5

Career GP wins – 68 (29 MGP, 13 500cc, 14 250cc, 12 125cc)

World Championships – 6 (3 MGP, 1 500cc, 1 250cc, 1 125cc)

Born 16 February, 1979, Urbino, Italy

2 MAKOTO TAMADA

EVERBODY must be measured against Rossi. Only three riders – Gibernau, Biaggi and Tamada – actually managed to defeat him in a straight fight. Of those who tried, the least fazed by Rossi's reputation was the Japanese charger. Simultaneously affable and inscrutable, Tamada's agenda had no room for compromise.

Tamada, a product of the All-Japan Superbike series and a former World Superbike winner, had almost everything necessary for a championship assault, in the shape of a factory Honda RC211V and a pocket full of confidence. The difference was his Bridgestone tyres. They were clearly good enough for three pole positions and two race wins, but were also bad enough early in the season to be chunking and disintegrating mid-race at Mugello. They improved rapidly, but still lacked the consistency of the dominant Michelins.

Tamada's first win came in Brazil, where both Gibernau and Rossi crashed out. The second was head-to-head with Rossi at Motegi. And he was consistent – although falling in the rain at Jerez, his only other no-scores were at Mugello, were his rear tyre chunked, and the next week at Catalunya, when his team called him in, fearful of it happening again.

He did badly at bad Bridgestone tracks. Tamada resented any notion that he did well only because Bridgestones were superior at others, and because their soft-compound qualifying tyres were better than their race rubber. There was truth in it all the same, though not all of the truth.

The smiling Japanese rider, who speaks little English, will switch to Michelin next year, all being well, so as to take on Rossi *et al* on equal terms. Then he *(and we)* will know whether his aggressive talent really has the depth that seemed to show in 2004.

Camel Honda

2003 World Championship: 6th (MotoGP)

Race wins: 2 • Pole positions: 3

Career GP wins: 2 (MGP)

Born: 4 November 1976, Ehime, Japan

3 SETE GIBERNAU

SETE'S good days in 2004 were very good indeed. He had the beating even of Rossi, at least in the second and third races and again at Brno. But Sete won only once after that, at Qatar, when Rossi crashed out. When it mattered, he was unable to prevent the Yamaha rider from taking control.

In his eighth year in the top class, the 32-year-old from Barcelona started out as a genuine title contender, and remained so until after the summer break. By the end of the year, he looked beaten, again.

Gibernau surely did enough, however, to shrug off a long-standing reputation for being a lucky rider, with a silver path to the top levels part of his Bultaco legacy (the firm was owned by his grandfather). The same legacy also makes Sete a cultured and refined gentleman racer, multi-lingual and highly articulate, to which he adds a penchant for wacky clothes and hair-styles, and a liking for the cameras. And while it is hard to see why this should be any barrier to success, it doesn't sit comfortably with everybody in the paddock.

It seems unfair when you look at how hard Sete has worked to achieve his position. Of all the Honda riders, it was Sete who led a rather confused fight against lone star Rossi. He rode better in 2004 than he had the year before, but he still lacked depth, when measured against his phenomenal rival.

At 31, there is still time for Gibernau to prove that the best is yet to come. Whether it will be good enough remains to be seen. At least, however, when he retires he will be able to recall that the only man who defeated him in 2004 was one of the world's greatest ever racers.

Telefónica MoviStar Honda
2004 World Championship – 2nd (MotoGP)
Race wins – 4
Pole positions – 5
Career GP wins – 9 (8 MGP, 1 500cc)
Born 15 December, 1972, Barcelona, Spain

4 MAX BIAGGI

MAX had a lot of bad luck in 2004... almost as much as he complained about. As when his gearshifter mechanism failed in Britain. He had arrived just one point behind Rossi, looking at last like a real contender, but departed 22 points adrift. Or in Portugal, knocked off in a first-lap collision with Capirossi. When the same thing happened again two weeks later in Japan, he did seem to be marked down as fortune's victim.

In fact, Max rode extremely well all year round. Every race was well judged and his accuracy remains inch-perfect. Also his assessment of what is possible. Those two innocent collisions were his only non-finishes all year.

Unfortunately, perhaps, Biaggi's estimation seems set in the belief that it is only possible to beat Rossi sometimes. Too often, Max seemed too eager to settle for second; most prefer their world champions to attempt the impossible, when called upon.

Max is also prone to accept and blame machine limitations, rather than overcoming them. This is another area where his long-standing Italian rival showed him up. At 33, he is vastly experienced, and seems more comfortable with his team and his profession than ever in the past. One hopes not too comfortable.

Biaggi's year was convincing enough for Honda to want him to lead the factory team next year. It marks the completion of a full circle. Max left Honda for Yamaha way back in 1998. This was his second year back, on satellite bikes. He said at the start of last year that: "If I'm a good boy, perhaps Honda will give me some cake." In the absence of any other available candidates, it seems in 2004 he was good enough.

Camel Honda
2004 World Championship – 3rd (MotoGP)
Race wins – 1 • Pole positions – 1
Career GP wins – 42 (5 MGP, 8 500cc, 29 250cc)
World Championships – 4 (250cc)
Born 26 June, 1971, Rome, Italy

5 SHINYA NAKANO

NAKANO and his green Kawasaki were a revelation of 2004. Almost a 250 champion, he had been promising on a two-stroke, but had slipped away towards obscurity in a satellite team, and was too late to get a chance on Yamaha's new four-stroke M1.

He was not unnoticed by other teams, however, and Kawasaki can count themselves very lucky to have secured his services.

He can count himself lucky that his arrival coincided with a significant upgrade of their also-ran machine, and a move from Dunlop to Bridgestone tyres. The rubber would almost kill Nakano when his rear tyre disintegrated at speed at Mugello, but Bridgestone's recovery and general rate of improvement was out of all proportion to that too-public disaster. And when the bike held together, Nakano would always be pushing as hard as he reasonably could, all the way to the end. In terms of lap times and results, he took the ZX-RR a massive step forward.

Nakano frequently qualified well, culminating in the marque's first MotoGP front-row grid position. More importantly he also raced very well. He showed consistency far greater than that of his blow-up-prone machine - his only crash all year was that Mugello loop-the-loop.

The rostrum at Motegi – achieved in the absence of six front runners, but still hard won – was the pay-off for the ex-student from near Tokyo.

Unfailingly polite and always cheerful, he has always been easy to underestimate, Nakano achieved a lot in 2004.

Kawasaki Racing Team

2004 World Championship – 10th (MotoGP)

Career GP wins – 6 (250cc)

Born 10 October, 1977, Chiba, Japan

6 COLIN EDWARDS

MUCH was expected of Edwards before the season. Obviously, as it transpired, too much. It seemed, one tame race after another, as though little was delivered. Yet Edwards was fifth overall, and his legendary consistency meant his only non-finish was as one of five Capirossi victims at Motegi.

It was by consistency that many thought he would be a serious title contender, back before the season, when nobody expected Rossi to win races until perhaps later in the year. Even then, they would need to be consistent rostrum finishes. That came only twice, in Britain and Qatar. Each of these second places was achieved in very convincing style.

He explained with his usual clarity that, when the bike is right, "it's a piece of cake." When the bike wasn't right, and this was more often than not, Edwards is too experienced and too intelligent to try to exceed its possibilities. And that's how he rode most races in 2004.

There was also a technical reason – the combination of the new big Michelins and the latest RCV chassis gave rise to chatter problems, obviously much exacerbated by his super-smooth style. And though he was quick to suggest a fix, he was the last to get the revised chassis... at the wrong end of the year. By then, he'd had enough of Honda's back burner, and decided to go to Yamaha.

For Colin, it's another chance to make good on all that latent promise. At 30, the popular wisecracking Texan still has time to prove his point.

Telefónica MoviStar Honda

2004 World Championship – 5th (MotoGP)

World Championships – 2 (World Superbike)

Born 27 February, 1974, Houston, USA

7 LORIS CAPIROSSI

HIS reputation may have been tarnished in 2004, firstly by the Ducati's technical missed shift, and secondly by yet more incidents of barging into other riders – at Motegi he skittled five in one go, and there has been a pattern of similar incidents in his long and spasmodically successful career.

The experienced Capirossi is still a quality article in MotoGP terms, and the greatest measure of his stature is the regard for his talents displayed by other riders.

Ducati's malaise was subtle but costly for the 31-year-old veteran of 216 GP starts. The new bike was more powerful, but it was not a happily balanced package, and it cost Capirossi the ability to back up his lightning starts with strong race finishes.

The bike lost time on fast corners, and also under braking. Time and again, we would see Capirossi losing one place after another as the race wore on, a sitting duck in spite of his generous top speed.

It wasn't until the penultimate race in Australia that he was rewarded by a rostrum, at a track where he could use the Ducati's power and his own riding skills.

Capirossi has been racing in the premier class for seven years on and off`, and in that time he can count only three wins. Yet his talent and status has never been in doubt.

Loris will stay on at Ducati next year, but the end is surely in sight for the former 125 and 250 champion.

2004 World Championship – 9th (MotoGP)

Career GP wins – 23 (1 MGP, 2 500cc, 12 250cc, 8 125cc)

World Championships – 3 (1 250cc, 2 125cc)

Born 4 April, 1973, Bologna, Italy

8 JOHN HOPKINS

THE youngest rider on the grid (after the departure of Fabrizio) had a difficult season, starting with breaking two ankles in a January Supercross crash, missing testing as a result. It went on in similar vein: if there was a multiple accident, Hopkins seemed to be in the firing line... at Le Mans and at Motegi. Each time the Anglo-American suffered more minor, but troublesome injuries.

Three more non-finishes were the result of machine failure. But although somewhat fragile, his Suzuki was not fast. Hopkins faced this problem like a real racer: determined to find ways around it from his own resources. Mainly this meant desperately hard braking and adventurously high corner speeds.

Gradual machine and Bridgestone tyre improvement gave Hopkins the team's best result, eighth at Donington Park, but race results are no measure of the potential he had underlined in the latter part of the season, taking his first front-row start at Motegi, and pushing hard whenever he could. Nor was 16th overall a reflection of how much he had learned during the season.

When he came GP racing, Hopkins was saddled with the tagline: "The next Kevin Schwantz". In three years he has shrugged off this heavy burden and is ready to progress further on his own account. There remains one similarity. Like Schwantz, Hopkins is not prepared to accept machine limitations as a hindrance to giving the racing everything he's got.

Team Suzuki

2004 World Championship – 16th (MotoGP)

Born 22 May, 1983, Ramona, USA

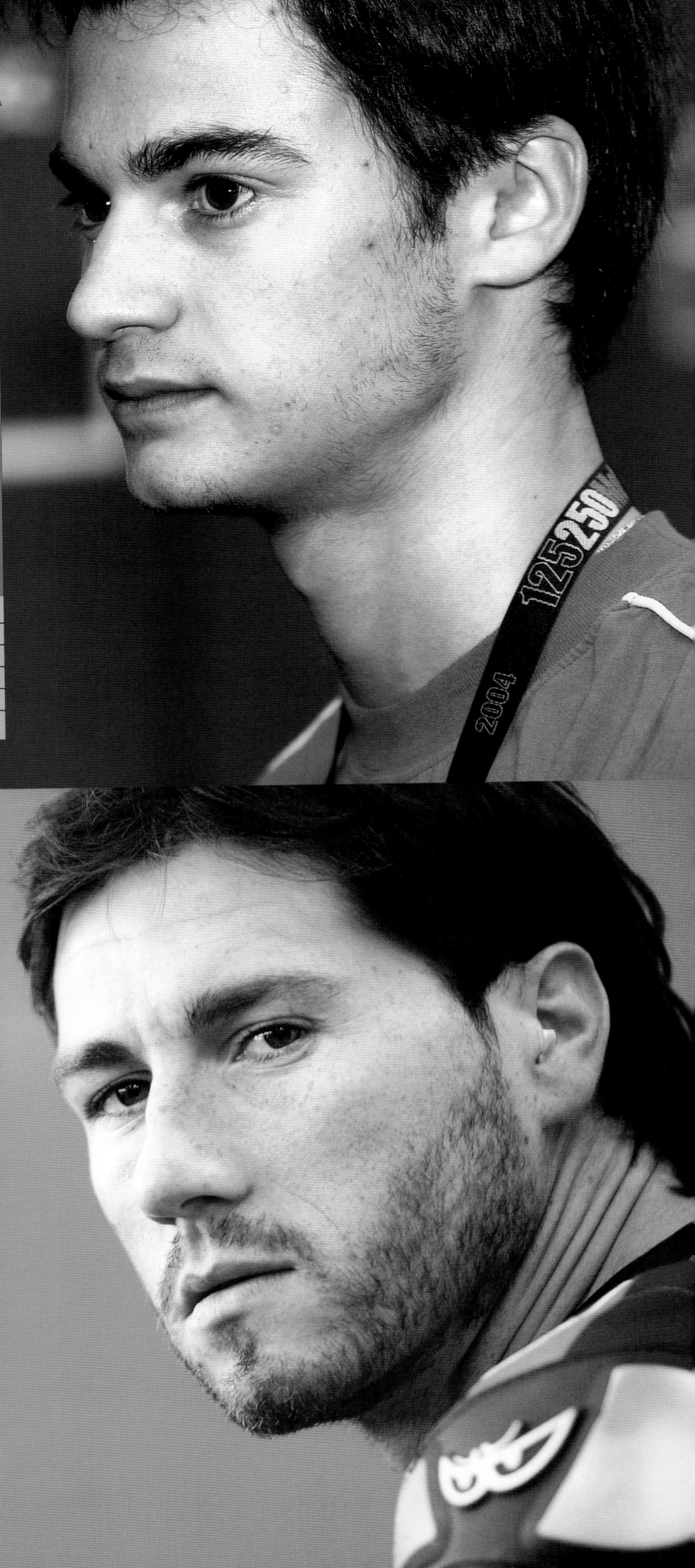

9 DANI PEDROSA

IT'S always hard to know whether or where to put riders from the smaller classes in a top ten list, but there's no question that Pedrosa should be on it. Still only 19, the hand-picked Spanish future megastar showed every ability in fulfilling his own and his mentor and racing guardian Alberto Puig's dreams of greatness.

In 2003, Dani swept to a dominant 125-class crown, but ended the year badly hurt. His racing return, on a factory 250 Honda, could hardly have been more convincing. He won the opening race, and proceeded to put together a year of strength and consistency that made his rivals look like also-rans. Only Porto put together a sustained challenge, but Pedrosa steadily drew ahead on points, as he frequently did at the racetracks.

Picked from among hundreds of applicants in a teenage recruiting drive, Pedrosa is still in the early stages of his journey towards racing maturity. Puig oversees everything, and it is impossible to fault the former 500-class GP winner's guidance.

Pedrosa has always shown a racing intelligence far beyond his years. He also has the ability to race like a demon. The combination is of course devastating.

Dani's only weakness is just that... weakness. He's still but a slip of a boy, weighing less than 50kg. His ultimate destination is MotoGP, but he will have to wait at least a year, and gain physical maturity to fulfil that goal.

Telefónica MoviStar Honda
2004 World Championship – 1st (250cc)
Race wins – 7 • Pole positions – 3
Career GP wins – 15 (7 250cc, 8 125cc)
World Championships – 2 (250cc, 125cc)
Born 29 September, 1985, Sabadell, Spain

10 RUBEN XAUS

RUBEN came from World Superbikes with a reputation as fast but dangerous, a frequent crasher who didn't know when to stop pushing. He lived up to this in his first MotoGP season. He recorded 15 crashes, the highest number (Melandri had only one less).

As the dust settled, however, it was obvious that Xaus was doing more than hanging on for dear life. At tracks new to him, he was learning fast and pushing to the maximum. At the few tracks he did know he was a serious threat, beating the factory machines at both Catalunya and Assen.

It all came together at Qatar, a track that nobody knew. He not only beat the factory Ducatis again, but finished on the rostrum to boot, after an impressively sustained fast ride.

Xaus is 26 years old, and has a lot on his side. He can be amusing in several languages, has a remarkable ability to walk away from crashes, and also has real speed. Perhaps he needed the stimulation of MotoGP's higher standard to help him mature as a racer.

After the end of the season, Xaus's plans for next year were not clear. One opportunity was a factory Yamaha. He deserves a better bike than the low-budget year-old Ducati he campaigned so ferociously in 2004.

D'Antin Ducati
2004 World Championship – 11th (MotoGP)
Born 18 February, 1978, Barcelona, Spain

IRTA BEST GRAND PRIX TROPHY

BRNO BEATS THE BEST

Right: IRTA's Mike Trimby.

Below: Brno's bustling paddock.
Photographs: Gold & Goose

THE superbly organised Czech Republic Grand Prix, held at the Brno circuit in Moravia, won the coveted IRTA 'Best Grand Prix Trophy' in 2004, ending three years of domination by Spanish circuits. It is the second time in the prestigious trophy's 21-year history that Brno has been victorious – the first was in 1999.

Brno fought off a strong challenge from Valencia, trophy winners in 2002 and 2003, with the Malaysian Sepang circuit in third place.

The award by the Teams' Association is an accolade highly valued by event and circuit organisers – a tribute from those who participated in 16 Grand Prix events in 2004. The poll takes into account all aspects of running a GP. IRTA members, comprising entrants in all three Grand Prix classes, vote on a points system that covers track safety, medical facilities, paddock and media facilities, event management, and on-track officials.

According to IRTA's official statement, Brno had a long history of well-run races, and the event showed "every indication of retaining its reputation as a top venue", with further improvements planned to the already excellent facilities.

Brno has a long motor sporting history, with the original 18-mile Masaryk open road track of 1930 replaced in 1950 with a shorter 11-mile public-roads circuit closer to the city centre. In the mid-Fifties Brno became an important venue for the 'Continental Circus', attracting top flight European riders, and in 1965 the CZ Federation was granted an FIM Grand Prix, at the revised 8.64-mile circuit.

By the Seventies, speeds and danger levels on the open roads rendered the circuit obsolete, and it was dropped from the GP calendar. Brno ceased road-race promotions in 1982, and set about building a permanent closed circuit, closer to the original Masaryk circuit.

The result is the present superbly laid out 3.357km closed circuit, situated ten miles from Brno city centre, opened in 1987.

Featuring six left hand corners and eight right handers the fifteen-metre wide track was designed with safety the overriding priority. The gravel traps are wide and deep and the track is ringed by an ambulance service road.

The wide, sweeping circuit has fast flowing downhill sections and a long uphill run to the final chicane just before the end of the lap. The downhill sweeps form a natural amphitheatre, a treat for spectators who crowd the area in their tens of thousands.

Facilities are among the very best, with 27 large, well-equipped pit boxes, extensive paddock area and good hospitality areas. Communications systems are good, and when the planned alterations to the media centre have been completed Brno will be the envy of all rivals, according to IRTA.

IRTA's report read:

"Ludek Starham, CEO and director of Automotodrom Brno and Events Manager Radka Dvorakova both have extensive international event promotion experience, and have established a mutually respectful rapport with the teams. With their staff they run a first class grand prix with style and efficiency.

"Clerk of the Course Vaclav Janek runs a solid operation, and his track marshals are among the best on the 16-race calendar – every emergency swiftly dealt with whether a minor crash or a more serious incident. "The medical staff, under the guidance of Dr Ivo Dedek, work from a state-of-the-art on-track mini-hospital, in total harmony with FIM Medical Director, Claudio Macchiagodena."

IRTA Trophy Roll of Honour

Year	Circuit
1984	Silverstone / GB
1985	Hockenheim / Germany
1986	Nurburgring / Germany
1987	Assen / Netherlands
1988	Suzuka / Japan
1989	Donington Park / GB
1990	Jerez / Spain
1991	Donington Park / GB
1992	Catalunya / Spain
1993	Eastern Creek / Australia
1994	Eastern Creek / Australia
1995	Mugello / Italy
1996	Mugello / Italy
1997	Mugello / Italy
1998	Phillip Island / Australia
1999	Brno / Czech Republic
2000	Mugello / Italy
2001	Catalunya / Spain
2002	Valencia / Spain
2003	Valencia / Spain
2004	Brno / Czech Republic

STATE OF RACING

RACING TO A DIFFERENT FUTURE

By MICHAEL SCOTT

ONLY time will tell how much of a landmark was the 2004 season, but viewed from close up, it gives every sign of having been pivotal in several respects.

In every outward aspect, motorcycle GP racing was booming in 2004. One clear indicator might be the crowds at the British GP. They overwhelmed the facilities. Only five years ago, it was the other way round, and the event appeared dead on its feet.

There are two significant reasons – Valentino Rossi, and the MotoGP fever generated by the new 990 four-strokes. Perhaps only one ... the motorbikes appeal only to those who already like motorcycles. Rossi appeals to everybody.

More importantly, the 25-year-old Italian is not merely good at playing the crowds. He also has talent of a stature seen but seldom in one's lifetime. The Virtuoso's switch to underdog Yamaha, his relentless defeat of the Honda hordes, and his manner of so doing massively and rightly reinforced the legend. Valentino, and those few others of his ilk, perform a rewarding function for humanity, and for the most human of all motor sports. They prove it is the rider who wins championships, not the bike.

Paradoxically, this does not undermine the technical interest. Three years old, the new-generation GP paragons have made major technical advances – weather permitting, there were faster poles almost everywhere, lap and race records at every track but one (the exception was Valencia). Along with increasing complexity, their engineers are correspondingly more secretive. This makes them more intriguing still.

So the crowds came.

At the same time, the TV show continued to add variety. The output varied depending on locality and personnel, but at best it was very good indeed, with sharp editing and replays, and a variety of new on-bike camera angles (some frankly a bit silly). There was even a revised soundtrack, as first the M1 Yamaha and by the year's end also Ducati, Suzuki and Proton revised firing intervals and sometimes firing order, finding ways to make better use of the already plentiful power. Never beyond criticism, Dorna's TV division nonetheless made much of what was generally a reliably spectacular year.

So the viewers switched on.

In the paddock, there was a proliferation of glass-fronted up-the-stairs posh hospitality units, hardly any of the chummy old open-sided tents remained – a major contribution to the pervasive new "them-and-us" mentality, along with other elements of F1 style and substance.

So the sponsors were happy.

The calendar was strong, mostly, and there was a new addition – Qatar. Next year will be even stronger, two of the world's greatest nations joining: China and the USA.

So Dorna were happy.

Perhaps that is why, in a paddock proliferating in a mode of business increasingly remote from the actual racing, it was easy to turn a blind eye to some disturbing realities.

It was easier for everyone to be happy.

SMOKE AND MIRRORED GLASS

As usual, not everything was quite as it seemed. A good illustration of precisely this came from World Superbikes, one year on from the much-derided switch to one-make Pirelli control tyres, and the withdrawal of the manufacturers (bar contract-bound Ducati). Perversely, SBK gained strength and credibility as a result. Where previously the Flammini Group management had been vilified as money-grubbing asset-strippers, now they were hailed as far-sighted visionaries. The manufacturers are sidling back to a production-based series that has successfully redefined itself by getting back in touch with its roots.

In Dorna's world, it was not so much that Qatar and China were on the calendar, but why. It is for the most cynical of reasons, and Qatar was among the most cynical of grand prix events. It rivalled those in Belgium and France in the Seventies (among others) that went ahead on bad tracks in spite of the withdrawal of all major teams and riders.

Qatar comprised a circuit – rather a good one if a touch dusty, fine pit and paddock buildings, an empty grandstand, and a spacious TV compound, for all the editing suites and outside-broadcast units. And a location where they really couldn't give a fig about tobacco advertising. China likewise. And Brazil, which stays on the calendar in place of South Africa, which has banned it.

This is a simple business strategy dictated by the EEC ban on tobacco logos, which comes into force midway through 2006, and follows the lead set by F1. The series needs to be expanded to add tobacco-friendly venues, from where the TV images are all branded, just like the good old days. Common talk was that the likes of Camel and Marlboro will put up with running unbranded in Europe, as long as they are guaranteed exposure from as few as a third of the total number of races. After all, where else will they have to spend their money?

Another alarming factor was the precarious look-no-hands state of some of the MotoGP teams. And a larger proportion in the 250 and 125 classes, increasingly the poor relations as market-think logic dictates that wider public appeal is to be gained by narrowing the focus to the major class. Just common sense, really, in a pyramid structure. But who could be sure which way up it was standing?

Except for survival specialists WCM, the teams tried to look as though they were generously sponsored. In the case of the new satellite Ducati team of Luis d'Antin, the Master Card livery turned out to be more smoke and mirrors. 2003 had seen desperate horse-trading of grid positions among the haves and have-nots, again involving d'Antin, as well as the heroic continuation of WCM, after losing Red Bull backing. 2004 saw variations of the same. And at the end of it, two significant teams (in stature, it not results) did not even know if they would be racing again in 2005.

One was Aprilia, for reasons beyond bike racing. The parent company had run into a cash crisis with the slump in scooter sales (the result of Italy's recent introduction of a helmet law); and while new owners Piaggio pledged to continue the 250 and 125 racing, months after the season there was still no word on Aprilia's MotoGP project. This had already suffered in 2004, with a Mk2 machine stalled at the testing stage, and riders obliged to soldier on with last year's fast but wayward bike.

The other was Proton Team KR, which will have to change its name if it does survive, because the generous Malaysian main backers Proton Cars no longer wished to continue the same level of sponsorship. This backing has sustained Kenny Roberts's England-based project since it began in 1997 as Modenas. Proton had smiled and forked up for year after year of almost-there. The two-stroke had its moments, the four-stroke V5 was different. And when the team firstly lost their Bridgestone tyres and were obliged to use bottom-of-the-class Dunlops; and secondly spent a fortune crafting a superbly finished chassis to house an engine that had less power than the previous year ... this was the last straw. The team were ready with the highly promising KTM V4 engine for next year, and even tested the bike impressively on Michelin tyres in late November. But they were searching for somebody to pay for this inevitably costly continuation of a so-far fruitless quest.

Some fear this is the thin end of an admittedly small but crucial wedge. Although casualties for different reasons, this would rob the grid of two out of seven different machines, with only the ambitious promise of a Czech-built WCM/Blata V6 to fill the gap. Technically speaking, all of these, plus the Kawasaki, Suzuki and, most of the time, the Ducati, are clearly not at the same level as Honda. Already dominating the grid on numbers, only Rossi prevented 2004 from being another Honda Cup – a big responsibility for one rider.

How much longer will the also-rans want to continue? More to the point, how much more money will their management be prepared to spend – for MotoGP, as predicted, chews up money much faster than the old two-strokes.

Above: On the outside, looking in ... Telefónica's fashionable glass-fronted mobile café was just one such in the burgeoning Hospitality Row.

Above left: To roar no more? Proton's badge is not likely to be seen on a MotoGP bike again.

Far left: Rossi's profile dominated the MotoGP landscape. What will happen when he is gone?

Below: Racing in Qatar was an isolated experience.

Photographs: Gold & Goose

SPONSOR TAKES ALL

An amenable sponsor with nice deep pockets could probably save Aprilia or Proton. At the same time, those who did have sponsors found this a mixed blessing. Sponsorship tied their hands in other crucial areas. Such as rider choice. This has been an element for a long time, but was more conspicuous in 2004 than anyone could remember. The case of the Honda team illustrates the point. Their original plan (and one of Rossi's original complaints) was to keep all their bikes as far as possible identical. Rossi felt a number one rider should have something better. Then Repsol insisted that the letter of their contract meant their team should have special equipment. More than that, the Spanish petroleum corporation (with strong Latin American interests) was more than just influential in putting Alex Barros onto the seat of the best of the best Hondas. Many felt there were other riders who might have done a better job. Not least Sete Gibernau. And this triggered another episode of Repsol muscle power.

HRC were interested in enlisting Sete for the factory team for 2005, but he has strong personal links with his team's sponsor Telefónica MoviStar. Couldn't an accommodation be reached ... perhaps for fairing space to be shared? After all, these two Spanish companies were not direct rivals. Repsol played hard-ball, according to leaks from meetings before Brno. They would only consider it if Telefónica agreed to pay the whole bill.

Yamaha were much under sponsor influence too. Although Valentino managed to overcome his objections to promoting cigarettes ("I'd rather have tobacco money than not race," he'd said the year before), there were suggestions that the retention of Checa as his team-mate, rather than say Melandri or Nakano, was dictated by Fortuna. (In the same way, the same rider would get a fair wind to Ducati for 2005; Marlboro Spain exerting a strong influence.)

This system of patronage blocks the path for younger riders. It was to Suzuki's credit then that, in spite of already having to foot the whole bill for the past two years, they resisted the temptation to take a welcome big sponsorship deal, because that sponsor wanted Hopkins replaced. Suzuki decided that keeping this talented young rider was more important, for the moment, than balancing the books.

If it is hard for the likes of Hopkins, already with a firm hold on the MotoGP ladder, how is it for other riders? There are numerous others whose talent is wasted or frustrated, while the support goes in favour of more sponsor-friendly (or more usually sponsorship-bearing) riders. Take 250 GP winner Anthony West. He has now at last been given a top-quality ride for 2005, debuting the KTM 250. Westy is 23 years old, and he deserved a chance like this two or more years ago. Compare the case of Chaz Davies, who finished the year with a run of best-ever top ten finishes on an ageing privateer machine. Davies (17) had an offer for 2005 to move up to the Campetella team, to a semi-

Top: Lots of money, well spent ... tobacco cash put Rossi on the Yamaha.

Centre left: Checa enjoys his status as a well-funded MotoGP rider.

Above left: Alex Barros, a MotoGP perennial, took Rossi's place at Honda.

Right: 250 charger Anthony West is one rider who has had to wait and wait. In 2005, he joins the KTM factory team.
Photographs: Gold & Goose

factory bike ... but only if he could bring more money to the deal than he could raise in his home country, where his exploits go largely unnoticed, certainly outside the specialist press. What a contrast to the career of Dani Pedrosa, just two years older, but nurtured from early teens, to sweep to two consecutive World Championships.

NEW RULES, NEW ARGUMENTS

Racing management had a bumpy ride. Although Race Director Paul Butler made a good job of explaining most decisions, his position means he can hardly expect to please everybody all the time. Especially when the rules give him the right, in some cases, to make it up as he goes along. One such was at Le Mans, where Rossi stalled before the warm-up lap. By the time IRTA boss Mike Trimby and two mechanics from Tech 3 had joined the party trying to get the M1 going again, this definitely breached the "one-helper" rule. But by now, Butler explained, the race was no longer under the start procedure, but under his direct control ... and "for sporting reasons" he elected to allow Rossi to come through from behind a suspiciously slow sweep safety car to take up his proper grid position. (Rossi did not question that decision, but was less sanguine when things went against him at Qatar, and he was pushed to the back of the grid. No win-some, lose-some philosophy in racing, where winning is everything.)

There were some important changes to the regulations. One dealt with the problem of overtaking under yellow caution flags. At Motegi a new system would allow a rider to expiate a possibly inadvertent sin. After appropriate signals, he had three laps to drop back and resume whatever position he held before the infringement. Again Rossi was a factor. Penalised twice last year, he found himself on the receiving end at Mugello, when he alleged Gibernau had passed him under the flags for Nakano's pit-straight crash (Gibernau claimed he had only pulled alongside, and dropped back at the first opportunity). Shortly afterwards, the race was stopped, and "neutralised" under current wet-race rules. The positions counted only for grid positions for the restart. Rossi felt that Gibernau should carry the penalty into the restart; but did not protest, and it was not put to the test. Butler's informal judgement was that since the race had been neutralised, so had any offence, real or imagined.

The second important change concerned rain-hit (or indeed drying) races. The new solution, finally accepted by a reluctant MSMA, is flag to flag with no interruption. Riders and teams will make their own decision on when or whether to stop to change from dry bikes to wet (or indeed vice versa). The prime objection had been not so much that tyre changes would be required, but also brake changes – from carbon to steel discs, pads included. Not the sort of work one wants doing in a hurry. The new plan, ratified at the Motegi round in September, allows teams to have a spare bike ready and waiting, already configured for the changed conditions. There are still some safety concerns. For example, a rider may decide it would cost more time to change bikes than to ride at reduced speed on slicks for a few remaining laps of a rain-hit race. This is a high-risk option, but has the virtue of putting the responsibility squarely in the hands of the person taking the risk, rather than some remote official wielding a reluctant red flag.

Next year, the MotoGP class maximum tank size drops from 24 to 22 litres (4.84 gallons).This requires a fuel consumption better than 15 mpg at GP speeds. HRC at least are convinced this can be achieved without any sacrifice in performance.

In 2005, the qualifying procedure will change radically: Saturday only will count – a TV inspired alteration. The smallest class has been singled out in another area, to emphasise its role as kindergarten. In addition to the existing maximum 125 class entry age of 25, from next year there's an overall maximum of 28, eliminating a number of senior riders including championship contender Roberto Locatelli.

Clears the deadwood, anyway. If only they could make a similar rule for superannuated sponsor favourites in the top class.

Is GP racing more precarious than the boom time suggests? We will find out, in time to come. Certainly the steep climb over the past three years means it has further to fall now than ever before. By the same token, grand prix motorcycle racing has survived far leaner times in the past.

And, in spite of the fastest ever accident in GP racing, there were no serious injuries all season. That shows that GP racing is better than ever at getting away with things.

TOO FAST TO RACE?

The 990cc capacity limit for MotoGP four-strokes was chosen largely to ensure that the new generation would not be beaten by the old 500cc two-strokes. Many people thought they went too far. Among them riders, some of whom felt the speeds had got out of control.

The Motor Sport Manufacturers Association – MSMA – were invited to address the problem. To engineers dedicated to maximising performance, looking for ways to do the opposite provoked a lot of disagreement, but a decision came early in the season.

"In the interests of safety," read the MSMA statement, they had agreed it was necessary to limit the increase in performance. The reduction in fuel capacity next year was a step, but this would not be sufficient in the long term.

"For this reason, the MSMA has decided to propose a reduction in engine capacity from 990cc to 900cc, starting from 2007.

"The intention is not to reduce performance, but to prevent a continuous improvement in speed and lap times."

This seemed a mere bagatelle – a ten-percent reduction in capacity to machines whose power output had already climbed by more than that in the first two years. By 2007, it is unlikely this change will even bring power back to 2004 levels.

HRC went public with their own opposition to this decision. New managing director Satoru Horiike affirmed they had suggested 700 to 800cc, but the association had decided differently.

The name of the class, MotoGP, was chosen to allow capacity changes; and while the 900cc limit of 2007 is a firm commitment, there are likely to be further changes in the future. Cynics wondered how long it would take to regain the base line ... 500cc.

For the too-fast/too-dangerous brigade, the new rule makes little sense. More radical changes will be needed. But for the moment, going slower will have to wait.

Photograph: Gold & Goose

GO!!!!!!!
YAMAHA
MOTUL

YAMADA

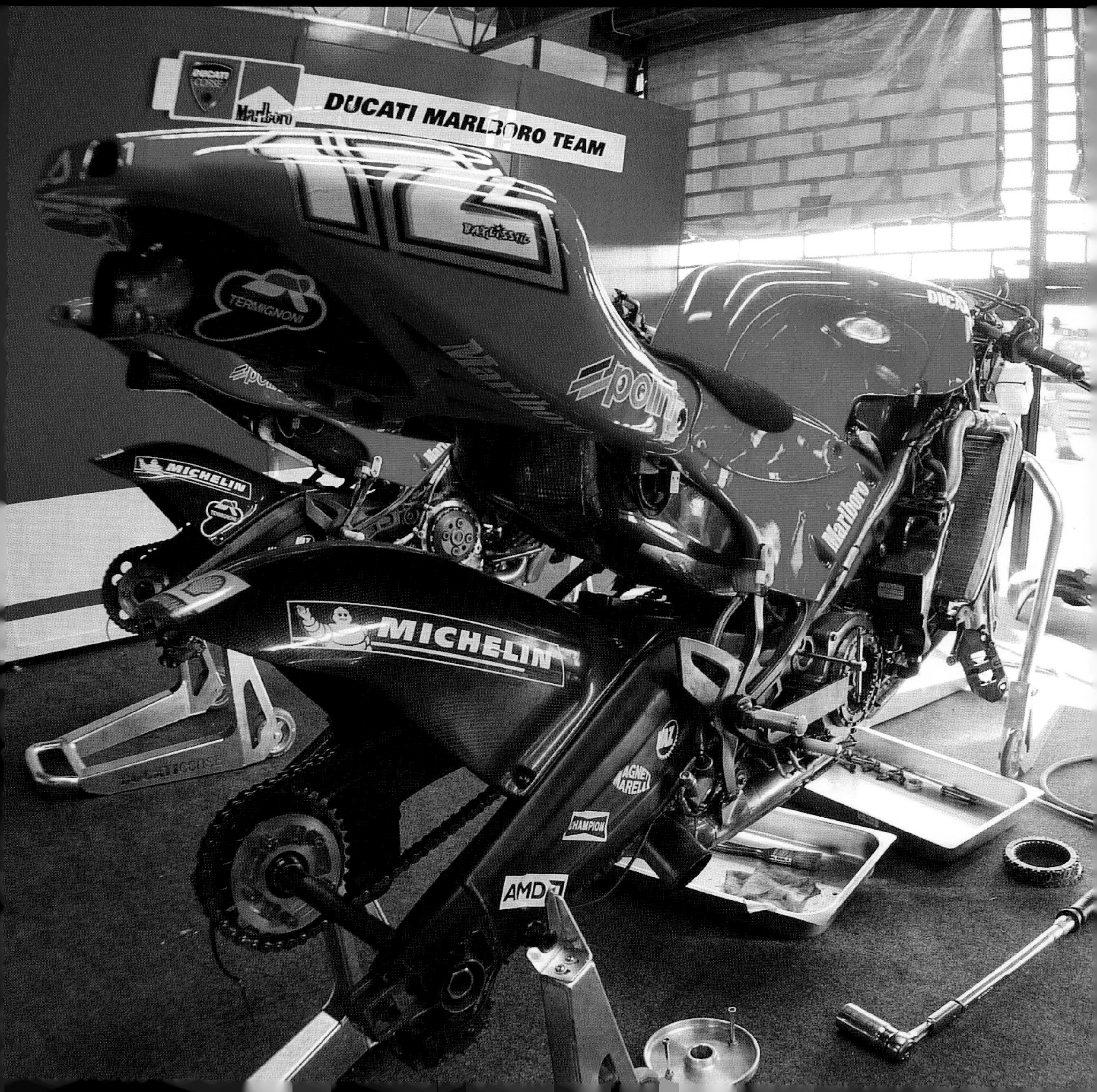

MOTOGP TECHNICAL REVIEW

A NEW GOLDEN AGE?

By NEIL SPALDING

Opposite page: Top marques – Rossi's M1 Yamaha (top left), Tamada's Honda RC211V (top right), and Bayliss's Ducati Desmosedici GP4.

Photographs: Gold & Goose

IN its third year MotoGP underlined the fact that motorcycling is in a Golden Age. New technology is coming in just as fast, if not faster, than when the class was announced.

Three years ago all the talk was that Formula One technology would take over. A lot of this car technology has indeed come into motorcycle racing, but now that technology is being scrutinised far more closely to see if it really fits the needs of the modern MotoGP bike. Two years ago large bores and short strokes were all the rage, and lightweight cranks with electronic fly-by-wire systems to control them were seen as a good way forward. In 2004, it became increasingly apparent that the all-important connection between the riders' right hand and the tiny tyre contact patch is far more important than sheer power.

The biggest single change of the year has been in the sounds coming out of pit lane; the exhaust-pipe orchestra gained a new bass line-up. Yamaha debuted a new firing interval motor for Valentino Rossi at the start of the season, by the middle of it every team except Kawasaki and WCM had changed their motor in some way too. The common aim has been to give the rider a more controllable, smoother, type of power. The common solution, achieved in various ways, is a firing order that lowers the number of torque fluctuations coming from the crank, essentially giving a reduced number of smoother, longer bangs, helping the tyre grip both on acceleration and into corners.

It is Long Bang rather than Big Bang, because that is how merged power pulses affect the crankshaft. As a piston approaches top dead centre to compress the mixture, it decelerates briefly. Then burning mixture accelerates the piston down again rapidly. Rather than a single strike, the main push on the piston lasts at least 50 degrees of crankshaft rotation. If two pistons fire separated by say 40 to 50 degrees, then these phases merge. The acceleration of the first piston counteracts the deceleration of the next. An in-line four (like the M1 Yamaha) can achieve this effect by timing the crankshaft with pairs of pistons separated by only 40 degrees rather than the conventional 180 degrees. Instead of four evenly spaced firing cycles, there are now two longer cycles ... each pair of pistons merging. So the crankshaft decelerates only once instead of twice per revolution, while the tyre gets one long shove, then a longer period to recover.

Longer-stroke engines and heavier crankshafts provide more sympathetic power delivery. Throttle systems that acknowledge that a rider is never going to use 100 percent throttle in first gear reduce the full 90 degrees of twist grip movement to move the butterfly just 50 degrees. In second and third gears the same system can provide 60, 70 or 80 degrees… as the rider prefers. This allows much more precise control of an engine that was previously putting out on average 2.8 more horsepower for each degree of movement at the handlebar!

Engine braking and the best ways of controlling it are becoming a little more formulaic. Most bikes use systems that make a fast idle, either by opening a butterfly, or a separate air bleed into the intake ports, using a slipper clutch to smooth out any remaining problems. Chassis flexibility, and the best ways of managing it are also getting similar responses from each factory. We are seeing more swing arms machined from solid, and the whole paddock has adopted lower front engine mounts, which allow the headstock to deflect sideways more readily at full lean, for the best front wheel grip.

Advancement doesn't stop there, however. There is a full-blown tyre war in progress with Michelin, Bridgestone and Dunlop scrapping out for the honours. Michelin did most of the winning, and Dunlop, without a really fast team, stayed relegated. Bridgestone's move last winter to sign both Suzuki and Kawasaki as well as Tamada's Honda paid off, with two GP wins and three pole positions too. This has not been without its drama however with Bridgestone's previous generation of tyres suffering a couple of embarrassingly public failures at Mugello, and others in private elsewhere. It will only take Bridgestone to sign with one of the current top teams for this war to intensify to levels seen between Dunlop and Michelin in Superbike several years ago.

MotoGP's favoured suspension supplier Ohlins also made big advances. From the start of the year, on the works Yamaha's, Ohlins debuted the new TT25 front fork, using slightly different technology from last year's gas forks. The new forks were available to all Ohlins teams from Brno onwards; a common theme from the riders was that as soon as they were fitted, half the bumps on the circuit disappeared.

New technical rules were announced, and from 2007 the capacity limit will be dropped to 900cc, with revised weight limits for each type of engine. At the current speed of development, it may well be that we will regret not taking the opportunity to lower the engine capacity to 800cc. What was particularly interesting was the statement that accompanied the new rules, which specifically noted that the manufacturers wished to maintain the high technology advances and didn't want to limit electronic controls or other systems. This series is indeed being used to develop the next generation of sporting motorcycles and to make sure that, even with new draconian emissions limits coming into force worldwide over the next few years, the sport of motorcycling will be able to continue.

Right: **Aprilia's deafening trumpets.**

Below: **McWilliams's Aprilia – still Mk1, with the replacement never arriving.**

Bottom: **Aprilias improved in detail, but basic design had flaws.**

Photographs: Gold & Goose

APRILIA: MotoGP ON A DIET

Aprilia has had a year of stagnation in the face of a financial crisis in the parent company. Several of the senior MotoGP engineers left in the winter, including eventually Jan Witteveen, Aprilia's race director. A believer in the philosophy that "first we get a good motorcycle and then we add the trick stuff," he had turned to basic engineering solutions to the bike's complex problems.

Over the course of the year quite a few new parts were fitted, but all quite simple items: a heavier crankshaft to slow throttle response, a new fairing for some easy speed, and halfway through the year a revised swing arm. All these things will help greatly once the chassis has been rearranged so that the chain pull doesn't impair the tyre grip off the corners. There is no doubt that the Aprilia Cube makes sufficient power, but it finds it impossible to put it down to the road when the bike is not completely upright.

The long term solution is the same as we predicted at the end of last year: a revised engine layout, with the output shaft lower. This requires a completely new gearbox and primary drive arrangement, together with a new chassis... not things you do when the very survival of your company is in the balance. We do know a prototype of this bike exists and that McWilliams has tested it, but it would send the wrong message to the financial markets if four brand new bikes suddenly popped up in the MotoGP garage.

Witteveen admitted earlier in the year that they had taken off most of the fly-by-wire throttle linkage systems that had given Colin Edwards such an adventurous 2003. This was replaced with a simple one-to-one relationship in the top three gears and an adjustable, but linear, system giving perhaps 50% of butterfly movement for all 90 degrees of twist grip travel in each of the first three gears. Additional weight on the crank slowed down its reaction speed, and gave the riders a better chance to tailor the acceleration of the engine to what their tyres could handle.

Michelin's new super grippy tyres have not worked well on this chassis however, with both riders complaining of really bad chatter problems, both tyres off the ground in some corners. Aprilia's already compromised chassis makes it more difficult than usual to dial this out.

DUCATI: THE NEW HONDA

Ducati's debut year with the Desmosedici in 2003 sent shockwaves around the sport. How could such a small factory get the very complex formula that makes a successful MotoGP bike so right so quickly? The 2004 Desmosedici was supposed to be an improvement all round - more rear tyre grip, better aerodynamics, more power, better weight distribution, the lot. What we saw though was a bike that the riders had extreme difficulty in riding.

At the pre-season Catalunya tests Capirossi set the highest top speeds seen in MotoGP, but on the track his bike just didn't look right. It appeared very stiff and tight, and it was clearly not as he wanted it to be. At the first GP in South Africa, the enormity of the problems struck home. Capirossi opted to keep his old favoured seventeen inch front tyre, Bayliss chose to use the new sixteen and a half. It didn't make any difference, as neither rider could get the bike to work for them. Both pleaded with Ducati for a milder motor and a change back to the handling they had got used to the year before, a call that echoed many a works Honda rider in the past.

Ducati held a press conference before the second round at Jerez to announce that they would increase their testing programme in the hope of finding a way out of their problems. Extraordinary scenes followed, with a back-to-back test of a pair of '03 bikes built from spares at Le Mans. By Mugello the riders had a choice of three bikes each over the weekend, starting with an '03 and an '04 bike each, then two '04 bikes; weight being visibly moved around the bikes every session. While these weight shifts clearly made a difference, Ducati were really waiting for their revised firing order motor, the "twin pulse", to allow them to have both their horsepower increase and a better feeling and level of grip for their riders.

Catalunya was the turning point. For this race there was a new traction-control system, this cut the ignition on individual cylinders as the rear tyre spun up, sounding as if the bike had been equipped with a hammer drill as the rider hit the throttle coming out of corners. In testing after the race, there was the new firing order motor. By Assen Capirossi had two of the deeper-toned engines, and Bayliss one. At Donington both riders' bikes were equipped with the new design.

The twin pulse motor had been tested alongside the four-pulse at the end of 2002, with the latter chosen by riders and technicians - the double-pulse engine proving fragile due to the extreme shock loadings. The new twin-pulse is similar mainly in name. The second incarnation is believed to have decoupled the cylinders by about 45 degrees, removing the peak shock loadings. It is Ducati's own Long Bang engine.

By the end of the year the bike was a lot better, and achieved a rostrum at last at Phillip Island, but the pace of development was less than expected after '03. The new bike still couldn't get into turns easily, nor was it easy to stop, but in terms of absolute power the Ducati's have been very good all year. It is obvious that they have not backed off in that department; if they can make the bike do all the other things it should do just a little bit better, then they will be seriously quick.

Above: Ducati's V4 engine ... still one of the most powerful.

Below left: revised exhausts and seats helped remove heat.

Photographs: Gold & Goose

Below, left and right: Honda's exhaust changed during the year, from the early single high pipe to a slant-cut pair.

Bottom: Strip-down view shows lower exhausts; note lack of adjustment for rear suspension pivot point.

Photographs: Gold & Goose

HONDA RC211V: V5's TRUE GENIUS SHOWS THROUGH

For its third year of racing Honda's RCV was given another update: a new swing arm and linkage, an increase in power and revs, and Michelin's new big tyres. Pre-season testing had gone very well for Honda, given that the departure of Jerry Burgess and his crew to Yamaha had left a gaping hole in the factory team personnel. The arrival at the end of testing of the increased-power motor and the new swing arm and tyres however upset the balance of the bike. Gibernau bounced back first finding settings he could use but it took to the middle of the season before revised parts were available that would allow some other riders to fully address some of the problems.

Sachsenring saw the debut of a frame with a revised swing arm pivot position, up five mm from the start of the year and actually higher than the earliest version. Raising the swing arm pivot like this ensures that the swing arm is pushed away from the bike by chain pull under acceleration, effectively lifting the back of the bike as the throttle is opened. This will change the pressure on the rear tyre, and quite possibly will allow it to spin. Either act would change the way the chassis is reacting to the increased levels of grip, and should allow the rider to eliminate some of the chatter using the throttle.

Also seen for the first time at Sachsenring was a revised exhaust system and engine, first for Barros and then within two rounds for the rest of the top riders. The changes were designed to provide better low-end response but did not meet with full approval. The works team and Biaggi adopted them immediately but Gibernau noticeably did not, preferring to race on a motorcycle with which he was familiar.

The move by the other manufacturers to revised firing orders brought home the underlying design superiority of Hondas 75.5 degree Vee five. Honda won't discuss the precise firing order, but it is sounding increasingly likely that the engine setup that all the other factories are now chasing has been built into the Honda all along. During the year several other RCV's secrets came out. The main one being a throttle system that allowed the rider to maintain a direct connection with his motor, but which allowed all 90 degrees of throttle movement at the handlebar to reduce to 50, 60 or 70 degrees as appropriate at the butterfly in the first three gears, much improving controllability in those low gears.

The Honda is the best overall bike on the track, but it is going to take some careful rethinking of their strategy for this to translate back into the wins the machine deserves. One of Honda's long term policies has been to provide bikes for customer teams that are set up for the top rider, but with minimal adjustment. This is to prevent teams becoming confused with too many variables. It now appears that some of the chatter that arrived with the new swing arm and new-generation Michelins could be partially controlled with a slightly higher swing arm pivot position. This is one of the variables that is not adjustable on the 'standard' race bike. If this had been adjustable, it is possible that satellite teams could have solved the chatter problems much earlier in the season, quite possibly significantly changing the year's results.

KAWASAKI: THE BEST M1 YAMAHA NEVER MADE

With the embarrassment of their 2003 efforts behind them Kawasaki came back with a bike that went a long way to showing just how good a motorcycle they could build. The '04 bike was small, flexible and had more power - it was virtually a new motorcycle. Acknowledging they had a problem early in 2003, development started in July of a replacement bike built with help from Suter Racing in Switzerland. Kawasaki also exchanged Dunlop for Bridgestone tyres at the end of 2003.

The new bike is much smaller than the old with a more centralised centre of gravity. Built like a 250, the bike has several interesting design features, including a combined seat and fuel tank unit that extends forwards to form the sides of the airbox. A bottom section attached to the motor and a lid above the injection units completes the airbox itself. The frame is now an all fabricated 'round the outside of the engine' aluminium beam unit, with front engine mounts that attach at the top of the crankcases in line with the latest fashion.

Although major progress has been made, the overall pace of development in MotoGP has if anything accelerated this year. Kawasaki's problems now come from having a motorcycle designed in two stages. The chassis is quite extreme in geometry terms, it makes up for the very conservative engine design; but the marriage of the two parts seems to be causing ongoing difficulties. On circuits where high corner speeds can be used the bikes are fast, but as soon as there is a combination of high and slow speed corners they are difficult to set up. The set-up needed to allow it to turn in the slower corners works against it in the faster ones.

Engine design and layout has a major influence on handling. Normal forward rotating engines endow the machine with a lot of gyroscopic stability, the crank's gyro effects being added to those of the wheels. This stability increases as the revs rise. It's worse on across the frame fours because you have to factor in the effort of rolling a long crankshaft over as the bike is leaned into a corner. Kawasaki are still trying to cure this with forward turning lightweight low inertia crankshafts. Yamaha's solution, to rotate the crank backwards to counteract some of the gyroscopic effects and therefore to make the bike more agile, seems increasingly attractive.

The engine's firing interval has remained the same old-fashioned 180-degree crank style, with evenly spaced firing strokes, abandoned by Yamaha at the end of last year. Given the success of Yamaha's new "virtual vee" configuration (which requires a balance shaft that the current Kawasaki lacks), Kawasaki are considering a similar solution.

But nobody could accuse the factory of not trying, with at least five different engine tunes being tried out during the year; unfortunately usually coinciding with piston, ring or valve failure, and leading to rather smoky DNFs. The most successful modification was the adoption of a Weber Marelli Fuel injection system. Tried at Motegi, it immediately gave the rider better feel and confidence, and was immediately adopted on all their bikes.

Top: Second-generation Kawasaki was significantly more compact, with weight centralised.

Inset: Team boss Harald Eckl.

Above: Plentiful power generates plentiful heat... Kawasaki radiator is typically huge.

Photographs: Gold & Goose

Top: **Proton: superlative quality of multi-tasking chassis construction.**

Above: **Proton airbox reveals upstream injectors, now commonly used in MotoGP.**

Right: **Narrow-angle V5 motor lacked horsepower.**

Photographs: Gold & Goose

PROTON KR - FLAWED MASTERPIECE

Kenny Roberts hired John Barnard for new ideas and execution. He certainly got what he wanted in the chassis and packaging of the 2004 Proton KR V5. Proton had finished 2003 with a motor they knew needed work, and ideas for a new chassis. In the complex world of tyre contracts they lost their preferred Bridgestones, and ended up with Dunlops instead – WCM was the only other Dunlop team.

With inventive use of materials and a careful rethink of basic concepts, the bike is very neat and nicely manufactured. It exudes quality with gorgeous machined-from-solid aluminium main-frame spars, headstock, rear subsection and swing arm, and carefully fabricated titanium triple clamps. The reasoning was to ensure accuracy, avoiding inevitable distortions that come with the welding and heat treatment of aluminium fabrications. The careful design was also apparent in the way every part did at least two jobs – the rear cylinder head, for example, also acted as a frame cross-brace; while water and oil were routed inside the frame spars.

The project also envisaged a major engine revision, to try and make the V5 act more like the Honda. It was decided to build new heads on to the old crankcases and that's where it all went horribly wrong. Barnard's design required that the rear cylinder head be part of the chassis structure, so design changes were irrevocable. And although computer simulations had promised otherwise, the redesigned motor simply didn't make the sort of power that had been projected.

The original choice of firing order encouraged wheel hop entering corners, unsettling the bike on its suspension in spite of the best efforts of engine management and slipper clutch. The original design of the engine used a 75 mm bore, with what is a relatively short stroke of 44.8 mm. A change was introduced early in the year, as soon as the limitations of the new design became apparent, with 72 X 48.7mm dimensions.

Depending on the stroke of the engine different exhaust pipes were tried. The team settled on a system for the 72mm version with a two-into-one and a one-into-one from the front 3 cylinders. The rear pair have an exhaust pipe each.

The final versions of the motor were all longer stroke, with the revised firing order, which gave the clutch an easier time, allowing the bike to roll into corners more smoothly; the longer stroke gave the riders a better feel.

By the end of the year the team was pretty much back where it had started. They could match the Suzukis for speed, but they could not get enough grip to stay with them on track.

Given the quality and thought behind its execution and the sheer effort put in by everybody involved the outcome has been extremely disappointing. Behind the scenes however the team tested the V4 engine from the aborted KTM MotoGP project in a variation of their chassis. Initial results were highly promising, and if this project bears fruit (and given resolution of tyre difficulties) it may not be long before Kenny Roberts's team is where it aims to be, in the front half of the field.

SUZUKI - UNFINISHED BUSINESS

For 2004 Suzuki took a step back from their almost fully automated 2003 bike. They also sat down and built a revised chassis and swing arm where the primary change was in the method of construction, allowing parts of different flexibility to be produced at will.

Other changes to the 65-degree V4 before the season included a simplified and refined electronic control package. The motor-drive clutch was replaced with a mechanical slipper; this complex electronic/mechanical device had been meant to control engine braking, but the riders found it unpredictable.

Engine designer Kunio Arase explained: "We did not so much reduce electronic control, but removed the motor-drive clutch. The fast idle system is very simple, but the control programme is very difficult." This solved difficulties in corner entry, and in testing the bike went startlingly quickly.

The major outward change was the different swing arm. The team also swapped to Bridgestones, which clearly suited their new chassis very well. Despite one or two unexpectedly good results in the first half year things didn't really get better until a 360 degree crank version arrived with new cylinder head internals and a new exhaust system. The new crank improved drive out of, and let the bike flow into, corners more easily.

At Motegi, yet another Yoshimura exhaust system arrived, which was another step forward - overall power remained the same, and somewhat short of the mark, as top speeds showed, but mid-range and general rideability were significantly improved.

Several very good qualifying performances on Bridgestones never really quite turned into the hoped-for race results. John Hopkins suffered several mechanical failures while in potentially good race positions. The Suzuki engine does seem to have a rather fragile top end, with cam followers and springs being particularly delicate. It is hoped that by 2005 a far more robust piece will have been developed.

Arase sums up the situation. "Our problem is very simple. We need more top speed. So there are two areas we need to improve... top end power and aerodynamics. We are concentrating now on developing more power, but at this stage we need a new engine," he said.

Left, top to bottom: **Suzuki used three different exhaust systems during the year, the topmost being the final version. Side-on view shows RGV's new swing-arm.**

Above: **Former (and future) Honda technical guru Erv Kanemoto joined Suzuki for one fruitful season.**

Photographs: Gold & Goose

WCM - BUDGET RACING

For the WCM team, this year's bikes were the same as those at the end of last year, and just being on track was a victory. WCM though got some fair results during the year, by having an effective and simple, if somewhat underpowered, race bike. In the wet Michel Fabrizio was extremely effective. At various times of year the Aprilias and the Protons, both far more generously funded projects by comparison, fell foul of the WCM's "never give up" attitude.

The bike uses a Harris twin-spar aluminium chassis and swing arm: two different swing arm lengths were available. Ohlins provide front and rear suspension; wheels vary from Marchesini magnesium through to BST carbon-fibre wheels.

In June this year WCM finally jettisoned the carbon-fibre AP slipper clutch it had been using since the project's inception. An STM clutch using proprietary technology gave a much smoother clutch release action than the temperature-sensitive and grabby carbon unit; the riders could finally get a cleaner run into the corners.

The WCM announcement at Brno that they would build a V6 for the 2005 series, along with the Czech mini-bike company Blata, caught everybody by surprise. Regardless of how it goes it's going to be a really interesting motorcycle to watch - and listen to - next year.

Below: Yamaha R1-based Harris WCM was thoroughly conventional – the greatest achievement was survival.

Bottom: WCM team boss Peter Clifford ponders his MotoGP racer.

Photographs: Gold & Goose

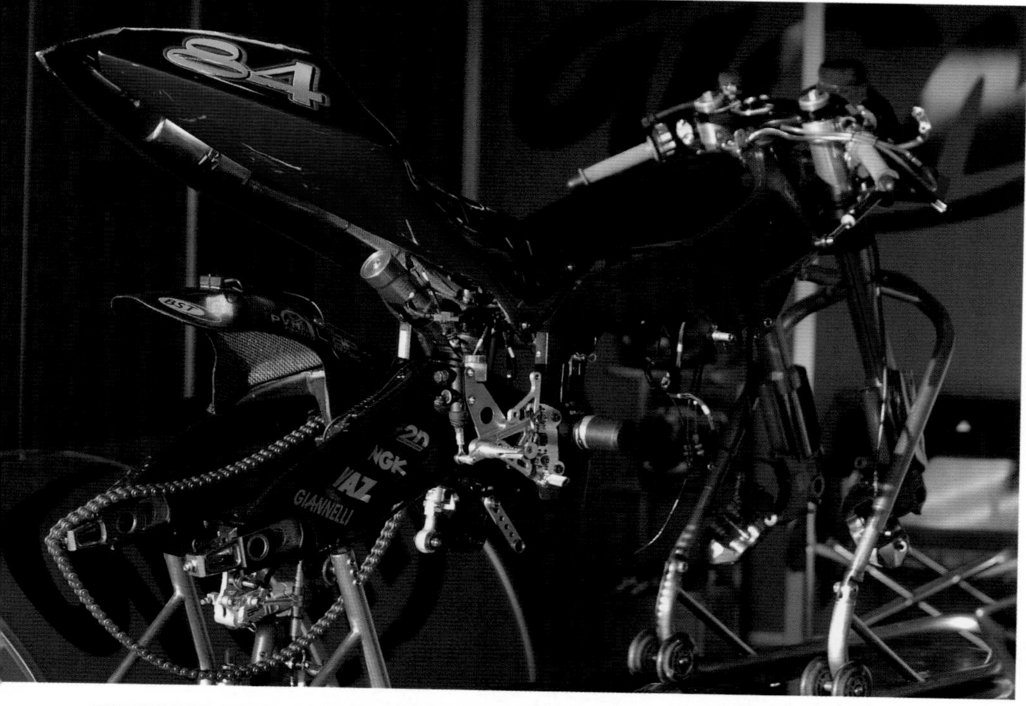

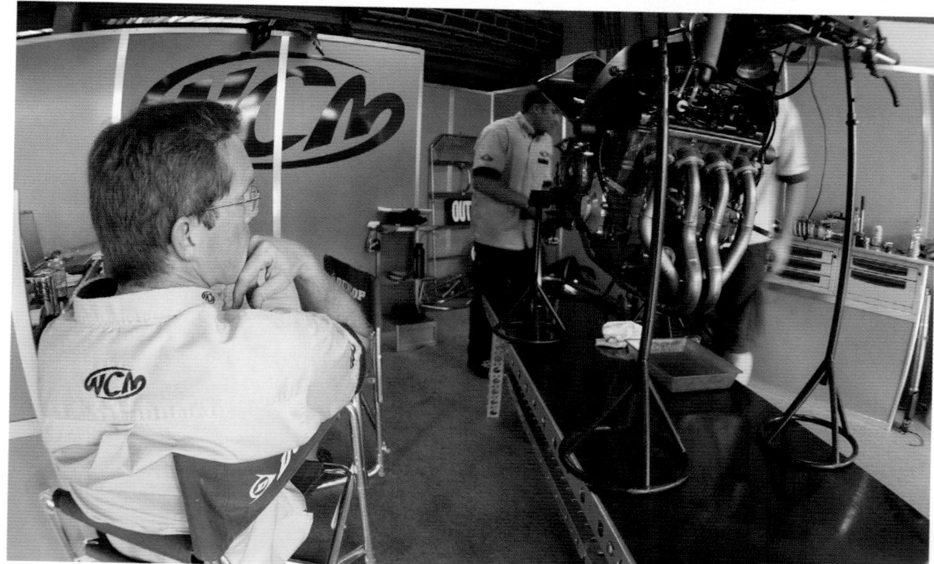

YAMAHA M1-UGLY DUCKLING NO MORE

Rossi and Burgess arrived at Yamaha to race a bike that had seriously under-performed for the previous two years. Yamaha were ready for them, though. Masao Furusawa, Yamaha's new race chief had been in place for over six months preparing for 2004. For what was supposed to be a testing year prior to an attempt on the title to coincide with Yamaha Motor's 50th anniversary in 2005, Furusawa had arranged for several different engine configurations to be available for Rossi to test. Rossi duly chose what Furusawa thought was their best motor package, a four-valve irregular-firing motor, and the project was on.

Once the engine spec was settled it was a question of Burgess finding a way for Valentino to use it. Most important was to find a way for the rider to initiate and recover from a slide progressively and smoothly. The Burgess belief was that grip and traction are everything, but when you have 240 horsepower you have to find a way to let it stop gripping in a controllable manner.

To achieve this, Burgess lengthened and raised the motorcycle, letting Valentino control grip by moving his weight around. Once they got a motorcycle that Valentino could ride fast and could slide at will, they set about finding the point of optimum grip, still allowing easy control of the resulting chassis behaviour. During the year they went back some way to a shorter wheelbase, putting more weight on the rear tyre, looking for more grip. To control the subsequent snappy behaviour, different swing-arms and chassis were used to try and find the right combinations of flexibility to give Rossi back the control he needed.

Furusawa describes his engine philosophy as "optimising" the power from an in-line four. Smooth power without unsettling torque fluctuations was his aim – he used the simile of an electric motor. The new M1 mimics Vee configuration engines in the way that pairs of power impulses follow one another closely, but it does so without the relative bulk of a vee configuration.

Yamaha built, in effect, a virtual vee-four, within the simpler and more compact architecture of an in-line four. It is also potentially lighter, with only two camshafts and associated drive, compared with four. The exhaust run is symmetrical, and small size allows more freedom in chassis dimensions and weight distribution.

In this way, Yamaha liberated the Long Bang, giving a new dimension to their well-developed in-line four. They confirmed that

Centre left: **Yamaha M1's single exhaust remained all year, in spite of late tests with a more compact system.**

Left: **Yamaha team manager Davide Brivio.**

Below: **Tech 3 Yamaha team boss Herve Poncharal.**

Bottom: **It was never the fastest, but Rossi's M1 Yamaha was unbeatable all the same.**

Photographs: Gold & Goose

the actual firing order was as normal in such an engine... 1-3-4-2, but never did disclose the exact timing of the crankshaft, believed to be between 40 and 50 degrees compared with the 180-degrees of a conventional in-line four. But they did reveal that this was an active area of research, and that they were still experimenting with different timings.

As the year went on Burgess worked his way through the entire motorcycle, making sure that they took all the advantages they could and converting them all into benefits. If a modification made one thing work better, and another worse, they worked on keeping the improvement and sorting out the problem rather than giving up on any possible benefits.

The M1 was not the best bike in pit lane, a fact Yamaha concedes, but with Rossi on board the combination was better than all the others. The 2005 "M1 evolution" bike was out at Valencia just days after the final GP, and was completely new, engine and all. The whole unit is more compact, with the cam drive now seemingly off the balance shaft, to allow a shorter crankshaft. On its fourth lap, Rossi matched his best race lap. It augured well ... Rossi, Burgess and Yamaha had almost six months to get it ready, and the benefit of one year's data on the 2004 machine, after coming in stone cold at the start of their first victorious season.

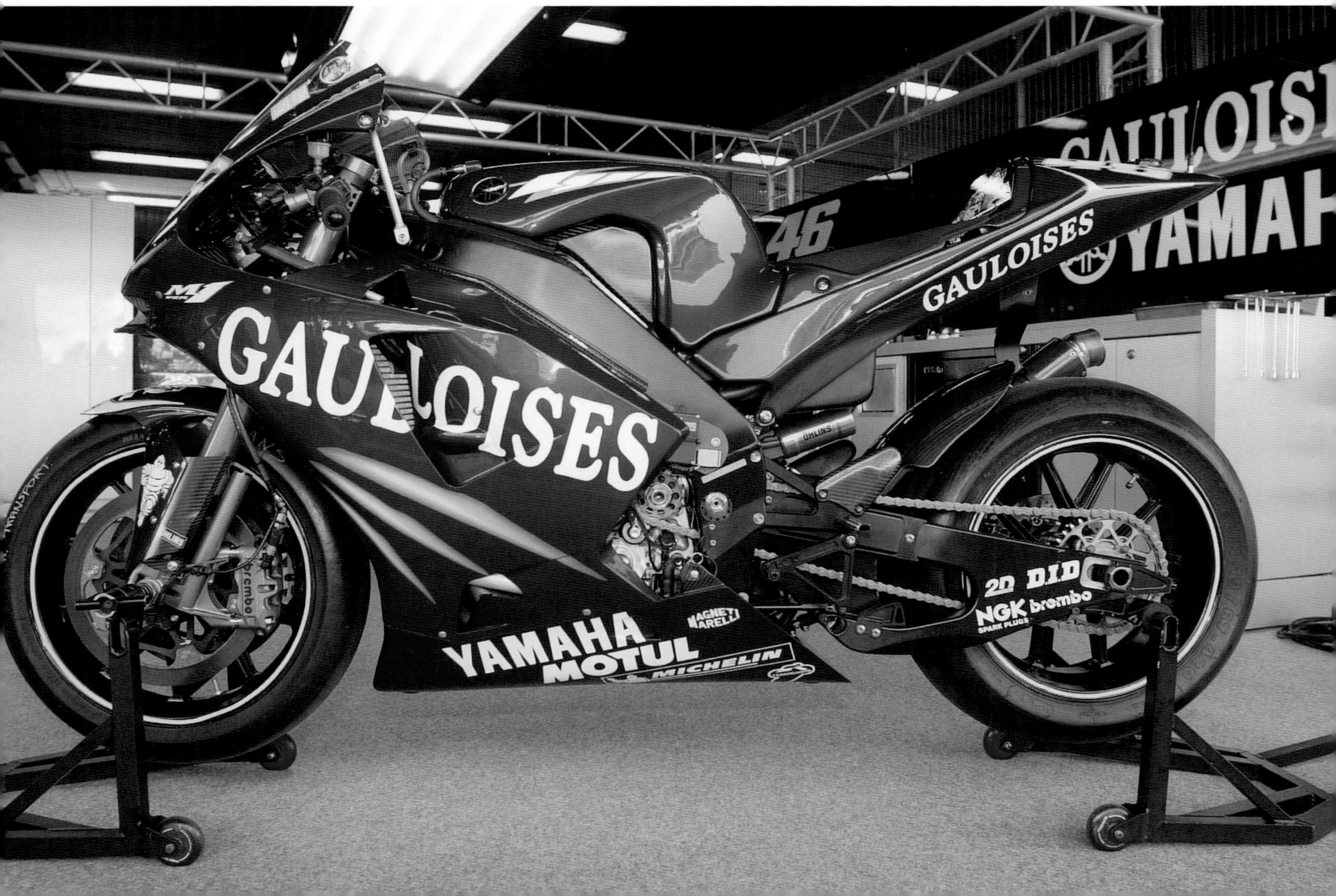

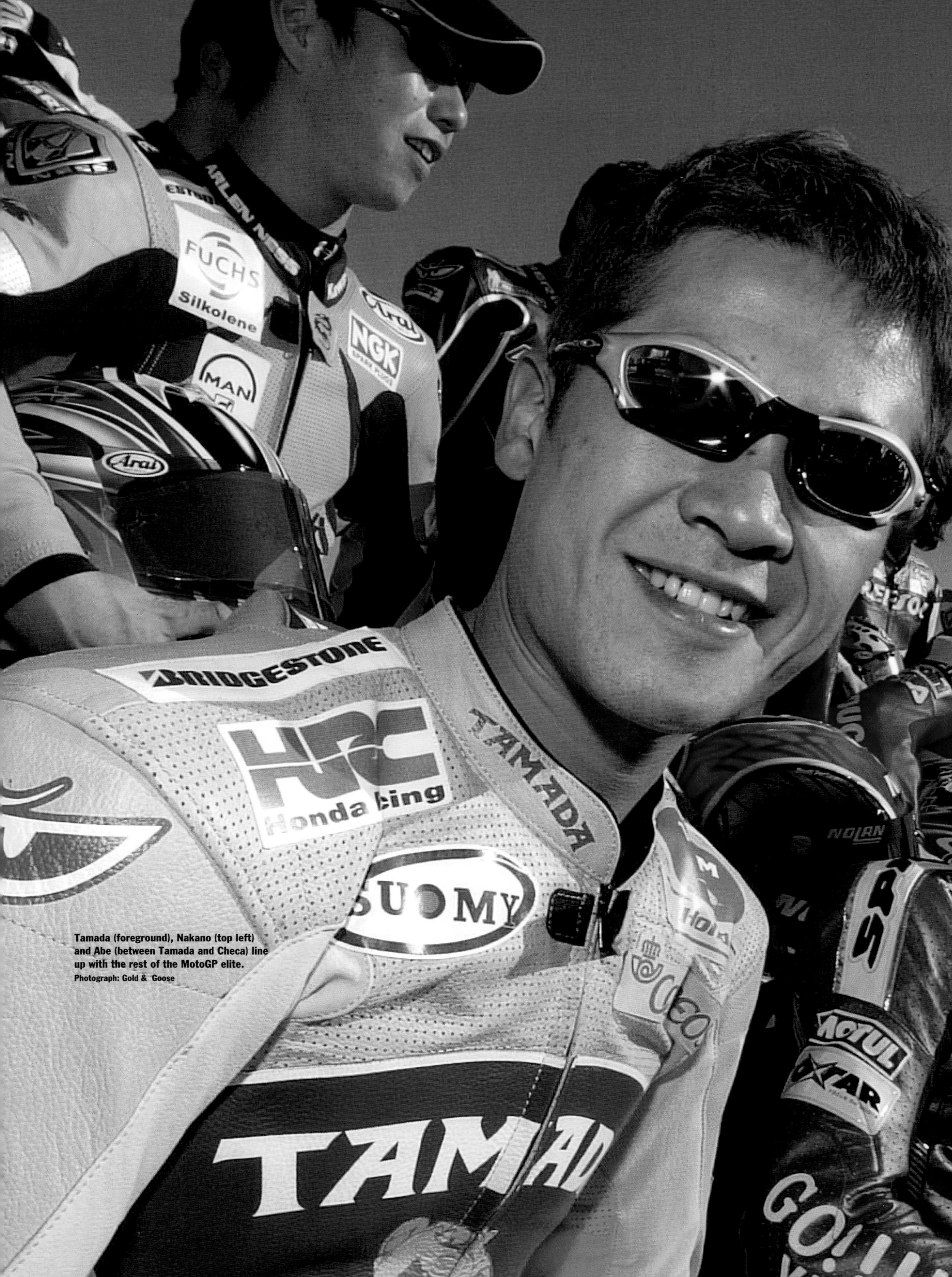

Tamada (foreground), Nakano (top left) and Abe (between Tamada and Checa) line up with the rest of the MotoGP elite.
Photograph: Gold & Goose

RE-TURNING JAPANESE

In 1993, with the rise of the likes of 250 champion Tetsuya Harada and 125 stars like Nobbie Ueda and Haru Aoki, MOTOCOURSE reported on the phenomenon of 'Turning Japanese'. The ensuing decade was disappointing. The momentum did not carry the new wave all the way to the highest level. With a new freedom for the stars like Makoto Tamada and Shinya Nakano, that, reports MARK GRAHAM, may be about to change...

JAPANESE riders have recently, and convincingly, lifted World 125 and 250 titles. But when it comes to performing in the big class, no one has yet mounted and sustained a credible season-long challenge. Now that is changing. The false dawns and failures just may be over.

When Hideo Kanaya notched the first 500cc Grand Prix win for a Japanese rider in 1975 on a Yamaha at the Salzburgring, it was his second GP of that season, in which team-mate Agostini went on to claim the first two-stroke title. Kanaya scored second at Paul Ricard in the opening round, winning in Austria at round two, then a fourth at Hockenheim and another second place at Imola – something like the form of a World Championship contender.

Then he vanished. Called back to Japan after just four rounds to continue the TZ500 development programme. That was how it was when there was no reason for a Japanese factory to have a Japanese rider winning races on a Japanese bike. Market forces dictated that Ago was the winning face needed to sell bikes in Europe – the Rossi of his time. A neo-feudal factory system tied rider employees to whatever task was required of them. Kanaya now runs a tearoom south of Tokyo.

Japan's first World Champion (in the 350 class) Takazumi Katayama finished fifth overall in 1978, then seventh in 1982. Tadahiko Taira managed sixth in the standings in 1987, but neither of them won a race. In 1993 Shinichi Itoh scored a third at Hockenheim, then a second at Brno in 1994, followed by another second at Catalunya in 1995. Nothing remotely remarkable. There was will and talent in Katayama's case, but not quite enough of one or the other in Taira and Itoh. Riders and factories generated negligible title impetus.

Back in Japan, however, interest in racing was fuelling a new breed of riders. Schooled on pocket bikes, they moved up to fierce factory-backed national competition, including until the late Nineties the 500cc class. At the Japanese GP, wild cards were to be feared and respected, especially in the smaller classes. The same Japanese riders were becoming a title force at GP level, in 125s and 250s. When Rossi came to the 125 class in 1996, he even adopted the Japanese nickname Rossifumi, to acknowledge their strength in depth and in numbers.

Norifumi Abe's showing at Suzuka in 1994 as a reigning 17-year-old all-Japan 500cc Champion was remarkable, unfazed by fighting with Mick Doohan. Then his win at Suzuka in 1996 seemed to confirm the arrival of a long-awaited and genuine contender. His fifth place overall that same year was mildly disappointing. But not quite as frustrating as the rest of his long career would prove to be.

Loyal Honda retainer Tadayuki Okada won at Sentul, Indonesia in 1997 and finished second overall in the title standings. But Mick Doohan was at the height of his powers, winning 12 races from 15. Taddy was in the right place at the wrong time.

It seemed the upward curve might continue when the Fireball Brothers exploded onto the scene. But they shone only for a moment. The stars that burned twice as bright burned only half as long: Takuma's career cut short by a grave testing crash, Nobu's by an ill-advised switch to Suzuki for 1998. Haruchika Aoki won two 125cc World Championships in 1995 and '96 before his 500cc efforts fizzled out. No one could stop Doohan in 1998. Taddy managed a third overall that year, Abe sixth. Aside from Norick's sporadic wins, any meaningful Japanese challenge had wilted.

Now the picture has changed. When Nobu Aoki jumped ship to Suzuki, Honda had trouble coping with the boldness of the move, to the extent that through the steely gaze of the corporate eye Nobu simply ceased to exist. He had broken the bonds and gone where he wanted to go – not where he was told to go. It was viewed almost as a desertion.

The current Japanese riders in MotoGP can now afford to employ a markedly more independent modus operandi. Tohru Ukawa and Norick Abe were probably the last of the truly 'tied' riders. Shinya Nakano and Makoto Tamada realise they are not part of a factory fiefdom – they are free agents – because they are good enough.

Nakano openly admits to being courted by Aprilia in 2003, before his switch from Yamaha to Kawasaki, and by Ducati this season before he opted to stay with the green team. When asked if this represented a long-term commitment to Kawasaki he replied, "Not really. What if I had an offer from Repsol Honda?"

Left: Shinya Nakano's combination of good cheer and racing talent lifted Kawasaki, and confirmed his own stature.

Below: Tamada – the first Japanese MotoGP winner.

Bottom: Norick Abe, in the twilight of a long career tied to Yamaha.

Photographs: Gold & Goose

Tamada, dismayed by the removal of long-time confidant Gianluca Montiron from his Camel squad last season, has now militated for a one-rider set-up in 2005, like he had in 2003. The resolute Japanese has also ditched Bridgestone in favour of Michelin tyres. "I wanted to have a strong end to the season after my win in Brazil," he said. "But I knew I'd never have the same level of consistency on Bridgestones that my chief rivals had with Michelin." Tamada now has Montiron and Michelin. Two years ago, he might have ended up with neither.

These riders are no longer listed under goods and chattels on a factory inventory. They ride the bikes. They also call some shots. The late Daijiro Kato, a Honda-raised rider, was no respecter of factory protocol. He had few qualms about refusing to use HRC prototype parts if he felt they'd be of little benefit to him. Such was his status that Honda often felt little reason to press the issue. European riders had done that before, but rarely a Japanese. This new autonomy caught on.

"People always had me marked as Yamaha rider," said Nakano. "Since I switched to Kawasaki things have been more open. There's a tendency for Japanese riders to become too closely identified with one factory."

Abe, in the fast-fading twilight of his career, knows all about doing time as a factory-man. He's now had nine years with Yamaha. Norick believes the best chance Japanese riders have to make a title-winning impact in MotoGP, is now, and that the future is less promising. "There are still no Japanese World Champions in MotoGP because it's still at a really high level. If you want to be a Japanese World Champion go to 250, or 125. I never had a 250 or 125 ride, only MotoGP," he said. "But the riding level in Japan isn't so high now because the factories are not there. Before it was all factory – Honda, Yamaha, Suzuki, Kawasaki. Now nothing. And the Japanese champions are now the same age group as me – not young riders. The future will be difficult in MotoGP for Japanese riders."

Nakano will apply all his innocent intensity to developing a new 'big bang' Kawasaki engine next year. He is also running erratic Bridgestone rubber. Two burdens too many for sustained success.

Tamada won two races and set three pole positions this season. He is no respecter of reputations. He has speed. His exploratory lines as he feints to make a pass on one side only to make the move elsewhere show a hyperactive racing brain at work. His time is now. And the motorcycle-marketing people might just have to work around him.

Above: Tamada's fortunes were linked to those of his Bridgestone tyres. In 2005 he would switch to Michelins, to be on equal footing with Rossi.

Left: Abe ponders over his M1.

Below: Nobu Aoki, here on a Proton KR, broke the mould by abandoning Honda.
Photographs: Gold & Goose

TECHNICAL FEATURE

BIG BANG REDUX

By KEVIN CAMERON

BIG Bang is back. This is the practice of firing two or more of an engine's cylinders together or nearly so, then leaving an extended interval until the next firing. The result is a pulsating delivery of torque to the rear wheel, rather than the otherwise desirable smooth delivery. In motorcycle GP racing, this idea dates to 1992-3 when Honda engineers, noticing some strange effects of firing order on 250 twin performance, decided to test the idea on a 500. In off-road racing, the idea is much older.

Evidence that such firing orders are being used in MotoGP comes from the ears, which noticed the deeper, rougher sound of certain engines this year. This has its counterpart in the early 1990s, when the usual high song of 4-cylinder 500s changed to obviously deeper tones. At 12,000-rpm, a 2-stroke 500 firing pairs of cylinders at 180-degree intervals (a common firing scheme) generates a 400-cycle tone, but when switched to fire all cylinders within 67 degrees, then wait 293-degrees before firing again, the fundamental tone is cut in half at once-per-revolution and 200 cycles.

You can be sure that engineers were concerned when these experiments began, for delivering torque in large pulses requires a higher-capacity clutch and wider, heavier gears to handle the pulsation without slippage or failure. And failures there were. Also, the lower the frequency of torque pulsation, the more likely it is to excite damaging torsional (twisting) vibrations in the crankshaft.

What benefit motivated teams to accept heavier parts and greater risk of mechanical failure? It was claimed that pulsed torque delivery actually increased rear tyre grip during the critical phase of off-corner acceleration. Soon every team had made sound recordings of the Hondas, displayed the sound's waveform on oscilloscope screens, and had measured the firing interval. Shortly, every team's 500 sounded deep and motocross-like.

Seemingly no sooner did everyone's 500 make the trendy new sound but Mick Doohan, Honda's five-times 500 champion, showed up with 90- or 180-degree-firing "screamer" engines and again won races on them, defeating those on Big Bangers. Had Big Bang been just one more proof of the "placebo effect", which reveals that ill persons mysteriously feel better when given pills of chalk by actors dressed as doctors? Was it all a fad, a kind of GP racing Hula-Hoop? Or was it 'the madness of crowds', a collective delusion?

Later, it was explained that 500 two-strokes only needed Big Bang traction when leaded gasoline enabled them to run knock-free at high compression ratios, generating high torque as a result. Just as Big Bang bikes were becoming general, the FIM mandated reduction of lead anti-knock additive in fuel.

When compression ratios came down in response, peak torque had to fall with them, making Big Bang less necessary. This made it possible for Mick Doohan to again win races with engines of normal firing order.

There are ample other reasons to be sceptical. If torque pulsation produces the extra grip claimed for it, why isn't it used by dragsters or Formula One cars? As it was explained to me, the shaft drivelines of such vehicles are torsionally so "soft" that they cannot transmit torque pulses at even the frequency that would result if cylinders were fired in sets of four or five at once.

At the time that Big Bang first hit the 500GP scene, there was concern over the many corner exit high-side crashes that were occurring. I wondered if perhaps pulsed torque delivery might usefully blur the transition from gripping to sliding, making bikes easier to control near the limit. But no, insiders insisted that grip was actually increased, and Honda's official explanation was that Big Bang was "like anti-lock brakes working in reverse". This was a very interesting idea, but its credibility was weakened by the fact that at that time, no anti-lock brake system gave as short stopping distances as an expert human driver. That has since changed, but not by a large percentage. This has still not been satisfactorily explained.

When old-time dirt-trackers and hill-climbers first heard about Big Bang they were amused – after all, everyone on the dirt circuit has always "known" that a single accelerates off turns or climbs hills better than a twin. Yet for engineers this was hard to swallow – like trying to persuade a mathematician that four is larger than 2 + 2. Why should it matter how you add the firing pulses if they are all the same size? At trackside such questions were shrugged off – it's faster this way, why question a useful technique, end of discussion.

Now think about friction. Two surfaces in frictional contact have been described as 'like turning Switzerland upside down and putting it on top of Austria'. Even surfaces which look smooth to the eye consist of profiles which are jagged in micro-scale, and the contact they make with each other is generally mountaintop-to-mountaintop, so the true area of contact is far smaller than it appears – only a few percent of the apparent gross contact area. At these limited points of contact, pressures are very high, leading to local welding in metals and to formation of lesser molecular bonds in other materials. Friction increases as we press the two surfaces together harder because the actual area of contact is increased as the peaks ("asperities" in tech talk) are more extensively crushed against each other. Is there anything here to suggest an explanation of Big Bang traction?

Maybe. The first point is the difference between static friction – the force required to start the surfaces sliding – and kine-

Man and machine – a complex harmony.
Photograph: Gold & Goose

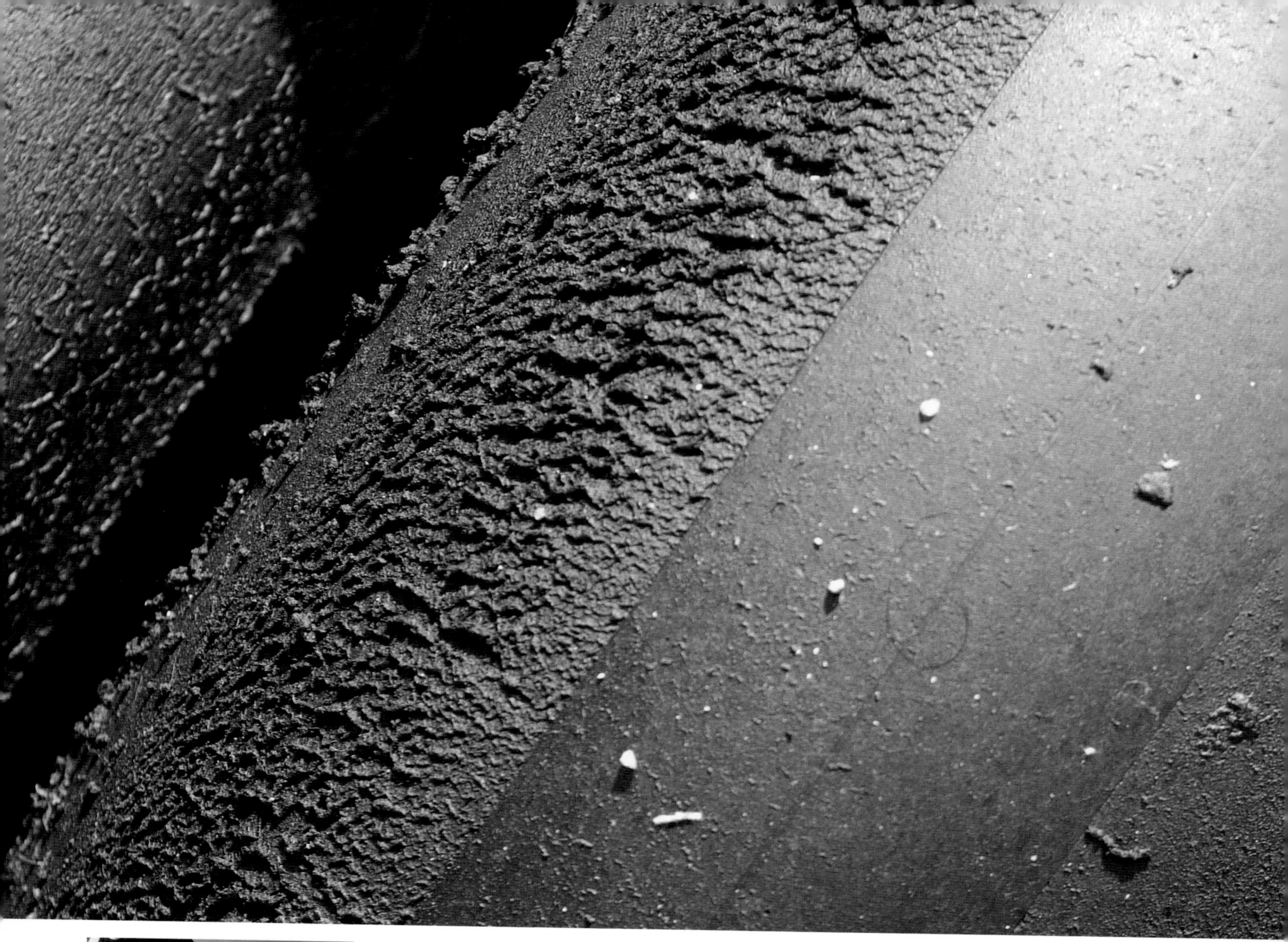

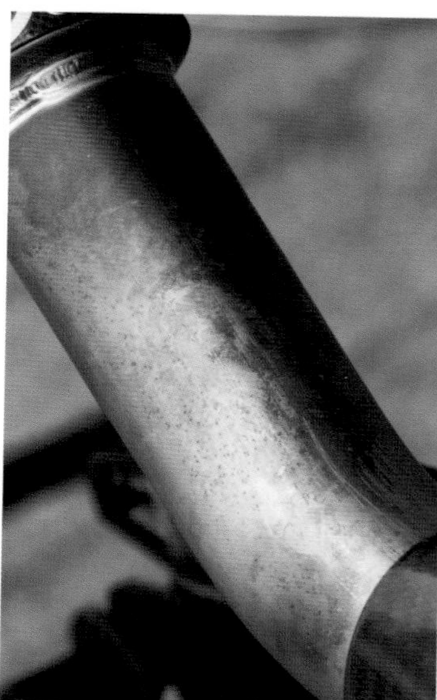

matic friction – the force required to keep them sliding once started. This difference exists because to start the sliding, you must break all the micro-welds or molecular bonds at once, while to maintain the motion, you break fewer bonds as some are always in the process of re-formation.

The second point is that rubber is a very non-linear material. If we support a bar of steel, aluminum, or titanium at its ends and hang weight at its middle, we discover that the bar sags in direct proportion to the weight supported. Rubber is different. Pull on a rubber band with one unit of force and you get a large deflection. But when you double the force, you get less than double the deflection. Rubber stiffens the more it is deformed, finally assuming a rigid, crystalline form at very high stress. This is the reason why wide tyres can deliver more grip than narrow ones – even though this violates the classical Amonton's law of friction, which says that area of contact shouldn't matter. The first pound of force pressing a square inch of rubber against the pavement produces significantly more area of actual contact than does the second pound, the third, and so on. Finally the rubber has infiltrated the pavement surface as deeply as it can and further load increases no longer produce increased grip. This condition is called 'stress saturation'. It is thus a better use of tyre load to spread it over a large area than over a small one.

The classic law of friction applies to materials with linear load-vs-deflection curves. Dragging a brick across a concrete floor generates a friction force that consists of the force necessary to break all the tiny points of actual contact between the two. If we add a second brick, the total number of points of contact is the same whether we stack the two or place them side-by-side; a given load generates a given area of true contact. This is why classical Amonton friction is independent of apparent contact area. But for rubber, which is very soft initially but grows stiffer as load increases, Amonton's Law is invalid. Wide tyres generate more grip than narrow tyres.

If we could somehow peer into the interface between tyre and road, and see the action there as a tyre grips during slow sliding, we would see rubber cling to an asperity, being stretched in the process, then letting go and snapping back to grip the next asperity, and so on. This is rather like what goes on as a cruise ship backs away from the pier – travellers extend their hands to those on the dock, holding on as long as the slow motion of the ship permits, then let go to grasp another friendly hand, and then another. This process of breaking local bonds, elastically snapping back when they are broken by the sliding motion, and forming new bonds does not happen instantly. It has a time constant that depends on an important property of the rubber – its internal damping or 'hysteresis'. This internal damping delays the snap-back of the rubber after a local bond is broken, and it also delays the motion of the rubber, being pressed downward by its load to fill in the hollows between asperities. The result is that it takes time for full grip to be established because it takes time for rubber – slowed by its own viscosity - to flow down among the asperities as far as it can under the prevailing load, establishing thereby its maximum total area of contact with the surface. This is why the static friction of rubber can be so very high, and is one reason among several as to why it is the perfect material for tyres.

Once rubber is forced to slide on pavement, some sliding speed will be high enough that there is no longer time for the sluggish material to fully invade the "valleys between the mountains" on the pavement's rough surface. By reducing the total area of actual contact, this reduces the grip. This reveals the mechanism of a high-side crash. The rider, accelerating hard out of a turn, overdoes the throttle by a tiny bit, causing the rear tyre to break loose and slide. The sliding takes place at reduced grip but, because the friction remains fairly high, the sliding velocity falls. When sliding slows enough for the rubber to again have time to fill the valleys between the mountains, grip rises sharply, sliding stops suddenly, and the bike's sideways momentum is near-instantly converted into a sharp rotation or 'flick' that throws the rider off.

What does this have to do with a possible grip increase with pulsating torque? As a motorcycle accelerates off a turn, its rear tyre must simultaneously transmit (1) cornering force to keep it turning and (2) driving force from the engine, to accelerate it. These two add to produce a net diagonal force. As the tyre rolls, the leading edge of its footprint has essentially no

stress on it as it is first laid down, but as the tyre rolls over a given tread element, stress on it rises, reaching a maximum somewhere near the trailing edge of the footprint. As a result, there is a steep stress gradient from the leading edge (zero stress) to somewhere near the trailing edge (maximum stress). This is an inefficient way to produce grip from the footprint because instead of stressing every element equally and maximally, the stress varies from zero to maximum and thus averages out to half or less of its whole potential.

Now consider the motorcycle accelerating off a turn, but with pulsating engine torque. During the low-torque part of the cycle, most of the stress on the tyre comes just from cornering, so it is oriented straight inward at the center of the turn circle. Because the bike is accelerating, it is not at maximum lean, so cornering stress is moderate. If the engine's firing interval is long enough, this may mean that the tyre has time to lay down a whole footprint of this low-stress type. Because little sliding is going on, the rubber has time to more fully fill in the valleys in the pavement profile, resulting in a large area of real contact.

Now the cylinders begin to fire, and torque rises, applying driving force to the tyre in addition to the cornering force it already feels. The footprint strongly resists being dragged across the pavement by the engine's torque pulse because:

(a) A very large area of true contact has been established, which is hard to break loose;

(b) This footprint, having been laid down with little stress, is ready to resist the engine's torque pulse almost equally over its whole area, rather than having a steep stress gradient across it, from zero stress at its leading edge to maximum stress near its trailing edge;

(c) The stress pattern and gradient already in the footprint as the torque pulse begins is oriented at right angles to the rising force from the torque pulse.

The low-stress footprint laid down between pulses can now have a large force applied to it without sliding because a larger, more uniform stress can be applied to all its elements.

As a result of these mechanisms, the footprint does not readily break loose and slide away, because just as it begins to do so, the engine's torque pulse begins to die away and a fresh, largely unstressed footprint begins to be laid down.

We can run one kind of rough plausibility check on the above by seeing how far apart are the firing impulses in terms of tyre advance. In lower gear the bike's speed is of the order of 100 feet per second (68-mph/75 kph), and at 10,000-rpm our close-firing-order 500-cc two-stroke engine is giving torque pulses 167 times per second. This means there will be a torque pulse every 100/167 foot of tyre advance, or about every seven inches (18-cm). This is roughly the length of one tyre footprint.

Close firing order is if anything made easier by the four-stroke cycle, since although four-strokes tend to rev somewhat higher than the 500 two-strokes they replace, they fire only one-half as often. Using an in-line four as our example, we can fire cylinders 1 and 4 together, then cylinders 2 and 3 together 180 degrees later, after which the engine will be silent for the remaining 540-degrees of its two-revolution, 720-degree cycle. If our four-stroke is turning 12,000 as we accelerate off a turn in lower gear, we have as above a notional speed of 100 feet per second but a pulsation frequency of 200 per second. This cuts our per-pulse tyre advance to 6 inches (150-mm), or roughly what we had before. Either way, the idea is at least plausible that Big Bang works by laying down a low-stress, high contact area footprint, then hitting it with a big torque pulse that dies away before the footprint is finally overstressed.

All this will be blurred by the fact that the torque pulses are not sharp but fuzzy, and torque almost certainly just oscillates above and below a mean value rather than dropping to zero between pulses. Everything gets complicated, but something like the above argument might have plausibility.

I won't blame anyone who finds all this arm-waving less than convincing. So do I, because what's missing are any hard facts. The argument is, as they say in Scots jurisprudence, "not proven". It will require the publication of actual scientific data as opposed to gas-bagging to support a plausible explanation that will fully define what happens in Big-Bang traction. But the above at least provides some means of thinking about the problem.

Will whoever has the real data please come forward and put the rest of us out of our collective misery?

Above: **Follow the stripes ... John Hopkins lays rubber at Valencia.**

Above left: **The point of contact; mixed-compound tyres, with a band of harder rubber in the centre, complicate the equation still further.**

Far left: **Yamaha's growler exhaust.**

Photographs: Gold & Goose

VAL THE IMPALER

THE NEW VALENTINO ROSSI

BY MICHAEL SCOTT

Main picture: Rossi broke long-standing barriers in 2004.

Bottom left: Elfin charm, or deep menace. Rossi could manage both.

Right: Rossi became one of a handful of riders to prove that the man is more important than the motorcycle.
Photographs: Gold & Goose

This racing season marked a transition in the life of Valentino Rossi. He moved from the hall of fame into the pantheon of the gods. There are many (especially those under 40) who believe he now outranks even Mike Hailwood, as the greatest motorcycle racer of all time. . .

GAULOISES
YAMAHA

46

KERAKOLL
46
YAMAHA

YAMAHA

Putting Rossi above Hailwood seems a bit premature. Rossi needs to distinguish himself also in car racing then return several years later to win ... well, perhaps not a TT, like Mike the Bike, but certainly a MotoGP race.

Nor has he yet equalled the feats of John Surtees, another multi-class two-wheel champion, who went on to win the F1 title. Knowing Rossi, who has already flirted impressively with a Ferrari at their private test track, this should not be ruled out.

But Rossi's step was still of huge significance – his stylish and commanding title victory on a bike no other rider could place higher than seventh overall was one for the history books. It's hard to imagine that any other rider might win it again next year. And hard to imagine that 2005 will be anything other than an anti-climax.

In the jubilant aftermath of his title win, Rossi admitted that they had just achieved a two-year plan in half that time, and that it would not be easy to find the same motivation in 2005. But he didn't anticipate anything like the slump in enthusiasm that marked the first half of his final year with Honda. "The target was for two years, to win the championship. We took only one year, but I will try to win it again next year," he said.

The rider, who turned 25 shortly before the start of the season, has pledged one more year after that. He will race on into 2006. MOTOCOURSE wonders whether his rivals can make it interesting enough for him to want to fulfil that promise.

There was another change in 2004; his outwardly rather childish and unsporting feud with Gibernau over the Qatar affair was one strong sign of it. There was a loss of innocence this season. The floppy-haired joker in the Robin Hood hat is a figure of a long-distant past.

Valentino's progress as the precociously talented son of former GP winner Graziano seemed until this year to have been blessed with innocence. Blessed also with good bikes, good teams, and a fine racing brain. In this way, with Rossano Brazzi at Aprilia then Jeremy Burgess at Honda, Rossi conquered the GP classes one by one – 125, then 250, 500, and MotoGP. He achieved it all with boyish charm intact, surviving the transition from a skinny androgynous teenager through all the hair-dye changes of the clowning years, into the adulthood of big bikes. And with the luck always somehow on his side.

Any illusions were shattered by his achievement in 2004. Even the post-race pantomimes now had a cutting edge of irony – the mocking brooming of the track at Australia, for instance. And his riding, his whole approach to racing, was both remorseless and inspired. This was a motorcycle racing giant, at full stretch.

Beyond the post-race pantomime and cheery on-camera waves, Valentino revealed himself as a staggeringly ferocious competitor, driven by a need to defeat his rivals that borders on the pathological. As he said, directly after that crucial maximum-risk final victory in Australia, where he could have let Gibernau have the race and still been champion: "I am racing against other riders, not against different kinds of motorbike."

And why would anyone want one of the greatest World Champions of all time to be any different?

Amazingly, however, a central core of Casual seems to have survived all the racing, and all the relentless pressures of a fame that far outstrips any of his predecessor World Champions. Rossi may be demonically driven, but he is not haunted by those demons, as happens to some riders. Perhaps that is because he has not yet met his match. Perhaps this search was the real single reason why he was driven to give his rivals a technical advantage in 2004.

The Rossi of 2004 was very different from the teenage 125 rider, forever underfoot in the paddock, certainly always courting the press. Blossoming fame reversed that equation several years ago. This year, encouraged by the lax terms they were able to negotiate with an eager-to-please Yamaha, Rossi's personal management team (still run by old family pal "Gibo" from the home town) introduced stringent and unprecedented conditions concerning access. In principal, each journalist got ten minutes, all year.

As it worked out, it wasn't quite that bad, and given the right approach Rossi was as lively and entertaining to talk to as ever. But interviews were conducted with PR personnel in close attendance, humming and ha-ing at any questions close to the bone. "Nothing about girls, religion, drugs or politics," MOTOCOURSE was injunctioned, only half-jokingly.

There were still other questions ... about Rossi's move to Yamaha. He'd already explained how he needed to boost his motivation, and reiterated: "To stay another year with Honda would have been a fight for me ... to work for something I had already done." Revenge against HRC, and their habit of valuing the machine more than the rider, had been a factor. Mainly, it was a desire to renew the challenge, a purely personal affair.

But there were crucial matters of timing, especially concerning the technical upgrade in the form of the new motor, which certainly made his task easier. Was the new motor a reason behind the switch?

"No. I didn't know about the engine when I decided to change. Only the next year, when we went to Malaysia for the first or second test." It was round about then that he had the first inkling that his two-year plan to turn the M1 into a title winner might be accomplished in half the time.

How crucial to the move was the presence of Jerry Burgess? Also not a key factor, he said. He and Yamaha had spoken during the year, and he had discussed the matter step by step with his crew chief. "I would have moved also without Jerry, but I wanted him. I wanted all the team. We spoke a lot, and I tried very hard to convince him," he said.

Could he have done it without the Australian's patient pragmatism, and clear-cut competitive motivation? "We'll never know. For sure Jerry is a great help, because of the relationship I have with him already. When you change the team, the bike, and all the guys that work with you ... in the end, maybe it's too much. It's enough to change the bike. So I fought to keep my team. All my team, because we had a great relationship.

"It was the same when I moved from Aprilia 250 to Honda 500, the big problem for me was I wanted to bring Rossano Brazzi with me (his former crew chief). And when I understood he would not come, it was difficult. But with Jerry, from the start I have a special relationship. Already we have been together four years. For me, it is important."

Rossi has brought to racing more than any other individual in recent years. The fact that sooner or later he will leave is a worrying prospect, for those whose love of bike racing is more concerned with TV viewing figures than what's occurring on the track. A great relief, however, to his competitors.

Racing his given him unprecedented earning power as well as unprecedented fame. In an age where many have done a great deal less than Valentino to achieve celebrity status, he is modern racing's first megastar. The personal cost has been high, forcing Valentino into a fugitive lifestyle at the tracks and in Italy. Even in his London refuge he is no longer perfectly safe.

MOTOCOURSE asked him if there was one thing he would change about his life. He gave his familiar spontaneous chuckle. "My face.

"It would be interesting to go around without Valentino Rossi, just like an ordinary person."

Not much chance of that. Especially after the 2004 racing season.

Above: Rossi's machine control is masterful.
Photograph: Malcolm Bryan/BPC

Opposite: In action at Rio... scene of one of his very rare race mistakes.

Insets, clockwise from top left: Valentino's ritual obeisance, practised every time he leaves the pits; Jerry Burgess, crucial ally; Rossi looks glazed after his hammering Malaysian win in the heat; mugging with childhood friend and companion Uccio; and getting ready for work.
Photographs: Gold & Goose

2004 TEAMS & RIDERS

MOTOGP: SMALL CHANGE, BIG DIFFERENCE

ONE man changed everything for 2004. When Valentino Rossi decided to abandon Honda and switch to Yamaha, the balance of power was altered, and the profile of the grid was redrawn.

For one thing, Yamaha's previous top rider took over the empty slot at Honda. To little avail, as it would turn out.

There were six Hondas on the 22-strong grid, one less than last year. Yamaha had also dropped one – just four M1s this year. Ducati took up the two slots: the satellite d'Antin team helping them fulfil their promise to have more than just two factory bikes on the grid ... as in World Superbikes. The remaining ten runners were made up of two-bike teams: Aprilia, Kawasaki, Proton KR, Suzuki and WCM.

As well as the minor but significant rider reshuffles, there were changes in the crucial matter of tyres also. Bridgestone revised and extended their operation. In 2003, they had supplied only Tamada's Pramac Honda team, and Proton Team KR. At the end of last season, they dropped the latter to join up with the two lesser Japanese factory teams ... Kawasaki and Suzuki.

With almost everybody else on Michelins, the French tyre company was unable to supply Kenny Roberts's Malaysian-backed team. In a classic case of Hobson's choice, they took over the Dunlops happily abandoned by Kawasaki. WCM also ran the least favoured tyre brand.

HONDA

After earlier saying they would have six equal machines on the grid, HRC affirmed that in fact the Repsol Honda team would, according to contract, be the official factory squad, first to be be favoured with development parts. They pledged that they would keep the satellite teams supplied with the most up to date equipment possible, and by and large they made good on this promise, with some exceptions.

The six-strong fleet gave Honda strength in numbers. The risk of such a strategy is that too many strong riders take points away from one another, allowing a lone star to defeat them all. In precisely this way, Honda were to lose the riders' title, but win the constructors'.

The principal team, operating out of HRC's traditional Belgian base, was almost as traditionally Repsol sponsored. Rossi's place was taken by Alex Barros; Nicky Hayden remained on the other side of the garage.

Barros, the man with the best job in racing, was 33 at the start of the season, third-oldest behind McWilliams and Bayliss on a grid with an average age of 25.8. The Brazilian veteran of 225 GP starts (next up Capirossi on 200) was fresh from a crash-happy year of pain and problems on the M1 Yamaha, and also from surgery on a long-lasting shoulder injury. Now he was back on the Honda four-stroke which he had raced four times in 2002, to two wins and two more rostrums. It should have been an auspicious union, but his physical condition at the start of the year was a poor omen.

Nicky Hayden (22 – only Fabrizio, Hopkins and Melandri were younger) was his team-mate, the popular Kentucky rider in his second year on a full factory Honda. Nicky had impressed especially towards the end of the previous season. More progress was expected this year from the friendly down-home youngster, former American champion.

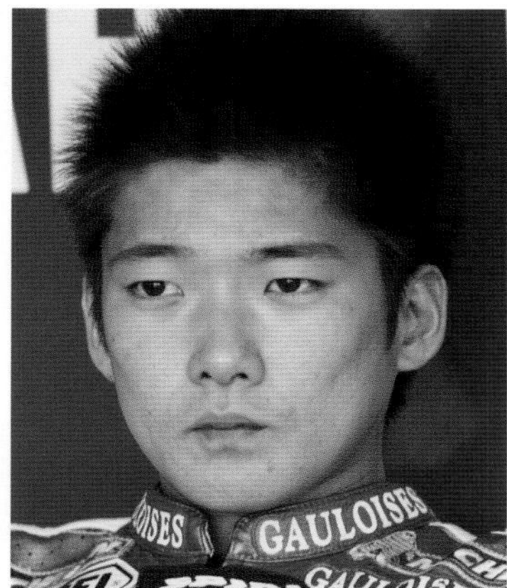

Two satellite teams – Telefónica MoviStar Gresini and Camel Honda Pons – each fielded two riders.

Based in Italy, the Telefónica team was part of ex-125 champion Fausto Gresini's growing empire (including also the 250 "Junior" team). They retained Sete Gibernau, who last year had finished second overall, helping the team recover from the loss of Daijiro Kato. Gibernau (31) was in his eighth top-class season, in a career that had accumulated momentum steadily.

Gresini's second rider was of a status to challenge the incumbent star ... double Superbike champion Colin Edwards (30), fresh from a difficult first MotoGP season on the Aprilia, and raring to be back on a Honda. Many favoured him to emerge as the senior rider.

The Camel team was a mish-mash, really two teams in one. Max Biaggi (32) and Makoto Tamada (27) ran out of the same pit in the same colours, but were independent to a large degree, not least in using different tyres .... Biaggi on Michelin, Tamada on Bridgestone. This complex deal allowed Pramac to retain a grid spot (in 2003 they leased one from d'Antin), as well as finding a place for Biaggi, contracted to Pramac rather than Pons or HRC.

Biaggi brought experience – four 250 titles and six years in the top class, with 12 wins. Tamada offered slightly more youthful aggression. By this and other contrasts, the two near-team-mates would remain friendly all year long.

YAMAHA

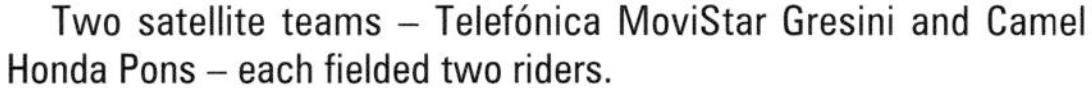

With four M1s, Yamaha had dropped numbers by one compared with the previous year, but had gained a great deal more, both in terms of the factory's own focus and commitment – and the consequent highly effective new engine configuration, and even more in terms of riding strength. Now they had the best of them all.

Sponsorship arrangements were another mish-mash, at least to the eye. The same tobacco firm, Altadis, backed both the two-man official factory team, now based in Italy, and the France-based Tech 3 satellite team. But complex national marketing considerations meant that each team ran one rider in Gauloises colours and the other in Fortuna. Team-mates did not look the same.

The factory bikes went of course to prize new signing Valentino Rossi (25), fresh from a hat-trick of top-class titles on both two- and four-stroke Hondas, and a remarkable top-class win rate of better than 50 percent: 33 wins from 64 500cc/MotoGP starts. Rossi ran a blue Gauloises bike, and had brought most of his Honda pit crew with him, most crucially the veteran chief Jeremy "Jerry" Burgess. Right from the first pre-season tests, Rossi showed he would far outclass all the other Yamaha riders.

His factory team-mate was Carlos Checa (31), in his sixth year with Yamaha, with his identical factory machine in the red-and-silver of Spanish cigarette brand Fortuna. Checa's record of 124 top-class starts equalled Rossi's total in three classes, but had yielded only two wins. His status with the sponsors seemed his strongest asset.

The Poncharal-run Tech 3 team had similarly liveried bikes, one rung down the ladder – although both riders had at least one of the new revised-firing-interval machines in time for the first race. The Fortuna-painted bike went to ex-250 champion Marco Melandri (21), demoted from the factory squad after a first year plagued by injury and crashes.

The second, in blue Gauloises colours, went to a most surprising choice, dictated by the factory: veteran Norick Abe (28), back after a year as a race-department tester. His popularity in the Far East was a factor in choosing him rather than pressing to keep Nakano.

Opposite page (top to bottom): Honda's seasoned troops, Max Biaggi, Alex Barros and Sete Gibernau.

Opposite bottom: The same trio in action, Gibernau from Barros and Biaggi.

This page, left hand column, from top: Colin Edwards, Nicky Hayden and Makoto Tamada – more Honda talent.

This page, clockwise from top centre: One-man army? Valentino Rossi, Norick Abe, Carlos Checa and Marco Melandri made up Yamaha's troops.

All photographs: Gold & Goose

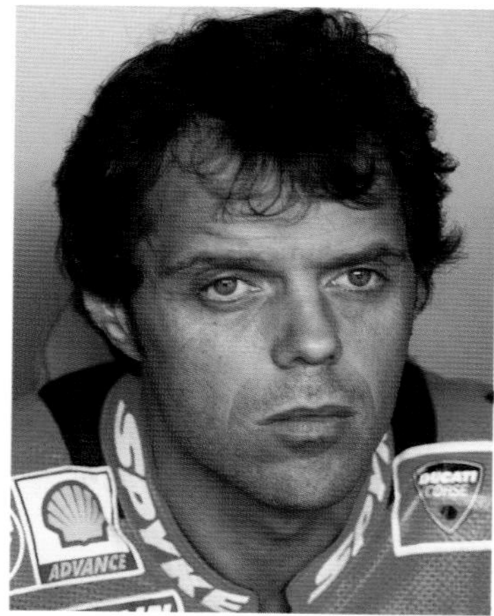

Above, from top: Loris Capirossi and Troy Bayliss were back on the factory Ducatis; Shinya Nakano was Kawasaki's new boy.

Right: Aprilia regular Jeremy McWilliams (top left) was joined by Garry McCoy (top right) at year's end, after Shane Byrne (bottom right) was injured.

Below right: Alex Hofmann went from Kawasaki tester to MotoGP full-timer.

Photographs: Gold & Goose

DUCATI MARLBORO TEAM

After their fine race-winning debut in 2004, Ducati were back with the same red-painted Marlboro bikes, the same pair of riders and essentially the same team as the year before. Only the machines were different. Crucially so.

The winner last year was all-Italian old favourite Loris Capirossi (31), a veteran of 200 starts, though only 89 (and three wins) in the biggest class. He had won titles on 125s and in 250, but though a frequent front-runner had not scaled the heights in MotoGP.

Alongside him Troy Bayliss, the archetypal Aussie battler, starting his second GP season at the age of 35. A fine Superbike champion, Bayliss had hardly been far behind Capirossi the previous year, and the late starter still had the press-on style of a teenager, in spite of his relatively advanced age.

Ducati's first satellite team came from left field ... the independent Spanish-based d'Antin squad, which last year ran Nakano on a Yamaha. Still hunting for significant sponsorship at the end of the year, it was a shoestring effort on year-old bikes. Even so, they would now and then beat the big-budget factory team.

As well as the machines, Ducati also provided the riders, in a manner of speaking. They were Superbike team-mates from the factory squad of the previous year. Neil Hodgson (30) had won that title; Ruben Xaus (26) had finished second.

It was a GP return for Hodgson, who campaigned a 125 in 1993, then as a 500-class privateer, before a tortuous career path that had led eventually to British and World Superbike championships. Xaus was a GP rookie, seeing many of the tracks for the first time.

APRILIA

The other Italian factory had plans for a step forward, but by the time the season was under way they were becoming increasingly hamstrung by the parent company's deepening financial crisis. They ended the year uncertain as to whether they would still have a team next year.

In the interim, they had shelved plans to introduce the Mk2 "Cube" (though they continued testing the prototype), leaving their two new riders struggling with what improvements could be wrought to the fast-but-wayward Mk1 machine, still wearing MS (cigarettes) livery.

Both riders were British. Jeremy McWilliams (40), old man of the paddock, came from two years with Proton Team KR, unwilling to stay when that team lost the chance of Bridgestone or Michelin tyres. An old Aprilia factory associate in his 250 days, he was expecting that although not ready to retire, this might be his last GP season.

The second recruit was wide-eyed Kentishman Shane "Shakey" Byrne, winner of the BSB title the previous year, and at 27 the oldest of four class rookies. Byrne would go to a difficult task with a will, but injuries to this gamest of riders saw him sitting out a number rounds. His replacement was the popular Australian Garry McCoy (31) who fitted in around his World Superbike committments.

KAWASAKI RACING TEAM

Reconstituted in terms of machinery, tyres and riders, former 250 GP racer Harald Eckl's Fuchs Kawasaki squad had taken advantage of Yamaha's lack of commitment to Shinya Nakano, snapping up the Japanese rider, in his fourth top-class season, and still only 26. The least-favoured factory bike of 2003 would seem to be an odd choice for a rider of his stature, but it turned out to be far-sighted and fruitful.

His team-mate was last year's test rider and sometime wild card entry Alex Hofmann (23), carrying the hopes of his nation as well as his Germany-based team, as the sole German in the class. A somewhat experienced rookie, Hofmann had nine class starts as well as four 250 years to his credit.

PROTON KR

The only true independent manufacturer in racing came out the losers in the close-season tyre shuffle. Dismayed at being informed by Bridgestone, after two years as development partners, that they would no longer be supplied, the team tried and failed to secure Michelins. In the end, it was Hobson's choice, and the England-based squad put a brave face on their task of developing tyres with Dunlop.

This process took some time and delayed rider choices. But they retained faithful rider Nobuatsu Aoki (32) for a third season, giving continuity to the V5 programme.

The second slot went to team principal Kenny Roberts's second son Kurtis (25), fresh from his first race wins in the AMA Superbike series. He would face a tough class rookie season, although at least vaguely familiar with some tracks, after racing an interrupted 250 year in 1997. Unfortunately for Kurtis injuries blighted his year and the experienced Brit James Haydon (30) stepped up from British Superbikes to deputise.

TEAM SUZUKI

Both Suzuki's 2003 riders were still under contract, 2000 World Champion Kenny Roberts Jr. for his sixth year with the team. At 30, Roberts had endured three bad seasons since his title win, but in between complaining of a lack of development continued to iterate his commitment to the team.

Team-mate John Hopkins (20), born in the USA to English parents, was in his third GP season, showing a promising combination of racing spirit and talent. His season started badly, after he broke both ankles in a Supercross crash in January. He missed most of the testing, and would require more surgery at the far end of the season.

Replacements for 'Hopper' included the Suzuki stalwarts Gregorio Lavilla (30) and Yukio Kagayama (29).

All riders were hampered by the GSV-R's shortcomings, though even before the season there were signs of more fruitful developments that would continue through the year.

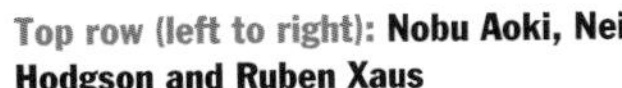

Top row (left to right): Nobu Aoki, Neil Hodgson and Ruben Xaus

Centre row (left to right): Kurtis and Kenny Roberts, John Hopkins

Below (left to right): Proton substitute James Haydon, and WCM part-timer David de Gea and James Ellison, and early quitter Michel Fabrizio.

Photographs: Gold & Goose

WCM

The smallest team's greatest strength was for survival, as they came back after a year of serial disqualification before they could finally get their R1-based MotoGP machine to comply with the letter of the prototype law, if not the spirit.

Now based in Belgium, lacking significant sponsorship, WCM returned British hopeful Chris Burns (23) for a second year. Their second rider was to be something of a revelation, but European Superstock champion Michel Fabrizio (19, from Italy) did not see out the season, ending it in dispute over his contract, and was replaced by British Superbike series privateer James Ellison (23). Other riders to don the blue and silver leathers were Spaniard David de Gea, and the diminuitive one-time Japanese 125cc winner Youichi Ui.

Moriwaki

Japanese race engineering firm Moriwaki again enjoyed HRC backing, with V5 RC211V engines for their heretical steel tube chassis. The other difference was to be the only Honda on Dunlop tyres. They ran a handful of wild card entries, with Andrew Pitt (28), replaced at year's end by Olivier Jacque (30) ... former World Champions both.

Above: Youichi Ui finished the year on the WCM.

Left: British racer Chris Burns and Moriwaki part-timers Olivier Jacque (above centre) Andrew Pitt (left).

Photographs: Gold & Goose

250cc: NEW BLOOD AT THE TOP

The 250 class continued on the path followed for the past few years – some interest from Honda, with four riders on factory-supported machines, a couple of Yamahas fighting a rearguard action without serious development and factory commitment. And the bulk of the field made up by Aprilias, ranging from five full factory machines to an assortment of mix-and-match private bikes. As always, there was room for a bewildering confection of chassis and engine combinations in both factory and private machines.

The rider pool had been stirred by a more-or-less straight swap of riders; Elias from Aprilia to Honda, and vice versa for Porto. It was also refreshed by high-level rookies: Pedrosa, Arnaud Vincent and de Angelis up from 125s; Aoyama from the All-Japan series.

The pace was to be fast for the year, but the racing rather spread out once again. At year's end, however, came the promise of a fresh wave of young talent from 125s – Dovizioso, Barbera, Lorenzo and Stoner all to move to 250s.

HONDA

Honda's RS250R-W (for works) is as close as they now get to a full factory 250, though nominally just a development version of the stock machine. There were four of these, with two major teams.

In the blue corner, the Telefónica MoviStar Honda team, with two class rookies. One of them was of a special calibre: Spaniard Dani Pedrosa (18) was on stage two of a carefully mapped career path, and fresh from a dominant 125-class title. His ever-present mentor Alberto Puig oversaw his side of things; Gresini Racing ran the team. Pedrosa switched early in the year from the latest version of the chassis, with full-floater rear suspension like the MotoGP bike, back to last year's chassis.

The second rider was rising Japanese star Hiroshi Aoyama (22), six times a domestic wild card with a best of second at Suzuka last year.

Fortuna also had a two-rider team. Much was expected of breakaway Spaniard Toni Elias (21), who had turned his back on the Telefónica fold and now also had left Repsol Aprilia for a factory Honda. His team-mate, in his second year, was Roberto Rolfo (24), runner up last year.

Honda's inroads into Aprilia's market were limited to four production-level machines (RS250R), Spaniard Alex Debon (28) and Andorra-based Eric Bataille (22) rode for the Wurth team; German Christian Gemmel (23) for Castrol Honda; and Czech rider Jakub Smrz (21) for Team Molenaar.

Top: Renewed rivalry between former 125 foes Toni Elias (left) and Dani Pedrosa (right).

Above centre: Roberto Rolfo, a second Honda season.

Above: Spain's Eric Bataille was a Honda privateer.

Right: Fast rookie Hiroshi Aoyama.

Far right: Alex Debon, also on a private Honda.

Photographs: Gold & Goose

Top row, from left: **Fonsi Nieto, Randy de Puniet and Manuel Poggiali.**

Centre row, from left: **Sebastian Porto, Alex de Angelis, Chaz Davies.**

Below centre: **Returnee Johan Stigefelt.**
Photographs: Gold & Goose

APRILIA

Heavily dominant in numbers, the Aprilias spanned the grid in terms of quality.

Even among the five factory machines, there was a pecking order. The factory team, sponsored again by MS, fielded just one rider, defending champion Manuel Poggiali (21), in his second season in the class. The San Marino youth was set for an extraordinarily disappointing season.

Team Repsol-Aspar had two factory machines, for Argentine ex-Honda turncoat Sebastian Porto (25), who had changed places with Elias. Porto was starting his tenth season in the class, and with 123 starts was by far the most experienced rider.

The second was for regular team member, Spaniard Fonsi Nieto (25, nephew of Angel), his sixth year in the class. Fonsi also preferred to switch back to older parts, racing a 2003/4 hybrid. The team was run by former 80cc and 125cc multi-champion Jorge Martinez.

Another factory bike was for French would-be-star Randy de Puniet (23), after three wins last year, his third in the class. He was the only rider in the newly retired 125 racer Lucio Cecchinello's Safilo LCR team.

The final works-bike beneficiary was Alex de Angelis (20), also from San Marino, and another rising star fresh from 125s.

The next level was a grey area, though several riders had ex-factory motors and/or chassis of varying vintages. Prominent among them Campatella riders Franco Battaini (31 – Italian veteran of more than 100 starts) and Frenchman Sylvain Guintoli (21), with third Spanish team-mate Joan Olive (19) taking the leftovers.

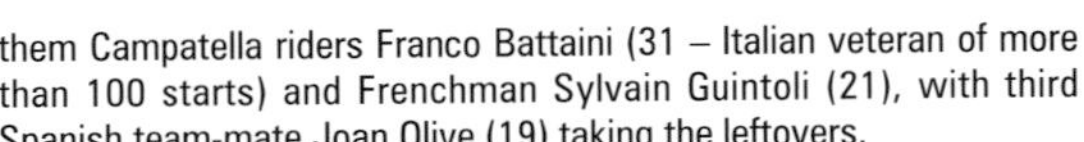

GP winner Anthony West (22) had a similar machine to Battaini, the Australian again in the Freesoul Abruzzo team; his team-mate was third-year Frenchman Hugo Marchand (22).

The Aprilia Germany team retained the very promising Welsh youngster Chaz Davies (17) for his second 250 season, joined for another try by Swedish racer Johan Stigefelt (28). France's Scrab team ran former 125 champion Arnaud Vincent (29) as a class rookie, and 24-year-old compatriot Gregory Lefort, also new in the class.

Italian Alex Baldolini (19) was with Matteoni Racing for a second season; the Grefusa-Aspar team ran German Dirk Heidolf (27) and Spaniard Hector Faubel (20), making up the total Aprilia strength of 17.

YAMAHA

Two teams and four riders made up the Yamaha contingent. Old faithful Naoki Matsudo (30), from Japan was starting his eighth year on the machine, still awaiting a first race win. His team-mate in the UGT Kurz squad was Erwan Nigon (20) from France, in his third year.

Diminutive Italian Max Sabbatani (28) making his class debut after a career in 125s; and Japan's Taro Sekiguchi (28) rode for the NC World Trade team, the latter for a second year.

Above: **Yamaha man Taro Sekiguchi.**

Bottom left: **Australian Anthony West.**

Left: **Veteran Naoki Matsudo.**
Photographs: Gold & Goose

125cc: YOUTH VERSUS EXPERIENCE, THE LAST SHOWDOWN

Top: Hector Barbera – a fast Aprilia.

Above centre: The Godfather – Roberto Locatelli.

Above: Finn Vesa Kallio.

Above right: Pablo Nieto, son of Angel.

Right: Alvaro Bautista, rising Spaniard.
Photographs: Gold & Goose

A grid numbering 34 was the most volatile of the year, with six different manufacturers – Aprilia, Honda, Derbi, Gilera, KTM and Malaguti – almost as many as MotoGP, though Derbi and Gilera were only nominally different.

Aprilia dominated the 34 entries on numbers, with the same tally as in the 250 class at 17. Nine more rode Hondas, the others had two bikes each. Only the two-bike teams were classified as factory entries. Neither Aprilia nor Honda support factory machines. However, in both cases a system of patronage means that top riders get considerably better equipment than the lowlier privateers.

The youthful bias of the class was reflected in an average age of 21.11 (25.8 for MotoGP, 23.4 for 250). Next year the profile will be even younger, with a maximum age of 28. This made 2004 the last chance for several fast riders, including Locatelli, Jenkner, Borsoi, Giansanti and Perugini.

Italian was the most widely spoken language on the grid, with 13 riders, eight more from Spain, and no more than two each for any other country. Only one spoke English – Australian Casey Stoner.

APRILIA

Italian patronage meant that returned 29-year-old former champion Roberto Locatelli (KTM last year) had special parts for his machine, entered by the Cecchinello team; although fellow-Italian team-mate Mateo Pasini (18) did not.

Of the following notable Aprilia riders, several also had various degrees of help.

The Seedorf team, owned by Dutch footballer Clarence, was back for a second and more serious year, this time with rising Spaniard Hector Barbera (17) and likewise promising compatriot Alvaro Bautista (19), the former with a notably fast machine.

Pablo Nieto (23, son of Angel) was back with a Repsol-backed effort. Former East German Steve Jenkner (27) was also on an Aprilia once more, for a last season, teamed in the Rauch Bravo squad with Marco Simoncelli (17), the Italian's second full season.

Veteran Gino Borsoi (30) was teamed with fellow-Italian Mike di Meglio, in his second season at 16, in the Globet team. Finn Vesa Kallio (23, Mika's older brother) joined the class, teamed with third-year Hungarian Imre Toth (18) in a Hungarian team. Mirko Giansanti (27) rode for the Matteoni team.

HONDA

Notable Honda riders were led in importance and in factory favour by Italian Andrea Dovizioso (18). The Team Scot rider had access to the machine on which Pedrosa won the title the previous year. The chassis was the biggest difference, after he switched to a longer version at the start of the year. That plus the engine marked him out for special favour.

His team-mate was old mini-bike rival and compatriot Simone Corsi (16).

Spaniard Julian Simon (17) was back for a second full year, likewise promising Swiss teenager Thomas Luthi (17).

FACTORY TEAMS

The bright orange KTMs were back after a promising first season, and had taken over bright hope (though frequent crasher) Casey Stoner (18). The second rider, Finn Mika Kallio (21) had joined them halfway through the previous season.

Malaguti's second year team was headed by Gabor Talmacsi (22), the Hungarian's fourth season in the class. He was joined by Italian rookie Manuel Manna (20).

Gilera had the services of the most experienced rider on the grid, Stefano Perugini (29), with 135 starts to Locatelli's 131. He was teamed with fellow-Italian Fabrizio Lai (25), in his second season.

The differently named but identically powered Derbis were ridden again by rising Spanish star Jorge Lorenzo (16), teamed with compatriot Angel Rodriguez (18).

Left: **Bound for glory, Andrea Dovizioso.**

Below: **Derbi duo Jorge Lorenzo (left) and Angel Rodriguez.**

Photographs: Gold & Goose

Above: **Marco Simoncelli.**

Left: **KTM pair Casey Stoner (left) and Mika Kallio.**

Bottom row, from left: **Aprilia rider Jordi Carchano, Stefano Perugini and Simone Corsi.**

Photographs: Gold & Goose

GRANDS PRIX 2004

SOUTH AFRICAN GP 52
SPANISH GP 58
FRENCH GP 64
ITALIAN GP 70
CATALAN GP 76
DUTCH TT 82
RIO GP 88
GERMAN GP 94
BRITISH GP 100
CZECH REPUBLIC GP 106
PORTUGUESE GP 112
JAPANESE GP 118
QATAR GP 124
MALAYSIAN GP 130
AUSTRALIAN GP 136
VALENCIA GP 142

Photograph: Gold & Goose

BIAGGI
SUOMY
SUOMY
SHIMANO
SHIMANO
CORREOS
TEAM
Honda
BIAGGI
CORREOS
HONDA
PRAMAC
3
BIAGGI
HONDA
BIAGGI
BIAGGI
TEAM
Honda

FIM WORLD CHAMPIONSHIP • ROUND 1

SOUTH AFRICAN GP

WELKOM

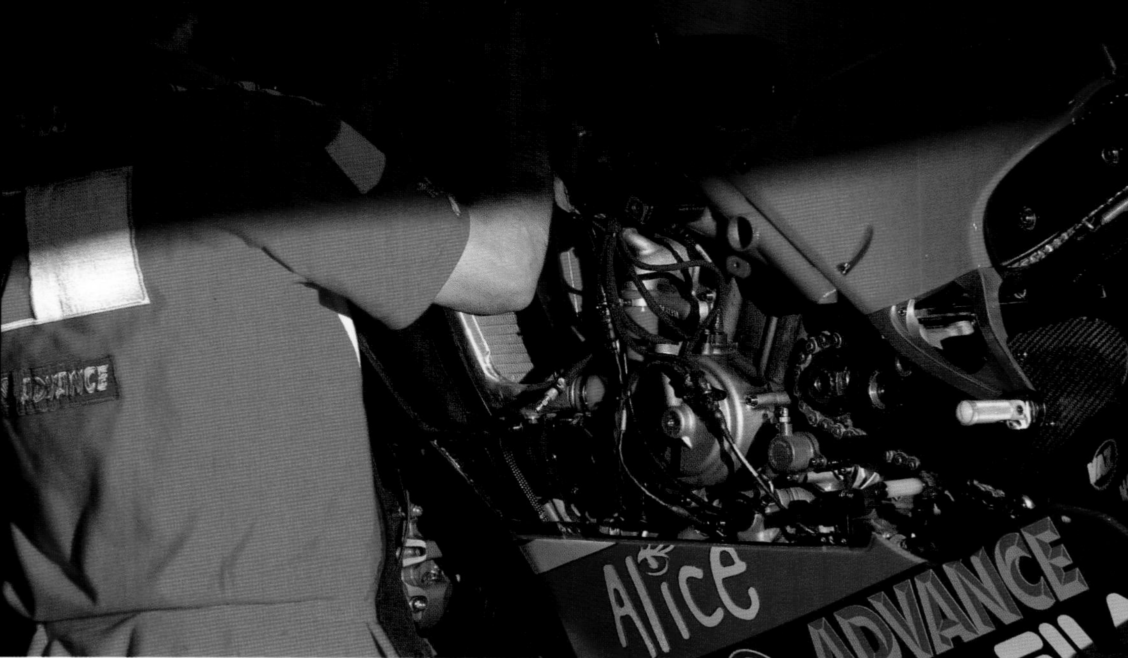

Main picture: "And then I changed to second gear ..." Eyes shining after his greatest ever victory, Rossi recounts his race to avid Italian pressmen.

Far left: Jerry Burgess, Rossi's invaluable ally in a historic feat.

Left: On the limit from flag to flag, Rossi narrowly heads the Hondas. Biaggi would fight to the bitter end; Gibernau (here third) couldn't match their pace.

Right: Red is the colour, but Ducati had the New Bike Blues.

Photographs: Gold & Goose

WITH Suzuka awaiting "safety improvements" that may never come, South Africa started the year for the first time since 1985... but this race too was under sentence of death. Built by the provincial government for the first race in 1999, and with the would-be grandiose banked section still awaiting serious use (except as a handy motorcycle escape road), the Phakisa Raceway hadn't so much run out of optimism or cash as political support. This, we learned even before arrival, was going to be the last South African GP. This lent a funereal feel to what was conversely the start of a new era.

This is a fun track, despite the bumps and the power-sapping high altitude and the local hospitality had a special feel, as well as a special hugely inflated price for foreigners. Nowhere else, apart from Japan itself, do earth tremors add a shaky edge to GP racing and nowhere do the barbecues or the clear night skies compare. By the end of the weekend, this had changed - nothing to do with the best-ever 45,000-strong crowd, but entirely local political shifts making the return of the race a distinct possibility.

Whether swan song or just a nervous tremor like those that from time to time shake the mine-shaft-riddled ground, this was a monumental event that will live on in the memory and in racing history. Valentino Rossi made it so. Among other facets, he was the first rider in history to win back-to-back GPs on different makes of machine.

The newly introduced mid-winter testing ban had further heated already feverish pre-season speculation, as racing contemplated both Rossi's short- and long-term futures. Most felt that the crash-happy M1 Yamaha would prove a tough nut even for him and Jerry Burgess. Not impossible, but taking a little time.

Rossi's early testing lap times in Malaysia and Australia had been impressively on the pace, but, well, you'd expect that, wouldn't you? Then, the formally timed Spanish group IRTA tests were hit by adverse weather and were therefore inconclusive; but when the chips were down and a prize was on the table (a BMW Z3 for the best of a special timed session), Rossi had come up with the goods. That was impressive. Again, that was Rossi.

What was new was the obvious strength of Yamaha's level of commitment, quite clearly expressed in the 2004 M1's growling exhaust note. The crucial details of crankshaft retiming remained shrouded in thought-provoking secrecy. Though Yamaha did admit that this year's M1, outwardly a close relative of last year's, had abandoned the company's pet five-valve configuration for racing-conventional four-valve - echoing a similar switch in Yamaha's F1 days, and itself a sign of a new approach. This time round, the engineers had been given the upper hand over the marketing department.

At first, the engine had been only for Rossi, he tested old and new back to back in Malaysia. There had never been any question which he preferred. Checa had to wait until the final tests, where he found "it's as though you're using a higher gear everywhere". Only now did satellite-team riders Melandri and Abe get the new Growler, although only one apiece. Which, needless to say, each rider infinitely preferred.

Yamaha's enthusiasm had not just appeared over the winter but over the past year or more. Honda had responded, said project leader Shogo Kanaumi in an unrevealing but immensely cheerful briefing, with electronics (including refined switchable traction control programmes), and by elevating the rev ceiling "about three percent". This made it around 16,000rpm, liberating power without compromising service life, he said. In its third season, the RCV still had potential to spare, and remained the best-balanced package.

An inverted design for the concertina rear suspension put the major mechanism at the top. This further improved the centralisation of mass, but gave the riders a problem. The latest swing-arm had arrived only for the weather-hit IRTA tests, and they lacked testing and set-up experience. Tamada and Edwards decided to stick with the familiar 2003 chassis as a result.

Ducati were in a not unfamiliar condition from their Superbike experiences: they had the New Bike Blues. We shall return to their plight.

Aprilia had all-new riders, but not the expected all-new bike as promised. The feisty Cube had supposedly been tamed, but still dangled too loosely on its fly-by-wire management as new rider McWilliams found, especially in its reluctance to shut off promptly for corners. New team-mate Shaky Byrne, green and keen, was having fun, impressively fast and taking a point in his first GP.

Suzuki and their commercial (if not racing) partners Kawasaki had both muddied the waters of their changes by signing up with Bridgestone, still something of an unknown quantity in their third year in the class. They had a few strong runs with Tamada last year, but Michelin (as we shall see) remained a moving target. But there was also the thought that Suzuki (whose best qualifying lap time improved by just under one percent) might have masked their own improvement by the switch from Michelin to Bridgestone, while Kawasaki (with a leap of almost two percent) might have flattered theirs by the move from Dunlop to Bridgestone.

In each case, the improvement had come from making their bikes more like motorbikes. Suzuki, with new man Masahito Imada in charge since the previous July, had fined up the chassis and backed off the electronics, and had engine revisions coming, including a revised-firing-order engine to be tested after the next round in Jerez. Kawasaki had already embarked on their forward path last year, with the compact Eskil Suter-designed chassis, and detail engine revisions, especially to mapping.

But, as ever, Michelin set a moving target. Two moving targets. At the rear a larger-then-ever slick, up front a grippier and quicker-turning 16.5-inch front to match. This saved weight for more or less the same contact patch and rolling diameter, but gave the tyre engineers more rubber to play with. And, said first-time rider Nicky Hayden, "gives you more confidence into the corner, especially when you're trail-braking the rear."

But for one of the size's pioneers, Michelin tester Colin Edwards - who used the 16.5 last year on the Aprilia and previously in Superbikes - the new front was just dandy, but the new rear pushed him into serious, eyeball-shaking chatter problems that half-the-year later would not be completely resolved.

Kurtis Roberts had a reverse-gear debut, after dislocating his right shoulder in his first outing on the new Proton chassis and Dunlop tyres in Valencia. The shakes and swerves of Welkom were simply too much for his still-weak shoulder, and he flew home early after pulling out of practice.

The paddock was saddened by the news that renowned and highly successful Barcelona engineer Antonio Cobas had succumbed two days before practice began, to the brain tumour that cut his career short suddenly the previous season. A stalwart of Team Pons, Cobas had been a valuable asset also to Honda, and an influential chassis designer credited with the first refinement of the now almost universal twin-spar design.

He would have been pleased to see that his influence on racing continued to contribute to ever-higher standards, better performance, faster lap times, and ever-improving understanding. In all classes, race averages were faster than last year, by 0.38 and 0.50 percent in the 250 and 125 classes, and a highly respectable 0.76 percent in MotoGP.

Below: Watch your back! Superbike champion Hodgson faced his GP return with the d'Antin team as a lone Lancastrian Rose in Spanish Harlem.

Below right: Hopkins in repose.

Bottom right: Shakey Byrne: green but keen.

Bottom: Abe is coming through the other Yamahas. He trails Melandri (33), Kawasaki new rider Nakano (56) in his wake, soon to succumb to Checa.

Photographs: Gold & Goose

MOTOGP RACE – 28 laps

Qualifying was a fitting climax to the waiting. Rossi had led day one, then came the final flurry, the last ten minutes, when everybody fitted soft tyres and showed their last cards. To the surprise of none more than his Kawasaki pit, Nakano was first to head the list. Biaggi was the next to go fastest, followed by Gibernau, then Hayden. Then came Rossi, straight to the top, followed by an even faster lap. His pole was just 35 hundredths ahead of last year's winner Gibernau, while Biaggi was alongside.

The new three-by-three grid formation saw Hayden dropped to the second row. There were dire predictions that the artificially spread field would bunch into the first tight corner, the back rows telescoping to disaster. Among those considered at risk was a puzzled and puzzling Bayliss, 21st to team-mate Capirossi's ninth, and faster only than the WCM of rookie Fabrizio at the track where last year he fought with Rossi up at the front.

There was a bit of a muddle at the back into Turn One, Ruben Xaus making an early impression in the thick of it... but nothing ter-

minal as Rossi took the early lead from Gibernau, ousted by Biaggi by the back straight. The yellow Honda proceeded to lean on Rossi, a process he was to continue for most of the race... to little avail. He was faster onto the back straight and along it, but Rossi was both braver at the end of that straight, and quicker through the tight final turns. Biaggi, he said later, had chatter there.

By lap four the leading trio had made a little ground on the pursuit (Hayden, Melandri, Edwards, Roberts and Capirossi at the end of lap one, Barros closing up), and now they had a minor skirmish, Biaggi nosing briefly into the lead then dropping just as briefly to third as Rossi and Gibernau pushed straight back ahead.

We had seen some strong rides from Rossi on the Honda, notably his fightback from the gravel in Catalunya and from a yellow-flag infringement in Australia, but neither was a patch on this. He was right on the limit, Biaggi looking smooth and comfortable by comparison. Rossi would continue to ride at the same pitch for the rest of the season - hopping under braking, sliding under power, out of the seat more often than since his days as a bold 125 learner. The display was never more magnificent than today.

After half distance, Gibernau's pursuit turned from waiting game to follow-my-leader, he was always close but never threatening for the front, later complaining of a lack of set-up time for the new chassis and swing-arm, supplied only in time for wet-stricken IRTA tests.

Biaggi moved with six laps to go. Inches behind on the preceding to-and-fro, he flew past Rossi down the back straight for a second time, and now managed to keep his advantage round the last corners. For three laps he worked at breaking away - but now it was obvious he too was right on the limit, running wide, and sliding everywhere. He was never as much as half-a-second ahead over the line.

With three laps left, Rossi replied, with a firm block pass into the last tight right, the penultimate corner. His efforts to break free were no more successful than Biaggi's. Rossi was just three tenths ahead at the start of the last lap. Biaggi gave it everything, and set a new record in the attempt. Rossi was just one tenth slower, and two tenths ahead at the end.

The tension was extraordinary, the win historic. There were no chicken costumes or doctor antics for Rossi this time. Instead, he parked his bike by the rail, kissed it, then crunched down, shoulders shaking with emotion. This was something quite new. He knew at once it was his greatest race so far in 60 GP wins.

The sideshow? They lost touch from lap four, Hayden still in front; Edwards "riding out of my skin" with the chatter to stay with him. Then came Melandri, with Capirossi and Barros closing behind, both passing Roberts. After two more laps, the Suzuki was out... for a strange reason. An "electrical problem" had been triggered when Roberts knocked the kill switch while trying to change the engine mapping, and the engine then declined to restart.

By now Capirossi and Barros had disposed of Melandri; before half distance Barros was ahead and closing on Edwards, hanging grimly onto Hayden. The official top Honda rider passed both in one lap.

Capirossi also passed Edwards with four laps to go, but Hayden just escaped the same fate at the flag. Tamada moved through to finish eight seconds behind Edwards; Abe and Checa were pushing him hard to the end, Melandri dropping back. Melandri had been with this group, but was still inches behind Checa over the line.

Hopkins was another 12 seconds away, then Bayliss, Byrne, McWilliams and Aoki's Proton. Fabrizio stopped for a tyre change on the Dunlop-shod WCM, finishing three laps down. Xaus had pitted after four spirited laps; Hodgson also retiring from the points after half distance. Hofmann crashed out after half-distance.

Above: All elbows and aggression, Rossi leads Gibernau, Biaggi and the rest on the first lap.
Photograph: Gold & Goose

Right: Reigning champion and precocious challenger. Dani Pedrosa (right) scored a debut win; Manuel Poggiali (left) missed the rostrum at the start of a dismal title defence.

Below: The leader's pace stretched the pursuit ... as would happen most of the year. Here Debon (6), chasing Porto through, heads Faubel, Battaini, Aoyama and Vincent.

Photograph: Gold & Goose

Above: Porto and Fonsi Nieto.

Right: Dovisioso just beat Locatelli to win the 125cc race.

Photographs: Gold & Goose

250 cc RACE – 26 laps

With new blood and the odd machine change, would 2004 bring a revival of the recently dormant close 250 racing? Yes, no, and in the end yes again. This was also a landmark race - a superbly judged and fiercely achieved class debut win for teenage hero Dani Pedrosa. The teenager had celebrated his 125 championship in a wheelchair after smashing both ankles in a practice crash at Phillip Island. Flawed, but hardly less impressive was ex-Honda rider Porto's debut on an Aprilia: his race took him from first to 22nd... and all the way back to the rostrum again.

Pedrosa had started at the far end of the front row, behind the Aprilias of de Puniet, Porto and defending champion Poggiali.

Porto led away, with a pile-up near the back eliminating Davies, Bataille and Baldolini on the first lap. On the second, Porto's front slid away on the fast kink out at the back. His recovery took him right off the track and onto the banking, where he stopped safely, and rejoined hastily to finish that lap 22nd. And on a mission, gaining four and even five positions a lap, setting a new lap record on the fifth. By the eighth he had his sights on a scuffle for fourth, between Elias, Rolfo, Nieto and de Angelis, and was soon setting about them.

Up front, de Puniet, Pedrosa and Poggiali had stretched away, and spread out somewhat. Then Pedrosa picked up his pace, and just before half distance powered past de Puniet on the back straight to pull away by more than a second. The Aprilia rider had elected to nurse his tyres, and save the battle for later. With six laps to go, he eased back into range and retook the lead.

The Frenchmen led laps 21 to 25, but under relentless pressure from the rookie. On the last lap, Pedrosa slipped past into the first section only for de Puniet to retake the lead directly. Pedrosa nosed ahead on the last fast corner, only for de Puniet to push past again on the inside into the last tight right.

One corner left, de Puniet swept in wide and fast. A mistake. It left room for Pedrosa to force his way inside, to lead over the line by half a second.

Porto was less than six seconds behind, having dealt with an off-form Poggiali and left him trailing by 20 seconds, though six seconds clear of the remnants of the race-long battle. De Angelis led from Debon, who had followed Porto at a little distance.

Both escaped a controversial contact that gave Nieto seventh from Elias, and reinforced the Spaniard's reputation for fighting dirty. It emerged that he had actually leaned over and grabbed Elias's brake lever on the way into the turn! Rolfo was close behind.

Old hand Battaini led the next gaggle, from factory Honda rookie Aoyama, Faubel and 250-rookie and ex-125 champion Arnaud Vincent.

Anthony West was two tenths out of the points, behind Guintoli.

125 cc RACE – 24 laps

Plenty of vitality in the smallest class, with a healthy crop of fast kids on fast bikes, and a smattering of old hands. Pole went to 18-year-old Dovizioso, from the well-seasoned 2000 champion Locatelli (29). They lined up next to Giansanti and di Meglio for an all-action race with a breathtaking finish.

Locatelli and Dovizioso led away from the start, the Aprilia leading over the line every lap, Dovizioso nosing ahead here and there, now and then.

Before half distance, Stoner had picked his way through to join them. The Australian's orange KTM also had a short time up front, but he was outpaced in the last few laps, by which time he had his hands full with Nieto, who had inched closer lap by lap.

The leaders were hard at it, Locatelli harried everywhere by Dovizioso. He managed to hold him off last time down the back straight, but there was one chance left, and the youngster was close enough to take it, forcing inside into the last tight corner. It meant running wide on the exit, with Locatelli closing up fast... but the finish line was just close enough, and Dovizioso took it by seven hundredths. A fine first win, and no flash in the pan.

Two seconds behind, Stoner and Nieto were scrapping it out; the Australian prevailing in the last close corners.

Fifth, ten seconds adrift, went to di Meglio from team-mate Borsoi and Giansanti, Jenkner at the back of the gang. Barbera lost the next battle, for ninth, to his team-mate Bautista.

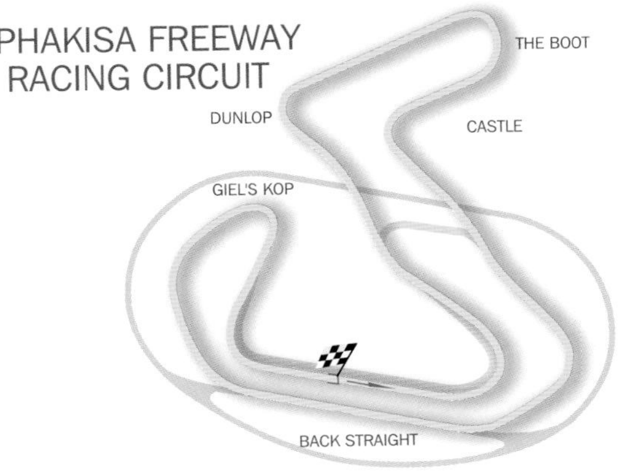

CIRCUIT LENGTH: 2.636 miles/4.242 km

MotoGP

28 laps, 73.808 miles/118.776 km

Pos.	Rider (Nat.)	No.	Machine	Laps	Time & speed
1	Valentino Rossi (I)	46	Yamaha	28	43m 50.218s 101.016 mph/ 162.569 km/h
2	Max Biaggi (I)	3	Honda	28	43m 50.428s
3	Sete Gibernau (E)	15	Honda	28	43m 57.473s
4	Alex Barros (BR)	4	Honda	28	44m 08.885s
5	Nicky Hayden (USA)	69	Honda	28	44m 14.312s
6	Loris Capirossi (I)	65	Ducati	28	44m 14.593s
7	Colin Edwards (USA)	45	Honda	28	44m 19.073s
8	Makoto Tamada (J)	6	Honda	28	44m 26.753s
9	Norick Abe (J)	17	Yamaha	28	44m 26.861s
10	Carlos Checa (E)	7	Yamaha	28	44m 29.502s
11	Marco Melandri (I)	33	Yamaha	28	44m 34.024s
12	Shinya Nakano (J)	56	Kawasaki	28	44m 34.138s
13	John Hopkins (USA)	21	Suzuki	28	44m 46.246s
14	Troy Bayliss (AUS)	12	Ducati	28	44m 46.776s
15	Shane Byrne (GB)	67	Aprilia	28	45m 04.049s
16	Jeremy McWilliams	99	Aprilia	28	45m 12.424s
17	Nobuatsu Aoki (J)	9	Proton KR	28	45m 17.151s
18	Michel Fabrizio (I)	84	Harris WCM	25	44m 05.911s
	Alex Hofmann (D)	66	Kawasaki	15	DNF
	Neil Hodgson (GB)	50	Ducati	15	DNF
	Kenny Roberts (USA)	10	Suzuki	6	DNF
	Ruben Xaus (E)	11	Ducati	4	DNF

Fastest lap: Biaggi, 1m 33.208s, 101.805 mph/163.840 km/h (record).

Previous record: Valentino Rossi, I (Honda), 1m 33.851s, 101.108 mph/162.717 km/h (2003).

Event best maximum speed: Hayden, 174.8 mph/281.3 km/h (qualifying practice no. 2).

Qualifying: 1 Rossi, 1m 32.647s; 2 Gibernau, 1m 32.682s; 3 Biaggi, 1m 32.919s; 4 Hayden, 1m 33.098s; 5 Edwards, 1m 33.111s; 6 Nakano, 1m 33.276s; 7 Melandri, 1m 33.296s; 8 Barros, 1m 33.359s; 9 Capirossi, 1m 33.522s; 10 Kenny Roberts, 1m 33.543s; 11 Hopkins, 1m 33.598s; 12 Tamada, 1m 33.679s; 13 Hofmann, 1m 33.815s; 14 Checa, 1m 33.884s; 15 Hodgson, 1m 33.977s; 16 Xaus, 1m 34.103s; 17 McWilliams, 1m 34.404s; 18 Abe, 1m 34.484s; 19 Byrne, 1m 34.703s; 20 Aoki, 1m 34.845s; 21 Bayliss, 1m 35.804s; 22 Fabrizio, 1m 36.982s.

Fastest race laps: 1 Biaggi, 1m 33.208s; 2 Rossi, 1m 33.269s; 3 Gibernau, 1m 33.511s; 4 Barros, 1m 33.836s; 5 Capirossi, 1m 33.922s; 6 Hayden, 1m 33.969s; 7 Edwards, 1m 34.254s; 8 Tamada, 1m 34.361s; 9 Kenny Roberts, 1m 34.525s; 10 Melandri, 1m 34.533s; 11 Checa, 1m 34.561s; 12 Abe, 1m 34.612s; 13 Xaus, 1m 34.738s; 14 Nakano, 1m 34.744s; 15 Hopkins, 1m 34.779s; 16 Bayliss, 1m 34.785s; 17 Hodgson, 1m 35.013s; 18 McWilliams, 1m 35.679s; 19 Hofmann, 1m 35.858s; 20 Byrne, 1m 35.900s; 21 Aoki, 1m 36.187s; 22 Fabrizio, 1m 38.138s.

World Championship: 1 Rossi, 25; 2 Biaggi, 20; 3 Gibernau, 16; 4 Barros, 13; 5 Hayden, 11; 6 Capirossi, 10; 7 Edwards, 9; 8 Tamada, 8; 9 Abe, 7; 10 Checa, 6; 11 Melandri, 5; 12 Nakano, 4; 13 Hopkins, 3; 14 Bayliss, 2; 15 Byrne, 1.

250 cc

26 laps, 68.536 miles/110.292 km

Pos.	Rider (Nat.)	No.	Machine	Laps	Time & speed
1	Daniel Pedrosa (E)	26	Honda	26	42m 04.690s 97.72 mph/ 157.267 km/h
2	Randy de Puniet (F)	7	Aprilia	26	42m 05.226s
3	Sebastian Porto (ARG)	19	Aprilia	26	42m 10.549s
4	Manuel Poggiali (RSM)	54	Aprilia	26	42m 29.251s
5	Alex de Angelis (RSM)	51	Aprilia	26	42m 34.708s
6	Alex Debon (E)	6	Honda	26	42m 35.343s
7	Fonsi Nieto (E)	10	Aprilia	26	42m 36.148s
8	Toni Elias (E)	24	Honda	26	42m 36.562s
9	Roberto Rolfo (I)	2	Honda	26	42m 36.630s
10	Franco Battaini (I)	21	Aprilia	26	42m 40.333s
11	Hiroshi Aoyama (J)	73	Honda	26	42m 41.108s
12	Hector Faubel (E)	33	Aprilia	26	42m 41.554s
13	Arnaud Vincent (F)	12	Aprilia	26	42m 43.795s
14	Dirk Heidolf (D)	28	Aprilia	26	42m 47.717s
15	Sylvain Guintoli (F)	50	Aprilia	26	42m 56.183s
16	Anthony West (AUS)	14	Aprilia	26	42m 56.389s
17	Joan Olive (E)	11	Aprilia	26	42m 57.573s
18	Naoki Matsudo (J)	8	Yamaha	26	43m 04.590s
19	Hugo Marchand (F)	9	Aprilia	26	43m 07.509s
20	Erwan Nigon (F)	36	Yamaha	26	43m 19.534s
21	Jakub Smrz (CZ)	96	Honda	26	43m 19.716s
22	Taro Sekiguchi (J)	44	Yamaha	26	43m 23.920s
23	Johan Stigefelt (S)	16	Aprilia	26	43m 26.317s
24	Max Sabbatani (I)	40	Yamaha	26	43m 33.680s
25	Gregory Lefort (F)	77	Aprilia	26	43m 34.522s
	Christian Gemmel (D)	15	Honda	24	DNF
	Alex Baldolini (I)	25	Aprilia	0	DNF
	Eric Bataille (F)	34	Honda	0	DNF
	Chaz Davies (GB)	57	Aprilia	0	DNF

Fastest lap: Porto, 1m 35.593s, 99.265 mph/159.752 km/h (record).

Previous record: Manuel Poggiali, RSM (Aprilia), 1m 36.649s, 98.180 mph/158.006 km/h (2003).

Event best maximum speed: Pedrosa, 153.9 mph/247.7 km/h (qualifying practice no. 2).

Qualifying: 1 de Puniet, 1m 35.300s; 2 Porto, 1m 35.379s; 3 Poggiali, 1m 35.596s; 4 Pedrosa, 1m 35.843s; 5 de Angelis, 1m 36.251s; 6 Nieto, 1m 36.447s; 7 Rolfo, 1m 36.611s; 8 Bataille, 1m 36.690s; 9 Aoyama, 1m 36.764s; 10 Battaini, 1m 36.819s; 11 Elias, 1m 36.884s; 12 Faubel, 1m 37.088s; 13 Davies, 1m 37.172s; 14 Matsudo, 1m 37.373s; 15 Debon, 1m 37.382s; 16 Marchand, 1m 37.386s; 17 Baldolini, 1m 37.418s; 18 Olive, 1m 37.605s; 19 Guintoli, 1m 37.614s; 20 West, 1m 37.633s; 21 Smrz, 1m 37.688s; 22 Heidolf, 1m 37.716s; 23 Nigon, 1m 37.739s; 24 Vincent, 1m 38.333s; 25 Gemmel, 1m 38.406s; 26 Stigefelt, 1m 38.735s; 27 Lefort, 1m 38.940s; 28 Sekiguchi, 1m 38.976s; 29 Sabbatani, 1m 39.143s.

Fastest race laps: 1 Porto, 1m 35.593s; 2 de Puniet, 1m 35.886s; 3 Pedrosa, 1m 35.933s; 4 Poggiali, 1m 36.497s; 5 Elias, 1m 36.994s; 6 Rolfo, 1m 37.322s; 7 de Angelis, 1m 37.322s; 8 Debon, 1m 37.428s; 9 Aoyama, 1m 37.432s; 10 Nieto, 1m 37.515s; 11 Battaini, 1m 37.566s; 12 Matsudo, 1m 37.649s; 13 Faubel, 1m 37.670s; 14 West, 1m 37.686s; 15 Guintoli, 1m 37.705s; 16 Heidolf, 1m 37.904s; 17 Vincent, 1m 37.932s; 18 Olive, 1m 38.082s; 19 Marchand, 1m 38.170s; 20 Smrz, 1m 38.335s; 21 Nigon, 1m 38.471s; 22 Lefort, 1m 38.902s; 23 Gemmel, 1m 39.139s; 24 Stigefelt, 1m 39.202s; 25 Sekiguchi, 1m 39.389s; 26 Sabbatani, 1m 39.406s.

World Championship: 1 Pedrosa, 25; 2 de Puniet, 20; 3 Porto, 16; 4 Poggiali, 13; 5 de Angelis, 11; 6 Debon, 10; 7 Nieto, 9; 8 Elias, 8; 9 Rolfo, 7; 10 Battaini, 6; 11 Aoyama, 5; 12 Faubel, 4; 13 Vincent, 3; 14 Heidolf, 2; 15 Guintoli, 1.

125 cc

24 laps, 63.264 miles/101.808 km

Pos.	Rider (Nat.)	No.	Machine	Laps	Time & speed
1	Andrea Dovizioso (I)	34	Honda	24	40m 34.318s 93.553 mph/ 150.559 km/h
2	Roberto Locatelli (I)	15	Aprilia	24	40m 34.389s
3	Casey Stoner (AUS)	27	KTM	24	40m 36.521s
4	Pablo Nieto (E)	22	Aprilia	24	40m 36.734s
5	Mike di Meglio (F)	63	Aprilia	24	40m 46.630s
6	Gino Borsoi (I)	23	Aprilia	24	40m 47.588s
7	Mirko Giansanti (I)	6	Aprilia	24	40m 48.775s
8	Steve Jenkner (D)	21	Aprilia	24	40m 49.364s
9	Alvaro Bautista (E)	19	Aprilia	24	40m 59.153s
10	Hector Barbera (E)	3	Aprilia	24	40m 59.584s
11	Julian Simon (E)	10	Honda	24	41m 03.674s
12	Mika Kallio (SF)	36	KTM	24	41m 07.452s
13	Mattia Pasini (I)	54	Aprilia	24	41m 07.555s
14	Simone Corsi (I)	24	Honda	24	41m 08.000s
15	Youichi Ui (J)	41	Aprilia	24	41m 11.295s
16	Jorge Lorenzo (E)	48	Derbi	24	41m 17.968s
17	Stefano Perugini (I)	7	Gilera	24	41m 19.548s
18	Robbin Harms (DK)	69	Honda	24	41m 19.707s
19	Dario Giuseppetti (D)	26	Honda	24	41m 19.908s
20	Lukas Pesek (CZ)	52	Honda	24	41m 20.033s
21	Fabrizio Lai (I)	32	Gilera	24	41m 20.279s
22	Imre Toth (H)	25	Aprilia	24	1m 20.447s
23	Sergio Gadea (E)	33	Aprilia	24	41m 39.308s
24	Vesa Kallio (SF)	55	Aprilia	24	41m 40.102s
25	Mattia Angeloni (I)	11	Honda	24	41m 57.859s
26	Manuel Manna (I)	8	Malaguti	24	41m 58.071s
27	Jordi Carchano (E)	28	Aprilia	24	41m 59.278s
	Thomas Luthi (CH)	12	Honda	17	DNF
	Marco Simoncelli (I)	58	Aprilia	16	DNF
	Andrea Ballerini (I)	50	Aprilia	13	DNF
	Angel Rodriguez (E)	47	Derbi	7	DNF
	Gioele Pellino (I)	42	Aprilia	7	DNF
	Raymond Schouten (NL)	16	Honda	4	DNF
	Gabor Talmacsi (H)	14	Malaguti	3	DNF

Fastest lap: Locatelli, 1m 40.711s, 94.220 mph/151.633 km/h (record).

Previous record: Daniel Pedrosa, E (Honda), 1m 41.006s, 93.946 mph/151.191 km/h (2003).

Event best maximum speed: Jenkner, 132.9 mph/213.9 km/h (race).

Qualifying: 1 Dovizioso, 1m 40.942s; 2 Locatelli, 1m 41.024s; 3 Giansanti, 1m 41.193s; 4 di Meglio, 1m 41.195s; 5 Stoner, 1m 41.204s; 6 Nieto, 1m 41.373s; 7 Simoncelli, 1m 41.483s; 8 Bautista, 1m 41.550s; 9 Ui, 1m 41.619s; 10 Simon, 1m 41.644s; 11 Barbera, 1m 41.682s; 12 Borsoi, 1m 41.754s; 13 Lorenzo, 1m 41.762s; 14 Talmacsi, 1m 41.866s; 15 M. Kallio, 1m 41.896s; 16 Giuseppetti, 1m 41.959s; 17 Lai, 1m 42.038s; 18 Jenkner, 1m 42.106; 19 Perugini, 1m 42.143s; 20 Pasini, 1m 42.194s; 21 Corsi, 1m 42.242s; 22 Harms, 1m 42.551s; 23 Luthi, 1m 42.634s; 24 Gadea, 1m 42.642s; 25 Toth, 1m 43.195s; 26 V. Kallio, 1m 43.301s; 27 Pesek, 1m 43.590s; 28 Rodriguez, 1m 43.864s; 29 Ballerini, 1m 44.014s; 30 Pellino, 1m 44.099s; 31 Manna, 1m 44.115s; 32 Angeloni, 1m 44.345s; 33 Carchano, 1m 44.560s; 34 S Schouten, 1m 44.741s.

Fastest race laps: 1 Locatelli, 1m 40.711s; 2 Dovizioso, 1m 40.737s; 3 Stoner, 1m 40.751s; 4 Nieto, 1m 40.795s; 5 Jenkner, 1m 40.903s; 6 di Meglio, 1m 41.013s; 7 Simoncelli, 1m 41.084s; 8 Barbera, 1m 41.093s; 9 Borsoi, 1m 41.149s; 10 Giansanti, 1m 41.228s; 11 Simon, 1m 41.232s; 12 Talmacsi, 1m 41.258s; 13 M. Kallio, 1m 41.390s; 14 Bautista, 1m 41.541s; 15 Ui, 1m 41.608s; 16 Pasini, 1m 41.747s; 17 Luthi, 1m 41.859s; 18 Corsi, 1m 41.874s; 19 Perugini, 1m 41.874s; 20 Lorenzo, 1m 41.948s; 21 Lai, 1m 42.008s; 22 Giuseppetti, 1m 42.115s; 23 Toth, 1m 42.187s; 24 Harms, 1m 42.308s; 25 Pesek, 1m 42.364s; 26 Gadea, 1m 42.605s; 27 Rodriguez, 1m 42.690s; 28 Ballerini, 1m 42.948s; 29 V. Kallio, 1m 43.205s; 30 Manna, 1m 43.661s; 31 Angeloni, 1m 43.715s; 32 Pellino, 1m 43.724s; 33 Carchano, 1m 44.128s; 34 Schouten, 1m 44.255s.

World Championship: 1 Dovizioso, 25; 2 Locatelli, 20; 3 Stoner, 16; 4 Nieto, 13; 5 di Meglio, 11; 6 Borsoi, 10; 7 Giansanti, 9; 8 Jenkner, 8; 9 Bautista, 7; 10 Barbera, 6; 11 Simon, 5; 12 M. Kallio, 4; 13 Pasini, 3; 14 Corsi, 2; 15 Ui, 1.

FIM WORLD CHAMPIONSHIP • ROUND 2

SPANISHGP
JEREZ

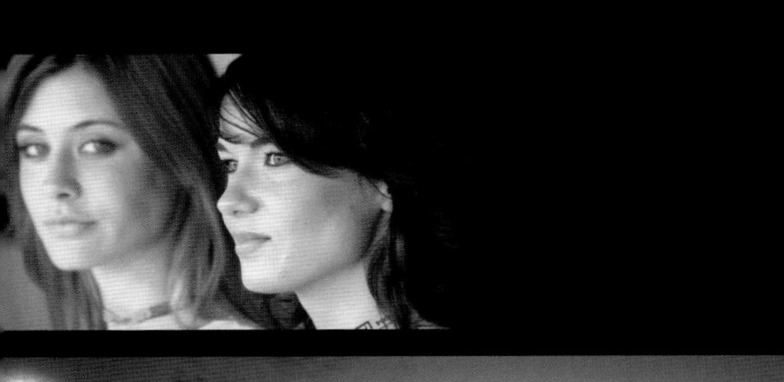

Above: Heavy skies loom over the reassembled GP paddock.

Left: Troy Bayliss and his Ducati teamsters had plenty to talk about. Help was coming.

Below: Jerez means fiesta to Spain's good-natured bike fans.

Bottom: Barros and crew chief Forcada have a last-minute word on the grid.

Far left: Gibernau's first win of the year put him in the points lead for the first time in his life.

Photographs: Gold & Goose

ONE could easily think of places that Ducati Corse's top brass would rather have been - anywhere, really, other than at the top table, hosting a formal press conference in Jerez's high-rolling "UFO"; the new VIP centre straddling the front straight. The time and place were pre-ordained by team sponsors Marlboro, canapes and cocktails all laid out, and a good attendance assured by the promise of a gift. Which wasn't necessary. There were plenty of questions for Ducati Corse.

The first was obvious. In that morning's first free training session, the 2003 Desmosedicis had been quicker than the new factory 2004 bikes. The old bikes ridden, forsooth, by class rookies Xaus and Hodgson, against seasoned factory man Capirossi and team-mate Bayliss. What on earth was going on?

"This is only temporary," said CEO Claudio Domenicali, smilingly acknowledging that he had been both dreading and expecting the question. He was right, but in fact it was not until the next day that a factory bike was the fastest Ducati, and that was in the wet, with Bayliss second both morning and afternoon. But starting times were set on Friday afternoon's dry-session times, with Xaus 12th on the grid, Capirossi 15th (admittedly just half-a-tenth slower), Bayliss and Hodgson behind.

He didn't just mean practice, however, but the overall poor performance of the Mk2 Desmosedici, disappointing not only in pre-season tests, but also in the opening round. More powerful it may be, but something was wrong with the balance and since the new motor/chassis combination had different mounting points, there was no easy way of getting back to last year's wayward, tail-happy, slower, but more effective motorcycle.

MOTOCOURSE's technical chapters analyse the Ducati's failings more deeply. Domenicali's explanation was more general. The bike had been changed because there was no more potential left in the first one, he said. But the extra power was hard to manage, while the handling had suffered particularly in fast corners, where data showed the new bike could not match the speed of the old. "Last year's bike had more weight on the front - which worked well, especially on fast corners. But the aim is to have a bike that works well on all different circuits," said Domenicali. They had a new swing-arm to try at the track, and he was confident. "This is still a test session for us," he said. "We only started the bike in January, it is still very early in its development."

The confident serenity belied frantic action back at Bologna, where they were already secretly testing a revived version of the Twin Pulse engine, discarded early in preliminary testing at the end of 2002, but due for a comeback in tests after the next race at Le Mans, and in action a few rounds after that. The first version had suffered internal breakages, doubtless due to the double-strength pounding of the aptly-named Twin Pulses power impulses. Ducati retained secrecy, but for now there was eager speculation that they had followed Honda's lead and dephased the pulses by a few degrees, retaining most of the basic V-twin character without overloading gear teeth and crankcases in the process.

This kind of lofty technical speculation was much in the air, imperfect understanding no barrier to long-winded analysis. Changing crankshaft layout and thus the intervals (and possibly also the order) between firing impulses was what Yamaha were assumed to have done to make their M1 not only growl, but also pick up better out of the corners and to feel more friendly. It was a return of the Big Bang revolution of the 500cc two-strokes of 1992. That blinding revelation was also set off by Honda, and close firing orders became an essential for a while, until a combination of tyre, suspension and electronic developments, and the sensitive throttle hand of Mick Doohan, revealed that it was not the final answer.

Suzuki had their own version of the same thing, to be tested after this race... their V4's previous 180-degree crank layout (adjacent pistons one-up/one-down) replaced with a 360-degree crank (adjacent pistons rise and fall together). This changed the firing intervals significantly, and - as we would later discover - engine character for the better.

There was more... also for post-race tests, with Proton following a similar path. With five cylinders to choose from, they didn't need to change the crankshaft, only cams and ignition, to shuffle the cylinder firing order and change the intervals between pulses. "We had it firing big bang, but maybe it was the wrong sort of big bang," said team owner Roberts.

All this would remain speculation, however, because the rain on Saturday heralded a streaming wet Sunday that would rewrite the rules after Rossi's revelation a fortnight before. This time they went in Honda's favour, with a rostrum full of RCVs and Gibernau leading the World Championship for the first time in his life. Was it something to do with machine balance, again? In the broadest sense, maybe so... because Rossi's problems in the race can basically be put down to a shortage of overall set-up time in the wet with the Yamaha. But the Hondas were still working out their new chassis/swingarm combination, with Edwards and Tamada joining the club for the second race. Later in the year, the same pair would get left behind again with another revised chassis.

Some paintwork action from WCM, who abandoned hope that new rider Michel Fabrizio would bring along some Italian sponsorship money. The R1 clones reverted to blue with white graphics, but enjoyed something else the teenager had brought with him: precocious talent and deep-end daring. In fact he'd failed to qualify in the sole dry session, but placed tenth in the wet on Saturday morning and was allowed to start under special concession. His lack of power a positive advantage in the wet, he managed a top-ten finish, lapping faster than a number of factory riders, in spite of falling when his primitive slipper clutch caught him out.

And new colours too from D'Antin Ducati, with their bikes painted in the orange white and blue of a famous credit card company. The colours remained, without any affirmative logos, for more than half the season, but the money never materialised, and after the summer break the Ducatis were painted generic red and black instead.

As usual, Jerez hosted a massive crowd, in spite of the dismal weather. The biggest surprise at Jerez came later in the season, when the track declared itself bankrupt, just two years after major rebuilding works. As in the case of Phakisa, this is a municipal track and there were local political ramifications.

Below: Front wheels gently hovering, the Hondas had their day in the rain. Biaggi's close pursuit of Gibernau went all the way.

Opposite, top left: Twice the bridesmaid, Biaggi remained in a challenging position.

Opposite, top right: Man inspired – Michel Fabrizio on the humble WCM heads factory riders Abe, Hofmann and Capirossi through the spray.

Opposite centre: Takes more than bad weather to dampen the ardour of GP racing's most numerous fans.

Opposite bottom, clockwise from top left: Rossi tests his luck severely one more time. It didn't let him down. Barros watches the lucky escape.

Photographs: Gold & Goose

MOTOGP RACE – 27 laps

As rain was predicted for Saturday, everyone knew Friday's first timed session might set grid positions. Rossi took pole in dominant style, a full second faster than last year, Gibernau four tenths behind; Checa making two Yamahas up front, and Biaggi leading row two. Nakano put in another Kawasaki flier, placing sixth.

With no fear of wet-and-dry race stoppages due to the steady rain almost all day long, Gibernau led away on a streaming track, Rossi chasing, Checa and Biaggi bickering behind.

Bayliss was on a mission, forging through from 17th on the grid to ninth at the end of lap one, only to fall on the second. Xaus also crashed out on the same lap. Byrne had fallen heavily on the first, breaking bones in his hand.

Up front, there was plenty of shuffling in the spray: Gibernau led lap two, but Rossi was now fifth, behind Biaggi, Checa and Barros. Next time round, Melandri had also got ahead of Rossi. All eyes were on Rossi, but it was too early to say if he was having trouble. Perhaps he was just biding his time.

Biaggi was pushing Gibernau hard, both pulling away to have a four-second gap after seven laps. They were engaged for the rest of the race, and the issue in doubt until the last. Biaggi nosed ahead at the end of the back straight on lap 16, upping the pace to try to break away. Gibernau was having none of it, and when the Italian ran wide one lap later he regained the lead, and stayed there to the finish. Both were on the limit and close to crashing as the rain continued and the puddles got deeper.

Before one third distance Melandri outpaced Checa for third, and on lap nine Rossi also passed his team-mate to move into fourth, bringing Barros along with him. Soon afterwards, Barros passed Rossi. Now it was clear that Valentino was definitely struggling.

Melandri had no hope of catching the leading pair, 13 seconds ahead on lap 18, but he was 10 seconds clear of Barros, Rossi was in turn five seconds behind the Brazilian. But Melandri's rostrum hopes were not to be fulfilled. On lap 19 he fell on the second of the two rights behind the paddock. "I wasn't pushing, and I didn't even have the throttle open when the back slid round," he said later.

Barros was now alone and safe in third. Rossi was not so comfortable. Checa, complaining later of a fogged visor, had fallen back into the hands of Edwards, but Hayden had passed them both, and with eight laps left he was less than five seconds behind Rossi, and closing fast. With five laps left the gap was less than a second, but the relative rookie found Rossi to be easier to catch than to overtake, with several attempts repulsed.

Checa managed to lose Edwards; a long way back came a slowing Kenny Roberts, in danger of being lapped but he was the best of the Bridgestone runners ... the Japanese wet tyres not showing well at this stage.

Nakano came next and then the remarkable Fabrizio on the low-end WCM on ill-favoured Dunlop tyres. He had climbed to 12th on lap 12 before sliding off. He kept it running and clambered straight back on, losing four places to rejoin ahead of Kurtis Roberts and Hopkins, all at sea in the wet. Not daunted, Fabrizio charged off again, closing up again on his erstwhile companions. He passed a slowing Aoki and Hofmann in one lap, then took three more to deal with Capirossi and Abe. Given a couple more laps, he might also have caught Nakano... a fine ride.

Abe was 11th, then Capirossi - he'd been forced off the track twice, and "by the end, I just wanted to finish," he said. Hofmann was 13th, complaining of aquaplaning problems, as did Dunlop-shod Aoki. Then came a downcast Hopkins, a long way back but, with only 15 finishers, still in the points. His wet confidence remained shaken by three crashes in one weekend at Le Mans last year; while his injured ankles were still far from full strength.

As well as the crashers, McWilliams retired with grip problems, after gambling on a hard rear tyre. Tamada had been left trailing, had pitted for a new tyre, then pulled in again. Kurtis Roberts retired, unsure of whether his sliding problems were of his own making or endemic to the bike.

Max
3
SUOMY
DAINESE
SHIMANO
CORREOS
CAMEL

Top: **Fonsi Nieto heads Anthony West to the rostrum, after a last-lap ramming.**

Above: **Rainmaster Rolfo stamped his authority on the 250 race, here heading Aoyama and de Puniet.**

Right: **First-time 125 winner Marco Simoncelli survived the conditions, where many others failed.**

Photographs: Gold & Goose

250 cc RACE – 26 laps

Porto survived a huge crash on the first day to claim a very fast pole, almost half-a-second ahead of champion Poggiali, with Pedrosa third on the grid. Rain changed everything, with a costly first lap eliminating Poggiali at the last hairpin, as his nightmare title defence took another downturn.

It was Rolfo, surging through from row two, who made the most of the conditions, for the first (and for a long while the last) time at ease with his new Honda. He led all the way to the end, but he was kept honest especially in the latter stages by de Puniet, who pushed steadily if from a distance to finish eight seconds adrift.

Pedrosa might have been among them, but he too fell victim to the treacherous surface. Second after one lap, he lost two places, and crashed out on the fifth. It was his own team-mate Aoyama, a wet specialist, who passed him on lap two, followed by de Puniet. But the Japanese rider was gone even before Pedrosa, crashing out on lap three. Conditions were appalling.

This left Rolfo and de Puniet to get on with it up front. Debon, so often fast away, was holding the rest back. Battaini had got by to third on lap six, only to crash out on lap ten. By then Guintoli had found a way past Nieto and was promoted to third briefly, but was back in fifth when he narrowly saved a big slide that dropped him to tenth, and led to an eventual retirement.

Nieto was always pushing, but the star of the pursuit was West, showing well once more on a slippery track. He finished lap one 14th after starting 13th, and moved through steadily into third by lap 11, passing both Guintoli and Nieto in the process.

Looking comfortable, he had no chance of catching the leaders, and (it seemed) a safe rostrum. But Nieto just wouldn't give up, and he was again riding beyond the call of duty. The pair had collided once early on in their battle; on the last lap they did so again at the Nieto Curve (named after Fonsi's uncle Angel), Nieto forcing inside West and using him as a barrier. It pushed a much-dismayed West wide, and "I wasn't able to get close enough to attack at the last hairpin," he said ruefully.

Splashing along behind, Debon was 30 seconds adrift; while de Angelis was a strong sixth, fending Porto off over the line. Arnaud Vincent lost touch with this pair at the finish. His rookie team-mate Gregory Lefort was miles behind in ninth, ahead of Matsudo. The rain really had shuffled the pack... but it was de Puniet ahead on points.

125 cc RACE – 23 laps

First out to test the streaming conditions, the 125s served more Australian heartbreak. Casey Stoner started from the front row and forged into an assured lead from the first lap. He was in complete control, almost nine seconds ahead with three laps left.

Next time at the final hairpin, off line passing backmarkers, he hit a puddle and slid off. "I wasn't going fast, but it was so dark I didn't even see it," he said later, after rapidly scrambling back to save fifth.

He'd leapt away from the line, to head a pursuit pack engaged in many dramas. Locatelli was fast away, but lost ground; after eight laps Barbera was second from Jenkner and Dovizioso, with first-time pole starter Simoncelli off the back of the group.

Jenkner was in eager mode after a slow start, but plans for improvement were scuppered when he hit a slick patch and all-but high-sided. He landed back in the seat, but was heading straight off the track towards the air-fence. A heroic save on wet grass saw him miss the corner of the fence by inches; he rejoined in sixth to begin again.

When Stoner fell, Simoncelli was well ahead of a battle involving Barbera, the returned Jenkner, Dovizioso and rookie Pasini, who also fell before the flag.

First-time-winner Simoncelli, just 17, came close to losing it. He started the final lap with a three-second advantage, and long before he finished he was celebrating, waving at the crowd and popping wheelies. Behind him, Jenkner was concentrating on racing, and came within almost half-a-second of snatching the race.

Barbera had also run off and recovered to rejoin battle earlier in the race. Now he narrowly held Dovizioso behind; Stoner passed Ballerini and Ui to finish fifth.

Three seconds down came Locatelli, outpaced this time by the new teenage chargers, well clear of Nieto and Giansanti. In a fraught race with 26 finishers from 35 starters, the kids had all the advantages.

FIM WORLD CHAMPIONSHIP • ROUND 2

MARLBORO SPANISH grand prix

2 MAY 2004

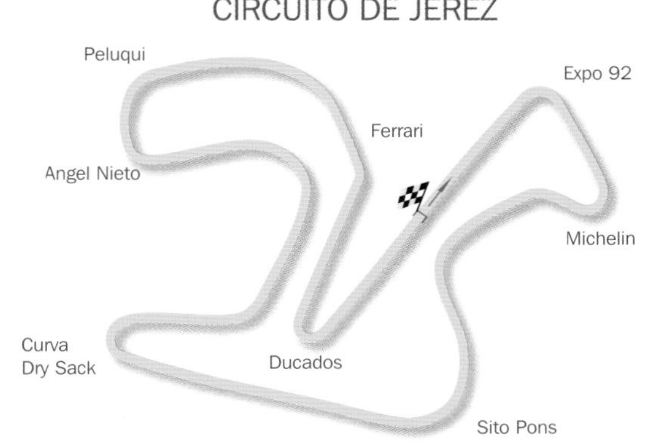

CIRCUIT LENGTH: 2.749 miles/4.424 km

MotoGP

27 laps, 74.196 miles/119.421 km

Pos.	Rider (Nat.)	No.	Machine	Laps	Time & speed
1	Sete Gibernau (E)	15	Honda	27	52m 01.293s 85.585 mph/ 137.736 km/h
2	Max Biaggi (I)	3	Honda	27	52m 06.745s
3	Alex Barros (BR)	4	Honda	27	52m 53.863s
4	Valentino Rossi (I)	46	Yamaha	27	52m 59.849s
5	Nicky Hayden (USA)	69	Honda	27	53m 00.576s
6	Carlos Checa (E)	7	Yamaha	27	53m 08.477s
7	Colin Edwards (USA)	45	Honda	27	53m 20.832s
8	Kenny Roberts (USA)	10	Suzuki	27	53m 46.350s
9	Shinya Nakano (J)	56	Kawasaki	26	52m 07.304s
10	Michel Fabrizio (I)	84	Harris WCM	26	52m 16.335s
11	Norick Abe (J)	17	Yamaha	26	52m 19.549s
12	Loris Capirossi (I)	65	Ducati	26	52m 22.550s
13	Alex Hofmann (D)	66	Kawasaki	26	52m 26.929s
14	Nobuatsu Aoki (J)	9	Proton KR	26	52m 39.533s
15	John Hopkins (USA)	21	Suzuki	26	52m 59.546s
	Marco Melandri (I)	33	Yamaha	18	DNF
	Neil Hodgson (GB)	50	Ducati	17	DNF
	Kurtis Roberts (USA)	80	Proton KR	13	DNF
	Makoto Tamada (J)	6	Honda	11	DNF
	Jeremy McWilliams (GB)	99	Aprilia	10	DNF
	Ruben Xaus (E)	11	Ducati	1	DN
	Troy Bayliss (AUS)	12	Ducati	1	DNF
	Shane Byrne (GB)	67	Aprilia	0	DNF
	Chris Burns (GB)	35	Harris WCM		DNQ

Fastest lap: **Gibernau,** 1m 53.508s, **87.165 mph/140.279 km/h.**

Lap record: **Valentino Rossi, I (Honda),** 1m 42.788s, **96.256 mph/154.909 km/h (2003).**

Event best maximum speed: **Xaus,** 180.6 mph/290.6 km/h **(qualifying practice no. 1).**

Qualifying: **1 Rossi,** 1m 40.818s; **2 Gibernau,** 1m 41.198s; **3 Checa,** 1m 41.427s; **4 Biaggi,** 1m 41.546s; **5 Tamada,** 1m 41.631s; **6 Nakano,** 1m 41.645s; **7 Hayden,** 1m 41.911s; **8 Edwards,** 1m 42.000s; **9 Barros,** 1m 42.141s; **10 Kenny Roberts,** 1m 42.312s; **11 Melandri,** 1m 42.479s; **12 Xaus,** 1m 42.945s; **13 Hopkins,** 1m 42.954s; **14 Hofmann,** 1m 43.004s; **15 Capirossi,** 1m 43.008s; **16 Byrne,** 1m 43.024s; **17 Bayliss,** 1m 43.349s; **18 Hodgson,** 1m 43.627s; **19 McWilliams,** 1m 43.730s; **20 Abe,** 1m 44.058s; **21 Aoki,** 1m 44.536s; **22 Kurtis Roberts,** 1m 45.899s; **23 Fabrizio,** 1m 48.485s; **24 Burns,** 1m 48.602s.

Fastest race laps: **1 Gibernau,** 1m 53.508s; **2 Biaggi,** 1m 53.542s; **3 Melandri,** 1m 54.405s; **4 Barros,** 1m 54.627s; **5 Rossi,** 1m 54.766s; **6 Hayden,** 1m 55.111s; **7 Checa,** 1m 55.134s; **8 Hodgson,** 1m 55.142s; **9 Edwards,** 1m 55.198s; **10 Kenny Roberts,** 1m 55.675s; **11 Fabrizio,** 1m 56.085s; **12 Abe,** 1m 56.651s; **13 Nakano,** 1m 57.361s; **14 Hofmann,** 1m 57.520s; **15 Capirossi,** 1m 57.632s; **16 Aoki,** 1m 58.095s; **17 McWilliams,** 1m 58.452s; **18 Hopkins,** 1m 58.935s; **19 Kurtis Roberts,** 1m 59.238s; **20 Tamada,** 2m 00.056s; **21 Xaus,** 2m 10.157s; **22 Bayliss,** 2m 10.254s.

World Championship: **1 Gibernau,** 41; **2 Biaggi,** 40; **3 Rossi,** 38; **4 Barros,** 29; **5 Hayden,** 22; **6 Edwards,** 18; **7 Checa,** 16; **8 Capirossi,** 14; **9 Abe,** 12; **10 Nakano,** 11; **11 Kenny Roberts and Tamada,** 8; **13 Fabrizio,** 6; **14 Melandri,** 5; **15 Hopkins,** 4; **16 Hofmann,** 3; **17 Aoki and Bayliss,** 2; **19 Byrne,** 1.

250 cc

26 laps, 71.448 miles/114.998 km

Pos.	Rider (Nat.)	No.	Machine	Laps	Time & speed
1	Roberto Rolfo (I)	2	Honda	26	52m 20.145s 81.920 mph/ 131.838 km/h
2	Randy de Puniet (F)	7	Aprilia	26	52m 28.885s
3	Fonsi Nieto (E)	10	Aprilia	26	52m 52.768s
4	Anthony West (AUS)	14	Aprilia	26	52m 52.989s
5	Alex Debon (E)	6	Honda	26	53m 19.029s
6	Alex de Angelis (RSM)	51	Aprilia	26	53m 24.095s
7	Sebastian Porto (ARG)	19	Aprilia	26	53m 25.467s
8	Arnaud Vincent (F)	12	Aprilia	26	53m 29.068s
9	Gregory Lefort (F)	77	Aprilia	26	54m 07.226s
10	Naoki Matsudo (J)	8	Yamaha	26	54m 09.336s
11	Alex Baldolini (I)	25	Aprilia	26	54m 15.173s
12	Toni Elias (E)	24	Honda	26	54m 21.901s
13	Hugo Marchand (F)	9	Aprilia	25	52m 24.419s
14	Johan Stigefelt (S)	16	Aprilia	25	52m 29.502s
15	Taro Sekiguchi (J)	44	Yamaha	25	52m 35.608s
16	Dirk Heidolf (D)	28	Aprilia	25	52m 39.046s
17	Hector Faubel (E)	33	Aprilia	25	52m 45.361s
18	Jarno Ronzoni (I)	63	Yamaha	25	53m 37.422s
19	Radomil Rous (CZ)	43	Aprilia	25	53m 39.812s
20	Joan Olive (E)	11	Aprilia	25	53m 58.276s
21	Gregory Leblanc (F)	42	Aprilia	24	52m 27.206s
	Alvaro Molina (E)	41	Aprilia	24	DNF
	Sylvain Guintoli (F)	50	Aprilia	23	DNF
	Franco Battaini (I)	21	Aprilia	23	DNF
	Christian Gemmel (D)	15	Honda	23	DNF
	Jakub Smrz (CZ)	96	Honda	17	DNF
	Chaz Davies (GB)	57	Aprilia	8	DNF
	Max Sabbatani (I)	40	Yamaha	5	DNF
	Daniel Pedrosa (I)	26	Honda	4	DNF
	Hiroshi Aoyama (J)	73	Honda	3	DNF
	Eric Bataille (F)	34	Honda	3	DNF
	Manuel Poggiali (RSM)	54	Aprilia	0	DNF

Fastest lap: **Rolfo,** 1m 58.815s, **83.272 mph/134.013 km/h.**

Lap record: **Daijiro Kato, J (Honda),** 1m 44.444s, **94.729 mph/152.452 km/h (2001).**

Event best maximum speed: **Pedrosa,** 152.5 mph/245.4 km/h **(qualifying practice no. 1).**

Qualifying: **1 Porto, 1**m 43.673s; **2 Poggiali,** 1m 44.054s; 3 **Pedrosa,** 1m 44.163s; **4 de Puniet,** 1m 44.196s; **5 Rolfo,** 1m 44.716s; **6 Elias,** 1m 44.989s; **7 Nieto,** 1m 45.222s; **8 de Angelis,** 1m 45.258s; **9 Battaini,** 1m 45.652s; **10 Aoyama,** 1m 45.822s; **11 Faubel,** 1m 45.976s; **12 Guintoli,** 1m 45.991s; **13 West,** 1m 46.075s; **14 Olive,** 1m 46.311s; **15 Debon,** 1m 46.429s; **16 Bataille,** 1m 46.514s; **17 Davies,** 1m 46.575s; **18 Smrz,** 1m 46.614s; **19 Matsudo,** 1m 46.657s; **20 Marchand,** 1m 46.966s; **21 Vincent,** 1m 47.158s; **22 Heidolf, 1m 47.214s; 23 Molina,** 1m 47.382s; **24 Baldolini,** 1m 47.411s; **25 Gemmel,** 1m 47.561s; **26 Sabbatani,** 1m 48.204s; **27 Stigefelt, 1m 48.376s; 28 Lefort,** 1m 48.452s; **29 Rous,** 1m 48.812s; **30 Sekiguchi, 1m 48.995s; 31 Leblanc,** 1m 49.144s; **32 Ronzoni,** 1m 50.311s.

Fastest race laps: **1 Rolfo,** 1m 58.815s; **2 de Puniet,** 1m 59.382s; **3 Nieto,** 2m 00.029s; **4 West,** 2m 00.096s; **5 Battaini,** 2m 00.732s; **6 Porto,** 2m 01.065s; **7 Debon,** 2m 01.158s; **8 Aoyama,** 2m 01.162s; **9 Lefort,** 2m 01.192s; 1**0 Guintoli, 2**m 01.329s; **11 de Angelis,** 2m 01.455s; **12 Baldolini,** 2m 01.477s; **13 Vincent,** 2m 01.986s; **14 Matsudo,** 2m 02.110s; **15 Stigefelt,** 2m 02.427s; **16 Molina,** 2m 02.628s; **17 Pedrosa,** 2m 02.917s; **18 Marchand,** 2m 03.301s; **19 Sekiguchi,** 2m 03.437s; **20 Heidolf,** 2m 03.442s; **21 Gemmel,** 2m 03.491s; **22 Rous,** 2m 03.852s; **23 Elias,** 2m 03.994s; **24 Faubel,** 2m 04.108s; **25 Ronzoni,** 2m 04.339s; **26 Bataille,** 2m 04.477s; **27 Smrz,** 2m 05.010s; **28 Davies,** 2m 06.370s; **29 Olive,** 2m 06.637s; **30 Leblanc,** 2m 07.981s; **31 Sabbatani,** 2m 08.348s.

World Championship: **1 de Puniet,** 40; **2 Rolfo,** 32; **3 Pedrosa, Nieto and Porto,** 25; **6 Debon and de Angelis,** 21; **8 Poggiali and West,** 13; **10 Elias, 12; 11 Vincent,** 11; **12 Lefort,** 7; **13 Battaini and Matsudo,** 6; **15 Aoyama and Baldolini,** 5; **17 Faubel,** 4; **18 Marchand,** 3; **19 Heidolf and Stigefelt,** 2; **21 Guintoli and Sekiguchi,** 1.

125 cc

23 laps, 63.204 miles/101.729 km

Pos.	Rider (Nat.)	No.	Machine	Laps	Time & speed
1	Marco Simoncelli (I)	58	Aprilia	23	47m 45.700s 79.408 mph/ 127.795 km/h
2	Steve Jenkner (D)	21	Aprilia	23	47m 46.460s
3	Hector Barbera (E)	3	Aprilia	23	47m 52.895s
4	Andrea Dovizioso (I)	34	Honda	23	47m 53.742s
5	Casey Stoner (AUS)	27	KTM	23	48m 00.312s
6	Andrea Ballerini (I)	50	Aprilia	23	48m 00.796s
7	Youichi Ui (J)	41	Aprilia	23	48m 02.776s
8	Roberto Locatelli (I)	15	Aprilia	23	48m 05.113s
9	Pablo Nieto (E)	22	Aprilia	23	48m 12.756s
10	Mirko Giansanti (I)	6	Aprilia	23	48m 16.133s
11	Julian Simon (E)	10	Honda	23	48m 18.402s
12	Simone Corsi (I)	24	Honda	23	48m 18.860s
13	Fabrizio Lai (I)	32	Gilera	23	48m 42.367s
14	Jordi Carchano (E)	28	Aprilia	23	48m 55.073s
15	Dario Giuseppetti (D)	26	Honda	23	49m 02.361s
16	Julian Miralles (E)	70	Aprilia	23	49m 05.767s
17	Sergio Gadea (E)	33	Aprilia	23	49m 05.841s
18	Vesa Kallio (SF)	66	Aprilia	23	49m 32.763s
19	Gino Borsoi (I)	23	Aprilia	23	49m 39.716s
20	Raymond Schouten (NL)	16	Honda	23	49m 47.188s
21	Mattia Angeloni (I)	11	Honda	23	49m 48.622s
22	Georg Frohlich (D)	20	Honda	22	47m 57.018s
23	Stefano Perugini (I)	7	Gilera	22	48m 01.589s
24	Manuel Manna (I)	8	Malaguti	22	48m 21.451s
25	Enrique Jerez (E)	71	Honda	22	49m 12.335s
26	Imre Toth (H)	25	Aprilia	20	49m 02.346s
	Thomas Luthi (CH)	12	Honda	21	DNF
	Lukas Pesek (CZ)	52	Honda	20	DNF
	Mattia Pasini (I)	54	Aprilia	19	DNF
	Angel Rodriguez (E)	47	Derbi	16	DNF
	Gabor Talmacsi (H)	14	Malaguti	15	DNF
	Mike di Meglio (F)	63	Aprilia	10	DNF
	Mika Kallio (SF)	36	KTM	7	DNF
	Robbin Harms (DK)	69	Honda	6	DNF
	Ismael Ortega (E)	81	Aprilia	6	DNF
	Gioele Pellino (I)	42	Aprilia	5	DNF
	Manuel Hernandez (E)	43	Aprilia	4	DNF
	Jorge Lorenzo (E)	48	Derbi	3	DNF
	Alvaro Bautista (E)	19	Aprilia	0	DNF

Fastest lap: **Jenkner,** 2m 00.510s, **82.101 mph/132.128 km/h.**

Lap record: **Stefano Perugini, I (Aprilia),** 1m 47.766s, **91.809 mph/147.753 km/h (2003).**

Event best maximum speed: **Ui,** 131.3 mph/211.3 km/h **(free practice no. 1).**

Qualifying: **1 Simoncelli,** 1m 48.106s; **2 Bautista,** 1m 48.245s; **3 Stoner,** 1m 48.302s; **4 Nieto,** 1m 48.363s; **5 Dovizioso,** 1m 48.392s; **6 Locatelli,** 1m 48.410s; **7 Ui,** 1m 48.485s; **8 M. Kallio,** 1m 48.600s; **9 Talmacsi,** 1m 48.653s; **10 Giansanti,** 1m 48.883s; **11 Jenkner,** 1m 49.177s; **12 Barbera,** 1m 49.184s; **13 Borsoi,** 1m 49.326s; **14 Lorenzo,** 1m 49.404s; **15 di Meglio, 1**m 49.423s; **16 Pasini,** 1m 49.774s; **17 Simon,** 1m 49.948s; **18 Toth,** 1m 50.051s; **19 Pesek,** 1m 50.203s; **20 Perugini,** 1m 50.243s; **21 Ballerini,** 1m 50.269s; **22 Lai,** 1m 50.371s; **23 Hernandez,** 1m 50.418s; **24 Gadea,** 1m 50.554s; **25 Carchano,** 1m 50.619s; **26 Pellino,** 1m 50.834s; **27 Corsi,** 1m 50.944s; **28 Luthi,** 1m 50.993s; **29 Harms,** 1m 51.185s; **30 Manna,** 1m 51.287s; **31 Schouten,** 1m 51.330s; **32 V. Kallio,** 1m 51.336; **33 Giuseppetti,** 1m 51.356s; **34 Rodriguez,** 1m 51.924s; **35 Miralles, 1m 52.290s; 36 Jerez,** 1m 52.408s; **37 Frohlich,** 1m 52.538s; **38 Angeloni,** 1m 53.018s; **39 Ortega,** 1m 53.219s.

Fastest race laps: **1 Jenkner,** 2m 00.510s; **2 Stoner,** 2m 00.514s; **3 Simoncelli,** 2m 00.867s; **4 di Meglio, 2**m 01.121s; **5 Dovizioso,** 2m 01.146s; **6 Barbera**, 2m 01.364s; **7 Pasini,** 2m 01.447s; **8 Ballerini, 2m** 01.813s; **9 Ui,** 2m 02.036s; **10 Pesek,** 2m 02.059s; **11 Corsi,** 2m 02.256s; **12 Harms,** 2m 02.264s; **13 Nieto,** 2m 02.283s; **14 Giansanti,** 2m 02.290s; **15 Talmacsi,** 2m 02.297s; **16 Locatelli,** 2m 02.425s; **17 M. Kallio,** 2m 02.513s; **18 Borsoi,** 2m 02.769s; **19 Simon,** 2m 02.896s; **20 Lai,** 2m 03.746s; **21 Ortega,** 2m 03.820s; **22 Luthi,** 2m 03.841s; **23 Carchano,** 2m 04.275s; **24 Rodriguez,** 2m 04.439s; **25 Pellino,** 2m 04.490s; **26 Miralles,** 2m 04.987s; **27 Gadea,** 2m 05.140s; **28 Hernandez,** 2m 05.752s; **29 Giuseppetti,** 2m 05.857s; **30 V. Kallio,** 2m 06.139s; **31 Perugini,** 2m 06.791s; **32 Schouten,** 2m 07.025s; **33 Toth,** 2m 07.159s; **34 Lorenzo,** 2m 07.182s; **35 Frohlich,** 2m 07.887s; **36 Angeloni,** 2m 07.905s; **37 Jerez,** 2m 09.079s; **38 Manna,** 2m 09.159s.

World Championship: **1 Dovizioso,** 38; **2 Jenkner and Locatelli,** 28; **4 Stoner,** 27; **5 Simoncelli,** 25; **6 Barbera,** 22; **7 Nieto,** 20; **8 Giansanti,** 15; **9 di Meglio,** 11; **10 Ballerini, Borsoi, Simon and Ui,** 10; **14 Bautista,** 7; **15 Corsi,** 6; **16 M. Kallio,** 4; **17 Lai and Pasini,** 3; **19 Carchano,** 2; **20 Giuseppetti,** 1.

FIM WORLD CHAMPIONSHIP • ROUND 3

FRENCHGP

LE MANS

VALENTINO Rossi was off the front row at Le Mans for the first time since Jerez last year (where he won). And he was off the rostrum again for a second successive race. Yet he remained the luckiest man in motorcycle racing.

The lack of form was for a tangible reason. "We made a Horlicks of the front fork settings," said crew chief Jerry Burgess later. This undermined braking stability, crucial at stop-and-go Le Mans, almost two seconds a lap faster after complete resurfacing. Rossi was, for once, outqualified and outraced by team-mate Checa.

But he was lucky not to have had a much harder race, as he escaped having to start from pit lane after stalling his engine at the start of the warm-up lap. The sequence of events that unfolded was both controversial and pure French farce.

On the line, green flag shown, everyone takes off for the warm-up lap. Except Rossi. Yamaha had switched to Marelli ignition, and he blamed "a bad feeling". He'd let the fire go out.

The regulations say only one mechanic can attend a rider on the line. This man and Rossi tried a bump-start, without success - the new growler engine is frequently rather reluctant. Another of his men joined in with the starter roller, but that chose this moment to conk out. Along came two Tech 3 mechanics with their roller. All the while, IRTA general secretary Mike Trimby had been in arm-waving attendance. Now he lent his gravitas on the back of the seat, to make sure the rollers wouldn't slip. With five people helping out, it finally burst back into life.

Rossi set off as if it were a race - it was a race, to catch the safety car at the back of the field before it got to the start line. The driver lingered obligingly in the final corners, and he made it. But instead of being motioned to the back of the grid, he was waved through to his second row position.

This appeared to have been just one of several breeches of the regulations, but Race Director Paul Butler put up a robust defence. The regs applied while the 60- and 30-second boards were displayed, but once the green flag had been shown, the race was under his direct control, and he was entitled to take whatever decision he saw fit. In any case the regulations were for safety, not to make it difficult for a rider to start. All his decisions had been taken for the good of the sport, he said, and it was hard to argue against that. Nor did any team offer an official protest. The catch in the throat came when wondering if the same positive discrimination would also be applied to, say, one of the Protons, or a Kawasaki.

The green bikes had a dramatic weekend anyway, with a timely reminder that four-strokes carry oil, and have the potential to drop it all, at very short notice.

The first bulletin was when Hofmann blew up dramatically on the fastest corner, the formidable Turn One at the end of the pit straight. This after two other big adventures there: Hopkins's Suzuki shed its chain at top speed on the entrance, for a scary trip through the gravel; Shakey Byrne - nursing right hand injuries from Jerez - was unable to hang on to the Aprilia Cube and followed suit, before withdrawing from the race.

Hofmann avoided this fate, and prompt red flags meant that his large oil slick didn't precipitate anybody else down the same route. Practice was delayed by 15 minutes as prodigious quantities of cement dust were strewn along his path. Soon after the restart, he did it again, elsewhere on the track, and this time without the oil. Hofmann had a third blow-up in the race as well, when Nakano brought the total of lunched engines to four in the weekend.

The first question concerned whether enough was done in MotoGP to prevent dangerous oil spills. American AMA bikes pack fairing belly pans with absorbent material; MotoGP requires only a sealed pan, though a drain plug may be removed in the wet. To be honest, the scale and speed of the leakage was such that it's hard to imagine how it might be contained, short of wrapping the whole bike in cotton wool.

Secondly, Kawasaki seemed to have taken a clear step forward this season, aided by their new Bridgestone tyres. Now, suddenly, it was Bastille Day, Fourth of July and Guy Fawkes Night all at once. They'd proved fragile in the past, but this was ridiculous.

The destruction was so complete that it was hard even to know where it had begun, project leader Naoyo Kaneko later told MOTOCOURSE. Probably piston, but they couldn't be sure. Patient investigation revealed a faulty batch of sensors deep in the engine management ECU, throwing ignition and injection out of kilter enough to trigger spectacular self-destruction.

No smokey blow-ups this time for the Proton KR V5, celebrating its first birthday with a new and painfully noisy flat five-pipe exhaust drone note from their retimed Mk2 V5. Another innovation during the weekend was a longer-stroke motor... plenty of increasingly desperate work back at Banbury.

Launched amid fine promises of "raising the bar", the British-built bike had succeeded in doing so only in limited areas. These included an integration of design (and a standard of fit and finish) in advance even of Honda, with an aerospace-standard chassis carved from solid, and highly specialised purpose-built parts, such as titanium brake hydraulic unions. Another area was in costs. "We're going to outspend everyone this year," said team principal Roberts, dryly.

Much was the trade-mark of F1 guru John Barnard, recruited to the team the previous season. The down-side came hand in hand as an unfortunate consequence: the chassis had required slimmer cylinder heads, and performance fell short of computer projections, robbing an already underpowered machine of some 15 horsepower, explained Roberts. The fruitless search for it was to occupy much of the rest of the season.

They were running the lathes late at Ducati's workshops too, the results under wraps... a pair of 2003 machines, to be tested back to back with the new bike after the race. Since the entire previous production was with the d'Antin team, this pair had to be specially made. There were no plans to race them, said team chief Livio Suppo. They were purely to provide a baseline comparison, and to show that Ducati "keep an open mind." In the event, that's how it turned out.

Different target, same old bulls eye in the 250 class, when Fonsi Nieto again appeared to attack another rider deliberately... this time the sainted Pedrosa, on a fast lap in the first timed session. He had passed Nieto, running slowly, into a turn, only for the older rider to stuff him back on the exit, almost causing both to fall. Fingers wagged on the track; in the pit afterwards an intended apology from Nieto turned into a stand-up row with Pedrosa's mentor, Alberto Puig. Passions ran high between the austere old-school former 500 GP winner (against Doohan) and the tinted-tips Nieto, a brash newcomer with a big name (he is Angel's nephew), but fisticuffs were avoided.

Top left: French tripods ... fans exploit all vantage points.

Above left: 100 podium finishes were a piece of cake for Max Biaggi.

Above: Helping hands include those of IRTA boss Mike Trimby (right) after Rossi stalled his engine on the line.

Right: Kenny Roberts – no smiles for Proton's first birthday.

Below: Fonsi Nieto's portrait looks over his shoulder.

Photographs: Gold & Goose

65
12

SHOEI
PROTON

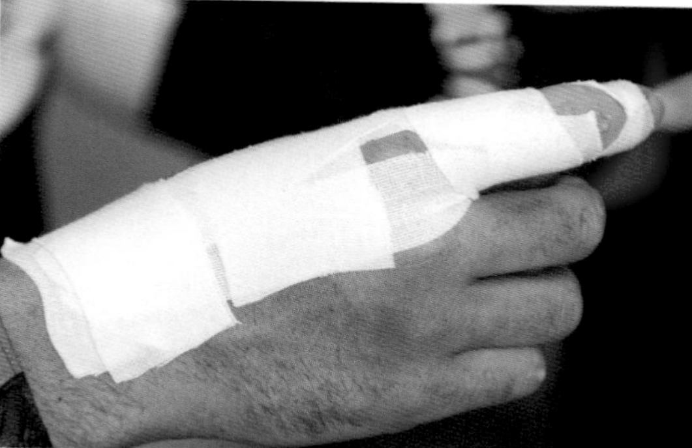

Movistar
Arai

MOTOGP RACE – 28 laps

With the first dozen within a second of pole, Rossi's second row was still only a quarter-of-a-second off. Gibernau was fastest, on fine form in spite of a fever that had him sweating and cursing. Checa and Biaggi were alongside.

Rossi had a little crash in morning warm-up - his first off since a similar incident in Germany last year. Then came the start-line shambles. He was under more pressure than the practice time interval suggested.

Aoki was starting from the pit lane, after switching to his spare for the warm-up, then coming back in for the other bike, the slipper clutch now readjusted. Rossi finally arrived, and off they went.

Three riders never made it back, after Hodgson high-sided on the last left-hander. That brought down Abe and Hopkins as well. Hodgson broke ribs in the melee; Hopkins his thumb. Barros narrowly avoided becoming involved, finishing lap one 13th.

Over the next two laps Checa stretched away, Gibernau with him and Rossi a second or so adrift. Biaggi led Edwards and Melandri a little way back.

By lap ten, Rossi was 2.5 seconds adrift and Biaggi was closing; Melandri had passed Edwards but couldn't match Biaggi's pace. Likewise Capirossi, losing ground on this group with Barros up to eighth, ahead of Bayliss, Hayden and Nakano, with Roberts dropping out of this gang behind. Hayden would soon also leave the party, after an off-track excursion.

At the long Garage Vert U-turn before the back straight, Checa made his first mistake, running wide. Gibernau was fault-free, pretty much, and certainly ready to slip inside for a lead he would keep to the end.

That was on lap 12; at the same time Biaggi had lined up Rossi, to surge past convincingly on the front straight, the pair then starting to work on a two-second cap to Checa. Rossi made one lunge past Max on brakes at the end of the back straight, but was wide mid-corner and behind on the exit again. His problems were starting to show as Max concentrated on applying pressure to Checa... until he ran over the kerbs at the first tight chicane, nearly colliding with the Yamaha as he regained the track, and easing off for a while to recover from a blow in the testicles.

Rossi was once again within a second, but he was right on the limit, as he showed when he straight-lined the left-right at the end of the back straight, actually gaining ground to end up Biaggi's tail. Checa had his work cut out to stay ahead of the pair, until on lap 26 Rossi was ahead of Biaggi again. But it was only for a moment, and Biaggi set a new record as he closed right up on Checa, his final attack spoiled when they ran up on a group of backmarkers in the final tight bends.

Rossi was 2.3 seconds adrift at the flag; Edwards emerged a comfortable victor over Melandri in the battle for fifth; Barros's climb ended at seventh; Bayliss pulling clear of the persistent Tamada, both leaving a troubled Capirossi trailing. Likewise Hayden and Roberts. McWilliams rode his Aprilia to 13th in spite of a ride-through penalty for jumping the start... the bike had a new heavier crank, making throttle responses less erratic.

The backmarkers who baulked Biaggi were in a battle for the final points. Xaus had fallen and remounted, and in the last lap passed Kurtis Roberts at the crucial last corner, with Fabrizio's WCM right behind. Aoki was out of the points.

Both Kawasakis had expired in clouds of smoke - Hofmann's third blow-up of the weekend on the fifth lap. Nakano lasted 11 more laps and was a fighting 11th when the same happened to him.

Gibernau had been faultless all race long. One more race, and still he led the World Championship. With high-speed Mugello coming up, and the long straight that should favour the Hondas, how long could it last?

Above: **On form and outranking Rossi, Checa leads eventual winner Gibernau, his illustrious team-mate, then Biaggi and Edwards.**

Top left: **Capirossi temporarily heads the Ducati formation from team-mate Bayliss; Tamada close behind.**

Bottom left: **Kurtis Roberts trying hard on the new noisier Proton.**

Centre left: **Byrne's finger ... he pulled out after losing control at speed.**

Bottom centre: **Edwards, still searching for his high-speed comfort zone.**

Photographs: Gold & Goose

Right: Pedrosa (26) would soon leave the 250 brawl behind; Rolfo (2) is off-line, and shortly off the track too.

Below: Last-corner drama as a close-to-crashing Dovizioso (34) steals Locatelli's line.

Bottom: Dovizioso claimed a second win in three races.

Photographs: Gold & Goose

250 cc Race – 26 laps

Pedrosa disputed pole with local hero de Puniet, and took it by three tenths; two more Aprilias completed the row ... Porto and Poggiali, for once looking stronger. Elias led row two, a little happier on the Honda on a real scratcher's track.

Pedrosa led away strongly, Rolfo started from the far end of row two, and demonstrated his Honda problems on the second corner, crashing to earth. Poggiali did the same thing one lap later. The older hands were finding the going tough.

Pedrosa was steadfast, his riding typically accurate - and his pace devastating. De Puniet was clinging on desperately; Porto led the next group, already two seconds behind after two laps.

In this way, Pedrosa's second win of his rookie year was totally dominant, five seconds ahead after ten laps, his only problem being to keep his focus. De Puniet had already given up, the previous day's hopes of becoming the first French 250 winner at Le Mans fading even after five laps. "I wanted to go with Dani, but I seemed to have a little problem at the rear. I don't know why," he said later.

Porto kept him honest, cutting the gap to less than a second after half distance, only to lose touch again with a little slip. He'd caught up again when he crashed out on lap 18.

Behind these three, Elias, Aoyama and de Angelis were locked in battle, Battaini and Nieto dropping back from it in the early laps. With six to go, Elias took control at the chicane, and started to edge away, a second clear of Aoyama at the end, with de Angelis snapping at the second blue Honda's back wheel.

Anthony West was having a strong race, starting from the third row on his ageing Aprilia, finishing lap one 11th and gaining places rapidly. Eight on lap five, he was closing on Nieto, who complained later of bad handling. He dogged his adversary from the previous race until lap 12, then passed him decisively. "I followed him, then made the pass stick, so he never had the chance to get back at me," he said.

Nieto fell back behind the next battle, but pulled back ahead of Battaini and Debon again by the finish. Chaz Davies scored his first points for 12th, in the thick of the next gang.

125 cc Race – 24 laps

Kids' stuff on the front row, with Dovizioso, Lorenzo and Barbera pushing veteran Locatelli to the far end.

Barbera led away, Jerez winner Simoncelli crashing out of the pursuit pack early on. They swamped the leader on lap five, Dovizioso surging past, Lorenzo with him. They stretched a little gap, but Locatelli was coming through the pack rapidly to attack, and on lap nine he flew past Dovizioso's Honda at the end of the straight.

This pair drew away from then on, the teenager shadowing the 29-year-old former champion. With two laps to go, Locatelli tried to persuade his companion to take a turn up front... but the Honda rider was saving everything for the final lap, attacking on the back straight to block the final twists. He nearly lost it into the last tight right, but his slip worked to his advantage, blocking Locatelli's line. He won by six tenths, like Pedrosa, his second of the year, extending to 26 a record run of 125 races without a back-to-back winner.

Lorenzo managed to get clear of a battle between Giansanti and Barbera. At the finish Nieto nosed in between the KTMs, Kallio sixth and Stoner eighth; Bautista close, Jenkner dropping back. De Meglio and Ui had crashed out of this battling group before half-distance.

16 MAY 2004

LE MANS – BUGATTI CIRCUIT

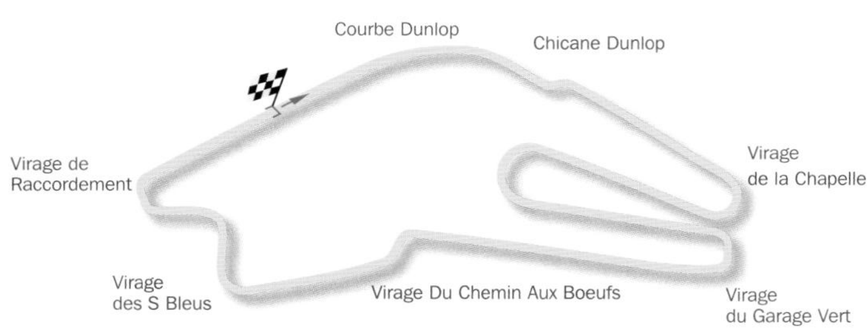

CIRCUIT LENGTH: 2.597 miles/4.180 km

Moto GP

28 laps, 72.716 miles/117.040 km

Pos.	Rider (Nat.)	No.	Machine	Laps	Time & speed
1	Sete Gibernau	15	Honda	28	44m 22.750s 98.323 mph/ 158.236 km/h
2	Carlos Checa (E)	7	Yamaha	28	44m 24.421s
3	Max Biaggi (I)	3	Honda	28	44m 24.658s
4	Valentino Rossi (I)	46	Yamaha	28	44m 27.022s
5	Colin Edwards (USA)	45	Honda	28	44m 38.505s
6	Marco Melandri (I)	33	Yamaha	28	44m 40.975s
7	Alex Barros (BR)	4	Honda	28	44m 50.406s
8	Troy Bayliss (AUS)	12	Ducati	28	44m 54.280s
9	Makoto Tamada (J)	6	Honda	28	44m 55.914s
10	Loris Capirossi (I)	65	Ducati	28	45m 02.262s
11	Nicky Hayden (USA)	69	Honda	28	45m 10.375s
12	Kenny Roberts (USA)	10	Suzuki	28	45m 34.890s
13	Jeremy McWilliams (GB)	99	Aprilia	28	45m 46.141s
14	Ruben Xaus (E)	11	Ducati	27	44m 23.773s
15	Kurtis Roberts (USA)	80	Proton KR	27	44m 24.402s
16	Michel Fabrizio (I)	84	Harris WCM	27	44n 24.563s
17	Nobuatsu Aoki (J)	9	Proton KR	27	44m 33.360s
	Shinya Nakano (J)	56	Kawasaki	16	DNF
	Chris Burns (GB)	35	Harris WCM	14	DNF
	Alex Hofmann (D)	66	Kawasaki	5	DNF
	Norick Abe (J)	17	Yamaha	0	DNF
	John Hopkins (USA)	21	Suzuki	0	DNF
	Neil Hodgson (GB)	50	Ducati	0	DNF
	Shane Byrne (GB)	67	Aprilia		DNS

Fastest lap: Biaggi, 1m 34.088s, 99.379 mph/159.935 km/h (record).

Previous record: Valentino Rossi, I (Honda), 1m 36.846s, 96.549 mph/155.380 km/h (2002).

Event best maximum speed: Capirossi, 191.8 mph/308.6 km/h (race).

Qualifying: 1 Gibernau, 1m 33.425s; 2 Checa, 1m 33.575s; 3 Biaggi, 1m 33.579s; 4 Rossi, 1m 33.668s; 5 Edwards, 1m 33.870s; 6 Melandri, 1m 33.920s; 7 Hayden, 1m 33.966s; 8 Tamada, 1m 34.057s; 9 Capirossi, 1m 34.095s; 10 Bayliss, 1m 34.211s; 11 Barros, 1m 34.342s; 12 Nakano, 1m 34.362s; 13 Kenny Roberts, 1m 34.459s; 14 Hodgson, 1m 34.526s; 15 Xaus, 1m 34.578s; 16 Hopkins, 1m 34.597s; 17 Abe, 1m 34.665s; 18 McWilliams, 1m 35.371s; 19 Hofmann, 1m 35.718s; 20 Aoki, 1m 36.044s; 21 Kurtis Roberts, 1m 36.373s; 22 Byrne, 1m 36.543s; 23 Fabrizio, 1m 37.710s; 24 Burns, 1m 38.097s.

Fastest race laps: 1 Biaggi, 1m 34.088s; 2 Gibernau, 1m 34.343s; 3 Rossi, 1m 34.486s; 4 Checa, 1m 34.500s; 5 Melandri, 1m 34.793s; 6 Edwards, 1m 35.004s; 7 Barros, 1m 35.144s; 8 Tamada, 1m 35.241s; 9 Capirossi, 1m 35.266s; 10 Bayliss, 1m 35.407s; 11 Hayden, 1m 35.594s; 12 Nakano, 1m 35.829s; 13 Kenny Roberts, 1m 35.895s; 14 Xaus, 1m 35.908s; 15 McWilliams, 1m 36.040s; 16 Hofmann, 1m 36.533s; 17 Aoki, 1m 37.322s; 18 Kurtis Roberts, 1m 37.584s; 19 Fabrizio, 1m 37.783s; 20 Burns, 1m 39.436s.

World Championship: 1 Gibernau, 66; 2 Biaggi, 56; 3 Rossi, 51; 4 Barros, 38; 5 Checa, 36; 6 Edwards, 29; 7 Hayden, 27; 8 Capirossi, 20; 9 Melandri and Tamada, 15; 11 Abe and Kenny Roberts, 12; 13 Nakano, 11; 14 Bayliss, 10; 15 Fabrizio, 6; 16 Hopkins, 4; 17 Hofmann and McWilliams, 3; 19 Aoki and Xaus, 2; 21 Byrne and Kurtis Roberts, 1.

250 cc

26 laps, 67.522 miles/108.680 km

Pos.	Rider (Nat.)	No.	Machine	Laps	Time & speed
1	Daniel Pedrosa (E)	26	Honda	26	43m 03.338s 94.107 mph/ 151.450 km/h
2	Randy de Puniet (F)	7	Aprilia	26	43m 11.049s
3	Toni Elias (E)	24	Honda	26	43m 22.571s
4	Hiroshi Aoyama (J)	73	Honda	26	43m 23.765s
5	Alex de Angelis (RSM)	51	Aprilia	26	43m 24.513s
6	Anthony West (AUS)	14	Aprilia	26	43m 27.607s
7	Fonsi Nieto (E)	10	Aprilia	26	43m 41.875s
8	Franco Battaini (I)	21	Aprilia	26	43m 43.165s
9	Alex Debon (E)	6	Honda	26	43m 45.927s
10	Joan Olive (E)	11	Aprilia	26	43m 50.879s
11	Jakub Smrz (CZ)	96	Honda	26	43m 51.212s
12	Chaz Davies (GB)	57	Aprilia	26	43m 54.961s
13	Hector Faubel (E)	33	Aprilia	26	43m 55.151s
14	Naoki Matsudo (J)	8	Yamaha	26	44m 02.218s
15	Alex Baldolini (I)	25	Aprilia	26	44m 06.599s
16	Dirk Heidolf (D)	28	Aprilia	26	44m 08.708s
17	Hugo Marchand (F)	9	Aprilia	26	44m 09.244s
18	Erwan Nigon (F)	36	Yamaha	26	44m 11.661s
19	Christian Gemmel (D)	15	Honda	26	44m 22.680s
20	Gregory Lefort (F)	77	Aprilia	26	44m 24.374s
21	Taro Sekiguchi (J)	44	Yamaha	26	44m 43.199s
22	Gregory Leblanc (F)	42	Aprilia	25	43m 28.918s
	Sebastian Porto (ARG)	19	Aprilia	17	DNF
	Arnaud Vincent (F)	12	Aprilia	11	DNF
	Sylvain Guintoli (F)	50	Aprilia	10	DNF
	Radomil Rous (CZ)	43	Aprilia	6	DNF
	Johan Stigefelt (S)	16	Aprilia	6	DNF
	Roberto Rolfo (I)	2	Honda	4	DNF
	Manuel Poggiali (RSM)	54	Aprilia	1	DNF
	Eric Bataille (F)	34	Honda	1	DNF
	Samuel Aubry (F)	45	Honda		DNQ
	Vincent Eisen (F)	46	Honda		DNQ
	Marc Antoine Scaccia (F)	47	Yamaha		DNQ

Fastest lap: Pedrosa, 1m 38.202s, 95.216 mph/153.235 km/h (record).

Previous record: Marco Melandri, I (Aprilia), 1m 39.648s, 93.834 mph/151.011 km/h (2002).

Event best maximum speed: Aoyama, 161.2 mph/259.4 km/h (qualifying practice no. 2).

Qualifying: 1 Pedrosa, 1m 37.123s; 2 de Puniet, 1m 37.407s; 3 Porto, 1m 37.436s; 4 Poggiali, 1m 38.007s; 5 Elias, 1m 38.536s; 6 Battaini, 1m 38.674s; 7 Nieto, 1m 38.903s; 8 Rolfo, 1m 39.085s; 9 Aoyama, 1m 39.088s; 10 de Angelis, 1m 39.151s; 11 Guintoli, 1m 39.163s; 12 West, 1m 39.314s; 13 Debon, 1m 39.360s; 14 Bataille, 1m 39.516s; 15 Faubel, 1m 39.775s; 16 Olive, 1m 39.828s; 17 Heidolf, 1m 39.936s; 18 Smrz, 1m 39.976s; 19 Davies, 1m 40.144s; 20 Matsudo, 1m 40.201s; 21 Nigon, 1m 40.249s; 22 Marchand, 1m 40.302s; 23 Vincent, 1m 40.616s; 24 Lefort, 1m 40.778s; 25 Baldolini, 1m 40.788s; 26 Gemmel, 1m 40.942s; 27 Rous, 1m 41.607s; 28 Leblanc, 1m 41.855s; 29 Stigefelt, 1m 42.182s; 30 Sekiguchi, 1m 42.214s; 31 Aubry, 1m 44.064s; 32 Eisen, 1m 44.524s; 33 Scaccia, 1m 45.659s.

Fastest race laps: 1 Pedrosa, 1m 38.202s; 2 Porto, 1m 38.590s; 3 de Puniet, 1m 38.764s; 4 Elias, 1m 39.012s; 5 West, 1m 39.213s; 6 de Angelis, 1m 39.312s; 7 Aoyama, 1m 39.347s; 8 Nieto, 1m 39.879s; 9 Battaini, 1m 39.913s; 10 Smrz, 1m 40.020s; 11 Debon, 1m 40.216s; 12 Davies, 1m 40.251s; 13 Guintoli, 1m 40.302s; 14 Faubel, 1m 40.364s; 15 Olive, 1m 40.453s; 16 Matsudo, 1m 40.498s; 17 Marchand, 1m 40.793s; 18 Vincent, 1m 40.863s; 19 Baldolini, 1m 40.887s; 20 Nigon, 1m 40.950s; 21 Heidolf, 1m 40.965s; 22 Rous, 1m 41.139s; 23 Lefort, 1m 41.167s; 24 Gemmel, 1m 41.354s; 25 Rolfo, 1m 41.433s; 26 Leblanc, 1m 41.610s; 27 Sekiguchi, 1m 42.227s; 28 Stigefelt, 1m 42.603s; 29 Poggiali, 1m 44.749s; 30 Bataille, 1m 49.921s.

World Championship: 1 de Puniet, 60; 2 Pedrosa, 50; 3 Nieto, 34; 4 Rolfo and de Angelis, 32; 6 Debon and Elias, 28; 8 Porto, 25; 9 West, 23; 10 Aoyama, 18; 11 Battaini, 14; 12 Poggiali, 13; 13 Vincent, 11; 14 Matsudo, 8; 15 Faubel and Lefort, 7; 17 Baldolini and Olive, 6; 19 Smrz, 5; 20 Davies, 4; 21 Marchand, 3; 22 Heidolf and Stigefelt, 2; 24 Guintoli and Sekiguchi, 1.

125 cc

24 laps, 62.328 miles/100.320 km

Pos.	Rider (Nat.)	No.	Machine	Laps	Time & speed
1	Andrea Dovizioso (I)	34	Honda	24	41m 26.747s 90.242 mph/ 145.230 km/h
2	Roberto Locatelli (I)	15	Aprilia	24	41m 27.341s
3	Jorge Lorenzo (E)	48	Derbi	24	41m 33.427s
4	Mirko Giansanti (I)	6	Aprilia	24	41m 36.409s
5	Hector Barbera (E)	3	Aprilia	24	41m 36.925s
6	Mika Kallio (SF)	36	KTM	24	41m 47.445s
7	Pablo Nieto (E)	22	Aprilia	24	41m 47.714s
8	Casey Stoner (AUS)	27	KTM	24	41m 47.905s
9	Alvaro Bautista (E)	19	Aprilia	24	41m 48.392s
10	Steve Jenkner (D)	21	Aprilia	24	41m 49.827s
11	Gino Borsoi (I)	23	Aprilia	24	41m 53.446s
12	Mattia Pasini (I)	54	Aprilia	24	41m 56.079s
13	Julian Simon (E)	10	Honda	24	41m 59.934s
14	Lukas Pesek (CZ)	52	Honda	24	42m 03.749s
15	Simone Corsi (I)	24	Honda	24	42m 06.986s
16	Gabor Talmacsi (H)	14	Malaguti	24	42m 07.051s
17	Gioele Pellino (I)	42	Aprilia	24	42m 18.666s
18	Angel Rodriguez (E)	47	Derbi	24	42m 21.270s
19	Dario Giuseppetti (D)	26	Honda	24	42m 21.322s
20	Fabrizio Lai (I)	32	Gilera	24	42m 21.669s
21	Imre Toth (H)	25	Aprilia	24	42m 32.205s
22	Sergio Gadea (E)	33	Aprilia	24	42m 32.357s
23	Manuel Manna (I)	8	Malaguti	24	42m 40.729s
24	Jordi Carchano (E)	28	Aprilia	24	42m 40.995s
25	Julian Miralles (E)	70	Aprilia	24	42m 41.286s
26	Vesa Kallio (SF)	66	Aprilia	24	42m 50.977s
27	Mattia Angeloni (I)	11	Honda	24	42m 54.354s
28	Raymond Schouten (NL)	16	Honda	24	43m 03.685s
29	Mathieu Gines (F)	74	Honda	23	42m 16.147s
30	Yannick Deschamps (F)	73	Honda	23	42m 29.764s
	Robbin Harms (DK)	69	Honda	22	DNF
	Youichi Ui (J)	41	Aprilia	12	DNF
	Mike di Meglio (F)	63	Aprilia	9	DNF
	Alexis Masbou (F)	72	Honda	9	DNF
	Andrea Ballerini (I)	50	Aprilia	7	DNF
	Stefano Perugini (I)	7	Gilera	7	DNF
	Marco Simoncelli (I)	58	Aprilia	1	DNF
	Thomas Luthi (CH)	12	Honda	0	DNF
	Georg Frohlich (D)	20	Honda		DNS

Fastest lap: Dovizioso, 1m 42.651s, 91.089 mph/146.593 km/h (record).

Previous record: Daniel Pedrosa, E (Honda), 1m 43.837s, 90.048 mph/144.919 km/h (2003).

Event best maximum speed: Borsoi, 135.5 mph/218.0 km/h (qualifying practice no. 2).

Qualifying: 1 Dovizioso, 1m 42.608s; 2 Lorenzo, 1m 42.990s; 3 Barbera, 1m 43.086s; 4 Locatelli, 1m 43.190s; 5 Giansanti, 1m 43.282s; 6 Jenkner, 1m 43.324s; 7 Ui, 1m 43.379s; 8 di Meglio, 1m 43.421s; 9 Simoncelli, 1m 43.441s; 10 Nieto, 1m 43.458s; 11 Bautista, 1m 43.515s; 12 Corsi, 1m 43.956s; 13 Stoner, 1m 43.975s; 14 Luthi, 1m 44.194s; 15 Borsoi, 1m 44.261s; 16 Perugini, 1m 44.324s; 17 Pasini, 1m 44.342s; 18 Simon, 1m 44.364s; 19 Lai, 1m 44.435s; 20 M. Kallio, 1m 44.652s; 21 Pesek, 1m 44.877s; 22 Talmacsi, 1m 44.977s; 23 Ballerini, 1m 45.067s; 24 Pellino, 1m 45.087s; 25 Toth, 1m 45.158s; 26 Giuseppetti, 1m 45.189s; 27 Gadea, 1m 45.492s; 28 Harms, 1m 45.553s; 29 Manna, 1m 45.625s; 30 V. Kallio, 1m 45.726s; 31 Rodriguez, 1m 46.134s; 32 Frohlich, 1m 46.181s; 33 Schouten, 1m 46.282s; 34 Miralles, 1m 46.366s; 35 Carchano, 1m 46.559s; 36 Masbou, 1m 47.004s; 37 Angeloni, 1m 47.304s; 38 Deschamps, 1m 48.700s; 39 Gines, 1m 49.152s.

Fastest race laps: 1 Dovizioso, 1m 42.651s; 2 Locatelli, 1m 42.662s; 3 Barbera, 1m 43.036s; 4 Lorenzo, 1m 43.052s; 5 di Meglio, 1m 43.079s; 6 Giansanti, 1m 43.164s; 7 Nieto, 1m 43.486s; 8 Bautista, 1m 43.491s; 9 Borsoi, 1m 43.552s; 10 M. Kallio, 1m 43.552s; 11 Ui, 1m 43.597s; 12 Stoner, 1m 43.660s; 13 Jenkner, 1m 43.738s; 14 Pasini, 1m 43.758s; 15 Simon, 1m 43.928s; 16 Pesek, 1m 44.049s; 17 Talmacsi, 1m 44.241s; 18 Corsi, 1m 44.317s; 19 Pellino, 1m 44.480s; 20 Perugini, 1m 44.562s; 21 Giuseppetti, 1m 44.575s; 22 Lai, 1m 44.664s; 23 Rodriguez, 1m 44.779s; 24 Gadea, 1m 44.853s; 25 Harms, 1m 44.874s; 26 Toth, 1m 45.044s; 27 Carchano, 1m 45.383s; 28 Ballerini, 1m 45.485s; 29 Miralles, 1m 45.574s; 30 Manna, 1m 45.583s; 31 V. Kallio, 1m 45.737s; 32 Angeloni, 1m 45.909s; 33 Schouten, 1m 46.448s; 34 Masbou, 1m 48.703s; 35 Gines, 1m 48.786s; 36 Deschamps, 1m 48.959s; 37 Simoncelli, 1m 51.527s.

World Championship: 1 Dovizioso, 63; 2 Locatelli, 48; 3 Stoner, 35; 4 Jenkner, 34; 5 Barbera, 33; 6 Nieto, 29; 7 Giansanti, 28; 8 Simoncelli, 25; 9 Lorenzo, 16; 10 Borsoi, 15; 11 Bautista and M. Kallio, 14; 13 Simon, 13; 14 di Meglio, 11; 15 Ballerini and Ui, 10; 17 Corsi and Pasini, 7; 19 Lai, 3; 20 Carchano and Pesek, 2; 22 Giuseppetti, 1.

FIM WORLD CHAMPIONSHIP • ROUND 4

ITALIANGP

MUGELLO

Far left: Rossi fans were out in force.

Centre left: The object of their fervour performs his ritual oblations before taking to the track.

Below left: Abe takes a flier in the restart, to power between Rossi and Biaggi, Gibernau on the right.

Right: Nakano before the start.

Inset right: The wreckage of his Kawasaki after his record-breaking high-speed crash.

Photographs: Gold & Goose

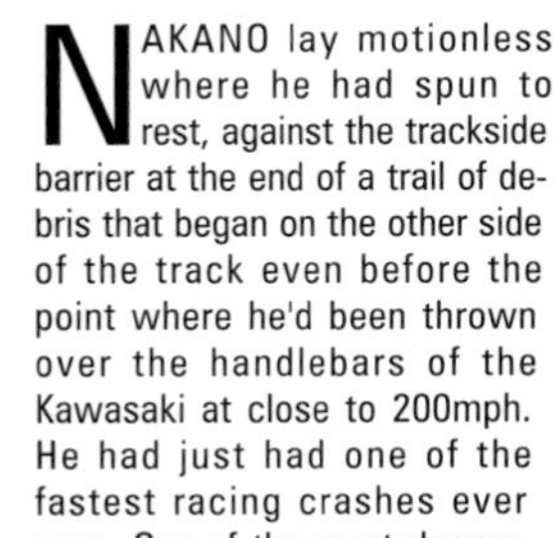

NAKANO lay motionless where he had spun to rest, against the trackside barrier at the end of a trail of debris that began on the other side of the track even before the point where he'd been thrown over the handlebars of the Kawasaki at close to 200mph. He had just had one of the fastest racing crashes ever seen. One of the most dangerous kind of crashes too, travelling in a straight line. Everybody feared the worst as officials ran to the fallen rider.

They clustered round his prone form, prepared a stretcher. Then, miraculously, the Japanese rider weakly raised an arm, to wave. "I wanted people to know I wasn't dead," he explained later.

It really was something of a miracle. Nakano was not only alive but had escaped serious injury, to the extent that he was able to race one weekend later, beating Biaggi for a fine seventh. His comment at that time was both charming and a little chilling. "A week ago I thought I was dead. Now I had a great race. That's why I love racing."

And it was a key moment for Bridgestone, who supplied the tyre that failed at close to 200mph... a fixed track camera showed a chunk flying off the rear as he passed the start line, still accelerating. The bike was wallowing so much by the end of the pit wall that it simply tripped over its front wheel. At that speed, it was like an air crash.

This "bitter experience" was not Bridgestone's first or only such failure this year... indeed, just one lap later Tamada had ended a promising race, when in the fight for the lead, pulling in to the trackside with a similarly chunking rear. His, at least, was still inflated. The same rider had rear failures at speed in pre-season testing, as had Kenny Roberts Jr., crashing heavily at Sepang. This was more serious, for several reasons. One was that Bridgestone thought they'd put those failures behind them; it took them "completely by surprise". The other that it was so fast, so dangerous, and so very public.

A week later, at Catalunya, sober-faced Bridgestone engineers spoke of how they had scrapped more than 300 tyres, and taken several backward steps in development and construction, losing "two or three months of progress", but determined to err on the side of safety, with much stronger if heavier tyre constructions. At the time, their teams and riders were in a state of some trepidation. As it transpired, if anything this low point acted as an even stronger spur to a tyre development team already setting a cracking pace in the drive to catch up with Michelin, leaving Dunlop looking nonplussed in their own serially unsuccessful quest to do the same.

It was speed rather than heat that did it; conditions were less than scorching by Mugello standards, and more especially by those of Sepang, where the pre-season failures had struck. Mugello didn't quite match Capirossi's 215 mph, set pre-season at Catalunya with a powerful tailwind, but it came very close. Top speeds are fudged by slipstreaming among other things, but remain revealing. Fastest of the weekend was Barros's factory Honda, at 213.13 mph (343.0 km/h), more than five mph up on last year; then Capirossi's Duke at 211.94, Biaggi fractionally slower, and then Rossi's Yamaha at 210.64. All these were race speeds. In practice, Capirossi had only been marginally slower riding alone, but Rossi's best was 206.7.

By comparison, the best by any other Yamaha all weekend was Melandri in the race, a whisker faster than that. Aprilia clocked a best of 206.91 (McWilliams), Aoki's Proton 204.62, Roberts's lone Suzuki 203.44 - Hopkins was out with his thumb not up to riding, fellow Le Mans injury victim Hodgson soldiering on, in much pain from rib and back injuries.

Five mph down in true top end, this track should not have suited Rossi. Compared with both Ducatis and Hondas, the M1 is short of numbers. Being Rossi, he won anyway. Being Rossi in Italy, he won twice - not only in the first leg in the dry, but then a very different restart of six laps. The first leg, counting in the end only for grid positions for the restart, was a fine game of high-speed tactics, draughting and swooping round the lovely old track. The second was a brawling sprint in club-race style, the world's finest on slick tyres on a half-wet circuit. They went back and forth on surges of courage, luck and skill, and in that six laps alone there were four different race leaders, including such unexpected candidates as Xaus and Bayliss.

The first such restart of this season again raised questions of the fairness of a system in which all the do-or-die of the first race means nothing more than a place on the grid. Certainly the race-in-itself restart had been successful in replacing the bewilderment of the previous amalgamated-time races with breathtaking excitement. The Mugello restart was a memorable race. But it would not have been belittled if only for half points, with the other half being awarded for the first part of the interrupted race. Before the end of the season, the debate was rendered irrelevant. No more race interruptions from 2005; they would go flag to flag.

Earlier promises of a new Aprilia for Mugello were only half fulfilled, with an upgraded bike distinguished by a slimmer fairing, now with winglets ... "to increase downforce", they said.

Winglets and downforce have a long and mainly dysfunctional history in bike racing, dating back to the Seventies or even earlier, and they keep popping up at intervals, though the same old questions never go away. One problem rises when the bike does a big wheelie: if they have any effect at all, the angle of attack of the winglets would now encourage the bike to take off. Another conundrum is the direction of operation of the downforce, if any. It acts with the axis of the bike, and when it is leaned over, it still acts in that direction, so instead of increasing tyre grip it would instead encourage side-slip. F1 and now road supercar design guru Gordon Murray, a lifelong motorcyclist and bike racing fan, was at the track, and mildly amused. "I'd love to try to find a way to get downforce on a bike in a corner, but it would have to act at 90 degrees to the ground, not in line with the machine, to improve tyre side-grip. But you'd have to persuade the riders to adopt exactly the same angle of lean through every corner. Change the lean and you change the downforce... and probably crash," he smiled.

MoviStar
HONDA

11

CAMEL
6
46
GAULOISES

teamkr.com

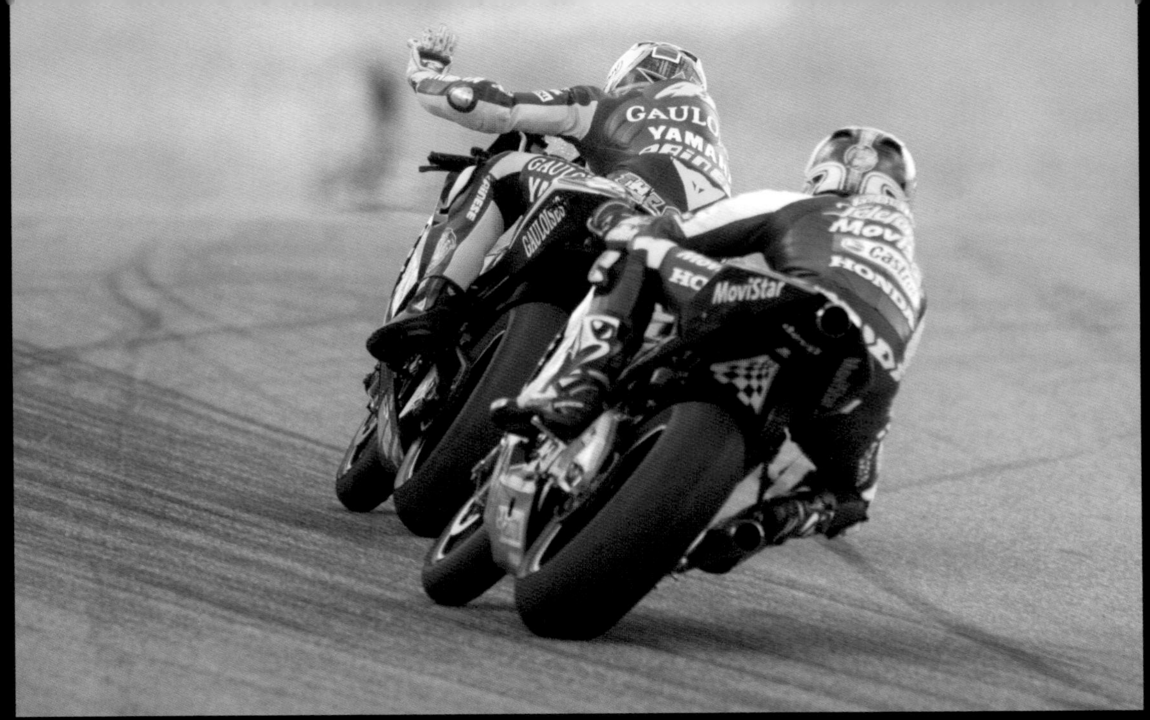

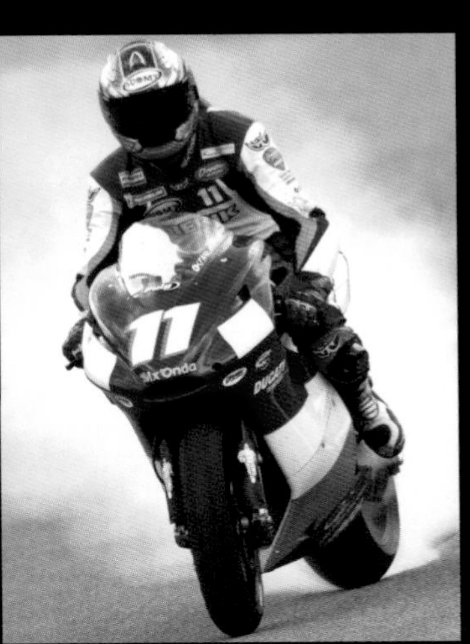

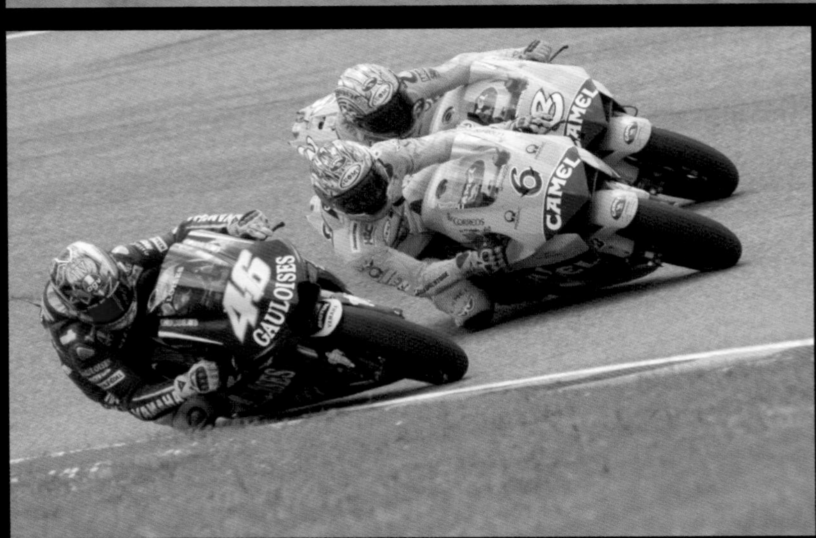

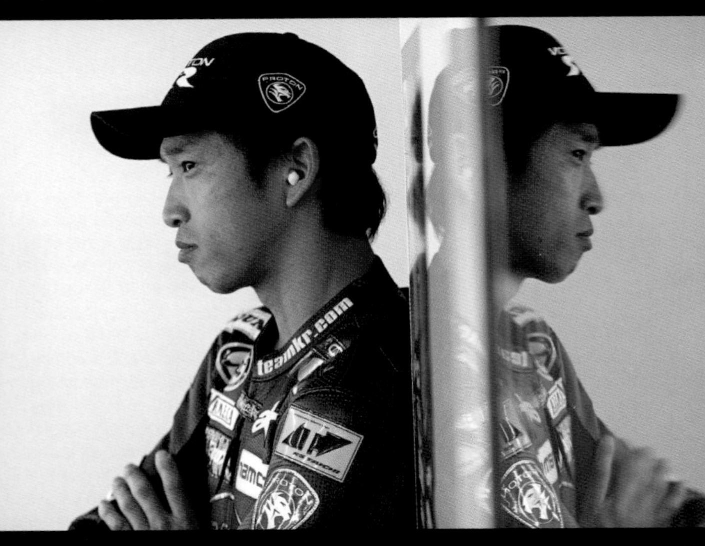

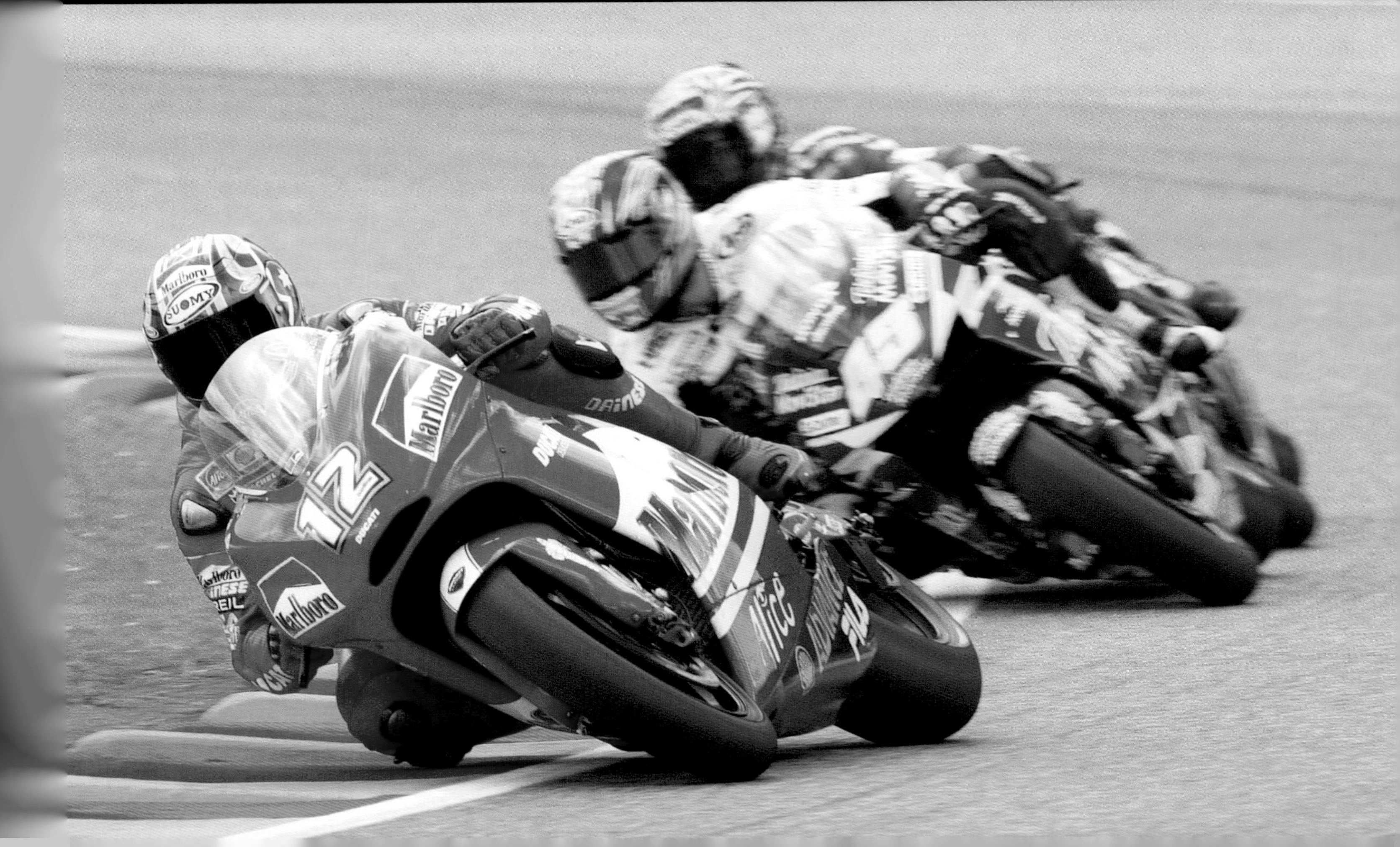
Marlboro
SUOMY
12
Marlboro
Marlboro

MOTOGP RACE – Six laps

Qualifying showed that Gibernau's form was clearly intact, reeling off fast laps to slash 2.4 seconds off Rossi's pole of last year. Kurtis Roberts had a fiery crash in the final session, bringing out the red flags and messing up timing and tactics. In the final sprint, Hayden followed Barros and ousted hard-riding Rossi from second; Barros led row two from Melandri and Biaggi.

The first 17 laps may not have been worth championship points, but they were well worth reporting. It certainly ranks among the best races any of the massive crowd, as well as seasoned paddock veterans, had ever seen.

Rossi was away fast, Biaggi powered past the first time down the front straight, Rossi pounced directly back into the first corner again. Sheer speed, versus sheer Rossi.

Capirossi was already losing ground in third, with Tamada shoving past on lap two, followed by Melandri, Hayden and Gibernau. Checa was also past the red Duke one lap later, but Barros pushed past both of them at once, and Checa slipped off soon afterwards, trying to get him back.

Rossi was manfully battling for every advantage over Max, but now Tamada had joined in, past Max on lap four and leading for the first time on lap five... only for Rossi to outbrake him into Turn One. Next time round Tamada was ready for it, and held the lead for the next six laps... over the line. But he and Rossi were changing places as much as six times a lap, corner after corner. Max was pushing between them now and then, and Gibernau had closed up. It was fearsomely close and fast battle.

At half distance, it was still anybody's race. Then suddenly Tamada wasn't there anymore. His tyre had started vibrating two corners from the end of lap 14. "It got worse on the straight. I preferred to stop," he said. Understandably, since one lap before Nakano's rear had exploded, and the track was covered with chunks of rubber and shards of unmistakably green bodywork.

Marshals dashed bravely among speeding bikes to retrieve this debris - it took three or four laps. Many were surprised that the race was not stopped. Meanwhile Kawasaki had hung a board out to Hofmann, the last remaining Bridgestone runner, to be cautious... whatever that might mean on a 200mph straight. They were about to call him in, under Bridgestone's recommendation, when the red flag came out as the leaders started lap eighteen.

By the end of the previous lap, Rossi and Gibernau were a second clear of Biaggi, while Barros had continued his progress, past Melandri on lap nine, and was closing steadily. A battle was looming, but it was forestalled by spots of rain.

The positions at lap 17 were: Rossi, Gibernau, Biaggi, Barros, Melandri, Bayliss, Abe, Edwards, Xaus, a fading Capirossi, Hodgson, Hofmann, Byrne, McWilliams, Aoki, Pitt and Fabrizio.

Out of the action were crashers Nakano, Checa and Hayden, who slipped out of a strong fifth on lap seven, and retirees Tamada and the Roberts brothers, Kenny on lap ten with a broken engine, Kurtis earlier still with a slipping clutch.

The rain was soon heavy if spasmodic and locally short-lived, and they lined up in that order for a restart of six laps.

MOTOGP RESTART

Parts of the track - notably Turn One - were still drenched, but the overall trend was drying, and slicks the tyre of choice. Biaggi led them as they tiptoed perilously into the first corner.

Bravery paid more dividends than cutting edge factory bikes in the early laps; rookies Xaus and Byrne both enjoying the effect. Barros led lap one, from Biaggi, Abe, Gibernau and Rossi. Xaus went piling past them all at Turn One to lead the whole of the second lap.

Bayliss was also making the most of conditions, and he pushed past his old Superbike adversary to lead lap three. At this point Gibernau was second, from Rossi, Biaggi and Xaus. It was still very up and down, but the more experienced riders were beginning to get the hang of things, and it was also drying out.

On lap four, Rossi took control, stretching almost a second advantage on the next lap, with Gibernau behind, poised for a last lap attack. His last lap was his fastest, but Rossi held on by three tenths for a second win of the day, and the one that counted for 25 points. Biaggi was a little way back, heading the notably determined Bayliss, Xaus and Barros, with Abe leading the next group from Capirossi, Melandri and the impressive Byrne. Hodgson, Edwards and Aoki followed on, then Hofmann and rain-tyre gamblers Fabrizio, McWilliams and Andrew Pitt, back for a first wild card on the Honda-powered but Dunlop-shod tube-frame Moriwaki Dream.

After two such exciting races, the rain-drenched crowd was at fever pitch. When Rossi took the lead with two laps to go, they started chanting his name in operatic unison, 85,000-strong. Even he could hear it, as he won on the fastest straight without needing to have the fastest bike.

Top left: Rain stops play – leader Rossi raises his hand, follower Gibernau is already slowing and sitting up.

Near left: Smoky celebration after rookie Xaus proved his prowess in the wet,

Centre far left: Rossi, Tamada, Biaggi – swapping paint and places for lap after lap.

Centre near left: Reflective Aoki ... the calm before the calm.

Bottom left: Bayliss, here leading Edwards and Abe, shone when the conditions were worst.

Below: Chanting crowds strive to get closer to national hero Rossi on the podium.

Photographs: Gold & Goose

Above: Pedrosa, de Puniet and Porto in close combat.

Top right: Porto set pole position on the first day ... and then had this massive crash.

Right: Casey Stoner, waiting for his first KTM win.

Below: The 125s were close all the way. Here Dovizioso leads Barbera and winner Locatelli; then Stoner, Pasini (54) and Jenkner; then Kallio and Pablo Nieto, Ui losing ground behind.

Photographs: Gold & Goose

250 cc RACE – 21 laps

Porto was on pole on day one when he had a huge high-side crash. Battered but with nothing broken, he was back the next day, his time still good enough to keep Pedrosa second, ahead of de Puniet and Elias on the front row.

Three riders were out in a turn one tangle, robbing the midfield of Vincent, Heidolf and Sabbatani. By the end of that lap, the front runners were already established: Pedrosa ahead, Porto and de Puniet tucked in behind, and Poggiali losing ground in fourth.

They seemed very evenly matched, changing places round the sweeping and plunging track, tucked in close down the straight. Pedrosa led over the line for six laps and de Puniet for five, but Porto had the most of it, leading the other ten, including the only one that really mattered.

By that stage, Pedrosa had dropped out of contention, settling for third after he started suffering front-wheel slides. De Puniet was right there and challenging, right until the final corner. Halfway through it, he suddenly slowed, his Aprilia down to just one cylinder, and that one not running very well.

Porto powered away for his first win of the year, the hapless Frenchman wagged at the throttle in vain, powerless as the following riders came barrelling into view over his shoulder.

First was Pedrosa, gifted a lucky second. Three seconds back, Poggiali had been fending off Elias and Nieto, and for a while also de Angelis, before he lost tyre grip and faded. The defending champion had prevailed for the last lap, and had enough of an advantage to be the only one to catch and pass de Puniet over the line.

Nieto was still ahead of Elias; Rolfo a lonely seventh. Three seconds behind the slowing de Angelis managed to hold off Aoyama, the GP rookie again picking up pace towards the end of the race.

West was tenth, just ahead of Joan Olive and two more Campetella Aprilias, Battaini and Guintoli. Davies was 17th, at the back of a close quartet disputing 14th. Bataille, Baldolini, Smrz and Ronzono all crashed out.

De Puniet's misfortune shrank his points lead. Pedrosa, ominously, was just three behind.

125 cc RACE – 20 laps

Jenkner found the Mugello rhythm to take pole from Stoner, fast rookie Pasini and Dovizioso. With Locatelli leading row two from Kallio and young guns Barbera and Lorenzo, and the first 11 within a second, it was going to be a close race.

And how. At the end there were still six, but experience prevailed over youthful enthusiasm. It was Locatelli's first 125 win since 2000.

The veteran led away for a crash-strewn race - three out on the first corner, with Harms stretchered away with broken ribs and internal injuries. Pasini ran well at first, but couldn't stand the pace of eight fast men, who had broken away before half distance.

With the tiniest GP bikes swarming in and out of one another's draught on the straight, one never knew who might lead over the line. It was Dovizioso on lap one, then Barbera for a few laps, and Locatelli again. Nieto was the first outsider to break through, on lap 17. Elsewhere on the long track there were puffs of tyre smoke and crunching bodywork, but amazingly no crashes, as they ran into corners three or four abreast.

There were six left at the end, Locatelli leading onto the last lap... until Nieto barged past at the first drop off the hill, only to run wide at the next left-hander to drop from first to sixth.

By the time they ran into the last corner, it looked as though Dovizioso might be on for a second successive win, breaking the 26-race record. A slip in the last long left had him out of the saddle, and down to fourth. Locatelli kept it together to head Stoner over the line by less than two tenths; Barbera almost alongside, then Dovizioso, Giansanti and Nieto in short order.

Jenkner dropped back to a lone seventh, likewise Pasini in eighth. Borsoi led Lorenzo, Corsi, Ballerini and Talmacsi in the next tight group over the line.

FIM WORLD CHAMPIONSHIP • ROUND 4

CINZANO ITALIAN grand prix

6 JUNE 2004

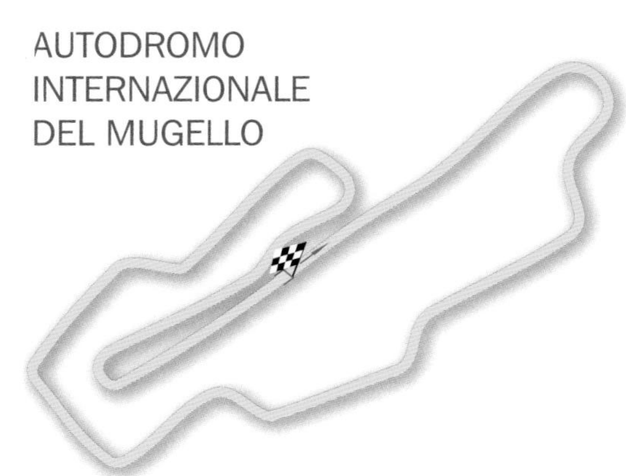

CIRCUIT LENGTH: 3.259 miles/5.245 km

MotoGP

Six laps, 19.554 miles/31.470 km*

Pos.	Rider (Nat.)	No.	Machine	Laps	Time & speed
1	Valentino Rossi (I)	46	Yamaha	6	12m 06.803s 96.857 mph/ 155.877 km/h
2	Sete Gibernau (E)	15	Honda	6	12m 07.164s
3	Max Biaggi (I)	3	Honda	6	12m 08.343s
4	Troy Bayliss (AUS)	12	Ducati	6	12m 08.585s
5	Ruben Xaus (E)	11	Ducati	6	12m 09.192s
6	Alex Barros (BR)	4	Honda	6	12m 09.249s
7	Norick Abe (J)	17	Yamaha	6	12m 12.645s
8	Loris Capirossi (I)	65	Ducati	6	12m 13.031s
9	Marco Melandri (I)	33	Yamaha	6	12m 13.264s
10	Shane Byrne (GB)	67	Aprilia	6	12m 14.001s
11	Neil Hodgson (GB)	50	Ducati	6	12m 15.851s
12	Colin Edwards (USA)	45	Honda	6	12m 16.429s
13	Nobuatsu Aoki (J)	9	Proton KR	6	12m 21.004s
14	Alex Hofmann (D)	66	Kawasaki	6	12m 54.894s
15	Michel Fabrizio (I)	84	Harris WCM	6	12m 57.301s
16	Jeremy McWilliams (GB)	99	Aprilia	6	13m 03.375s
17	Andrew Pitt (AUS)	88	Moriwaki	6	13m 06.070s
	Did not start Race Part 2:				
	Makoto Tamada (J)	6	Honda	DNS	
	Shinya Nakano (J)	56	Kawasaki	DNS	
	Nicky Hayden (USA)	69	Honda	DNS	
	Kenny Roberts (USA)	10	Suzuki	DNS	
	Carlos Checa (E)	7	Yamaha	DNS	
	Kurtis Roberts (USA)	80	Proton KR	DNS	
	Chris Burns (GB)	35	Harris WCM	DNQ	

*Race Part 1: 17 laps, result neutralised.

Fastest lap: Gibernau, 1m 51.133s, 105.573 mph/169.904 km/h (unofficial record set in Race Part 1).

Lap record: Tohru Ukawa, J (Honda), 1m 52.601s, 104.197 mph/167.689 km/h (2002).

Event best maximum speed: Barros, 213.1 mph/343.0 km/h (race Part 2).

Qualifying: 1 Gibernau, 1m 49.553s; 2 Hayden, 1m 49.922s; 3 Rossi, 1m 49.926s; 4 Barros, 1m 50.058s; 5 Melandri, 1m 50.315s; 6 Biaggi, 1m 50.445s; 7 Tamada, 1m 50.584s; 8 Capirossi, 1m 50.699s; 9 Kenny Roberts, 1m 50.736s; 10 Nakano, 1m 50.807s; 11 Checa, 1m 50.858s; 12 Edwards, 1m 50.970s; 13 Hofmann, 1m 51.303s; 14 Xaus, 1m 51.405s; 15 Bayliss, 1m 51.647s; 16 Abe, 1m 51.659s; 17 Byrne, 1m 52.355s; 18 McWilliams, 1m 52.368s; 19 Hodgson, 1m 52.496s; 20 Aoki, 1m 52.904s; 21 Kurtis Roberts, 1m 54.066s; 22 Pitt, 1m 54.556s; 23 Fabrizio, 1m 54.695s; 24 Burns, 1m 58.174s.

Fastest race laps (after Race Part 2): 1 Gibernau, 1m 52.891s; 2 Rossi, 1m 53.513s; 3 Biaggi, 1m 53.603s; 4 Bayliss, 1m 54.015s; 5 Melandri, 1m 54.200s; 6 Barros, 1m 54.319s; 7 Xaus, 1m 54.645s; 8 Abe, 1m 55.046s; 9 Capirossi, 1m 55.425s; 10 Hodgson, 1m 56.119s; 11 Edwards, 1m 56.296s; 12 Byrne, 1m 56.410s; 13 Aoki, 1m 57.761s; 14 Hofmann, 1m 58.152s; 15 Pitt, 2m 03.720s; 16 Fabrizio, 2m 07.328s; 17 McWilliams, 2m 08.542s.

World Championship: 1 Gibernau, 86; 2 Rossi, 76; 3 Biaggi, 72; 4 Barros, 48; 5 Checa, 36; 6 Edwards, 33; 7 Capirossi, 28; 8 Hayden, 27; 9 Bayliss, 23; 10 Melandri, 22; 11 Abe, 21; 12 Tamada, 15; 13 Xaus, 13; 14 Kenny Roberts, 12; 15 Nakano, 11; 16 Byrne and Fabrizio, 7; 18 Aoki, Hodgson and Hofmann, 5; 21 Hopkins, 4; 22 McWilliams, 3; 23 Kurtis Roberts, 1.

250 cc

21 laps, 68.439 miles/110.145 km

Pos.	Rider (Nat.)	No.	Machine	Laps	Time & speed
1	Sebastian Porto (ARG)	19	Aprilia	21	40m 32.672s 101.282 mph/ 162.998 km/h
2	Daniel Pedrosa (E)	26	Honda	21	40m 38.819s
3	Manuel Poggiali (RSM)	54	Aprilia	21	40m 41.087s
4	Randy de Puniet (F)	7	Aprilia	21	40m 43.898s
5	Fonsi Nieto (E)	10	Aprilia	21	40m 44.548s
6	Toni Elias (E)	24	Honda	21	40m 44.560s
7	Roberto Rolfo (I)	2	Honda	21	40m 57.070s
8	Alex de Angelis (RSM)	51	Aprilia	21	41m 00.222s
9	Hiroshi Aoyama (J)	73	Honda	21	41m 00.798s
10	Anthony West (AUS)	14	Aprilia	21	41m 10.697s
11	Joan Olive (E)	11	Aprilia	21	41m 10.879s
12	Franco Battaini (I)	21	Aprilia	21	41m 18.460s
13	Sylvain Guintoli (F)	50	Aprilia	21	41m 33.822s
14	Hector Faubel (E)	33	Aprilia	21	41m 39.559s
15	Alex Debon (E)	6	Honda	21	41m 39.694s
16	Naoki Matsudo (J)	8	Yamaha	21	41m 39.709s
17	Chaz Davies (GB)	57	Aprilia	21	41m 39.868s
18	Gregory Lefort (F)	77	Aprilia	21	41m 50.136s
19	Johan Stigefelt (S)	16	Aprilia	21	41m 52.327s
20	Christian Gemmel (D)	15	Honda	21	41m 57.784s
21	Taro Sekiguchi (J)	44	Yamaha	21	42m 05.760s
	Jarno Ronzoni (I)	63	Yamaha	15	DNF
	Jakub Smrz (CZ)	96	Honda	11	DNF
	Erwan Nigon (F)	36	Yamaha	10	DNF
	Alex Baldolini (I)	25	Aprilia	8	DNF
	Eric Bataille (F)	34	Honda	8	DNF
	Hugo Marchand (F)	9	Aprilia	8	DNF
	Arnaud Vincent (F)	12	Aprilia	0	DNF
	Dirk Heidolf (D)	28	Aprilia	0	DNF
	Max Sabbatani (I)	40	Yamaha	0	DNF

Fastest lap: Porto, 1m 54.599s, 102.380 mph/164.765 km/h.

Lap record: Shinya Nakano, J (Yamaha), 1m 54.462s, 102.503 mph/164.963 km/h (2000).

Event best maximum speed: Nieto, 172.6 mph/277.7 km/h (free practice no. 2).

Qualifying: 1 Porto, 1m 53.691s; 2 Pedrosa, 1m 53.979s; 3 de Puniet, 1m 54.180s; 4 Elias, 1m 54.635s; 5 de Angelis, 1m 54.643s; 6 Poggiali, 1m 54.670s; 7 Battaini, 1m 54.815s; 8 Rolfo, 1m 55.157s; 9 Nieto, 1m 55.158s; 10 Olive, 1m 55.502s; 11 Aoyama, 1m 55.627s; 12 Smrz, 1m 55.972s; 13 Faubel, 1m 56.057s; 14 Matsudo, 1m 56.247s; 15 Guintoli, 1m 56.328s; 16 West, 1m 56.381s; 17 Marchand, 1m 56.510s; 18 Baldolini, 1m 56.704s; 19 Bataille, 1m 56.752s; 20 Davies, 1m 56.926s; 21 Lefort, 1m 57.146s; 22 Vincent, 1m 57.330s; 23 Nigon, 1m 57.363s; 24 Heidolf, 1m 57.515s; 25 Debon, 1m 57.568s; 26 Stigefelt, 1m 57.796s; 27 Gemmel, 1m 58.477s; 28 Ronzoni, 1m 58.643s; 29 Sekiguchi, 1m 58.690s; 30 Sabbatani, 2m 01.051s.

Fastest race laps: 1 Porto, 1m 54.599s; 2 de Puniet, 1m 54.945s; 3 Pedrosa, 1m 55.112s; 4 Poggiali, 1m 55.265s; 5 de Angelis, 1m 55.301s; 6 Nieto, 1m 55.365s; 7 Elias, 1m 55.429s; 8 Battaini, 1m 56.070s; 9 West, 1m 56.086s; 10 Rolfo, 1m 56.188s; 11 Aoyama, 1m 56.288s; 12 Olive, 1m 56.661s; 13 Smrz, 1m 56.748s; 14 Matsudo, 1m 57.118s; 15 Baldolini, 1m 57.135s; 16 Guintoli, 1m 57.270s; 17 Bataille, 1m 57.363s; 18 Faubel, 1m 57.387s; 19 Debon, 1m 57.674s; 20 Lefort, 1m 57.742s; 21 Davies, 1m 57.926s; 22 Sekiguchi, 1m 57.939s; 23 Marchand, 1m 57.945s; 24 Stigefelt, 1m 58.374s; 25 Gemmel, 1m 58.449s; 26 Nigon, 1m 58.628s; 27 Ronzoni, 1m 59.518s.

World Championship: 1 de Puniet, 73; 2 Pedrosa, 70; 3 Porto, 50; 4 Nieto, 45; 5 Rolfo, 41; 6 de Angelis, 40; 7 Elias, 38; 8 Debon, Poggiali and West, 29; 11 Aoyama, 25; 12 Battaini, 18; 13 Olive and Vincent, 11; 15 Faubel, 9; 16 Matsudo, 8; 17 Lefort, 7; 18 Baldolini, 6; 19 Smrz, 5; 20 Davies and Guintoli, 4; 22 Marchand, 3; 23 Heidolf and Stigefelt, 2; 25 Sekiguchi, 1.

125 cc

20 laps, 65.180 miles/104.900 km

Pos.	Rider (Nat.)	No.	Machine	Laps	Time & speed
1	Roberto Locatelli (I)	15	Aprilia	20	40m 13.158s 97.240 mph/ 156.492 km/h
2	Casey Stoner (AUS)	27	KTM	20	40m 13.310s
3	Hector Barbera (E)	3	Aprilia	20	40m 13.355s
4	Andrea Dovizioso (I)	34	Honda	20	40m 13.731s
5	Mirko Giansanti (I)	6	Aprilia	20	40m 13.753s
6	Pablo Nieto (E)	22	Aprilia	20	40m 14.037s
7	Steve Jenkner (D)	21	Aprilia	20	40m 19.138s
8	Mattia Pasini (I)	54	Aprilia	20	40m 32.364s
9	Gino Borsoi (I)	23	Aprilia	20	40m 41.814s
10	Jorge Lorenzo (E)	48	Derbi	20	40m 41.829s
11	Simone Corsi (I)	24	Honda	20	40m 41.875s
12	Andrea Ballerini (I)	50	Aprilia	20	40m 41.989s
13	Gabor Talmacsi (H)	14	Malaguti	20	40m 42.113s
14	Dario Giuseppetti (D)	26	Honda	20	40m 57.924s
15	Lukas Pesek (CZ)	52	Honda	20	40m 58.033s
16	Imre Toth (H)	25	Aprilia	20	40m 58.840s
17	Alessio Aldrovandi (I)	75	Honda	20	41m 09.486s
18	Stefano Bianco (I)	53	Aprilia	20	41m 09.816s
19	Michaele Pirro (I)	61	Aprilia	20	41m 09.832s
20	Julian Simon (E)	10	Honda	20	41m 20.449s
21	Jordi Carchano (E)	28	Aprilia	20	41m 41.818s
22	Youichi Ui (J)	41	Aprilia	20	42m 42.784s
23	Sergio Gadea (E)	33	Aprilia	19	41m 09.845s
	Mika Kallio (SF)	36	KTM	17	DNF
	Mattia Angeloni (I)	11	Honda	12	DNF
	Alvaro Bautista (E)	19	Aprilia	10	DNF
	Marco Simoncelli (I)	58	Aprilia	8	DNF
	Raymond Schouten (NL)	16	Honda	8	DNF
	Vesa Kallio (SF)	66	Aprilia	8	DNF
	Angel Rodriguez (E)	47	Derbi	8	DNF
	Lorenzo Zanetti (I)	77	Honda	8	DNF
	Gioele Pellino (I)	42	Aprilia	6	DNF
	Fabrizio Lai (I)	32	Gilera	6	DNF
	Stefano Perugini (I)	7	Gilera	6	DNF
	Mike di Meglio (F)	63	Aprilia	2	DNF
	Thomas Luthi (CH)	12	Honda	2	DNF
	Robbin Harms (DK)	69	Honda	0	DNF
	Michele Danese (I)	76	Aprilia	0	DNF
	Manuel Manna (I)	8	Malaguti	0	DNF

Fastest lap: Nieto, 1m 59.400s, 98.264 mph/158.140 km/h.

Lap record: Gino Borsoi, I (Aprilia), 1m 58.969s, 98.620 mph/158.713 km/h (2003).

Event best maximum speed: Barbera, 146.2 mph/235.3 km/h (race).

Qualifying: 1 Jenkner, 1m 58.575s; 2 Stoner, 1m 58.877s; 3 Pasini, 1m 58.941s; 4 Dovizioso, 1m 58.964s; 5 Locatelli, 1m 59.132s; 6 M. Kallio, 1m 59.260s; 7 Barbera, 1m 59.324s; 8 Lorenzo, 1m 59.341s; 9 di Meglio, 1m 59.387s; 10 Lai, 1m 59.451s; 11 Giansanti, 1m 59.527s; 12 Nieto, 1m 59.578s; 13 Pesek, 1m 59.618s; 14 Ui, 1m 59.623s; 15 Simon, 1m 59.899s; 16 Simoncelli, 2m 00.016s; 17 Ballerini, 2m 00.029s; 18 Bautista, 2m 00.120s; 19 Borsoi, 2m 00.155s; 20 Luthi, 2m 00.476s; 21 Corsi, 2m 00.481s; 22 Talmacsi, 2m 00.500s; 23 Rodriguez, 2m 00.565s; 24 Pellino, 2m 00.582s; 25 Aldrovandi, 2m 00.727s; 26 Perugini, 2m 00.780s; 27 Toth, 2m 00.862s; 28 Danese, 2m 01.316s; 29 Manna, 2m 01.319s; 30 Harms, 2m 01.320s; 31 V. Kallio, 2m 01.332s; 32 Bianco, 2m 01.598s; 33 Gadea, 2m 01.786s; 34 Giuseppetti, 2m 01.923s; 35 Schouten, 2m 02.055s; 36 Pirro, 2m 02.704s; 37 Carchano, 2m 03.296s; 38 Zanetti, 2m 03.357s; 39 Angeloni, 2m 04.178s.

Fastest race laps: 1 Nieto, 1m 59.400s; 2 Jenkner, 1m 59.433s; 3 Stoner, 1m 59.435s; 4 Barbera, 1m 59.464s; 5 Locatelli, 1m 59.493s; 6 Dovizioso, 1m 59.501s; 7 Giansanti, 1m 59.581s; 8 Bautista, 1m 59.624s; 9 Simoncelli, 1m 59.658s; 10 Ui, 1m 59.699s; 11 Pasini, 1m 59.924s; 12 Pellino, 1m 59.983s; 13 M. Kallio, 2m 00.133s; 14 Ballerini, 2m 00.235s; 15 Borsoi, 2m 00.329s; 16 di Meglio, 2m 00.376s; 17 Lorenzo, 2m 00.478s; 18 Lai, 2m 00.556s; 19 Talmacsi, 2m 00.719s; 20 Rodriguez, 2m 00.723s; 21 Corsi, 2m 00.828s; 22 Toth, 2m 00.928s; 23 Pesek, 2m 01.073s; 24 Giuseppetti, 2m 01.230s; 25 Perugini, 2m 01.460s; 26 Pirro, 2m 01.496s; 27 Bianco, 2m 01.634s; 28 Luthi, 2m 01.720s; 29 Aldrovandi, 2m 01.807s; 30 Gadea, 2m 01.869s; 31 Simon, 2m 01.871s; 32 V. Kallio, 2m 01.876s; 33 Schouten, 2m 02.017s; 34 Zanetti, 2m 02.742s; 35 Carchano, 2m 03.262s; 36 Angeloni, 2m 04.988s.

World Championship: 1 Dovizioso, 76; 2 Locatelli, 73; 3 Stoner, 55; 4 Barbera, 49; 5 Jenkner, 43; 6 Giansanti and Nieto, 39; 8 Simoncelli, 25; 9 Borsoi and Lorenzo, 22; 11 Pasini, 15; 12 Ballerini, Bautista and M. Kallio, 14; 15 Simon, 13; 16 Corsi, 12; 17 di Meglio, 11; 18 Ui, 10; 19 Giuseppetti, Lai, Pesek and Talmacsi, 3; 23 Carchano, 2.

Right: Rossi takes control into turn one, from Gibernau (15), Biaggi, Tamada (6) and Barros (4). Hopkins (21) is away well from row three, alongside Melandri (33).
Photograph: Gold & Goose

Bottom: Sealed with a kiss - Sete's fans get up close and personal.
Photograph: Malcom Bryan/BPC

FIM WORLD CHAMPIONSHIP • ROUND 5

CATALANGP

BARCELONA

Top: Rossi, tossing a knee-slider to the adoring multitude, fully enjoyed another narrow victory.

Above: Past masters all. Wayne Rainey, Kevin Schwantz, Mick Doohan and Alex Criville shared ten titles between them.

Left: A slider's circuit, Catalunya needs dual-compound tyres, and punishes them severely.

Photographs: Gold & Goose

"IF we were still racing, Valentino would be fifth." The remark, from Kevin Schwantz, drew laughter and applause, in a packed conference room where Schwantz was one of a quartet of former 500-class heroes, with 118 GP victories and ten World Championships between them. His companions were Mick Doohan, Alex Criville and Wayne Rainey, visiting his first four-stroke GP race. The adulation was well deserved.

After the race, however, Schwantz revised his comment. "I guess he'd be top three, behind me and Rainey obviously - if we were at one of our favourite tracks."

The gathering of past gods put an interesting perspective on the comparison of the old class and new. All commented on the relative docility of the four-strokes compared with their 500 two-strokes, but Rainey declined to agree with contemporary Christian Sarron's comment, a couple of years ago, that the MotoGP monsters were "beautiful bikes... for a girl." Rainey said: "I don't believe there's less risk at all. They're for men. They can still bite you very hard. You see Valentino out of the seat trying to win races." Schwantz added: "I don't want to pick on Christian, but I bet he - and myself - could find a way to crash one of these things." Doohan had a similar perspective. "They are a bit more docile. In qualifying the average rider looks fairly good, on fresh rubber. Come the race, those guys aren't anywhere to be seen. There's only one or two guys out the front like there's always been."

And he was right. Just one winner, and we all know who. Once again at a track that should have favoured the faster Hondas, Rossi proved that the right rider can still prevail. To muddy the waters still further, there were three Yamahas in the top five.

Top speed and long straights aren't everything though, as the Ducati riders continue to prove. The more important character of Catalunya is the nature of the corners... long and mostly fairly fast, with the bikes spending a lot of time leaned right over. The pace has increased exponentially - the first 12 in practice not just inside the lap record, but faster than last year's pole, and achieved with more power-on slides than you'd see anywhere outside a flat-track or speedway race.

This is where the Yamaha has an edge on the Hondas, and as a result Gibernau chose softer tyres than Rossi, in the hope that he'd be able to get enough of a gap earlier on to make up for any loss of performance later in the race. Not so, and when Rossi saw him slide, he realised the race was starting to go his way.

The other story of the weekend concerned Bridgestone, galvanised into remarkable action by last weekend's failures, and flying in top brass as well as 100 tyres with "reinforced construction". This would cost grip, they said, but would finish the race. Their riders felt some unease all the same. Tamada pitted with a rear vibration, though his team said afterwards the tyre had been fine; Roberts did the same, and again no tyre problem was in evidence. "I must have hit something in the track," he said. With a new rear he rejoined right with the two leaders, and ran with Rossi and Gibernau to the end, proving that, with new tyres at least, the Suzuki was as fast as Hondas and Yamahas on old tyres. "I had a grandstand seat, but I made sure not to influence the outcome of the race," he said.

With Honda and the new Yamaha setting a cracking pace, the rival teams had little to do but mind their own business. Literally, in the case of Aprilia. News had broken in the days before the race that the factory was in serious financial trouble, hit hard by a slump in scooter sales in Italy. Racing manager Jan Witteveen was determinedly upbeat, insisting it would not affect the racing programme. "What is Aprilia without racing?" he asked. "To lose it would reduce the value of the company." At a time when they were seeking a buyer, this would not help. And though the three-cylinder MotoGP Cube had developed but little since last year, they were testing a revised engine, with altered shaft positions, that promised more for the future.

Suzuki's big changes were already at the track, at least for one rider. Roberts's GSV-R had a different sound from the soulful previous version, and a pair of mismatched exhausts to go with it. Inside, the crankshaft and firing intervals had been radically altered. Gone was the original 180-degree crank, replaced with a 360-degree unit. It had, said Roberts, cost a little top speed and gained nothing in acceleration, but throttle responses and engine braking were both improved. "In a lot of areas it's much better," he said. "I can go through the corners with more control." Kinder to the tyres, it would improve the poor-relation Suzuki's race performance, if not its top-speed deficit.

Ducati were fresh from revealing tests of their own. At Mugello they had given Xaus a run on this year's bike, and the ex-Superbike rider had been quicker than both team regulars, until they put on soft tyres. If the purpose had been to put a rocket up Capirossi and Bayliss, the result was not as productive as might have been hoped. Bayliss crashed heavily in the race, ironically enough after colliding with Xaus while trying to pass; last year's winner Capirossi was tenth after running off on the first lap. Xaus, at the first track where he had any prior knowledge and experience, was a strong sixth, and top Ducati in practice, in spite of three tumbles. "I'm learning, and when you're learning, you make mistakes," he said. It would not be the last time the rookie would outclass the big-timers. But the most important news was that factory tester Vittorio Guareschi had been testing the revised and rephased Twin Pulse at the same time. This bike would soon be the Ducati of choice for the factory men.

No matter that Spain had already seen MotoGP five weeks before, the crowd was vast; 68,000 grandstand tickets sold out well in advance, and another 23,000 crowded the hillsides.

Above: For a couple of laps, Hodgson enjoyed showing factory Ducati rider Capirossi the way on his year-old bike. He finished in the points again.
Photograph: Gold & Goose

MOTOGP RACE – 25 laps

Gibernau's third pole in succession came with dominance throughout. Rossi had one off-track excursion and one on-track breakdown before he moved to second. Hayden took a second front-row in succession. He was half-a-second down on pole, Biaggi another four tenths behind him. Xaus, top Ducati, led row three.

Hayden went from third to 12th on the run to the first corner, "spinnin' all the way". Gibernau had led the charge, but Rossi had the line to slip inside to lead the rest of the lap. Capirossi, trying to compensate for his fifth-row start, had a bump and a bang and a wild ride across the gravel trap. At this point Biaggi and Tamada were third and fourth, Barros pushing hard behind.

Rossi's only mistake of the race, at the end of the back straight on lap two, saw him almost out of the seat under braking. The quality of his riding was plain to all. Instead of running off into the dirt like anyone else, he kept cool and merely ran a little wide. Gibernau got past, but Rossi slotted right in behind him before Biaggi could follow suit.

From then on the two leaders had it their own way; Rossi close to the Spaniard and holding tighter lines. Then on lap 14 Gibernau ran wide once too often, at the looping right-hand Turn Four. Rossi needed no second invitation.

It wasn't over yet. Gibernau powered past down the main straight, only to run wide again at the start of the back straight a lap later, letting Rossi by for six laps. Gibernau was looking desperate, nearly hitting the back of the Yamaha once, but was finally able to use his speed advantage to regain the lead on lap 22. For only two more laps, however.

With two laps to go, Rossi hung in the Honda's draft and went flying past into the first corner. On the limit and with better corner speed, he held on to the end, the frustrated Gibernau just two tenths behind over the line. "We changed the bike all weekend," said Rossi. "The last change was in the morning - and it was very, very good to ride. When I got to the first corner of the last lap without him coming by, I knew I could win."

The rest were in another race. Biaggi had lost touch early on, Barros was past Tamada and leaning on him when he slid to earth, losing the front. By now Melandri was ahead of Tamada and chasing the Brazilian. A lap later he was past Biaggi, who complained later of a sliding rear. The leaders were still only two seconds ahead, but it was more than Melandri could deal with, and in any case third was his first rostrum, making him (at 21 years, ten months and six days) the youngest ever to stand there. This after he had been doubtful about starting, after suffering arm-pump problems - three days later he went under the knife to solve them. It was also the first time since 2001 that there was more than one Yamaha in the top three.

Tamada was now back behind Biaggi; then came Xaus, going strong ahead of Checa, Bayliss, Roberts, Hopkins and slow-starting Edwards. Checa passed his compatriot on lap seven, with a brawling gang behind the Ducati rider - Bayliss from Edwards; Nakano's Kawasaki ahead of Roberts, Hopkins close behind. Hayden was coming through from behind, and had passed both Suzukis when he pulled off on the back straight after a radiator leak.

A fine battle raged until there were seven laps to go: Xaus holding Bayliss at bay while closing on Biaggi - Tamada had already pitted. Roberts slipped out of touch, fading tyres meant he couldn't use corner speed to make up for his acceleration and speed deficit; soon afterward he would pit, with team-mate Hopkins following him in with a blown engine. Roberts rejoined to get some TV time, with the leaders.

With four laps left, both Ducatis were ahead of Biaggi, and clearly on the limit. Bayliss was closer to it than Xaus, apparently. He saved a big high-sider on Turn Four, only to touch Xaus and crash properly soon afterwards - a nasty-looking end-over-end tumble, and was lucky to escape with a grazed face (his visor came off), a wrenched neck and ankle, and a few bruises. This shuffled the pack, with Edwards getting to the front of it and taking a small gap as Biaggi, Xaus and Nakano scrapped back and forth. Xaus prevailed, Biaggi was the loser.

Abe was lonely in ninth; Capirossi never got up to any real speed, but managed to snitch tenth ahead of Hofmann. Then came Hodgson, Byrne, Moriwaki wild card Pitt, with Aoki taking the last point, inches ahead of Fabrizio's WCM. Roberts was 17th; Burns on the other WCM five laps down, after pitting three times to adjust his clutch. Lavilla on the wild-card Suzuki ran out of gas on the last lap, but was never in the picture. McWilliams did not start, after breaking ribs in a morning warm-up tumble.

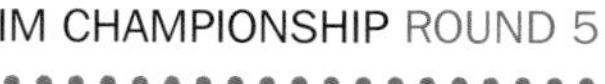

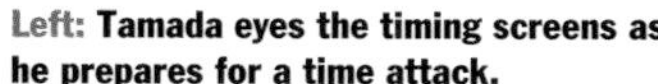

Left: Tamada eyes the timing screens as he prepares for a time attack.

Below: Melandri's third made him the youngest-ever podium finisher in the top class.

Photographs: Gold & Goose

Bottom: Hayden qualified well again, started badly ... and then ran out of luck.

Photograph: Malcolm Bryan/BPC

Above: De Puniet holds off Pedrosa for the lead, Elias in close attendance, as he heads for his first win of the year.

Below: Trade-mark 125 racing, as Dovizioso (34) moves inside Bautista, ahead of Stoner (27) and Locatelli, under hard braking.

Photographs: Gold & Goose

250 cc RACE – 23 laps

De Puniet was narrowly ahead of Pedrosa, Porto more than half-a-second down from de Angelis; Elias heading row two from Nieto, Guintoli and Rolfo.

It was another race with fairly sparse action up front. Pedrosa got away first but de Puniet dived underneath him into Turn One to lead for the next ten laps, with Elias losing ground in third from the off.

Just before half-distance Pedrosa showed his cards, leading for one lap. Elias had also closed up again, just a second away. It was only temporary. De Puniet regained the lead next time round, and with the pace increasing Elias dropped out of touch once again.

Pedrosa simply wouldn't give up, and the pair touched as they swapped once again. Then on lap 18 Pedrosa ran into the first corner at blinding speed, staying ahead for two laps as they scythed through backmarkers. But de Puniet had the speed, and when he got in front once more, it was for good. Elias was a lonely third; Porto ditto in fourth.

Rolfo had taken control of the next group early on, losing almost a second a lap on the leaders but holding Nieto, Porto, de Angelis and Poggiali at bay. De Angelis came through to harry Rolfo, but crashed in the attempt. Poggiali was next up, Nieto on his rear, and the defending champion attacked at the end of the main straight. It was hopelessly over-ambitious, and he was still upright and trying to get it slowed as Rolfo peeled across in front of him. They collided, and though Rolfo shook his fist as he picked himself up out of the gravel, when Poggiali apologised he gave him a friendly hug.

This left a lucky fifth to Nieto, who had Aoyama closing to within three seconds in the final laps. Guintoli was seventh, then Debon prevailed over West and Battaini for eighth. Davies was 13th, ahead of Matsudo's increasingly outclassed Yamaha.

125 cc RACE – 22 laps

Lorenzo took a massive pole, seven tenths ahead of Barbera. Stoner was close in third, Nieto completed the front row, and Dovizioso was eighth. The race was to be a lot closer, with half-a-dozen riders crossing the line within the same interval of seven tenths.

Barbera and Nieto were left at the start as Locatelli led away from the second row. It was all action from the start, Dovizioso taking over the lead for a couple of laps, then Lorenzo for a long spell, his rapid Derbi threatening to break away down the straight, but never managing it.

Corsi had been with the front men, but crashed out on lap two after colliding with Barbera, making his way back from his bad start. This put Barbera all the way back to 23rd. Jenkner was another, until he had a big slide on lap ten and he dropped out of touch. Then Simoncelli lost touch, unable to stand the furious pace.

Nieto took his place in the lead group after half distance; the amazing Barbera also came back again, setting the lap record as he stormed through to join the gang on lap 16.

Up front, Lorenzo waved Locatelli past for a couple of laps until Nieto barged through to lead. Locatelli promptly high-sided spectacularly out of the race.

Barbera gained the lead for the first time with three laps to go, the other five still within inches, changing to and fro round the loops and twirls.

On the last lap, Nieto led again briefly, Stoner and Dovizioso both pushing him hard. They were two or three abreast into the final turns, and it looked as though points leader Dovizioso had timed it perfectly as he pushed past Nieto to second, then got a flying exit from the last corner to rocket past Barbera. If the line had been only a few yards further he would have made it, but Barbera was hero of the day, by just 0.016 of a second.

Nieto was third, Stoner fourth, Lorenzo fifth and the increasingly impressive Bautista sixth.

CATALUNYA CIRCUIT – BARCELONA

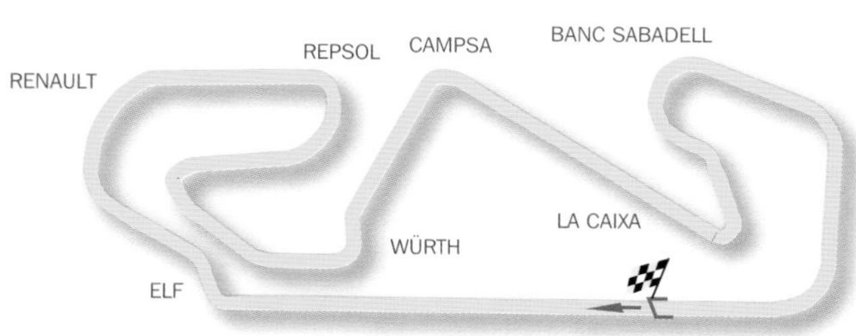

CIRCUIT LENGTH: 2.937 miles/4.727 km

MotoGP

25 laps, 73.425 miles/118.175 km

Pos.	Rider (Nat.)	No.	Machine	Laps	Time & speed
1	Valentino Rossi (I)	46	Yamaha	25	44m 03.255s 100.009 mph/ 160.949 km/h
2	Sete Gibernau (E)	15	Honda	25	44m 03.414s
3	Marco Melandri (I)	33	Yamaha	25	44m 17.178s
4	Carlos Checa (E)	7	Yamaha	25	44m 22.468s
5	Colin Edwards (USA)	45	Honda	25	44m 24.460s
6	Ruben Xaus (E)	11	Ducati	25	44m 26.102s
7	Shinya Nakano (J)	56	Kawasaki	25	44m 27.269s
8	Max Biaggi (I)	3	Honda	25	44m 27.359s
9	Norick Abe (J)	17	Yamaha	25	44m 38.931s
10	Loris Capirossi (I)	65	Ducati	25	44m 44.030s
11	Alex Hofmann (D)	66	Kawasaki	25	44m 44.117s
12	Neil Hodgson (GB)	50	Ducati	25	44m 59.412s
13	Shane Byrne (GB)	67	Aprilia	25	45m 06.934s
14	Andrew Pitt (AUS)	88	Moriwaki	25	45m 09.188s
15	Nobuatsu Aoki (J)	9	Proton KR	25	45m 21.454s
16	Michel Fabrizio (I)	84	Harris WCM	25	45m 21.770s
17	Kenny Roberts (USA)	10	Suzuki	24	44m 03.684s
18	Chris Burns (GB)	35	Harris WCM	20	44m 58.331s
	Gregorio Lavilla (E)	32	Suzuki	24	DNF
	Troy Bayliss (AUS)	12	Ducati	21	DNF
	John Hopkins (USA)	21	Suzuki	18	DNF
	Nicky Hayden (USA)	69	Honda	16	DNF
	Makoto Tamada (J)	6	Honda	12	DNF
	Kurtis Roberts (USA)	80	Proton KR	5	DNF
	Alex Barros (BR)	4	Honda	4	DNF
	Jeremy McWilliams (GB)	99	Aprilia		DNS

Fastest lap: Gibernau, 1m 44.641s, 101.050 mph/162.624 km/h (record).

Previous record: Valentino Rossi, I (Honda), 1m 45.472s, 100.254 mph/161.343 km/h (2003).

Event best maximum speed: Barros, 210.9 mph/339.4 km/h (race).

Qualifying: 1 Gibernau, 1m 42.596s; 2 Rossi, 1m 42.959s; 3 Hayden, 1m 43.124s; 4 Biaggi, 1m 43.563s; 5 Melandri, 1m 43.601s; 6 Barros, 1m 43.647s; 7 Xaus, 1m 43.680s; 8 Hopkins, 1m 43.693s; 9 Tamada, 1m 43.708s; 10 Bayliss, 1m 43.793s; 11 Edwards, 1m 43.832s; 12 Checa, 1m 43.860s; 13 Nakano, 1m 43.948s; 14 Hofmann, 1m 44.126s; 15 Capirossi, 1m 44.131s; 16 Kenny Roberts, 1m 44.175s; 17 Hodgson, 1m 44.761s; 18 Abe, 1m 44.988s; 19 McWilliams, 1m 45.108s; 20 Byrne, 1m 45.200s; 21 Lavilla, 1m 46.142s; 22 Pitt, 1m 46.327s; 23 Kurtis Roberts, 1m 46.399s; 24 Aoki, 1m 46.957s; 25 Fabrizio, 1m 47.503s; 25 Burns, 1m 48.684s.

Fastest race laps: 1 Gibernau, 1m 44.641s; 2 Melandri, 1m 44.708s; 3 Barros, 1m 44.735s; 4 Rossi, 1m 44.791s; 5 Biaggi, 1m 44.792s; 6 Tamada, 1m 44.964s; 7 Xaus, 1m 45.119s; 8 Checa, 1m 45.186s; 9 Kenny Roberts, 1m 45.477s; 10 Hayden, 1m 45.524s; 11 Nakano, 1m 45.532s; 12 Edwards, 1m 45.629s; 13 Bayliss, 1m 45.897s; 14 Abe, 1m 46.027s; 15 Hofmann, 1m 46.213s; 16 Hopkins, 1m 46.223s; 17 Hodgson, 1m 46.296s; 18 Capirossi, 1m 46.382s; 19 Lavilla, 1m 46.797s; 20 Byrne, 1m 47.038s; 21 Pitt, 1m 47.138s; 22 Fabrizio, 1m 47.651s; 23 Aoki, 1m 47.739s; 24 Kurtis Roberts, 1m 47.920s; 25 Burns, 1m 51.519s.

World Championship: 1 Gibernau, 106; 2 Rossi, 101; 3 Biaggi, 80; 4 Checa, 49; 5 Barros, 48; 6 Edwards, 44; 7 Melandri, 38; 8 Capirossi, 34; 9 Abe, 28; 10 Hayden, 27; 11 Bayliss and Xaus, 23; 13 Nakano, 20; 14 Tamada, 15; 15 Kenny Roberts, 12; 16 Byrne and Hofmann, 10; 18 Hodgson, 9; 19 Fabrizio, 7; 20 Aoki, 6; 21 Hopkins, 4; 22 McWilliams, 3; 23 Pitt, 2; 24 Kurtis Roberts, 1.

250 cc

23 laps, 67.551 miles/108.721 km

Pos.	Rider (Nat.)	No.	Machine	Laps	Time & speed
1	Randy de Puniet (F)	7	Aprilia	23	41m 29.955s 97.673 mph/ 157.189 km/h
2	Daniel Pedrosa (E)	26	Honda	23	41m 30.064s
3	Toni Elias (E)	24	Honda	23	41m 39.476s
4	Sebastian Porto (ARG)	19	Aprilia	23	41m 50.826s
5	Fonsi Nieto (E)	10	Aprilia	23	42m 04.292s
6	Hiroshi Aoyama (J)	73	Honda	23	42m 07.524s
7	Sylvain Guintoli (F)	50	Aprilia	23	42m 12.042s
8	Alex Debon (E)	6	Honda	23	42m 15.805s
9	Anthony West (AUS)	14	Aprilia	23	42m 15.893s
10	Franco Battaini (I)	21	Aprilia	23	42m 16.190s
11	Eric Bataille (F)	34	Honda	23	42m 20.649s
12	Alex Baldolini (I)	25	Aprilia	23	42m 20.935s
13	Chaz Davies (GB)	57	Aprilia	23	42m 26.740s
14	Naoki Matsudo (J)	8	Yamaha	23	42m 26.850s
15	Jakub Smrz (CZ)	96	Honda	23	42m 27.321s
16	Hector Faubel (E)	33	Aprilia	23	42m 28.119s
17	Erwan Nigon (F)	36	Yamaha	23	43m 02.277s
18	Taro Sekiguchi (J)	44	Yamaha	22	41m 42.664s
19	Jarno Ronzoni (I)	63	Honda	22	42m 05.431s
20	David Fouloi (F)	72	Aprilia	22	42m 05.504s
	Roberto Rolfo (I)	2	Honda	14	DNF
	Manuel Poggiali (RSM)	54	Aprilia	14	DNF
	Alex de Angelis (RSM)	51	Aprilia	14	DNF
	Joan Olive (E)	11	Aprilia	12	DNF
	Gregory Lefort (F)	77	Aprilia	12	DNF
	Hugo Marchand (F)	9	Aprilia	7	DNF
	Johan Stigefelt (S)	16	Aprilia	7	DNF
	Dirk Heidolf (D)	28	Aprilia	6	DNF
	Max Sabbatani (I)	40	Yamaha		DNS
	Jose Luis Cardoso (E)	30	Yamaha		DNQ

Fastest lap: Pedrosa, 1m 47.302s, 98.544 mph/158.591 km/h (record).

Previous record: Valentino Rossi, I (Aprilia), 1m 47.585s, 98.285 mph/158.174 km/h (1998).

Event best maximum speed: de Angelis, 172.7 mph/278.0 km/h (qualifying practice no. 2).

Qualifying: 1 de Puniet, 1m 46.292s; 2 Pedrosa, 1m 46.434s; 3 Porto, 1m 46.976s; 4 de Angelis, 1m 47.184s; 5 Elias, 1m 47.377s; 6 Nieto, 1m 47.628s; 7 Guintoli, 1m 47.725s; 8 Rolfo, 1m 47.738s; 9 Poggiali, 1m 47.823s; 10 Battaini, 1m 48.115s; 11 Olive, 1m 48.115s; 12 Lefort, 1m 48.190s; 13 Aoyama, 1m 48.299s; 14 Bataille, 1m 48.488s; 15 Matsudo, 1m 48.533s; 16 Debon, 1m 48.553s; 17 Marchand, 1m 48.569s; 18 Smrz, 1m 48.659s; 19 West, 1m 48.808s; 20 Faubel, 1m 49.085s; 21 Davies, 1m 49.122s; 22 Nigon, 1m 49.319s; 23 Stigefelt, 1m 49.484s; 24 Baldolini, 1m 49.552s; 25 Heidolf, 1m 49.659s; 26 Sekiguchi, 1m 49.773s; 27 Ronzoni, 1m 51.937s; 28 Sabbatani, 1m 52.745s; 29 Fouloi, 1m 52.796s; 30 Cardoso, 1m 54.924s.

Fastest race laps: 1 Pedrosa, 1m 47.302s; 2 de Puniet, 1m 47.518s; 3 Elias, 1m 47.755s; 4 de Angelis, 1m 48.213s; 5 Porto, 1m 48.332s; 6 Poggiali, 1m 48.344s; 7 Rolfo, 1m 48.380s; 8 Nieto, 1m 48.395s; 9 Aoyama, 1m 48.823s; 10 Olive, 1m 48.921s; 11 Guintoli, 1m 48.973s; 12 Battaini, 1m 49.174s; 13 West, 1m 49.219s; 14 Debon, 1m 49.373s; 15 Matsudo, 1m 49.461s; 16 Baldolini, 1m 49.505s; 17 Marchand, 1m 49.550s; 18 Davies, 1m 49.592s; 19 Bataille, 1m 49.616s; 20 Lefort, 1m 49.620s; 21 Faubel, 1m 49.726s; 22 Smrz, 1m 49.913s; 23 Nigon, 1m 51.007s; 24 Heidolf, 1m 51.501s; 25 Sekiguchi, 1m 51.530s; 26 Ronzoni, 1m 51.570s; 27 Stigefelt, 1m 52.590s; 28 Fouloi, 1m 52.957s.

World Championship: 1 de Puniet, 98; 2 Pedrosa, 90; 3 Porto, 63; 4 Nieto, 56; 5 Elias, 54; 6 Rolfo, 41; 7 de Angelis, 40; 8 Debon, 37; 9 West, 26; 10 Aoyama, 35; 11 Poggiali, 29; 12 Battaini, 24; 13 Guintoli, 13; 14 Olive and Vincent, 11; 16 Baldolini and Matsudo, 10; 18 Faubel, 9; 19 Davies and Lefort, 7; 21 Smrz, 6; 22 Bataille, 5; 23 Marchand, 3; 24 Heidolf and Stigefelt, 2; 26 Sekiguchi, 1.

125 cc

22 laps, 64.614 miles/103.994 km

Pos.	Rider (Nat.)	No.	Machine	Laps	Time & speed
1	Hector Barbera (E)	3	Aprilia	22	41m 17.986s 93.877 mph/ 151.081 km/h
2	Andrea Dovizioso (I)	34	Honda	22	41m 18.002s
3	Pablo Nieto (E)	22	Aprilia	22	41m 18.328s
4	Casey Stoner (AUS)	27	KTM	22	41m 18.386s
5	Jorge Lorenzo (E)	48	Derbi	22	41m 18.534s
6	Alvaro Bautista (E)	19	Aprilia	22	41m 18.719s
7	Marco Simoncelli (I)	58	Aprilia	22	41m 25.893s
8	Mike di Meglio (F)	63	Aprilia	22	41m 28.779s
9	Mika Kallio (SF)	36	KTM	22	41m 31.417s
10	Mirko Giansanti (I)	6	Aprilia	22	41m 31.499s
11	Mattia Pasini (I)	54	Aprilia	22	41m 32.228s
12	Steve Jenkner (D)	21	Aprilia	22	41m 32.319s
13	Gioele Pellino (I)	42	Aprilia	22	41m 34.195s
14	Julian Simon (E)	10	Honda	22	41m 40.591s
15	Angel Rodriguez (E)	47	Derbi	22	41m 40.641s
16	Dario Giuseppetti (D)	26	Honda	22	41m 40.759s
17	Gabor Talmacsi (H)	14	Malaguti	22	41m 40.947s
18	Youichi Ui (J)	41	Aprilia	22	41m 41.561s
19	Imre Toth (H)	25	Aprilia	22	41m 58.655s
20	Andrea Ballerini (I)	50	Aprilia	22	42m 00.915s
21	Sergio Gadea (E)	33	Aprilia	22	42m 09.432s
22	Stefano Perugini (I)	7	Gilera	22	42m 16.894s
23	Jordi Carchano (E)	28	Aprilia	22	42m 16.981s
24	Manuel Hernandez (E)	43	Aprilia	22	42m 17.534s
25	Mikko Kyyhkynen (SF)	38	Honda	22	42m 35.213s
26	Enrique Jerez (E)	71	Honda	22	42m 54.624s
27	Vesa Kallio (SF)	66	Aprilia	22	43m 06.604s
28	Jordi Planas (E)	78	Honda	21	41m 50.975s
	Lukas Pesek (CZ)	52	Honda	21	DNF
	Mattia Angeloni (I)	11	Honda	21	DNF
	Roberto Locatelli (I)	15	Aprilia	17	DNF
	Gino Borsoi (I)	23	Aprilia	16	DNF
	Fabrizio Perren (ARG)	68	Honda	12	DNF
	Manuel Manna (I)	8	Malaguti	4	DNF
	Simone Corsi (I)	24	Honda	1	DNF
	Fabrizio Lai (I)	32	Gilera		DNS

Fastest lap: Barbera, 1m 50.903s, 95.344 mph/153.442 km/h (record).

Previous record: Casey Stoner, AUS (Aprilia), 1m 51.190s, 95.098 mph/153.046 km/h (2003).

Event best maximum speed: Barbera, 149.8 mph/241.0 km/h (race).

Qualifying: 1 Lorenzo, 1m 50.497s; 2 Barbera, 1m 51.219s; 3 Stoner, 1m 51.260s; 4 Nieto, 1m 51.315s; 5 Pesek, 1m 51.357s; 6 Locatelli, 1m 51.388s; 7 Giansanti, 1m 51.451s; 8 Dovizioso, 1m 51.465s; 9 di Meglio, 1m 51.579s; 10 Jenkner, 1m 51.623s; 11 Simon, 1m 51.639s; 12 Bautista, 1m 51.658s; 13 Simoncelli, 1m 51.666s; 14 Talmacsi, 1m 51.918s; 15 M. Kallio, 1m 51.928s; 16 Corsi, 1m 51.972s; 17 Pasini, 1m 51.999s; 18 Ui, 1m 52.204s; 19 Toth, 1m 52.923s; 20 Perugini, 1m 52.982s; 21 Lai, 1m 53.080s; 22 Pellino, 1m 53.136s; 23 Giuseppetti, 1m 53.158s; 24 Borsoi, 1m 53.168s; 25 Ballerini, 1m 53.357s; 26 Hernandez, 1m 53.653s; 27 Gadea, 1m 53.669s; 28 Rodriguez, 1m 54.004s; 29 Carchano, 1m 54.223s; 30 V. Kallio, 1m 54.243s; 31 Kyyhkynen, 1m 55.045s; 32 Perren, 1m 55.114s; 33 Manna, 1m 55.182s; 34 Angeloni, 1m 55.238s; 35 Jerez, 1m 55.282s; 36 Planas, 1m 56.875s.

Fastest race laps: 1 Barbera, 1m 50.903s; 2 Simoncelli, 1m 51.114s; 3 Lorenzo, 1m 51.420s; 4 Bautista, 1m 51.488s; 5 Jenkner, 1m 51.634s; 6 Dovizioso, 1m 51.642s; 7 Stoner, 1m 51.657s; 8 Nieto, 1m 51.676s; 9 Locatelli, 1m 51.705s; 10 Giansanti, 1m 51.753s; 11 Pellino, 1m 51.862s; 12 Pasini, 1m 51.862s; 13 di Meglio, 1m 51.940s; 14 M. Kallio, 1m 51.952s; 15 Talmacsi, 1m 52.012s; 16 Pesek, 1m 52.200s; 17 Borsoi, 1m 52.308s; 18 Ui, 1m 52.389s; 19 Simon, 1m 52.390s; 20 Rodriguez, 1m 52.463s; 21 Giuseppetti, 1m 53.546s; 22 Ballerini, 1m 52.706s; 23 Toth, 1m 52.955s; 24 Perugini, 1m 53.088s; 25 Hernandez, 1m 53.513s; 26 Carchano, 1m 53.618s; 27 Gadea, 1m 53.728s; 28 Perren, 1m 54.427s; 29 Angeloni, 1m 54.502s; 30 Kyyhkynen, 1m 54.518s; 31 V. Kallio, 1m 54.671s; 32 Jerez, 1m 54.969s; 33 Manna, 1m 55.655s; 34 Planas, 1m 56.746s; 35 Corsi, 1m 59.217s.

World Championship: 1 Dovizioso, 96; 2 Barbera, 74; 3 Locatelli, 73; 4 Stoner, 68; 5 Nieto, 55; 6 Jenkner, 47; 7 Giansanti, 45; 8 Simoncelli, 34; 9 Lorenzo, 33; 10 Bautista, 24; 11 Borsoi, 22; 12 M. Kallio, 21; 13 Pasini, 20; 14 di Meglio, 19; 15 Simon, 15; 16 Ballerini, 14; 17 Corsi, 12; 18 Ui, 10; 19 Giuseppetti, Lai, Pellino, Pesek and Talmacsi, 3; 24 Carchano, 2; 25 Rodriguez, 1.

FIM WORLD CHAMPIONSHIP • ROUND 6

DUTCH TT

ASSEN

Above: Checa leads the thunder of the MotoGP class.

Right: Roberts tried hard and qualified better than usual, only for yet more Suzuki problems to spoil his race.

Centre right: Fearless Tamada explores the limits on his Bridgestone wets.

Far right: Michele Fabrizio was again fast in the wet, but fell in the race.

Photographs: Gold & Goose

NEWCOMERS and track changes notwithstanding, Assen remains the cathedral of motorcycle racing. Or, to some, the university. Once again this year it set hard tasks for its students. Those who graduated needed all their skill and wits. And sheer chutzpah.

The handling advantage of the Yamaha may not have been as obvious as expected, and Gibernau may have been still on top form, leading 18 out of 19 laps. But Rossi had an eye for the front, and his last-lap move was so daring it left his rival not only breathless, but also minus a few bits of bodywork after the Italian (inadvertently, he insisted) used the Spaniard's Honda to help him make it round the next corner. Rossi's win was an amazing 37 seconds faster than the last dry race here two years before; Gibernau's deficit less than half a second. But there can be only one doctorate awarded, and it went to The Doctor.

This year's examinations were invigilated under typically austere conditions, with drenching rain providing a sharp contrast to baking Catalunya, where several teams had stayed on to test. Among them Ducati, again, where the new version of the V-twin-like Twin Pulse found favour with both riders. "After 18 laps I was still doing good lap times and the tyre was cooler and in better condition than in the race," said Capirossi. "The lap times come easier, without having to go too much above yourself," he added. A shortage of parts kept Bayliss switching back and forth between old and new machines in practice. And in the race, Xaus beat them both again, on last year's machine.

Three out of four practice sessions were sodden, leaving everyone complaining of a lack of dry set-up time. Never mind, it looked as though it would rain again on race day. But it never materialised, a bonus for the 90,000 crowd. The rain had given the ill-favoured WCM team and their Dunlops another chance to shine... rookie Fabrizio was fourth in the first timed wet session. "He obviously hasn't read the script," said delighted team manager Peter Clifford.

It was the former European Supersport champion's sixth GP. At the other end of the scale, Alex Barros was recording his 200th start, to become the most experienced GP rider in history, next on the list is Jack Findlay, who clocked up 165 in 20 years, when there were considerably fewer races each year. The 33-year-old Brazilian lied about his age to embark on his career in the 80cc class in 1986, and has finished in the top ten of the top-class World Championship for the past 11 years straight, with more points than anyone except Doohan, one of the pastmasters to join in the champagne toast in the paddock. But he did not cover himself with glory as he racked up his double century. Though he ran with the leading pair and even nosed ahead of Rossi briefly, the man on the top factory Honda - who had harried Rossi without mercy two years go, on a two-stroke against the much fasted four-stroke - crashed heavily soon afterwards when he hooked first instead of second into the first right-hander.

Melandri was rather more impressive. Nine days after surgery to his right arm to cure armpump problems, the 20-year-old claimed a second successive rostrum, so that Yamahas again out-numbered Hondas on the box. Surgery to cure the dreaded Racers' Wrist syndrome is usually reserved for the winter, but Melandri's problems had struck suddenly early in the season, and become rapidly worse.

Over at Suzuki, Roberts was still the only one with the new motor. Hopkins, in his second race back since breaking his thumb at Le Mans, said: "It only motivates me to try harder on the old one," and he out-pointed his senior team-mate for a second time this year, continuing to make a strong impression in a season where injuries dogged his efforts. To be fair, the senior rider might have had a much better weekend than usual, after qualifying seventh and running in the same position in morning warm-up, had he not suffered an electronic glitch that robbed him of horsepower all race long.

Bridgestone's problems were still not over. Another rear tyre had failed in post-race tests at Catalunya, Tamada in the saddle again, and on one of the new generation tyres. Then came a scary moment in qualifying, when Nakano's Kawasaki shed a large black chunk at speed. He didn't crash, however, or even slow down much. It turned out to be a piece of seat padding that had come adrift.

Briton Chris Burns also had a bad moment. The WCM rider fell in practice, slithered through the wet grass to end up in several inches of standing water and in danger of drowning after water had sluiced into his helmet and up his nose. "I didn't even know which way was up," the beleaguered Geordie said later.

Assen's stature is partly because of the nature of the bikes-only circuit, partly because of its position at or at least near the middle of the season, partly because of the vast crowds it draws - although eclipsed nowadays by some Spanish races, and partly because of its history, the only circuit that has been used continuously since the start of the World Championships in 1949. Fittingly the northernmost venue of the year was pivotal in the world championships. In the top class, Rossi took the lead from Gibernau... although equal on points, he has more race wins. In the 250s, Pedrosa closed to within just one point of early leader de Puniet. The points closed up also in the 125 class, with Locatelli closing to within 14 points of Dovizioso. This last, however, was to prove a false dawn.

Right: Assen fans in good cheer and unexpected good weather.

Below: Barros – with chief mechanic Ramon Forcada – had an unhappy 200th grand prix.

Bottom: A close fight for the rostrum saw Biaggi and Melandri trading blows to the end.

Photographs: Gold & Goose

MOTOGP RACE – 19 laps

There was just one dry practice session, the last, and that looked as though it would soon get wet again, so everyone tried to put in fast laps early. Names heading the list included Roberts, Checa, Gibernau and Rossi. At the finish Checa was ahead... until a devastating run by Rossi, the first to break the 1:59 barrier.

Three of the top four were Yamahas, with Checa second, Gibernau slotting in to the last front-row position, and Melandri leading row two.

The MotoGP pack roared away on a dry track, though the threat of another shower was ever-present. Checa led through the first corners, but both Rossi and Gibernau were past before half a lap was completed, and the Spaniard was slipping away on the second, blaming a lack of rear grip.

Barros took advantage to move to third, and was soon with the leading pair as they pulled ahead for the first half of the race. At the end of lap nine Barros managed a cleaner exit from the chicane and surged past Rossi as they passed the pits. He was still ahead next time round, but as they peeled into the track's first serious corner his Honda snapped sideways and he crashed heavily, lucky to emerge without serious injury.

Gibernau forged on ahead, but there was naught for his comfort. Rossi looked menacing and ready to attack at any moment. He nosed alongside on lap 15, but Gibernau kept tucked in and held the position.

He stayed in front for most of the final lap. Rossi's move came just before they turned for the final run through Duikersloot and to the finish line. And it was devastating, pushing past on the outside of a right-hander. Gibernau tried to resist and stayed alongside, but Rossi had the line for the next left. And he left his braking stunningly late. Too late, perhaps, under normal circumstances, but as his bike slid towards the outside he collided with the usefully placed blue Honda, breaking a chunk off the front mudguard but bouncing back onto line.

"I didn't mean to hit him... I lost the front," said Rossi later, adding: "It was a great race between us." A grim-faced Gibernau, who declined to join in the usual champagne-spraying podium fun and games, could only say: "If that's true, then these things sometime happen in racing."

Not too far behind, Checa had been caught by an all-action trio. Biaggi had been leading Melandri and Xaus, the last-named once again at a familiar track. Melandri led the trio as they closed on the Yamaha, and he was the first to get past, gaining a small advantage as the other two worked on finding their way ahead. Biaggi caught up again once he'd moved past, but Xaus had lost touch as he traded blows with his compatriot.

The pair of Italians were locked in battle for the rest of the race, swapping places several times, but with Melandri always getting back ahead, to claim his second third place in two races in fine fighting style.

Capirossi led the next group as they closed on the Checa-Xaus confrontation. Hopkins had been with them until losing ground with sliding tyres; the Hondas of Hayden and Edwards kept with the red factory Desmosedici. In the confusion Xaus managed to escape, with the Honda pair taking three more laps to dispose first of Capirossi and then Checa. They were clear and uncatchable by the time Capirossi also got ahead of Rossi's team-mate.

Hopkins continued to lose places, overtaken first by Bayliss, and then dropping back into the hands of a battling pair, Hodgson finally ahead of Abe after a slow start. The so-far lacklustre World Superbike Champion said afterwards: "This was my first real race of the season," after all sorts of minor technical and/or team problems had spoiled every other race so far.

The pair were closing on Bayliss, but the battle they expected in the last laps never happened, with Bayliss suddenly missing. A gearbox bearing had failed... perhaps the revived Twin Pulse was still too punishing for its components.

Hodgson held his advantage to the flag for his first top ten. Tamada was a little way back at the finish, then Hofmann, with Hopkins hanging on behind as best he could. McWilliams was another ten seconds back to take the last point.

Kenny Roberts was 16th after losing ground all race long, blaming an electronic gremlin that cost him power after qualifying seventh at a track where the latest Suzuki might have gone better than usual. Burns was almost 40 seconds adrift.

Nakano retired after seven laps, his engine seized; Byrne pitted with handling problems. Both Protons failed to finish, Aoki suffering terminal clutch slip and Roberts a broken crankshaft. Fabrizio crashed out after four laps.

Top: Rossi was again untouchable, for a third win in a row.

Above: Gibernau grim, after losing the championship lead.

Photographs: Gold & Goose

Above: **Porto took control for a clear win.**

Below: **Lorenzo leads the 125s past the packed stands.**

Photographs: Gold & Goose

250 cc RACE – 18 laps

Assen wet-weather winner West was fastest in the wet practice, but he dropped to 11th in the single dry session as the faster bikes took over, Porto taking his third pole of the year from Pedrosa, de Puniet and Elias. Poggiali headed row two from de Angelis and Rolfo.

Pedrosa bogged off the line, getting to the first corner 17th, immediately starting to forge his way through backmarkers and midfielders alike.

Porto seized the early advantage, taking a second out of Rolfo and de Puniet, but when the Frenchman moved to second on lap two he started to chip away at the margin slowly but remorselessly, and by lap seven he was on the Argentinean's tail, and Elias had come through to join in.

Remarkably, Pedrosa was up to fourth, his last victim being de Angelis. West had got ahead of a skirmish with Nieto, Rolfo and Poggiali. One lap later Pedrosa was ahead of Elias in third, the top five all closing up as the race passed half distance.

Porto had a second attempt at escaping, and gradually he got a little gap - still less than a second after 11 laps, but another second more next time as the pursuers slowed one another, de Angelis dropping off the back of the group, Elias and Pedrosa trading blows, de Puniet hanging on to the Spanish pair.

Porto was now in control, and with three laps to go de Puniet lost touch with Pedrosa and Elias, who scrapped to the finish, Pedrosa claiming a new lap record on the last lap as he prevailed once and for all.

De Puniet was four seconds back, five more found de Angelis, West a similar distance behind for this underrated rider's best of the year so far.

Behind them Rolfo and Nieto had been fighting over seventh, but Poggiali was poised close behind, and passed them both on the last lap.

Aoyama was a distant tenth, prevailing narrowly over Baldolini and Debon, with Matsudo, Bataille and Davies taking the last points.

The major significance was how the balance of the title battle had changed.

125 cc RACE – 17 laps

The smallest class got the worst of the weather in practice. Although the end of the final session was somewhat drier, pole was still eight seconds down on last year, claimed for the first time this season by Stoner's KTM. He shaded Nieto by half-a-second, then came Dovizioso and Jenkner, with Locatelli leading row two.

There was watery sunshine as the Australian took off in the lead, with Locatelli passing him before the end of the lap, and the pair opening up a small gap. Lorenzo was eighth, but working his way through to third by the end of lap four, quickly closing the gap to the leading pair.

Dovizioso led the next group, Barbera dropping off the back. It included Kallio and Jenkner, who went with the young Italian Honda star as he closed on the front three to make it six disputing the lead.

Lorenzo took the lead for the first time on lap ten, but it was only narrowly. Kallio and Jenkner were losing touch, the former to retire before the end.

Lorenzo led the start of the last lap, Dovizioso nosing ahead, triggering a brawl through the circuit's sweeping bends, the lead changing hands twice more during the lap. But Lorenzo was the strongest while Dovizioso for once got the worst of it, Locatelli and Stoner inches behind for the rostrum.

Jenkner hung on to a lonely fifth; Barbera got the better of Simoncelli, Nieto and Giansanti for sixth.

FIM WORLD CHAMPIONSHIP • ROUND 6

ASSEN TT RACING CIRCUIT

26 JUNE 2004

CIRCUIT LENGTH: 3.745 miles/6.027 km

MotoGP

19 laps, 71.155 miles/114.513 km

Pos.	Rider (Nat.)	No.	Machine	Laps	Time & speed
1	Valentino Rossi (I)	46	Yamaha	19	38m 11.831s 111.770 mph/ 179.876 km/h
2	Sete Gibernau (E)	15	Honda	19	38m 12.287s
3	Marco Melandri (I)	33	Yamaha	19	38m 21.740s
4	Max Biaggi (I)	3	Honda	19	38m 22.014s
5	Nicky Hayden (USA)	69	Honda	19	38m 22.131s
6	Colin Edwards (USA)	45	Honda	19	38m 22.632s
7	Ruben Xaus (E)	11	Ducati	19	38m 25.536s
8	Loris Capirossi (I)	65	Ducati	19	38m 25.922s
9	Carlos Checa (E)	7	Yamaha	19	38m 26.990s
10	Neil Hodgson (GB)	50	Ducati	19	38m 45.897s
11	Norick Abe (J)	17	Yamaha	19	38m 46.245s
12	Makoto Tamada (J)	6	Honda	19	38m 51.017s
13	Alex Hofmann (D)	66	Kawasaki	19	38m 53.337s
14	John Hopkins (USA)	21	Suzuki	19	39m 06.400s
15	Jeremy McWilliams (GB)	99	Aprilia	19	39m 16.592s
16	Kenny Roberts (USA)	10	Suzuki	19	39m 34.097s
17	Chris Burns (GB)	35	Harris WCM	19	40m 12.300s
	Troy Bayliss (AUS)	12	Ducati	17	DNF
	Alex Barros (BR)	4	Honda	10	DNF
	Shane Byrne (GB)	67	Aprilia	8	DNF
	Shinya Nakano (J)	56	Kawasaki	7	DNF
	Nobuatsu Aoki (J)	9	Proton KR	7	DNF
	Kurtis Roberts (USA)	80	Proton KR	5	DNF
	Michel Fabrizio (I)	84	Harris WCM	4	DNF

Fastest lap: Rossi, 1m 59.472s, 112.847 mph/181.609 km/h (record).

Previous record: Valentino Rossi, I (Honda), 2m 00.973s, 111.446 mph/179.355 km/h (2002).

Event best maximum speed: Biaggi, 196.4 mph/316.1 km/h (qualifying practice no. 2).

Qualifying: 1 Rossi, 1m 58.758s; 2 Checa, 1m 59.440s; 3 Gibernau, 1m 59.903s; 4 Melandri, 2m 00.724s; 5 Nakano, 2m 00.755s; 6 Barros, 2m 00.977s; 7 Kenny Roberts, 2m 01.182s; 8 Tamada, 2m 01.212s; 9 Xaus, 2m 01.312s; 10 Hopkins, 2m 01.593s; 11 Hofmann, 2m 01.617s; 12 Biaggi, 2m 01.635s; 13 Edwards, 2m 01.642s; 14 Bayliss, 2m 01.707s; 15 Capirossi, 2m 02.029s; 16 Hayden, 2m 02.062s; 17 Abe, 2m 02.427s; 18 Byrne, 2m 02.580s; 19 McWilliams, 2m 02.613s; 20 Hodgson, 2m 02.896s; 21 Fabrizio, 2m 03.852s; 22 Aoki, 2m 03.912s; 23 Kurtis Roberts, 2m 05.311s; 24 Burns, 2m 06.137s.

Fastest race laps: 1 Rossi, 1m 59.472s; 2 Gibernau, 1m 59.473s; 3 Biaggi, 1m 59.983s; 4 Barros, 2m 00.042s; 5 Melandri, 2m 00.063s; 6 Xaus, 2m 00.172s; 7 Hayden, 2m 00.260s; 8 Checa, 2m 00.284s; 9 Edwards, 2m 00.296s; 10 Capirossi, 2m 00.606s; 11 Hopkins, 2m 00.919s; 12 Tamada, 2m 00.957s; 13 Bayliss, 2m 00.970s; 14 Abe, 2m 01.020s; 15 Hodgson, 2m 01.240s; 16 Nakano, 2m 01.531s; 17 Hofmann, 2m 01.680s; 18 Kenny Roberts, 2m 02.129s; 19 McWilliams, 2m 02.407s; 20 Byrne, 2m 03.288s; 21 Aoki, 2m 03.695s; 22 Fabrizio, 2m 03.807s; 23 Burns, 2m 04.586s; 24 Kurtis Roberts, 2m 05.437s.

World Championship: 1 Rossi, 126; 2 Gibernau, 126; 3 Biaggi, 93; 4 Checa, 56; 5 Edwards and Melandri, 54; 7 Barros, 48; 8 Capirossi, 42; 9 Hayden, 38; 10 Abe, 33; 11 Xaus, 32; 12 Bayliss, 23; 13 Nakano, 20; 14 Tamada, 19; 15 Hodgson, 15; 16 Hofmann, 13; 17 Kenny Roberts, 12; 18 Byrne, 10; 19 Fabrizio, 7; 20 Aoki and Hopkins, 6; 22 McWilliams, 4; 23 Pitt, 2; 24 Kurtis Roberts, 1.

250 cc

18 laps, 67.410 miles/108.468 km

Pos.	Rider (Nat.)	No.	Machine	Laps	Time & speed
1	Sebastian Porto (ARG)	19	Aprilia	18	37m 26.576s 108.020 mph/ 173.842 km/h
2	Daniel Pedrosa (E)	26	Honda	18	37m 29.142s
3	Toni Elias (E)	24	Honda	18	37m 30.614s
4	Randy de Puniet (F)	7	Aprilia	18	37m 34.600s
5	Alex de Angelis (RSM)	51	Aprilia	18	37m 40.172s
6	Anthony West (AUS)	14	Aprilia	18	37m 46.981s
7	Manuel Poggiali (RSM)	54	Aprilia	18	37m 53.053s
8	Fonsi Nieto (E)	10	Aprilia	18	37m 53.878s
9	Roberto Rolfo (I)	2	Honda	18	37m 53.933s
10	Hiroshi Aoyama (J)	73	Honda	18	38m 10.269s
11	Alex Baldolini (I)	25	Aprilia	18	38m 10.521s
12	Alex Debon (E)	6	Honda	18	38m 10.757s
13	Naoki Matsudo (J)	8	Yamaha	18	38m 19.214s
14	Eric Bataille (F)	34	Honda	18	38m 19.344s
15	Chaz Davies (GB)	57	Aprilia	18	38m 19.476s
16	Franco Battaini (I)	21	Aprilia	18	38m 26.441s
17	Hector Faubel (E)	33	Aprilia	18	38m 30.352s
18	Hugo Marchand (F)	9	Aprilia	18	38m 30.570s
19	Taro Sekiguchi (J)	44	Yamaha	18	38m 44.632s
20	Johan Stigefelt (S)	16	Aprilia	18	38m 44.704s
21	Klaus Nöhles (D)	17	Honda	18	39m 27.512s
22	Ivan Silva (E)	22	Aprilia	17	37m 41.578s
	Gregory Lefort (F)	77	Aprilia	8	DNF
	Gregory Lefort (F)	77	Aprilia	8	DNF
	Arnaud Vincent (F)	12	Aprilia	7	DNF
	Joan Olive (E)	11	Aprilia	6	DNF
	Sylvain Guintoli (F)	50	Aprilia	5	DNF
	Erwan Nigon (F)	36	Yamaha	4	DNF
	Jakub Smrz (CZ)	96	Honda	1	DNF
	Hans Smees (NL)	59	Honda		DNQ
	Randy Gevers (NL)	61	Aprilia		DNQ
	Patrick Lakerveld (NL)	58	Yamaha		DNQ
	Emile Litjens (NL)	60	Aprilia		DNQ
	Max Sabbatani (I)	40	Yamaha		DNQ
	Jan Roelofs (NL)	62	Yamaha		DNQ

Fastest lap: Pedrosa, 2m 03.469s, 109.193 mph/175.729 km/h (record).

Previous record: Roberto Rolfo, I (Honda), 2m 04.824s, 108.008 mph/173.822 km/h (2002).

Event best maximum speed: de Angelis, 164.8 mph/265.2 km/h (race).

Qualifying: 1 Porto, 2m 03.668s; 2 Pedrosa, 2m 04.451s; 3 de Puniet, 2m 04.529s; 4 Elias, 2m 04.838s; 5 Poggiali, 2m 04.903s; 6 de Angelis, 2m 04.959s; 7 Rolfo, 2m 05.956s; 8 Olive, 2m 06.107s; 9 Nieto, 2m 06.131s; 10 Debon, 2m 06.149s; 11 West, 2m 06.311s; 12 Battaini, 2m 06.386s; 13 Baldolini, 2m 06.548s; 14 Aoyama, 2m 06.595s; 15 Matsudo, 2m 06.799s; 16 Guintoli, 2m 06.885s; 17 Davies, 2m 07.520s; 18 Vincent, 2m 07.546s; 19 Bataille, 2m 07.699s; 20 Faubel, 2m 07.869s; 21 Smrz, 2m 07.937s; 22 Stigefelt, 2m 08.315s; 23 Marchand, 2m 08.316s; 24 Nigon, 2m 09.456s; 25 Sekiguchi, 2m 10.238s; 26 Lefort, 2m 10.933s; 27 Silva, 2m 11.067s; 28 Nöhles, 2m 11.793s; 29 Smees, 2m 12.734s; 30 Gevers, 2m 13.220s; 31 Lakerveld, 2m 13.451s; 32 Litjens, 2m 14.169s; 33 Sabbatani, 2m 15.180s; 34 Roelofs, 2m 16.335s.

Fastest race laps: 1 Pedrosa, 2m 03.469s; 2 Porto, 2m 03.541s; 3 Elias, 2m 03.718s; 4 de Puniet, 2m 03.852s; 5 de Angelis, 2m 04.191s; 6 West, 2m 04.959s; 7 Poggiali, 2m 05.207s; 8 Rolfo, 2m 05.441s; 9 Nieto, 2m 05.463s; 10 Bataille, 2m 05.941s; 11 Baldolini, 2m 06.027s; 12 Davies, 2m 06.175s; 13 Matsudo, 2m 06.224s; 14 Debon, 2m 06.264s; 15 Aoyama, 2m 06.282s; 16 Battaini, 2m 06.492s; 17 Guintoli, 2m 07.207s; 18 Olive, 2m 07.361s; 19 Faubel, 2m 07.493s; 20 Marchand, 2m 07.525s; 21 Stigefelt, 2m 07.649s; 22 Sekiguchi, 2m 07.672s; 23 Vincent, 2m 08.129s; 24 Nigon, 2m 08.890s; 25 Silva, 2m 10.287s; 26 Nöhles, 2m 10.320s; 27 Lefort, 2m 11.576s; 28 Smrz, 2m 19.186s.

World Championship: 1 de Puniet, 111; 2 Pedrosa, 110; 3 Porto, 88; 4 Elias, 70; 5 Nieto, 64; 6 de Angelis, 51; 7 Rolfo, 48; 8 West, 46; 9 Aoyama and Debon, 41; 11 Poggiali, 38; 12 Battaini, 24; 13 Baldolini, 15; 14 Guintoli and Matsudo, 13; 16 Olive and Vincent, 11; 18 Faubel, 9; 19 Davies, 8; 20 Bataille and Lefort, 7; 22 Smrz, 6; 23 Marchand, 3; 24 Heidolf and Stigefelt, 2; 26 Sekiguchi, 1.

125 cc

17 laps, 63.665 miles/102.459 km

Pos.	Rider (Nat.)	No.	Machine	Laps	Time & speed
1	Jorge Lorenzo (E)	48	Derbi	17	37m 13.859s 102.600 mph/ 165.118 km/h
2	Roberto Locatelli (I)	15	Aprilia	17	37m 14.094s
3	Casey Stoner (AUS)	27	KTM	17	37m 14.423s
4	Andrea Dovizioso (I)	34	Honda	17	37m 14.465s
5	Steve Jenkner (D)	21	Aprilia	17	37m 17.724s
6	Hector Barbera (E)	3	Aprilia	17	37m 25.309s
7	Marco Simoncelli (I)	58	Aprilia	17	37m 25.615s
8	Pablo Nieto (E)	22	Aprilia	17	37m 25.623s
9	Mirko Giansanti (I)	6	Aprilia	17	37m 25.772s
10	Imre Toth (H)	25	Aprilia	17	37m 43.198s
11	Mattia Pasini (I)	54	Aprilia	17	37m 43.710s
12	Mike di Meglio (F)	63	Aprilia	17	37m 44.253s
13	Gioele Pellino (I)	42	Aprilia	17	37m 44.287s
14	Stefano Perugini (I)	7	Gilera	17	37m 53.092s
15	Angel Rodriguez (E)	47	Derbi	17	37m 53.205s
16	Alvaro Bautista (E)	19	Aprilia	17	37m 53.442s
17	Gabor Talmacsi (H)	14	Malaguti	17	37m 53.636s
18	Simone Corsi (I)	24	Honda	17	37m 53.917s
19	Julian Simon (E)	10	Honda	17	37m 54.570s
20	Andrea Ballerini (I)	50	Aprilia	17	38m 13.236s
21	Sergio Gadea (E)	33	Aprilia	17	38m 21.414s
22	Raymond Schouten (NL)	16	Honda	17	38m 21.574s
23	Vesa Kallio (SF)	66	Aprilia	17	38m 40.608s
24	Jarno van der Marel (NL)	82	Honda	17	39m 04.919s
25	Mikko Kyyhkynen (SF)	38	Honda	16	37m 16.649s
26	Adri den Bekker (NL)	79	Honda	16	37m 16.822s
27	Marketa Janakova (CZ)	9	Honda	16	37m 50.487s
	Dario Giuseppetti (D)	26	Honda	16	DNF
	Manuel Manna (I)	8	Malaguti	16	DNF
	Lukas Pesek (CZ)	52	Honda	16	DNF
	Mika Kallio (SF)	36	KTM	15	DNF
	Youichi Ui (J)	41	Aprilia	7	DNF
	Gino Borsoi (I)	23	Aprilia	7	DNF
	Fabrizio Lai (I)	32	Gilera		DNS
	Gert-Jan Kok (NL)	83	Honda		DNQ
	Mark van Kreij (NL)	80	Honda		DNQ
	Frank van den Dragt (NL)	44	Honda		DNQ
	Jordi Carchano (E)	28	Aprilia		DNQ

Fastest lap: Lorenzo, 2m 10.123s, 103.609 mph/166.743 km/h (record).

Previous record: Joan Olive, E (Honda), 2m 11.209s, 102.752 mph/165.363 km/h (2002).

Event best maximum speed: Stoner, 142.6 mph/229.5 km/h (race).

Qualifying: 1 Stoner, 2m 18.592s; 2 Nieto, 2m 19.046s; 3 Dovizioso, 2m 19.972s; 4 Jenkner, 2m 20.168s; 5 Locatelli, 2m 20.656s; 6 Ui, 2m 20.689s; 7 Lorenzo, 2m 21.041s; 8 Corsi, 2m 21.551s; 9 Ballerini, 2m 21.727s; 10 Toth, 2m 22.180s; 11 Giansanti, 2m 22.318s; 12 Simon, 2m 22.724s; 13 Barbera, 2m 22.746s; 14 Simoncelli, 2m 22.837s; 15 Pesek, 2m 23.117s; 16 di Meglio, 2m 23.142s; 17 V. Kallio, 2m 23.363s; 18 Gadea, 2m 23.431s; 19 van der Marel, 2m 23.462s; 20 M. Kallio, 2m 23.823s; 21 Pasini, 2m 24.329s; 22 Manna, 2m 24.347s; 23 Giuseppetti, 2m 24.455s; 24 Bautista, 2m 24.865s; 25 Schouten, 2m 24.897s; 26 Borsoi, 2m 25.119s; 27 Lai, 2m 25.152s; 28 Pellino, 2m 25.176s; 29 Rodriguez, 2m 25.595s; 30 Talmacsi, 2m 25.604s; 31 Janakova, 2m 25.736s; 32 Perugini, 2m 25.876s; 33 den Bekker, 2m 26.785s; 34 Kyyhkynen, 2m 27.325s; 35 Kok, 2m 28.941s; 36 van Kreij, 2m 29.005s; 37 van den Dragt, 2m 29.010s; 38 Carchano, 2m 29.923s.

Fastest race laps: 1 Lorenzo, 2m 10.123s; 2 Stoner, 2m 10.221s; 3 Dovizioso, 2m 10.247s; 4 M. Kallio, 2m 10.319s; 5 Locatelli, 2m 10.376s; 6 Jenkner, 2m 10.384s; 7 Barbera, 2m 10.413s; 8 Giansanti, 2m 10.478s; 9 Nieto, 2m 10.713s; 10 Simoncelli, 2m 10.742s; 11 Toth, 2m 11.810s; 12 Pasini, 2m 11.828s; 13 Talmacsi, 2m 11.893s; 14 Pellino, 2m 11.996s; 15 di Meglio, 2m 12.096s; 16 Simon, 2m 12.130s; 17 Rodriguez, 2m 12.144s; 18 Ui, 2m 12.216s; 19 Perugini, 2m 12.228s; 20 Bautista, 2m 12.406s; 21 Corsi, 2m 12.433s; 22 Ballerini, 2m 12.646s; 23 Pesek, 2m 13.170s; 24 Manna, 2m 13.715s; 25 Gadea, 2m 13.728s; 26 Giuseppetti, 2m 13.962s; 27 Schouten, 2m 14.117s; 28 Borsoi, 2m 14.437s; 29 V. Kallio, 2m 15.179s; 30 van der Marel, 2m 16.450s; 31 Kyyhkynen, 2m 17.881s; 32 den Bekker, 2m 18.161s; 33 Janakova, 2m 19.529s.

World Championship: 1 Dovizioso, 109; 2 Locatelli, 93; 3 Barbera, 84; 4 Stoner, 84; 5 Nieto, 63; 6 Lorenzo, 58; 7 Jenkner, 58; 8 Giansanti, 52; 9 Simoncelli, 43; 10 Pasini, 25; 11 Bautista, 24; 12 di Meglio, 23; 13 Borsoi, 22; 14 M. Kallio, 21; 15 Simon, 15; 16 Ballerini, 14; 17 Corsi, 12; 18 Ui, 10; 19 Pellino and Toth, 6; 21 Giuseppetti, Lai, Pesek and Talmacsi, 3; 25 Carchano, Perugini and Rodriguez, 2.

FIM WORLD CHAMPIONSHIP • ROUND 7

BRAZILGP

RIO DE JANEIRO

Left: Me happy! Tamada's first win redoubled the Japanese rider's habitual grin.

Bottom left: Me angry! Gibernau walks the line, after his early race exit.

Below: Me too! Rossi strikes sparks as he copies Gibernau's crash.

Bottom: Me? Roberts was as surprised as anyone to qualify on pole.
Photographs: Gold & Goose

HRC gave themselves some difficult questions for 2004. The main one was which rider to favour with the best equipment and support. Contractually they are obliged to favour Repsol, but from the start the satellite team riders were making the running in the fight against Rossi and Yamaha... and they had already confirmed that the difference between the Repsol factory bikes of Barros and Hayden and the satellite machines would be minimal.

Everyone had thought the dilemma would come between Gibernau and Edwards, the latter many people's pre-season favourite for the title. The former Superbike champion had shown trade-mark consistency, but not yet front-running form. By the time they left Brazil, the question was between Gibernau and Biaggi. Max didn't win the race. Instead it was a historic first win for Makoto Tamada, the Bridgestone rider breaking a run of 92 consecutive Michelin victories. But Max was second, and closed up to within 13 points of Rossi in the title chase.

It could have been very different, of course. Rossi had one of those rare weekends when he gets it all wrong. It's easy to fall off at the Nelson Piquet circuit, both slippery and bumpy, as Gibernau proved on only the second lap. It was Rossi's big chance to extend his newly-won lead. Instead he hit the same bump as Sete, and fell in exactly the same spot. Proving himself human and fallible after all.

Perhaps it was the fatigue. Rossi had complained before the weekend about the punishing schedule, echoing the general feeling that six races in eight weekends was too many. Rio was the fourth of them, and a long way away. Although the earlier date for the race this year did confer one benefit... midsummer in Assen might have been rainy and cold, but midwinter in Rio was a benign almost-30 degrees, settled and dry, at a race which previously (in spring) had been at the mercy of the rainy season.

But it was also possible not to fall off, at a circuit that is unique. Although it has a long straight and looks sterile on the map, the corners are wide, bumpy, long and difficult, for technicians as well as riders, seeking a balance with suspension soft enough to ride the bumps and grip the slippery sections but firm enough for stability at speed. Carlos Checa: "When we get rid of a problem in one area we find another problem in another area. It's difficult to find a good compromise without losing something important somewhere else."

The track certainly rewards accurate riding. And, apparently, the Bridgestone tyres, just four weeks after their disaster at Mugello, benefitted. If this was the result of being put a few months back in development, it was pretty impressive. Then again, it's a track where they work. Last year Tamada gave them their first front row start and their first podium here.

One other beneficiary, of both tyres and track, was Kenny Roberts Jr. Off the front row since his championship year of 2000, Roberts put the GSV-R Suzuki on pole position, six tenths faster than Rossi's pole last year, and almost 3.5 seconds faster than his own qualifying time on the Suzuki. Junior was wreathed in somewhat unfamiliar smiles afterwards, in spite of expressing his usual reservations about the difficulties of maintaining it all over race distance. "It's nice to have a day of sunshine like this... to ride through the corners as one of the fastest and end up with a faster time, instead of doing it for the third or fourth row. There was no way I could ride that lap harder and I expected to come in to see ninth or tenth... and it was first! It shows everybody that if we get some engine underneath us, we're going to be right there," he said. The figures bore him out. Second qualifier Biaggi's Honda clocked 205.4 mph, against Kenny's 196.4.

Team-mate Hopkins had one of the new engines for the first time, but was finding it hard to set, and for once was way off Kenny's pace. Ducati also had more of the new Twin Pulse motors, with a pair for Capirossi, though still just one for Bayliss.

Tamada had the engine as well as the tyres, and explained afterwards: "I chose a new-profile Bridgestone introduced at Assen. The settings and tyres were as good as they could be. The team did a magnificent job... and I did the rest." The race was on the fourth of July, a special day for more than just the Americans, because it was the late Kato's birthday, and Tamada dedicated his first win to his fallen friend.

At the other end of the tyre spectrum, Dunlop's troops were disappointed that new tyres that had been promising in tests after Catalunya failed to do the job, with the fastest on the tyres, Aoki, suffering bad chatter. Desperate measures for desperate times... they cut a groove round the circumference of the sidewall to make it more flexible. "It improves the chatter on the exits, but grip is still a problem," said Aoki.

For once, the day started with the main event, so that the MotoGP class could take the benefit of a gap in a busy European TV schedules, slotting in between the French F1 car GP and the Euro 2004 football cup final. Just one of all sorts of things that are different in Rio. Where else, for instance, would you expect the paddock to be abuzz with stories of muggings in the city. The bloke who tried it on with Troy Bayliss, however, got short shrift rather than a bulging wallet. "I told them to f*** off and go and get a job," he said. Apparently they took his advice. Where else would the press room have to be evacuated at the height of the qualifying action, because of an electrical fire. And where else would riders McWilliams, Byrne, Hopkins, Hofmann and Davies run into world cup superstar Ronaldinho, playing a sophisticated game of hands-free volleyball on the beach. They posed with him for the family album, once they'd paid their respects.

The 125 class remained more exciting than the 250s, with Barbera bouncing back from a heavy crash in practice that put him in a neck brace to win his second race of the year. This brought the record without a back-to-back victory to 30.

The paddock was shocked by the news that former 250 rider Jaroslav Hules, without a ride this year, had attempted suicide at home in the Czech Republic on his 30th birthday. Although taken to hospital, he succumbed soon afterwards.

Right: Vast stands gave the crowd plenty of room, beneath encroaching new apartments.

Far right Tamada's Bridgestones gave him a commanding edge in the closing laps.
Photographs: Gold & Goose

Below: The growling new Twin-Pulse Ducati was now starting to assert itself – fourth was Capirossi's best so far.
Photograph: Malcolm Bryan/BPC

Bottom: Biaggi leads Hayden and the pack in the early stages.
Photographs: Gold & Goose

MOTOGP RACE – 24 laps

Two tenths covered the front row - Roberts, Biaggi and Hayden for a second successive race. Gibernau led row two from Barros and Capirossi, and Rossi was in the middle of the third, and still scratching to get his Yamaha settled even after morning warm-up. "It'll be good to take off with people like Max. They'll blow the stickers off my bike on the straight, but at least they won't hold me up in the turns, like in the middle of the field," said Roberts.

Max led away, Roberts dived underneath at the first chance, riding very hard to try and get a gap before reaching the straight. This he achieved, still in front at the end of lap one. Next time he was third, with Biaggi and Hayden both blowing past on the straight, and almost Barros as well.

Rossi had finished lap one behind Gibernau, and had a grandstand seat as the Spaniard lost the front at the last left, sliding off gracefully, on lap two, his first race crash for more than a year. By now Tamada was on the Yamaha's back wheel, and attacking.

After five laps Rossi had followed Barros past Roberts; Tamada also one lap later. The leading pack were more than 1.5 seconds ahead of Edwards leading the next group, and by the time Capirossi got past the Honda the gap had grown. Only Roberts was dropping back, behind the Ducati on lap nine and engaged with old AMA adversary Edwards, a battle he would eventually lose.

Up front, Biaggi and Hayden were setting the pace, while Barros was having trouble with a sliding front, and fell victim to Rossi. The hardest charger was Tamada, who followed Rossi up to the leading duo. Then Rossi ran wide at the start of lap 12, and Tamada was past to start working on Hayden.

At the start of lap 13 Rossi was already losing touch, and the feeling wasn't to his liking. But he could see the leaders, and wanted to get there. Crew chief Jerry Burgess explained what happened next. "He wheelied out of (Turn) Ten and was a little off line into Eleven when he got the wheel down. There's a bump there, and you can see a little more fork stroke before he loses the front." He had a copycat crash right at the same place as Gibernau. He'd thrown away an easy chance to stretch his title lead.

By now Tamada was past Hayden and hounding Biaggi. With ten laps left, Hayden started to lose touch a few tenths at a time. Biaggi knew the writing was on the wall. "I could hear him opening the throttle behind me earlier that I was able to do, so I knew what was coming," he said later. It came with less than five laps to go, on the exit of the corner where Gibernau and Rossi had crashed. Tamada exited faster than Biaggi and nipped past on the short straight. From then on he stretched away little by little until the end, for a very convincing first win.

The rest were stretching out. On lap 12 Edwards got past Roberts, gradually shaking him off. Ahead of them, Barros succumbed to Capirossi on lap 15, getting away easily. Barros was now under threat from Edwards, who closed a four-second gap with eight laps left to less than a second at the flag.

Safely behind Roberts, Abe fended off Nakano to the end. Checa closed towards the end, but was out of touch again at the finish. Behind, Hopkins and Hofmann (both Bridgestone-shod) were battling back and forth for 11th, both passing Xaus early on the way to their last-lap climax at the end of the long straight. Hofmann had been ahead at the start of it, Hopkins tried to outbrake him, and they collided. The German survived, but Hopkins had to take to the banking of the adjoining oval track, where he fell at low speed, scrambling back hastily to finish 15th.

This was to the benefit of Xaus, who managed to get back at Melandri - victim of a collision with Checa on lap one that put him off the track - after a spirited battle. Behind them McWilliams had emerged victor from a long fight with Hodgson, the latter fading at the finish, still troubled by his arm injury from Le Mans, ceding the last point to Hopkins.

Byrne was 17th, complaining of a mysterious power loss; Aoki was a distant 18th, well ahead of team-mate Roberts, both suffering tyre problems; Burns was a lap behind and last... WCM team-mate Fabrizio missed the race, suffering foot fractures when he fell at Assen.

Bayliss had yet another misfortune, crashing out on the fourth lap.

Left: Barros's home GP led yet again to disappointment.

Left: Hayden's trade-mark wave celebrates his long-awaited first rostrum of the year.

Photographs: Gold & Goose

Above: **A hard-fought win was welcome relief for puzzlingly off-form defending 250 champion Poggiali, here holding off Pedrosa, Elias and de Puniet. It was his only win of the year.**

Below: **Tucking in for the long straight, Barbera leads Stoner, Dovizioso and Locatelli. They finished in this order, and as close.**

All photographs: Gold & Goose

250 cc RACE – 22 laps

Porto snatched pole at the finish from Elias at the closest thing he has to a home GP. De Puniet and Poggiali completed the front row.

Pedrosa led away from the second row, from Elias, Poggiali and de Puniet, then came West after a flyer from row three. Nieto passed the Australian on lap two, who crashed out on the third lap, punching himself repeatedly as he stalked away from his fallen machine.

Porto was losing touch with the five leaders, but de Angelis was coming fast after being pushed wide at the first corner after the start, and set fastest lap as he passed the Argentinean to push up and join the leaders.

Poggiali was now leading from Pedrosa, and on lap six Elias also got ahead of the Honda... only for three laps, before Pedrosa galloped past down the straight to set about the leader. For the first time all year, however, Poggiali was at full strength, and resisted manfully.

Elias was on the limit, and ran wide to lose touch with the leaders. Behind him, de Puniet had run into rear tyre problems and was dropping away; Porto was again ahead of de Angelis, and by half distance had passed Elias as well, starting to work on closing the gap to the leading pair. He was within less than a second when suddenly he slowed, his Aprilia on one cylinder and cruised towards a bitterly disappointing retirement.

Pedrosa had one last attack on the last lap, closing on the factory Aprilia, slipstreaming him down the straight to try to outbrake him at the end. The champion, for the first time all year, was riding perfectly, with the benefit of a new exhaust and revised engine mapping. Pedrosa never gave up, and was less than a tenth behind over the line.

Almost four seconds back Elias managed to fend off de Angelis, for whom fourth was a best-yet result in his rookie season. Another 15 seconds, and then came Nieto, holding Aoyama narrowly at bay. Some way back came Rolfo, complaining later at the puzzle that made his Honda slower than the others down the straight. Another gap, then de Puniet, almost caught by race-long combatants Debon and Battaini.

Davies was 13th, his second best of the year, behind the French pair of Marchand (his best so far) and Guintoli, but ahead of last points-scorers Matsudo and Heidolf.

125 cc RACE – 21 laps

Barbera took pole in spite of his morning crash and neck injuries, from Dovizioso, Lorenzo and Pasini, with Stoner leading row two.

Stoner pushed through to lead the first two laps, but there was a typical swarm of six changing positions back and forth at other points on the track, and though Barbera took over for a spell of six more laps and Stoner for another four, the issue remained in doubt. But this pair seemed the strongest, exchanging the lead over the line until the second-to-last, when it was Dovizioso up front.

By that point there were just five, with Lorenzo slipping off just before half distance. Stoner was a little down on top speed, and determined he needed to get to the back straight first if he was to have any chance. "I knew there were a few capable of passing me down the straight, and I knew I didn't want to be second when I got there," he said later. "I tried to get a good run, but it wasn't enough."

He had achieved that first ambition, but not with enough clear air to compete the lap first. He was less than a tenth behind Barbera over the line, but still ahead of Dovizioso, Locatelli and Giansanti.

Simoncelli beat Nieto for sixth.

FIM WORLD CHAMPIONSHIP • ROUND 7

RIO - JACAREPAGUÁ

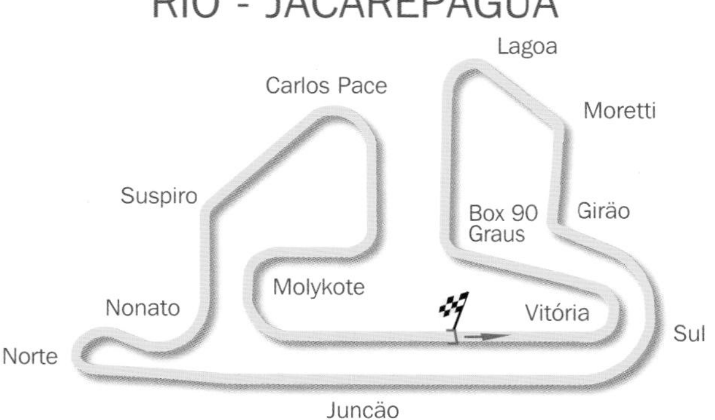

CIRCUIT LENGTH: 3.065 miles/4.932 km

MotoGP

24 laps, 73.560 miles/118.392 km

Pos.	Rider (Nat.)	No.	Machine	Laps	Time & speed
1	Makoto Tamada (J)	6	Honda	24	44m 21.976s 99.488 mph/ 160.110 km/h
2	Max Biaggi (I)	3	Honda	24	44m 23.995s
3	Nicky Hayden (USA)	69	Honda	24	44m 27.740s
4	Loris Capirossi (I)	65	Ducati	24	44m 33.121s
5	Alex Barros (BR)	4	Honda	24	44m 34.927s
6	Colin Edwards (USA)	45	Honda	24	44m 35.880s
7	Kenny Roberts (USA)	10	Suzuki	23	44m 45.469s
8	Norick Abe (J)	17	Yamaha	24	44m 49.474s
9	Shinya Nakano (J)	56	Kawasaki	24	44m 49.778s
10	Carlos Checa (E)	7	Yamaha	24	44m 58.784s
11	Alex Hofmann (D)	66	Kawasaki	24	44m 59.689s
12	Ruben Xaus (E)	11	Ducati	24	45m 10.900s
13	Marco Melandri (I)	33	Yamaha	24	45m 19.078s
14	Jeremy McWilliams (GB)	99	Aprilia	24	45m 25.022s
15	John Hopkins (USA)	21	Suzuki	24	45m 32.272s
16	Neil Hodgson (GB)	50	Ducati	24	45m 34.524s
17	Shane Byrne (GB)	67	Aprilia	24	45m 41.710s
18	Nobuatsu Aoki (J)	9	Proton KR	24	45m 53.488s
19	Kurtis Roberts (USA)	80	Proton KR	24	46m 05.603s
20	Chris Burns (GB)	35	Harris WCM	23	44m 34.854s
	Valentino Rossi (I)	46	Yamaha	12	DNF
	David de Gea (E)	52	Harris WCM	7	DNF
	Troy Bayliss (AUS)	12	Ducati	3	DNF
	Sete Gibernau(E)	15	Honda	1	DNF

Fastest lap: Tamada, 1m 49.789s, 100.509 mph/161.753 km/h (record).

Previous record: Valentino Rossi, I (Honda), 1m 50.453s, 99.905 mph/160.781 km/h (2003).

Event best maximum speed: Biaggi, 205.4 mph/330.5 km/h (qualifying practice no. 2).

Qualifying: 1 Kenny Roberts, 1m 48.418s; 2 Biaggi, 1m 48.572s; 3 Hayden, 1m 48.580s; 4 Gibernau, 1m 48.618s; 5 Barros, 1m 48.675s; 6 Capirossi, 1m 48.844s; 7 Tamada, 1m 48.848s; 8 Rossi, 1m 49.075s; 9 Nakano, 1m 49.153s; 10 Bayliss, 1m 49.546s; 11 Edwards, 1m 49.648s; 12 Checa, 1m 49.673s; 13 Melandri, 1m 49.773s; 14 Hofmann, 1m 49.853s; 15 Abe, 1m 50.128s; 16 Xaus, 1m 50.240s; 17 Hopkins, 1m 50.350s; 18 McWilliams, 1m 50.942s; 19 Hodgson, 1m 51.031s; 20 Byrne, 1m 51.792s; 21 Aoki, 1m 51.955s; 22 Kurtis Roberts, 1m 52.054s; 23 Burns, 1m 54.092s; 24 de Gea, 1m 54.116s.

Fastest race laps: 1 Tamada, 1m 49.789s; 2 Hayden, 1m 49.799s; 3 Biaggi, 1m 49.905s; 4 Rossi, 1m 50.026s; 5 Barros, 1m 50.031s; 6 Capirossi, 1m 50.139s; 7 Kenny Roberts, 1m 50.292s; 8 Edwards, 1m 50.557s; 9 Checa, 1m 50.606s; 10 Abe, 1m 50.752s; 11 Nakano, 1m 50.812s; 12 Bayliss, 1m 50.982s; 13 Melandri, 1m 51.198s; 14 Xaus, 1m 51.521s; 15 Hofmann, 1m 51.521s; 16 Hopkins, 1m 51.619s; 17 Hodgson, 1m 52.037s; 18 McWilliams, 1m 52.049s; 19 Byrne, 1m 52.870s; 20 Aoki, 1m 53.363s; 21 Kurtis Roberts, 1m 53.523s; 22 Gibernau, 1m 54.715s; 23 Burns, 1m 54.769s; 24 de Gea, 1m 54.887s.

World Championship: 1 Rossi, 126; 2 Gibernau, 126; 3 Biaggi, 113; 4 Edwards, 64; 5 Checa, 62; 6 Barros, 59; 7 Melandri, 57; 8 Capirossi, 55; 9 Hayden, 54; 10 Tamada, 44; 11 Abe, 41; 12 Xaus, 36; 13 Nakano, 27; 14 Bayliss, 23; 15 Kenny Roberts, 21; 16 Hofmann, 18; 17 Hodgson, 15; 18 Byrne, 10; 19 Fabrizio and Hopkins, 7; 21 Aoki and McWilliams, 6; 23 Pitt, 2; 24 Kurtis Roberts, 1.

250 cc

22 laps, 67.430 miles/108.526 km

Pos.	Rider (Nat.)	No.	Machine	Laps	Time & speed
1	Manuel Poggiali (RSM)	54	Aprilia	22	41m 56.561s 96.467 mph/ 155.249 km/h
2	Daniel Pedrosa (E)	26	Honda	22	41m 56.637s
3	Toni Elias (E)	24	Honda	22	42m 00.353s
4	Alex de Angelis (RSM)	51	Aprilia	22	42m 01.239s
5	Fonsi Nieto (E)	10	Aprilia	22	42m 16.954s
6	Hiroshi Aoyama (J)	73	Honda	22	42m 17.137s
7	Roberto Rolfo (I)	2	Honda	22	42m 26.960s
8	Randy de Puniet (F)	7	Aprilia	22	42m 31.303s
9	Alex Debon (E)	6	Honda	22	42m 32.582s
10	Franco Battaini (I)	21	Aprilia	22	42m 33.037s
11	Hugo Marchand (F)	9	Aprilia	22	42m 47.552s
12	Sylvain Guintoli (F)	50	Aprilia	22	42m 48.757s
13	Chaz Davies (GB)	57	Aprilia	22	42m 50.137s
14	Naoki Matsudo (J)	8	Yamaha	22	42m 58.202s
15	Dirk Heidolf (D)	28	Aprilia	22	42m 58.575s
16	Klaus Nöhles (D)	17	Honda	22	43m 08.317s
17	Erwan Nigon (F)	36	Yamaha	22	43m 08.560s
18	Gregory Lefort (F)	77	Aprilia	22	43m 16.787s
19	Arnaud Vincent (F)	12	Aprilia	22	43m 18.598s
20	Taro Sekiguchi (J)	44	Yamaha	21	42m 05.957s
	Jakub Smrz (CZ)	96	Honda	21	DNF
	Sebastian Porto (ARG)	19	Aprilia	20	DNF
	Joan Olive (E)	11	Aprilia	11	DNF
	Max Sabbatani (I)	40	Yamaha	6	DNF
	Anthony West (AUS)	14	Aprilia	2	DNF
	Johan Stigefelt (S)	16	Aprilia	1	DNF
	Alex Baldolini (I)	25	Aprilia	1	DNF
	Eric Bataille (F)	34	Honda	0	DNF
	Hector Faubel (E)	33	Aprilia		DNS

Fastest lap: Porto, 1m 53.573s, 97.160 mph/156.364 km/h (record).

Previous record: Manuel Poggiali, RSM (Aprilia), 1m 54.215s, 96.614 mph/155.485 km/h (2003).

Event best maximum speed: Poggiali, 167.8 mph/270.1 km/h (qualifying practice no. 1).

Qualifying: 1 Porto, 1m 52.503s; 2 Elias, 1m 52.823s; 3 de Puniet, 1m 52.929s; 4 Poggiali, 1m 52.981s; 5 de Angelis, 1m 53.157s; 6 Pedrosa, 1m 53.227s; 7 Guintoli, 1m 53.602s; 8 Battaini, 1m 53.682s; 9 Rolfo, 1m 53.776s; 10 Nieto, 1m 53.872s; 11 West, 1m 53.962s; 12 Debon, 1m 54.392s; 13 Olive, 1m 54.617s; 14 Matsudo, 1m 54.666s; 15 Aoyama, 1m 54.738s; 16 Baldolini, 1m 54.791s; 17 Smrz, 1m 54.992s; 18 Vincent, 1m 54.998s; 19 Davies, 1m 55.017s; 20 Nöhles, 1m 55.059s; 21 Lefort, 1m 55.105s; 22 Bataille, 1m 55.109s; 23 Marchand, 1m 55.215s; 24 Heidolf, 1m 55.723s; 25 Nigon, 1m 55.799s; 26 Stigefelt, 1m 56.029s; 27 Faubel, 1m 56.375s; 28 Sekiguchi, 1m 56.550s; 29 Sabbatani, 2m 00.125s.

Fastest race laps: 1 Porto, 1m 53.573s; 2 Poggiali, 1m 53.673s; 3 de Angelis, 1m 53.726s; 4 Pedrosa, 1m 53.777s; 5 Elias, 1m 53.848s; 6 de Puniet, 1m 53.868s; 7 West, 1m 54.194s; 8 Nieto, 1m 54.219s; 9 Aoyama, 1m 54.691s; 10 Rolfo, 1m 54.824s; 11 Battaini, 1m 55.051s; 12 Debon, 1m 55.255s; 13 Guintoli, 1m 55.707s; 14 Davies, 1m 55.756s; 15 Olive, 1m 55.790s; 16 Marchand, 1m 55.818s; 17 Heidolf, 1m 55.907s; 18 Matsudo, 1m 56.023s; 19 Smrz, 1m 56.399s; 20 Nigon, 1m 56.433s; 21 Vincent, 1m 56.441s; 22 Nöhles, 1m 56.616s; 23 Lefort, 1m 56.767s; 24 Sekiguchi, 1m 58.587s; 25 Sabbatani, 1m 59.669s; 26 Stigefelt, 2m 05.632s.

World Championship: 1 Pedrosa, 130; 2 de Puniet, 119; 3 Porto, 88; 4 Elias, 86; 5 Nieto, 75; 6 de Angelis, 64; 7 Poggiali, 63; 8 Rolfo, 57; 9 Aoyama, 51; 10 Debon, 48; 11 West, 46; 12 Battaini, 30; 13 Guintoli, 17; 14 Baldolini and Matsudo, 15; 16 Davies, Olive and Vincent, 11; 19 Faubel, 9; 20 Marchand, 8; 21 Bataille and Lefort, 7; 23 Smrz, 6; 24 Heidolf, 3; 25 Stigefelt, 2; 26 Sekiguchi, 1.

125 cc

21 laps, 64.365 miles/103.593 km

Pos.	Rider (Nat.)	No.	Machine	Laps	Time & speed
1	Hector Barbera (E)	3	Aprilia	21	41m 41.459s 92.638 mph/ 149.086 km/h
2	Casey Stoner (AUS)	27	KTM	21	41m 41.555s
3	Andrea Dovizioso (I)	34	Honda	21	41m 41.661s
4	Roberto Locatelli (I)	15	Aprilia	21	41m 41.818s
5	Mirko Giansanti (I)	6	Aprilia	21	41m 42.196s
6	Marco Simoncelli (I)	58	Aprilia	21	41m 49.073s
7	Pablo Nieto (E)	22	Aprilia	21	41m 49.228s
8	Mika Kallio (SF)	36	KTM	21	41m 54.184s
9	Alvaro Bautista (E)	19	Aprilia	21	41m 55.409s
10	Mattia Pasini (I)	54	Aprilia	21	42m 01.397s
11	Andrea Ballerini (I)	50	Aprilia	21	42m 07.442s
12	Mike di Meglio (F)	63	Aprilia	21	42m 08.092s
13	Simone Corsi (I)	24	Honda	21	42m 08.455s
14	Julian Simon (E)	10	Honda	21	42m 08.590s
15	Lukas Pesek (CZ)	52	Honda	21	42m 12.156s
16	Gioele Pellino (I)	42	Aprilia	21	42m 12.265s
17	Gino Borsoi (I)	23	Aprilia	21	42m 20.050s
18	Imre Toth (H)	25	Aprilia	21	42m 33.964s
19	Gabor Talmacsi (H)	14	Malaguti	21	42m 41.052s
20	Steve Jenkner (D)	21	Aprilia	21	42m 48.792s
21	Vesa Kallio (SF)	66	Aprilia	21	43m 01.524s
22	Stefano Perugini (I)	7	Gilera	21	43m 29.696s
23	Manuel Manna (I)	8	Malaguti	21	43m 29.770s
24	Raymond Schouten (NL)	16	Honda	21	43m 30.864s
	Jordi Carchano (E)	28	Aprilia	11	DNF
	Jorge Lorenzo (E)	48	Derbi	10	DNF
	Youichi Ui (J)	41	Aprilia	7	DNF
	Mikko Kyyhkynen (SF)	38	Honda	6	DNF
	Marketa Janakova (CZ)	9	Honda	6	DNF
	Angel Rodriguez (E)	47	Derbi	1	DNF
	Fabrizio Lai (I)	32	Gilera	0	DNF
	Sergio Gadea (E)	33	Aprilia	0	DNF

Fastest lap: Barbera, 1m 57.789s, 93.682 mph/150.767 (record).

Previous record: Daniel Pedrosa, E (Honda), 1m 58.121s, 93.419 mph/150.344 km/h (2003).

Event best maximum speed: de Angelis, 143.6 mph/231.1 km/h (qualifying practice no. 1).

Qualifying: 1 Barbera, 1m 57.323s; 2 Dovizioso, 1m 57.683s; 3 Lorenzo, 1m 57.793s; 4 Pasini, 1m 57.923s; 5 Stoner, 1m 58.055s; 6 Locatelli, 1m 58.162s; 7 Giansanti, 1m 58.254s; 8 Nieto, 1m 58.639s; 9 Ballerini, 1m 58.664s; 10 Ui, 1m 58.726s; 11 Jenkner, 1m 58.779s; 12 Borsoi, 1m 58.782s; 13 Simon, 1m 58.806s; 14 Bautista, 1m 58.828s; 15 Corsi, 1m 58.847s; 16 di Meglio, 1m 58.979s; 17 Pesek, 1m 59.073s; 18 M. Kallio, 1m 59.094s; 19 Toth, 1m 59.180s; 20 Simoncelli, 1m 59.201s; 21 Talmacsi, 1m 59.663s; 22 Pellino, 1m 59.817s; 23 Gadea, 1m 59.845s; 24 Perugini, 2m 00.118s; 25 Rodriguez, 2m 00.352s; 26 Lai, 2m 00.392s; 27 V. Kallio, 2m 01.415s; 28 Manna, 2m 02.226s; 29 Schouten, 2m 02.229s; 30 Carchano, 2m 02.363s; 31 Janakova, 2m 02.885s; 32 Kyyhkynen, 2m 03.481s.

Fastest race laps: 1 Barbera, 1m 57.789s; 2 Simoncelli, 1m 58.032s; 3 Giansanti, 1m 58.037s; 4 Dovizioso, 1m 58.125s; 5 Stoner, 1m 58.166s; 6 Locatelli, 1m 58.231s; 7 Lorenzo, 1m 58.296s; 8 Jenkner, 1m 58.549s; 9 Nieto, 1m 58.569s; 10 M. Kallio, 1m 58.622s; 11 Pasini, 1m 58.802s; 12 Ballerini, 1m 58.850s; 13 Bautista, 1m 58.941s; 14 Simon, 1m 59.089s; 15 Corsi, 1m 59.136s; 16 Borsoi, 1m 59.145s; 17 Pesek, 1m 59.163s; 18 Pellino, 1m 59.388s; 19 Ui, 1m 59.618s; 20 di Meglio, 1m 59.671s; 21 Toth, 1m 59.935s; 22 Talmacsi, 2m 00.020s; 23 Carchano, 2m 01.249s; 24 V. Kallio, 2m 01.961s; 25 Perugini, 2m 02.486s; 26 Manna, 2m 03.181s; 27 Schouten, 2m 03.208s; 28 Kyyhkynen, 2m 03.647s; 29 Janakova, 2m 03.855s; 30 Rodriguez, 2m 06.819s.

World Championship: 1 Dovizioso, 125; 2 Barbera, 109; 3 Locatelli, 106; 4 Stoner, 104; 5 Nieto, 72; 6 Giansanti, 63; 7 Jenkner and Lorenzo, 58; 9 Simoncelli, 53; 10 Bautista and Pasini, 31; 12 M. Kallio, 29; 13 di Meglio, 27; 14 Borsoi, 22; 15 Ballerini, 19; 16 Simon, 17; 17 Corsi, 15; 18 Ui, 10; 19 Pellino and Toth, 6; 21 Pesek, 4; 22 Giuseppetti, Lai and Talmacsi, 3; 25 Carchano, Perugini and Rodriguez, 2.

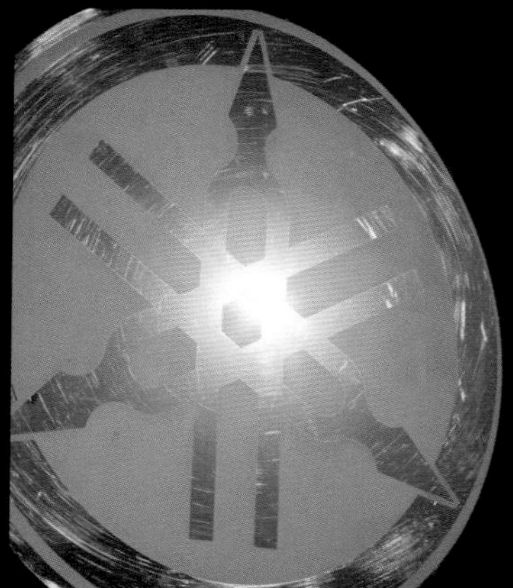

FIM WORLD CHAMPIONSHIP • ROUND 8

GERMANGP
SACHSENRING

NO circuit and no event more clearly indicated the changes to GP racing over the past five years than the German GP at the Sachsenring. A phoenix project born on the back of failure the Hockenheim- and Nurburgrings, at a car-park track not only below minimum length but also absurdly twisting for a 990cc racing prototype or for the previous 500cc two-strokes, it has in the course of seven years gone from strength to strength.

The first GP at the cramped venue outside Chemnitz, (Karlmarx-Stadt, in the communist era) was in 1999, at a makeshift little circuit that had come into being by sleight of hand. Civic funds were made available not for a race-track, on the hillside bordering a new industrial estate, but for a driver training centre. This included a skid pan, and some handy links to a short section of the old public roads circuit. The former was ideal for a makeshift paddock; the latter could be turned into a short and desperately tight circuit.

To cut a long story short, the crowds that had shunned the Nurburgring swarmed to the new Sachsenring, and since then full state support has been forthcoming to give the little twister an improved layout, large permanent pits and a working paddock area inside the circuit. The skid-pan on the outside houses the overflow – hospitality row, team canteens, and riders' motorhomes.

By a trick of smoke and mirrors, it not only looks like a real grand prix, but is one of the European season's sell-out events.

The message is simple. To riders, engineers, and insider hangers on, GP racing may be an exalted pastime, a purist sport of excellence; and this little crazy-golf track no place to race 210mph prototypes. To the 93,000 people packing the stands crammed around the loops and swirls, it's just entertainment. And damned fine entertainment it was, in a MotoGP race that brought winner Max back into the title battle with a vengeance.

There was another indicator of the widening divide in racing – between on-track reality and the quite different high-rolling one-upmanship game played out where racing's reason for being is as an element of the entertainment industry. The shibboleth was the Suzuki team's new "unit". Yamaha maintained a semblance, but Suzuki had been the last factory team to feed riders, team and guests in a true old-style tent, sides open to the breezes, and to the tide of humanity passing by. Now Suzuki (or, to be precise, their catering company Cator) had not just joined the trend towards glass-sided edifices, already followed by Marlboro, Repsol, Camel, Telefónica, Aprilia, Kawasaki etc. This one was taller, wider, more cleverly self-stowing … and more imposingly remote, a frosted-glass designer restaurant, reached by a staircase and a sliding door. Inside, guests ate aloof, self-contained. As elsewhere, the only evidence of racing came from the TV monitors. A splendid new addition to what increasingly resembled the high street of a low-rise new-town. All it lacked was clusters of smokers outside the doorways … but so far the likes of Gauloises and Camel still allow their guests to light up.

Fittingly, the scandal of the meeting had to do with marketing and sponsorship. News had leaked that Yamaha were planning to run next year without sponsorship – Rossi to sweep to his second championship with the marque in their own corporate livery, as a 50-year celebration. That this argument, still going back and forth at this time, should command any interest is another clear illustration of how the tail can so easily be allowed to wag the dog.

The racing, at least, retained its core values. Numerically, Germany marked the end of the first half of the season, and it was a significant race in terms of half-term improvements, both for Honda and Ducati. The latter had disposed of the Four-Pulse motors, with the latest Twin Pulse Desmos for both riders, and were it seemed finding a bit of momentum in terms of development.

Honda had an important chassis change with a higher swing-arm pivot height, not only for Barros but also Hayden, Gibernau and Biaggi. This firmly addressed the chatter generated by the new big Michelin tyres. More visibly, and audibly, Barros had a new exhaust system – distinguished by a new seat tail containing a pair of slash-cut big-bore tailpipes, with a fruitier rasp. The central exhaust still had its own pipe at low level; HRC said the new layout improved the mid-range power and response, without costing anything at the top.

Once again, the question arose of who should really be the top Honda rider, with both factory riders beaten (albeit narrowly) by Max's satellite bike. But for a while at least it seemed that Honda's broad-front attack might be fruitful, as Biaggi moved past Gibernau to take up the title fight with Rossi. It was to prove a false dawn.

Rossi had one of his bad weekends – a continuation of the conundrum that had allowed the out-paced M1 to win at fast tracks, but left the supposedly nimble machine struggling at tighter tracks, like Le Mans and now the Sachsenring. It wasn't a handling issue or a horsepower issue as such, but a combination of each that left the M1 feeling out of sorts and hard to get settled at these tracks. Rossi's post-practice comment summed it up. "It feels wild. I think I need a lion tamer." The consequence was not that he was out-paced but that he used his tyres harder, and ran out of the wherewithal to take part in the final battle. His was the only M1 to finish, after a desperate-looking Melandri tangled with Abe in a nasty-looking late-race collision.

Opposite: Back in contention after his first win, ecstatic Max kisses his trophy.

Bottom far left: All stubbed out. Yamaha were rumoured to be ditching tobacco sponsorship next year, to celebrate their half-centenary.

Bottom centre: Biaggi fans – when bad hair days turn good.

Below: "What the !!!!" The Roberts clan, King Kenny flanked by Kurtis and Kenny Junior.

Photographs: Gold & Goose

Bottom right: Barros shows a clean pair of pipes – the new exhaust system gave him his best result of a so-far rather barren season.

Photograph: Malcolm Bryan/BPC

Above: What, me worry? Byrne found the Aprilia a handful on the twists.

Far right: A capacity crowd and a fine view for all.

Photographs: Gold & Goose

Opposite: Winner Biaggi leads Rossi, Gibernau struggles to stay in touch. Soon he will be gone, and Rossi all tyred out.
Photograph: Gold & Goose

Below: Moment of truth. Capirossi's charge through to third ended in this crash.
Photograph: Malcolm Bryan/BPC

MOTOGP RACE – 30 laps

Practice times could hardly have been closer: 14 within a second, and last year's pole man Biaggi on top, for the first time this year and a full second faster than last. Rossi was next, then Roberts on the Suzuki, survivor of a hair-raising on-the-grass slide at the bottom of the roller-coaster hill, showing again that he was still prepared to ride hard and fast, if only in short bursts. Gibernau was fourth, Nakano fifth in the best yet for the Kawasaki.

All survived the funnelling into the first corner, not without some pushing and shoving. The front row men all held formation – Biaggi, Rossi and Roberts; Capirossi bullied his way to fourth from the fourth row, Gibernau right behind, and quickly ahead once more.

Roberts was soon dropping back, simply overpowered. Gibernau was first past, then a flying Checa, who then passed his Spanish rival as well, before his over-enthusiasm got the better of him on the second-last left-hander at the bottom of the hill. Down he went.

Biaggi, Rossi and Gibernau were already a little ahead when Capirossi also passed Roberts on lap six. They were fully engaged in some high-class close combat, until suddenly Gibernau was gone. His front tucked under early on the ninth lap, where the track starts to open up. A second crash in two consecutive weekends dealt a crucial blow to his title campaign.

Capirossi was now third, 2.5 seconds adrift, but his race was going smoothly enough, he felt. And he was closing up. Then he too slipped off, victim of the high lean angles and low gearing of a track that makes any MotoGP bike a handful.

There were just the two left up front, a familiar pattern it seemed – Biaggi ahead, Rossi breathing down his neck, just waiting for his moment. The short corners and the Honda's stronger acceleration meant that time and again Max would arrive at the next corner first, and going fast enough to block Rossi's teasing attacks … but at the start of the 17th lap Rossi got a good run down the front straight and dived past under braking for the first corner.

Once and for all? On past performance, that would be about it … Rossi would dominate in demoralising fashion. But now things were a little different. Not only did Max stay right on target, but a new dynamic was coming into play. The factory Hondas had both suffered in the first corner scrummage, finishing the lap with Barros eighth and Haydon 12th. The American had led the orange charge through the survivors, past Roberts on lap seven, gifted third by Capirossi on lap ten, and already closing a 2.5 second gap. He'd taken plenty of chances. "I had to pass two at a time," he said later.

One had been his senior team-mate, who had then hooked on behind, to overtake him once again as Rossi took the lead from Biaggi. Four of them, all up close. And no escape for Rossi, suffering excessive tyre wear on the left.

Biaggi attacked at the bottom of the downhill back straight at the end of lap 23, and immediately gained a small but stable cushion. Rossi, short of grip in the faster corners and down on acceleration, was having trouble keeping up.

A bigger-than-usual slide on lap 24 gave Barros his chance to get by. Directly afterwards, Rossi was wide into Turn One, leaving the way open to Hayden as well. This was about as close as we would ever get to seeing him flustered.

Up front, Biaggi's fast corner speeds and defensive riding were enough to protect his only win of the season from Barros. A little way back, Rossi mounted a spirited last-lap attack on Hayden, almost succeeding in getting by. "He's not the kind of guy you want behind you at that stage of the race," drawled the gratified young American later.

The next group had found their way past Roberts, Abe setting the pace, with Edwards behind, coming under attack from Tamada at half distance, the pair back and forth. The battle carried them past Abe. At the same time Melandri was coming back after dropping out of the top ten in the first third of the race. On lap 20 he passed his Tech 3 team-mate, shortly thereafter hit the grass and tumbled right in front of the Japanese rider, whose bike hit Melandri's, sending him flying head over heels through the air.

Edwards narrowly prevailed over Tamada at the finish; behind them Nakano had got ahead of Roberts on lap 18. Second Suzuki rider Hopkins was closing after finishing lap one 14th, and his arrival gave Roberts a new lease of life, and he speeded up to keep him safely at bay, the pair spread out again by the finish.

Hofmann was well adrift, passing Xaus after half distance and preserving the gap to the end. Behind them, McWilliams managed to fend off Hodgson. Byrne was finding the Aprilia a handful at a brand-new track. Kurtis Roberts had been exchanging blows with him before falling back to retire with a blistered tyre as well as clutch problems, leaving the last point to Fabrizio, with Chris Burns a lap down.

Aoki had crashed out after three laps, over-excited perhaps at the rare chance of battling with Hodgson's Ducati, at a track where his Proton's power deficit was less of a drawback than elsewhere. Bayliss had also gone west, disputing tenth with Nakano and Hopkins at one-third distance when he once more hit the gravel. A fourth crash in eight races triggered a shouting match between the frustrated rider and team manager Suppo. "We're a family, and sometimes families argue," he smoothly explained later.

Above: **Close racing is a Sachsenring given ... de Puniet leads de Angelis, Aoyama and Rolfo through the tricky final turn onto the crucial front straight.**

Right: **Battle for the final point ... Matsudo leads Smrz and Vincent. Smrz took it.**

Below: **A swarm of 125s, with winner Locatelli leading Kallio, Ui and the rest.**

250 cc RACE – 26 laps

Porto took a third pole in succession, with two more Aprilias up front, and Rolfo the top Honda for once, third. Pedrosa led the second row from Poggiali, two champions together.

Rolfo led away, but was immediately under pressure. Pedrosa took over after one lap, and set off for another bravura performance, taking full benefit of a clear track and his own great gifts of speed, talent and race-craft, now as clear in the 250 class after half a season as they had been in 125s. Riding with rhythmic precision, he just kept pulling away. By lap 22, he had more than six seconds in hand.

He probably didn't need any help, but Rolfo did delay the pursuit briefly. De Puniet took another lap to get by him; then both Porto and de Angelis piled past, the former promptly seizing second on lap four. He was already a second behind Pedrosa, and try as he might over the next four laps he could make no impression on that. With de Angelis

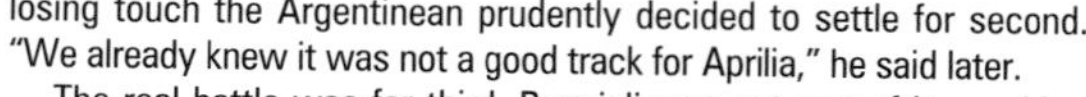

losing touch the Argentinean prudently decided to settle for second. "We already knew it was not a good track for Aprilia," he said later.

The real battle was for third. Poggiali was not part of it, crashing out on the sixth lap while struggling to regain the leading pack after a mediocre start. Rather an ethereal personality, he had superstitiously been wearing the same (not so) lucky boots since the first race. They had a hole in the side ... and it got caught in his gearlever.

De Puniet was in front of de Angelis, Elias, Rolfo and Aoyama at this point. The action was relentless, the challenges constant. Elias clawed his way to the front briefly on lap 16, but was back in the thick of it when he fell on lap 18, remounting right at the back. De Puniet led the survivors as they started the last lap, but the efforts of staying there had depleted his tyres. De Angelis timed his run perfectly to surge past for a first rostrum. Aoyama followed him by three tenths, a frustrated de Puniet two tenths behind him. Rolfo was a second behind.

West came in seventh after another strong ride on his ageing bike, after an almost race-long to-and-fro with frequent sparring partner Nieto, equipped with a factory Aprilia. He held him over the line by seven tenths.

It was close for the lower points; Battaini holding off Guintoli. Then Debon, under severe pressure from Davies, enjoying the levelling effect of the track as he followed Guintoli through, then got caught up behind the Spaniard.

125 cc RACE – 24 laps

Dovizioso led a tight front row, covered by two tenths, his Honda ahead of Barbera, Jenkner and Giansanti.

The pack was close on the tight twists; 13 in the leading group after eight laps. Then Sanna crashed in the middle of it, and subsequent yellow flags took out two more – erstwhile leader Simoncelli and a little later home hero Jenkner were given ride-through penalties.

At half distance Barbera, Dovizioso and Nieto broke away, Nieto leading briefly after Barbera slowed. The loss of pace helped Locatelli to halve a 2.4-second gap, and he redoubled his efforts. With three laps left the veteran had caught and passed them all.

The last lap was typically hectic; Barbera moving from fourth to second; Nieto elbowed his way to third past Dovizioso, almost putting him on the grass in the scramble to the finish line.

The next group was now four-strong, Ui having crashed out of it with four laps left. They closed right up as the leaders slowed one another. Kallio ended up in control, from Lorenzo, Bautista and Giansanti. The first eight crossed the line within an amazing 1.4 seconds. Simon was ninth, with Simoncelli and Jenkner recovering from their penalties to complete the top ten.

Locatelli's win had been "the best race of my life," he said later, and it revived his championship threat as he closed to within seven points of Dovizioso. The weekend was a disaster for Stoner's title hopes. The Australian's KTM had been fastest in session on Saturday morning when he crashed, and broke his right collarbone, out for this and the next race.

FIM WORLD CHAMPIONSHIP • ROUND 8

VELTINS GERMAN grand prix

18 JULY 2004

SACHSENRING GRAND PRIX CIRCUIT

CIRCUIT LENGTH:
2.281 miles/3.671 km

MotoGP

30 laps, 68.430 miles/110.130 km

Pos.	Rider (Nat.)	No.	Machine	Laps	Time & speed
1	Max Biaggi (I)	3	Honda	30	42m 23.287s 96.864 mph/ 155.888 km/h
2	Alex Barros (BR)	4	Honda	30	42m 23.636s
3	Nicky Hayden (USA)	69	Honda	30	42m 27.580s
4	Valentino Rossi (I)	46	Yamaha	30	42m 27.787s
5	Colin Edwards (USA)	45	Honda	30	42m 39.424s
6	Makoto Tamada (J)	6	Honda	30	42m 39.769s
7	Shinya Nakano (J)	56	Kawasaki	30	42m 41.764s
8	Kenny Roberts (USA)	10	Suzuki	30	42m 46.622s
9	John Hopkins (USA)	21	Suzuki	30	42m 53.992s
10	Alex Hofmann (D)	66	Kawasaki	30	43m 03.827s
11	Ruben Xaus (E)	11	Ducati	30	43m 06.999s
12	Jeremy McWilliams (GB)	99	Aprilia	30	43m 16.078s
13	Neil Hodgson (GB)	50	Ducati	30	43m 16.977s
14	Shane Byrne (GB)	67	Aprilia	30	43m 36.502s
15	Michel Fabrizio (I)	84	Harris WCM	30	43m 43.337s
16	Chris Burns (GB)	35	Harris WCM	29	42m 48.726s
	Kurtis Roberts (USA)	80	Proton KR	26	DNF
	Marco Melandri (I)	33	Yamaha	20	DNF
	Norick Abe (J)	17	Yamaha	20	DNF
	Troy Bayliss (AUS)	12	Ducati	10	DNF
	Loris Capirossi (I)	65	Ducati	9	DNF
	Sete Gibernau (E)	15	Honda	8	DNF
	Carlos Checa (E)	7	Yamaha	4	DNF
	Nobuatsu Aoki (J)	9	Proton KR	3	DNF

Fastest lap: Barros, 1m 24.056s, 97.694 mph/157.223 km/h (record).

Previous record: Max Biaggi, I (Honda), 1m 24.630s, 97.031 mph/156.157 km/h (2003).

Event best maximum speed: Bayliss, 180.8 mph/290.9 km/h (qualifying practice no. 1).

Qualifying: 1 Biaggi, 1m 22.756s; 2 Rossi, 1m 22.840s; 3 Kenny Roberts, 1m 22.961s; 4 Gibernau, 1m 22.969s; 5 Nakano, 1m 23.009s; 6 Barros, 1m 23.154s; 7 Checa, 1m 23.336s; 8 Bayliss, 1m 23.372s; 9 Hayden, 1m 23.453s; 10 Capirossi, 1m 23.475s; 11 Edwards, 1m 23.583s; 12 Hopkins, 1m 23.622s; 13 Tamada, 1m 23.623s; 14 Melandri, 1m 23.692s; 15 Abe, 1m 24.151s; 16 Hofmann, 1m 24.172s; 17 McWilliams, 1m 24.322s; 18 Xaus, 1m 24.377s; 19 Hodgson, 1m 24.599s; 20 Aoki, 1m 25.038s; 21 Fabrizio, 1m 25.310s; 22 Kurtis Roberts, 1m 25.478s; 23 Byrne, 1m 25.614s; 24 Burns, 1m 26.665s.

Fastest race laps: 1 Barros, 1m 24.056s; 2 Gibernau, 1m 24.168s; 3 Rossi, 1m 24.185s; 4 Checa, 1m 24.223s; 5 Biaggi, 1m 24.264s; 6 Hayden, 1m 24.281s; 7 Tamada, 1m 24.382s; 8 Capirossi, 1m 24.428s; 9 Bayliss, 1m 24.595s; 10 Hopkins, 1m 24.597s; 11 Kenny Roberts, 1m 24.662s; 12 Melandri, 1m 24.740s; 13 Edwards, 1m 24.784s; 14 Nakano, 1m 24.805s; 15 Abe, 1m 24.814s; 16 Hofmann, 1m 25.272s; 17 McWilliams, 1m 25.292s; 18 Xaus, 1m 25.359s; 19 Hodgson, 1m 25.731s; 20 Kurtis Roberts, 1m 26.410s; 21 Fabrizio, 1m 26.411s; 22 Byrne, 1m 26.545s; 23 Aoki, 1m 26.609s; 24 Burns, 1m 27.815s.

World Championship: 1 Rossi, 139; 2 Biaggi, 138; 3 Gibernau, 126; 4 Barros, 79; 5 Edwards, 75; 6 Hayden, 70; 7 Checa, 62; 8 Melandri, 57; 9 Capirossi, 55; 10 Tamada, 54; 11 Abe and Xaus, 41; 13 Nakano, 36; 14 Kenny Roberts, 29; 15 Hofmann, 24; 16 Bayliss, 23; 17 Hodgson, 18; 18 Hopkins, 14; 19 Byrne, 12; 20 McWilliams, 10; 21 Fabrizio, 8; 22 Aoki, 6; 23 Pitt, 2; 24 Kurtis Roberts, 1.

250 cc

29 laps, 66.149 miles/106.459 km

Pos.	Rider (Nat.)	No.	Machine	Laps	Time & speed
1	Daniel Pedrosa (E)	26	Honda	29	41m 37.239s 95.362 mph/ 153.470 km/h
2	Sebastian Porto (ARG)	19	Aprilia	29	41m 41.518s
3	Alex de Angelis (RSM)	51	Aprilia	29	41m 53.642s
4	Hiroshi Aoyama (J)	73	Honda	29	41m 54.008s
5	Randy de Puniet (F)	7	Aprilia	29	41m 54.205s
6	Roberto Rolfo (I)	2	Honda	29	41m 55.374s
7	Anthony West (AUS)	14	Aprilia	29	42m 09.380s
8	Fonsi Nieto (E)	10	Aprilia	29	42m 10.005s
9	Franco Battaini (I)	21	Aprilia	29	42m 14.965s
10	Sylvain Guintoli (F)	50	Aprilia	29	42m 15.327s
11	Alex Debon (E)	6	Honda	29	42m 28.021s
12	Chaz Davies (GB)	57	Aprilia	29	42m 28.173s
13	Joan Olive (E)	11	Aprilia	29	42m 38.185s
14	Eric Bataille (F)	34	Honda	29	42m 39.649s
15	Jakub Smrz (CZ)	96	Honda	29	42m 39.766s
16	Naoki Matsudo (J)	8	Yamaha	29	42m 39.793s
17	Taro Sekiguchi (J)	44	Yamaha	29	42m 55.474s
18	Dirk Heidolf (D)	28	Aprilia	29	42m 55.625
19	Erwan Nigon (F)	36	Yamaha	29	42m 58.394s
20	Johan Stigefelt (S)	16	Aprilia	29	42m 58.813s
21	Klaus Nöhles (D)	17	Honda	29	42m 59.287s
22	Toni Elias (E)	24	Honda	28	42m 26.928s
	Hugo Marchand (F)	9	Aprilia	19	DNF
	Gregory Lefort (F)	77	Aprilia	16	DNF
	Arnaud Vincent (F)	12	Aprilia	12	DNF
	Alex Baldolini (I)	25	Aprilia	11	DNF
	Max Sabbatani (I)	40	Yamaha	8	DNF
	Manuel Poggiali (RSM)	54	Aprilia	6	DNF

Fastest lap: Porto, 1m 25.118s, 96.476 mph/155.262 km/h (record).

Previous record: Fonsi Nieto, E (Aprilia), 1m 26.469s, 94.968 mph/152.836 km/h (2003).

Event best maximum speed: Poggiali, 151.7 mph/244.1 km/h (qualifying practice no. 1).

Qualifying: 1 Porto, 1m 25.078s; 2 de Angelis, 1m 25.236s; 3 Rolfo, 1m 25.386s; 4 de Puniet, 1m 25.535s; 5 Pedrosa, 1m 25.633s; 6 Poggiali, 1m 25.652s; 7 Elias, 1m 25.719s; 8 Nieto, 1m 25.783s; 9 Matsudo, 1m 26.195s; 10 Battaini, 1m 26.256s; 11 Guintoli, 1m 26.260s; 12 Aoyama, 1m 26.300s; 13 Debon, 1m 26.353s; 14 West, 1m 26.405s; 15 Heidolf, 1m 26.511s; 16 Olive, 1m 26.530s; 17 Davies, 1m 26.714s; 18 Baldolini, 1m 26.720s; 19 Nöhles, 1m 26.795s; 20 Marchand, 1m 27.133s; 21 Smrz, 1m 27.180s; 22 Sekiguchi, 1m 27.403s; 23 Nigon, 1m 27.663s; 24 Bataille, 1m 27.731s; 25 Vincent, 1m 27.752s; 26 Stigefelt, 1m 27.845s; 27 Lefort, 1m 29.194s; 28 Sabbatani, 1m 29.384s.

Fastest race laps: 1 Porto, 1m 25.118s; 2 Pedrosa, 1m 25.124s; 3 de Puniet, 1m 25.600s; 4 de Angelis, 1m 25.666s; 5 Elias, 1m 25.946s; 6 Rolfo, 1m 26.062s; 7 Aoyama, 1m 26.109s; 8 Poggiali, 1m 26.239s; 9 Nieto, 1m 26.252s; 10 Debon, 1m 26.412s; 11 Battaini, 1m 26.478s; 12 West, 1m 26.532s; 13 Guintoli, 1m 26.596s; 14 Davies, 1m 26.700s; 15 Baldolini, 1m 26.811s; 16 Heidolf, 1m 27.202s; 17 Matsudo, 1m 27.237s; 18 Smrz, 1m 27.354s; 19 Bataille, 1m 27.396s; 20 Nigon, 1m 27.486s; 21 Olive, 1m 27.638s; 22 Sekiguchi, 1m 27.872s; 23 Vincent, 1m 27.961s; 24 Marchand, 1m 27.997s; 25 Stigefelt, 1m 28.007s; 26 Nöhles, 1m 28.095s; 27 Lefort, 1m 29.499s; 28 Sabbatani, 1m 30.633s.

World Championship: 1 Pedrosa, 155; 2 de Puniet, 130; 3 Porto, 108; 4 Elias, 86; 5 Nieto, 83; 6 de Angelis, 80; 7 Rolfo, 67; 8 Aoyama, 64; 9 Poggiali, 63; 10 West, 55; 11 Debon, 53; 12 Battaini, 37; 13 Guintoli, 23; 14 Baldolini, Davies and Matsudo, 15; 17 Olive, 14; 18 Vincent, 11; 19 Bataille and Faubel, 9; 21 Marchand, 8; 22 Lefort and Smrz, 7; 24 Heidolf, 3; 25 Stigefelt, 2; 26 Sekiguchi, 1.

125 cc

27 laps, 61.587 miles/99.117 km

Pos.	Rider (Nat.)	No.	Machine	Laps	Time & speed
1	Roberto Locatelli (I)	15	Aprilia	27	40m 03.511s 92.248 mph/ 148.458 km/h
2	Hector Barbera (E)	3	Aprilia	27	40m 03.676s
3	Pablo Nieto (E)	22	Aprilia	27	40m 04.217s
4	Andrea Dovizioso (I)	34	Honda	27	40m 04.226s
5	Mika Kallio (SF)	36	KTM	27	40m 04.584s
6	Jorge Lorenzo (E)	48	Derbi	27	40m 04.687s
7	Alvaro Bautista (E)	19	Aprilia	27	40m 04.794s
8	Mirko Giansanti (I)	6	Aprilia	27	40m 04.970s
9	Julian Simon (E)	10	Honda	27	40m 13.147s
10	Marco Simoncelli (I)	58	Aprilia	27	40m 15.332s
11	Steve Jenkner (D)	21	Aprilia	27	40m 21.478s
12	Simone Corsi (I)	24	Honda	27	40m 23.818s
13	Gioele Pellino (I)	42	Aprilia	27	40m 35.309s
14	Sergio Gadea (E)	33	Aprilia	27	40m 35.438s
15	Stefano Perugini (I)	7	Gilera	27	40m 41.067s
16	Gabor Talmacsi (H)	14	Malaguti	27	40m 41.231s
17	Lukas Pesek (CZ)	52	Honda	27	40m 41.422s
18	Thomas Luthi (CH)	12	Honda	27	40m 41.431s
19	Robbin Harms (DK)	69	Honda	27	40m 58.861s
20	Mattia Pasini (I)	54	Aprilia	27	40m 58.895s
21	Patrick Unger (D)	39	Aprilia	27	41m 02.453s
22	Vesa Kallio (SF)	66	Aprilia	27	41m 03.413s
23	Georg Frohlich (D)	20	Honda	27	41m 21.234s
24	Jordi Carchano (E)	28	Aprilia	27	41m 21.508s
25	Vaclav Bittman (CZ)	35	Honda	27	41m 21.808s
26	Manuel Manna (I)	8	Malaguti	27	41m 22.061s
27	Manuel Mickan (D)	40	Honda	26	40m 21.999s
	Youichi Ui (J)	41	Aprilia	23	DNF
	Gino Borsoi (I)	23	Aprilia	23	DNF
	Julian Miralles (E)	70	Aprilia	17	DNF
	Imre Toth (H)	25	Aprilia	16	DNF
	Fabrizio Lai (I)	32	Gilera	13	DNF
	Mike di Meglio (F)	63	Aprilia	13	DNF
	Simone Sanna (I)	18	Aprilia	9	DNF
	Angel Rodriguez (E)	47	Derbi	9	DNF
	Raymond Schouten (NL)	16	Honda	0	DNF
	Casey Stoner (AUS)	27	KTM		DNS

Fastest lap: Barbera, 1m 27.680s, 93.656 mph/150.725 km/h (record).

Previous record: Pablo Nieto, E (Aprilia), 1m 28.490s, 92.799 mph/149.345 km/h (2003).

Event best maximum speed: Barbera, 128.8 mph/207.3 km/h (race).

Qualifying: 1 Dovizioso, 1m 27.836s; 2 Barbera, 1m 27.870s; 3 Jenkner, 1m 27.881s; 4 Giansanti, 1m 28.030s; 5 Nieto, 1m 28.061s; 6 Simoncelli, 1m 28.106s; 7 Simon, 1m 28.202s; 8 Ui, 1m 28.333s; 9 Borsoi, 1m 28.404s; 10 Locatelli, 1m 28.448s; 11 M. Kallio, 1m 28.542s; 12 Stoner, 1m 28.570s; 13 Lorenzo, 1m 28.577s; 14 Pesek, 1m 28.882s; 15 Corsi, 1m 28.942s; 16 Lai, 1m 28.986s; 17 Bautista, 1m 28.994s; 18 Gadea, 1m 29.055s; 19 Pellino, 1m 29.217s; 20 Talmacsi, 1m 29.273s; 21 di Meglio, 1m 29.366s; 22 Sanna, 1m 29.416s; 23 Toth, 1m 29.552s; 24 Pasini, 1m 29.568s; 25 Harms, 1m 29.693s; 26 Perugini, 1m 29.940s; 27 Luthi, 1m 30.123s; 28 V. Kallio, 1m 30.439s; 29 Rodriguez, 1m 30.475s; 30 Unger, 1m 30.476s; 31 Carchano, 1m 30.553s; 32 Schouten, 1m 30.909s; 33 Mickan, 1m 31.096s; 34 Frohlich, 1m 31.280s; 35 Miralles, 1m 31.376s; 36 Bittman, 1m 31.388s; 37 Manna, 1m 31.790s.

Fastest race laps: 1 Barbera, 1m 27.680s; 2 Bautista, 1m 28.055s; 3 Lorenzo, 1m 28.076s; 4 Ui, 1m 28.083s; 5 Locatelli, 1m 28.176s; 6 Giansanti, 1m 28.184s; 7 Nieto, 1m 28.195s; 8 M. Kallio, 1m 28.209s; 9 Simon, 1m 28.211s; 10 Simoncelli, 1m 28.222s; 11 Dovizioso, 1m 28.256s; 12 Jenkner, 1m 28.294s; 13 Corsi, 1m 28.375s; 14 Sanna, 1m 28.681s; 15 Talmacsi, 1m 29.040s; 16 Gadea, 1m 29.075s; 17 Pasini, 1m 29.170s; 18 Pellino, 1m 29.173s; 19 Pesek, 1m 29.250s; 20 Perugini, 1m 29.307s; 21 Lai, 1m 29.365s; 22 Harms, 1m 29.495s; 23 Luthi, 1m 29.551s; 24 di Meglio, 1m 29.712s; 25 Borsoi, 1m 29.775s; 26 Toth, 1m 29.921s; 27 V. Kallio, 1m 29.955s; 28 Unger, 1m 29.961s; 29 Manna, 1m 30.198s; 30 Rodriguez, 1m 30.377s; 31 Bittman, 1m 30.781s; 32 Frohlich, 1m 30.822s; 33 Carchano, 1m 30.845s; 34 Mickan, 1m 31.518s; 35 Miralles, 1m 31.544s.

World Championship: 1 Dovizioso, 138; 2 Locatelli, 131; 3 Barbera, 129; 4 Stoner, 104; 5 Nieto, 88; 6 Giansanti, 71; 7 Lorenzo, 68; 8 Jenkner, 63; 9 Simoncelli, 59; 10 Bautista and M. Kallio, 40; 12 Pasini, 31; 13 di Meglio, 27; 14 Simon, 24; 15 Borsoi, 22; 16 Ballerini and Corsi, 19; 18 Ui, 10; 19 Pellino, 9; 20 Toth, 6; 21 Pesek, 4; 22 Giuseppetti, Lai, Perugini and Talmacsi, 3; 26 Carchano, Gadea and Rodriguez, 2.

FIM WORLD CHAMPIONSHIP • ROUND 9

BRITISHGP

DONINGTON PARK

Left: Just one Valentino – Rossi pays homage to himself after defiantly regaining winning form.

Below: Fans packed the greensward at the revived British GP. Not long ago, the hillsides were all but empty.
Photographs: Gold & Goose

Above: Never keen on his livery, Hodgson was pleased to auction off a set of leathers for Riders for Health.

Above centre: "Sparkling, or still?" No shortage of water for the Gauloises-Fortuna hospitality staff.
Photographs: Gold & Goose

ANY illusions of new paddock opulence fostered in Germany were soon laid to rest at Donington. The circuit had hosted a record-breaking Day of Champions on Thursday, with £145,000 raised in near perfect weather, only for the heavens to open that night. The paddock was comprehensively flooded, to a depth of almost two feet in some areas. Some brave souls even went swimming outside Yamaha's VIP tent. And in the media centre, an old paddock saying – "It never rains in the press room," – was perforce brought up to date. A whopping leak in the roof threatened computers and tangled electrical connections among the trestle tables and garden chairs that Britain's premier bike racing event provides pressmen. One dedicated Italian continued working beneath an umbrella; and the proverb gained an extra sentence: "Except at Donington Park."

There is much to criticise at Britain's GP venue. The fans might have started with the shambolic traffic arrangements that kept them gridlocked for well over three hours when they were trying to go home – something to add to the list of shabby facilities and food, soggy campgrounds, and a general Sunday boot-sale air.

They couldn't complain about the racing, for whatever is wrong with Donington, the circuit itself remains a fascination, with its dual character a special challenge to riders and engineers alike. On a good day, it is also something of a leveller. And Sunday was a very good day.

The pits may be the same as on the first visit here in 1987, but there was one important change: the full 2.5-mile lap had been resurfaced. The complexities remained – how to seek a balance between the delicate steering feel and responses needed for the fast downhill Hollywood and Craner Curves and the rest of the sweeping lap, and the very different motorcycle needed for the fierce-braking hard-accelerating brawl at the chicane and the last two hairpins. This time, however, the bumps had gone, and the grip was consistent all the way round.

This factor changed everything for Colin Edwards. So far his second MotoGP year had fallen short of pre-season expectations. Never better than fifth, he had never been a factor for the lead. There was an explanation. Edwards was plagued with chatter – worse, it seems, than any other Honda rider. Whether this is a matter of his riding style or simply his response to it is impossible to say, but one comment at Donington might be suggestive: "When things are not so good, I'm not the rider to push hard for bad results."

The problem had been triggered by the big new Michelins that arrived at Welkom; Edwards had been nagging HRC for chassis changes ever since (the Honda being notoriously non-adjustable in this regard). The new chassis had come at the last race, apparently along the lines he had requested. But there still wasn't one for Colin, and wouldn't be for several races yet. It seemed he was still, as he had described himself before moving to Aprilia, Honda's "red-headed stepson".

Donington came to him instead. Now the only question was whether or not he wanted to beat his team-mate Gibernau. Edwards didn't pause for a minute ...

Already a firm favourite with British fans (his leathers earned the biggest money at the Riders for Health charity auction, £5,000), Edwards found the new surface's grip levels, along with his latest settings, just exactly right to deal with the chatter, and at last allow him the chance to employ his unique combination of aggression and precision. "We found a good setting in Germany to make the rear work, and I asked my guys for something that would keep the front wheel ahead of me instead of over there... (pointing wide). When we got here on Friday, it felt like a new motorcycle. Everything just worked. It's easy when it works – a piece of cake."

Edwards had finished second, even challenging Rossi at certain points of a race interrupted by a spatter of rain, though not officially stopped. Earlier, he had been more outspoken, giving a defiant gesture on the rostrum to critics who had been looking perhaps unkindly at the poor record of the ex-Superbike champions. These included also Bayliss and the hapless Hodgson, a floundering foreigner in a team that sometimes fell short in even the most basic areas. Edwards spoke for them all: "To the nay-sayers – up yours."

It was an impressive performance, though – as with Biaggi's last-weekend win – Edwards's access to the front was to be short-lived. Biaggi followed up his day in the sun with a dismal weekend, failing to find the right settings then suffering a gearshift failure that consigned him to a lowly 12th. This day actually belonged to Rossi, who showed that when a bad result – for whatever reason – puts him under pressure, he responds magnificently.

It wouldn't be England if the weather didn't prove a talking point, and after several years of balmy conditions Sunday dawned rainy for morning warm-up and the race – one-and-a-half hours late to avoid a TV clash with the German car GP – was run under skies that did more than merely lower. Short sharp showers did actually touch the far side of the circuit, but they were over as soon as they began, and barely wet the track. This led to some confusion. Rossi, leading, slowed but elected not to raise his hand. Better, he reasoned, to try and get the race over if possible. His ninth lap was eight tenths slower. Some behind him took his slackening of pace as a signal, including Edwards, whose time dropped by 1.7 seconds. The concertina effect meant that a few places back Capirossi and Checa lost fully four seconds. Afterwards they insisted the race should have been stopped, but in fact conditions proved Rossi, and Race Direction, to be right in continuing, albeit by the narrowest of margins.

With the summer break coming up, abbreviated to three weekends this year, there was an end-of-term feeling –a rather fragile gaiety. Just the spirit to absorb the news that the WCM team, currently hanging on by their fingernails, would be racing MotoGP's first V6 next season. Although still very much in the planning stage, they aimed to be testing in January. An ambitious target for the Czech Republic's Blata company, currently thriving on mini-bikes and a new scooter. At least, unlike independent manufacturers Proton KR, they have their own foundry. And everyone was delighted at what even team boss Peter Clifford admitted was more for novelty value than a serious vision of actually challenging the factories. Except on noise.

And then each of the three championship leaders went off on their holidays with another win, and an extended points lead. Had their rivals but known, it was already effectively all over.

Above: Edwards at last found form and fulfilled expectations at Donington, having no scruples in heading team-mate Gibernau, and pushing Rossi hard.
Photograph: Gold & Goose

MOTOGP RACE – 30 laps

Rossi and his crew were back on sizzling form; the track had rhythm and he had the beat. His fourth pole was two seconds quicker than last year's, half-a-second clear of the rest, all bunched up tight. Gibernau and Capirossi completed the front row, the Ducati's first of the year, with Bayliss leading row two.

Melandri withdrew from the race – he'd fractured a bone at the base of his thumb crashing under braking for the Melbourne hairpin when a very contrite Hofmann moved right across in front of him at much slower speed. Had the new entry kerb been longer, fulminated safety-commission rep Roberts Jr., Melandri would not have crashed.

The weather looked dangerous; everyone was keen to get the late-starting race under way. Nobody more so than leader Rossi, who plays the rain game better than most. When his screen and visor were spattered slightly on lap nine and then again later, he pressed on without raising his hand, though slowing enough to put those behind off their stride.

The pattern of the race was established over some fraught first laps. Rossi led into Redgate, but was cautious on the treacherous sweeps leading off downhill. Capirossi dived past before the Old Hairpin; Gibernau also two corners later. Rossi waited until the Melbourne Loop hairpin to regain second. Bayliss was all elbows and aggression in fourth; Edwards all over him, then Biaggi, Checa, Hayden, Barros and Xaus headed a close pack.

Capirossi led only one lap. Rossi and Gibernau ran one each side under braking for the chicane. Edwards was by now ahead of Bayliss and looking for his chance to do the same to Capirossi. It took one more lap, and then he was right up on his team-mate Gibernau. He stayed there three laps before slipping by to pursue Rossi, a clear target just over a second ahead.

The gap grew, shrank and grew over the next laps, hovering at just over a second, Edwards setting a new record on the eighth, before the rain slowed them both for a couple of laps. It was only after half-distance that Rossi started to draw away significantly – two seconds ahead on lap 17, three on lap 21, four on lap 24. A master at work.

Capirossi complained later of braking problems, and both Bayliss and Hayden took advantage of this, the Ducati rider taking up a spirited if ultimately unsuccessful chase of Gibernau. Before half distance, Hayden had closed him down again, passing into the chicane on lap 15. Bayliss fought back, and was attacking hard on lap 19 when a massive front-wheel slide at Craner Curves took him onto wet grass at some 120mph. Somehow he stayed on to rejoin past the Old Hairpin ... by then Hayden had gone.

Hopkins was the surprise in the next group. Thirteenth on lap one, he followed team-mate Roberts past Abe, then got ahead of him as well before setting about and disposing of Xaus. The Suzuki rider closed up now on Checa, somewhat dispirited after slowing right down in the rain, and Hopkins followed the Spaniard as he made up ground again, catching first Capirossi and then Barros on his way to an eventual sixth. Hopkins took a little longer to get past each of these, and was behind Capirossi once more at the finish. It was a highly impressive ride all the same.

Barros was happy just to finish, albeit only ninth, after getting well knocked about in a typical high-speed Craner Curves spill the day before. He was back on the same bike, and it didn't feel right, he said.

Hodgson got tenth at home, equalling his best so far. Might have been better but for all-too-familiar machine problems, this time erratic electronics in the lower gears. At least he'd beaten team-mate Xaus, by three seconds.

And then, in a lowly 12th place – costly both in terms of points and in self-esteem – came erstwhile championship challenger Biaggi. Later he showed bleeding toes; his quick-shift had failed, and he'd been obliged to change manually ... not as easy as a road-bike rider might think. Biaggi uses a road-pattern, with an up-for-down pedal, and had a punishing race to the doldrums.

Byrne grew more and more comfortable with his Aprilia on an achingly familiar track as the fuel load burned off, and the crowd cheered him on to a storming finish in 13th, closing to within three seconds of Biaggi. Tamada was ten seconds down, at sea with tyre choice; likewise fellow-Bridgestone user Nakano, equally distant but salvaging the final point.

McWilliams was the last rider on the same lap, with a now-touring Kenny Roberts (too-soft tyre choice), Aoki, Hofmann and Fabrizio. Abe was the only rider to crash – another big high-sider at Craner. He'd repassed Hopkins and was closing on Capirossi when he went down with two laps to go. Burns and Kurtis Roberts retired.

Left: Capirossi complained of braking problems. Here's the proof. Bayliss (12) and Hayden are ready to pounce.

Below: Tousle-haired and goggle-eyed, Valentino could do no wrong.

Bottom: Two pairs – The Aprilias of McWilliams and Byrne head the Protons of Aoki and Kurtis Roberts. They were not the most valuable cards in the pack.

Photographs: Gold & Goose

Right: You take the high road, and I'll take the hairpin. Porto is framed by an East Midlands airport jet.

Below: 250 title leader Pedrosa was flawless again, already drawing away from Porto, Aoyama and Debon (6), with Elias, de Angelis (51) and de Puniet (7) behind.
Photographs: Gold & Goose

Above: Raring to go – the 125s wait for the green light in qualifying. Left to right, Bautista (19), Lorenzo (48), Manna (8), Rodriguez (47) and Pellino (42).

Right: Spanish tempers flare as Gadea squares up to fellow 125 rookie Carchano after a practice tangle.
Both photographs: Gold & Goose

250 cc RACE – 27 laps

De Angelis took his first pole, narrowly ousting Porto. Wide-eyed Aoyama was a best-ever third, the rookie well on the pace and ahead of Pedrosa. De Puniet led row two.

Pedrosa's pace was devastating from the start. Porto and Nieto stayed with him for a while, Debon heading the increasingly distant pursuit. Nieto dropped away after just three laps; Porto kept trying for a couple more, but it was a repeat of the weekend before in Germany, and once again he settled for second. Not without some complaints afterwards at the unfair advantage of Pedrosa's much lighter weight, a major help in accelerating out of the last tight corners.

Aoyama's race had been short – T-boned in the last hairpin of the first lap by Elias and knocked flying. He remounted, right at the back. One lap later, Poggiali crashed out in the same place, for a second successive race. Bad to worse for the champion.

By this stage, de Puniet had got past Debon – soon to crash out – and was closing on Nieto, losing pace in a familiar style. By lap seven he was ahead, and he continued to the end without any more excitement.

Nieto fell back into the next group, where de Angelis and Elias were playing a leading role, until Elias suddenly slowed to retire.

This inspired de Angelis to get ahead of Nieto once and for all, and he closed up to within 1.5 seconds of a slowing de Puniet by the end.

It was not an exciting race. Nieto was another 18 seconds away; West had got ahead of Battaini and was still slowly closing on Nieto by the finish, but two seconds adrift.

Battaini was seventh, Matsudo alone behind him, and then the remounted Aoyama, who came through to take ninth from Guintoli in the closing laps of a well-spread race. Chaz Davies had crashed out after just two laps, pushing hard towards the top ten of his home GP.

125 cc RACE – 25 laps

Dovizioso took a slender pole from Barbera, Kallio and Corsi filling the front row; but come race day his advantage was greater, and he ran away from the start to stretch a disconsolate field out in his wake – there was to be no big 125 brawl for the Donington fans.

The fact that it was the 200th Italian victory in the class may have been neither here nor there to the teenager; more importantly his third win of the year was at a race where both Locatelli and Barbera crashed out. The latter went on the first lap, one of three victims of the treachery of Craner Curves on cold tyres, along with regular front-runner Pablo Nieto and frequent faller Pasini.

More than a second ahead after lap one, Dovizioso kept on pulling away. Locatelli headed the next group, just clear of Kallio, Corsi and Bautista. The last-named was fastest, and after a few narrow squeaks he got to third on lap five, and quickly closed up to harry Locatelli, to pass him too on the eighth lap, although nowhere near getting even a distant scent of the leader.

Locatelli was alone behind him, then came Kallio, outdistancing Corsi but now under pressure from the quickening Lorenzo.

Locatelli crashed out with three laps to go at Coppice, onto the straight. "Maybe my concentration slipped for a second," he said later. This meant Kallio and Lorenzo were battling for third, and the latter made it by four tenths, after a daring last corner attack.

Corsi managed to save fifth from late-arrival Jenkner, who had escaped Ui, Simon and Borsoi in the closing laps.

Rising youngster Bautista, in footballer Clarence Seedorf's team in its second year, took the lap record; Dovizioso went off on holiday with a comforting 32-point lead.

FIM WORLD CHAMPIONSHIP • ROUND 9

CINZANO BRITISH grand prix

25 JULY 2004

DONINGTON PARK

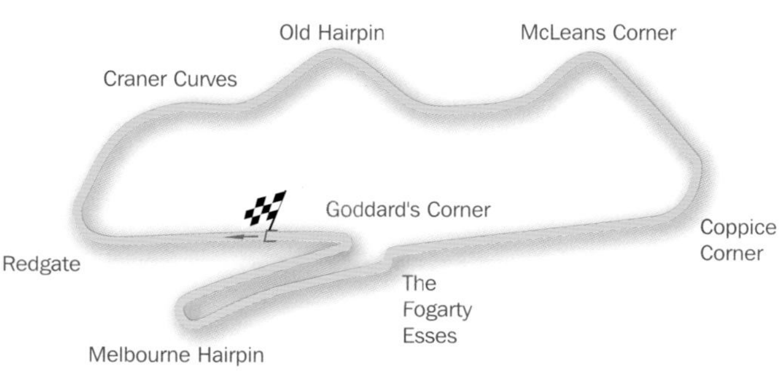

CIRCUIT LENGTH: 2.500 miles/4.023 km

MotoGP

30 laps, 75.000 miles/120.690 km

Pos.	Rider (Nat.)	No.	Machine	Laps	Time & speed
1	Valentino Rossi (I)	46	Yamaha	30	45m 30.473s 98.875 mph/ 159.124 km/h
2	Colin Edwards (USA)	45	Honda	30	45m 33.418s
3	Sete Gibernau (E)	15	Honda	30	45m 34.899s
4	Nicky Hayden (USA)	69	Honda	30	45m 36.569s
5	Troy Bayliss (AUS)	12	Ducati	30	45m 45.184s
6	Carlos Checa (E)	7	Yamaha	30	45m 47.583s
7	Loris Capirossi (I)	65	Ducati	30	45m 53.786s
8	John Hopkins (USA)	21	Suzuki	30	45m 58.594s
9	Alex Barros (BR)	4	Honda	30	46m 05.853s
10	Neil Hodson (GB)	50	Ducati	30	46m 14.941s
11	Ruben Xaus (E)	11	Ducati	30	46m 17.963s
12	Max Biaggi (I)	3	Honda	30	46m 24.477s
13	Shane Byrne (GB)	67	Aprilia	30	46m 27.851s
14	Makoto Tamada (J)	6	Honda	30	46m 37.631s
15	Shinya Nakano (J)	56	Kawasaki	30	46m 46.268s
16	Jeremy McWilliams (GB)	99	Aprilia	30	46m 56.958s
17	Kenny Roberts (USA)	10	Suzuki	29	45m 39.070s
18	Nobuatsu Aoki (J)	9	Proton KR	29	45m 51.868s
19	Alex Hofmann (D)	66	Kawasaki	29	45m 55.289s
20	Michel Fabrizio (I)	84	Harris WCM	29	45m 56.509s
	Norick Abe (J)	17	Yamaha	28	DNF
	Kurtis Roberts (USA)	80	Proton KR	11	DNF
	Chris Burns (GB)	35	Harris WCM	2	DNF
	Marco Melandri (I)	33	Yamaha		DNS

Fastest lap: Edwards, 1m 29.973s, 100.021 mph/160.968 km/h (record).

Previous record: Valentino Rossi, I (Honda), 1m 31.023s, 98.867 mph/159.111 km/h (2003).

Event best maximum speed: Capirossi, 177.1 mph/285.0 km/h (race).

Qualifying: 1 Rossi, 1m 28.720s; 2 Gibernau, 1m 29.152s; 3 Capirossi, 1m 29.209s; 4 Bayliss, 1m 29.214s; 5 Edwards, 1m 29.250s; 6 Hayden, 1m 29.295s; 7 Checa, 1m 29.329s; 8 Biaggi, 1m 29.502s; 9 Barros, 1m 29.801s; 10 Xaus, 1m 29.840s; 11 Melandri, 1m 29.900s; 12 Nakano, 1m 30.214s; 13 Kenny Roberts, 1m 30.239s; 14 Hodgson, 1m 30.297s; 15 Tamada, 1m 30.371s; 16 Hopkins, 1m 30.442s; 17 Abe, 1m 30.460s; 18 Byrne, 1m 30.502s; 19 McWilliams, 1m 30.595s; 20 Fabrizio, 1m 31.353s; 21 Hofmann, 1m 31.486s; 22 Aoki, 1m 31.491s; 23 Kurtis Roberts, 1m 32.222s; 24 Burns, 1m 33.285s.

Fastest race laps: 1 Edwards, 1m 29.973s; 2 Hayden, 1m 30.021s; 3 Rossi, 1m 30.023s; 4 Bayliss, 1m 30.121s; 5 Gibernau, 1m 30.367s; 6 Hopkins, 1m 30.511s; 7 Barros, 1m 30.518s; 8 Checa, 1m 30.640s; 9 Abe, 1m 30.722s; 10 Capirossi, 1m 30.791s; 11 Xaus, 1m 31.405s; 12 Tamada, 1m 31.425s; 13 Hodgson, 1m 31.471s; 14 Byrne, 1m 31.472s; 15 Nakano, 1m 31.868s; 16 McWilliams, 1m 31.915s; 17 Biaggi, 1m 32.024s; 18 Kenny Roberts, 1m 32.272s; 19 Hofmann, 1m 32.476s; 20 Kurtis Roberts, 1m 33.112s; 21 Aoki, 1m 33.310s; 22 Fabrizio, 1m 33.419s; 23 Burns, 1m 45.293s.

World Championship: 1 Rossi, 164; 2 Gibernau, 142; 3 Biaggi, 142; 4 Edwards, 95; 5 Barros, 86; 6 Hayden, 83; 7 Checa, 72; 8 Capirossi, 64; 9 Melandri, 57; 10 Tamada, 56; 11 Xaus, 46; 12 Abe, 41; 13 Nakano, 37; 14 Bayliss, 34; 15 Kenny Roberts, 29; 16 Hodgson and Hofmann, 24; 18 Hopkins, 22; 19 Byrne, 15; 20 McWilliams, 10; 21 Fabrizio, 8; 22 Aoki, 6; 23 Pitt, 2; 24 Kurtis Roberts, 1.

250 cc

27 laps, 67.500 miles/108.621 km

Pos.	Rider (Nat.)	No.	Machine	Laps	Time & speed
1	Daniel Pedrosa (E)	26	Honda	27	42m 17.705s 95.747 mph/ 154.090 km/h
2	Sebastian Porto (ARG)	19	Aprilia	27	42m 23.708s
3	Randy de Puniet (F)	7	Aprilia	27	42m 29.168s
4	Alex de Angelis (RSM)	51	Aprilia	27	42m 30.427s
5	Fonsi Nieto (E)	10	Aprilia	27	42m 48.135s
6	Anthony West (AUS)	14	Aprilia	27	42m 50.712s
7	Franco Battaini (I)	21	Aprilia	27	43m 09.636s
8	Naoki Matsudo (J)	8	Yamaha	27	43m 12.760s
9	Hiroshi Aoyama (J)	73	Honda	27	43m 15.127s
10	Sylvain Guintoli (F)	50	Aprilia	27	43m 17.161s
11	Joan Olive (E)	11	Aprilia	27	43m 23.975s
12	Alex Baldolini (I)	25	Aprilia	27	43m 24.271s
13	Hugo Marchand (F)	9	Aprilia	27	43m 38.730s
14	Johan Stigefelt (S)	16	Aprilia	27	43m 39.505s
15	Jakub Smrz (CZ)	96	Honda	27	43m 46.825s
16	David de Gea (E)	52	Honda	27	43m 50.438s
17	Dirk Heidolf (D)	28	Aprilia	27	43m 50.860s
18	Klaus Nöhles (D)	17	Honda	26	42m 27.973s
19	Taro Sekiguchi (J)	44	Yamaha	26	43m 01.102s
20	Lee Dickinson (GB)	65	Honda	26	43m 06.553s
21	Radomil Rous (CZ)	43	Yamaha	26	43m 06.985s
	Arnaud Vincent (F)	12	Aprilia	24	DNF
	Toni Elias (E)	24	Honda	13	DNF
	Alex Debon (E)	6	Honda	3	DNF
	Manuel Poggiali (RSM)	54	Aprilia	2	DNF
	Chaz Davies (GB)	57	Aprilia	2	DNF
	Erwan Nigon (F)	36	Aprilia	0	DNF
	Roberto Rolfo (I)	2	Honda		DNS
	Frederik Watz (S)	64	Yamaha		DNS
	Hector Faubel (E)	33	Aprilia		DNS
	Max Sabbatani (I)	40	Yamaha		DNS
	Tony Campbell (GB)	66	Yamaha		DNQ
	Bruce Dunn (GB)	67	Honda		DNQ

Fastest lap: Pedrosa, 1m 33.217s, 96.540 mph/155.366 km/h (record).

Previous record: Daijiro Kato, J (Honda), 1m 34.096s, 95.638 mph/153.915 km/h (2001).

Event best maximum speed: Aoyama, 152.7 mph/245.8 km/h (qualifying practice no. 2).

Qualifying: 1 de Angelis, 1m 32.430s; 2 Porto, 1m 32.493s; 3 Aoyama, 1m 32.557s; 4 Pedrosa, 1m 32.643s; 5 de Puniet, 1m 32.870s; 6 Elias, 1m 33.002s; 7 Poggiali, 1m 33.176s; 8 West, 1m 33.213s; 9 Nieto, 1m 33.503s; 10 Debon, 1m 33.550s; 11 Matsudo, 1m 33.724s; 12 Davies, 1m 33.927s; 13 Battaini, 1m 34.132s; 14 Olive, 1m 34.281s; 15 Guintoli, 1m 34.457s; 16 Stigefelt, 1m 34.921s; 17 Smrz, 1m 34.982s; 18 Rolfo, 1m 35.090s; 19 de Gea, 1m 35.171s; 20 Vincent, 1m 35.403s; 21 Baldolini, 1m 35.543s; 22 Marchand, 1m 35.697s; 23 Heidolf, 1m 35.721s; 24 Nöhles, 1m 35.823s; 25 Nigon, 1m 36.184s; 26 Sekiguchi, 1m 36.739s; 27 Watz, 1m 37.504s; 28 Dickinson, 1m 37.622s; 29 Rous, 1m 37.795s; 30 Faubel, 1m 38.294s; 31 Sabbatani, 1m 38.438s; 32 Campbell, 1m 39.646s; 33 Dunn, 1m 39.994s.

Fastest race laps: 1 Pedrosa, 1m 33.217s; 2 de Angelis, 1m 33.478s; 3 Porto, 1m 33.736s; 4 de Puniet, 1m 33.826s; 5 Elias, 1m 33.998s; 6 Nieto, 1m 34.326s; 7 West, 1m 34.518s; 8 Aoyama, 1m 34.584s; 9 Battaini, 1m 34.668s; 10 Debon, 1m 34.918s; 11 Olive, 1m 35.100s; 12 Baldolini, 1m 35.144s; 13 Guintoli, 1m 35.270s; 14 Matsudo, 1m 35.426s; 15 Poggiali, 1m 35.571s; 16 Stigefelt, 1m 35.651s; 17 Marchand, 1m 35.926s; 18 Smrz, 1m 36.167s; 19 Heidolf, 1m 36.477s; 20 de Gea, 1m 36.572s; 21 Nöhles, 1m 36.914s; 22 Sekiguchi, 1m 37.071s; 23 Vincent, 1m 37.286s; 24 Davies, 1m 37.381s; 25 Rous, 1m 37.580s; 26 Dickinson, 1m 38.229s.

World Championship: 1 Pedrosa, 180; 2 de Puniet, 146; 3 Porto, 128; 4 Nieto, 94; 5 de Angelis, 93; 6 Elias, 86; 7 Aoyama, 71; 8 Rolfo, 67; 9 West, 65; 10 Poggiali, 63; 11 Debon, 53; 12 Battaini, 46; 13 Guintoli, 29; 14 Matsudo, 23; 15 Baldolini and Olive, 19; 17 Davies, 15; 18 Marchand and Vincent, 11; 20 Bataille and Faubel, 9; 22 Smrz, 8; 23 Lefort, 7; 24 Stigefelt, 4; 25 Heidolf, 3; 26 Sekiguchi, 1.

125 cc

25 laps, 62.500 miles/100.575 km

Pos.	Rider (Nat.)	No.	Machine	Laps	Time & speed
1	Andrea Dovizioso (I)	34	Honda	25	41m 14.592s 90.916 mph/ 146.315 km/h
2	Alvaro Bautista (E)	19	Aprilia	25	41m 18.399s
3	Jorge Lorenzo (E)	48	Derbi	25	41m 22.842s
4	Mika Kallio (SF)	36	KTM	25	41m 23.233s
5	Simone Corsi (I)	24	Honda	25	41m 31.298s
6	Steve Jenkner (D)	21	Aprilia	25	41m 31.585s
7	Youichi Ui (J)	41	Aprilia	25	41m 36.712s
8	Julian Simon (E)	10	Honda	25	41m 37.662s
9	Gino Borsoi (I)	23	Aprilia	25	41m 38.452s
10	Gioele Pellino (I)	42	Aprilia	25	41m 44.585s
11	Stefano Perugini (I)	7	Gilera	25	41m 45.067s
12	Lukas Pesek (CZ)	52	Honda	25	41m 45.185s
13	Gabor Talmacsi (H)	14	Malaguti	25	41m 55.094s
14	Fabrizio Lai (I)	32	Gilera	25	41m 55.732s
15	Mike di Meglio (F)	63	Aprilia	25	41m 59.887s
16	Sergio Gadea (E)	33	Aprilia	25	42m 00.762s
17	Robbin Harms (DK)	69	Honda	25	42m 03.917s
18	Thomas Luthi (CH)	12	Honda	25	42m 09.264s
19	Imre Toth (H)	25	Aprilia	25	42m 31.815s
20	Georg Frohlich (D)	20	Honda	25	42m 35.026s
21	Christian Elkin (GB)	49	Honda	25	42m 37.618s
22	Simone Sanna (I)	18	Aprilia	25	42m 39.028s
23	Vaclav Bittman (CZ)	35	Honda	25	42m 43.525s
24	Raffaele de Rosa (I)	30	Honda	25	42m 48.342s
25	Eugene Laverty (GB)	85	Honda	24	41m 14.875s
26	Kris Weston (GB)	51	Honda	23	41m 23.822s
27	Thomas Bridewell (GB)	84	Honda	23	41m 25.261s
	Angel Rodriguez (E)	47	Derbi	24	DNF
	Roberto Locatelli (I)	15	Aprilia	24	DNF
	Vesa Kallio (SF)	66	Aprilia	22	DNF
	Mirko Giansanti (I)	6	Aprilia	17	DNF
	Manuel Manna (I)	8	Malaguti	16	DNF
	Raymond Schouten (NL)	16	Honda	9	DNF
	Marco Simoncelli (I)	58	Aprilia	4	DNF
	Pablo Nieto (E)	22	Aprilia	0	DNF
	Hector Barbera (E)	3	Aprilia	0	DNF
	Mattia Pasini (I)	54	Aprilia	0	DNF
	Jordi Carchano (E)	28	Aprilia		DNS

Fastest lap: Bautista, 1m 38.263s, 91.583 mph/147.388 km/h (record).

Previous record: Lucio Cecchinello, I (Aprilia), 1m 38.312s, 91.537 mph/147.314 km/h (2002).

Event best maximum speed: M. Kallio, 133.0 mph/214.1 km/h (qualifying practice no. 2).

Qualifying: 1 Dovizioso, 1m 37.211s; 2 Barbera, 1m 37.245s; 3 M. Kallio, 1m 37.687s; 4 Corsi, 1m 37.697s; 5 Ui, 1m 37.781s; 6 Lorenzo, 1m 37.797s; 7 Locatelli, 1m 37.831s; 8 Simon, 1m 37.907s; 9 Bautista, 1m 37.912s; 10 Simoncelli, 1m 37.974s; 11 Jenkner, 1m 38.064s; 12 Giansanti, 1m 38.089s; 13 Lai, 1m 38.278s; 14 Nieto, 1m 38.283s; 15 Borsoi, 1m 38.425s; 16 di Meglio, 1m 38.473s; 17 Luthi, 1m 38.521s; 18 Perugini, 1m 38.834s; 19 Pasini, 1m 39.071s; 20 Pesek, 1m 39.135s; 21 Harms, 1m 39.185s; 22 Talmacsi, 1m 39.270s; 23 Pellino, 1m 39.365s; 24 Gadea, 1m 39.442s; 25 Rodriguez, 1m 39.462s; 26 Carchano, 1m 39.886s; 27 Sanna, 1m 40.010s; 28 V. Kallio, 1m 40.346s; 29 Bittman, 1m 40.379s; 30 Toth, 1m 40.410s; 31 Elkin, 1m 40.631s; 32 Laverty, 1m 40.717s; 33 de Rosa, 1m 40.936s; 34 Schouten, 1m 41.417s; 35 Manna, 1m 41.589s; 36 Frohlich, 1m 41.659s; 37 Weston, 1m 42.689s; 38 Bridewell, 1m 43.906s.

Fastest race laps: 1 Bautista, 1m 38.263s; 2 Dovizioso, 1m 38.335s; 3 Locatelli, 1m 38.407s; 4 Lorenzo, 1m 38.475s; 5 Simon, 1m 38.495s; 6 M. Kallio, 1m 38.563s; 7 Ui, 1m 38.590s; 8 Rodriguez, 1m 38.690s; 9 Jenkner, 1m 38.701s; 10 Borsoi, 1m 38.743s; 11 Giansanti, 1m 38.767s; 12 Corsi, 1m 38.815s; 13 Pellino, 1m 38.848s; 14 Pesek, 1m 38.921s; 15 Perugini, 1m 38.939s; 16 di Meglio, 1m 39.013s; 17 Talmacsi, 1m 39.193s; 18 Gadea, 1m 39.229s; 19 Lai, 1m 39.272s; 20 Harms, 1m 39.362s; 21 Simoncelli, 1m 39.669s; 22 Luthi, 1m 39.971s; 23 Toth, 1m 40.511s; 24 Sanna, 1m 40.524s; 25 Frohlich, 1m 40.736s; 26 V. Kallio, 1m 40.887s; 27 Elkin, 1m 41.055s; 28 de Rosa, 1m 41.328s; 29 Bittman, 1m 41.473s; 30 Manna, 1m 41.499s; 31 Laverty, 1m 41.769s; 32 Weston, 1m 42.439s; 33 Schouten, 1m 43.359s; 34 Bridewell, 1m 43.770s.

World Championship: 1 Dovizioso, 163; 2 Locatelli, 131; 3 Barbera, 129; 4 Stoner, 104; 5 Nieto, 88; 6 Lorenzo, 84; 7 Jenkner, 73; 8 Giansanti, 71; 9 Bautista, 60; 10 Simoncelli, 59; 11 M. Kallio, 53; 12 Simon, 32; 13 Pasini, 31; 14 Corsi, 30; 15 Borsoi, 29; 16 di Meglio, 28; 17 Ballerini and Ui, 19; 19 Pellino, 15; 20 Perugini and Pesek, 8; 22 Talmacsi and Toth, 6; 24 Lai, 5; 25 Giuseppetti, 3; 26 Carchano, Gadea and Rodriguez, 2.

FIM WORLD CHAMPIONSHIP • ROUND 10

CZECH REPUBLICGP

BRNO

Above: Brno is almost the perfect track for spectators.
Photograph: Gold & Goose

Right: Gravel-scraped and fuming, Hodgson stopped short of physically attacking Biaggi, who had caused his crash. Team owner Sito Pons (right) looks on with trepidation.
Photograph: Malcolm Bryan/BPC

Below: Shakey by name ... Byrne's heavy crash severely injured his wrist.
Photograph: Gold & Goose

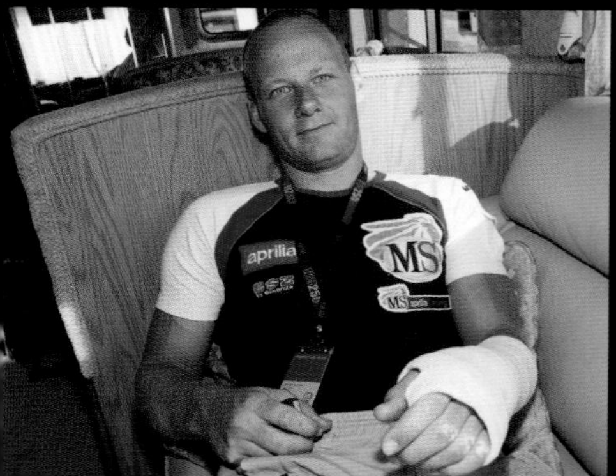

IT was very much back to business at Brno, in all sorts of ways. There were important announcements ... next year's calendar was revealed (China and the USA added, Rio or South Africa to be dropped); while HRC chose the resumption of what was left of the European season to launch a new friendship offensive. A senior management shuffle had brought in a new regime, promising to be "open and candid", and guaranteeing a smiling face for the most august of the Japanese racing companies. (Or there'll be trouble, quipped a rival team manager.)

It was back to motorbike racing too, and with pre-race testing banned most teams had their hotel rooms held to stay on after the race. This included not only the usual big names, with Lavilla on hand to join Suzuki tests; but also Moriwaki, with a new rider ... jobless Olivier Jacque would take over from Andrew Pitt, here for one last race on the machine before thankfully leaving for a substitute Supersport 600 ride.

It was not an auspicious time for those espousing technical adventure. In the Moriwaki's case it is the anachronistic tubular steel frame. For the Proton KR, it is just about everything. But team principal Kenny Roberts had taken a policy decision before the summer break. From now on they would stop trying to coax the missing 15-odd horsepower from their Mk2 V5 engine. Instead they would accept its limitations, and those of the Dunlop tyres, and concentrate on making what they had go round the race-track as well and as reliably as possible. Among other things, a new supplier solved the persistent clutch seal oil leaks, and in terms of reliability the bike made impressive strides from now on. The basic fact remained: the quest to challenge the Japanese factories had foundered expensively, with too little of everything. Anything else would be good money after bad. The V5 had reached the end of the line, with half-a-season left to go. Proton's last hope lay in forthcoming tests with the so-far still-born KTM V4 MotoGP motor. They would be back at Brno within the week, for Aoki to shake this bike down, at an open public track day!

Blata must have been taking all this in, and they announced they were to seek EEC funding for their V6 project, to be built at a new factory at Blansko, just 25km away from traditional racing base Brno. They showed drawings of the proposed bike, distinguished by six tailpipes. They must also have noticed the Proton V5's sole and brief moment of glory, when Kurtis Roberts put it sixth fastest in wet practice on Friday. That didn't last, however. In the wet the next day, Roberts had a vicious corner-entry high-side, and among other injuries broke his left wrist badly enough to put him out for the rest of the season.

Another such victim was Shakey Byrne. His fall came in dry weather, but was nasty. It was on Saturday morning, on the first of the downhill double lefts of the natural stadium section. His Aprilia tossed him over the high side in spectacular fashion rivalling the height record set by Kagayama some years ago at Paul Ricard, and he landed badly, face first. Concussion and other injuries were added to a serious double wrist fracture and dislocations in his left wrist. The courageous Kentishman was to return at Motegi in four weeks, but this would turn out to be not just premature but to make the injury much worse.

On the injury theme, Stoner returned one race earlier than expected, wearing an extraordinary contraption purpose-made by German off-road body-armour firm Ortema. This used a moulding of his shoulders as basis for a framework worn under the leathers, designed to protect his still-healing collarbone in case of an accident. The crash-prone Australian made it through practice okay, but crashed after less than two laps of the race ... without ill effects.

Honda now had more of the new exhaust system and engine mods Barros had debuted in Germany, and Max bolted them straight on. Gibernau however eschewed the change, preferring to stick with what he knew, at least until post-race tests. In any case Brno is a fast track where mid-range throttle response is of limited interest, but in fact Sete was to stay with the original system for the rest of the year.

Kawasaki's changes entailed continuing experiments with crankshaft weights, switching back to a unit lighter by some 15 percent. This was a mixed blessing; reduced gyroscopic effects improved handling, but reduced flywheel weight also made the engine more lively in throttle response. Since it already erred towards an excess of this characteristic, the payoff for easier handling in high-speed direction changes was a less friendly machine, harder to ride. "We will have to try to solve this problem with electronics," said project leader Naoyo Kaneko. This they proceeded to do over the forthcoming races.

Biaggi's reputation for on-track arrogance was bolstered on Saturday morning, when he was blamed for a nasty collision. Aiming for the pits, he swung right across the racing line of the last corner right in front of Hodgson, on a fast lap. Max escaped with a damaged seat, Hodgson bit the dirt. He marched straight to Biaggi's pit for a session of blunt Northern finger-wagging. Aware that the cameras were on him, Hodgson stopped short of physical assault. "Talk about road rage," he said later. "Racing is dangerous enough, and I wanted him to know he had just screwed my weekend." Biaggi blamed a gear-selection problem, and was not contrite.

A sad note from the 125 class, where Ui was sacked from the Abruzzo team. Eleven times a GP winner Ui had struggled on the low-level Aprilia; his place went to more sponsorship-friendly 21-year-old Italian Gioele Pellino.

And controversy in the 250 race, where twice two different leading riders tried to have it stopped for rain, only to be ignored. Race Director Paul Butler said later: "We take our information from other sources than only riders, and reports from the corners and the helicopter were that the track was safe and the rain not setting in. Lap times only dropped on the laps the riders held up their hands." This reinforced his authority, and proved once again that unity among riders is very hard to achieve. And once again his decision was proved correct by circumstances. But many wondered what would have happened had it been the MotoGP class, and Rossi or Biaggi holding up their hands.

Above: Above: Kurtis, sixth-fastest in the rain, chats to Kenny Jr. and John Hopkins, their Suzukis fast only in the dry. It would be the younger Roberts's last race of the year.

Left: Still a sketchy proposition, the Blata V6 had tailpipes galore.

Photographs: Gold & Goose

Above: **Winner Gibernau leads lap one, from Barros (4), Biaggi (3), Rossi (46) and Edwards (half-hidden, 45). Also prominent are Abe (17) and Capirossi (65). Gibernau would also lead the last lap, and most of them in between.**

Opposite top right: **Five-times champion Mick Doohan, HRC's general manager of racing, is dwarfed by new icon Hayden.**

Opposite centre right: **Team owner and ex-racer Luis d'Antin.**

Bottom right: **Capirossi paints rubber with a surge of Ducati power.**

Photographs: Gold & Goose

MOTOGP RACE – 22 laps

All qualifying times were set in wet afternoon sessions; dry times in the mornings had been somewhat different, with Hopkins on fire on the Suzuki, fastest both Friday and Saturday, with team-mate Roberts third. When it counted in the rain, they felt the opposite effect from their Bridgestones, and were placed 21st and 16th respectively.

Gibernau claimed his fourth pole; Barros alongside, and then Rossi, who was second-quickest in the dry in the morning. He pushed Bayliss back onto row two.

The weather cleared; Gibernau took the first corner from Barros, Biaggi and Edwards, set for a two-lap run with the leaders before his tyres wore enough for his demon chatter to depress his progress. By lap six Barros had made a slip to let Biaggi and Rossi past; Hayden had closed up behind them. Capirossi was losing ground, Edwards behind him.

Six laps later, after half distance, Rossi upped the pace. He dived inside Biaggi at the first Esses, and started to loom closer to Gibernau. A couple of slides showed he was on the limit, but not about to slack off.

Barros had collected himself by now, and also got past Biaggi, and promptly got ahead of Rossi as well, as the Yamaha took another jinking slide. Rossi fought straight back; Barros was lining him up for another go when his front wheel slid away and he fell in a heap in the gravel trap. An all too frequent event, once aptly described by Rossi's crew chief Burgess. "It looked like amateur hour out there."

Biaggi was straining to catch up as Rossi closed up to attack Gibernau. At the first Esses on lap 17 he pushed past into the first section; Gibernau got him straight back at the second. The same thing happened two corners later. Down at the bottom of the hill Rossi nosed alongside again ... but it was for the last time. Gibernau had everything under control, and from then on he started to pull away gradually for an impressively well-measured win.

At the start of the next lap Biaggi tried to get past Rossi, but his entry was too fast and he ran wide on the exit. Hayden followed him, "a bit mesmerised", and promptly slid off as the front tucked under.

Tamada had been picking up places after his poor qualification on the wet Bridgestones, down in 16th. Before one third distance he had caught fast starter Hopkins and Checa, piled up behind Edwards. Hopkins was looking to move further forward when he suddenly slowed on lap 12, blowing up next time round in a cloud of smoke ... another valve spring gone.

Tamada got past Edwards three laps after that, and now he had Capirossi five seconds ahead. With seven laps left it seemed a tall order, but his Bridgestones were working better and better, and he caught up after only five laps, flying past the Ducati, Capirossi later complaining of stability problems.

Checa also passed the trailing Edwards with three laps to go; close behind Melandri and Roberts were battling back and forth. Abe was soon to close up after disposing of Bayliss (a rostrum finisher here last year); Hodgson also getting ahead of the newer Ducati and tagging on to Abe. With four laps to go, the pair caught the two in front, for a final sort-out.

Abe won out; Melandri on his heels, then Roberts and Hodgson.

With three laps to go, Xaus's Ducati blew up at the last corner, spilling oil that tipped its own rider off. Bayliss and then Dean Ellison (the British Superbike ace riding in place of injured Burns) fell off on the oil next time round.

The yellow flags were still out when the Kawasakis arrived on the final lap, Hofmann poised to attack his team-mate. Instead he had to stay behind, and he finished just one tenth adrift. McWilliams was three seconds away; some way back Aoki managed to fend off Pitt and the Moriwaki for the final point.

GAS

D'ANTIN
MotoGP
DUCATI

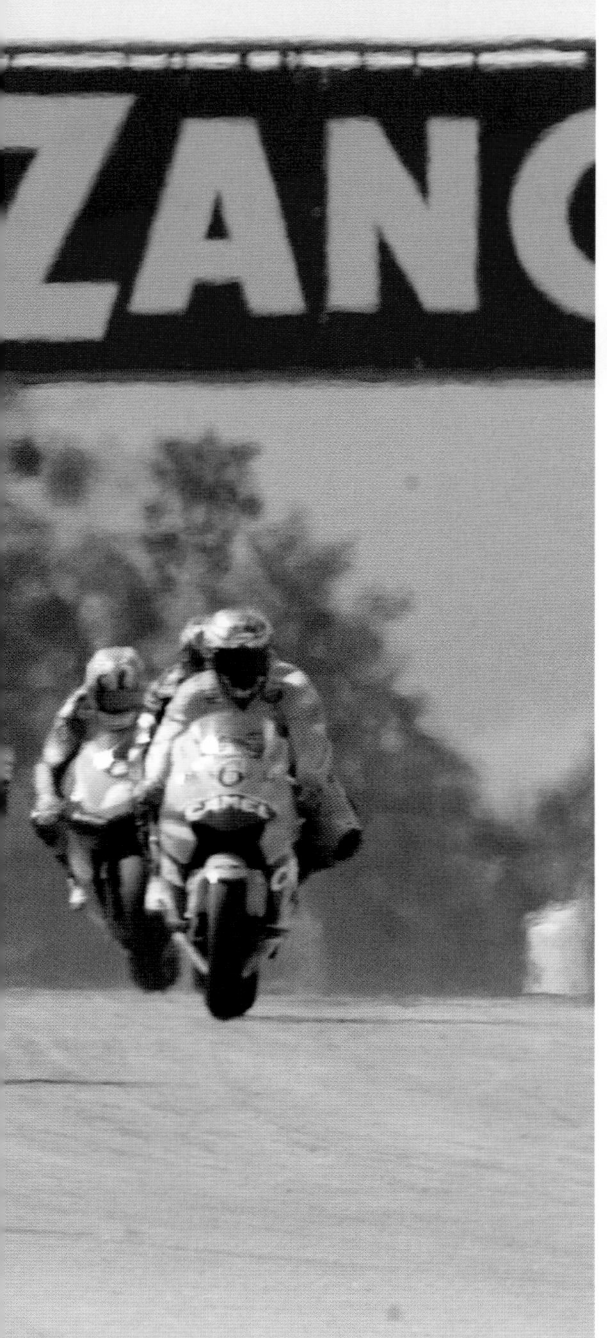

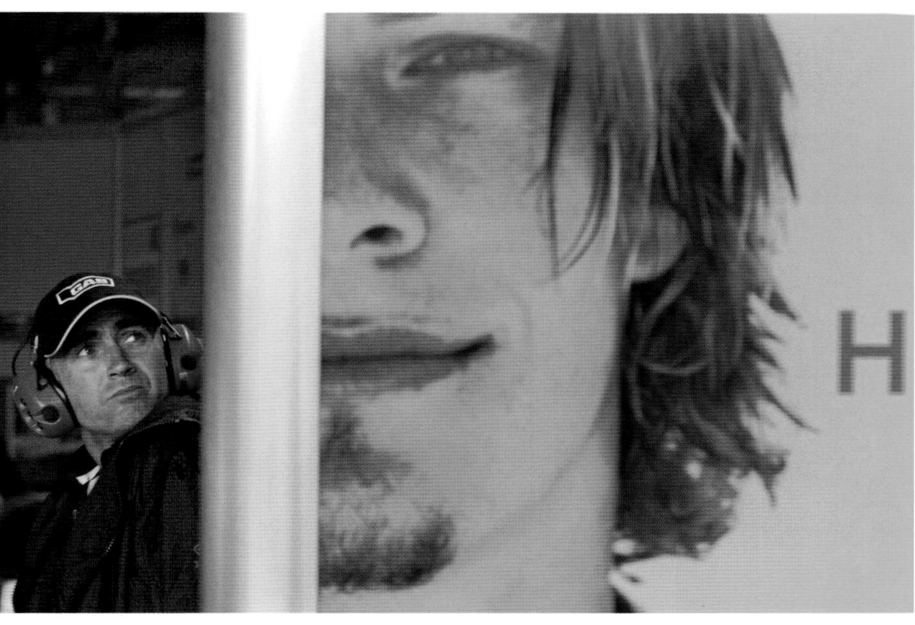

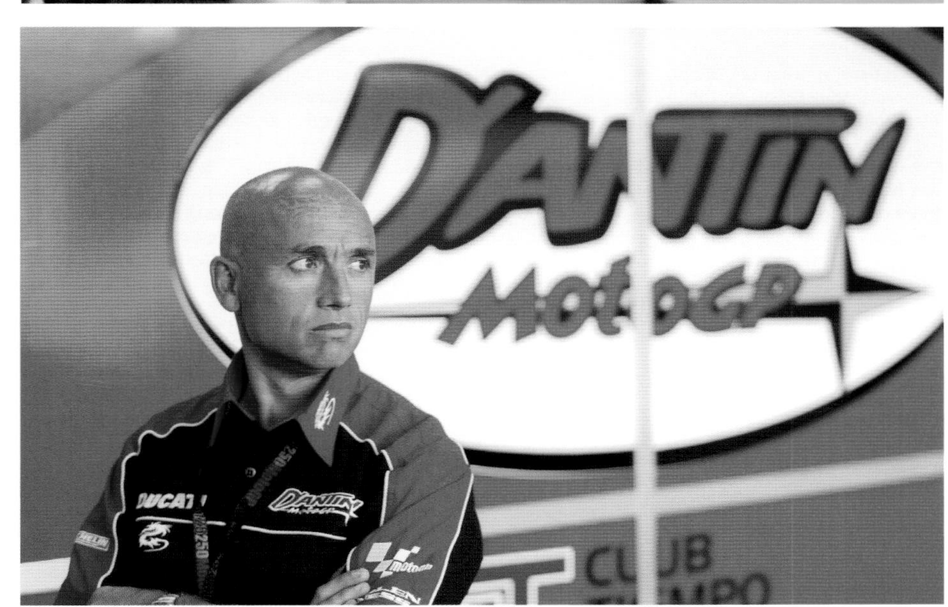

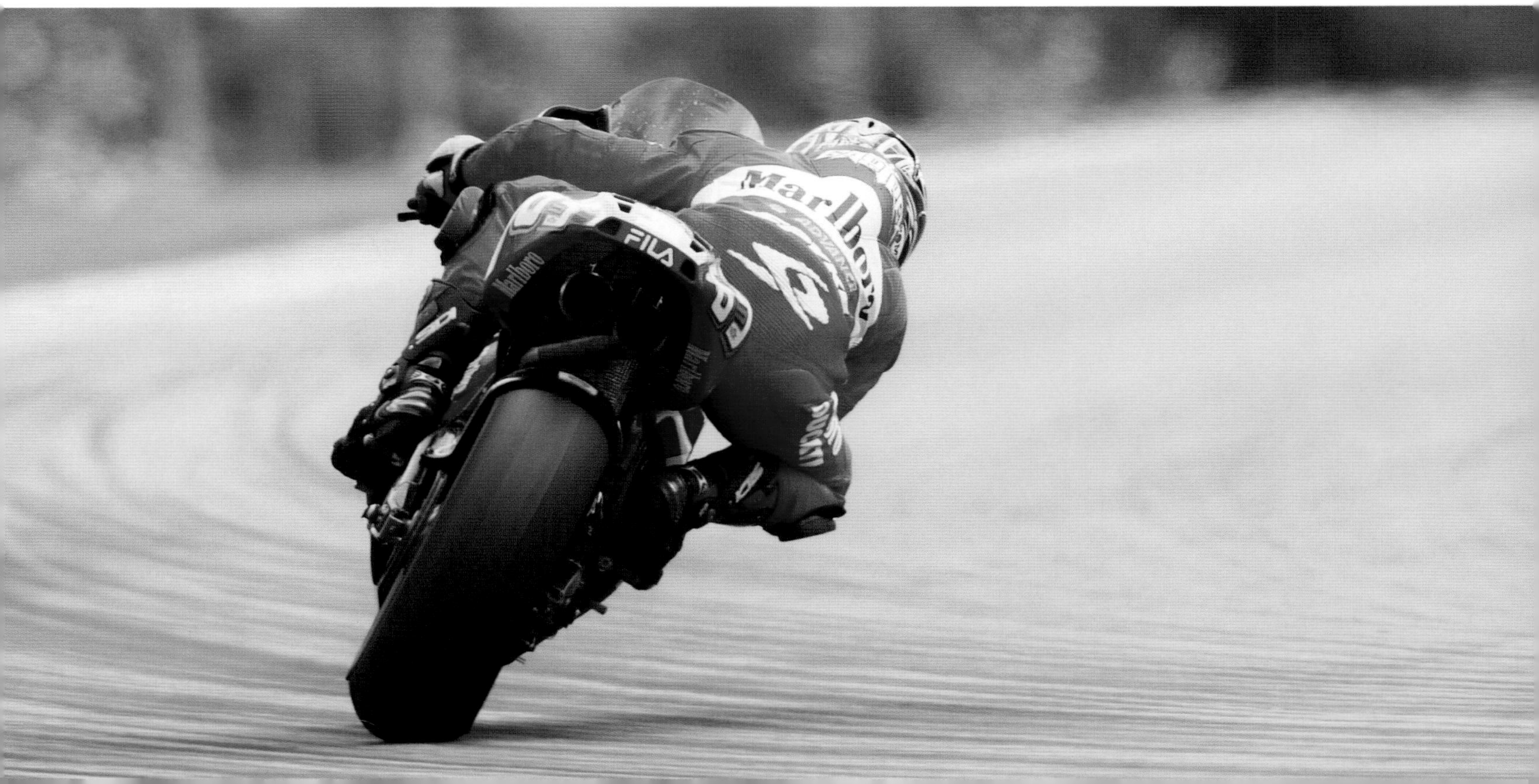
Marlboro
FILA

Above: Sebastian Porto read the rules and the weather, and took control of a controversial 250 race.

Below: Derbi snitches the 125 race – Lorenzo beating Dovizioso, Locatelli and Nieto to the flag.

Opposite page: Gibernau's sigh of relief was blatant, as he got back on top of Rossi one more time.

Photographs: Gold & Goose

250 cc RACE – 20 laps

Already short of time compared with MotoGP, the 250s were even harder hit by weather in qualifying. It would get worse in the race.

Brno suits Aprilias, and they dominated the front row– Porto, Nieto, de Angelis and Guintoli, times well spread; Pedrosa was struggling, 20th on day one and only up to the fourth row by the end.

A shower had swept through after the 125 race, but the track was dry for the start: Porto heading Aoyama into the first section. De Angelis was second by the end of the lap and promptly took the lead on the next, as de Puniet and Pedrosa both got past the Japanese rookie.

De Angelis was still up front when rain spotted in on one section on lap six, and he immediately put his hand up and slowed. So did some others ... the foolish virgins. The wise virgins had read the rules, and knew that the race leader had no right to stop the race. Porto was one, and he swept into the lead as the first half-dozen all closed up, de Angelis at the back. Aoyama was second, then de Puniet, Pedrosa, and now also Elias. Next time round Aoyama slithered wide and dropped behind not only these but also an on-form West, ninth on lap one but moving forward steadily.

De Angelis rapidly moved through to third again, Pedrosa with him, Elias losing ground once more. After five laps of this, Pedrosa and de Angelis trading blows over third, de Puniet took the lead for the first time. One lap later and Porto was down to fourth, cautious on sections of track that were increasingly slippery, as spots of rain fell here and there.

It was now lap 16, and Pedrosa thought the race might be stopped at any moment. It was time to take control. He picked his way from third to first, and next time round had taken a second out of de Angelis, now up to second, but shortly to fall victim to his own pace and the tricky conditions, sliding out. This increased Pedrosa's lead still further.

On lap 18, Pedrosa twice put his hand up, slowing his pace. His rivals did the same to him as to de Angelis: Porto and de Puniet surging past and Porto making the most of it to keep pulling away, to win by four seconds.

Pedrosa was flabbergasted, coming in another six seconds adrift, and saying: "I'm amazed they didn't stop the race." His anger abated somewhat under the stern tutelage of his patron Alberto Puig, and a week later he resolved that next time, he would keep on racing.

West had caught and passed Elias, fending off his strong attack on the final lap. Rolfo was seven seconds away, keeping Aoyama back.

Another ten seconds away Davies scored a career-best eighth after a strong ride, the privateer dealing with defending champion Poggiali convincingly mid-race to cross the line 15 seconds clear.

Eight riders crashed out, none more spectacularly than Guintoli, with Rolfo and Aoyama when he was flicked over the high side. His bike snapped off the rear suspension as it landed, and promptly exploded. Nieto took a leading role in a tragi-comic series of crashes at the first left-hander just after half distance. Lying 11th after a bad start, he slipped off on the corner entry. He blamed some spillage – fuel, oil or water, and was born out when two more, Bataille and Baldolini, crashed out at the same spot. An incensed Nieto ran to the marshal point and seized an oil flag to run back to the trackside with it. He was later fined US $5,000 for his pains.

125 cc RACE – 19 laps

Dry weather led to a storming race – the lead changed hands six times, including one collision, on the last lap alone.

Simoncelli ousted Dovizioso for his second pole; Simon and Lorenzo completing row one. Bad weather kept Barbera, Locatelli and Nieto on the sixth and seventh rows.

Dovizioso got the jump for an early lead from Stoner and Lorenzo, Stoner crashing out second time round. Barbera was up to seventh; two laps later he was second. Nieto was sixth and Locatelli the fastest on the track, though only just in the top 15.

Dovizioso's lead stretched to three seconds, but soon Barbera was taking four or five tenths out of this every lap, Jenkner and home runner Lukas Pesek with him, nine laps of glory before he seized in a cloud of smoke. A little way back Lorenzo was caught up with Borsoi and Nieto

After half distance, Barbera took the lead and Jenkner pushed Dovizioso to third. Nieto was close, Lorenzo three seconds behind, but soon to close.

Nieto made a lunge for the lead, only to drop to eighth. With two laps left, Barbera led Dovizioso, Lorenzo, Jenkner, Locatelli, Borsoi and Nieto, Giansanti close behind in an eight-strong pack.

Lorenzo led onto the last lap. He and Barbera changed places four times over the first run to the bottom of the hill. At that lowest corner they collided hard enough to send Barbera way out wide.

As they reached the last left-right combination, Dovizioso made the final move, taking control on the entry. But no! Hard charger Lorenzo pushed straight back past into the second part of the corner, to the Italian's dismay, to lead over the line by less than four hundredths. The wily Locatelli was a tenth behind that, then Nieto and a small gap to Borsoi, Jenkner, Barbera and Giansanti.

FIM WORLD CHAMPIONSHIP • ROUND 10

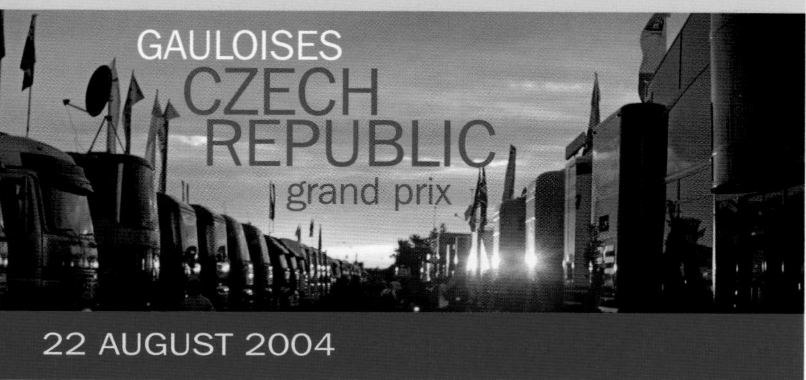

GAULOISES CZECH REPUBLIC grand prix

22 AUGUST 2004

AUTODROM BRNO – CZECH REPUBLIC

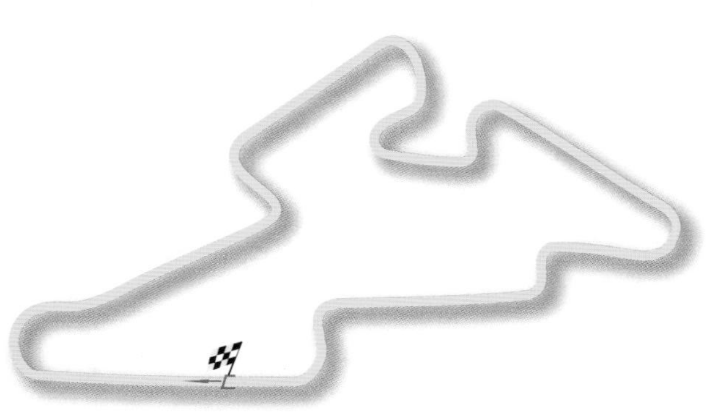

CIRCUIT LENGTH: 3.357 miles/5.403 km

MotoGP

22 laps, 73.854 miles/118.866 km

Pos.	Rider (Nat.)	No.	Machine	Laps	Time & speed
1	Sete Gibernau (E)	15	Honda	22	44m 03.480s 100.585 mph/ 161.876 km/h
2	Valentino Rossi (I)	46	Yamaha	22	44m 06.994s
3	Max Biaggi (I)	3	Honda	22	44m 07.810s
4	Makoto Tamada (J)	6	Honda	22	44m 19.737s
5	Loris Capirossi (I)	65	Ducati	22	44m 21.410s
6	Carlos Checa (E)	7	Yamaha	22	44m 24.661s
7	Colin Edwards (USA)	45	Honda	22	44m 25.951s
8	Norick Abe (J)	17	Yamaha	22	44m 34.559s
9	Marco Melandri (I)	33	Yamaha	22	44m 34.638s
10	Kenny Roberts (USA)	10	Suzuki	22	44m 35.105s
11	Neil Hodgson (GB)	50	Ducati	22	44m 37.574s
12	Shinya Nakano (J)	56	Kawasaki	22	44m 57.604s
13	Alex Hofmann (D)	66	Kawasaki	22	44m 57.768s
14	Jeremy McWilliams (GB)	99	Aprilia	22	45m 00.951s
15	Nobuatsu Aoki (J)	9	Proton KR	22	45m 21.995s
16	Andrew Pitt (AUS)	88	Moriwaki	22	45m 22.171s
17	Michel Fabrizio (I)	84	Harris WCM	22	45m 56.618s
	Troy Bayliss (AUS)	12	Ducati	20	DNF
	James Ellison (GB)	77	Harris WCM	20	DNF
	Ruben Xaus (E)	11	Ducati	19	DNF
	Nicky Hayden (USA)	69	Honda	18	DNF
	Alex Barros (BR)	4	Honda	14	DNF
	John Hopkins (USA)	21	Suzuki	12	DNF
	Gregorio Lavilla (E)	32	Suzuki	4	DNF
	Kurtis Roberts (USA)	80	Proton KR		DNS
	Shane Byrne (GB)	67	Aprilia		DNS

Fastest lap: Barros, 1m 59.302s, 101.307 mph/163.038 km/h (record).

Previous record: Valentino Rossi, I (Honda), 1m 59.966s, 100.746 mph/162.135 km/h (2003).

Event best maximum speed: Biaggi, 193.4 mph/311.2 km/h (race).

Qualifying: 1 Gibernau, 2m 09.782s; 2 Barros, 2m 10.090s; 3 Rossi, 2m 10.470s; 4 Bayliss, 2m 10.923s; 5 Edwards, 2m 11.096s; 6 Checa, 2m 11.188s; 7 Hayden, 2m 11.662s; 8 Biaggi, 2m 11.737s; 9 Capirossi, 2m 11.821s; 10 Xaus, 2m 12.073s; 11 Melandri, 2m 12.685s; 12 Hodgson, 2m 13.008s; 13 Abe, 2m 13.327s; 14 Kurtis Roberts, 2m 13.345s; 15 McWilliams, 2m 13.781s; 16 Kenny Roberts, 2m 13.817s; 17 Tamada, 2m 14.031s; 18 Fabrizio, 2m 14.223s; 19 Byrne, 2m 14.304s; 20 Pitt, 2m 14.397s; 21 Hopkins, 2m 14.727s; 22 Aoki, 2m 15.682s; 23 Lavilla, 2m 16.150s; 24 Ellison, 2m 16.715s; 25 Nakano, 2m 16.723s; 26 Hofmann, 2m 17.157s.

Fastest race laps: 1 Barros, 1m 59.302s; 2 Gibernau, 1m 59.403s; 3 Rossi, 1m 59.416s; 4 Biaggi, 1m 59.477s; 5 Hayden, 1m 59.547s; 6 Capirossi, 1m 59.595s; 7 Tamada, 1m 59.638s; 8 Hopkins, 1m 59.759s; 9 Checa, 1m 59.947s; 10 Kenny Roberts, 2m 00.087s; 11 Edwards, 2m 00.140s; 12 Melandri, 2m 00.514s; 13 Abe, 2m 00.817s; 14 Hodgson, 2m 00.853s; 15 Bayliss, 2m 00.854s; 16 McWilliams, 2m 01.134s; 17 Hofmann, 2m 01.311s; 18 Nakano, 2m 01.566s; 19 Xaus, 2m 02.176s; 20 Pitt, 2m 02.747s; 21 Lavilla, 2m 02.995s; 22 Aoki, 2m 03.119s; 23 Fabrizio, 2m 03.607s; 24 Ellison, 2m 04.948s.

World Championship: 1 Rossi, 184; 2 Gibernau, 167; 3 Biaggi, 158; 4 Edwards, 104; 5 Barros, 86; 6 Hayden, 83; 7 Checa, 82; 8 Capirossi, 75; 9 Tamada, 69; 10 Melandri, 64; 11 Abe, 49; 12 Xaus, 46; 13 Nakano, 41; 14 Kenny Roberts, 35; 15 Bayliss, 34; 16 Hodgson, 29; 17 Hofmann, 27; 18 Hopkins, 22; 19 Byrne, 15; 20 McWilliams, 12; 21 Fabrizio, 8; 22 Aoki, 7; 23 Pitt, 2; 24 Kurtis Roberts, 1

250 cc

20 laps, 67.140 miles/108.060 km

Pos.	Rider (Nat.)	No.	Machine	Laps	Time & speed
1	Sebastian Porto (ARG)	19	Aprilia	20	42m 03.061s 95.805 mph/ 154.184 km/h
2	Randy de Puniet (F)	7	Aprilia	20	42m 07.370s
3	Daniel Pedrosa (E)	26	Honda	20	42m 13.980s
4	Anthony West (AUS)	14	Aprilia	20	42m 16.853s
5	Toni Elias (E)	24	Honda	20	42m 17.193s
6	Roberto Rolfo (I)	2	Honda	20	42m 24.231s
7	Hiroshi Aoyama (J)	73	Honda	20	42m 25.101s
8	Chaz Davies (GB)	57	Aprilia	20	42m 36.487s
9	Manuel Poggiali (RSM)	54	Aprilia	20	42m 51.387s
10	Hector Faubel (E)	33	Aprilia	20	43m 06.522s
11	Dirk Heidolf (D)	28	Aprilia	20	43m 06.861s
12	Hugo Marchand (F)	9	Aprilia	20	43m 07.193s
13	Gregory Leblanc (F)	42	Aprilia	20	43m 07.691s
14	Jakub Smrz (CZ)	96	Honda	20	43m 14.021s
15	Joan Olive (E)	11	Aprilia	20	43m 14.493s
16	Naoki Matsudo (J)	8	Yamaha	20	43m 26.229s
17	Johan Stigefelt (S)	16	Aprilia	20	43m 27.726s
18	Radomil Rous (CZ)	43	Yamaha	20	43m 36.091s
19	Henk vd Lagemaat (NL)	71	Aprilia	19	42m 56.383s
	Alex de Angelis (RSM)	51	Aprilia	17	DNF
	Klaus Nöhles (D)	17	Honda	17	DNF
	Sylvain Guintoli (F)	50	Aprilia	15	DNF
	Taro Sekiguchi (J)	44	Yamaha	15	DNF
	Gergo Talmacsi (H)	88	Yamaha	13	DNF
	Eric Bataille (F)	34	Honda	10	DNF
	Fonsi Nieto (E)	10	Aprilia	10	DNF
	Alex Baldolini (I)	25	Aprilia	10	DNF
	Erwan Nigon (F)	36	Aprilia	6	DNF
	Arnaud Vincent (F)	12	Aprilia	4	DNF
	Franco Battaini (I)	21	Aprilia	0	DNF
	Alex Debon (E)	6	Honda		DNS
	Valerio Anghetti (I)	27	Aprilia		DNS

Fastest lap: Pedrosa, 2m 03.332s, 97.996 mph/157.710 km/h (record).

Previous record: Marco Melandri, I (Aprilia), 2m 03.836s, 97.598 mph/157.069 km/h (2001).

Event best maximum speed: de Angelis, 158.4 mph/255.0 km/h (race).

Qualifying: 1 Porto, 2m 14.261s; 2 Nieto, 2m 14.457s; 3 de Angelis, 2m 14.528s; 4 Guintoli, 2m 15.846s; 5 Rolfo, 2m 15.952s; 6 Battaini, 2m 16.216s; 7 Elias, 2m 16.257s; 8 Aoyama, 2m 16.639s; 9 Vincent, 2m 16.965s; 10 Matsudo, 2m 17.385s; 11 de Puniet, 2m 17.542s; 12 West, 2m 17.656s; 13 Pedrosa, 2m 18.061s; 14 Debon, 2m 18.149s; 15 Baldolini, 2m 19.057s; 16 Smrz, 2m 19.477s; 17 Poggiali, 2m 19.873s; 18 Stigefelt, 2m 20.175s; 19 Davies, 2m 21.027s; 20 Bataille, 2m 21.244s; 21 Nigon, 2m 22.220s; 22 Marchand, 2m 22.305s; 23 Heidolf, 2m 22.508s; 24 Rous, 2m 22.858s; 25 Faubel, 2m 23.339s; 26 Olive, 2m 23.502s; 27 Leblanc, 2m 23.526s; 28 vd Lagemaat, 2m 23.799s; 29 Nöhles, 2m 24.350s; 30 Sekiguchi, 2m 24.696s; 31 Talmacsi, 2m 25.252s; 32 Anghetti, 2m 36.226s.

Fastest race laps: 1 Pedrosa, 2m 03.332s; 2 de Angelis, 2m 03.984s; 3 de Puniet, 2m 04.125s; 4 Porto, 2m 04.422s; 5 Elias, 2m 04.657s; 6 West, 2m 04.814s; 7 Aoyama, 2m 05.314s; 8 Poggiali, 2m 05.354s; 9 Rolfo, 2m 05.549s; 10 Bataille, 2m 05.559s; 11 Guintoli, 2m 05.656s; 12 Davies, 2m 05.668s; 13 Nieto, 2m 05.999s; 14 Baldolini, 2m 06.302s; 15 Matsudo, 2m 06.870s; 16 Nigon, 2m 06.928s; 17 Heidolf, 2m 06.965s; 18 Leblanc, 2m 07.123s; 19 Faubel, 2m 07.211s; 20 Nöhles, 2m 07.349s; 21 Smrz, 2m 07.568s; 22 Marchand, 2m 07.599s; 23 Olive, 2m 07.846s; 24 Stigefelt, 2m 07.928s; 25 Rous, 2m 08.541s; 26 Vincent, 2m 10.768s; 27 Sekiguchi, 2m 10.835s; 28 vd Lagemaat, 2m 13.259s; 29 Talmacsi, 2m 16.906s.

World Championship: 1 Pedrosa, 196; 2 de Puniet, 166; 3 Porto, 153; 4 Elias, 97; 5 Nieto, 94; 6 de Angelis, 93; 7 Aoyama, 80; 8 West, 78; 9 Rolfo, 77; 10 Poggiali, 70; 11 Debon, 53; 12 Battaini, 46; 13 Guintoli, 29; 14 Davies and Matsudo, 23; 16 Olive, 20; 17 Baldolini, 19; 18 Faubel and Marchand, 15; 20 Vincent, 11; 21 Smrz, 10; 22 Bataille, 9; 23 Heidolf, 8; 24 Lefort, 7; 25 Stigefelt, 4; 26 Leblanc, 3; 27 Sekiguchi, 1.

125 cc

19 laps, 63.783 miles/102.657 km

Pos.	Rider (Nat.)	No.	Machine	Laps	Time & speed
1	Jorge Lorenzo (E)	48	Derbi	19	41m 19.475s 92.615 mph/ 149.049 km/h
2	Andrea Dovizioso (I)	34	Honda	19	41m 19.511s
3	Roberto Locatelli (I)	15	Aprilia	19	41m 19.621s
4	Pablo Nieto (E)	22	Aprilia	19	41m 19.661s
5	Gino Borsoi (I)	23	Aprilia	19	41m 20.580s
6	Steve Jenkner (D)	21	Aprilia	19	41m 20.672s
7	Hector Barbera (E)	3	Aprilia	19	41m 21.054s
8	Mirko Giansanti (I)	6	Aprilia	19	41m 21.062s
9	Simone Corsi (I)	24	Honda	19	41m 31.963s
10	Julian Simon (E)	10	Honda	19	41m 31.998s
11	Robbin Harms (DK)	69	Honda	19	41m 35.422s
12	Andrea Ballerini (I)	50	Aprilia	19	41m 35.562s
13	Alvaro Bautista (E)	19	Aprilia	19	41m 35.661s
14	Mattia Pasini (I)	54	Aprilia	19	41m 44.559s
15	Fabrizio Lai (I)	32	Gilera	19	41m 47.746s
16	Michael Ranseder (A)	88	KTM	19	41m 47.804s
17	Stefano Perugini (I)	7	Gilera	19	41m 53.370s
18	Thomas Luthi (CH)	12	Honda	19	41m 57.229s
19	Marco Simoncelli (I)	58	Aprilia	19	42m 04.016s
20	Dario Giuseppetti (D)	26	Honda	19	42m 06.302s
21	Lorenzo Zanetti (I)	45	Aprilia	19	42m 14.880s
22	Tomoyoshi Koyama (J)	89	Yamaha	19	42m 14.920s
23	Vesa Kallio (SF)	66	Aprilia	19	42m 15.133s
24	Mike di Meglio (F)	63	Aprilia	19	42m 18.495s
25	Georg Frohlich (D)	20	Honda	19	42m 43.559s
26	Raymond Schouten (NL)	16	Honda	19	43m 12.547s
27	Patrik Vostarek (CZ)	87	Honda	19	43m 33.689s
28	Marketa Janakova (CZ)	9	Honda	18	41m 44.627s
	Sergio Gadea (E)	33	Aprilia	16	DNF
	Vaclav Bittman (CZ)	35	Honda	15	DNF
	Jordi Carchano (E)	28	Aprilia	15	DNF
	Lukas Pesek (CZ)	52	Honda	9	DNF
	Imre Toth (H)	25	Aprilia	7	DNF
	Gabor Talmacsi (H)	14	Malaguti	6	DNF
	Mika Kallio (SF)	36	KTM	4	DNF
	Manuel Manna (I)	8	Malaguti	3	DNF
	Casey Stoner (AUS)	27	KTM	1	DNF
	Angel Rodriguez (E)	47	Derbi	1	DNF
	Gioele Pellino (I)	42	Aprilia	1	DNF

Fastest lap: Jenkner, 2m 08.891s, 93.770 mph/150.908 km/h.

Lap record: Lucio Cecchinello, I (Aprilia), 2m 07.836s, 94.544 mph/152.154 km/h (2003).

Event best maximum speed: Barbera, 137.0 mph/220.5 km/h (race).

Qualifying: 1 Simoncelli, 2m 24.458s; 2 Dovizioso, 2m 24.638s; 3 Simon, 2m 25.218s; 4 Lorenzo, 2m 25.549s; 5 Talmacsi, 2m 25.831s; 6 Stoner, 2m 25.967s; 7 Corsi, 2m 26.232s; 8 Zanetti, 2m 26.390s; 9 Pesek, 2m 26.516s; 10 Borsoi, 2m 26.605s; 11 Ballerini, 2m 26.805s; 12 Harms, 2m 26.855s; 13 Jenkner, 2m 26.978s; 14 Giansanti, 2m 27.128s; 15 Koyama, 2m 27.131s; 16 Bautista, 2m 27.402s; 17 M. Kallio, 2m 27.607s; 18 Ranseder, 2m 27.613s; 19 Lai, 2m 28.731s; 20 Gadea, 2m 28.819s; 21 Luthi, 2m 28.886s; 22 Toth, 2m 29.063s; 23 Pasini, 2m 29.123s; 24 Barbera, 2m 29.160s; 25 Locatelli, 2m 29.562s; 26 Nieto, 2m 29.753s; 27 di Meglio, 2m 30.189s; 28 Pellino, 2m 30.390s; 29 Carchano, 2m 31.002s; 30 Bittman, 2m 31.190s; 31 Perugini, 2m 31.320s; 32 Janakova, 2m 33.028s; 33 Giuseppetti, 2m 33.158s; 34 Vostarek, 2m 33.650s; 35 Schouten, 2m 33.722s; 36 Frohlich, 2m 33.729s; 37 Manna, 2m 34.575s; 38 V. Kallio, 2m 34.601s; 39 Rodriguez, 2m 34.619s.

Fastest race laps: 1 Jenkner, 2m 08.891s; 2 Locatelli, 2m 08.972s; 3 Barbera, 2m 08.986s; 4 Nieto, 2m 09.015s; 5 Giansanti, 2m 09.220s; 6 Pesek, 2m 09.248s; 7 Borsoi, 2m 09.249s; 8 Simon, 2m 09.282s; 9 Corsi, 2m 09.299s; 10 Dovizioso, 2m 09.404s; 11 Lorenzo, 2m 09.506s; 12 Pasini, 2m 09.872s; 13 Simoncelli, 2m 09.954s; 14 Harms, 2m 10.033s; 15 Ballerini, 2m 10.036s; 16 Bautista, 2m 10.052s; 17 Gadea, 2m 10.388s; 18 Ranseder, 2m 10.599s; 19 Perugini, 2m 10.771s; 20 Lai, 2m 10.859s; 21 Luthi, 2m 10.860s; 22 Talmacsi, 2m 11.579s; 23 Giuseppetti, 2m 11.659s; 24 Toth, 2m 11.805s; 25 Zanetti, 2m 11.912s; 26 V. Kallio, 2m 11.994s; 27 Koyama, 2m 12.255s; 28 M. Kallio, 2m 12.305s; 29 di Meglio, 2m 12.504s; 30 Frohlich, 2m 12.929s; 31 Bittman, 2m 13.451s; 32 Carchano, 2m 14.088s; 33 Schouten, 2m 15.387s; 34 Vostarek, 2m 15.677s; 35 Stoner, 2m 17.220s; 36 Janakova, 2m 17.296s; 37 Manna, 2m 17.792s; 38 Rodriguez, 2m 21.887s; 39 Pellino, 2m 21.920s.

World Championship: 1 Dovizioso, 183; 2 Locatelli, 147; 3 Barbera, 138; 4 Lorenzo, 109; 5 Stoner, 104; 6 Nieto, 101; 7 Jenkner, 83; 8 Giansanti, 79; 9 Bautista, 63; 10 Simoncelli, 59; 11 M. Kallio, 53; 12 Borsoi, 40; 13 Simon, 38; 14 Corsi, 37; 15 Pasini, 33; 16 di Meglio, 28; 17 Ballerini, 23; 18 Ui, 19; 19 Pellino, 15; 20 Perugini and Pesek, 8; 22 Lai, Talmacsi and Toth, 6; 25 Harms, 5; 26 Giuseppetti, 3; 27 Carchano, Gadea and Rodriguez, 2.

FIM WORLD CHAMPIONSHIP • ROUND 11

PORTUGUESE GP

ESTORIL

Biaggi's race was short and inglorious, after he collided with Capirossi on the first lap. Capirossi had moved wide to let Rossi through to lead … and the Yamaha rider sailed serenely away as Biaggi sprinted back to his bike.
Photographs: Gold & Goose

THERE was a time when GP racing was only part of a top rider's season. There were also major national and international events, often paying much bigger money than GPs, and for some the Isle of Man TT. The practice came to an end when 1983 World Champion Freddie Spencer jeopardised his title chances crashing in the pre-season Trans-Atlantic Match Races at Donington Park two years later. Riders were too valuable to risk in this way. But racers are by nature risk-takers … and accidents will happen.

The victim this time was Nicky Hayden, and like fellow-American John Hopkins earlier in the year his accident came riding off-road. The younger rider had missed tests after breaking both ankles in a January Supercross race, earning the opprobrium of the Suzuki team, and requiring further surgery mid-season. Hayden hadn't been racing. It was almost worse … he'd crashed a Supermoto bike at an Alpinestars promotional event, breaking his right collarbone and injuring his left knee. The first injury was rapidly plated at Costa's clinic, the second troubled him right up until the final race. In any case, he was pulled out of this round without turning a wheel. "Tell the truth, I wanted to ride," he said ruefully, spectating on the first day. "But Honda said no."

It was not a particularly good time to be upsetting Honda, because the president of the Honda Motor Corporation was present – Mr Takeo Fukui. The former paddock regular was greyer. the impish look now more gnomic than when he headed HRC in the Eighties, or even earlier that decade, as one of the leading engineers behind the NR500 oval-piston four-stroke GP bike. That bike was seen as a debacle, but HRC were to revise the history somewhat in a presentation in the coming weeks. Although racing success was elusive, the lessons learned had been of vast value since, in areas both specific (like slipper-clutch experience) and in general understanding of how to create successful racing motorcycles. And in training engineers for the future – several others involved in that project had gone on to greater heights.

Fukui-San's role at Estoril, he explained, was to "energise all the Honda riders … especially in MotoGP". The boss of bosses was careful not to be drawn on specifics, and professed that he cared little that the official factory team had not won a race so far this year (and in fact would not do so all season), "as long as it is a Honda winning". But he was unequivocal when asked who his favourite Honda rider was. Not Doohan, the biggest winner; not Rossi, the most recent; not even Hailwood, their first big star. "Freddie Spencer. We need Freddie now."

Yamaha had another super-hero: Melandri was attempting to offset his bad second year on the bike with the return of the lucky Spiderman leathers he had worn to win the 250 GP in Italy in 2002. Those had been auctioned off for charity; this second incarnation extended to the fairing of his M1 and his helmet, and would also come under the hammer. Minutes after taking to the track, he had crashed. That was patched up; in the race a massive crash left the bodywork in shards and tatters. He sold it piece by piece, realising more than he had the previous occasion.

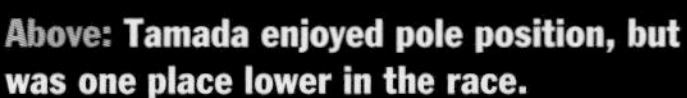

Above: Tamada enjoyed pole position, but was one place lower in the race.

Top: Fabrizio took over the Aprilia for one race – but even with bandages it was literally too much of a handful.

Left: What a tangled web … Melandri's Spiderman bodywork was shattered in a heavy race crash.
Photographs: Gold & Goose

Fellow Italian Michel Fabrizio had impressed on the WCM; now he was drafted in to the Aprilia team to take the place of Byrne. (Ellison remained for a second race on the WCM.) A shake-down test at Mugello had left him deeply impressed at the power – always a striking feature of the RS3; by the end of the weekend in Portugal its wayward handling and tendency to wheelie then land with a big tank-slapper had beaten up his wrists so badly he was unable to finish the race. Bear that in mind, for when Byrne climbs back on the Aprilia in two weeks time …

The race was another Rossi triumph, for more reasons than just his strong return to form and almost start-to-finish victory. Not only did closest rival Gibernau manage no better than fourth, but Biaggi's title challenge that had sparked up in Germany was now firmly extinguished. Max became yet another of Capirossi's victims (the way he saw it), a list that spans the years and includes not only 250 rivals Romboni, Lucchi and Harada (who lost the title as a result) but also Biaggi on a prior occasion. Two weeks later, Capirossi was to add another five names at Motegi. This time, the case was arguable.

It happened on lap one, as Rossi pushed inside Capirossi into the tight uphill corner early on the lap. Capirossi obligingly went wide, Biaggi tried to follow Rossi through … as Capirossi slammed back across onto the racing line. The Ducati rider was merely pushed off the track, to rejoin at the back, but Biaggi was off and his race over. "Was he trying to win the race on the first lap," he said later; to which Capirossi would respond: "He could have waited for a safer place to pass me."

In any case, it meant Rossi could go off to the flyaways with a handsomely increased advantage – a 29-point cushion that meant he could miss a race and still retain the lead for the first time all season. A different measure showed just how close it had all been – BMW's contest to win a 645 coupe totted up practice times from all races, plus those recorded pre-season at the IRTA tests. After 11 races, Rossi had spent a total of 20 minutes and 32.488 seconds setting his fastest laps. Gibernau had spent just 0.126 seconds longer.

Estoril is the slowest circuit of the season, in spite of a long downhill straight where the MotoGP bikes were handsomely exceeding 200 mph – eventually Biaggi's Honda was fastest, at 341.8km/h (212.4 mph) – and one fast (almost 140 mph) corner. The other corners are slow enough to make up for it, and make it a somewhat acrobatic affair for a MotoGP bike.

Rossi in perfect harmony – another bravura performance gave him a one-race points cushion before the flyaway races. He would use it.

Photograph: Gold & Goose

MOTOGP RACE – 28 laps

With rain forecast for Saturday, everybody put on qualifiers and went for a time on Friday afternoon. In fact, the final timed session was dry, but by then torrential rain had washed the rubber off the line, and almost half the riders – including Rossi – failed to improve. Not so a rampant Tamada, who ousted Rossi off pole, his career first, Bridgestone's second of the year. Gibernau was a close third; a second Bridgestone rider, Hopkins, was at the far end of the second row, his best ever qualifying.

Capirossi blasted into the lead from row four, using all the Desmosedici's power to outdrag everybody into the first slow corner. Rossi, Biaggi and Tamada followed on, Gibernau sixth behind Melandri.

Rossi had no margin, and wanted an early advantage, "in case the tyres went bad later," he explained. His attack on Capirossi was assured and effective, and brought a bit of breathing space right away, as Capirossi and Biaggi tangled in his wake. The Doctor continued to build on his advantage over Tamada, running a blistering pace as he stretched by three or four tenths a lap, to have more than a second after four of the 28.

From then on he and his pursuer continued to move steadily away from the rest, neither putting a wheel wrong. It was a fine display, and just one winner. Rossi didn't see another bike all race long, except when he lapped Ellison.

Melandri had been third at the end of the first lap, but was promptly mobbed by Barros and Gibernau, the pair already embroiled in a race-long battle for third that was fierce but static, in that they never did change places. Gibernau later complained that set-up problems spoiled his braking; he did come alongside Barros out of the final corner, only to be pushed firmly onto the paint.

Spiderman was still close as they started lap eight, his hands full resisting strong pressure from Checa. Halfway round the young Italian went flying again, this time in spectacular fashion, touching the dirt under braking at the end of the back straight. His bike somersaulted to destruction, the custom-painted bodywork shattered. After the accident, Melandri was walking around picking up bits and pieces, to salvage what he could.

Checa was now fifth. He had taken two laps to get ahead of fast-starting Hopkins, but the Suzuki rider was going strong, though he complained afterwards about how hard he was having to ride to make up for the sluggish Suzuki's acceleration and top speed problems.

A second behind him, Edwards headed a close group, Roberts and Bayliss right with him, Xaus closing up for a while, before losing ground gradually. Bayliss pushed to the front of it, and all of them closed up on Hopkins.

At the same time, Capirossi was making up places rapidly from the back, and had picked up slow-starting Abe on the way through. By lap 12 he was past Roberts for ninth and hounding Edwards; taking two laps to pick him off, the same again to get ahead of Bayliss.

By now Hopkins was three seconds clear, a second behind Checa and closing. With seven laps left, he would prove an impossible target for the factory Ducati. But though he pushed and shoved at Checa's faster Yamaha, and even nosed ahead on the back straight on the final lap, it was to no avail, for he ran onto the paint under braking and was wide for the next corner, and finished just over half-a-second behind.

Bayliss was content to follow Capirossi, and in the final laps had his hands full keeping old SBK rival Edwards behind; Abe was just over a second adrift. A long way back, Nakano headed McWilliams; then Hofmann and Roberts – he complained later that his engine had gone off song, affecting responses and handling, causing him to drop back. A distant Aoki's Proton was weeping oil again, but still going for the final point. Ellison, in his second race as a substitute on the WCM, was the only other finisher, a lap down.

Aside from Biaggi and Melandri, Fabrizio retired after wrenching his wrists. And the two d'Antin Ducati riders ran into problems indicative of the low-rent nature of the team, still without a major sponsor. Hodgson had a perished fuel pipe burst, almost blinding him with fuel … he had little option but to run off at the next turn, all but taking McWilliams with him. Two laps later Xaus's rear brake caliper came adrift.

Left: As close as paint – de Puniet took the last rostrum place from Pedrosa by just this much.
Photograph: Gold & Goose

250 cc RACE – 26 laps

Pedrosa was the only one of the top five to better his time on Saturday, right at the end, snatching pole from Porto by two tenths. Elias was alongside, switched to the old Honda chassis, and happy for the first time all year.

Porto led away, pushing hard and a second clear of Pedrosa, Elias, Nieto and de Puniet at the end of lap one. He continued to draw away; it looked like another processional 250 race was in store.

Not so. Elias was not about to pass up the opportunity offered by his improved handling. Both he and de Puniet got ahead of Pedrosa next time round, and the Spaniard quickly got to work on closing the gap. De Puniet was a couple of seconds adrift already, Pedrosa a little further behind him, soon to face pressure from de Angelis, before the rookie's tyres went off and dropped away again.

Elias attacked Porto for the first time onto the front straight on lap ten. Porto slipstreamed him past the pits and outbraked him at the next corner. Battle was commenced, and the next time Elias nosed ahead he stayed there for seven laps. He was clearly close to the limit; Porto looked the more comfortable, poised close behind.

Elias had a particularly lurid slide on lap 18, and Porto took advantage to slip ahead, and he led for the next three laps. On the 19th, Elias outbraked him at the end of the back straight, only to lose the place again directly. He was just practising, it turned out – part of a strategically clever race.

With five laps to go, he did it again. This time he made it stick, but it still seemed that Porto had something left, and particularly that he was faster through and out of the crucial last corner. There would be room for him to surge past over the line. Instead it was Elias who had speed to spare. His last lap was his fastest, a new record, and Porto was never close enough to challenge. He did complain later about his rival's aggressive riding, and had pulled alongside to wag his finger at one point of the race.

Almost ten seconds behind, de Puniet and Pedrosa had been hard at it. The Frenchman had lost touch with Elias only on the 20th lap, saving a big slide. This allowed Pedrosa to close up again, and he pushed hard to the finish, culminating in a last slingshot attempt out of the last corner. He failed to make it by just two hundredths. His points lead was slightly diminished, but he too still had a race in hand.

A lone de Angelis followed; six more seconds away West managed to keep Poggiali at bay by two tenths, another strong ride for the privateer. Debon had lost touch with them in the closing stages; Aoyama recovered from an off-track excursion for ninth; Rolfo trailed in tenth. Nieto had dropped back to retire after running strongly in the early laps; Davies just missed the points.

Above: Elias bounced back with a win, after an unproductive first Honda season. Porto, chasing hard, was still there at the finish.

Left: 125 winner Barbera is flanked by Kallio and Lorenzo.

Below: Dovizioso holds an early lead from the KTMs of Stoner (27) and Kallio (36), with Lai (32) and Simoncelli (58) chasing hard. Shortly afterwards, he would collide with Stoner.
Photographs: Gold & Goose

125 cc RACE – 23 laps

Dovizioso took pole on a Friday time; Stoner was fastest in the wet, and third in the dry. Second-fastest Corsi led away, but Stoner and fellow KTM rider Kallio were ahead by the end of the lap. Dovizioso, slow off the line, finished that lap ninth, but closing on the bumping and barging rabble disputing the lead.

By lap three he was in front, the rest back and forth behind him. Two laps later Kallio was in second, dogged by Stoner and Corsi, as they accelerated up to sixth gear onto the front straight. Then Stoner missed a gear, Corsi ran right into the back of him, and fell right under the wheels of the pursuing pack. Mercifully, nobody hit him, and he escaped serious injury. Stoner made it to the end of the straight, pulling off at turn one, his exhaust sticking out at 90 degrees.

Dovizioso was already clearing off; Barbera was making progress after a bad start. Fourteenth on lap one, he was third by lap six, setting a new record on the way. He was engaged with Kallio for the rest of the race, for what would turn out to be first place, won by Barbera by just two tenths.

Dovizioso's strong early lead had seemed safe enough, but suddenly he slowed, cruising to the pits after ten laps. A 4cm woodscrew had punctured his rear tyre ... his pit crew blamed workers erecting advertising signage for this piece of bad luck, the points leader's only non-finish of the year.

This meant third for a distant Locatelli, until he ran onto the gravel one lap later. Simoncelli took over, to be swamped by the next group, with Nieto heading Lorenzo and a fierce gang.

In the sprint to the line, Lorenzo triumphed over Nieto by mere hundredths, Bautista close, Simoncelli a second adrift, then Talmacsi and Pesek, with Locatelli narrowly taking ninth from Perugini.

Marlboro
SUOMY
FOG CITY
SUOMY
Alice
12
DUCATI
DUCATI
Marlboro

FIM WORLD CHAMPIONSHIP • ROUND 11

MARLBORO PORTUGUESE grand prix

5 SEPTEMBER 2004

ESTORIL CIRCUIT

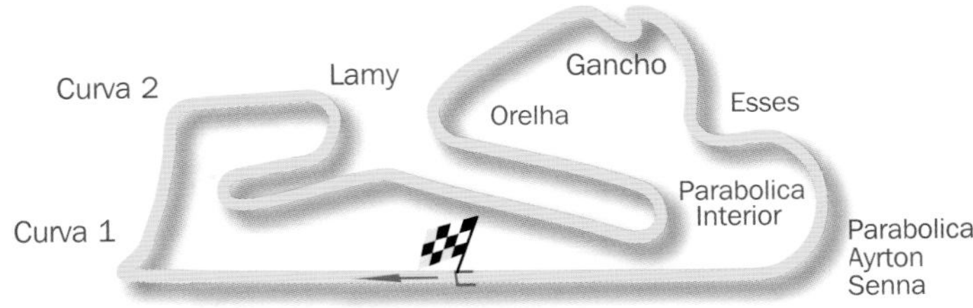

CIRCUIT LENGTH: 2.599 miles/4.183 km

MotoGP

28 laps, 72.772 miles/117.096 km

Pos.	Rider (Nat.)	No.	Machine	Laps	Time & speed
1	Valentino Rossi (I)	46	Yamaha	28	46m 34.911s 93.719 mph/ 150.826km/h
2	Makoto Tamada (J)	6	Honda	28	46m 40.022s
3	Alex Barros (BR)	4	Honda	28	46m 43.068s
4	Sete Gibernau (E)	15	Honda	28	46m 43.223s
5	Carlos Checa (E)	7	Yamaha	28	46m 52.877s
6	John Hopkins (USA)	21	Suzuki	28	46m 53.542s
7	Loris Capirossi (I)	65	Ducati	28	46m 58.581s
8	Troy Bayliss (AUS)	12	Ducati	28	47m 00.037s
9	Colin Edwards (USA)	45	Honda	28	47m 00.522s
10	Norick Abe (J)	17	Yamaha	28	47m 01.638s
11	Shinya Nakano (J)	56	Kawasaki	28	47m 19.615s
12	Jeremy McWilliams (GB)	99	Aprilia	28	47m 25.422s
13	Alex Hofmann (D)	66	Kawasaki	28	47m 29.283s
14	Kenny Roberts (USA)	10	Suzuki	28	47m 34.429s
15	Nobuatsu Aoki (J)	9	Proton KR	28	48m 07.764s
16	James Ellison (GB)	77	Harris WCM	27	46m 49.825s
	Ruben Xaus (E)	11	Ducati	18	DNF
	Neil Hodgson (GB)	50	Ducati	16	DNF
	Michel Fabrizio (I)	84	Aprilia	11	DNF
	Marco Melandri (I)	33	Yamaha	7	DNF
	Max Biaggi (I)	3	Honda	0	DNF
	Chris Burns (GB)	35	Harris WCM		DNS

Fastest lap: Rossi, 1m 38.423s, 95.047 mph/152.964 km/h (record).

Previous record: Valentino Rossi, I (Honda), 1m 39.189s, 94.313 mph/151.782 km/h (2003).

Event best maximum speed: Biaggi, 212.4 mph/341.8 km/h (qualifying practice no. 1).

Qualifying: 1 Tamada, 1m 37.933s; 2 Rossi, 1m 38.036s; 3 Gibernau, 1m 38.067s; 4 Biaggi, 1m 38.069s; 5 Barros, 1m 38.215s; 6 Hopkins, 1m 38.323s; 7 Melandri, 1m 38.367s; 8 Edwards, 1m 38.438s; 9 Kenny Roberts, 1m 38.740s; 10 Checa, 1m 38.862s; 11 Capirossi, 1m 39.071s; 12 Nakano, 1m 39.157s; 13 Bayliss, 1m 39.279s; 14 Abe, 1m 39.635s; 15 Hodgson, 1m 39.677s; 16 McWilliams, 1m 39.815s; 17 Hofmann, 1m 39.852s; 18 Xaus, 1m 40.259s; 19 Fabrizio, 1m 40.586s; 20 Aoki, 1m 41.279s; 21 Ellison, 1m 42.284s; 22 Burns, 1m 43.293s.

Fastest race laps: 1 Rossi, 1m 38.423s; 2 Tamada, 1m 38.920s; 3 Gibernau, 1m 39.077s; 4 Barros, 1m 39.081s; 5 Melandri, 1m 39.219s; 6 Checa, 1m 39.372s; 7 Capirossi, 1m 39.617s; 8 Bayliss, 1m 39.834s; 9 Hopkins, 1m 39.855s; 10 Abe, 1m 39.858s; 11 Kenny Roberts, 1m 40.017s; 12 Edwards, 1m 40.031s; 13 Xaus, 1m 40.043s; 14 Nakano, 1m 40.442s; 15 McWilliams, 1m 40.476s; 16 Hodgson, 1m 40.560s; 17 Hofmann, 1m 40.945s; 18 Fabrizio, 1m 41.333s; 19 Aoki, 1m 42.038s; 20 Ellison, 1m 42.193s.

World Championship: 1 Rossi, 209; 2 Gibernau, 180; 3 Biaggi, 158; 4 Edwards, 111; 5 Barros, 102; 6 Checa, 93; 7 Tamada, 89; 8 Capirossi, 84; 9 Hayden, 83; 10 Melandri, 64; 11 Abe, 55; 12 Nakano and Xaus, 46; 14 Bayliss, 42; 15 Kenny Roberts, 37; 16 Hopkins, 32; 17 Hofmann, 30; 18 Hodgson, 29; 19 McWilliams, 16; 20 Byrne, 15; 21 Aoki and Fabrizio, 8; 23 Pitt, 2; 24 Kurtis Roberts, 1.

250 cc

26 laps, 67.574 miles/108.732 km

Pos.	Rider (Nat.)	No.	Machine	Laps	Time & speed
1	Toni Elias (E)	24	Honda	26	44m 23.399s 91.322 mph/ 146.968 km/h
2	Sebastian Porto (ARG)	19	Aprilia	26	44m 23.722s
3	Randy de Puniet (F)	7	Aprilia	26	44m 33.317s
4	Daniel Pedrosa (E)	26	Honda	26	44m 33.334s
5	Alex de Angelis (RSM)	51	Aprilia	26	44m 44.840s
6	Anthony West (AUS)	14	Aprilia	26	44m 51.037s
7	Manuel Poggiali (RSM)	54	Aprilia	26	44m 51.265s
8	Alex Debon (E)	6	Honda	26	44m 58.072s
9	Hiroshi Aoyama (J)	73	Honda	26	45m 09.322s
10	Roberto Rolfo (I)	2	Honda	26	45m 17.637s
11	Hector Faubel (E)	33	Aprilia	26	45m 22.150s
12	Franco Battaini (I)	21	Aprilia	26	45m 22.522s
13	Eric Bataille (F)	34	Honda	26	45m 35.019s
14	Jakub Smrz (CZ)	96	Honda	26	45m 35.184s
15	Dirk Heidolf (D)	28	Aprilia	26	45m 35.704s
16	Chaz Davies (GB)	57	Aprilia	26	45m 38.324s
17	Taro Sekiguchi (J)	44	Yamaha	26	45m 38.381s
18	Joan Olive (E)	11	Aprilia	26	45m 45.654s
19	Hugo Marchand (F)	9	Aprilia	26	45m 48.470s
20	Johan Stigefelt (S)	16	Aprilia	26	45m 49.972s
21	Erwan Nigon (F)	36	Aprilia	26	45m 52.139s
22	Gregory Leblanc (F)	42	Aprilia	25	44m 23.660s
23	Klaus Nöhles (D)	17	Honda	25	44m 25.453s
	Sylvain Guintoli (F)	50	Aprilia	24	DNF
	Radomil Rous (CZ)	43	Yamaha	23	DNF
	Fonsi Nieto (E)	10	Aprilia	21	DNF
	Alex Baldolini (I)	25	Aprilia	3	DNF
	Naoki Matsudo (J)	8	Yamaha	2	DNF
	Arnaud Vincent (F)	12	Aprilia	1	DNF
	Gergo Talmacsi (H)	88	Yamaha		DNQ

Fastest lap: Elias, 1m 41.595s, 92.080 mph/148.188 km/h (record).

Previous record: Manuel Poggiali, RSM (Aprilia), 1m 42.215s, 91.521 mph/147.289 km/h (2003).

Event best maximum speed: Aoyama, 174.6 mph/281.0 km/h (qualifying practice no. 2).

Qualifying: 1 Pedrosa, 1m 41.417s; 2 Porto, 1m 41.638s; 3 Elias, 1m 41.645s; 4 de Puniet, 1m 41.814s; 5 de Angelis, 1m 42.226s; 6 Nieto, 1m 42.488s; 7 Debon, 1m 42.516s; 8 Poggiali, 1m 42.520s; 9 Aoyama, 1m 42.709s; 10 Battaini, 1m 42.769s; 11 West, 1m 42.781s; 12 Baldolini, 1m 43.171s; 13 Matsudo, 1m 43.191s; 14 Rolfo, 1m 43.298s; 15 Guintoli, 1m 43.491s; 16 Davies, 1m 43.507s; 17 Heidolf, 1m 43.561s; 18 Olive, 1m 43.810s; 19 Faubel, 1m 44.039s; 20 Marchand, 1m 44.088s; 21 Smrz, 1m 44.175s; 22 Nigon, 1m 44.187s; 23 Stigefelt, 1m 44.226s; 24 Sekiguchi, 1m 44.312s; 25 Vincent, 1m 44.318s; 26 Leblanc, 1m 44.704s; 27 Bataille, 1m 44.733s; 28 Nöhles, 1m 45.269s; 29 Rous, 1m 46.649s; 30 Talmacsi, 1m 48.666s.

Fastest race laps: 1 Elias, 1m 41.595s; 2 Porto, 1m 41.652s; 3 Pedrosa, 1m 41.978s; 4 de Angelis, 1m 42.019s; 5 de Puniet, 1m 42.043s; 6 Debon, 1m 42.632s; 7 Poggiali, 1m 42.742s; 8 West, 1m 42.859s; 9 Aoyama, 1m 43.224s; 10 Nieto, 1m 43.262s; 11 Faubel, 1m 43.465s; 12 Battaini, 1m 43.819s; 13 Rolfo, 1m 43.892s; 14 Bataille, 1m 44.009s; 15 Sekiguchi, 1m 44.154s; 16 Smrz, 1m 44.195s; 17 Baldolini, 1m 44.202s; 18 Davies, 1m 44.211s; 19 Heidolf, 1m 44.282s; 20 Nigon, 1m 44.665s; 21 Stigefelt, 1m 44.695s; 22 Marchand, 1m 44.720s; 23 Guintoli, 1m 44.809s; 24 Olive, 1m 44.863s; 25 Nöhles, 1m 45.259s; 26 Rous, 1m 45.482s; 27 Leblanc, 1m 45.583s; 28 Matsudo, 1m 55.191s; 29 Vincent, 1m 56.739s.

World Championship: 1 Pedrosa, 209; 2 de Puniet, 182; 3 Porto, 173; 4 Elias, 122; 5 de Angelis, 104; 6 Nieto, 94; 7 West, 88; 8 Aoyama, 87; 9 Rolfo, 83; 10 Poggiali, 79; 11 Debon, 61; 12 Battaini, 50; 13 Guintoli, 29; 14 Davies and Matsudo, 23; 16 Faubel and Olive, 20; 18 Baldolini, 19; 19 Marchand, 15; 20 Bataille and Smrz, 12; 22 Vincent, 11; 23 Heidolf, 9; 24 Lefort, 7; 25 Stigefelt, 4; 26 Leblanc, 3; 27 Sekiguchi, 1.

125 cc

23 laps, 59.777 miles/96.186 km

Pos.	Rider (Nat.)	No.	Machine	Laps	Time & speed
1	Hector Barbera (E)	3	Aprilia	23	41m 01.272s 87.419 mph/ 140.687 km/h
2	Mika Kallio (SF)	36	KTM	23	41m 01.423s
3	Jorge Lorenzo (E)	48	Derbi	23	41m 10.096s
4	Pablo Nieto (E)	22	Aprilia	23	41m 10.160s
5	Alvaro Bautista (E)	19	Aprilia	23	41m 10.938s
6	Marco Simoncelli (I)	58	Aprilia	23	41m 11.619s
7	Gabor Talmacsi (H)	14	Malaguti	23	41m 13.191s
8	Lukas Pesek (CZ)	52	Honda	23	41m 13.234s
9	Roberto Locatelli (I)	15	Aprilia	23	41m 20.458s
10	Stefano Perugini (I)	7	Gilera	23	41m 20.820s
11	Mike di Meglio (F)	63	Aprilia	23	41m 28.253s
12	Fabrizio Lai (I)	32	Gilera	23	41m 32.980s
13	Sergio Gadea (E)	33	Aprilia	23	41m 33.764s
14	Dario Giuseppetti (D)	26	Honda	23	41m 34.168s
15	Gino Borsoi (I)	23	Aprilia	23	41m 36.092s
16	Thomas Luthi (CH)	12	Honda	23	41m 36.117s
17	Mattia Pasini (I)	54	Aprilia	23	41m 59.681s
18	Vesa Kallio (SF)	66	Aprilia	23	42m 01.431s
19	Lorenzo Zanetti (I)	45	Aprilia	23	42m 27.634s
20	Jordi Carchano (E)	28	Aprilia	23	42m 27.770s
21	Raymond Schouten (NL)	16	Honda	23	42m 37.926s
22	Manuel Manna (I)	8	Malaguti	23	42m 37.988s
23	Manuel Hernandez (E)	43	Aprilia	22	41m 44.933s
24	Marketa Janakova (CZ)	9	Honda	22	41m 46.712s
	Imre Toth (H)	25	Aprilia	14	DNF
	Gioele Pellino (I)	42	Aprilia	12	DNF
	Angel Rodriguez (E)	47	Derbi	11	DNF
	Andrea Dovizioso (I)	34	Honda	11	DNF
	Casey Stoner (AUS)	27	KTM	5	DNF
	Simone Corsi (I)	24	Honda	4	DNF
	Robbin Harms (DK)	69	Honda	4	DNF
	Mirko Giansanti (I)	6	Aprilia	2	DNF
	Andrea Ballerini (I)	50	Aprilia	2	DNF
	Steve Jenkner (D)	21	Aprilia	0	DNF
	Vincent Braillard (CH)	91	Honda		DNQ
	Carlos Ferreira (P)	90	Honda		DNQ

Fastest lap: Barbera, 1m 45.573s, 88.610 mph/142.604 km/h (record).

Previous record: Hector Barbera, E (Aprilia), 1m 46.225s, 88.066 mph/141.729 km/h (2003).

Event best maximum speed: Barbera, 149.8 mph/241.1 km/h (qualifying practice no. 1).

Qualifying: 1 Dovizioso, 1m 46.280s; 2 Corsi, 1m 46.338s; 3 Stoner, 1m 46.380s; 4 Locatelli, 1m 46.496s; 5 Simoncelli, 1m 46.572s; 6 Giansanti, 1m 46.691s; 7 Lorenzo, 1m 46.735s; 8 Jenkner, 1m 46.851s; 9 M. Kallio, 1m 46.877s; 10 Barbera, 1m 46.965s; 11 Nieto, 1m 47.111s; 12 Lai, 1m 47.132s; 13 Pesek, 1m 47.251s; 14 Perugini, 1m 47.270s; 15 Talmacsi, 1m 47.320s; 16 Bautista, 1m 47.452s; 17 Rodriguez, 1m 47.508s; 18 Pasini, 1m 47.533s; 19 Borsoi, 1m 47.544s; 20 Gadea, 1m 47.861s; 21 Luthi, 1m 47.875s; 22 Ballerini, 1m 48.135s; 23 di Meglio, 1m 48.693s; 24 Toth, 1m 48.751s; 25 Harms, 1m 48.782s; 26 Giuseppetti, 1m 48.818s; 27 V. Kallio, 1m 48.876s; 28 Pellino, 1m 48.998s; 29 Zanetti, 1m 50.346s; 30 Manna, 1m 50.716s; 31 Carchano, 1m 51.210s; 32 Schouten, 1m 51.489s; 33 Hernandez, 1m 51.834s; 34 Janakova, 1m 52.777s; 35 Braillard, 1m 54.414s; 36 Ferreira, 1m 57.086s.

Fastest race laps: 1 Barbera, 1m 45.573s; 2 Dovizioso, 1m 45.936s; 3 Locatelli, 1m 46.069s; 4 Nieto, 1m 46.102s; 5 M. Kallio, 1m 46.207s; 6 Perugini, 1m 46.229s; 7 Bautista, 1m 46.239s; 8 Lorenzo, 1m 46.499s; 9 Talmacsi, 1m 46.519s; 10 Simoncelli, 1m 46.559s; 11 Pesek, 1m 46.572s; 12 Lai, 1m 46.745s; 13 di Meglio, 1m 46.850s; 14 Stoner, 1m 47.030s; 15 Corsi, 1m 47.094s; 16 Rodriguez, 1m 47.221s; 17 Borsoi, 1m 47.393s; 18 Ballerini, 1m 47.394s; 19 Giuseppetti, 1m 47.424s; 20 Gadea, 1m 47.488s; 21 Harms, 1m 47.515s; 22 Luthi, 1m 47.534s; 23 Pasini, 1m 47.905s; 24 Giansanti, 1m 48.029s; 25 Toth, 1m 48.406s; 26 V. Kallio, 1m 48.690s; 27 Pellino, 1m 49.338s; 28 Carchano, 1m 49.450s; 29 Zanetti, 1m 49.877s; 30 Schouten, 1m 50.201s; 31 Manna, 1m 50.221s; 32 Hernandez, 1m 51.417s; 33 Janakova, 1m 52.325s.

World Championship: 1 Dovizioso, 183; 2 Barbera, 163; 3 Locatelli, 154; 4 Lorenzo, 125; 5 Nieto, 114; 6 Stoner, 104; 7 Jenkner, 83; 8 Giansanti, 79; 9 Bautista, 74; 10 M. Kallio, 73; 11 Simoncelli, 69; 12 Borsoi, 41; 13 Simon, 38; 14 Corsi, 37; 15 di Meglio and Pasini, 33; 17 Ballerini, 23; 18 Ui, 19; 19 Pesek, 16; 20 Pellino and Talmacsi, 15; 22 Perugini, 14; 23 Lai, 10; 24 Toth, 6; 25 Gadea, Giuseppetti and Harms, 5; 28 Carchano and Rodriguez, 2.

Left: The piercing stare of Troy Bayliss, concentrating hard in wet practice ... a powerful image usually hidden behind tinted visors.

Photograph: Malcolm Bryan/BPC

FIM WORLD CHAMPIONSHIP • ROUND 12

JAPANESEGP

MOTEGI

Above: Capirossi's caper causes carnage: Hopkins's bike is already upside down and the rider about to hit the ground; Capirossi also spinning through the air, Edwards (45) and Biaggi (3) with nowhere to go.

Right: Sequence shows the destruction, with Hayden (69) about to hit trouble as luckier riders slip through behind. The worst-hurt was Kenny Roberts Jr., clutching his dislocated left arm (bottom right).

Photographs: Gold & Goose

Left: Nakano's unexpected podium was Kawasaki's first since 1981.
Photograph: Gold & Goose

Above: Above: Barros's beauty – the top dog factory Honda unclad.

Left: Kawasaki's new exhaust, part of a continuing programme.

Below: Olivier Jacque – the ex-250 champion was rewarded with Moriwaki's best-ever finish.
Photographs: Gold & Goose

THE PR machine's image-laundering can sometimes make one forget that Moto GP heroes are only motorbike racers. Highly skilled hooligans on a Sunday afternoon. Until every so often one or another departs from the script, and proves the point.

On this occasion it was Loris Capirossi. (Again, you might say.) Qualified on the third row, blessed with lots of horsepower, he was intent on seizing the lead into the first corner, as in Portugal. But the straight was too short. Rossi peeled in, Hopkins on his wheel, as the Ducati scythed up the inside of the pack, back wheel in the air, already out of control. He piled straight into first-time front-row starter Hopkins, to trigger a devastating chain reaction.

By the time the looping bikes and tumbling riders had come to rest in the dust, six were out of the race. Capirossi and Hopkins, obviously; but also Biaggi, Edwards, Roberts and Hayden ... the last-named fell only after coming to rest, only for his feeble knee to cave in under him.

Capirossi was stretchered off with foot injuries, Hopkins with broken ribs and a deep gash in his backside ("I'm only glad whatever hit my bum didn't hit my spine," he said later); Roberts was hurt more badly. His arm had been trapped by Biaggi's back wheel, pulling him in to the bike so the exhaust burned his neck, and also dislocating his left elbow. He would be out for the rest of the season.

It was uncannily similar to last year. That time, Hopkins had knocked Edwards, Bayliss and Checa off at the same spot. He had been severely punished by Race Direction, with a hefty fine and suspension for one race. This time, Capirossi went unpunished. The difference? Hard for outsiders to see, but two points were apparent to Race Direction, defending themselves against allegations of inconsistency and even hypocrisy.

The first was that Hopkins, immediately afterwards, had owned up, and apologised to the other riders. After that, there could be no question of his guilt, said Race Director Paul Butler. One might only take issue with the severity of his punishment.

The second was that nobody had lodged a protest. Race Direction had viewed the tapes and decided it was a racing incident; in the absence of any contrary opinion from other riders or teams, this decision had not been called into question.

All seemed a bit slender, certainly to Hopkins who had been too honest; but Capirossi did the right thing, saying simply: "I don't know what happened."

It was unlucky for Edwards, for a second year in a row. At last he had been given the new chassis, and found it a revelation. It was his only non-finish of the year.

Rossi, typically lucky, missed it all, but for once got beaten fair and square. Makoto Tamada had two things to avenge – his disqualification last year, part of the same post-race draconian crackdown, after he'd squeezed Gibernau on the final lap; and also his defeat at Estoril. "Valentino had some fun with me there, I plan to have some fun with him here," he said before the race.

It was lucky also for the survivors, with six front-runners missing. None took more benefit than Nakano, who rode a blinding race to third, Kawasaki's first podium since Finland in 1981, where Kork Ballington was third on the monocoque square-four 500.

Kawasaki had an exhaust change, their four-into-one replaced with an equally shrill four-into-two system by Akrapovic, on both of Hofmann's machines. More importantly they were using Magneti Marelli engine management electronics for the first time, which proved to be a big improvement in terms of rider feel compared with the previous Mitsubishi system. The biggest contribution was Nakano's riding, and it was not without heart-in-the-mouth moments, particularly when the bike started smoking heavily in the early stages ... heavy oil consumption meant the sump had been over-filled, and the smoke stopped when the surplus had burned off.

Exhausts were a theme ... Rossi had been testing a compact four-into-four system in the interim, which was among other things better aerodynamically than the M1's current slant-mounted single silencer pipe. It wasn't ready to race, and though he said he hoped it would soon be on the bike, in fact it didn't reappear until the very last race.

Suzuki's new Yoshimura system was in place. Longer than the previous stubby system, the pipes looped back and forth to end in a tailpipe each side. They brought a significant mid-range boost to the still-disappointing V4 motor – as much as 10 horsepower – and made the bike easier to ride, as well as giving it a welcome increase in "grunt" (according to Hopkins) on the corner exits.

Shane Byrne was back, promising to give it a go to see how his wrist felt. He could hardly have picked a circuit with more hard braking, which was more punishing than he realised. "I'm okay in the corners, but under braking my arm just folds up. I'm worried about getting hit from behind. I always hope nobody's drafting me. Not that that happens very often." Full marks for bravery and three points for 13th place. But the fractured bone in his wrist rotated during the race, and he left Motegi in far worse condition than he had arrived, and did not race again all year.

His one-race replacement Fabrizio was scheduled to return to WCM, but didn't turn up. WCM are used to making do, and quickly replaced him with jobless 125 rider Youichi Ui. The tiny rider couldn't even reach the ground, and failed to qualify, though he was allowed to start anyway. His biggest problem, he said, at a track with low gearing and lots of hard acceleration, had simply been wheelspin, because of his lack of weight.

Ukawa was on a wild card factory Honda – a prototype for next year, they said, which had achieved better fuel economy without losing speed – as the trap figures showed (he was second-fastest Honda). The bike was fitted with a 22-litre fuel tank, to prove the point that even at a fuel-thirsty track like this, they could go the distance. Sadly, the rider crashed out long before that.

Jacque was back on the Moriwaki, and had the quote of the meeting, after the interposition of some of the PR spin mentioned in the first paragraph (not all of it, as you shall see, done to a very high standard). Under the mystifying headline "OLIVIER JACQUE SHOWING A PROCE", the statement read: "I am happy to have come back to the GP paddock, and I am really enjoying the joint with Moriwaki Racing Team." Fine, as long as nobody finds out.

Right: "Now where did I put that boot?" Xaus stretches self and leathers.

Below: Nakano's Kawasaki heads Gibernau's Honda and Checa's Yamaha.
Both photographs: Gold & Goose

MOTOGP RACE – 24 laps

Times were fast, 18 riders inside the lap record, and obviously Bridgestone's testing here had paid big dividends, as they took two out of three front row slots. Until the very end, it was Hopkins on pole; Tamada snatched it with a real flyer at the finish, fully half a second faster. Rossi was third, but looking strong on race tyres, with a string of fast laps.

Hopkins's hopes for glory were scuppered by Capirossi at Turn One, along with those of Edwards, Roberts, Biaggi and Hayden. The depleted field left the carnage behind, Tamada already pressing Rossi hard. Almost two seconds adrift Melandri led Nakano, Abe, Gibernau, Checa, Xaus and the other survivors.

As in Portugal, the two leaders kept on pulling away, more than five seconds clear after just eight laps. The difference this time was the order. On lap five, Tamada set a new lap record as he closed right up; on the sixth he firmly outbraked the Yamaha at the end of the back straight. Rossi stayed with him, and until shortly before half distance nobody would have bet against another win. After ten laps, the gap was still half a second ... but it was starting to stretch inexorably by a few tenths each lap. Rossi had no answer to Tamada's sustained high pace, and at the finish he was six seconds adrift.

The Japanese rider was beaming. Abe was the first of his countryman to win his home GP, at Suzuka in 1996 and 2000; Tamada the first to do so at Motegi. "Victory was everything to me today, and my bike and my tyres were perfect," he smiled.

Rossi was impressed by his pace, and especially his tyres. "When I tried to follow him, it was impossible. I was sliding everywhere – he seemed glued to the track," he said.

The battle for third was close for most of the race. Melandri kept control for the first 18 laps, with Abe slipping past the at-first ominously smoky Nakano. But it was the Yamaha that suffered mechanical failure, Abe suddenly slowing on lap ten to tour back to his garage. Gibernau had been following on, but now started dropping away; likewise Checa behind him, who soon came into the clutches of Bayliss, picking up the pace, and then also Barros, 15th after lap one after threading his way through the first-corner mish-mash.

The pair kept on going, closing rapidly on the troubled Gibernau, again at sea with set-up. Bayliss got by on lap 15 under braking for Turn One; Barros copied the same move next time round, and they now started to close a two-second gap on Nakano and Melandri, who had swapped places on lap 19.

Bayliss was poised to pounce on Melandri when he lost the front and slipped off into the gravel, once again all too literally the gritty Australian. Barros managed to get by safely one lap later, but Nakano was again a couple of seconds clear, and maintained the gap to the finish. A fine ride on the obviously fast-progressing Bridgestones, only seven seconds behind Rossi. For the first time since Brazil in 1995 Michelin occupied only one of the three rostrum slots.

Checa lost touch with this group after an off-track excursion, and was almost ten seconds adrift of the lonely Gibernau at the finish. A similar distance behind came Hodgson in eighth, his best of the year. He'd followed Barros past team-mate Xaus on lap six, and the Spaniard stayed with him and kept pushing for the full race, still less than two seconds behind at the end. Hofmann had in turn been pressing Xaus, but dropped away in the later stages.

There were lucky points for riders promoted by the early carnage. Jacque, miles back, scored the Moriwaki's best-ever 11th; McWilliams was next, after remounting following a tumble on lap three, last rider not to be lapped. Then came Byrne, struggling to the finish, a lone and distant Aoki, and eventually also Ui, all in the points.

Wild card Tohru Ukawa, riding an development prototype RC211V, failed to impress, and crashed out of ninth place with 15 laps still to go.

It had been an extraordinary race with a highly enjoyable result. And a lucky one for Gibernau, as Rossi pointed out. "The six who crashed would have all finished in front of him, but the only one who might have changed my result was Max. He got more points than he should have." A peevish observation that presaged a growing feud.

Above: Ui couldn't touch the ground at rest, suffered wheelspin on the move, but scored a point on the WCM.

Right: Wild card Tohru Ukawa's demonstration of the 2005 prototype RCV Honda was cut short when he crashed out.
Photographs: Gold & Goose

Tamada was in no mood to be trifled with; for once Rossi (inset) was left short.
Both photographs: Gold & Goose

Above: **250 class rookie Aoyama for once knew the circuit, and claimed a first top three finish.**

Right: **Gilera rider Fabrizio Lai, here heading Kallio's KTM, is working his way towards second place.**

Below: **Lai, Dovizioso and Corsi made an all-Italian 125 rostrum.**

Photographs: Gold & Goose

250 cc RACE – 23 laps

Pedrosa fell heavily on Friday, but came back to claim pole by two tenths from Aoyama, at last on a familiar track. De Puniet was close, Elias completing the front row. Porto led row two, the first time all year he had not been in the top four.

It was Elias who led away, de Puniet and Pedrosa close, Aoyama and Anthony West behind. Next time round, Pedrosa was ahead, and started to attack the Honda rider straight away for the lead.

On the third lap, he took it through the Ess-bends on the back straight. Elias outbraked him as soon as they got to the other end. It was a rivalry rejoined from their 125 days, as well as an important national struggle. And a revival of the way 250 racing used to be, even though there were just the two protagonists.

Two laps later Elias waved Pedrosa past, and settled down to hound him relentlessly. He was within a few tenths right up until lap 17, but it was a hopeless struggle, at a track where slow corners and short straights put a premium on acceleration. He lost touch over the remaining laps to finish three seconds adrift. "I don't think Dani was faster than me today," Elias complained later. "But he weighs 44 kilos and I weigh 67. There's nothing I can do about that." Pedrosa was quick to respond. "I want everyone to know my weight is actually 49kg," he said.

It was clearly a Honda circuit, he added. As De Puniet found, hanging on valiantly in third for five laps before starting to drop away. Now he found himself under attack from the Hondas of Aoyama and wild card Yuki Takahashi. Aoyama had just got ahead when the Frenchman crashed on the exit of the first corner on lap nine, hurriedly scrambling back on board to rejoin in 19th.

Heading the next group, fast-starter West now had some fast riders climbing all over him, including Porto and de Angelis. Porto was ahead on lap eight, but West held the young factory rider at bay for the next seven laps, before crashing at the bottom of the hill.

Porto kept driving hard, passing the slowing Takahashi on lap 14, but nowhere near being able to catch Aoyama.

The rest were mainly spaced out: de Angelis a lonely sixth, well clear of Rolfo, busy fending off another Honda wild card rider, Shuhei Aoyama. Battaini had eventually passed and outdistanced Debon. De Puniet was 11th after a spirited recovery ride. Chaz Davies crashed out of a battle for the final points, with three laps to go. Poggiali was a lowly 17th, never anywhere near being in the picture.

125 cc RACE – 13 laps

Dovizioso was on pole again from Locatelli, for an extraordinary race, stopped after nine laps after a crash left debris across the track over the finish line – Ballerini had fallen, Toth ploughed into his bike, lucky not to be hurt.

It was restarted for a 13-lap sprint, the first race counting only for grid positions. Stoner was already out – leading the first lap, then pulling off with gearshift problems again; and Nieto had also pitted.

A handsome lead put Dovizioso on pole for the restart, but Locatelli set the pace for the first seven laps, until the Honda rider drafted past on the pit straight. Locatelli did it back to him next time, but two laps later Dovizioso was in front again.

Locatelli mounted a convincing last-lap attack, only for his front wheel to tuck under at a slow corner for a graceful low-side slide. "It was a shame for him, but good for me," said the teenage four-times winner, who left with a handsome boost to his title lead, now a massive 45 points.

Barbera did not score, stricken with bike trouble on the second warm-up that put him on the back row of the grid. He retired after getting no higher than 19th. Locatelli got just two points, after scrambling back for a glum finish in 14th. The next-closest challenger Lorenzo also had to restart from the back, though he salvaged nine points.

A close battle for second went to Lai's Gilera, from Corsi, Giansanti and Jenkner, covered by less than half a second. Simoncelli was off the back of this; Lorenzo passing Talmacsi on the final lap, wild card Tomoyoshi Koyama's Yamaha close behind, while another – Toshihisa Kuzuhara (Honda) – heading the next group of regulars for tenth.

FIM WORLD CHAMPIONSHIP • ROUND 12

19 SEPTEMBER 2004

TWIN RING MOTEGI

CIRCUIT LENGTH: 2.983 miles/4.801 km

MotoGP

24 laps, 71.592 miles/115.224 km

Pos.	Rider (Nat.)	No.	Machine	Laps	Time & speed
1	Makoto Tamada (J)	6	Honda	24	43m 43.220s 98.256 mph/ 158.128 km/h
2	Valentino Rossi (I)	46	Yamaha	24	43m 49.388s
3	Shinya Nakano (J)	56	Kawasaki	24	43m 56.616s
4	Alex Barros (BR)	4	Honda	24	43m 58.655s
5	Marco Melandri (I)	33	Yamaha	24	44m 06.797s
6	Sete Gibernau (E)	15	Honda	24	44m 10.598s
7	Carlos Checa (E)	7	Yamaha	24	44m 19.054s
8	Neil Hodgson (GB)	50	Ducati	24	44m 31.196s
9	Ruben Xaus (E)	11	Ducati	24	44m 33.101s
10	Alex Hofmann (D)	66	Kawasaki	24	44m 39.327s
11	Olivier Jacque (F)	19	Moriwaki	24	45m 04.457s
12	Jeremy McWilliams (GB)	99	Aprilia	24	45m 10.903s
13	Shane Byrne (GB)	67	Aprilia	23	43m 49.679s
14	Nobuatsu Aoki (J)	9	Proton KR	23	44m 09.870s
15	Youichi Ui (J)	41	Harris WCM	23	45m 35.067s
	Troy Bayliss (AUS)	12	Ducati	19	DNF
	Norick Abe (J)	17	Yamaha	9	DNF
	Tohru Ukawa (J)	72	Honda	8	DNF
	Kenny Roberts (USA)	10	Suzuki	0	DNF
	John Hopkins (USA)	21	Suzuki	0	DNF
	Max Biaggi (I)	3	Honda	0	DNF
	Colin Edwards (USA)	45	Honda	0	DNF
	Loris Capirossi (I)	65	Ducati	0	DNF
	Nicky Hayden (USA)	69	Honda	0	DNF

Fastest lap: Tamada, 1m 48.524s, 98.960 mph/159.260 km/h (record).

Previous record: Valentino Rossi, I (Honda), 1m 48.885s, 98.631 mph/158.732 km/h (2003).

Event best maximum speed: Ukawa, 192.7 mph/310.1 km/h (qualifying practice no. 1).

Qualifying: 1 Tamada, 1m 46.673s; 2 Hopkins, 1m 47.230s; 3 Rossi, 1m 47.275s; 4 Biaggi, 1m 47.401s; 5 Edwards, 1m 47.821s; 6 Melandri, 1m 47.845s; 7 Capirossi, 1m 47.886s; 8 Roberts, 1m 47.929s; 9 Hayden, 1m 47.940s; 10 Barros, 1m 47.963s; 11 Checa, 1m 47.982s; 12 Nakano, 1m 48.042s; 13 Gibernau, 1m 48.107s; 14 Ukawa, 1m 48.154s; 15 Abe, 1m 48.154s; 16 Bayliss, 1m 48.174s; 17 Hodgson, 1m 48.656s; 18 Xaus, 1m 48.859s; 19 Hofmann, 1m 48.885s; 20 McWilliams, 1m 49.139s; 21 Jacque, 1m 49.545s; 22 Aoki, 1m 51.388s; 23 Byrne, 1m 51.466s; 24 Ui, 1m 54.743s.

Fastest race laps: 1 Tamada, 1m 48.524s; 2 Rossi, 1m 48.535s; 3 Ukawa, 1m 48.745s; 4 Melandri, 1m 48.823s; 5 Barros, 1m 48.834s; 6 Abe, 1m 48.861s; 7 Nakano, 1m 49.100s; 8 Bayliss, 1m 49.110s; 9 Gibernau, 1m 49.136s; 10 Checa, 1m 49.549s; 11 Hodgson, 1m 49.785s; 12 McWilliams, 1m 50.145s; 13 Hofmann, 1m 50.424s; 14 Xaus, 1m 50.441s; 15 Jacque, 1m 51.156s; 16 Byrne, 1m 51.939s; 17 Aoki, 1m 53.223s; 18 Ui, 1m 55.813s.

World Championship: 1 Rossi, 229; 2 Gibernau, 190; 3 Biaggi, 158; 4 Barros, 115; 5 Tamada, 114; 6 Edwards, 111; 7 Checa, 102; 8 Capirossi, 84; 9 Hayden, 83; 10 Melandri, 75; 11 Nakano, 62; 12 Abe, 55; 13 Xaus, 53; 14 Bayliss, 42; 15 Hodgson and Kenny Roberts, 37; 17 Hofmann, 36; 18 Hopkins, 32; 19 McWilliams, 20; 20 Byrne, 18; 21 Aoki, 10; 22 Fabrizio, 8; 23 Jacque, 5; 24 Pitt, 2; 25 Kurtis Roberts and Ui, 1.

250 cc

23 laps, 68.609 miles/110.423 km

Pos.	Rider (Nat.)	No.	Machine	Laps	Time & speed
1	Daniel Pedrosa (E)	26	Honda	23	43m 36.798s 94.393 mph/ 151.911 km/h
2	Toni Elias (E)	24	Honda	23	43m 39.972s
3	Hiroshi Aoyama (J)	73	Honda	23	44m 52.789s
4	Sebastian Porto (ARG)	19	Aprilia	23	43m 56.873s
5	Yuki Takahashi (J)	55	Honda	23	44m 02.248s
6	Alex de Angelis (RSM)	51	Aprilia	23	44m 10.249s
7	Roberto Rolfo (I)	2	Honda	23	44m 19.882s
8	Shuhei Aoyama (J)	76	Honda	23	44m 20.068s
9	Franco Battaini (I)	21	Aprilia	23	44m 25.571s
10	Alex Debon (E)	6	Honda	23	44m 28.798s
11	Randy de Puniet (F)	7	Aprilia	23	44m 37.505s
12	Yuzo Fujioka (J)	78	Honda	23	44m 38.270s
13	Naoki Matsudo (J)	8	Yamaha	23	44m 38.918s
14	Hugo Marchand (F)	9	Aprilia	23	44m 43.286s
15	Hector Faubel (E)	33	Aprilia	23	44m 45.868s
16	Choujun Kameya (J)	70	Honda	23	44m 48.889s
17	Manuel Poggiali (RSM)	54	Aprilia	23	44m 52.242s
18	Taro Sekiguchi (J)	44	Yamaha	23	44m 54.282s
19	Sylvain Guintoli (F)	50	Aprilia	23	44m 54.551s
20	Katsuyuki Nakasuga (J)	79	Yamaha	23	45m 04.092s
21	Dirk Heidolf (D)	28	Aprilia	23	45m 21.044s
22	Erwan Nigon (F)	36	Aprilia	23	45m 22.623s
	Joan Olive (E)	11	Aprilia	22	DNF
	Chaz Davies (GB)	57	Aprilia	20	DNF
	Anthony West (AUS)	14	Aprilia	18	DNF
	Klaus Nöhles (D)	17	Honda	17	DNF
	Radomil Rous (CZ)	43	Yamaha	13	DNF
	Johan Stigefelt (S)	16	Aprilia	12	DNF
	Fonsi Nieto (E)	10	Aprilia	11	DNF
	Alex Baldolini (I)	25	Aprilia	6	DNF
	Jakub Smrz (CZ)	96	Honda	5	DNF
	Arnaud Vincent (F)	12	Aprilia	1	DNF
	Eric Bataille (F)	34	Honda		DNS
	Gergo Talmacsi (H)	88	Yamaha		DNQ

Fastest lap: Pedrosa, 1m 52.788s, 95.218 mph/153.239 km/h.

Lap record: Shinya Nakano, J (Yamaha), 1m 52.253s, 95.673 mph/153.970 km/h (2000).

Event best maximum speed: H. Aoyama, 158.1 mph/254.5 km/h (qualifying practice no. 1).

Qualifying: 1 Pedrosa, 1m 52.137s; 2 H. Aoyama, 1m 52.366s; 3 de Puniet, 1m 52.453s; 4 Elias, 1m 52.534s; 5 Porto, 1m 52.550s; 6 Takahashi, 1m 52.638s; 7 de Angelis, 1m 52.809s; 8 West, 1m 53.642s; 9 Battaini, 1m 53.694s; 10 Poggiali, 1m 53.786s; 11 Nieto, 1m 53.798s; 12 Rolfo, 1m 53.835s; 13 S. Aoyama, 1m 53.893s; 14 Debon, 1m 54.027s; 15 Fujioka, 1m 54.242s; 16 Matsudo, 1m 54.423s; 17 Kameya, 1m 54.571s; 18 Faubel, 1m 54.655s; 19 Davies, 1m 54.670s; 20 Nigon, 1m 54.784s; 21 Smrz, 1m 54.811s; 22 Bataille, 1m 54.867s; 23 Heidolf, 1m 55.135s; 24 Guintoli, 1m 55.143s; 25 Marchand, 1m 55.286s; 26 Olive, 1m 55.606s; 27 Vincent, 1m 55.678s; 28 Nakasuga, 1m 55.721s; 29 Stigefelt, 1m 55.795s; 30 Sekiguchi, 1m 55.813s; 31 Baldolini, 1m 56.020s; 32 Rous, 1m 56.949s; 33 Nöhles, 1m 57.256s; 34 Talmacsi, 2m 02.836s.

Fastest race laps: 1 Pedrosa, 1m 52.788s; 2 Elias, 1m 52.936s; 3 Porto, 1m 53.593s; 4 Takahashi, 1m 53.711s; 5 H. Aoyama, 1m 53.783s; 6 de Angelis, 1m 53.907s; 7 de Puniet, 1m 53.923s; 8 West, 1m 54.189s; 9 S. Aoyama, 1m 54.284s; 10 Rolfo, 1m 54.967s; 11 Battaini, 1m 54.987s; 12 Debon, 1m 55.069s; 13 Matsudo, 1m 55.080s; 14 Fujioka, 1m 55.330s; 15 Faubel, 1m 55.516s; 16 Poggiali, 1m 55.645s; 17 Kameya, 1m 55.742s; 18 Marchand, 1m 55.765s; 19 Nieto, 1m 55.824s; 20 Davies, 1m 55.906s; 21 Sekiguchi, 1m 56.039s; 22 Olive, 1m 56.099s; 23 Heidolf, 1m 56.107s; 24 Guintoli, 1m 56.167s; 25 Smrz, 1m 56.236s; 26 Nakasuga, 1m 56.559s; 27 Stigefelt, 1m 56.715s; 28 Nigon, 1m 56.887s; 29 Baldolini, 1m 57.312s; 30 Nöhles, 1m 58.098s; 31 Rous, 1m 58.617s; 32 Vincent, 2m 07.313s.

World Championship: 1 Pedrosa, 234; 2 de Puniet, 187; 3 Porto, 186; 4 Elias, 142; 5 de Angelis, 114; 6 H. Aoyama, 103; 7 Nieto, 94; 8 Rolfo, 92; 9 West, 88; 10 Poggiali, 79; 11 Debon, 67; 12 Battaini, 57; 13 Guintoli, 29; 14 Matsudo, 26; 15 Davies, 23; 16 Faubel, 21; 17 Olive, 20; 18 Baldolini, 19; 19 Marchand, 17; 20 Bataille and Smrz, 12; 22 Takahashi and Vincent, 11; 24 Heidolf, 9; 25 S. Aoyama, 8; 26 Lefort, 7; 27 Fujioka and Stigefelt, 4; 29 Leblanc, 3; 30 Sekiguchi, 1.

125 cc

13 laps, 38.779 miles/62.413 km*

Pos.	Rider (Nat.)	No.	Machine	Laps	Time & speed
1	Andrea Dovizioso (I)	34	Honda	13	25m 52.175s 89.947 mph/ 144.756 km/h
2	Fabrizio Lai (I)	32	Gilera	13	26m 03.257s
3	Simone Corsi (I)	24	Honda	13	26m 03.276s
4	Mirko Giansanti (I)	6	Aprilia	13	26m 03.516s
5	Steve Jenkner (D)	21	Aprilia	13	26m 03.694s
6	Marco Simoncelli (I)	58	Aprilia	13	26m 06.666s
7	Jorge Lorenzo (E)	48	Derbi	13	26m 17.454s
8	Gabor Talmacsi (H)	14	Malaguti	13	26m 17.495s
9	Tomoyoshi Koyama (J)	89	Yamaha	13	26m 18.038s
10	Toshihisa Kuzuhara (J)	62	Honda	13	26m 22.347s
11	Gino Borsoi (I)	23	Aprilia	13	26m 22.607s
12	Thomas Luthi (CH)	12	Honda	13	26m 22.737s
13	Sergio Gadea (E)	33	Aprilia	13	26m 24.345s
14	Roberto Locatelli (I)	15	Aprilia	13	26m 25.146s
15	Vesa Kallio (SF)	66	Aprilia	13	26m 34.125s
16	Gioele Pellino (I)	42	Aprilia	13	26m 34.233s
17	Suhathai Chaemsap (THA)	67	Honda	13	26m 36.711s
18	Manuel Hernandez (E)	43	Aprilia	13	26m 43.409s
19	Jordi Carchano (E)	28	Aprilia	13	26m 43.458s
20	Raymond Schouten (NL)	16	Honda	13	26m 56.894s
21	Lorenzo Zanetti (I)	45	Aprilia	13	27m 04.004s
22	Manuel Manna (I)	8	Malaguti	13	27m 06.069s
23	Marketa Janakova (CZ)	9	Honda	13	27m 28.425s
	Angel Rodriguez (E)	47	Derbi	11	DNF
	Shigeki Norikane (J)	64	Yamaha	10	DNF
	Hector Barbera (E)	3	Aprilia	8	DNF
	Mika Kallio (SF)	36	KTM	7	DNF
	Lukas Pesek (CZ)	52	Honda	3	DNF
	Stefano Perugini (I)	7	Gilera	1	DNF
	Alvaro Bautista (E)	19	Aprilia	0	DNF
	Dario Giuseppetti (D)	26	Honda	0	DNF
	Did not start Race Part 2:				
	Pablo Nieto (E)	22	Aprilia		DNS
	Imre Toth (H)	25	Aprilia		DNS
	Casey Stoner (AUS)	27	KTM		DNS
	Andrea Ballerini (I)	50	Aprilia		DNS
	Mattia Pasini (I)	54	Aprilia		DNS
	Mike di Meglio (F)	63	Aprilia		DNS
	Yuki Hatano (J)	95	Honda		DNS
	Did not start Race Part 1:				
	Robbin Harms (DK)	69	Honda		DNS

*Race Part 1: 8 laps, result nullified.

Fastest lap: Dovizioso, 1m 58.766s, 90.426 mph/145.526 km/h.

Lap record: Daniel Pedrosa, E (Honda) 1m 58.354s, 90.741 mph/146.033 km/h (2002).

Event best maximum speed: Barbera, 137.9 mph/221.9 km/h (qualifying practice no. 1).

Qualifying: 1 Dovizioso, 1m 58.385s; 2 Locatelli, 1m 58.427s; 3 Stoner, 1m 58.576s; 4 Barbera, 1m 58.678s; 5 M. Kallio, 1m 58.750s; 6 Lorenzo, 1m 58.964s; 7 Talmacsi, 1m 58.997s; 8 Pesek, 1m 59.174s; 9 Nieto, 1m 59.243s; 10 Corsi, 1m 59.622s; 11 Simoncelli, 1m 59.627s; 12 Lai, 1m 59.694s; 13 Borsoi, 1m 59.735s; 14 Jenkner, 1m 59.827s; 15 Giansanti, 1m 59.905s; 16 Ballerini, 1m 59.919s; 17 Koyama, 1m 59.944s; 18 Bautista, 2m 00.271s; 19 Luthi, 2m 00.296s; 20 Pasini, 2m 00.324s; 21 di Meglio, 2m 00.477s; 22 Rodriguez, 2m 00.589s; 23 Perugini, 2m 00.687s; 24 Kuzuhara, 2m 00.773s; 25 Gadea, 2m 01.281s; 26 Harms, 2m 01.322s; 27 Giuseppetti, 2m 01.330s; 28 Toth, 2m 01.607s; 29 Norikane, 2m 01.941s; 30 V. Kallio, 2m 01.942s; 31 Carchano, 2m 02.092s; 32 Chaemsap, 2m 02.128s; 33 Hernandez, 2m 02.129s; 34 Zanetti, 2m 02.151s; 35 Hatano, 2m 02.286s; 36 Schouten, 2m 02.857s; 37 Manna, 2m 02.972s; 38 Pellino, 2m 02.990s; 39 Janakova, 2m 04.002s.

Fastest race laps: (after Race Part 2): 1 Dovizioso, 1m 58.766s; 2 Locatelli, 1m 58.803s; 3 Jenkner, 1m 59.301s; 4 Corsi, 1m 59.313s; 5 Simoncelli, 1m 59.388s; 6 M. Kallio, 1m 59.398s; 7 Giansanti, 1m 59.411s; 8 Lai, 1m 59.515s; 9 Pesek, 1m 59.603s; 10 Lorenzo, 2m 00.042s; 11 Borsoi, 2m 00.365s; 12 Rodriguez, 2m 00.384s; 13 Koyama, 2m 00.393s; 14 Talmacsi, 2m 00.471s; 15 Gadea, 2m 00.630s; 16 Kuzuhara, 2m 00.775s; 17 Luthi, 2m 00.917s; 18 Barbera, 2m 01.277s; 19 V. Kallio, 2m 01.344s; 20 Chaemsap, 2m 01.522s; 21 Pellino, 2m 01.526s; 22 Norikane, 2m 02.013s; 23 Carchano, 2m 02.102s; 24 Hernandez, 2m 02.150s; 25 Zanetti, 2m 02.324s; 26 Schouten, 2m 03.138s; 27 Manna, 2m 03.738s; 28 Janakova, 2m 05.062s; 29 Perugini, 2m 11.289s.

World Championship: 1 Dovizioso, 208; 2 Barbera, 163; 3 Locatelli, 156; 4 Lorenzo, 134; 5 Nieto, 114; 6 Stoner, 104; 7 Jenkner, 94; 8 Giansanti, 92; 9 Simoncelli, 79; 10 Bautista, 74; 11 M. Kallio, 73; 12 Corsi, 53; 13 Borsoi, 46; 14 Simon, 38; 15 di Meglio and Pasini, 33; 17 Lai, 30; 18 Ballerini and Talmacsi, 23; 20 Ui, 19; 21 Pesek, 16; 22 Pellino, 15; 23 Perugini, 14; 24 Gadea, 8; 25 Koyama, 7; 26 Kuzuhara and Toth, 6; 28 Giuseppetti and Harms, 5; 30 Luthi, 4; 31 Carchano and Rodriguez, 2; 33 V. Kallio, 1.

GAULOISES GAULOISES
FIM WORLD CHAMPIONSHIP • ROUND 13
QATARGP
DOHA

Main picture: Fine stage, no audience. Qatar showed once and for all that fans are not necessary in modern multimedia MotoGP.

Clockwise from top left: Astroturf kept dust down, was just as slippery as grass; track like a mirage in the lone and level sands; TV made Qatar make sense; fans flocked elsewhere; Nakano's and Capirossi's steeds really do handle like camels.

Right: TV cameras and pressmen congregate at the back of the grid for once, where Rossi and Biaggi are side by side.

All photographs: Gold & Goose

THE first ever motorcycle GP in the Middle East was extraordinary in every way – the venue, the desert location, the atmosphere, the temperature, and also the train of events.

Many things seemed symbolic. One was the grass lining the track, a shocking green against the uniformly dun desert. It was of course Astroturf, but – as Rossi discovered – you could fall off on it just as easily as grass. Another was the level of local involvement. A hundred marshals had been flown in from Valencia, an even larger number of back-ups recruited world-wide. A few eager Qatari volunteers added to the numbers. Their interest didn't last until the first qualifying session. After all, they knew a lot better than to stand around in the open desert in the full heat of the day. They went home instead.

The track, built in record time at a cost of US $58-million, was hard to fault. Dusty and very slippery, yes, but that was only to be expected. The same is true, though to a lesser extent, of any "green" surface, and of other little-used circuits, like Welkom. It's the same for everybody, and this is after all a World Championship. Sometimes these conditions prevail in the world. But the layout was well-considered and technically interesting, the lap fast and generous in length, the facilities top-rate. Oil-rich countries tend not to do these things by halves.

The most pervasive feeling was of isolation. There was a single grandstand opposite the pits, with a seating capacity of 5,000. It was not even one third full for the race. There were hardly any motorcycles in the car park. It was the same in the capital Doha. Not even delivery bikes. Half an hour out of town, the whole MotoGP family was assembled, to celebrate, bicker and play amongst themselves. Alongside the paddock, there was the usual massive TV compound – trucks and offices, editing suites and technical equipment and outside broadcast units. It's all you really need for a race: participants, motorcycles and the TV feed.

And no silly fuss about cigarette logos, on trackside signage or the motorcycles. In that respect, it was just like the good old days. For the same reason, it also provided a glimpse of a barren sort of future. The bad new days?

Family bickering was the story of the weekend. It centred, like most things, on Rossi. Or, to be more precise, his crew. By the end of it, they had been convicted of cheating (if you saw it that way); and so had Biaggi's crew. And Rossi left the track injured and angry, and blaming his closest rival (and race winner) Sete Gibernau for everything.

It began on race eve, after Rossi had unusually qualified on the third row. With the track still slippery off line and overtaking thus difficult, Jerry Burgess wanted to give him the best and cleanest possible run to the first corner. The plan was for him to ride over and over his grid position along the intended line in morning warm-up. But the one-kilometre-plus straight meant speeds well over 200 mph at that point. And a 2004 grid is a mess of paint and boxes – four per row for the smaller classes, three per row for MotoGP. Hard to spot. So Rossi's crew took a paddock scooter out to the grid position, and then held it over the track while spinning the rear wheel, skimming the surface to lay down a big black mark for Rossi to aim for. There was no secrecy involved.

Marking was the main reason, said Burgess later. Another, thought rivals, was to lay rubber for extra launch grip. Nearby, Pons team members were tackling the matter differently, giving Biaggi's fourth-row spot a good brooming.

Trouble was, Burgess left the track without telling the team manager Davide Brivio what they had done. Brivio takes up the story. "At about eight o'clock on the evening before the race, I was with Valentino at the track. We saw the mark, and we thought that someone had done something to damage our grid position. We immediately called the circuit manager. He wondered if it was paint, or possibly oil. He promised to do something, and we left. It is a bit embarrassing that we didn't know how it happened."

Now it got messy. For one thing, the acetone the circuit staff had used for cleaning improved the grip very significantly.

Rossi would later blame Gibernau for instigating it all, but it was HRC MotoGP manager Shoji Tachikawa who blew the whistle, showing racing manager Carlo Fiorani a photograph of the big rubber slick. Shortly afterwards Gibernau's team boss Fausto Gresini and Ducati manager Livio Suppo joined the discussion about the now scrubbed black mark. They called an impromptu pit-lane meeting with Brivio. The result was that both Honda teams and Ducati prepared written protests. Since each requires a 1,000 Swiss Franc guarantee, Race Direction persuaded them that just one would suffice. It was HRC's that went in.

Rossi's team hadn't broken any specific rule, but officials decided they had infringed the general sporting code. Their chosen penalty was a back-row start. This was implemented by adding an otherwise arbitrary six seconds to Rossi's practice time.

Yamaha, tit for tat, had protested Biaggi's team sweepers. This too was upheld (there is a specific rule against this), and he was given the same penalty for a different offence.

The implications were complex and far-reaching. For one thing, it is common practice for teams to dry the paint in front of their riders on a wet grid. That will have to stop, in spite of the safety implications. On another side, as Burgess later told MOTOCOURSE: "You used to be rewarded for doing something clever. Now you get penalised." But making these two start from the back certainly spiced up the race, and ultimately also the championship.

Earlier plans to run the race at night under floodlights had been shelved; naturally it was blazing hot – 40 degrees on race day, the track more than ten degrees higher. Low humidity made it more bearable for the riders, but the machines suffered a high failure rate: Kawasaki had at least three engine blow-ups with a bad batch of pistons, while in the race only one Yamaha made it to the end – Abe's. Rossi crashed out, but the other two suffered fuel vaporisation and pump cavitation problems in the heat, so it's possible he might have run into the same thing. Abe, fortuitously, had just had a new fuel pump fitted.

Ellison was joined by two more BSB riders, and 2004 race winners. Yukio Kagayama had postponed final corrective surgery to take Roberts's place on the Suzuki; former 500 GP (and WSB) rider James Haydon took over kid brother Kurtis's Proton. He gladdened the team with his unbridled enthusiasm. Especially when he said the back-of-the-grid V5 was "the fastest bike I've ever ridden". His bike kept going all the way, and he was rewarded with the V5's best finish of the year.

Above: Checa led out in the early stages, Xaus (11), Gibernau (15), Nakano (56), Capirossi (65), Edwards (45) and Hayden (69) prominent in the pursuit. But just look at Rossi (46), already ahead of Melandri (33) and the rest.
Photograph: Gold & Goose

MOTOGP RACE – 22 laps

Qualifying had been fraught on the slippery surface: everyone had at least one trip through the vast gravel traps, most a lot more – Rossi ran off eight times. Amazingly, nobody fell, and times improved by fully eight seconds over four sessions.

Times were close, Checa taking his third pole of his career, from Barros and Gibernau. Edwards had been fast, but ran wide on his qualifying tyres. Hayden, Nakano and Capirossi made row two; Rossi in the middle of row three, slower than Xaus, though only half a second off pole. He'd also wrecked his qualifying run with another gravel gallop. It made little difference. He started at the back, ahead only of Biaggi, who had qualified 12th.

Checa led away but Gibernau powered past on the straight, the pair soon pulling clear of Nakano and the rest ... but all eyes were on Rossi, hurtling through. Even on the first short straight, on the slippery side of the track, he'd passed 12 riders, up to ninth into Turn One.

Nakano's engine lasted one more lap before piston problems struck. In the middle of the early twists, the green bike spewed out a smokescreen of military proportions. Luckily, only Barros actually ran off the track. The Honda rider had already lost two places after Rossi bounced into him off Xaus at Turn One. He at least waved an apology.

In this way, Rossi was fourth after four laps. Now he was with Edwards, and both were closing a gap of four seconds to the leaders.

Rossi could have settled for a bit of wait-and-see, but his blood was up and he was riding right on the limit, using the kerbs on the corner exits to stop his slides. On lap six, he did it again on the exit of the last left-hander. Were the kerbs too short, as some riders suggested? Or Rossi a bit too aggressive, as others felt? Either way, the result was the same.

His bike flicked sideways as it hit the Astroturf, and in an instant he was sliding along behind it down the short straight, in a shower of sparks. Quickly on his feet, he clutched his helmet in despair, then ran off the track stripping off his left glove. His little finger had been bashed and gashed.

Gibernau had now put a second on Checa, who was starting to suffer the heat-triggered fuel vaporisation problem that would eventually consign him and later Melandri to the pits. Edwards was now fastest, and on lap nine he had caught and surged past the Yamaha. He was just four seconds behind Gibernau, , with 14 laps to go ... less than three tenths a lap.

Edwards set one fastest lap after another as he tried to close the gap, and he made some progress. Gibernau, however, had it under control, and made sure it never shrunk much below two seconds.

Biaggi's progress had been less dramatic (if more consistent) than Rossi's, and he was up to seventh by lap six. Ahead of him, ten seconds behind Edwards, the consistently impressive Xaus (for once equal with his peers on track knowledge) was narrowly ahead of a pressing Melandri, who did manage to get ahead at mid-distance, but only for a couple of laps. Hayden was four-odd seconds adrift, making no impression on those ahead, but holding Biaggi back until lap ten.

Barros was catching up fast. Seventeenth after his gravel trip, he too rubbished fears of impossible overtaking as he sliced through. He passed Hayden on lap 15, Biaggi two laps later, the latter staying with him as he continued to close gradually on the steadfast and ultimately uncatchable Xaus.

In fact, Biaggi was poised for a last-lap attack, but lost the front in the attempt, running off to let Hayden ahead again.

By then Melandri had stuttered to retirement. This left Abe, 15 seconds behind, the only Yamaha. He'd been engaged with Hopkins for much of the race, until the Suzuki rider's tyres started chattering and he had to concede to a bike significantly faster down the long straight. The pair had been joined by Capirossi mid-race, catching up after running off on lap five. He never got ahead, then retired to the pits after another excursion, blaming engine problems. Team-mate Bayliss retired early on with sliding tyres.

Hofmann nursed his Kawasaki to ninth; a long way back came Tamada, oddly never getting to grips with things all weekend. Kagayama was a distant 11th, two seconds clear of James Haydon in an impressive Proton debut; Ellison was 13th and last.

Points were a reward for simply surviving in the baking heat. Aoki had crashed out after five laps; as well as two Yamahas, both factory Ducatis and one Kawasaki, Hodgson and McWilliams also retired with sundry mechanical ills.

Left: Gibernau gets the taste of victory again.

Below centre: Battle of the BSB pair; Ellison (77) and Haydon were engaged to the end. The latter prevailed.

Below right: Ruben Xaus fought hard for a first rostrum, and put himself firmly on the map.

Photographs: Gold & Goose

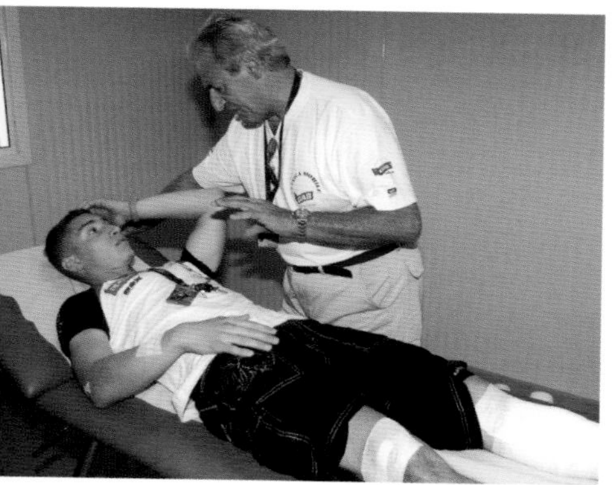

Above: **Luckless defending 250 champion Manuel Poggiali, injured in a freak off-track accident.**

Top: **Pedrosa led Porto (19) briefly, but the Argentine rider went on for a clear victory. Aoyama (73), de Angelis and Rolfo are still close; Nieto (10) losing touch ahead of Battaini.**

Below: **The first-ever photo-finish of the electronic era, after the computers timed a dead heat between Lorenzo (left) and Dovizioso. The judges gave it to Lorenzo.**

Photographs: Gold & Goose

250 cc RACE – 20 laps

Porto skated along the narrow grippy line to claim pole by the impressive margin of more than half a second. Pedrosa was next from de Angelis and de Puniet; Elias heading row two.

Poggiali was absent, his disastrous luck taking a turn for the worse with a freak accident at his hotel – playing squash he had bumped the glass back wall of the court. It shattered, cutting his legs badly enough to require 50 stitches.

Pedrosa led off the line, but on lap two Porto blasted by on the long straight. The Honda rider stayed close for next five laps, but Porto's pace was telling, and from the ninth lap he was already building on a gap of more than one second. He was never troubled again.

Seven fast laps were all de Angelis could manage, an impressive enough early charge, closing on the leaders, but then he was also dropping back, his tyres feeling the heat. He seemed safe enough in third, however, until heartbreak struck with two laps remaining. A wheel weight, thought mechanics, had come adrift, and punctured his radiator. Suddenly he dropped to touring speeds, and didn't make the finish.

This trio had rapidly pulled away from Aoyama, who had his hands full with Battaini. This battle lasted for the rest of the race, even though at the end Aoyama was fighting a phantom.

In the early stages, de Puniet had closed on the pair after getting by Nieto, but before he could join battle he slid and fell, after (as he explained with simple clarity) "I opened the gas too early out of the corner".

Aoyama was in front as they started the final lap, now fighting for a place on the rostrum. Battaini dived inside into the first corner, but directly ran wide, letting the blue Honda ahead again. In fact Battaini lost two seconds, but Aoyama had no idea, tucked behind the bubble for the rest of the lap, and weaving from side to side to block any last-minute passes on the finishing straight, only to discover he was alone.

Nieto was still close; Elias a long way behind after a sad story of the vanishing knee slider. He'd lost one on the sighting lap, another on the warm-up lap. He pulled in for a third, starting the race from pit lane, and charged through to seventh on lap eight, only for the same slider to come off again. That was the end of his attack, but pressing on valiantly, his leathers soon in tatters, he managed to hold the position, promoted to sixth at the finish by de Angelis's retirement.

For the final laps he'd been behind West, but was ahead again when the unlucky Australian privateer retired on the final lap.

Rolfo was seventh, fading on sliding tyres; Debon won a long battle with Frenchman Marchand; Olive completed the top ten. Chaz Davies missed the final point by just three tenths.

125 cc RACE – 18 laps

Stoner led away again, and for three laps, only to drop to fourth and then retire, his engine losing power – his third such non-finish in a row, and his sixth non-score. Just not his year …

Lorenzo had started from pole, with Dovizioso, Jenkner and Stoner completing the first row, Locatelli heading the second. The last-named bogged down on the line, and his motor never did clear properly. He finished 20th. Barbera was also in trouble, qualifying 14th and hardly improving in the race.

Lorenzo displaced Stoner from the front on lap five, Bautista in second, Dovizioso fourth. Kallio was losing ground in fourth, but gaining on the next gang, headed by Jenkner.

Stoner dropped out by the trackside soon afterwards, leaving the other three to battle it out all the way. All took turns at leading, but Bautista ran wide with two laps left, dropping out of contention. Lorenzo controlled the last lap; Dovizioso saving it all for a slingshot last run down the long straight. He so nearly made it that the transponders could not distinguish any difference in timing. The judges gave the race to Lorenzo, in the first photo finish of the electronic era.

Bautista was well clear of Kallio; after another long gap Lai's Gilera won out over Nieto, Simon and Borsoi. Jenkner dropped back to 11th, inches ahead of Barbera at the flag.

Lorenzo got the win and fastest lap, but again Dovizioso's lead had stretched, to an imposing 61 points, with only 75 more on the table.

MARLBORO QATAR grand prix

2 OCTOBER 2004

QATAR - LOSAIL GRAND PRIX CIRCUIT

CIRCUIT LENGTH: 3.343 miles/5.380 km

MotoGP

22 laps, 73.546 miles/118.360 km

Pos.	Rider (Nat.)	No.	Machine	Laps	Time & speed
1	Sete Gibernau (E)	15	Honda	22	44m 01.741s 100.223 mph/ 161.293 km/h
2	Colin Edwards (USA)	45	Honda	22	44m 03.056s
3	Ruben Xaus (E)	11	Ducati	22	44m 25.585s
4	Alex Barros (BR)	4	Honda	22	44m 27.199s
5	Nicky Hayden (USA)	69	Honda	22	44m 33.158s
6	Max Biaggi (I)	3	Honda	22	44m 40.950s
7	Norick Abe (J)	17	Yamaha	22	44m 55.114s
8	John Hopkins (USA)	21	Suzuki	22	44m 59.747s
9	Alex Hofmann (D)	66	Kawasaki	22	45m 06.061s
10	Makoto Tamada (J)	6	Honda	22	45m 20.259s
11	Yukio Kagayama (J)	71	Suzuki	22	45m 51.179s
12	James Haydon (GB)	36	Proton KR	22	45m 53.899s
13	James Ellison (GB)	77	Harris WCM	22	45m 55.641s
	Carlos Checa (E)	7	Yamaha	19	DNF
	Marco Melandri (I)	33	Yamaha	13	DNF
	Loris Capirossi (I)	65	Ducati	13	DNF
	Jeremy McWilliams (GB)	99	Aprilia	12	DNF
	Neil Hodgson (GB)	50	Ducati	10	DNF
	Nobuatsu Aoki (J)	9	Proton KR	6	DNF
	Valentino Rossi (I)	46	Yamaha	5	DNF
	Troy Bayliss (AUS)	12	Ducati	5	DNF
	Shinya Nakano (J)	56	Kawasaki	3	DNF
	Youichi Ui (J)		Harris WCM		DNQ

Fastest lap: Edwards, 1m 59.293s, 100.883 mph/162.356 km/h (record).
Previous record: none (new circuit).

Event best maximum speed: Biaggi, 207.8 mph/334.4 km/h (qualifying practice no. 2).

Qualifying: 1 Checa, 1m 58.988s; 2 Barros, 1m 59.119s; 3 Gibernau, 1m 59.126s; 4 Hayden, 1m 59.187s; 5 Nakano, 1m 59.232s; 6 Capirossi, 1m 59.281s; 7 Xaus, 1m 59.352s; 8*Rossi, 1m 59.494s; 9 Bayliss, 1m 59.551s; 10 Edwards, 1m 59.582s; 11 Hopkins, 1m 59.944s; 12*Biaggi, 2m 00.063s; 13 Tamada, 2m 00.638s; 14 McWilliams, 2m 00.660s; 15 Hodgson, 2m 00.826s; 16 Melandri, 2m 00.924s; 17 Abe, 2m 01.303s; 18 Hofmann, 2m 01.531s; 19 Kagayama, 2m 02.151s; 20 Aoki, 2m 03.281s; 21 Haydon, 2m 03.845s; 22 Ellison, 2m 04.627s; 23 Ui, 2m 07.466s.

*Both riders had 6 seconds added to their qualifying times for rule infringements and started the race from the back of the grid.

Fastest race laps: 1 Edwards, 1m 59.293s; 2 Gibernau, 1m 59.401s; 3 Rossi, 1m 59.630s; 4 Barros, 1m 59.768s; 5 Checa, 1m 59.835s; 6 Capirossi, 1m 59.875s; 7 Biaggi, 1m 59.952s; 8 Hayden, 2m 00.112s; 9 Melandri, 2m 00.208s; 10 Xaus, 2m 00.234s; 11 Abe, 2m 00.976s; 12 Nakano, 2m 01.006s; 13 Hopkins, 2m 01.095s; 14 Hofmann, 2m 01.629s; 15 McWilliams, 2m 01.779s; 16 Hodgson, 2m 01.980s; 17 Tamada, 2m 02.168s; 18 Bayliss, 2m 02.607s; 19 Kagayama, 2m 03.444s; 20 Haydon, 2m 03.572s; 21 Aoki, 2m 03.759s; 22 Ellison, 2m 04.195s.

World Championship: 1 Rossi, 229; 2 Gibernau, 215; 3 Biaggi, 168; 4 Edwards, 131; 5 Barros, 128; 6 Tamada, 120; 7 Checa, 102; 8 Hayden, 94; 9 Capirossi, 84; 10 Melandri, 75; 11 Xaus, 69; 12 Abe, 64; 13 Nakano, 62; 14 Hofmann, 43; 15 Bayliss, 42; 16 Hopkins, 40; 17 Hodgson and Kenny Roberts, 37; 19 McWilliams, 20; 20 Byrne, 18; 21 Aoki, 10; 22 Fabrizio, 8; 23 Jacque and Kagayama, 5; 25 Haydon, 4; 26 Ellison, 3; 27 Pitt, 2; 28 Kurtis Roberts and Ui, 1.

250 cc

20 laps, 66.860 miles/107.600 km

Pos.	Rider (Nat.)	No.	Machine	Laps	Time & speed
1	Sebastian Porto (ARG)	19	Aprilia	20	41m 17.343s 97.158 mph/ 156.361 km/h
2	Daniel Pedrosa (E)	26	Honda	20	41m 18.957s
3	Hiroshi Aoyama (J)	73	Honda	20	42m 00.655s
4	Franco Battaini (I)	21	Aprilia	20	42m 02.470s
5	Fonsi Nieto (E)	10	Aprilia	20	42m 04.525s
6	Toni Elias (E)	24	Honda	20	42m 16.814s
7	Roberto Rolfo (I)	2	Honda	20	42m 28.756s
8	Alex Debon (E)	6	Honda	20	42m 39.463s
9	Hugo Marchand (F)	9	Aprilia	20	42m 39.505s
10	Joan Olive (E)	11	Aprilia	20	42m 46.381s
11	Sylvain Guintoli (F)	50	Aprilia	20	42m 57.464s
12	Erwan Nigon (F)	36	Aprilia	20	43m 00.359s
13	Taro Sekiguchi (J)	44	Yamaha	20	43m 00.399s
14	Johan Stigefelt (S)	16	Aprilia	20	43m 08.227s
15	David de Gea (E)	52	Honda	20	43m 10.370s
16	Chaz Davies (GB)	57	Aprilia	20	43m 10.678s
17	Jakub Smrz (CZ)	96	Honda	20	43m 12.214s
18	Alex Baldolini (I)	25	Aprilia	20	43m 42.931s
19	Klaus Nöhles (D)	17	Honda	19	41m 30.648s
	Anthony West (AUS)	14	Aprilia	19	DNF
	Alex de Angelis (RSM)	51	Aprilia	18	DNF
	Naoki Matsudo (J)	8	Yamaha	15	DNF
	Dirk Heidolf (D)	28	Aprilia	8	DNF
	Radomil Rous (CZ)	43	Yamaha	5	DNF
	Randy de Puniet (F)	7	Aprilia	4	DNF
	Hector Faubel (E)	33	Aprilia	2	DNF
	Gregory Leblanc (F)	42	Aprilia	0	DNF
	Gergo Talmacsi (H)	88	Yamaha		DNQ

Fastest lap: de Angelis, 2m 03.015s, 97.831 mph/157.444 km/h (record).

Previous record: none (new circuit).

Event best maximum speed: Aoyama, 172.9 mph/278.2 km/h (qualifying practice no. 1).

Qualifying: 1 Porto, 2m 02.710s; 2 Pedrosa, 2m 03.181s; 3 de Angelis, 2m 03.894s; 4 de Puniet, 2m 04.385s; 5 Elias, 2m 04.391s; 6 Aoyama, 2m 04.568s; 7 Battaini, 2m 04.837s; 8 Nieto, 2m 05.364s; 9 Guintoli, 2m 05.998s; 10 West, 2m 06.244s; 11 Debon, 2m 06.425s; 12 Faubel, 2m 06.513s; 13 Davies, 2m 06.531s; 14 Olive, 2m 06.817s; 15 Baldolini, 2m 06.842s; 16 Rolfo, 2m 06.862s; 17 Smrz, 2m 06.971s; 18 Nigon, 2m 07.067s; 19 Heidolf, 2m 07.180s; 20 Matsudo, 2m 07.290s; 21 Sekiguchi, 2m 07.322s; 22 Stigefelt, 2m 07.359s; 23 Marchand, 2m 08.185s; 24 de Gea, 2m 08.345s; 25 Leblanc, 2m 08.815s; 26 Nöhles, 2m 09.014s; 27 Rous, 2m 11.115s; 28 Talmacsi, 2m 12.963s.

Fastest race laps: 1 de Angelis, 2m 03.015s; 2 Porto, 2m 03.041s; 3 Pedrosa, 2m 03.104s; 4 Elias, 2m 04.645s; 5 de Puniet, 2m 05.010s; 6 Battaini, 2m 05.111s; 7 Aoyama, 2m 05.251s; 8 West, 2m 05.319s; 9 Nieto, 2m 05.413s; 10 Rolfo, 2m 06.358s; 11 Marchand, 2m 06.584s; 12 Faubel, 2m 06.883s; 13 Debon, 2m 06.918s; 14 Olive, 2m 07.280s; 15 Sekiguchi, 2m 07.517s; 16 Stigefelt, 2m 07.537s; 17 Nigon, 2m 07.668s; 18 Guintoli, 2m 07.790s; 19 Heidolf, 2m 07.812s; 20 Matsudo, 2m 07.940s; 21 de Gea, 2m 08.000s; 22 Baldolini, 2m 08.092s; 23 Smrz, 2m 08.139s; 24 Nöhles, 2m 08.225s; 25 Davies, 2m 08.227s; 26 Rous, 2m 10.713s.

World Championship: 1 Pedrosa, 254; 2 Porto, 211; 3 de Puniet, 187; 4 Elias, 152; 5 H. Aoyama, 119; 6 de Angelis, 114; 7 Nieto, 105; 8 Rolfo, 101; 9 West, 88; 10 Poggiali, 79; 11 Debon, 75; 12 Battaini, 70; 13 Guintoli, 34; 14 Matsudo and Olive, 26; 16 Marchand, 24; 17 Davies, 23; 18 Faubel, 21; 19 Baldolini, 19; 20 Bataille and Smrz, 12; 22 Takahashi and Vincent, 11; 24 Heidolf, 9; 25 S. Aoyama, 8; 26 Lefort, 7; 27 Stigefelt, 6; 28 Fujioka, Nigon and Sekiguchi, 4; 31 Leblanc, 3; 32 de Gea, 1.

125 cc

18 laps, 60.174 miles/96.840 km

Pos.	Rider (Nat.)	No.	Machine	Laps	Time & speed
1	Jorge Lorenzo (E)	48	Derbi	18	39m 11.620s 92.117 mph/ 148.248 km/h
2	Andrea Dovizioso (I)	34	Honda	18	39m 11.620s
3	Alvaro Bautista (E)	19	Aprilia	18	39m 15.638s
4	Mika Kallio (SF)	36	KTM	18	39m 30.373s
5	Fabrizio Lai (I)	32	Gilera	18	39m 47.078s
6	Pablo Nieto (E)	22	Aprilia	18	39m 49.510s
7	Julian Simon (E)	10	Honda	18	39m 50.643s
8	Gino Borsoi (I)	23	Aprilia	18	39m 51.029s
9	Mattia Pasini (I)	54	Aprilia	18	39m 54.521s
10	Mirko Giansanti (I)	6	Aprilia	18	39m 54.538s
11	Steve Jenkner (D)	21	Aprilia	18	39m 59.045s
12	Hector Barbera (E)	3	Aprilia	18	39m 59.635s
13	Thomas Luthi (CH)	12	Honda	18	40m 04.272s
14	Andrea Ballerini (I)	50	Aprilia	18	40m 14.712s
15	Gioele Pellino (I)	42	Aprilia	18	40m 18.424s
16	Stefano Perugini (I)	7	Gilera	18	40m 18.663s
17	Lukas Pesek (CZ)	52	Honda	18	40m 32.338s
18	Sergio Gadea (E)	33	Aprilia	18	40m 35.428s
19	Dario Giuseppetti (D)	26	Honda	18	40m 38.489s
20	Roberto Locatelli (I)	15	Aprilia	18	40m 40.102s
21	Lorenzo Zanetti (I)	45	Aprilia	18	40m 41.399s
22	Jordi Carchano (E)	28	Aprilia	18	40m 49.015s
23	Manuel Manna (I)	8	Malaguti	18	40m 49.160s
24	Raymond Schouten (NL)	16	Honda	18	40m 50.021s
25	Imre Toth (H)	25	Aprilia	18	41m 06.237s
	Simone Corsi (I)	24	Honda	15	DNF
	Gabor Talmacsi (H)	14	Malaguti	9	DNF
	Casey Stoner (AUS)	27	KTM	8	DNF
	Max Sabbatani (I)	31	Honda	2	DNF
	Angel Rodriguez (E)	47	Derbi	0	DNF
	Vesa Kallio (SF)	66	Aprilia	0	DNF
	Marco Simoncelli (I)	58	Aprilia		DNS
	Marketa Janakova (CZ)	9	Honda		DNQ
	Mike di Meglio (F)	63	Aprilia		DNQ

Fastest lap: Lorenzo, 2m 09.569s, 92.883 mph/149.480 km/h (record).

Previous record: none (new circuit).

Event best maximum speed: Barbera, 146.6 mph/236.0 km/h (qualifying practice no. 1).

Qualifying: 1 Lorenzo, 2m 09.644s; 2 Dovizioso, 2m 09.928s; 3 Jenkner, 2m 10.496s; 4 Stoner, 2m 10.519s; 5 Locatelli, 2m 10.807s; 6 Nieto, 2m 10.875s; 7 Simoncelli, 2m 10.956s; 8 Simon, 2m 11.466s; 9 Giansanti, 2m 11.615s; 10 M. Kallio, 2m 11.784s; 11 Corsi, 2m 11.878s; 12 Bautista, 2m 11.977s; 13 Luthi, 2m 12.067s; 14 Barbera, 2m 12.139s; 15 Pasini, 2m 12.408s; 16 Lai, 2m 12.414s; 17 Talmacsi, 2m 12.606s; 18 Perugini, 2m 12.759s; 19 Gadea, 2m 12.760s; 20 V. Kallio, 2m 12.820s; 21 Ballerini, 2m 13.249s; 22 Borsoi, 2m 13.403s; 23 Rodriguez, 2m 13.432s; 24 Giuseppetti, 2m 14.088s; 25 Zanetti, 2m 14.628s; 26 Carchano, 2m 15.659s; 27 Pellino, 2m 15.659s; 28 Toth, 2m 16.050s; 29 Schouten, 2m 16.056s; 30 Pesek, 2m 16.406s; 31 Manna, 2m 17.474s; 32 Sabbatani, 2m 17.569s; 33 Janakova, 2m 19.184s; 34 di Meglio, 2m 30.098s.

Fastest race laps: 1 Lorenzo, 2m 09.569s; 2 Dovizioso, 2m 09.633s; 3 Bautista, 2m 09.648s; 4 M. Kallio, 2m 10.211s; 5 Stoner, 2m 10.376s; 6 Jenkner, 2m 10.841s; 7 Locatelli, 2m 11.111s; 8 Borsoi, 2m 11.178s; 9 Lai, 2m 11.281s; 10 Corsi, 2m 11.360s; 11 Simon, 2m 11.411s; 12 Nieto, 2m 11.419s; 13 Giansanti, 2m 11.526s; 14 Barbera, 2m 11.555s; 15 Luthi, 2m 11.628s; 16 Pasini, 2m 11.711s; 17 Ballerini, 2m 12.272s; 18 Perugini, 2m 12.433s; 19 Pesek, 2m 12.887s; 20 Gadea, 2m 12.972s; 21 Pellino, 2m 13.080s; 22 Talmacsi, 2m 13.252s; 23 Giuseppetti, 2m 13.257s; 24 Zanetti, 2m 14.000s; 25 Schouten, 2m 14.390s; 26 Toth, 2m 14.476s; 27 Carchano, 2m 14.506s; 28 Manna, 2m 14.580s; 29 Sabbatani, 2m 18.791s.

World Championship: 1 Dovizioso, 228; 2 Barbera, 167; 3 Lorenzo, 159; 4 Locatelli, 156; 5 Nieto, 124; 6 Stoner, 104; 7 Jenkner, 99; 8 Giansanti, 98; 9 Bautista, 90; 10 M. Kallio, 86; 11 Simoncelli, 79; 12 Borsoi, 54; 13 Corsi, 53; 14 Simon, 47; 15 Lai, 41; 16 Pasini, 40; 17 di Meglio, 33; 18 Ballerini, 25; 19 Talmacsi, 23; 20 Ui, 19; 21 Pellino and Pesek, 16; 23 Perugini, 14; 24 Gadea, 8; 25 Koyama and Luthi, 7; 27 Kuzuhara and Toth, 6; 29 Giuseppetti and Harms, 5; 31 Carchano and Rodriguez, 2; 33 V. Kallio, 1.

FIM WORLD CHAMPIONSHIP • ROUND 14

MALAYSIANGP
SEPANG

Above: Rossi, on pole and serious for the start of his ride to revenge.

Right: Not on speaking terms ... Gibernau and Rossi at a tense pre-race press conference.

Centre right: McCoy looked happy to be back.

Far right: Max was happier than he looked.

Photographs: Gold & Goose

ROSSI had left Qatar with the words: "I've been looking for an excuse not to talk to Sete. Today he gave me one." He flew back to Italy for treatment to his left little finger – it was the site of his only previous visible injury, sustained in 1995; the rest of the paddock reassembled at Sepang after a few days of R&R in Malaysia, agog to see how the row had developed.

When Rossi and Biaggi had a spat at Catalunya in 2001, the PR machine clicked into gear to stifle it. The pair shared cheesy grins and handshakes for the cameras at Assen, but continue to this day to avoid one another's eyes and company. Would this row be sanitised as well?

No chance of that. At a packed pre-race press conference, Rossi affirmed that he stuck by everything he said (that, among other things, Gibernau was "a bastard and a spy"), and steadfastly avoided acknowledging the Spaniard, sat one chair away. Sete, for his part, dealt articulately with a persistent line of questioning, insisting that he was innocent in every detail of having prosecuted the protest at Qatar (in fact his team was one of three – with Repsol Honda and Ducati, but this need not necessarily mean that Gibernau was personally behind it). As for the formerly more than cordial relationship with his title rival. "That is between me and Valentino," he said. Or not, suggested MOTOCOURSE, since he won't be speaking to you. "Then," smiled Gibernau to general laughter; "it is between Valentino and himself."

It was generally agreed that Gibernau had won the press conference. The race, rather more importantly, went the other way – another bravura performance by the virtuoso Valentino, magnificent under pressure. After the flag, Gibernau pulled alongside to congratulate him, holding out his hand. Again, as steadfastly, Rossi ignored him.

This public snub triggered some debate. Surely a great champion should also be enough of a sportsman and a gentleman to accept a beaten rival's congratulations? Rossi was accused of schoolboyish petulance. Or was he simply being true to himself, and a genuine hard-as-nails motorbike racer to boot? The verdict depended on mood, culture and other factors. The lack of pretence at least was refreshing.

Speculation was intensifying about who would go where next year, riders and managers to be seen slaloming secretively in and out of the row of temporary offices behind the pits. Much was already decided, with Edwards firmly set on switching to Yamaha after a year on Honda's back-burner, his return unrewarded; Melandri aiming to make the reverse move to Honda; and Bayliss given his marching orders by Ducati at the end of the weekend (an ill-timed move, it seemed, especially after the best they could find to replace him turned out to be Checa. The Australian was promptly offered several jobs, in and out of MotoGP, including both Kawasaki and Camel Honda). At that time, however, Ducati were still flirting with Hopkins; a bigger question concerned the fate of the factory Hondas. Hayden was well on the way to finalising another two-year deal, but plans to absorb Telefónica-backed Gibernau into the factory team had already come to naught (Repsol had offered the Spanish mobile telephone company co-sponsorship only on the most punishing terms, with Telefónica to pay all for half the fairing space). Now the choice was between Biaggi and Tamada, and in the end it would go to the former.

This was just the riders. It was a time of change at other paddock levels, with blood-letting in almost every major team. Suzuki team manager Garry Taylor had already announced his retirement the previous weekend; BSB Rizla Suzuki team boss Paul Denning would take his place from 2005, and already some members of the predominately British team had been told they would not be required next year. There were more mechanics axed at Yamaha, with long-serving Britons to be replaced by Italians, and team management also to move down to the Italian Belgarda base. At HRC also, most of Hayden's crew was to be replaced (more British victims), almost certainly to make way for the return of Erv Kanemoto, after a year with Suzuki. There was a strong feeling that the MotoGP class had not only changed life for the riders, but also significantly altered the overall balance in subtle ways. Perhaps it is too soon to know exactly how.

Sunday was blazing, but qualifying wasn't quite as hot as Qatar, though a lot steamier (or, as one of HRC's keenly awaited press releases would have it, "SWEALTERING"). And it rained, both evenings, though mercifully not on race day. This time, the machines survived. Yamaha had been taken by surprise by the fuel pump failures in the dry desert heat, and had revised internal airflow to prevent it happening again.

Proton had expected Kurtis Roberts to return for their main sponsor's home race, but he was still unfit. James Haydon had already flown home, but turned straight round. The team was hoping to convince Proton Cars to continue their generous backing in spite of poor results. Tests with the KTM engine after Portugal had been very promising – the V4 was not only more reliable than their own V5, but also more powerful and faster round the track, making better use of the advanced chassis. "It would be a pity if we put a good package together next year and Proton aren't with us. They've spent a lot of money to get to this point," said Kenny Roberts, sounding wistful but not looking it, chomping on a big cigar. Later, after a zero-points race, he added: "It was a good day, because it's one day closer to putting the bikes into the museum."

Gary McCoy made a GP return, taking over Byrne's Aprilia. Three times a two-stroke winner and once revered as the Sultan of Slide, the Australian had fallen on hard times with Kawasaki and escaped to Superbikes, where he saw the chequered flag again. Glad to be back, he was fully aware of the Aprilia's shortcomings and the stop-gap nature of the exercise, emphasised when his leathers failed to arrive until day two, and he had to borrow some from team-mate McWilliams. He taped over part of the name, and said: "You can just call me Mac."

The health of the 125 class was proven again by a 37th race without a back-to-back win. This only reinforced the status of 2004's first World Champion Andrea Dovizioso. To shine in such close company is the mark of true talent.

Above: **Rossi dives inside Barros at the last hairpin, only to run wide on the exit. Behind, Hayden (69) is lining up for a more successful move on Checa (7).**
Photograph: Gold & Goose

MOTOGP RACE – 21 laps

Rossi's post-race explanation of his weekend's strategy was devastatingly clear. "I've worked with Jerry (Burgess) for four years, through good and bad times, but I've never seen him so deflated as in Qatar. I told him not to worry: we would go to Sepang and spank everybody's arse.

"I had a very precise plan – to work to the maximum on Friday so we could get to Saturday with the bike perfect, and then to show everybody what I was capable of on Sunday. I wanted to destroy their morale.

"I had no strategy for the race, except to go to the front and pull away, like a hammer, for lap after lap."

Final qualifying had been hit by weather, damp at the start; a sudden sprinkling right at the end, spoiling qualifying laps for a number: Gibernau and then Hopkins set fastest section times earlier in that lap. Rossi had already secured pole with one fastest lap after another, Barros second and Nakano (turning 27 on race day) third – the Kawasaki's first front row.

Race day was much hotter – 40 degrees and sweaty, track temperatures soaring to 57, hotter even than Qatar, making grip a scarcity.

Barros led away; Rossi attacked at the final hairpin on lap two, but ran wide. In their wake Biaggi had come through, and Checa was about to get repassed by Hayden.

Two laps later, Rossi had a second try at the slow left halfway round, and managed to hang on through the ensuing right. He was where he wanted to be, and stayed there for the rest of the afternoon. His plan worked to the letter. He rubbed salt in seventh-placed Sete's wounds, after snubbing his handshake: "I would have liked a fight, but I didn't even see him. It was extraordinary. For me, he did the best race of his season. He gave me a lot of points, and I'm very grateful."

Gibernau was suffering badly in the changed conditions as Rossi edged away from Barros and Biaggi, the trio in turn outpacing the pursuit. On lap seven Biaggi's persistent attacks finally paid off, and he was second, still less than a second behind Rossi.

The gap stretched and shrank over the next laps, the tension high. On lap 14 Max was again within a second. But then "I made a couple of mistakes, and realised how close to the limit we were … both of us. Rossi was riding very well, and so was I." He chose a safe second.

Barros had dropped away steadily after saving a couple of front-end slides. Hayden had dealt with Checa early on, then kept a briefly challenging Gibernau at bay, with the big-slide dirt-track technique he'd been enjoying all weekend. The Spaniard's pace slackened after eight laps, and Hayden was free for fourth.

Four seconds behind Checa in the early laps, Capirossi led a mob: Tamada and Nakano, Bayliss and Edwards, the last pair soon to lose touch. By lap 13 Capirossi had closed on Checa, who in turn was on the fading Gibernau. The Japanese riders watched closely as Capirossi passed first Checa then Gibernau on consecutive laps.

Left: **Edwards keeps cool on the grid.**

Below: **Close quarters for Xaus, Hodgson, McWilliams and Hofmann.**

Below centre: **Aoki chases Kagayama in the early stages.**

Bottom: **Shade seekers, McWilliams, McCoy and Hodgson before the start.**

Photographs: Gold & Goose

Tamada was now ahead of Checa and hounding Gibernau, his tyres coming good. He not only disposed of the Honda rider with three laps to go, but annihilated a two-second gap to Capirossi, pouncing on the Ducati through the last corner for fifth.

Gibernau just managed to keep Nakano behind him, Checa losing ground towards the end, then Bayliss and Edwards spread out in his wake. Abe had dropped out of a run with the Superbike rivals, but was well clear of Xaus.

Second-time Suzuki rider Kagayama and the Aprilias had battled over the last points, the Japanese rider finally prevailing as both McWilliams and first-timer McCoy suffered chatter, the latter dropping away by the finish.

Aoki soldiered on with his rear tyre shifted on the rim, vibrating badly; the WCMs were a lap behind.

Retirements started with Hopkins, angrily into the pits with another broken valve spring after a good start and only two laps. Hodgson had another strange afternoon, his d'Antin Ducati catching fire on the sighting lap, extinguished on the grid using his water bottle! Unsurprisingly, he did not finish. Hofmann also pitted, with "electronic problems". Melandri crashed out of 12th with 12 laps left, another to stalk off in a rage.

Haydon had a comedic race. Creeping on the grid, he was penalised for a jump start with a ride-through, then his crew missed him with his pit board a bit later. "I thought it meant they were calling me in," he said, after pitting, by now little point in rejoining.

Right: Porto gives it everything to hold off Elias on the run to the final hairpin.

Below: On-form Alvaro Bautista shaded Locatelli (15) on his way to the rostrum.
Photographs: Gold & Goose

250 cc RACE – 20 laps

Porto's slender title hopes were preserved with his seventh pole after a rain-hit final session; Pedrosa second, then de Puniet and de Angelis; Elias again leading the second row.

Pedrosa made an immaculate start to an immaculate race. Immediately in the lead, he started to draw away directly, the pursuit piled up behind Elias. On the first lap, second-row starter West was lying fifth when he and Rolfo tangled and both crashed out, the Australian breaking his left wrist in a heavy fall.

This thinned the pursuit, and in any case Pedrosa was piling it on, a new record on lap three, three seconds clear after one more, and still going away. By half distance, he was ten seconds clear.

In the early laps, Elias had Porto close behind, de Angelis hovering also – then a big gap to the next group, lead by Aoyama from slow-away de Puniet, Nieto and Debon.

Elias and Porto were back and forth, and after half-distance de Angelis joined in the scrap – but it didn't last, and he lost touch again. Porto resolved matters in his favour with an all-or-nothing final lap, gaining enough advantage not to be mugged at the final hairpin.

De Angelis was more than ten seconds away, the rest spaced out even more, for the most part ... de Puniet half a minute adrift in fifth, inheriting the position from misfortunate lap-16 crasher Aoyama, who had earlier seen the Frenchman off.

Battaini hung on to sixth from Nieto some way behind; they'd swapped places after half distance. Davies and Marchand been with them, and were still hard at it to the finish, now six seconds adrift. Marchand took eighth by just over a tenth ... but it was the start of a run of improving top tens for the young Welsh rider.

Debon had crashed out on lap nine, while tussling with Nieto.

Marcellino Lucchi, now a full-time Aprilia tester, made a GP return in place of Poggiali, at 46 displacing 40-year-old McWilliams as the oldest rider. Lucchi, who had spent the year testing the still-born Mk2 version of the MotoGP RS3, qualified on the fourth row, and found himself in a four-bike battle for 13th, finishing at the back of it behind Faubel, Smrz and Stigefelt. The racing may have been processional, but the pace in the class is high.

It was not a thrilling 250 race, but it was important enough. Porto managed to stop Pedrosa tying up the championship with two races to spare, but by such a narrow margin it was merely mathematical. The class rookie was already looking very much a champion.

Above: Second was good enough for Dovizioso to become the first World Champion of 2004.

Right: Casey Stoner finally claimed a first win.

Opposite page: Rossi sweeps the track in ironic post-race theatricals.
Photographs: Gold & Goose

125 cc RACE – 19 laps

Dry practice put Dovizioso on pole by almost a second. His last remaining title rival Barbera was next, then Stoner and Simoncelli.

Barbera's paper-thin hopes were shredded on lap two, after taking off on the lead. In the first sharp left he was flicked over the high-side. He ran to his bike, then fell theatrically backwards onto the track, luckily far enough away from the others not to be run over.

Stoner took over and held the lead to the finish. He was never alone, however. Dovizioso shadowed him all the way, only for his last-lap attack to fall short of his usual commitment. He came almost alongside, but second was good enough for the title.

They had outdistanced the pursuit by more than a second a lap from the start. Kallio crashed out of that group after two laps, leaving Lorenzo to lead the pack of eight for a spell, before Lai took over on lap five.

The pack diminished, Lorenzo pitting angrily after eight laps. By now Locatelli was in control, but Bautista pushed through before half distance and gradually pulled away to a second successive rostrum.

The remnants were led by a now lonely Locatelli, with Lai narrowly ahead of Simon, then Pasini prevailing after a long battle with Talmacsi and Borsoi. Jenkner had been with them, but dropped back at the finish.

FIM WORLD CHAMPIONSHIP • ROUND 14

SEPANG

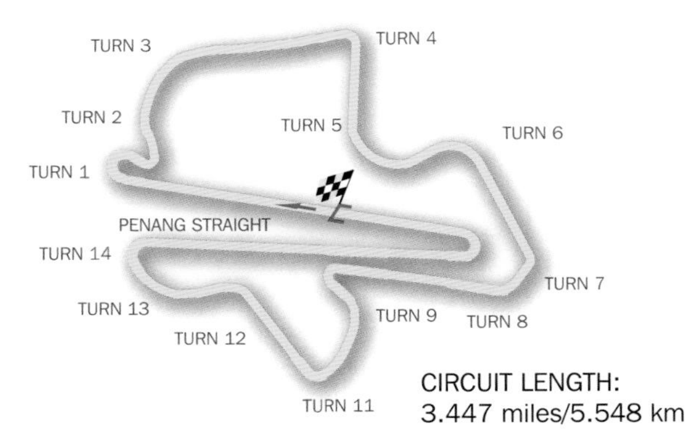

MotoGP

21 laps, 72.387 miles/116.508 km

Pos.	Rider (Nat.)	No.	Machine	Laps	Time & speed
1	Valentino Rossi (I)	46	Yamaha	21	43m 29.146s 99.775 mph/ 160.573 km/h
2	Max Biaggi (I)	3	Honda	21	43m 32.812s
3	Alex Barros (BR)	4	Honda	21	43m 38.445s
4	Nicky Hayden (USA)	69	Honda	21	43m 48.215s
5	Makoto Tamada (J)	6	Honda	21	43m 50.301s
6	Loris Capirossi (I)	65	Ducati	21	43m 50.414s
7	Sete Gibernau (E)	15	Honda	21	43m 51.027s
8	Shinya Nakano (J)	56	Kawasaki	21	43m 51.313s
9	Carlos Checa (E)	7	Yamaha	21	43m 52.296s
10	Troy Bayliss (AUS)	12	Ducati	21	44m 01.761s
11	Colin Edwards (USA)	45	Honda	21	44m 03.104s
12	Norick Abe (J)	17	Yamaha	21	44m 13.448s
13	Ruben Xaus (E)	11	Ducati	21	44m 24.381s
14	Yukio Kagayama (J)	71	Suzuki	21	44m 38.726s
15	Jeremy McWilliams (GB)	99	Aprilia	21	44m 39.522s
16	Garry McCoy (AUS)	24	Aprilia	21	44m 45.280s
17	Nobuatsu Aoki (J)	9	Proton KR	21	45m 24.243s
18	James Ellison (GB)	77	Harris WCM	20	43m 30.948s
19	Youichi Ui (J)	41	Harris WCM	20	44m 00.615s
	Marco Melandri (I)	33	Yamaha	9	DNF
	James Haydon (GB)	36	Proton KR	8	DNF
	Alex Hofmann (D)	66	Kawasaki	7	DNF
	Neil Hodgson (GB)	50	Ducati	6	DNF
	John Hopkins (USA)	21	Suzuki	2	DNF

Fastest lap: Rossi, 2m 03.253s, 100.691 mph/162.047 km/h (record).

Previous record: Valentino Rossi, I (Honda), 2m 03.822s, 100.228 mph/161.302 km/h (2003).

Event best maximum speed: Biaggi, 197.4 mph/317.7 km/h (race).

Qualifying: 1 Rossi, 2m 01.833s; 2 Barros, 2m 02.228s; 3 Nakano, 2m 02.278s; 4 Gibernau, 2m 02.283s; 5 Tamada, 2m 02.394s; 6 Hayden, 2m 02.399s; 7 Biaggi, 2m 02.446s; 8 Hopkins, 2m 02.588s; 9 Checa, 2m 02.602s; 10 Melandri, 2m 02.852s; 11 Capirossi, 2m 02.860s; 12 Edwards, 2m 03.014s; 13 Hofmann, 2m 03.321s; 14 Bayliss, 2m 03.384s; 15 Xaus, 2m 03.956s; 16 Abe, 2m 04.284s; 17 Hodgson, 2m 04.738s; 18 McWilliams, 2m 04.830s; 19 McCoy, 2m 04.875s; 20 Kagayama, 2m 05.285s; 21 Aoki, 2m 06.126s; 22 Haydon, 2m 06.443s; 23 Ellison, 2m 08.554s; 24 Ui, 2m 08.995s.

Fastest race laps: 1 Rossi, 2m 03.253s; 2 Biaggi, 2m 03.281s; 3 Barros, 2m 03.636s; 4 Hayden, 2m 03.790s; 5 Capirossi, 2m 04.048s; 6 Tamada, 2m 04.084s; 7 Gibernau, 2m 04.147s; 8 Nakano, 2m 04.264s; 9 Checa, 2m 04.277s; 10 Edwards, 2m 04.563s; 11 Melandri, 2m 04.669s; 12 Bayliss, 2m 04.703s; 13 Abe, 2m 04.808s; 14 Hopkins, 2m 04.879s; 15 Xaus, 2m 05.566s; 16 McWilliams, 2m 05.661s; 17 Hofmann, 2m 06.193s; 18 McCoy, 2m 06.280s; 19 Kagayama, 2m 06.415s; 20 Hodgson, 2m 06.587s; 21 Aoki, 2m 08.104s; 22 Haydon, 2m 08.460s; 23 Ellison, 2m 09.324s; 24 Ui, 2m 10.083s.

World Championship: 1 Rossi, 254; 2 Gibernau, 224; 3 Biaggi, 188; 4 Barros, 144; 5 Edwards, 136; 6 Tamada, 131; 7 Checa, 109; 8 Hayden, 107; 9 Capirossi, 94; 10 Melandri, 75; 11 Xaus, 72; 12 Nakano, 70; 13 Abe, 68; 14 Bayliss, 48; 15 Hofmann, 43; 16 Hopkins, 40; 17 Hodgson and Kenny Roberts, 37; 19 McWilliams, 21; 20 Byrne, 18; 21 Aoki, 10; 22 Fabrizio, 8; 23 Kagayama, 7; 24 Jacque, 5; 25 Haydon, 4; 26 Ellison, 3; 27 Pitt, 2; 28 Kurtis Roberts and Ui, 1.

250 cc

20 laps, 68.940 miles/110.960 km

Pos.	Rider (Nat.)	No.	Machine	Laps	Time & speed
1	Daniel Pedrosa (E)	26	Honda	20	43m 03.507s 96.075 mph/ 154.617 km/h
2	Sebastian Porto (ARG)	19	Aprilia	20	43m 17.020s
3	Toni Elias (E)	24	Honda	20	43m 17.092s
4	Alex de Angelis (RSM)	51	Aprilia	20	43m 28.534s
5	Randy de Puniet (F)	7	Aprilia	20	43m 53.485s
6	Franco Battaini (I)	21	Aprilia	20	44m 06.089s
7	Fonsi Nieto (E)	10	Aprilia	20	44m 06.177s
8	Hugo Marchand (F)	9	Aprilia	20	44m 12.867s
9	Chaz Davies (GB)	57	Aprilia	20	44m 12.999s
10	Naoki Matsudo (J)	8	Yamaha	20	44m 24.501s
11	Alex Baldolini (I)	25	Aprilia	20	44m 28.612s
12	Dirk Heidolf (D)	28	Aprilia	20	44m 31.537s
13	Hector Faubel (E)	33	Aprilia	20	44m 34.253s
14	Jakub Smrz (CZ)	96	Honda	20	44m 34.728s
15	Johan Stigefelt (S)	16	Aprilia	20	44m 35.068s
16	Marcellino Lucchi (I)	37	Aprilia	20	44m 35.726s
17	David de Gea (E)	52	Honda	20	44m 47.009s
18	Joan Olive (E)	11	Aprilia	20	44m 52.116s
19	Gregory Leblanc (F)	42	Aprilia	20	44m 52.319s
20	Radomil Rous (CZ)	43	Yamaha	20	45m 10.529s
	Hiroshi Aoyama (J)	73	Honda	15	DNF
	Alex Debon (E)	6	Honda	9	DNF
	Taro Sekiguchi (J)	44	Yamaha	5	DNF
	Anthony West (AUS)	14	Aprilia	0	DNF
	Roberto Rolfo (I)	2	Honda	0	DNF
	Erwan Nigon (F)	36	Aprilia	0	DNF
	Sylvain Guintoli (F)	50	Aprilia	0	DNF
	Gergo Talmacsi (H)	88	Yamaha		DNQ

Fastest lap: Pedrosa, 2m 08.015s, 96.946 mph/156.019 km/h (record).

Previous record: Toni Elias, E (Aprilia), 2m 08.566s, 96.530 mph/155.350 km/h (2003).

Event best maximum speed: de Angelis, 161.6 mph/260.0 km/h (warm-up).

Qualifying: 1 Porto, 2m 06.940s; 2 Pedrosa, 2m 07.644s; 3 de Puniet, 2m 08.287s; 4 de Angelis, 2m 08.345s; 5 Elias, 2m 08.501s; 6 Aoyama, 2m 08.510s; 7 Nieto, 2m 08.905s; 8 West, 2m 08.948s; 9 Battaini, 2m 09.051s; 10 Rolfo, 2m 09.364s; 11 Debon, 2m 09.760s; 12 Marchand, 2m 09.892s; 13 Lucchi, 2m 10.010s; 14 Nigon, 2m 10.494s; 15 Smrz, 2m 10.533s; 16 Baldolini, 2m 10.847s; 17 Matsudo, 2m 10.902s; 18 Davies, 2m 11.043s; 19 Stigefelt, 2m 11.084s; 20 Faubel, 2m 11.114s; 21 Heidolf, 2m 11.160s; 22 de Gea, 2m 11.231s; 23 Guintoli, 2m 11.518s; 24 Olive, 2m 11.707s; 25 Leblanc, 2m 12.364s; 26 Sekiguchi, 2m 12.623s; 27 Rous, 2m 14.901s; 28 Talmacsi, 2m 15.922s.

Fastest race laps: 1 Pedrosa, 2m 08.015s; 2 Elias, 2m 08.726s; 3 de Angelis, 2m 08.932s; 4 Porto, 2m 08.938s; 5 de Puniet, 2m 09.995s; 6 Aoyama, 2m 10.147s; 7 Debon, 2m 10.849s; 8 Nieto, 2m 10.978s; 9 Battaini, 2m 11.255s; 10 Marchand, 2m 11.482s; 11 Davies, 2m 11.489s; 12 Baldolini, 2m 12.091s; 13 Heidolf, 2m 12.135s; 14 Matsudo, 2m 12.254s; 15 Faubel, 2m 12.267s; 16 Stigefelt, 2m 12.436s; 17 Smrz, 2m 12.448s; 18 Lucchi, 2m 12.453s; 19 Sekiguchi, 2m 12.857s; 20 Olive, 2m 13.047s; 21 de Gea, 2m 13.163s; 22 Leblanc, 2m 13.357s; 23 Rous, 2m 13.771s.

World Championship: 1 Pedrosa, 279; 2 Porto, 231; 3 de Puniet, 198; 4 Elias, 168; 5 de Angelis, 127; 6 H. Aoyama, 119; 7 Nieto, 114; 8 Rolfo, 101; 9 West, 88; 10 Battaini, 80; 11 Poggiali, 79; 12 Debon, 75; 13 Guintoli, 34; 14 Marchand and Matsudo, 32; 16 Davies, 30; 17 Olive, 26; 18 Baldolini and Faubel, 24; 20 Smrz, 14; 21 Heidolf, 13; 22 Bataille, 12; 23 Takahashi and Vincent, 11; 25 S. Aoyama, 8; 26 Lefort and Stigefelt, 7; 28 Fujioka, Nigon and Sekiguchi, 4; 31 Leblanc, 3; 32 de Gea, 1.

125 cc

19 laps, 65.493 miles/105.412 km

Pos.	Rider (Nat.)	No.	Machine	Laps	Time & speed
1	Casey Stoner (AUS)	27	KTM	19	43m 10.360s 91.030 mph/ 146.498 km/h
2	Andrea Dovizioso (I)	34	Honda	19	43m 10.389s
3	Alvaro Bautista (E)	19	Aprilia	19	43m 16.907s
4	Roberto Locatelli (I)	15	Aprilia	19	43m 21.939s
5	Fabrizio Lai (I)	32	Gilera	19	43m 27.496s
6	Julian Simon (E)	10	Honda	19	43m 27.506s
7	Mattia Pasini (I)	54	Aprilia	19	43m 35.345s
8	Gabor Talmacsi (H)	14	Malaguti	19	43m 35.417s
9	Gino Borsoi (I)	23	Aprilia	19	43m 35.622s
10	Steve Jenkner (D)	21	Aprilia	19	43m 37.265s
11	Thomas Luthi (CH)	12	Honda	19	43m 47.179s
12	Sergio Gadea (E)	33	Aprilia	19	43m 55.918s
13	Dario Giuseppetti (D)	26	Honda	19	43m 58.357s
14	Andrea Ballerini (I)	50	Aprilia	19	43m 58.801s
15	Toshihisa Kuzuhara (J)	62	Honda	19	44m 17.286s
16	Jordi Carchano (E)	28	Aprilia	19	44m 29.214s
17	Mike di Meglio (F)	63	Aprilia	19	44m 29.258s
18	Imre Toth (H)	25	Aprilia	19	44m 34.421s
19	Raymond Schouten (NL)	16	Honda	19	44m 37.489s
20	Lorenzo Zanetti (I)	45	Aprilia	16	44m 17.158s
	Vesa Kallio (SF)	66	Aprilia	17	DNF
	Gioele Pellino (I)	42	Aprilia	15	DNF
	Angel Rodriguez (E)	47	Derbi	10	DNF
	Jorge Lorenzo (E)	48	Derbi	8	DNF
	Max Sabbatani (I)	31	Honda	8	DNF
	Marketa Janakova (CZ)	9	Honda	7	DNF
	Mirko Giansanti (I)	6	Aprilia	5	DNF
	Manuel Manna (I)	8	Malaguti	3	DNF
	Stefano Perugini (I)	7	Gilera	2	DNF
	Marco Simoncelli (I)	58	Aprilia	2	DNF
	Pablo Nieto (E)	22	Aprilia	2	DNF
	Hector Barbera (E)	3	Aprilia	1	DNF
	Mika Kallio (SF)	36	KTM	1	DNF
	Lukas Pesek (CZ)	52	Honda	1	DNF
	Simone Corsi (I)	24	Honda	0	DNF

Fastest lap: Stoner, 2m 14.928s, 91.978 mph/148.025 km/h.

Lap record: Lucio Cecchinello, I (Aprilia), 2m 13.919s, 92.671 mph/149.140 km/h (2002).

Event best maximum speed: Barbera, 139.3 mph/224.2 km/h (warm-up).

Qualifying: 1 Dovizioso, 2m 12.684s; 2 Barbera, 2m 13.576s; 3 Stoner, 2m 13.718s; 4 Simoncelli, 2m 13.843s; 5 Lorenzo, 2m 13.969s; 6 M. Kallio, 2m 14.346s; 7 Locatelli, 2m 14.479s; 8 Nieto, 2m 14.487s; 9 Giansanti, 2m 14.534s; 10 Lai, 2m 14.568s; 11 Talmacsi, 2m 14.664s; 12 Perugini, 2m 14.680s; 13 Bautista, 2m 14.915s; 14 Corsi, 2m 15.015s; 15 Simon, 2m 15.281s; 16 Jenkner, 2m 15.316s; 17 Pasini, 2m 15.379s; 18 Borsoi, 2m 15.379s; 19 Luthi, 2m 15.519s; 20 Pesek, 2m 15.876s; 21 Rodriguez, 2m 16.123s; 22 Ballerini, 2m 16.150s; 23 Gadea, 2m 16.358s; 24 di Meglio, 2m 16.428s; 25 Pellino, 2m 16.444s; 26 Giuseppetti, 2m 16.552s; 27 Zanetti, 2m 16.649s; 28 Kuzuhara, 2m 17.058s; 29 Toth, 2m 17.741s; 30 V. Kallio, 2m 17.751s; 31 Manna, 2m 18.154s; 32 Carchano, 2m 18.516s; 33 Schouten, 2m 18.554s; 34 Sabbatani, 2m 18.902s; 35 Janakova, 2m 19.389s.

Fastest race laps: 1 Stoner, 2m 14.928s; 2 Simon, 2m 14.955s; 3 Bautista, 2m 15.206s; 4 Dovizioso, 2m 15.532s; 5 Locatelli, 2m 15.675s; 6 Jenkner, 2m 15.772s; 7 Borsoi, 2m 15.993s; 8 Luthi, 2m 16.233s; 9 Pasini, 2m 16.263s; 10 Lai, 2m 16.268s; 11 Talmacsi, 2m 16.307s; 12 Giansanti, 2m 16.564s; 13 Lorenzo, 2m 16.658s; 14 Gadea, 2m 16.918s; 15 Nieto, 2m 16.991s; 16 Giuseppetti, 2m 17.117s; 17 Ballerini, 2m 17.311s; 18 Pellino, 2m 17.682s; 19 V. Kallio, 2m 17.712s; 20 Zanetti, 2m 17.883s; 21 di Meglio, 2m 18.015s; 22 Perugini, 2m 18.021s; 23 Sabbatani, 2m 18.211s; 24 Rodriguez, 2m 18.262s; 25 Kuzuhara, 2m 18.362s; 26 Carchano, 2m 19.044s; 27 Toth, 2m 19.204s; 28 Schouten, 2m 19.369s; 29 Simoncelli, 2m 20.780s; 30 Barbera, 2m 21.939s; 31 Manna, 2m 21.970s; 32 M. Kallio, 2m 23.073s; 33 Janakova, 2m 26.947s; 34 Pesek, 2m 27.607s.

World Championship: 1 Dovizioso, 248; 2 Locatelli, 169; 3 Barbera, 167; 4 Lorenzo, 159; 5 Stoner, 129; 6 Nieto, 124; 7 Bautista, 106; 8 Jenkner, 105; 9 Giansanti, 98; 10 M. Kallio, 86; 11 Simoncelli, 79; 12 Borsoi, 61; 13 Simon, 57; 14 Corsi, 53; 15 Lai, 52; 16 Pasini, 49; 17 di Meglio, 18 Talmacsi, 31; 19 Ballerini, 27; 20 Ui, 19; 21 Pellino and Pesek, 16; 23 Perugini, 14; 24 Gadea and Luthi, 12; 26 Giuseppetti, 8; 27 Koyama and Kuzuhara, 7; 29 Toth, 6; 30 Harms, 5; 31 Carchano and Rodriguez, 2; 33 V. Kallio, 1.

FIM WORLD CHAMPIONSHIP • ROUND 15

AUSTRALIANGP

PHILLIP ISLAND

Above: There were many destructive crashes on the "safer" track – this is James Ellison off the WCM.

Main picture: Early scramble in an epic race ... Capirossi leads Bayliss (12), with Hayden (69) in between. Edwards, Barros (4) and Biaggi (3) are also in the frame.

Photographs: Gold & Goose

WHERE as last year, ennui had spoiled the middle of his season, the whole of this year had been intensely emotional for Rossi, ever since his tear-jerking first win at Welkom. And not least because of the previous two flyaway races. He arrived in Australia on the brink of making history, after crushing his rival, Gibernau, both on and off the track. All he had to do now was to make sure he followed Gibernau home to become the third rider in history (after Duke and Lawson) to win premier-class titles on different makes of machine, and the second to do so back-to-back.

It would also be his fourth consecutive title in the premier class; a goal achieved one year earlier than he had planned or expected when he made the decision to abandon dominant Honda and join underdogs Yamaha. "I had thought it would take to the end of the season before we would be winning races," he affirmed, in the afterglow of an epic Australian GP.

All three of Valentino's previous top-class titles had been sealed with a race win, as had his 250 crown, though not his first 125 title of 1997. He saw no reason to change the habit now.

His first lap was executed at maximum risk (understand that when a rider of his calibre is at maximum risk, most other riders are already crashing). And it looked on that first lap, as he ran onto the dirt after attempting a simply impossible pass on the two Ducatis, as though he would crash.

Rossi's last lap was hardly lower on the scale of risk. His adversary, Gibernau, was riding a faster motorcycle as well as he ever has, but Rossi's sheer determination would not be denied. He won it like a true champion, as if there was any doubt.

The fine seaside circuit, a favourite among most riders, provided a fitting finale not only for Rossi's signal achievement but also for that of Pedrosa, who laid the ghosts of his bad practice crash here with a cautious ride to a debut-season 250 title. And the future of the classic track seemed assured. Earlier in the year the prime seaside property had been reprieved from the threat of housing development, with new owners intent on developing its motor sporting potential.

But there were some jarring notes. One early act had been to implement, at considerable cost (two-million Australian dollars), the requests of the riders' safety commission, a self-appointed body formed in the wake of Kato's fatal crash at Suzuka last year, but convened and ratified by race management including Dorna and the FIM. One alteration was a long-extended pit exit lane, which took traffic all the way down the rest of the front straight to the entry of the very fast Turn One before joining the main circuit. Another was the introduction of new gravel traps, and the considerable extension of some existing ones.

Things went wrong almost from the start. Those riders who crashed, often at high speed (such is the nature of the circuit), were hitting gravel instead of sliding along grass, and getting flicked end over end. It proved ruinous to motorcycles, and very dangerous to their fallen riders. Then there was a coming together among front-row starters for a national 125 support race. Instead of there being room on the left-hand-side of the track, there was now the extended pit wall. At least one rider hit it where previously he might have found room to regain control, and three went down, to be stretchered away. In this type of crash, it is always a mercy when the worst injuries are broken limbs.

The worst case was Anthony West, who was playing the role of local hero to the hilt. His left wrist strapped up to reinforce the fresh fractures, he was "giving it a go" in true blue style when he crashed at Turn One on the first day of practice. The loss of control, almost certainly because of physical weakness, came just as he started braking, at a speed of around 170 mph.

Westy was lucky that nobody was filtering in from pit lane at the time, because he would have collected them fair and square. Unhindered, he and his Aprilia went skimming off the track, and appeared to be launched by the lip of the new gravel trap, where before there was just a huge area of greensward. From there on, West and Aprilia went looping to mutual destruction. For the second time in a week the Queenslander was stretchered away, this time lucky to escape with only further wrist fractures, and to be cleared after a precautionary scan for head and neck injuries.

The circuit owners declined to comment, beyond saying that the changes were absolutely as dictated by the FIM. In fact, it was the four-man riders' commission that had laid down the requirements, and this had been approved by, among others, FIM Road Racing Commission boss Claude Danis. "We must all take responsibility, and we will look carefully at the situation after the race," he told MOTOCOURSE. "But it is hard to say that the gravel traps are a mistake. There are places – like Turn Eight – where without the gravel trap you could not guarantee a fallen rider would not hit the tyre wall. That is on dry grass... it's worse on wet grass."

Disagreement elsewhere centred on a radical proposal signed by all three tyre suppliers to the top class – Michelin, Bridgestone and Dunlop – presenting strict controls over the numbers and types of tyres to be supplied – a maximum of 18 front and 24 rear tyres per event. Further restrictions in the allowable variations effectively ended the use of qualifying tyres. This proposal had been rejected out of hand by the teams, but aspects were still under consideration by the GP Commission. Something needs to be done to control spiralling costs, and the fact that teams that, for whatever reason, cannot get Michelins (or now and then Bridgestones) simply don't have a hope in hell of a good result.

Above: Ten-cylinder symphony – Edwards and Hayden scythe their Hondas through the sweepers.
Photograph: Gold & Gose

MOTOGP RACE – 27 laps

For the first time all year, in comparable conditions, practice times were slower than last year, partly perhaps because a wet first morning cut set-up time at a track of fast corners, where the right balance is crucial. Times were very close, with 11 riders within the first second. Gibernau won pole from Rossi by just a tenth, with Capirossi alongside, for the second time in the year, and Edwards the best of the rest.

It was fierce from the start; Capirossi in front into the first corner, Gibernau sweeping round the outside of Rossi on the next, then outbraking the Ducati to lead at Honda Hairpin, where Rossi ran wide and dropped to fourth behind Bayliss. Just half a lap gone, and the drama was already beginning.

Two corners later and Rossi was on the dirt and almost off the bike. Undaunted he then passed both Ducatis on the swoop down to MG hairpin to regain second.

The confusion had given Gibernau a handy lead of 1.3 seconds. Rossi whittled it down steadily, while Barros got ahead of Bayliss to join Capirossi. By lap six the first four were together.

Gibernau and Rossi started moving away directly. Barros pulled the hairpin move on Capirossi on lap ten, but he was by now too far behind to close up again, and was, in any case, troubled with sliding tyres.

Gibernau said later his throttle mechanism wasn't working correctly. "I had to anticipate the throttle, and think about that rather than fighting Valentino." All the same, he was lapping fast and consistently. Rossi, for his part, was hounding him steadily, but when he did sweep past into the first corner on lap 19, Gibernau said he'd let him through. Sure enough, he powered alongside on the straight as they started lap 23, and took the lead again at the same place.

The battle grew increasingly fierce; and then came the last lap. Gibernau led, Rossi nosed ahead at the second corner, but ran wide at the next hairpin to let Gibernau through once more. Rossi couldn't bear to wait until the usual overtaking spot, the next heavy braking zone for MG, to attack again. With genuine flair, he created his own opportunity over the preceding hill, and held Gibernau at bay to the flag.

Once again, it was a masterful demonstration, rewarded by the ultimate prize. At a track he loves, Rossi had proved everything there was to prove. Asked afterwards how it felt to have beaten Honda at the first attempt, he said: "For me, the most important thing is to beat the other riders. For sure it is a great pleasure to beat Honda, but I don't fight for Yamaha against Honda. I am fighting for myself against Gibernau and Biaggi, and Capirossi, and if they are riding for Ducati or something else, I don't mind."

Capirossi had set a new record earlier on; in the closing stages he moved in again on Barros, with a gang of five coming up behind him. This had formed after Biaggi took fifth from Bayliss early on, though already troubled with traction problems. Edwards, Melandri, Tamada, Hayden and the two Kawasakis were battling behind him. Bayliss was heading the group again by half distance with Edwards all over him and the Kawasakis dropping away, but everyone else still up close. Then Melandri dropped out, blaming a mystery infection for vision problems.

Bayliss was losing places from lap 14, Biaggi now making the running but Edwards and Tamada both pushing hard. Then on lap 20 Hayden got between them, at which point Edwards took off, Biaggi following along and Tamada once again ahead of the younger American. A proper motorbike race.

Hayden was getting stronger, passing Tamada and Biaggi but not close enough to menace Edwards who was closing on the battle for third, where Capirossi had caught Barros on lap 23, and passed him one lap later. The order was resolved on the final set of fast left-handers; Barros running wide after a desperate lunge at the Ducati, letting Edwards through for fourth. Close behind Hayden shaded Biaggi for sixth, with Tamada a tenth behind. Bayliss ended up ninth, six seconds adrift; then came Checa, harried almost all race long by the persistent Xaus after a slow start.

Nakano was three seconds adrift, then came Hofmann, almost ten seconds behind. McWilliams had been enjoying one of his favourite tracks and a long battle with Hopkins, which he won by a tenth.

Lavilla and Abe were not far behind, but out of the points, the latter closing almost all the way at the end; Hodgson was miles behind and both the Protons and the WCMs had been lapped.

Left: **Checa on the grid – not a favourite circuit.**

Below: **Doohan looks wry as new champion Rossi consoles the crestfallen Gibernau, their feud over ... for now.**

Bottom: **Rossi was not to be beaten, and there was nothing the pursuing Gibernau could do about it.**

Photographs: Gold & Goose

Above: A cautious ride conquered Pedrosa's Island fears, and won him a classic maiden-season 250 title.

Below: Every which way for the 125s ... Lorenzo heading Dovizioso, Stoner and Locatelli.

Photographs: Gold & Goose

250 cc RACE – 25 laps

Pedrosa's title-winning style was the opposite of Rossi's – but who could blame him, when luck seemed weighed heavily against him. Back at the track where he broke both ankles last year, he crashed at speed on the second day, luckily unhurt but damaging his best bike beyond repair, and was heavily outqualified at this fast track by the long-legged Aprilias. Then his bike failed in race-morning warm-up, and he had to run back to the pits for a second hastily built spare.

Porto took pole by a huge margin from de Angelis and Poggiali, with Pedrosa retaining fourth in spite of his big crash. His teammate Aoyama also went end over end in the gravel traps.

Pedrosa led off the line, only for de Angelis and Porto to pass at the first and second corners respectively. Come the hairpin and he outbraked both to lead again. On lap two Porto made sure his move was permanent, and started to pull away. When de Angelis also passed the Honda two laps later the Argentinean was almost 1.5 seconds clear. He kept building the gap, up to six seconds by the end, with de Angelis also stretching away.

Pedrosa was riding carefully. Poggiali followed closely and finally powered past down the straight with four laps to go, Pedrosa tamely following him from then on.

With West out and Nieto colliding with Debon with a wildly over-ambitious inside-line attack at MG, the chasing group was much depleted. Elias was fifth, but losing ground gradually.

Most of the excitement came from Chaz Davies, with a best-ever tenth qualifying slot. He finished lap one eighth, passed Rolfo one lap later, then closed on practice crasher Aoyama. At the same time, de Puniet came flying past from a slow start, passing Davies and then Aoyama before crashing out again.

Now Davies took up the challenge on the factory Hondas, taking sixth and then proceeding to close within a second of Elias, before the pace began to tell and he lost time again. Sixth was his career best, and came at a good time for this increasingly promising British youngster.

The rest trailed in; Aoyama, then Guintoli and Stigefelt, with Rolfo another two seconds away. Debon remounted to win the battle for 11th from Marchand and Smrz, and de Gea saved 14th from Matsudo.

125 cc RACE – 23 laps

Locatelli led away from pole with Stoner pushing ahead halfway round, but Dovizioso was in command by the end of the first lap. Lorenzo was in third and Locatelli watched from a short distance behind.

The youthful trio traded the lead back and forth over the next lap, Lorenzo having a spell up front, then Dovizioso, and Stoner taking the lead only occasionally. As the end drew near, Locatelli closed up again, making it a four-way battle, only for him to drop away as the pace increased again.

Dovizioso led on to the last lap but Stoner dived past at Turn One. The Italian repaid the compliment at the distant Siberia corner, with Lorenzo following him through. Then Stoner regained second on the scramble down into MG.

Just the last lefts remained: a choice of lines for the smallest bikes, and then the sprint to the line. Dovizioso had enough to retain the narrowest of leads, and Stoner seemed safe in second... until Lorenzo pulled alongside in a familiar final gallop, to take the place by inches.

Thus was Stoner denied not only the chance to win his home GP, but also to break the run of races without a consecutive winner, which now stretched to 38.

Locatelli was fourth; then came Jenkner at the head of a three-strong Aprilia group disputing fifth – the German narrowly beating Barbera and Borsoi. Di Meglio won the next big battle, shading Bautista, Gadea, Talmacsi, Pesek, Giansanti, Ballerini and Nieto – eighth to 15th spanned by less than two seconds.

FIM WORLD CHAMPIONSHIP • ROUND 15

CINZANO AUSTRALIAN grand prix

17 OCTOBER 2004

PHILLIP ISLAND

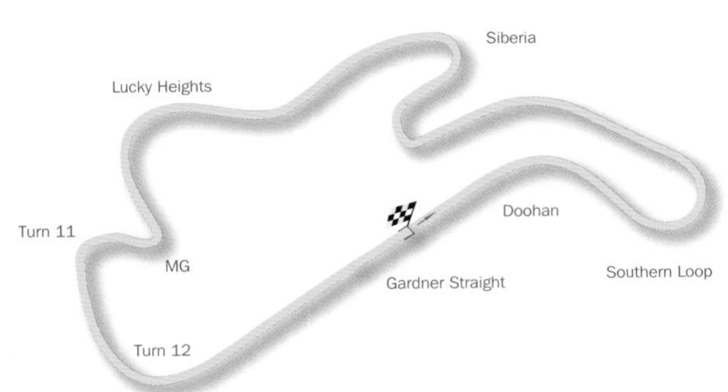

CIRCUIT LENGTH: 2.764 miles/4.448 km

MotoGP

27 laps, 74.624 miles/120.096 km

Pos.	Rider (Nat.)	No.	Machine	Laps	Time & speed
1	Valentino Rossi (I)	46	Yamaha	27	41m 25.819s 108.071 mph/ 173.924 km/h
2	Sete Gibernau (E)	15	Honda	27	41m 25.916s
3	Loris Capirossi (I)	65	Ducati	27	41m 36.305s
4	Colin Edwards (USA)	45	Honda	27	41m 36.636s
5	Alex Barros (BR)	4	Honda	27	41m 36.670s
6	Nicky Hayden (USA)	69	Honda	27	41m 38.029s
7	Max Biaggi (I)	3	Honda	27	41m 38.666s
8	Makoto Tamada (J)	6	Honda	27	41m 38.784s
9	Troy Bayliss (AUS)	12	Ducati	27	41m 44.426s
10	Carlos Checa (E)	7	Yamaha	27	41m 47.064s
11	Ruben Xaus (E)	11	Ducati	27	41m 48.992s
12	Shinya Nakano (J)	56	Kawasaki	27	41m 51.537s
13	Alex Hofmann (D)	66	Kawasaki	27	42m 00.956s
14	Jeremy McWilliams (GB)	99	Aprilia	27	42m 10.974s
15	John Hopkins (USA)	21	Suzuki	27	42m 11.016s
16	Gregorio Lavilla (E)	32	Suzuki	27	42m 18.024s
17	Norick Abe (J)	17	Yamaha	27	42m 18.484s
18	Neil Hodgson (GB)	50	Ducati	27	42m 37.213s
19	Nobuatsu Aoki (J)	9	Proton KR	26	41m 33.128s
20	James Haydon (GB)	36	Proton KR	26	41m 43.861s
21	Youichi Ui (J)	41	Harris WCM	26	42m 41.480s
22	James Ellison (GB)	77	Harris WCM	24	42m 52.400s
	Marco Melandri (I)	33	Yamaha	15	DNF
	Garry McCoy (AUS)	24	Aprilia	4	DNF

Fastest lap: Capirossi, 1m 31.102s, 109.217 mph/175.767 km/h (record).

Previous record: Valentino Rossi, 1m 31.421s, 108.836 mph/175.154 km/h (2003).

Event best maximum speed: Capirossi, 205.1 mph/330.0 km/h (qualifying practice no. 2).

Qualifying: 1 Gibernau, 1m 30.122s; 2 Rossi, 1m 30.222s; 3 Capirossi, 1m 30.613s; 4 Edwards, 1m 30.625s; 5 Tamada, 1m 30.716s; 6 Barros, 1m 30.757s; 7 Biaggi, 1m 30.767s; 8 Hofmann, 1m 30.819s; 9 Bayliss, 1m 30.873s; 10 Melandri, 1m 30.927s; 11 Nakano, 1m 31.093s; 12 Xaus, 1m 31.191s; 13 Checa, 1m 31.359s; 14 Hayden, 1m 31.377s; 15 McWilliams, 1m 31.491s; 16 Lavilla, 1m 31.846s; 17 Hopkins, 1m 31.911s; 18 Abe, 1m 32.452s; 19 Hodgson, 1m 32.531s; 20 McCoy, 1m 32.712s; 21 Aoki, 1m 32.857s; 22 Haydon, 1m 33.317s; 23 Ellison, 1m 33.608s; 24 Ui, 1m 35.280s.

Fastest race laps: 1 Capirossi, 1m 31.102s; 2 Barros, 1m 31.137s; 3 Gibernau, 1m 31.211s; 4 Rossi, 1m 31.334s; 5 Bayliss, 1m 31.374s; 6 Edwards, 1m 31.443s; 7 Hayden, 1m 31.561s; 8 Tamada, 1m 31.580s; 9 Melandri, 1m 31.607s; 10 Biaggi, 1m 31.610s; 11 Xaus, 1m 31.969s; 12 Checa, 1m 32.084s; 13 Nakano, 1m 32.096s; 14 Hopkins, 1m 32.235s; 15 Hofmann, 1m 32.344s; 16 McWilliams, 1m 32.499s; 17 Lavilla, 1m 32.908s; 18 Abe, 1m 33.292s; 19 Hodgson, 1m 33.459s; 20 Aoki, 1m 34.596s; 21 Ellison, 1m 34.784s; 22 Haydon, 1m 34.887s; 23 McCoy, 1m 35.711s; 24 Ui, 1m 36.606s.

World Championship: 1 Rossi, 279; 2 Gibernau, 244; 3 Biaggi, 197; 4 Barros, 155; 5 Edwards, 149; 6 Tamada, 139; 7 Hayden, 117; 8 Checa, 115; 9 Capirossi, 110; 10 Xaus, 77; 11 Melandri, 75; 12 Nakano, 74; 13 Abe, 68; 14 Bayliss, 55; 15 Hofmann, 46; 16 Hopkins, 41; 17 Hodgson and Kenny Roberts, 37; 19 McWilliams, 23; 20 Byrne, 18; 21 Aoki, 10; 22 Fabrizio, 8; 23 Kagayama, 7; 24 Jacque, 5; 25 Haydon, 4; 26 Ellison, 3; 27 Pitt, 2; 28 Kurtis Roberts and Ui, 1.

250 cc

25 laps, 69.096 miles/111.200 km

Pos.	Rider (Nat.)	No.	Machine	Laps	Time & speed
1	Sebastian Porto (ARG)	19	Aprilia	25	39m 24.604s 105.196 mph/ 169.296 km/h
2	Alex de Angelis (RSM)	51	Aprilia	25	39m 30.545s
3	Manuel Poggiali (RSM)	54	Aprilia	25	39m 37.893s
4	Daniel Pedrosa (E)	26	Honda	25	39m 39.570s
5	Toni Elias (E)	24	Honda	25	40m 10.687s
6	Chaz Davies (GB)	57	Aprilia	25	40m 19.744s
7	Hiroshi Aoyama (J)	73	Honda	25	40m 25.618s
8	Sylvain Guintoli (F)	50	Aprilia	25	40m 29.288s
9	Johan Stigefelt (S)	16	Aprilia	25	40m 32.260s
10	Roberto Rolfo (I)	2	Honda	25	40m 34.493s
11	Alex Debon (E)	6	Honda	25	40m 38.176s
12	Hugo Marchand (F)	9	Aprilia	25	40m 38.212s
13	Jakub Smrz (CZ)	96	Honda	25	40m 39.285s
14	David de Gea (E)	52	Honda	25	40m 46.077s
15	Naoki Matsudo (J)	8	Yamaha	25	40m 46.119s
16	Hector Faubel (E)	33	Aprilia	25	40m 51.464s
17	Gregory Leblanc (F)	42	Aprilia	25	40m 54.921s
18	Joshua Waters (AUS)	82	Honda	24	39m 54.031s
19	Radomil Rous (CZ)	43	Yamaha	24	39m 55.031s
	Dirk Heidolf (D)	28	Aprilia	21	DNF
	Alex Baldolini (I)	25	Aprilia	17	DNF
	Joan Olive (E)	11	Aprilia	15	DNF
	Taro Sekiguchi (J)	44	Yamaha	12	DNF
	Franco Battaini (I)	21	Aprilia	7	DNF
	Randy de Puniet (F)	7	Aprilia	4	DNF
	Fonsi Nieto (E)	10	Aprilia	0	DNF
	Erwan Nigon (F)	36	Aprilia		EXC
	Gergo Talmacsi (H)	88	Yamaha		DNQ
	Mark Rowling (AUS)	81	Yamaha		DNQ
	Peter Taplin (AUS)	80	Honda		DNQ
	Ben Ried (AUS)	84	Yamaha		DNQ

Fastest lap: Porto, 1m 33.381s, 106.551 mph/171.478 km/h (record).

Previous record: Valentino Rossi, I (Aprilia), 1m 33.556s, 106.352 mph/171.157 km/h (1999).

Event best maximum speed: de Angelis, 168.3 mph/270.9 km/h (warm-up).

Qualifying: 1 Porto, 1m 32.099s; 2 de Angelis, 1m 32.986s; 3 Poggiali, 1m 33.210s; 4 Pedrosa, 1m 33.225s; 5 de Puniet, 1m 33.764s; 6 Nieto, 1m 34.240s; 7 Aoyama, 1m 34.358s; 8 Battaini, 1m 34.576s; 9 Elias, 1m 34.583s; 10 Davies, 1m 35.027s; 11 Debon, 1m 35.084s; 12 Stigefelt, 1m 35.217s; 13 Guintoli, 1m 35.339s; 14 Smrz, 1m 35.568s; 15 Matsudo, 1m 35.574s; 16 Nigon, 1m 35.658s; 17 Rolfo, 1m 35.824s; 18 de Gea, 1m 35.863s; 19 Marchand, 1m 35.890s; 20 Baldolini, 1m 36.227s; 21 Olive, 1m 36.675s; 22 Leblanc, 1m 36.814s; 23 Rous, 1m 37.090s; 24 Heidolf, 1m 37.144s; 25 Sekiguchi, 1m 37.249s; 26 Faubel, 1m 37.376s; 27 Waters, 1m 38.149s; 28 Talmacsi, 1m 38.728s; 29 Rowling, 1m 41.268s; 30 Taplin, 1m 44.428s; 31 Ried, 1m 48.308s.

Fastest race laps: 1 Porto, 1m 33.381s; 2 de Angelis, 1m 33.650s; 3 Poggiali, 1m 34.089s; 4 Pedrosa, 1m 34.302s; 5 de Puniet, 1m 34.647s; 6 Elias, 1m 34.986s; 7 Davies, 1m 35.376s; 8 Aoyama, 1m 35.806s; 9 Debon, 1m 35.880s; 10 Rolfo, 1m 36.136s; 11 Smrz, 1m 36.176s; 12 Guintoli, 1m 36.272s; 13 Stigefelt, 1m 36.374s; 14 Marchand, 1m 36.532s; 15 Battaini, 1m 36.622s; 16 Baldolini, 1m 36.722s; 17 de Gea, 1m 36.808s; 18 Nigon, 1m 36.842s; 19 Matsudo, 1m 36.858s; 20 Heidolf, 1m 36.878s; 21 Faubel, 1m 36.999s; 22 Sekiguchi, 1m 37.008s; 23 Leblanc, 1m 37.196s; 24 Olive, 1m 37.621s; 25 Rous, 1m 38.013s; 26 Waters, 1m 38.450s.

World Championship: 1 Pedrosa, 292; 2 Porto, 256; 3 de Puniet, 198; 4 Elias, 179; 5 de Angelis, 147; 6 H. Aoyama, 128; 7 Nieto, 114; 8 Rolfo, 107; 9 Poggiali, 95; 10 West, 88; 11 Battaini and Debon, 80; 13 Guintoli, 42; 14 Davies, 40; 15 Marchand, 36; 16 Matsudo, 33; 17 Olive, 26; 18 Baldolini and Faubel, 24; 20 Smrz, 17; 21 Stigefelt, 14; 22 Heidolf, 13; 23 Bataille, 12; 24 Takahashi and Vincent, 11; 26 S. Aoyama, 8; 27 Lefort, 7; 28 Fujioka, Nigon and Sekiguchi, 4; 31 de Gea and Leblanc, 3.

125 cc

23 laps, 63.572 miles/102.304 km

Pos.	Rider (Nat.)	No.	Machine	Laps	Time & speed
1	Andrea Dovizioso (I)	34	Honda	23	38m 01.877s 100.289 mph/ 161.399 km/h
2	Jorge Lorenzo (E)	48	Derbi	23	38m 02.000s
3	Casey Stoner (AUS)	27	KTM	23	38m 02.000s
4	Roberto Locatelli (I)	15	Aprilia	23	38m 04.357s
5	Steve Jenkner (D)	21	Aprilia	23	38m 07.213s
6	Hector Barbera (E)	3	Aprilia	23	38m 07.292s
7	Gino Borsoi (I)	23	Aprilia	23	38m 07.325s
8	Mike di Meglio (F)	63	Aprilia	23	38m 19.853s
9	Alvaro Bautista (E)	19	Aprilia	23	38m 20.281s
10	Sergio Gadea (E)	33	Aprilia	23	38m 20.304s
11	Gabor Talmacsi (H)	14	Malaguti	23	38m 20.378s
12	Lukas Pesek (CZ)	52	Honda	23	38m 20.407s
13	Mirko Giansanti (I)	6	Aprilia	23	38m 20.616s
14	Andrea Ballerini (I)	50	Aprilia	23	38m 21.208s
15	Pablo Nieto (E)	22	Aprilia	23	38m 21.703s
16	Simone Corsi (I)	24	Honda	23	38m 29.848s
17	Gioele Pellino (I)	42	Aprilia	23	38m 29.860s
18	Mattia Pasini (I)	54	Aprilia	23	38m 29.873s
19	Thomas Luthi (CH)	12	Honda	23	38m 29.883s
20	Julian Simon (E)	10	Honda	23	38m 30.769s
21	Imre Toth (H)	25	Aprilia	23	38m 42.820s
22	Dario Giuseppetti (D)	26	Honda	23	38m 42.957s
23	Vesa Kallio (SF)	66	Aprilia	23	38m 50.004s
24	Lorenzo Zanetti (I)	45	Aprilia	23	38m 57.316s
25	Max Sabbatani (I)	31	Honda	23	39m 30.351s
26	Raymond Schouten (NL)	16	Honda	23	39m 30.533s
27	Matthew Kuhne (AUS)	46	Honda	23	39m 30.607s
28	Jordi Carchano (E)	28	Aprilia	23	39m 38.794s
29	Bryan Staring (AUS)	92	Honda	20	38m 46.611s
	Mika Kallio (SF)	36	KTM	17	DNF
	Stefano Perugini (I)	7	Gilera	11	DNF
	Fabrizio Lai (I)	32	Gilera	11	DNF
	Manuel Manna (I)	8	Malaguti	7	DNF
	Angel Rodriguez (E)	47	Derbi	6	DNF
	Brent Rigoli (AUS)	94	Honda		DNQ
	Malcolm Esler (AUS)	93	Honda		DNQ
	Brett Simmonds (AUS)	56	Honda		DNQ

Fastest lap: Dovizioso, 1m 38.024s, 101.504 mph/163.355 km/h.

Lap record: Daniel Pedrosa, E (Honda), 1m 37.983s, 101.547 mph/163.424 km/h (2002).

Event best maximum speed: Ballerini, 147.5 mph/237.4 km/h (race).

Qualifying: 1 Locatelli, 1m 37.417s; 2 Lorenzo, 1m 37.543s; 3 Stoner, 1m 37.590s; 4 Jenkner, 1m 38.147s; 5 Dovizioso, 1m 38.238s; 6 Borsoi, 1m 38.375s; 7 M. Kallio, 1m 38.386s; 8 Barbera, 1m 38.389s; 9 Giansanti, 1m 38.643s; 10 Simon, 1m 38.674s; 11 Pesek, 1m 38.725s; 12 Talmacsi, 1m 38.790s; 13 Nieto, 1m 38.854s; 14 Gadea, 1m 38.865s; 15 Perugini, 1m 38.870s; 16 di Meglio, 1m 38.907s; 17 Rodriguez, 1m 39.072s; 18 Lai, 1m 39.263s; 19 Ballerini, 1m 39.298s; 20 Toth, 1m 39.357s; 21 Corsi, 1m 39.366s; 22 Luthi, 1m 39.637s; 23 Pasini, 1m 39.708s; 24 Bautista, 1m 39.865s; 25 Zanetti, 1m 39.938s; 26 Giuseppetti, 1m 40.135s; 27 V. Kallio, 1m 40.264s; 28 Manna, 1m 40.801s; 29 Pellino, 1m 41.265s; 30 Kuhne, 1m 41.792s; 31 Staring, 1m 41.896s; 32 Schouten, 1m 42.237s; 33 Sabbatani, 1m 42.563s; 34 Carchano, 1m 42.592s; 35 Rigoli, 1m 44.503s; 36 Esler, 1m 45.397s; 37 Simmonds, 1m 45.803s.

Fastest race laps: 1 Dovizioso, 1m 38.024s; 2 Borsoi, 1m 38.121s; 3 Lorenzo, 1m 38.240s; 4 Stoner, 1m 38.309s; 5 Locatelli, 1m 38.415s; 6 Jenkner, 1m 38.545s; 7 Giansanti, 1m 38.620s; 8 Bautista, 1m 38.626s; 9 Gadea, 1m 38.662s; 10 Barbera, 1m 38.675s; 11 Simon, 1m 38.765s; 12 Perugini, 1m 38.810s; 13 Corsi, 1m 38.893s; 14 Ballerini, 1m 38.925s; 15 Pesek, 1m 38.959s; 16 Lai, 1m 39.074s; 17 di Meglio, 1m 39.082s; 18 Luthi, 1m 39.143s; 19 Nieto, 1m 39.143s; 20 Talmacsi, 1m 39.156s; 21 Pellino, 1m 39.274s; 22 Pasini, 1m 39.288s; 23 M. Kallio, 1m 39.436s; 24 Zanetti, 1m 39.540s; 25 Toth, 1m 39.638s; 26 V. Kallio, 1m 39.875s; 27 Rodriguez, 1m 39.946s; 28 Giuseppetti, 1m 39.961s; 29 Sabbatani, 1m 41.186s; 30 Staring, 1m 41.443s; 31 Carchano, 1m 41.667s; 32 Schouten, 1m 41.834s; 33 Kuhne, 1m 42.063s; 34 Manna, 1m 42.434s.

World Championship: 1 Dovizioso, 273; 2 Locatelli, 182; 3 Lorenzo, 179; 4 Barbera, 177; 5 Stoner, 145; 6 Nieto, 125; 7 Jenkner, 116; 8 Bautista, 113; 9 Giansanti, 101; 10 M. Kallio, 86; 11 Simoncelli, 79; 12 Borsoi, 70; 13 Simon, 57; 14 Corsi, 53; 15 Lai, 52; 16 Pasini, 49; 17 di Meglio, 41; 18 Talmacsi, 36; 19 Ballerini, 29; 20 Pesek, 20; 21 Ui, 19; 22 Gadea, 18; 23 Pellino, 16; 24 Perugini, 14; 25 Luthi, 12; 26 Giuseppetti, 8; 27 Koyama and Kuzuhara, 7; 29 Toth, 6; 30 Harms, 5; 31 Carchano and Rodriguez, 2; 33 V. Kallio, 1.

FIM WORLD CHAMPIONSHIP • ROUND 16

VALENCIA GP

VALENCIA

Above: "I am standing up." Dorna's Carmelo Ezpeleta meets US basketball giant and MotoGP virgin Michael Jordan.

Left: Last race for Garry Taylor, whose career began with Barry Sheene.

Below: Biaggi and Tamada took the first two places in qualifying.

Bottom: Brothers Tommy and Roger Lee join Nicky Hayden on the grid.

Opposite: Rostrum-bound, Bayliss gave full value in his last ride for Ducati.

Photographs: Gold & Goose

THE championships all settled, this may once have seemed like one race too many. Indeed, that feeling was still there, but eclipsed by another of excitement and preparation for the 2005 series, such is the extent to which one season now overlaps the next.

This has been reinforced by the extended testing ban over the winter, and the need and desire of all to get going early with developments for 2005, be they new motorcycle parts – as in the case of Rossi – or changed team personnel – as in the case of his new team-mate for next year, Colin Edwards, as well as Ducati-bound Carlos Checa. The track was booked up for the week after the race, not only for press tests of the obsolete 2004 MotoGP machines, but also for the much more serious matter of next year's championship. And Edwards, unlike Rossi the year before, was to be released early by Honda for his new job with Yamaha – one advantage to being at the back of their minds.

Still, this race had to be got out of the way first, and it was accomplished in an end-of-term atmosphere that was heightened by the arrival of the biggest sporting star yet to visit a MotoGP – US basketball legend Michael Jordan. An amiable giant, Jordan is a genuine enthusiast, to the extent of declining a ride on the two-seater Ducati behind Randy Mamola in favour of riding it himself. He circulated after qualifying along with Sete Gibernau and most of the American riders: Kurtis Roberts and Colin Edwards on their GP machines, and Kenny Roberts Jr. on a hastily borrowed street Suzuki GSX-R1000. The lap time was certainly slow enough, with the professionals whizzing either side of the star on their back wheels often as not, but Jordan rode neatly and with some spirit, and the first to congratulate him was Dorna CEO Carmelo Ezpeleta. No wonder... the American had just got wider publicity for MotoGP in a few minutes than Valentino Rossi had in an entire season.

Both Roberts boys were back for a last stab at 2004, but neither made the race. Kenny was there, as much as anything, for Suzuki team manager Garry Taylor – the longest-serving manager in the paddock, whose tenure with the team goes back to the days of double champion Barry Sheene in the mid-Seventies. He ran the first untimed session, fitting a qualifying tyre to record the fastest time, then pulled out, handing his bike to the waiting Lavilla, his arm still not strong enough to cope with the heavy braking of this excessively tortuous circuit. Kurtis lasted a day longer before his wrist gave out, bringing his last Proton ride to a premature end.

Bayliss was lining up for his last Ducati ride, and also intent on a blaze of glory, handsomely outqualifying and out-racing Capirossi to claim his first rostrum of the season. Ironically enough, the sacked rider had finally been allowed to try the latest forks he had been asking for almost all year, after the last round in Australia. They transformed the feel. "It's like a new bike," he enthused. It had come a little late for him, but his reputation had obviously survived, because now news broke that he had an even better choice available to him than Kawasaki in the form of a Camel Honda on Sito Pons's team, in place of factory-bound Max Biaggi. Any prospective employers must have been impressed to see him give full value to his previous one.

Not so John Hopkins, who finally signed with Suzuki, but whose hopes of giving Taylor a good result as a farewell came to nothing, scuppered by Bridgestones that clearly didn't suit the track, at least not on the down-on-power Suzuki, which relies on corner speed to make up the deficit.

Some were preparing for their last GP, and not all unwillingly – one such was Neil Hodgson, whose year with the d'Antin team had been a nightmare of poor machines and preparation, hampered all the way by a lack of communication with the very Spanish team. "When people used to say it wasn't just the rider but the team as well, I wasn't so sure as I am now," he said.

The futures of both Aprilia and Proton teams were in serious jeopardy, leaving their riders in limbo for the time being.

The Hayden family were present in strength, with both of Nicky's AMA racing brothers, Tommy and Roger Lee, joining father Earl for the last race. However. the Kentucky family had the misfortune to be robbed at the huge shopping mall near the track, leaving Nicky "with only the clothes on his back", as well as minus lap top, camera, iPod and all their passports. Getting new ones from US officials intent on high war-footing security eventually required a trip to Madrid, some 200 miles away. They took a taxi there and back, the driver offering a special price after recognising Nicky from the Repsol billboards displaying his face.

The victorious Rossi, meanwhile, was understandably jubilant. "The finish of the season was perfect for us – three in a row. Today was harder for me than Sepang and Phillip Island, because for me this track is difficult. I was scared with Tamada, because he had great grip... but then he slowed down. After that, Biaggi was very strong. I needed to push 100 percent to the end," he said.

"This year has been unforgettable for me, my team and Yamaha. I think we all did a great job. Next year Honda will want to come back stronger, but I think we will also be more strong. We have some data now. We are not starting from zero," he added.

Honda tied up the constructors' title in MotoGP and 250 classes – in 125s it went to Aprilia; the MotoGP team prize went to Rossi and Checa in spite of the latter's uninspired overall results, but just seven points from the privateer Gresini Honda team of Gibernau and Edwards. The factory Honda team was fourth, behind also Camel Honda.

Above: Tamada made the early running, but Rossi was ready to take over.

Top right: McCoy (24) and Hodgson dispute the final point of the year.

Centre right: Below: The Rossi fan club went home happy.

Bottom right: End of the road: long-term V5 rider Nobu Aoki takes the Proton to its final race finish.

MOTOGP RACE – 30 laps

For a second successive race, times were slower than the previous year, though once again very close with 13 qualifying within the space of one second. Race and lap records would remain unbroken as well at a track where surface grip had deteriorated in cool temperatures.

Tamada was on pole, for the third time in six races, with fellow Camel rider Biaggi only narrowly missing out, pushing Rossi to the far end of the first row, and Gibernau onto row two.

The yellow Hondas led away with Tamada shoving past Biaggi into Turn One. Aware that his tyres would deteriorate, the Japanese rider tried to break away. More than a second clear after two laps, he now had Gibernau in second, followed by Biaggi, Rossi and Hayden, with Bayliss dropping to the back of the group.

The next development came on lap three, when Biaggi took Gibernau, only to be almost brought down as the Spaniard came steaming back up the inside too fast to make the turn. This gifted second and third to Rossi and Hayden – the pair now closing steadily on Tamada – though Rossi's Yamaha was visibly slower onto the winding track's long straight.

Rossi took the lead on lap six. But two laps later Tamada used his speed to line up to outbrake him at Turn One to lead for seven more laps. However, Rossi retaliated, finding a way past again at the Esses on lap 15.

Biaggi, finally past Gibernau, caught the leaders and passed Hayden by half distance. Then on lap 17 Tamada had a big slide onto the straight, and both Biaggi and Hayden went by him – his time up front was over, and Rossi started to stretch his narrow advantage.

Gibernau, more than three seconds adrift, had his hands full with a charging Bayliss. The Ducati rider outbraked him at Turn One, and was the fastest man on the track as he consumed the gap. By lap 17 he took fourth off Tamada, and was hounding Hayden when the American was caught out under braking for the first corner, almost hitting Biaggi, running wide, and dropping behind Tamada again. Shortly afterwards, trying to regain ground, he lost the front on a left-hander, failing to save it with his still weak knee, and he was out.

Biaggi closed to within a second of Rossi as they started the last lap, but Rossi comfortably retained a narrow advantage to the flag for a ninth win of the year, equalling his tally of last year.

While Gibernau's hard tyre choice was finally coming good Tamada was struggling, and the Spaniard took fourth with three laps to go, too far behind Bayliss to improve any further. The Australian took a first rostrum of the year with his last ride for Ducati.

Tamada finished almost two seconds down; seven seconds later came Barros, cutting steadily through the crowd after finishing the first lap 14th. The rest were more or less evenly spaced out – Nakano comfortably clear of a wheelspinning Edwards. Capirossi passed Abe with five laps left. Hofmann was well down, after passing Hopkins, who was again kept honest by McWilliams.

Checa was seventh when he fell on lap eight, rejoining to work his way up from 20th to 14th, passing Hodgson with four laps to go. The Superbike champion has been between a scrapping Lavilla and McCoy, but escaped with Checa. Aoki was a lap down, with Ellison's WCM even further behind.

Xaus had a spectacular crash after 11 laps, lying in 13th. By then Melandri had crashed out yet again, in what was probably his last Yamaha ride. Jacque pitted the Moriwaki.

CAMEL

Above: Chaz Davies ended his year with a best-ever fifth.

Top: Pedrosa heads de Angelis, de Puniet, Elias and Aoyama, shortly before the second-placed rider crashed.

Below right: Spanish teenagers: Bautista (left) celebrates his fourth rostrum of the year with winner Barbera.

Photographs: Gold & Goose

250 cc RACE – 27 laps

Another triumph for Pedrosa was aided by two crashes. The first, on the fourth lap, took out one pursuer and did for two others; the second spiked a strong challenge from Porto. It was de Angelis who fell first, right in front of Elias, who only just managed to find his way between the sliding bike and rider, while de Puniet was also put off the track and out of contention for the lead.

Pedrosa had bounced back from a final-session crash to take pole from Porto, de Angelis and de Puniet, with Elias in familiar position heading row two.

Porto was first away, he and Pedrosa already gaining a little gap from de Angelis, de Puniet, Elias and Aoyama. When de Angelis fell, at the exit of Turn Two on lap four, that gap stretched to almost five seconds; Aoyama inheriting third ahead of Elias and de Puniet dropping to sixth behind Battaini.

Up front, Pedrosa shadowed the Aprilia, diving underneath at the third corner on lap 11. Porto took him again on the exit. Later that same lap Pedrosa did it again and started to stretch away gradually. After eight more laps the gap was more than two seconds as Porto proved how hard he was trying, losing the front and going flying.

This left Pedrosa with a lead of some 15 seconds, and he was able to nurse his tyres over the rest of the race, wave to the crowd on the final lap, and still win his seventh race of the year comfortably.

Further down the field, Aoyama and Elias had been disputing third. The Spaniard quickly pulled back ahead, but Aoyama regained the place and fended off every one of Elias's frequent attacks – he did get ahead, but never for long. With three laps to go, he did make it for good, pulling out a margin by the finish. But it hardly mattered. After the race, Aoyama's bike was found to be 500 grams – just over a pound – under the weight limit, and he was disqualified.

De Puniet was next; never back in touch, but defeating Battaini.

Once again, Davies was the other hero of the afternoon. He qualified tenth but finished the first lap 18th. After five he was up to 11th and starting work on his faster rivals; first Faubel, then Rolfo, and then Nieto. He closed on the factory rider, got past with five laps to go, and managed to keep him behind over the line. Rolfo followed, then came Matsudo ahead of Faubel.

Poggiali's dismal title defence ended with another crash, on the second lap. Debon and Guintoli also crashed out.

125 cc RACE – 24 laps

A crop of youngsters faced their last 125 race – Dovizioso, Lorenzo, Stoner and Barbera all moving up to 250s next year. Some older riders – Giansanti, Jenkner, Borsoi, Sabbatani and Ballerini – were also coming to the end, over next year's age limit of 28.

Dovizioso took pole from Barbera, Lorenzo and Borsoi, with Stoner on row two.

Borsoi led away, making the most of his last run to lead two laps, with Dovizioso second. On lap three both he and Barbera outbraked Borsoi into Turn One, with Lorenzo also ahead at the end of that lap and Stoner and Bautista leading the pursuing pack.

Barbera took the lead on lap four, setting a cracking pace. Three laps later Dovizioso had a massive slide, narrowly recovering to rejoin in 12th. This gave Barbera a gap of almost a second, which stretched to more than two as Borsoi and Lorenzo scrapped back and forth for second.

Lorenzo got clear on lap 11, and he was working on the interval to some effect when he slipped off three laps later, leaving the home-town hero a clear run to his fourth win of the year.

Gadea took over second for a spell, but his teammate Nieto and Locatelli were coming through as the field spread out. Dovizioso was also back up to eighth by half distance. By the final lap Dovizioso was in front of them all, with Bautista chasing hard followed by Nieto and Gadea, Locatelli dropping back behind.

Stoner had dropped back to ninth, struggling to keep the pace, when he crashed out on lap 15.

Barbera's win moved him to second overall, overtaking erstwhile title challenger Locatelli; Lorenzo stayed fourth in spite of no score.

FIM WORLD CHAMPIONSHIP • ROUND 16

MARLBORO VALENCIA grand prix

31 OCTOBER 2004

CIRCUITO DE LA COMUNITAT VALENCIANA

CIRCUIT LENGTH: 2.489 miles/4.005 km

MotoGP

30 laps, 74.670 miles/120.150 km

Pos.	Rider (Nat.)	No.	Machine	Laps	Time & speed
1	Valentino Rossi (I)	46	Yamaha	30	47m 16.145s 94.765 mph/ 152.509 km/h
2	Max Biaggi (I)	3	Honda	30	47m 16.570s
3	Troy Bayliss (AUS)	12	Ducati	30	47m 19.278s
4	Sete Gibernau (E)	15	Honda	30	47m 22.273s
5	Makoto Tamada (J)	6	Honda	30	47m 23.913s
6	Alex Barros (BR)	4	Honda	30	47m 30.820s
7	Shinya Nakano (J)	56	Kawasaki	30	47m 39.460s
8	Colin Edwards (USA)	45	Honda	30	47m 43.586s
9	Loris Capirossi (I)	65	Ducati	30	47m 45.548s
10	Norick Abe (J)	17	Yamaha	30	47m 47.682s
11	Alex Hofmann (D)	66	Kawasaki	30	47m 57.096s
12	John Hopkins (USA)	21	Suzuki	30	48m 18.159s
13	Jeremy McWilliams (GB)	99	Aprilia	30	48m 20.782s
14	Carlos Checa (E)	7	Yamaha	30	48m 24.187s
15	Neil Hodgson (GB)	50	Ducati	30	48m 25.509s
16	Garry McCoy (AUS)	24	Aprilia	30	48m 31.167s
17	Gregorio Lavilla (E)	32	Suzuki	30	48m 31.419s
18	Nobuatsu Aoki (J)	9	Proton KR	29	47m 35.559s
19	James Ellison (GB)	77	Harris WCM	29	47m 41.074s
	Olivier Jacque (F)	19	Moriwaki	24	DNF
	Nicky Hayden (USA)	69	Honda	22	DNF
	Chris Burns (GB)	35	Harris WCM	11	DNF
	Marco Melandri (I)	33	Yamaha	10	DNF
	Ruben Xaus (E)	11	Ducati	10	DNF
	Kurtis Roberts (USA)	80	Proton KR		DNS

Fastest lap: Biaggi, 1m 33.582s, 95.733 mph/154.068 km/h.

Lap record: Valentino Rossi, I (Honda), 1m 33.317s, 96.005 mph/154.505 km/h (2003).

Event best maximum speed: Bayliss, 199.5 mph/321.1 km/h (race).

Qualifying: 1 Tamada, 1m 32.815s; 2 Biaggi, 1m 32.831s; 3 Rossi, 1m 32.913s; 4 Gibernau, 1m 32.936s; 5 Hayden, 1m 32.999s; 6 Bayliss, 1m 33.083s; 7 Hopkins, 1m 33.422s; 8 Edwards, 1m 33.438s; 9 Checa, 1m 33.504s; 10 Nakano, 1m 33.557s; 11 Hofmann, 1m 33.723s; 12 Barros, 1m 33.773s; 13 Capirossi, 1m 33.781s; 14 McWilliams, 1m 34.104s; 15 Abe, 1m 34.175s; 16 Melandri, 1m 34.209s; 17 Xaus, 1m 34.280s; 18 Hodgson, 1m 34.602s; 19 Lavilla, 1m 34.974s; 20 McCoy, 1m 35.064s; 21 Aoki, 1m 35.082s; 22 Jacque, 1m 36.394s; 23 Ellison, 1m 37.143s; 24 Kurtis Roberts, 1m 37.922s; 25 Burns, 1m 38.661s.

Fastest race laps: 1 Biaggi, 1m 33.582s; 2 Rossi, 1m 33.641s; 3 Bayliss, 1m 33.790s; 4 Hayden, 1m 33.799s; 5 Tamada, 1m 33.854s; 6 Gibernau, 1m 33.855s; 7 Barros, 1m 34.093s; 8 Checa, 1m 34.335s; 9 Abe, 1m 34.398s; 10 Nakano, 1m 34.437s; 11 Xaus, 1m 34.462s; 12 Capirossi, 1m 34.474s; 13 Edwards, 1m 34.590s; 14 Melandri, 1m 34.656s; 15 Hofmann, 1m 35.003s; 16 Hopkins, 1m 35.144s; 17 McWilliams, 1m 35.498s; 18 Lavilla, 1m 35.523s; 19 McCoy, 1m 35.719s; 20 Hodgson, 1m 35.761s; 21 Aoki, 1m 36.799s; 22 Jacque, 1m 37.134s; 23 Ellison, 1m 37.307s; 24 Burns, 1m 38.435s.

Final MotoGP World Championship points: see page 148.

250 cc

27 laps, 67.203 miles/108.135 km

Pos.	Rider (Nat.)	No.	Machine	Laps	Time & speed
1	Daniel Pedrosa (E)	26	Honda	27	44m 10.176s 91.273 mph/ 146.890 km/h
2	Toni Elias (E)	24	Honda	27	44m 18.262s
3	Randy de Puniet (F)	7	Aprilia	27	44m 37.588s
4	Franco Battaini (I)	21	Aprilia	27	44m 41.796s
5	Chaz Davies (GB)	57	Aprilia	27	44m 44.235s
6	Fonsi Nieto (E)	10	Aprilia	27	44m 44.960s
7	Roberto Rolfo (I)	2	Honda	27	44m 50.528s
8	Naoki Matsudo (J)	8	Yamaha	27	44m 56.937s
9	Hector Faubel (E)	33	Aprilia	27	44m 56.946s
10	Alex Baldolini (I)	25	Aprilia	27	45m 08.411s
11	David de Gea (E)	52	Honda	27	45m 13.463s
12	Arnaud Vincent (F)	12	Aprilia	27	45m 15.791s
13	Jakub Smrz (CZ)	96	Honda	27	45m 16.200s
14	Alex Debon (E)	6	Honda	27	45m 17.034s
15	Joan Olive (E)	11	Aprilia	27	45m 21.018s
16	Alvaro Molina (E)	41	Aprilia	27	45m 24.122s
17	Johan Stigefelt (S)	16	Aprilia	27	45m 24.797s
18	Dirk Heidolf (D)	28	Aprilia	27	45m 25.279s
19	Radomil Rous (CZ)	43	Yamaha	27	45m 50.221s
20	Gregory Leblanc (F)	42	Aprilia	26	44m 54.950s
21	Hans Smees (NL)	75	Aprilia	26	45m 04.536s
22	Jarno Ronzoni (I)	63	Aprilia	26	45m 20.330s
	Sebastian Porto (ARG)	19	Aprilia	18	DNF
	Sylvain Guintoli (F)	50	Aprilia	18	DNF
	Frederik Watz (S)	64	Honda	17	DNF
	Taro Sekiguchi (J)	44	Yamaha	14	DNF
	Alex de Angelis (RSM)	51	Aprilia	3	DNF
	Manuel Poggiali (RSM)	54	Aprilia	1	DNF
	Hiroshi Aoyama (J)	73	Honda		DSQ*
	Hugo Marchand (F)	9	Aprilia		DNS
	Erwan Nigon (F)	36	Aprilia		DNS
	Gergo Talmacsi (H)	88	Yamaha		DNQ

*Rider disqualified due to bike weight irregularities.

Fastest lap: Pedrosa, 1m 36.957s, 92.401 mph/148.705 km/h.

Lap record: Shinya Nakano, J (Yamaha), 1m 36.398s, 92.937 mph/149.567 km/h (2000).

Event best maximum speed: Porto, 162.4 mph/261.4 km/h (race).

Qualifying: 1 Pedrosa, 1m 36.367s; 2 Porto, 1m 36.535s; 3 de Angelis, 1m 36.800s; 4 de Puniet, 1m 36.813s; 5 Elias, 1m 36.900s; 6 Battaini, 1m 37.071s; 7 Aoyama, 1m 37.123s; 8 Poggiali, 1m 37.307s; 9 Matsudo, 1m 37.446s; 10 Davies, 1m 37.461s; 11 Debon, 1m 37.482s; 12 de Gea, 1m 37.944s; 13 Faubel, 1m 38.184s; 14 Smrz, 1m 38.354s; 15 Olive, 1m 38.383s; 16 Nieto, 1m 38.541s; 17 Guintoli, 1m 38.684s; 18 Rolfo, 1m 38.688s; 19 Heidolf, 1m 38.916s; 20 Vincent, 1m 38.952s; 21 Baldolini, 1m 39.021s; 22 Marchand, 1m 39.590s; 23 Stigefelt, 1m 39.680s; 24 Sekiguchi, 1m 39.748s; 25 Nigon, 1m 39.905s; 26 Leblanc, 1m 40.043s; 27 Molina, 1m 40.329s; 28 Watz, 1m 40.384s; 29 Rous, 1m 40.712s; 30 Smees, 1m 40.916s; 31 Ronzoni, 1m 41.369s; 32 Talmacsi, 1m 43.375s.

Fastest race laps: 1 Pedrosa, 1m 36.957s; 2 Porto, 1m 37.042s; 3 Elias, 1m 37.232s; 4 de Angelis, 1m 37.235s; 5 de Puniet, 1m 37.340s; 6 Aoyama, 1m 37.582s; 7 Debon, 1m 38.206s; 8 Battaini, 1m 38.420s; 9 Davies, 1m 38.421s; 10 Nieto, 1m 38.696s; 11 Rolfo, 1m 38.856s; 12 Matsudo, 1m 38.979s; 13 Faubel, 1m 38.988s; 14 Baldolini, 1m 39.141s; 15 Guintoli, 1m 39.375s; 16 Heidolf, 1m 39.537s; 17 Vincent, 1m 39.659s; 18 Sekiguchi, 1m 39.671s; 19 Olive, 1m 39.690s; 20 de Gea, 1m 39.799s; 21 Smrz, 1m 39.800s; 22 Molina, 1m 39.825s; 23 Stigefelt, 1m 39.961s; 24 Watz, 1m 40.285s; 25 Rous, 1m 40.500s; 26 Leblanc, 1m 40.714s; 27 Ronzoni, 1m 41.938s; 28 Smees, 1m 42.159s; 29 Poggiali, 1m 48.017s.

Final 250 cc World Championship points: see page 149.

125 cc

24 laps, 59.736 miles/96.120 km

Pos.	Rider (Nat.)	No.	Machine	Laps	Time & speed
1	Hector Barbera (E)	3	Aprilia	24	40m 45.283s 87.930 mph/ 141.510 km/h
2	Andrea Dovizioso (I)	34	Honda	24	40m 46.044s
3	Alvaro Bautista (E)	19	Aprilia	24	40m 46.262s
4	Pablo Nieto (E)	22	Aprilia	24	40m 46.568s
5	Sergio Gadea (E)	33	Aprilia	24	40m 46.621s
6	Roberto Locatelli (I)	15	Aprilia	24	40m 48.991s
7	Gino Borsoi (I)	23	Aprilia	24	40m 54.065s
8	Simone Corsi (I)	24	Honda	24	40m 57.708s
9	Gabor Talmacsi (H)	14	Malaguti	24	40m 57.798s
10	Steve Jenkner (D)	21	Aprilia	24	41m 01.938s
11	Mattia Pasini (I)	54	Aprilia	24	41m 05.219s
12	Mirko Giansanti (I)	6	Aprilia	24	41m 05.359s
13	Julian Simon (E)	10	Honda	24	41m 05.410s
14	Thomas Luthi (CH)	12	Honda	24	41m 16.284s
15	Fabrizio Lai (I)	32	Gilera	24	41m 23.323s
16	Michaele Pirro (I)	37	Aprilia	24	41m 24.893s
17	Lorenzo Zanetti (I)	45	Aprilia	24	41m 25.234s
18	Michael Ranseder (A)	88	KTM	24	41m 31.167s
19	Julian Miralles (E)	70	Aprilia	24	41m 31.454s
20	Gioele Pellino (I)	42	Aprilia	24	41m 31.640s
21	Imre Toth (H)	25	Aprilia	24	41m 31.686s
22	Nicolas Terol (E)	59	Aprilia	24	41m 32.086s
23	Vesa Kallio (SF)	66	Aprilia	24	41m 41.819s
24	Aleix Espargaro (E)	57	Honda	24	41m 41.840s
25	Manuel Hernandez (E)	43	Aprilia	24	41m 45.214s
26	Enrique Jerez (E)	71	Honda	24	41m 47.474s
27	Jordi Carchano (E)	28	Aprilia	24	41m 47.567s
	Jorge Lorenzo (E)	48	Derbi	14	DNF
	Casey Stoner (AUS)	27	KTM	14	DNF
	Dario Giuseppetti (D)	26	Honda	9	DNF
	Raymond Schouten (NL)	16	Honda	6	DNF
	Mika Kallio (SF)	36	KTM	5	DNF
	Manuel Manna (I)	8	Malaguti	5	DNF
	Max Sabbatani (I)	31	Honda	2	DNF
	Lukas Pesek (CZ)	52	Honda	1	DNF
	Stefano Perugini (I)	7	Gilera	1	DNF
	Angel Rodriguez (E)	47	Derbi	0	DNF
	Andrea Ballerini (I)	50	Aprilia	0	DNF
	Marketa Janakova (CZ)	9	Honda		DNQ

Fastest lap: Nieto, 1m 40.581s, 89.072 mph/143.347 km/h.

Lap record: Steve Jenkner, D (Aprilia), 1m 40.252s, 89.364 mph/143.817 km/h (2002).

Event best maximum speed: Dovizioso, 140.4 mph/226.0 km/h (race).

Qualifying: 1 Dovizioso, 1m 39.927s; 2 Barbera, 1m 40.146s; 3 Lorenzo, 1m 40.413s; 4 Borsoi, 1m 40.461s; 5 Gadea, 1m 40.523s; 6 Stoner, 1m 40.562s; 7 Locatelli, 1m 40.571s; 8 Simon, 1m 40.662s; 9 Jenkner, 1m 40.726s; 10 Talmacsi, 1m 40.909s; 11 Bautista, 1m 40.971s; 12 Lai, 1m 41.023s; 13 Corsi, 1m 41.116s; 14 Nieto, 1m 41.333s; 15 Pasini, 1m 41.473s; 16 Pesek, 1m 41.487s; 17 Luthi, 1m 41.705s; 18 Ballerini, 1m 41.736s; 19 Giuseppetti, 1m 41.766s; 20 M. Kallio, 1m 41.881s; 21 Zanetti, 1m 42.229s; 22 Hernandez, 1m 42.236s; 23 Rodriguez, 1m 42.278s; 24 Terol, 1m 42.363s; 25 Giansanti, 1m 42.468s; 26 Toth, 1m 42.471s; 27 Perugini, 1m 42.508s; 28 Pirro, 1m 42.647s; 29 Espargaro, 1m 42.759s; 30 Manna, 1m 42.949s; 31 V. Kallio, 1m 43.019s; 32 Pellino, 1m 43.110s; 33 Miralles, 1m 43.444s; 34 Jerez, 1m 43.578s; 35 Carchano, 1m 43.594s; 36 Ranseder, 1m 43.620s; 37 Schouten, 1m 45.069s; 38 Sabbatani, 1m 45.161s; 39 Janakova, 1m 48.282s.

Fastest race laps: 1 Nieto, 1m 40.581s; 2 Barbera, 1m 40.730s; 3 Gadea, 1m 40.820s; 4 Dovizioso, 1m 40.841s; 5 Lorenzo, 1m 40.904s; 6 Locatelli, 1m 40.998s; 7 Bautista, 1m 41.096s; 8 Simon, 1m 41.107s; 9 Borsoi, 1m 41.187s; 10 Corsi, 1m 41.229s; 11 Jenkner, 1m 41.239s; 12 Stoner, 1m 41.369s; 13 Pasini, 1m 41.373s; 14 Talmacsi, 1m 41.386s; 15 Giansanti, 1m 41.668s; 16 Luthi, 1m 41.760s; 17 M. Kallio, 1m 41.854s; 18 Giuseppetti, 1m 42.101s; 19 Lai, 1m 42.124s; 20 Pirro, 1m 42.232s; 21 Ranseder, 1m 42.274s; 22 Zanetti, 1m 42.309s; 23 Hernandez, 1m 42.356s; 24 Toth, 1m 42.364s; 25 Pellino, 1m 42.370s; 26 Miralles, 1m 42.420s; 27 Terol, 1m 42.449s; 28 Espargaro, 1m 42.797s; 29 Carchano, 1m 42.891s; 30 V. Kallio, 1m 43.134s; 31 Jerez, 1m 43.200s; 32 Manna, 1m 44.704s; 33 Schouten, 1m 45.704s; 34 Sabbatani, 1m 47.410s.

Final 125 cc World Championship points: see page 149.

WORLD CHAMPIONSHIP POINTS 2004

MOTO GP

Position	Rider	Nationality	Machine	South Africa	Spain	France	Italy	Catalunya	Netherlands	Rio	Germany	Great Britain	Czech Repubic	Portugal	Japan	Qatar	Malaysia	Australia	Valencia	Points total
1	Valentino Rossi	I	Yamaha	25	13	13	25	25	25	-	13	25	20	25	20	-	25	25	25	304
2	Sete Gibernau	E	Honda	16	25	25	20	20	20	-	-	16	25	13	10	25	9	20	13	257
3	Max Biaggi	I	Honda	20	20	16	16	8	13	20	25	4	16	-	-	10	20	9	20	217
4	Alex Barros	BR	Honda	13	16	9	10	-	-	11	20	7	-	16	13	13	16	11	10	165
5	Colin Edwards	USA	Honda	9	9	11	4	11	10	10	11	20	9	7	-	20	5	13	8	157
6	Makoto Tamada	J	Honda	8	-	7	-	-	4	25	10	2	13	20	25	6	11	8	11	150
7	Carlos Checa	E	Yamaha	6	10	20	-	13	7	6	-	10	10	11	9	-	7	6	2	117
8	Nicky Hayden	USA	Honda	11	11	5	-	-	11	16	16	13	-	-	-	11	13	10	-	117
9	Loris Capirossi	I	Ducati	10	4	6	8	6	8	13	-	9	11	9	-	-	10	16	7	117
10	Shinya Nakano	J	Kawasaki	4	7	-	-	9	-	7	9	1	4	5	16	-	8	4	9	83
11	Ruben Xaus	E	Ducati	-	-	2	11	10	9	4	5	5	-	-	7	16	3	5	-	77
12	Marco Melandri	I	Yamaha	5	-	10	7	16	16	3	-	-	7	-	11	-	-	-	-	75
13	Norick Abe	J	Yamaha	7	5	-	9	7	5	8	-	-	8	6	-	9	4	-	6	74
14	Troy Bayliss	AUS	Ducati	2	-	8	13	-	-	-	-	11	-	8	-	-	6	7	16	71
15	Alex Hofmann	D	Kawasaki	-	3	-	2	5	3	5	6	-	3	3	6	7	-	3	5	51
16	John Hopkins	USA	Suzuki	3	1	-	-	-	2	1	7	8	-	10	-	8	-	1	4	45
17	Neil Hodgson	GB	Ducati	-	-	-	5	4	6	-	3	6	5	-	8	-	-	-	1	38
18	Kenny Roberts	USA	Suzuki	-	8	4	-	-	-	9	8	-	6	2	-	-	-	-	-	37
19	Jeremy McWilliams	GB	Aprilia	-	-	3	-	-	1	2	4	-	2	4	4	-	1	2	3	26
20	Shane Byrne	GB	Aprilia	1	-	-	6	3	-	-	2	3	-	-	3	-	-	-	-	18
21	Nobuatsu Aoki	J	Proton KR	-	2	-	3	1	-	-	-	-	1	1	2	-	-	-	-	10
22	Michel Fabrizio	I	Harris WCM	-	6	-	1	-	-	-	1	-	-	-	-	-	-	-	-	8
23	Yukio Kagayama	J	Suzuki	-	-	-	-	-	-	-	-	-	-	-	-	5	2	-	-	7
24	Olivier Jacque	F	Moriwaki	-	-	-	-	-	-	-	-	-	-	-	5	-	-	-	-	5
25	James Haydon	GB	Proton KR	-	-	-	-	-	-	-	-	-	-	-	-	4	-	-	-	4
26	James Ellison	GB	Harris WCM	-	-	-	-	-	-	-	-	-	-	-	-	3	-	-	-	3
27	Andrew Pitt	AUS	Moriwaki	-	-	-	-	2	-	-	-	-	-	-	-	-	-	-	-	2
28=	Kurtis Roberts	USA	Proton KR	-	-	1	-	-	-	-	-	-	-	-	-	-	-	-	-	1
28=	Youichi Ui	J	Harris WCM	-	-	-	-	-	-	-	-	-	-	-	1	-	-	-	-	1

Above: **Champions all. Dani Pedrosa, Valentino Rossi and Andrea Dovisioso**
Photograph: Gold & Goose

250 cc

Position	Rider	Nationality	Machine	South Africa	Spain	France	Italy	Catalunya	Netherlands	Rio	Germany	Great Britain	Czech Republic	Portugal	Japan	Qatar	Malaysia	Australia	Valencia	Points total
1	Daniel Pedrosa	E	Honda	25	-	25	20	20	20	20	25	25	16	13	25	20	25	13	25	317
2	Sebastian Porto	ARG	Aprilia	16	9	-	25	13	25	-	20	20	25	20	13	25	20	25	-	256
3	Randy de Puniet	F	Aprilia	20	20	20	13	25	13	8	11	16	20	16	5	-	11	-	16	214
4	Toni Elias	E	Honda	8	4	16	10	16	16	16	-	-	11	25	20	10	16	11	20	199
5	Alex de Angelis	RSM	Aprilia	11	10	11	8	-	11	13	16	13	-	11	10	-	13	20	-	147
6	Hiroshi Aoyama	J	Honda	5	-	13	7	10	6	10	13	7	9	7	16	16	-	9	-	128
7	Fonsi Nieto	E	Aprilia	9	16	9	11	11	8	11	8	11	-	-	-	11	9	-	10	124
8	Roberto Rolfo	I	Honda	7	25	-	9	-	7	9	10	-	10	6	9	9	-	6	9	116
9	Manuel Poggiali	RSM	Aprilia	13	-	-	16	-	9	25	-	-	7	9	-	-	-	16	-	95
10	Franco Battaini	I	Aprilia	6	-	8	4	6	-	6	7	9	-	4	7	13	10	-	13	93
11	Anthony West	AUS	Aprilia	-	13	10	6	7	10	-	9	10	13	10	-	-	-	-	-	88
12	Alex Debon	E	Honda	10	11	7	1	8	4	7	5	-	-	8	6	8	-	5	2	82
13	Chaz Davies	GB	Aprilia	-	-	4	-	3	1	3	4	-	8	-	-	-	7	10	11	51
14	Sylvain Guintoli	F	Aprilia	1	-	-	3	9	-	4	6	6	-	-	-	5	-	8	-	42
15	Naoki Matsudo	J	Yamaha	-	6	2	-	2	3	2	-	8	-	-	3	-	6	1	8	41
16	Hugo Marchand	F	Aprilia	-	3	-	-	-	-	5	-	3	4	-	2	7	8	4	-	36
17	Hector Faubel	E	Aprilia	4	-	3	2	-	-	-	-	-	6	5	1	-	3	-	7	31
18	Alex Baldolini	I	Aprilia	-	5	1	-	4	5	-	-	4	-	-	-	-	5	-	6	30
19	Joan Olive	E	Aprilia	-	-	6	5	-	-	-	3	5	1	-	-	6	-	-	1	27
20	Jakub Smrz	CZ	Honda	-	-	5	-	1	-	-	1	1	2	2	-	-	2	3	3	20
21	Arnaud Vincent	F	Aprilia	3	8	-	-	-	-	-	-	-	-	-	-	-	-	-	4	15
22	Johan Stigefelt	S	Aprilia	-	2	-	-	-	-	-	-	2	-	-	-	2	1	7	-	14
23	Dirk Heidolf	D	Aprilia	2	-	-	-	-	-	1	-	-	5	1	-	-	4	-	-	13
24	Eric Bataille	F	Honda	-	-	-	-	5	2	-	2	-	-	3	-	-	-	-	-	12
25	Yuki Takahashi	J	Honda	-	-	-	-	-	-	-	-	-	-	-	11	-	-	-	-	11
26	Shuhei Aoyama	J	Honda	-	-	-	-	-	-	-	-	-	-	-	8	-	-	-	-	8
27	David de Gea	E	Honda	-	-	-	-	-	-	-	-	-	-	-	-	1	-	2	5	8
28	Gregory Lefort	F	Aprilia	-	7	-	-	-	-	-	-	-	-	-	-	-	-	-	-	7
29=	Yuzo Fujioka	J	Honda	-	-	-	-	-	-	-	-	-	-	-	4	-	-	-	-	4
29=	Erwan Nigon	F	Aprilia	-	-	-	-	-	-	-	-	-	-	-	-	4	-	-	-	4
31	Taro Sekiguchi	J	Yamaha	-	1	-	-	-	-	-	-	-	-	-	-	3	-	-	-	4
32	Gregory Leblanc	F	Aprilia	-	-	-	-	-	-	-	-	-	3	-	-	-	-	-	-	3

125 cc

Position	Rider	Nationality	Machine	South Africa	Spain	France	Italy	Catalunya	Netherlands	Rio	Germany	Great Britain	Czech Republic	Portugal	Japan	Qatar	Malaysia	Australia	Valencia	Points total
1	Andrea Dovizioso	1	Honda	25	13	25	13	20	13	16	13	25	20	-	25	20	20	25	20	293
2	Hector Barbera	E	Aprilia	6	16	11	16	25	10	25	20	-	9	25	-	4	-	10	25	202
3	Roberto Locatelli	I	Aprilia	20	8	20	25	-	20	13	25	-	16	7	2	-	13	13	10	192
4	Jorge Lorenzo	E	Derbi	-	-	16	6	11	25	-	10	16	25	16	9	25	-	20	-	179
5	Casey Stoner	AUS	KTM	16	11	8	20	13	16	20	-	-	-	-	-	-	25	16	-	145
6	Pablo Nieto	E	Aprilia	13	7	9	10	16	8	9	16	-	13	13	-	10	-	1	13	138
7	Alvaro Bautista	E	Aprilia	7	-	7	-	10	-	7	9	20	3	11	-	16	16	7	16	129
8	Steve Jenkner	D	Aprilia	8	20	6	9	4	11	-	5	10	10	-	11	5	6	11	6	122
9	Mirko Giansanti	I	Aprilia	9	6	13	11	6	7	11	8	-	8	-	13	6	-	3	4	105
10	Mika Kallio	SF	KTM	4	-	10	-	7	-	8	11	13	-	20	-	13	-	-	-	86
11	Marco Simoncelli	I	Aprilia	-	25	-	-	9	9	10	6	-	-	10	10	-	-	-	-	79
12	Gino Borsoi	I	Aprilia	10	-	5	7	-	-	-	-	7	11	1	5	8	7	9	9	79
13	Simone Corsi	I	Honda	2	4	1	5	-	-	3	4	11	7	-	16	-	-	-	8	61
14	Julian Simon	E	Honda	5	5	3	-	2	-	2	7	8	6	-	-	9	10	-	3	60
15	Mattia Pasini	I	Aprilia	3	-	4	8	5	5	6	-	-	2	-	-	7	9	-	5	54
16	Fabrizio Lai	I	Gilera	-	3	-	-	-	-	-	-	2	1	4	20	11	11	-	1	53
17	Gabor Talmacsi	H	Malaguti	-	-	-	3	-	-	-	-	3	-	9	8	-	8	5	7	43
18	Mike di Meglio	F	Aprilia	11	-	-	-	8	4	4	-	1	-	5	-	-	-	8	-	41
19	Sergio Gadea	E	Aprilia	-	-	-	-	-	-	-	2	-	-	3	3	-	4	6	11	29
20	Andrea Ballerini	I	Aprilia	-	10	-	4	-	-	5	-	-	4	-	-	2	2	2	-	29
21	Lukas Pesek	CZ	Honda	-	-	2	1	-	-	1	-	4	-	8	-	-	-	4	-	20
22	Youichi Ui	J	Aprilia	1	9	-	-	-	-	-	-	9	-	-	-	-	-	-	-	19
23	Gioele Pellino	I	Aprilia	-	-	-	-	3	3	-	3	6	-	-	-	1	-	-	-	16
24	Stefano Perugini	I	Gilera	-	-	-	-	-	2	-	1	5	-	6	-	-	-	-	-	14
25	Thomas Luthi	CH	Honda	-	-	-	-	-	-	-	-	-	-	-	4	3	5	-	2	14
26	Dario Giuseppetti	D	Honda	-	1	-	2	-	-	-	-	-	-	2	-	-	3	-	-	8
27	Tomoyoshi Koyama	J	Yamaha	-	-	-	-	-	-	-	-	-	-	-	7	-	-	-	-	7
28	Toshihisa Kuzuhara	J	Honda	-	-	-	-	-	-	-	-	-	-	-	6	-	1	-	-	7
29	Imre Toth	H	Aprilia	-	-	-	-	-	6	-	-	-	-	-	-	-	-	-	-	6
30	Robbin Harms	DK	Honda	-	-	-	-	-	-	-	-	-	5	-	-	-	-	-	-	5
31	Jordi Carchano	E	Aprilia	-	2	-	-	-	-	-	-	-	-	-	-	-	-	-	-	2
32	Angel Rodriguez	E	Derbi	-	-	-	-	1	1	-	-	-	-	-	-	-	-	-	-	2
33	Vesa Kallio	SF	Aprilia	-	-	-	-	-	-	-	-	-	-	-	1	-	-	-	-	1

WORLD SUPERBIKES REVIEW • By GORDON RITCHIE

HAPPY FAMILIES

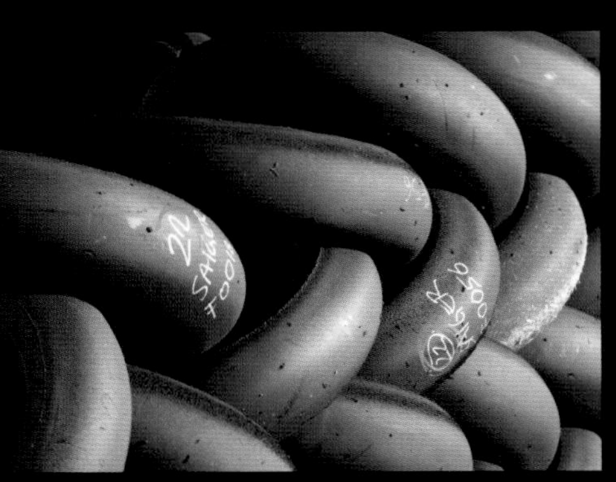

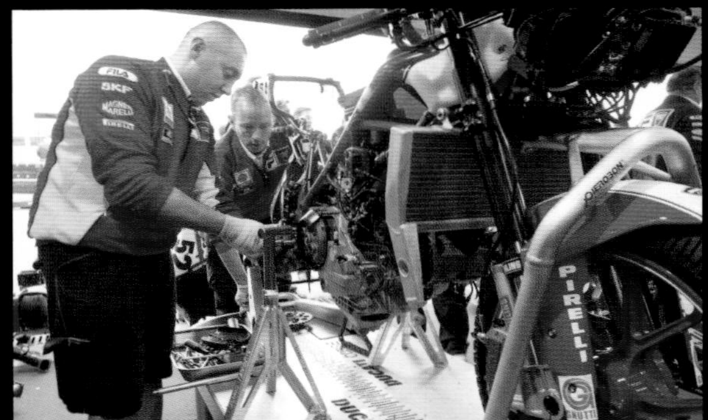

Above: Pirellis for all – the new rubber regime.

Above centre: Fila Ducati was the only official factory squad.

Above right: Paolo Flammini – a visionary after all?

Photographs: Gold & Goose

If controversy were a World Championship event the World Superbike series would simply disappear under its own haul of trophies.

This year was a classic example, as SBK risked and then ably survived suffocation by a combination its own brinksmanship and a removal of the oxygen of Japanese factory involvement.

Since its 1988 inception, steady motion in World Superbike's tectonic plates had evolved whole new continents and ever-higher plateaus, against a continual background rumble of aftershocks and occasional floodwaters at each new level of growth.

The advent of the four-stroke MotoGP class changed all of that for World Supers. Volcanic eruptions in politics, technical regulations and – most controversially – a single make Pirelli tyre initiative combined with an effective (or at least nominal) factory boycott for 2004 brought the other World Championship to what could be thought of as its lowest level for over ten years.

Nonetheless, against the gloomier predictions, two years of seeming freefall reached an end in 2004. The proof was multifaceted.

First: SBK's supposed self-inflicted wounds are looking more and more every day like a visionary realisation that lavish spending on factory efforts is now the sole preserve of MotoGP. If the price for SBK' s long haul survival and future growth is to take itself to a lower level of operations, then it's a sacrifice worth making.

Second: the single tyre supplier rule has, in the aforementioned circumstances at least, been the making of consistently close racing, with lavish tyre smoking and multi-rider battles. SBK 2004 was, whatever else, a spectacle in its own right, complete with a cliffhanging ending and two genuine title contenders in their early 20s - one ultimately crowned champ. Regeneration from within the SBK family, so to speak.

Last, and by no means least: the new technical rules have created the happy irony that just as the Japanese moved out *en masse,* the 1000cc four-cylinder machines immediately became the new heirs apparent. Little wonder that the Big Four are now queuing up to return, albeit via importer, dealer and private teams.

Left: The World Superbike teams pose before the opening round at Valencia.

Below: Pirelli's Ugo Former.

Bottom: Close racing was the consequence of controversial changes – here veteran Pier-Francesco Chili leads Laconi.

Photographs: Gold & Goose

SUOMY
FILA
52
FILA
DUCATI 999
FILA
FILA
PIRELLI
DATACOL
ADVANCE
CM composit
PIRELLI
PIRELLI
PIRELLI
SKF
brembo
CHAMPION

NEW AND IMPROVED

UNLIKE MotoGP, World Superbike seems to produce more than its fair share of champions who have had to stage a major recovery or two during their careers. History repeated itself this year, as James Toseland joined the likes of Colin Edwards (2000 and 2002), Neil Hodgson (2003) and maybe even John Kocinski (1997) as riders who have merited ultimate SBK honours after some heavy knocks and reversals.

How can this be so for Toseland, when he is the youngest rider ever to have won the full SBK crown? Well, despite taking the title two days shy of his 24th birthday, Toseland has been through a number of harsh racing mills, been physically and emotionally bruised, both on and off track, and yet has always bounced back harder, faster and smarter than ever.

Toseland has arguably taken the title at such an age partly because – and especially for a British rider – he started early on tarmac. Winning the Junior Road Racing Series in 1995 but making no particular mark on the self-explanatory Superteens series one year later, Toseland went racing in the one make Honda CB500 Cup in the UK in 1997, under the experienced eye of a fellow Sheffield native, Mick Corrigan.

Nothing less than domination ensued and soon enough he entered arguably the toughest British Championship class of all - Supersport. On a CBR600 Honda he secured four wins in eight outings, crashed while leading two others, finished third overall, and was snapped up by Castrol Honda's fledgling Supersport squad for 1998 and 1999.

It proved to be one long, agonising trial for JT, riding bewilderingly uncompetitive bikes in a cut-throat class, finishing 18th in year one, enduring the death of his team-mate Michael Paquay in '98 and suffering severe fractures to both ankles in a racing smash. Without a guiding fatherly hand this was a lot for a teenage lad to handle.

Back to the UK Scene on a VTR1000 in 2000, James was to ride yet another not-quite competitive Honda, suffering the agonising setback of a broken femur at mid-season.

Seeing the talent and grit that lay beneath this so far troubled race career, and seeing through his image in some quarters as a piano-playing oddity, the GSE team inducted James into the World Superbike paddock, on 998RS machines in 2001 and 2002. Even better 998F02 twins came around in 2003, and he duly finished third, behind only the factory 999s of Hodgson and Xaus, while he also took his first race win.

A sometimes seriously unconvincing 2004 season, with Laconi frequently showing him up, was put to rest over the final three rounds. Toseland, who had been desperate for a test to perform some iron horse-whispering to his uncooperative works bike, finally found a righteous set-up at Mugello, post Brands. Marrying that to a seriously dedicated physical and mental approach to training and preparation, King James was rock solid in all the last jousts.

His record of two wins, three seconds and a third was enough to give him a one-time improbable title. The fact that he made the biggest mark of all in front of his team-mate and rival Laconi's home crowd, reversing the Frenchman's points advantage under intense pressure, showed that Toseland may be a slower learner than some, but a surer learner than most.

How else do you suffer so many setbacks and still manage to be the youngest ever SBK champion, after the most evenly matched year on record?

2004 TEAMS AND RIDERS

gerrit ten kate

davide tardozzii

carl fogarty

james toseland

garry mccoy

leon haslam

noriyuki haga

chris walker

pierfrancesco chili

steve martin

troy corser

Photographs: Gold & Goose

Below: Top-level Ducati debate, as big boss Claudio Domenicali joins Toseland and crew.
Photograph: Gold & Goose

regis laconi

chris vermeulen

Fila Ducati

The combined talents of James Toseland (23) and Regis Laconi (29) were garnered by Ducati Corse racing Director Paolo Ciabatti and Team Manager Davide Tardozzi. The management's simple precept was that with Hodgson and Xaus off to MotoGP, they should get 2003's third and fourth placed riders on their side.

It wasn't too hard to persuade them, as each was a Ducati rider anyway, and the only two factory saddles of note in SBK were being offered. Toseland brought a mechanic with him from his defunct GSE team, but the swap to Pirellis was a serious challenge for the whole squad. Nonetheless, the Fila team finished 1-2, even if it was a damn close run thing.

Renegade Ducati Koji

Noriyuki Haga (29) and Leon Haslam (21) both felt the benefit of Ducati's decision to make the first release of the customer 999RS machines so close to the factory bike spec. Team owner Mark Griffiths had an outstanding first taste of World Superbike, winning at the first round. He also had a big bill to pay to keep the avaricious 999s in parts and loving care, the spanner work taken care of by his Anglo-Japanese crew. Koji was a late season sponsorship package that confused many, but was a welcome splash of colour thanks to an urban graffiti theme.

Ten Kate Honda

Rookies of the year, without question, as all three main parts of the equation – bike, rider and team – were new to World Superbike. The general pedigree was also unquestioned with Chris Vermeulen (22), the reigning Supersport championship, the CBR1000RR proving very race-ready, and Ten Kate's experience at making faster Hondas than the factory.

The status of the team was non-factory in terms of equipment and Japanese blessing. Supported by Honda Europe of course, but otherwise largely ignored by HRC and Honda in general. Results would dictate that they could not be ignored for long.

PSG1 Ducati

The oldest rider in the pack Pierfrancesco Chili (40) was largely a one-man band again this year, but after adopting a 998 baseline his 999RS went begging, and the odd race was completed with Giancarlo De Matteis (35).

A semi-acrimonious fall out underlined the year, when the team announced that they would be running Kawasakis in 2005, a decision from which Chili felt he had been excluded.

DFX Ducati Sterilgarda Extreme

Steve Martin (35) and Marco Borciani (28) were back again, but on privateer 999RS machines. Almost as much as the Renegade team, the DFX squad showed what the levelling of the tyres could do for a privateer squad. Martin drafted in former SBK race winner Peter Goddard to apply his analytical mind and experience to improve set-up and reliability but mid-season injury put Martin down the order from what many thought was his natural position.

DeCecco Racing

Giovanni Bussei (32), somewhat unimpressed with his SL Racing Ducati 749R in Supersport, left the class and enlisted the assistance of experienced race engineer Nando DeCecco's team, in Superbike - the same DeCecco who helped look after the factory Aprilias in 1999.

Some serious highpoints - sixth in Brands race two - proved that Bussei has talent under the beard, and that the 998RS was not quite finished yet.

Scuderia Caracchi Xerox Ducati

A big step up in sponsorship funds and personal fiscal commitment from boss Stefano Caracchi had two main effects. One was the adoption of Garry McCoy (32) into the squad; the other was the sponsor's choice of second rider, Miguel Praia (26).

On 999s, McCoy was to have some success, Praia was eventually relegated to the team's older 998s, and 2003 rider Davide Garcia (26) would be given a run out at Oschersleben and Silverstone. Ultimately, Gianluca Nannelli (31) came over to make a three-man team from Imola onwards.

Bertocchi Kawasaki

The only Kawasaki squad in the series once more had some fleeting highlights to remember, as Stefano Cruciani (25) lit up a wet and slippery Misano for a time, and Ivan Clementi (29) toiled away manfully, bouncing into the top ten a handful of times.

Team Pedercini Ducati

Mixing in World Superbike with the Italian Championship Lucio Pedercini (32) and Gianluca Nannelli (31) rode most of the year, until Nannelli headed off to the Caracchi squad and the warm embrace of a 999RS. This made way for Alessio Velini (25) to leave the Unionbike Yamaha team, to take over on the surprisingly competitive 998RS machines. Probably in their last year with Ducatis.

JM SBK Team

Hardy SBK annual that he is, Jiri Mrkykvka (30) returned with his impossibly compact team, and the usual seriously unreliable 998RS, only outperforming Miguel Praia in the SBK table.

MIR Racing Suzuki

Sergio Fuertes (25) was back again, once more at the controls of the big Suzuki, and other than the occasional ride from Davide Garcia, he was the only Spaniard in the SBK mix.

UnionBike Gi Motorsports Yamaha

In a year when other four-cylinder machines were to shine, Alessio Velini (25) found the R1 less than competitive. He rode a Pedercini Ducati in the final rounds of Imola and Magny Cours, leaving his R1 to Paolo Blora (35) in Imola and Polish privateer Teodor Myszkowski (31) at Magny-Cours.

Foggy Petronas Racing

Troy Corser (32) and Chris Walker (32) were this year's aspirants in the Foggy Petronas team, the latter the new boy in a new team for the fifth successive season. There were rewards, with podium finishes for each rider, and an outstanding brace of pole positions for Corser, at Oschersleben and Magny Cours.

The team swapped engine partners, to some measurable effect, but it was an uphill assault once more. Three years into a five-year contract, the Petronas team will be back in the mix in 2005.

Zongshen Suzuki

Old SBK hand Piergiorgio Bontempi (36) and World Endurance maestro Warwick Nowland (31) embarked on a new era for Chinese Motorsport, with the long term World Endurance squad stepping up to World Superbike. Running Suzukis, with absolutely zero Suzuki involvement, made this an unusual team for a whole host of reasons.

THE BIKES OF 2004

Ducati 999 F04

With one year of experience turning the 999F03 into a world championship-winner, the outside world felt that Ducati's 999F04 would be a much-improved beast. Despite the odd bhp here and weight saving mod there, plus detail changes inside the engine and 42mm gas-charged Öhlins forks as standard, the factory bike was not the usual heavy winter revamp. That was the official Ducati line at least, and it looked very much like it when the racing started.

Thus the 189bhp, 12,500rpm, 90° vee-twin featured a different design of Termignoni pipe, and a kilo less weight. The 104 x 58.8mm bore and stroke was shared with every other customer 999, and the F02/998RS of Chili.

Fuelled and ignited by a Magneti Marelli MF5 single injector per cylinder, the F04 proved finicky on the chassis side, and the seeming advantage of the gas forks was purely a financial consideration. If privateers wanted to buy them, then Öhlins would be delighted to sell them.

Gabriele Raccio tended James Toseland's bikes while Laconi's were looked after by Luigi Mitolo, with the technical side of things overseen by Ernesto Marinelli.

Ducati 999 RS04

So similar to the factory bike that you could hardly put a desmo shim between them, the 999RS was an expensive, exquisite but fickle way to win SBK races. It also proved to have key engine components with a relatively short life. Ducati claim to have warned their long client list to use only official parts and change them as directed, but there were numerous early and late mechanical retirements.

Certainly, at the first round, there seemed to be few enough cycle parts for the considerable numbers of riders who had opted to use Ducati's latest customer offering.

As Haga and co proved, the 999RS04 really was capable of winning, and as Haga himself frequently underlined, you did not have to even resort to the expensive add-on of gas-charged forks. He seldom used them, sticking most often with standard oil/air units.

Ducati 998RS

The 'old' 100 x 63.5mm bore and stroke of the 998RS limited the revs to 12,000 and power to around 180bhp – at best.

Used by the Pedercini, DeCecco and JM teams, the 998 was at least a known quantity, with much more available data and nicer track manners at speed than the flighty 999. Hence its occasional good showings, when few expected it.

PSG-1 Ducati 998 F02

Hating his 999RS from the outset, Chili's PSG-1 team commissioned Febur to make a 998-style single swingarm for it, to see if that improved things.

Desirous of the 999's outright power and higher revving engine, but needing the precise feel of the 998RS, what Chili really lusted after was the unobtainable – a 999F02, like those used by Bayliss in 2002 and the GSE boys in 2003.

His team then struck on the idea of buying one of the limited edition road bikes Ducati had to produce in order to meet homologation criteria. That engine had the same oversquare 104mm bore as the 999s, fitted into a legit 998F02 roadbike chassis. After all the mods allowed by the normal SBK technical rules, Chili had created what he liked to call a 998.5, basically a home brewed 998F02.

A captivating and wholly unexpected technical offshoot of the Ducati family tree.

Petronas FP-1

Back for another go with a revamped engine, the 889.5cc FP-1 went through two changes of background fettlers, as Ricardo Engineering became the new Petronas Engine Development Team, taking over from Suter Racing Technologies. At least three engine specs were the result in 2004. More power was found, 185 HP @ 13,500rpm, albeit at the crank, with a 14:1 compression ratio the highest in SBK.

Marelli DAS4 data acquisition took care of the data recording, and the seemingly ubiquitous Marelli supplied the 'MF4M' injection/ignition module. 55mm throttle bodies inside the airbox were fitted with double injectors, spitting fuel into the fire.

A gorgeously curvaceous 3:1:2:3 exhaust system featured serpent-head downpipes; flattened to improve throttle response and gas scavenging, without affecting the overall tuned length.

Transmission was via a dry SRT variable slipper clutch, operated hydraulically. Öhlins upside down fork 43mm forks kept the front end under control, but season-long chatter was only helped when Pirelli made a new construction of rear tyre, which was also taken up by the Bertocchi team.

Yamaha YZF1000R1

The uncompetitive 2004 UnionBike Gi Motorsport R1 was most noticeable by its perimeter braking system, supplied by the Braking company. With 12.8:1 compression ratio the bike produced a claimed 182 bhp at 11,500 rpm and the chassis featured a Yamaha France-designed swingarm.

Honda CBR1000RR

The universal Japanese Motorcycle came of age this year, as the 998cc, 73 x 56.5 mm Ten Kate Honda proved to be right on the Superbike pace, even without the loving mercies of HRC's factory backing - beyond regular race kit parts, of course.

In the early races the brand new bike, delivered only a scant few months before the season started, was no more than 80% towards being a full Superbike spec article. And yet right away the Fireblade had proved adept, with only mild tuning and small chassis changes.

The bike just got better as the year went on, breathing in through an HRC kit PGM - DSFI electronic fuel injection system and out via a (regularly modified) Arrow underseat exhaust.

WP Suspension graced the front and rear, even if standard fork outers were used right at the beginning. SBS brakepads gripped Braking disc rotors at season end. Depending on the track and set-up time, a standard clutch, with uprated plates and springs, usurped the STM slipper clutch.

As the year progressed the 200bhp engine output figure was gradually increased, with most of the benefits coming in rideability, and tweaking the power curve circuit to circuit.

Another impressive Superbike class rookie.

Kawasaki ZX-10

The most radical of the new clutch of litre streetbikes, in feel and ferocity at least, the ZX-10 proved itself adept in many aspects, and with a Toseland or Corser on board, may have proved even more successful.

Running the usual Bitubo suspension equipment the Bertocchi team is so fond of, the ZX-10 ploughed a lone technical path in that regard. Nonetheless, with assistance from the British Hawk Racing squad, and unofficial advice from Christian Bourgeois, the Bertocchi bike was not as alone as it seemed. The Zongshen team even ran a single ZX-10 for two races, allowing Stephane Duterne a bite at SBK racing.

Suzuki GSX-R1000

The 73 x 59mm bore and stroke of the Suzuki was, like all other four cylinder machines, unfettered by any intake restrictors, and thus it was theoretically capable of over 200bhp. The MIR Suzuki team were supposedly on ex-BSB Crescent Suzuki machines, the Zongshen Suzukis running lots of Yoshimura kit, with their engines tended by the French-based Akira technologies.

Top left: **Ten Kate Honda – fast out of the box.**

Top right: **New Kawasaki ZX10 – a lone presence.**

Above left: **Zongshen Suzuki – China's first team.**

Above right: **Team Caracchi's 999 Ducati.**

Left and opposite page: **The factory 999 Ducati, open and closed.**

Bottom left: **Chili ran hybrid 998/999 Ducatis with many variations. This is mainly 998.**

Bottom right: **Petronas FP1, upgraded in its third year.**

Photographs: Gold & Goose

Round 1
VALENCIA, Spain

29 February 2004, 2.489-mile/4.005-km km circuit

Race 1 23 laps, 57.247 miles/92.115 km

Pl.	Name Nat.(Machine)	No.	Time & gap	Laps
1	James Toseland, GB (Ducati)	52	42m 39.266s	23
			80.514 mph/129.574 km/h	
2	Pierfrancesco Chili, I (Ducati)	7	4.698s	23
3	Chris Walker, GB (Petronas)	9	22.109s	23
4	Marco Borciani, I (Ducati)	20	53.304s	23
5	Leon Haslam, GB (Ducati)	91	1m 02.286s	23
6	Gianluca Nannelli, I (Ducati)	69	1m 11.269s	23
7	Garry McCoy, AUS (Ducati)	24	1m 25.257s	23
8	Sergio Fuertes, E (Suzuki)	16	1m 26.590s	23
9	Horst Saiger, A (Yamaha)	22	1 lap	22
10	Jiri Mrkyvka, CZ (Ducati)	23	1 lap	22
11	Warwick Nowland, AUS (Suzuki)	12	1 lap	22
12	Chris Vermeulen, AUS (Honda)	17	1 lap	22
13	Miguel Praia, P (Ducati)	50	1 lap	22
14	Mauro Sanchini, I (Kawasaki)	6	3 laps	20
15	Piergiorgio Bontempi, I (Suzuki)	5	3 laps	20

DNF: Steve Martin, AUS (Ducati) 99, 21 laps; Ivan Clementi, I (Kawasaki) 8, 6 laps; Noriyuki Haga, J (Ducati) 41, 5 laps; Lucio Pedercini, I (Ducati) 19, 4 laps; Alessio Velini, I (Yamaha) 25, 3 laps; Troy Corser, AUS (Petronas) 4, 2 laps; Regis Laconi, F (Ducati) 55, 0 laps.

Fastest lap: McCoy, 1m 43.323s, 86.708 mph/139.543 km/h.

Race 2 23 laps, 57.247 miles/92.115 km

Pl.	Name Nat.(Machine)	No.	Time & gap	Laps
1	Noriyuki Haga, J (Ducati)	41	37m 32.364s	23
			91.484 mph/147.229 km/h	
2	James Toseland, GB (Ducati)	52	1.769s	23
3	Steve Martin, AUS (Ducati)	99	10.021s	23
4	Pierfrancesco Chili, I (Ducati)	7	10.138s	23
5	Chris Vermeulen, AUS (Honda)	17	17.067s	23
6	Garry McCoy, AUS (Ducati)	24	21.140s	23
7	Chris Walker, GB (Petronas)	9	21.584s	23
8	Marco Borciani, I (Ducati)	20	21.626s	23
9	Leon Haslam, GB (Ducati)	91	33.387s	23
10	Mauro Sanchini, I (Kawasaki)	6	33.537s	23
11	Troy Corser, AUS (Petronas)	4	36.556s	23
12	Sergio Fuertes, E (Suzuki)	16	40.458s	23
13	Lucio Pedercini, I (Ducati)	19	43.819s	23
14	Ivan Clementi, I (Kawasaki)	8	46.515s	23
15	Horst Saiger, A (Yamaha)	22	57.694s	23
16	Piergiorgio Bontempi, I (Suzuki)	5	1m 03.975s	23
17	Warwick Nowland, AUS (Suzuki)	12	1m 06.674s	23
18	Alessio Velini, I (Yamaha)	25	1m 09.952s	23
19	Miguel Praia, P (Ducati)	50	1 lap	22

DNF: Jiri Mrkyvka, CZ (Ducati) 23, 1 lap; Gianluca Nannelli, I (Ducati) 69, 0 laps; Regis Laconi, F (Ducati) 55, 0 laps.

Fastest lap: Haga, 1m 36.763s, 92.586 mph/149.003 km/h.

Superpole: Laconi, 1m 35.935s, 93.385 mph/150.289 km/h.

Lap record: Neil Hodgson, GB (Ducati), 1m 35.007s, 94.297 mph/151.757 km/h (2003).

Championship points: 1 Toseland, 45; 2 Chili, 33; 3 Haga and Walker, 25; 5 Borciani, 21; 6 McCoy, 19; 7 Haslam, 18; 8 Martin, 16; 9 Vermeulen, 15; 10 Fuertes, 12; 11 Nannelli, 10; 12 Saiger and Sanchini, 8; 14 Mrkyvka, 6; 15 Corser and Nowland, 5.

Top: Laconi takes a short-lived lead in the first race, as the season gets under way.

Above right: New Petronas rider Chris Walker gave them their first podium.

Above far right: Steve Martin retired from race one, but made sure of a top three in the second.

Photographs: Gold & Goose

VALENCIA

Late February was hellish early in the year to be starting a whole new era of World Superbike, and there were signs that several teams simply were not ready. A lack of spares for the 999s saw horse-trading in the paddock, a handlebar here for a footrest assembly there as the appetite for destruction proved as insatiable as ever.

Predictably, the factory Ducati Team (actually the only factory team) was the most prepared, despite a relative lack of testing time for new riders James Toseland and Regis Laconi. Laconi duly secured Superpole number one, the French/Italian rider on song to the tune of a second faster than his team-mate.

The Pirelli control tyres, with the same choices available to all, had an immediate effect. With lap times slower from earlier seasons, pre-race at least, the spec tyres seemed to do nothing to close the gap between the best factory bike rider and the rest.

There would indeed be a clear leader from the factory team on Sunday night, but it would not be Laconi. His race one crash and second race DNF, due to a chain jumping the sprockets, was a disaster of Alpine altitude for the Swiss resident. Before his luck changed, rain had suddenly appeared across the previously sunny Valencia on race morning, throwing tyre choice for race one right across the spectrum of available Pirellis.

Race Direction made a snap decision to hold a 15 minute wet session, postponing the Superstock race until later in the day, but no top riders dared venture out on what was already drying tarmac. Further ructions would come when the race was declared neither wet nor dry, and riders such as McCoy were up in arms at what they saw as an abdication of control on first day of school.

A cocktail of tyre solutions appeared for race one, plus another tyre-inspired controversy, when Ron Haslam was seen cutting his son Leon's front tyre by hand on the grid, a situation which, it was explained later, would not be tolerated again.

Laconi, starting a dismal day, fell in warm-up, restarted on his spare bike, and then promptly fell in the second corner of the race. On a bizarre and slick track surface, such little-known SBK entities as local boy Sergio Fuertes had a chance to lead, and rookie 998 rider Gianluca Nannelli (Pedercini Ducati) to threaten the podium places.

On the third lap of a contest which was as fascinating as it was incongruous, there were three riders abreast at one point, and during a rash move Corser crashed on the fast final corner as he tried to ride around the outside of Haga. Never an advisable move in the dry, but it showed Corser was at least there for more than the big bucks.

The Foggy Petronas team were nonetheless to get their first podium finish, as Chris Walker secured third when Steve Martin's bike blew up and Chili sailed home second, not bad on an old 998RS Ducati, with 17 bhp less than his new but unloved 999RS. With Toseland on an intermediate rear and having led for most of the race, he resisted the pressure of Martin and finally Chili (and even the return of the rain) to win the first 23-lapper by an almost easy 4.698 seconds, with Walker third.

Race two was the personal property of Haga, and indeed (with the exception of a missing Laconi, who lost his chain) the second outing was a relatively good flag up of how the first races would be conducted, with Toseland second, Martin a joyous third, and Chili fourth.

PHILLIP ISLAND

After Laconi took Superpole, it was surely a case of the same old/new faces, ready to hit the front come the races themselves

Laconi was indeed a big hit at Phillip Island, as he bounced onto the top podium step after race one, then bounced off down the track in race two. A folding front end for the Fila factory 999 fliers? *Quelle surprise.*

The opener was a virtual start-to-finish display of supremacy by Laconi, winner by over seven seconds. Behind him, it was a whole new story, as four riders battled away in the latter stages, finishing in the order Vermeulen, Toseland, Martin and McCoy. Martin was disappointed to finish just off the podium in race one, simply heart-broken after his battle for the lead in the follow up with eventual winner McCoy, came to naught. His bike expired in spectacular fashion with only three laps to go.

McCoy, former MotoGP race winner extraordinaire, finally found his feet, one for each cylinder, and gave the old NCR (now Xerox Scuderia Caracchi) Ducati team its first race win since the days of Doug Polen. McCoy's big rear end slides and charging pace (314kmph down the main straight!) were welcome in race two, but they may even have been eclipsed by the double second place finishes of Chris Vermeulen, and his Honda CBR1000RR, still largely a road bike. The yellow Ten Kate Fireblade had proved, in two weekends, what the often pilloried FGSport organisers had been trying to convince all of since day one; that their new technical rules, which had so riled the Japanese, really could put a potential race win your way for about $70,000 a bike, plus $45,000 a year for the same choice of rubber as anyone else. Unfancied Italian privateer Mauro Sanchini underlined it in light pencil with a pretty stock Bertocchi Kawasaki ZX-10, taking a sixth and the seventh.

After the first go at Valencia, the Pirelli experiment once more showed that even if the tyres could not match the pace of previous Dunlop and Michelin offerings, they could at least take the extremes of start-to-finish tail sliding meted out by McCoy, Vermeulen, Laconi and Toseland, with so much smoke produced that on occasions we were all convinced someone's engine must have blown. What we lost on the stopwatch, we gained on the spectacle.

PI brought about a bizarre sight, Pierfrancesco Chili on a 999RS with a 916-style single swingarm... a modification carried out with the intention of introducing some 998 feel to the 999's now notoriously sensitive yet remote front end. He was ninth on this set-up, behind a slowing Noriyuki Haga, the Japanese pilot having an invisible weekend, with eighth and sixth. Even with the hybrid 999 ditched in race two for the charms of his seriously outdated 998RS, with a less oversquare engine and a power deficit of almost 20bhp, the result was a third place for the old man on his old bike.

There have been faster races around PI, there have even been a few better ones, but there have seldom been such wide open and entertaining affairs as these, with quite so much demonstrable use of the throttle at key points of the track.

Four races into the season there were now four different winners, only one less than the whole of 2003, and almost double that of 2002, the classic Bayliss v Edwards face off.

The dynamics of the title charge were such that even though Toseland fell three times over the weekend, one of them in race two, he led the championship, from Chili.

Round 2
PHILLIP ISLAND, Australia
28 March 2004, 2.762-mile/ 4.445-km circuit

Race 1 22 laps, 60.764 miles/97.790 km

Pl.	Name Nat.(Machine)	No.	Time & gap	Laps
1	Regis Laconi, F (Ducati)	55	35m 04.598s	22
			103.939 mph/167.274 km/h	
2	Chris Vermeulen, AUS (Honda)	17	7.145s	22
3	James Toseland, GB (Ducati)	52	7.536s	22
4	Steve Martin, AUS (Ducati)	99	7.617s	22
5	Garry McCoy, AUS (Ducati)	24	7.808s	22
6	Mauro Sanchini, I (Kawasaki)	6	27.838s	22
7	Marco Borciani, I (Ducati)	20	27.924s	22
8	Noriyuki Haga, J (Ducati)	41	28.240s	22
9	Pierfrancesco Chili, I (Ducati)	7	36.040s	22
10	Chris Walker, GB (Petronas)	9	36.147s	22
11	Ivan Clementi, I (Kawasaki)	8	36.263s	22
12	Gianluca Nannelli, I (Ducati)	69	1m 02.542s	22
13	Troy Corser, AUS (Petronas)	4	1m 09.110s	22
14	Alessio Velini, I (Yamaha)	25	1m 23.898s	22
15	Warwick Nowland, AUS (Suzuki)	12	1 lap	21
16	Miguel Praia, P (Ducati)	50	1 lap	21

DNF: Sergio Fuertes, E (Suzuki) 16, 10 laps; Lucio Pedercini, I (Ducati) 19, 4 laps; Leon Haslam, GB (Ducati) 91, 0 laps.

NC: Piergiorgio Bontempi, I (Suzuki) 5, 6 laps.

DNS: Jiri Mrkyvka, CZ (Ducati) 23.

Fastest lap: Laconi, 1m 34.742s, 104.950 mph/168.901 km/h.

Race 2 22 laps, 60.764 miles/97.790 km

Pl.	Name Nat.(Machine)	No.	Time & gap	Laps
1	Garry McCoy, AUS (Ducati)	24	35m 10.023s	22
			103.672 mph/166.844 km/h	
2	Chris Vermeulen, AUS (Honda)	17	4.951s	22
3	Pierfrancesco Chili, I (Ducati)	7	6.439s	22
4	Marco Borciani, I (Ducati)	20	8.829s	22
5	Troy Corser, AUS (Petronas)	4	11.824s	22
6	Noriyuki Haga, J (Ducati)	41	12.223s	22
7	Mauro Sanchini, I (Kawasaki)	6	19.236s	22
8	Chris Walker, GB (Petronas)	9	19.323s	22
9	Ivan Clementi, I (Kawasaki)	8	19.478s	22
10	Leon Haslam, GB (Ducati)	91	35.352s	22
11	Piergiorgio Bontempi, I (Suzuki)	5	35.709s	22
12	Gianluca Nannelli, I (Ducati)	69	36.279s	22
13	Alessio Velini, I (Yamaha)	25	1m 10.305s	22
14	Warwick Nowland, AUS (Suzuki)	12	1m 10.545s	22

DNF: Steve Martin, AUS (Ducati) 99, 19 laps; Regis Laconi, F (Ducati) 55, 14 laps; Lucio Pedercini, I (Ducati) 19, 8 laps; James Toseland, GB (Ducati) 52, 3 laps; Miguel Praia, (Ducati) 50, 2 laps; Segio Fuertes, E (Suzuki) 16, 1 lap.

DNS: Jiri Mrkyvka, CZ (Ducati) 23.

Fastest lap: McCoy, 1m 34.514s, 105.203 mph/169.308 km/h.

Superpole: Laconi, 1m 33.427s, 106.427 mph/171.278 km/h.

Lap record: Troy Corser, AUS (Ducati), 1m 33.019s, 106.894 mph/172.029 km/h (1999).

Championship points: 1 Toseland, 61; 2 Chili, 56; 3 McCoy and Vermeulen, 55; 5 Borciani and Haga, 43; 7 Walker, 39; 8 Martin, 29; 9 Sanchini, 27; 10 Laconi, 25; 11 Haslam, 24; 12 Corser, 19; 13 Nannelli, 18; 14 Clementi, 14; 15 Fuertes, 12.

Top: Chili rang the machine changes – he leads the Kawasakis of Sanchini and Clementi.

Above left: Joy for McCoy in his second Superbike outing, the ex-GP winner taking the flag at home.

Far left: Chris Vermeulen underlined his new Honda threat with two second places.

Left: McCoy's win meant goodbye to his beard.

Photographs: Gold & Goose

Round 3
MISANO, Italy
18 April 2004, 2.523-mile/4.060-km circuit

Race 1 17 laps, 42.891 miles/69.020 km

Pl.	Name Nat.(Machine)	No.	Time & gap	Laps
1	Regis Laconi, F (Ducati)	55	28m 18.586s	17
			90.895 mph/146.282 km/h	
2	Troy Corser, AUS (Petronas)	4	1.944s	17
3	Pierfrancesco Chili, I (Ducati)	7	7.459s	17
4	Noriyuki Haga, J (Ducati)	41	9.728s	17
5	Chris Vermeulen, AUS (Honda)	17	12.310s	17
6	Chris Walker, GB (Petronas)	9	14.130s	17
7	Steve Martin, AUS (Ducati)	99	14.445s	17
8	Gianluca Nannelli, I (Ducati)	69	36.960s	17
9	Piergiorgio Bontempi, I (Suzuki)	5	37.379s	17
10	James Toseland, GB (Ducati)	52	37.501s	17
11	Leon Haslam, GB (Ducati)	91	42.064s	17
12	Ivan Clementi, I (Kawasaki)	8	54.642s	17
13	Alessio Velini, I (Yamaha)	25	1m 02.408s	17
14	Ivan Sala, I (Suzuki)	45	1m 05.352s	17
15	Gianmaria Liverani, I (Ducati)	11	1m 05.397s	17
16	Giancarlo de Matteis, I (Ducati)	27	1m 05.416s	17
17	Giuseppe Zannini, I (Ducati)	31	1m 05.557s	17
18	Warwick Nowland, AUS (Suzuki)	12	1m 27.317s	17
19	Jiri Mrkyvka, CZ (Ducati)	23	1m 28.314s	17
20	Berto Camlek, SLO (Yamaha)	77	1m 34.139s	17
21	Marco Borciani, I (Ducati)	20	2 laps	15

DNF: Lucio Pedercini, I (Ducati) 19, 16 laps; Mauro Sanchini, I (Kawasaki) 6, 14 laps; Luca Pini, I (Suzuki) 29, 8 laps; Garry McCoy, AUS (Ducati) 24, 7 laps; Sergio Fuertes, E (Suzuki) 16, 2 laps.

DNS: Doriano Romboni, I (Yamaha) 28.

Fastest lap: Laconi, 1m 38.339s, 92.354 mph/ 148.629 km/h.

Race 2 25 laps, 63.075 miles/101.500 km

Pl.	Name Nat.(Machine)	No.	Time & gap	Laps
1	Pierfrancesco Chili, I (Ducati)	7	44m 29.370s	25
			85.057 mph/136.886 km/h	
2	Regis Laconi, F (Ducati)	55	1.484s	25
3	Steve Martin, AUS (Ducati)a	99	32.259s	25
4	Norikyuki Haga, J (Ducati)	41	38.088s	25
5	Leon Haslam, GB (Ducati)	91	41.031s	25
6	James Toseland, GB (Ducati)	52	45.176s	25
7	Troy Corser, AUS (Petronas)	4	48.557s	25
8	Lucio Pedercini, I (Ducati)	19	1m 01.446s	25
9	Luca Pini, I (Suzuki)	29	1m 04.891s	25
10	Marco Borciani, I (Ducati)	20	1m 17.110s	25
11	Mauro Sanchini, I (Kawasaki)	6	1m 37.339s	25
12	Chris Vermeulen, AUS (Honda)	17	1m 37.760s	25
13	Chris Walker, GB (Petronas)	9	1m 44.683s	25
14	Gianmaria Liverani, I (Ducati)	11	1m 44.940s	25
15	Piergiorgio Bontempi, I (Suzuki)	5	1 lap	24
16	Jiri Mrkyvka, CZ (Ducati)	23	1 lap	24
17	Garry McCoy, AUS (Ducati)	24	1 lap	24
18	Sergio Fuertes, E (Suzuki)	16	1 lap	24
19	Giuseppe Zannini, I (Ducati)	31	1 lap	24
20	Ivan Sala, I (Suzuki)	45	2 laps	23

DNF: Alessio Velini, I (Yamaha) 25, 16 laps; Warwick Nowland, AUS (Suzuki) 12, 14 laps; Ivan Clementi, I (Kawasaki) 8, 2 laps; Gianluca Nannelli, I (Ducati) 69, 1 lap; Giancarlo de Matteis, I (Ducati) 27, 0 laps; Berto Camlek, SLO (Yamaha) 77, 0 laps.

DNS: Doriano Romboni, I (Yamaha) 28.

Fastest lap: Chili, 1m 42.997s, 88.177 mph/141.907 km/h.

Superpole: Martin, 1m 36.823s, 93.800 mph/ 150.956 km/h.

Lap record: John Kocinski, USA (Ducati), 1m 34.296s, 96.313 mph/155.001 km/h (1996).

Championship points: 1 Chili, 97; 2 Toseland, 77; 3 Laconi and Vermeulen, 70; 5 Haga, 69; 6 McCoy, 55; 7 Martin, 54; 8 Walker, 52; 9 Borciani, 49; 10 Corser, 48; 11 Haslam, 40; 12 Sanchini, 32; 13 Nannelli, 26; 14 Clementi, 18; 15 Bontempi, 14.

Top right: Laconi leads Haga and the rest in race one, bound for victory.

Above right: Maurizio Flammini with Lucio Pedercini and son.

Above far right: Chili in full flight, on his way to a fine win.

Photographs: Gold & Goose

MISANO

A chaotic start to the first race, held on a day of changeable weather conditions after Misano moved from its traditional midsummer slot, saw Piergiorgio Bontempi's Zong Shen Suzuki fail to fire on the start line. The race was at first delayed and then docked a lap.

Pierfrancesco Chili was a short-term leader, having stunned the paddock with the ruse of buying one of the 998R homologation special streetbikes (the model that allowed the Factory and GSE teams to run 104mm bore, high revving Testastrettas in previous seasons) and then fitting all the race bits from the 999RS he had otherwise abandoned.

This mix of 998 handling and 999 power meant Chili was about to leave Misano with a 20-point lead - thanks to a third and an emotional race two win.

The Misano peculiarities were many and diverse. They included a Superpole win for Martin, and a near race win for Corser, whose FP1 was second in race one to Laconi. A new high water mark for the aquamarine dream team.

Rains that waned then waxed through the opening race determined much of the final story, but with Mauro Sanchini fighting for a podium for much of the race, out-jousting even Laconi at times, and with James Toseland qualifying 20th on his Fila Ducati, before finishing tenth, it was a trip into the twilight zone, Adriatic style. In fairness, Sanchini was fast in practice too, showing local knowledge and the big Kawasaki in a good light.

Lucio Pedercini, sharing the front row after Superpole with Martin, Laconi and Chili, was in good form in race one, passing first Haga and then Laconi on one lap, shortly before a crash punctured his dream. With only Corser to go, Laconi made the best of it before the rains re-appeared, passing the 14-lap leader and then pulling away. The race was scheduled for 25 laps, then cut to 24, but with more rain it was stopped after 17. Thus Laconi took a win again.

On a pretty much fully wet track in race two, Chili, as he so often does, went his own way, rejecting full wet tyres. Slithering in the early stages, he soon made ground as it dried, going two seconds per lap faster than the opposition, stalking Laconi and then pouncing to win by 1.484 seconds. Steve Martin, in third, was 32 seconds down, a fact that showed both Chili's cleverness in tyre choice, and Laconi's persistent pace after some devilish early season luck.

Toseland, so desperately down the order in race one, salvaged a sixth in race two, four places away from Laconi. In third, Martin got a reward for his Superpole, while Haga, in fourth, was followed home by his aggressive and burgeoning team-mate, Leon Haslam, taking his second top five of the year.

Chili, emotional after the recent death of his grandmother, was visibly moved by his experience - a win on his own doorstep not being that common an occurrence.

The Ducati bosses were highly miffed by his rejection of their current model for the combination of the older chassis and newer engine. There was little they could do, except pray for the resurgence of Laconi and Toseland. Their wait was short for manna to be delivered, again at home, by a swift pair of one-twos. That was Monza, one race and four weekends away.

MONZA

The recent trend of unpredictability was rebuffed at Monza by the Fila Ducati red army's iron curtain of dominance, thanks to a double Laconi-Toseland one-two. And the rising tide of crimson engulfed the rostrum, with McCoy's Xerox Ducati third in both races. There might have been a splash of Ten Kate yellow too, but for once the Dutch were not the masters of the four-cylinder show. Neither factory Ducati rider fell off all weekend, something of a novelty in itself, as the factory effort began to look like the great double acts of yore.

Vermeulen's chance of third ran into problems – with his clutch in race one and a non-functioning ignition cut-out switch in post-race scrutineering after leg two. He had finished second on track, showing that the Honda had a huge turn of speed for a bike that was still only 85 percent towards being a race bike, despite some engine mods for the Monza speed bowl.

In good positions for a spell in both races, Haga also had two technical problems, ruling him out of the action. Local god Chili had two bike failures in a single race. His hybrid 999/998R blew up – spectacularly – on the warm up lap and he was stranded out at the first chicane until he borrowed a scooter, made it back to pit lane, and hopped on his unloved single-sided swing arm 999.

Away last and with a Monza mountain to climb, he was 14th by lap five, shortly before his second engine went pop. His day would get worse, as he fell in race two, pushing the front too hard into the Parabolica on lap five.

Zero points put Frankie from championship leader to third over one miserable home weekend. A poor reward for the large Monza crowd, enjoying the revamped facilities at this gloriously evocative track.

Toseland's plumes of rubber smoke from his rear Pirelli told how hard he was trying, but Laconi proved untouchable, to the tune of almost ten seconds in race one and a comprehensive 18 in the second.

At another fast track, as when he won at Phillip Island, McCoy was on song all the way through, earning third in each race, just behind Toseland.

Well behind the leaders but impressive nonetheless, Haslam had two fifths on track, and then a personal SBK best of fourth, after Vermeulen's exit by officialdom in race two.

With Ricardo Engineering now tending the needs of the Foggy Petronas 900cc triple some rewards were instantaneous, with Corser fifth in race two at this ultimate horsepower track, while each triple finished each race in the top ten.

With the Honda up there fighting there was another ray of hope for the new world of the 1000cc four-cylinders: Sergio Fuertes, sixth in race one, on his private MIR Suzuki.

After suffering a big crash in qualifying, Steve Martin did not finish race one and was a lowly 11th in the second running. He was one of many who failed to negotiate fully the high-rev engine culling grounds of Monza. Ten riders were out in race one, nine plus the excluded Vermeulen in race two.

Below: Laconi maintained form with double victory.

Below centre: Former champion Corser was fifth on the improving Petronas.

Photographs: Gold & Goose

Round 4
MONZA, Italy
16 May 2004, 3.600-mile/ 5.793-km circuit

Race 1 18 laps, 64.800 miles/104.274 km

Pl.	Name Nat.(Machine)	No.	Time & gap	Laps
1	Regis Laconi, F (Ducati)	55	32m 53.859s	1
			118.172 mph/190.179 km/h	
2	James Toseland, GB (Ducati)	52	9.800s	18
3	Garry McCoy, AUS (Ducati)	24	11.891s	18
4	Chris Vermeulen, AUS (Honda)	17	34.055s	18
5	Leon Haslam, GB (Ducati)	91	38.021s	18
6	Sergio Fuertes, E (Suzuki)	16	41.980s	18
7	Marco Borciani, I (Ducati)	20	42.117s	18
8	Chris Walker, GB (Petronas)	9	42.405s	18
9	Troy Corser, AUS (Petronas)	4	44.983s	18
10	Piergiorgio Bontempi, I (Suzuki)	5	57.215s	18
11	Ivan Clementi, I (Kawasaki)	8	57.408s	18
12	Giancarlo de Matteis, I (Ducati)	27	1m 10.048s	18
13	Horst Saiger, A (Yamaha)	22	1m 18.059s	18
14	Ivan Sala, I (Suzuki)	45	1m 33.348s	18

DNF: Mauro Sanchini, I (Kawasaki) 6, 15 laps; Alessio Velini, I (Yamaha) 25, 10 laps; Noriyuki Haga, J (Ducati) 41, 9 laps; Steve Martin, AUS (Ducati) 99, 6 laps; Pierfrancesco Chili, I (Ducati) 7, 4 laps; Miguel Praia, P (Ducati) 50, 4 laps; Jiri Mrkyvka, CZ (Ducati) 23, 4 laps; Gianluca Nannelli, I (Ducati) 69, 3 laps; Lucio Pedercini, I (Ducati) 19, 2 laps; Paolo Blora, I (Ducati) 113, 0 laps.

Fastest lap: Laconi, 1m 49.110s, 118.766 mph/191.136 km/h.

Race 2 18 laps, 64.800 miles/104.274 km

Pl.	Name Nat.(Machine)	No.	Time & gap	Laps
1	Regis Laconi, F (Ducati)	55	32m 48.901s	18
			118.469 mph/190.658 km/h	
2	James Toseland, GB (Ducati)	52	18.281s	18
3	Garry McCoy, AUS (Ducati)	24	19.403s	18
4	Leon Haslam, GB (Ducati)	91	34.611s	18
5	Troy Corser, AUS (Petronas)	4	40.665s	18
6	Marco Borciani, I (Ducati)	20	41.256s	18
7	Chris Walker, GB (Petronas)	9	42.485s	18
8	Steve Martin, AUS (Ducati)	99	48.936s	18
9	Mauro Sanchini, I (Kawasaki)	6	49.012s	18
10	Ivan Clementi, I (Kawasaki)	8	51.042s	18
11	Piergiorgio Bontempi, I (Suzuki)	5	1m 02.321s	18
12	Lucio Pedercini, I (Ducati)	19	1m 09.516s	18
13	Alessio Velini, I (Yamaha)	25	1m 09.573s	18
14	Horst Saiger, A (Yamaha)	22	1m 20.873s	18

DNF: Paolo Blora, I (Ducati) 113, 12 laps; Ivan Sala, I (Suzuki) 45, 7 laps; Noriyuki Haga, J (Ducati) 41, 6 laps; Pierfrancesco Chili, I (Ducati) 7, 5 laps; Giancarlo de Matteis, I (Ducati) 27, 3 laps; Jiri Mrkyvka, CZ (Ducati) 23, 1 lap; Gianluca Nannelli, I (Ducati) 69, 0 laps; Sergio Fuertes, E (Suzuki) 16, 0 laps; Miguel Praia, P (Ducati) 50, 0 laps.

EXC: Chris Vermeulen, AUS (Honda) 17, 18 laps (12.392s gap to winner).

Fastest lap: Laconi, 1m 48.773s, 119.134 mph/191.728 km/h.

Superpole: Laconi, 1m 48.258s, 119.701 mph/192.640 km/h.

Lap record: Troy Bayliss, AUS (Ducati), 1m 47.434s, 120.619 mph/194.117 km/h (2002).

Championship points: 1 Laconi, 120; 2 Toseland, 117; 3 Chili, 97; 4 McCoy, 87; 5 Vermeulen, 83; 6 Haga and Walker, 69; 8 Borciani, 68; 9 Corser, 66; 10 Haslam, 64; 11 Martin, 62; 12 Sanchini, 39; 13 Clementi, 29; 14 Nannelli, 26; 15 Bontempi, 25.

Above left: Marco Borciani was twice in the top ten.

Left: The same rostrum, twice ... from left Toseland, Laconi and McCoy.

Photographs: Gold & Goose

Round 5

OSCHERSLEBEN, Germany

30 May 2004, 2.279-mile/3.667-km circuit

Race 1 28 laps, 63.812 miles/102.676 km

Pl.	Name Nat.(Machine)	No.	Time & gap	Laps
1	Noriyuki Haga, J (Ducati)	41	41m 49.906s	28
			91.509 mph/147.270 km/h	
2	James Toseland, GB (Ducati)	52	5.164s	28
3	Pierfrancesco Chili, I (Ducati)	7	5.323s	28
4	Troy Corser, AUS (Petronas)	4	13.024s	28
5	Steve Martin, AUS (Ducati)	99	20.182s	28
6	Regis Laconi, F (Ducati)	55	24.754s	28
7	Leon Haslam, GB (Ducati)	91	27.300s	28
8	Jurgen Oelschläger, D (Honda)	72	30.508s	28
9	Garry McCoy, AUS (Ducati)	24	32.261s	28
10	Mauro Sanchini, I (Kawasaki)	6	37.660s	28
11	Ivan Clementi, I (Kawasaki)	8	45.800s	28
12	Gianluca Nannelli, I (Ducati)	69	48.708s	28
13	Andy Meklau, A (Suzuki)	34	52.478s	28
14	Piergiorgio Bontempi, I (Suzuki)	5	1m 01.527s	28
15	Chris Vermeulen, AUS (Honda)	17	1m 03.796s	28
16	Alessio Velini, I (Yamaha)	25	1m 06.945s	28
17	Miguel Praia, P (Ducati)	50	1 lap	27
18	Carl Berthelsen, N (Suzuki)	33	1 lap	27

DNF: Lucio Pedercini, I (Ducati) 19, 22 laps; Marco Borciani, I (Ducati) 20, 10 laps; Jiri Mrkyvka, CZ (Ducati) 23, 10 laps; David Garcia, E (Ducati) 48, 8 laps; Michael Schulten, D (Honda) 71, 6 laps; Chris Walker, GB (Petronas) 9, 5 laps.

Fastest lap: Haga, 1m 28.789s, 92.386 mph/ 148.681 km/h.

Race 2 28 laps, 63.812 miles /102.676 km

Pl.	Name Nat.(Machine)	No.	Time & gap	Laps
1	Regis Laconi, F (Ducati)	55	41m 50.459s	28
			91.489 mph/147.237 km/h	
2	James Toseland, GB (Ducati)	52	21.549s	28
3	Leon Haslam, GB (Ducati)	91	24.685s	28
4	Garry McCoy, AUS (Ducati)	24	27.413s	28
5	Gianluca Nannelli, I (Ducati)	69	30.621s	28
6	Mauro Sanchini, I (Kawasaki)	6	36.000s	28
7	Chris Walker, GB (Petronas)	9	42.083s	28
8	Chris Vermeulen, AUS (Honda)	17	46.944s	28
9	Ivan Clementi, I (Kawasaki)	8	47.021s	28
10	Andy Meklau, A (Suzuki)	34	47.239s	28
11	Piergiorgio Bontempi, I (Suzuki)	5	55.920s	28
12	Alessio Velini, I (Yamaha)	25	57.480s	28
13	Jiri Mrkyvka, CZ (Ducati)	23	1 lap	27
14	Carl Berthelsen, N (Suzuki)	33	1 lap	27

DNF: Noriyuki Haga, J (Ducati) 41, 22 laps; Steve Martin, AUS (Ducati) 99, 17 laps; Miguel Praia, P (Ducati) 50, 16 laps; Troy Corser, AUS (Petronas) 4, 14 laps; Jurgen Oelschläger, D (Honda) 72, 13 laps; Michael Schulten, D (Honda) 71, 11 laps; Pierfrancesco Chili, I (Ducati) 7, 6 laps; Lucio Pedercini, I (Ducati) 19, 6 laps; David Garcia, E (Ducati) 48, 3 laps.

NC: Marco Borciani, I (Ducati) 20, 8 laps.

Fastest lap: Haga, 1m 28.629s, 92.553 mph/ 148.949 km/h.

Superpole: Corser, 1m 27.687s, 93.547 mph/ 150.549 km/h.

Lap record: Colin Edwards, USA (Honda), 1m 26.549s, 94.777 mph/152.529 km/h (2002).

Championship points: 1 Toseland, 157; 2 Laconi, 155; 3 Chili, 113; 4 McCoy, 107; 5 Haga, 94; 6 Vermeulen, 92; 7 Haslam, 89; 8 Corser, 79; 9 Walker, 78; 10 Martin, 73; 11 Borciani, 68; 12 Sanchini, 55; 13 Clementi and Nannelli, 41; 15 Bontempi, 32.

Top right: Haga won the first race, and led Laconi in the second, only to retire.

Above right: His team-mate Haslam made his first podium.

Right: A long-awaited return to the top step had Haga beaming.

Photographs: Gold & Goose

OSCHERSLEBEN

Given his prowess at a similarly slow and tortuous Valencia on the first day of the season, Haga surprised no-one by securing the race one win with some aplomb, with a five second advantage over the hard working Toseland. Given his machine unreliability in practice, it was no surprise either that he retired from race two. Nonetheless, irritating beyond measure when you're forced to retire from the lead.

Race two was not all disaster for the Renegade team. Leon Haslam, 21 years old the day after the race, eighth on lap one, moved inexorably forward as his rivals dropped off the pace. He became yet another 2004 SBK podium placer, in third.

His fellow Brit Toseland may have won his first ever SBK race at Oschersleben last year. It was two seconds this time, still making him the best rider over the two legs. Happier with his bike set-up, he could lap consistently.

Chili, regenerating himself once more, made good use of a fast start in race one to finish third, a fair result in a race where all of the top riders but Walker finished. Some not without incident of course. Chili chased Toseland hard in the latter stages of the opener, losing the battle by a couple of tenths. In race two he repeated his Monza action, falling while cranked over on a corner entry.

Corser, a surprise Superpole winner, romped to fourth despite an imperfect set-up, even if he was to retire in race two. Like so many others... it was another contest where there were points going begging, as only 14 finishers went staggering, wheezing and clunking over the line.

Laconi, penalised with a ride through in race one, lost around 18 seconds in the pitlane, less than his team had originally feared. His transgression? Once again the issue of a non-functioning ignition cut out switch, for the umpteenth time in recent history. Crashing in practice, his bike plainly did not cut out, and thus he took the punishment. Fastest in regulation pre-Superpole qualifying, Laconi ended up in needless trouble.

Oschersleben is not an easy place to pass at, but Laconi went through the order in rapid and impressive fashion. He was thus good value for sixth. His staggering margin of victory in race two – a crushing 21 seconds, was mostly thanks to the retirement of leader Haga, but it showed how much the Frenchman had to give when bike set-up and tyres were pointing in the right direction.

Fast qualifying wild card Michael Schulten (Alpha Technik Honda Fireblade) gave Vermeulen a hard time in the opener, the Ten Kate rider suffering from a tyre which had spun on the rim, and a slipping slipper clutch. He would slither down to 15th at the flag; make a partial recovery to eighth in race two, fighting against handling problems due to an unnamed malfunction in the steering head assembly.

Clutch problems put Walker out of the first leg; he was seventh in race two. McCoy, quiet and relatively blunted since his PI win and Monza high points, went ninth and then fourth. With the 999 proving a finicky thing in both factory and privateer forms, even those with the lower revving 998 machines could show at a track like Oschersleben. Gianluca Nannelli, a natural born charger of impressive credentials, determined to make a name for himself again, and duly took fifth in race two on his Pedercini bike.

SILVERSTONE

Blessed with sunshine, the crowd was not blessed with a home win for Toseland. In fact, the Englishman's weekend was cursed in many ways. He DNF race one, and took only fifth in race two, after an off-track tango with Chili.

A close Superpole had gone to Laconi, the regulation qualifying to Chili; yet they would each only score a single third place podium finish each – Chili in race one and Laconi in race two.

Haga and Vermeulen were to duke it out for the real-time wins: the Japanese rider winning the first classic by 0.150; Vermeulen giving the Ten Kate Team, the Honda Fireblade and not least himself a first win in the top category of proddy racing – if by only 0.228.

It was also the first 1000cc four-cylinder SBK win... Gregorio Lavilla's Suzuki never quite managed such a feat in 2003. Talking of landmarks, it was achieved at the 400th SBK race, where Pier-Francisco Chili finally eclipsed previous record holder Aaron Slight, with his 229th start.

Silverstone features mostly fast and flowing corners, and then some comically slow sections, allowing bikes with differing abilities to keep up over the whole 5km lap. If their riders were up to it, that is. That the best of the leading trios in each race were over 20 seconds clear of their competitors showed once more that just because there are control tyres now, not everyone is going to make best use of them.

In the slow bits Haga's Ducati was best, and he overcame the usually leading Vermeulen in the last few corners of leg one. Race two was just as pugilistic, laden with risk and audacity from the leading pair, who proved their season-long credentials in just one afternoon.

The Fila Ducati squad was in hot and bitterly spiced water, as Toseland and Laconi both fell after running somewhat unwise front tyre choices in race one. Laconi recovered well to post third place in race two; Toseland, riding since practice with a severely ground down thumb, recovered somewhat...

Chili was pivotal to Toseland's race-two result. Earlier, he'd been an amazing third in race one. Clutch problems in Superpole meant a fourth-row start. He was up to seventh after one lap, and third before three had been completed. Soon after that, he was even catching the leading duo.

But he had a poor end to the day. As he tried to pass Toseland in race two, his rear rim hit the rumble strip, smashing the tyre seal so that he crashed at once, taking Toseland off track with him. The factory team rider recovered to an eventual fifth, ahead of Martin. Some harsh words from Chili to Toseland completed the Fila Ducati team's misery in the sun, and also a yin-yang weekend for Chili, who dropped to fifth overall in the points.

Behind the podium action, McCoy was a best of fourth in race one, dropping behind Haga and Vermeulen in the rankings. On home turf, the Renegade Team were ecstatic with Haga, and of course Haslam, fifth in race one, and fourth in race two.

No wildcards? For the second race in succession a local bike was in the top rider mix. James Ellison, on a very stock Yamaha R1 may have fallen in race one, pushing his front Pirelli too hard, but he was seventh in race two. Up to fifth at one stage, he was unfazed by the whole SBK faradiddle, and gained many admirers.

Round 6
SILVERSTONE, Great Britain

13 June 2004, 3.129-mile/5.036-km circuit

Race 1 20 laps, 62.580 miles/100.720 km

Pl.	Name Nat.(Machine)	No.	Time & gap	Laps
1	Noriyuki Haga, J (Ducati)	41	38m 43.657s	20
			96.961 mph/156.044 km/h	
2	Chris Vermeulen, AUS (Honda)	17	0.150s	20
3	Pierfrancesco Chili, I (Ducati)	7	6.583s	20
4	Garry McCoy, AUS (Ducati)	24	27.263s	20
5	Leon Haslam, GB (Ducati)	91	27.580s	20
6	Steve Martin, AUS (Ducati)	99	27.606s	20
7	Troy Corser, AUS (Petronas)	4	32.321s	20
8	Marco Borciani, I (Ducati)	20	38.956s	20
9	Piergiorgio Bontempi, I (Suzuki)	5	39.293s	20
10	Ivan Clementi, I (Kawasaki)	8	48.255s	20
11	Warwick Nowland, AUS (Suzuki)	12	1m 16.875s	20
12	Jiri Mrkyvka, CZ (Ducati)	23	1m 29.690s	20
13	Sergio Fuertes, E (Suzuki)	16	1m 30.546s	20
14	Miguel Praia, P (Ducati)	50	2m 00.074s	20

DNF: Regis Laconi, F (Ducati) 55, 17 laps; Mauro Sanchini, I (Kawasaki) 6, 15 laps; Gianluca Nannelli, I (Ducati) 69, 12 laps; James Toseland, GB (Ducati) 52, 11 laps; Chris Walker, GB (Petronas) 9, 7 laps; David Garcia, E (Ducati) 48, 3 laps; James Ellison, GB (Yamaha) 100, 2 laps; Lucio Pedercini, I (Ducati) 19, 1 lap; Alessio Velini, I (Yamaha) 25, 1 lap.

Fastest lap: Laconi, 1m 55.388s, 97.629 mph/157.119 km/h.

Race 2 20 laps, 62.580 miles/100.720 km

Pl.	Name Nat.(Machine)	No.	Time & gap	Laps
1	Chris Vermeulen, AUS (Honda)	17	38m 35.608s	20
			97.298 mph/156.586 km/h	
2	Noriyuki Haga, J (Ducati)	41	0.228s	20
3	Regis Laconi, F (Ducati)	55	6.155s	20
4	Leon Haslam, GB (Ducati)	91	20.895s	20
5	James Toseland, GB (Ducati)	52	27.504s	20
6	Steve Martin, AUS (Ducati)	99	28.491s	20
7	James Ellison, GB (Yamaha)	100	32.668s	20
8	Garry McCoy, AUS (Ducati)	24	33.518s	20
9	Troy Corser, AUS (Petronas)	4	36.312s	20
10	Ivan Clementi, I (Kawasaki)	8	38.114s	20
11	Marco Borciani, I (Ducati)	20	41.206s	20
12	Chris Walker, GB (Petronas)	9	41.536s	20
13	Mauro Sanchini, I (Kawasaki)	6	52.325s	20
14	Piergiorgio Bontempi, I (Suzuki)	5	1m 04.719s	20
15	Lucio Pedercini, I (Ducati)	19	1m 13.860s	20
16	Jiri Mrkyvka, CZ (Ducati)	23	1m 30.570s	20

DNF: Warwick Nowland, AUS (Suzuki) 12, 19 laps; Sergio Fuertes, E (Suzuki) 16, 19 laps; Miguel Praia, P (Ducati) 50, 18 laps; Gianluca Nannelli, I (Ducati) 69, 6 laps; Pierfrancesco Chili, I (Ducati) 7, 5 laps; David Garcia, E (Ducati) 48, 3 laps; Alessio Velini, I (Yamaha) 25, 1 lap.

Fastest lap: Vermeulen, 1m 54.919s, 98.028 mph/157.760 km/h.

Superpole: Laconi, 1m 54.331s, 98.531 mph/158.571 km/h.

Lap record: Gregorio Lavilla, E (Suzuki), 1m 53.629s, 99.140 mph/159.551 km/h (2003).

Championship points: 1 Laconi, 171; 2 Toseland, 168; 3 Haga, 139; 4 Vermeulen, 137; 5 Chili, 129; 6 McCoy, 128; 7 Haslam, 113; 8 Corser, 95; 9 Martin, 93; 10 Walker, 82; 11 Borciani, 81; 12 Sanchini, 58; 13 Clementi, 53; 14 Bontempi and Nannelli, 41.

Above left: Vermeulen leads Haga as they draw away from the start. Behind the factory Ducatis of Toseland (52) and Laconi (55) will both crash out; Haslam (91) will take fifth.

Far left: Nice and close – the Petronas pair mix it with the Ducatis.

Left: Vermeulen after his and Ten Kate's first SBK win.

Photographs: Gold & Goose

Round 7

Laguna Seca

11 July 2004, 2.243-mile/3.610-km circuit

Race 1 28 laps, 62.804 miles/101.080 km

Pl.	Name Nat.(Machine)	No.	Time & gap	Laps
1	Chris Vermeulen, AUS (Honda)	17	41m 03.371s	28
			91.789 mph/147.720 km/h	
2	Pierfrancesco Chili, I (Ducati)	7	4.127s	28
3	Steve Martin, AUS (Ducati)	99	5.707s	28
4	James Toseland, GB (Ducati)	52	8.347s	28
5	Regis Laconi, F (Ducati)	55	8.390s	28
6	Noriyuki Haga, J (Ducati)	41	18.560s	28
7	Garry McCoy, AUS (Ducati)	24	21.290s	28
8	Mauro Sanchini, I (Kawasaki)	6	31.795s	28
9	Leon Haslam, GB (Ducati)	91	34.166s	28
10	Troy Corser, AUS (Petronas)	4	8.175s	28
11	Marco Borciani, I (Ducati)	20	43.554s	28
12	Lucio Pedercini, I (Ducati)	19	57.948s	28
13	Piergiorgio Bontempi, I (Suzuki)	5	1m 18.252s	28
14	Horst Saiger, A (Yamaha)	22	1m 22.532s	28

DNF: Chris Walker, GB (Petronas) 9, 26 laps; Warwick Nowland, AUS (Suzuki) 12, 26 laps; Gianluca Nannelli, I (Ducati) 69, 17 laps; Ivan Clementi, I (Kawasaki) 8, 15 laps; Alessio Velini, I (Yamaha) 25, 9 laps; Jiri Mrkyvka, CZ (Ducati) 23, 7 laps.

DNS: Miguel Praia, P (Ducati) 50.

Fastest lap: Vermeulen, 1m 26.798s, 93.036 mph/149.727 km/h.

Race 2 28 laps, 62.804 miles/101.080 km

Pl.	Name Nat.(Machine)	No.	Time & gap	Laps
1	Chris Vermeulen, AUS (Honda)	17	40m 56.568s	28
			92.043 mph/148.129 km/h	
2	James Toseland, GB (Ducati)	52	0.465s	28
3	Regis Laconi, F (Ducati)	55	13.520s	28
4	Noriyuki Haga, J (Ducati)	41	13.742s	28
5	Pierfrancesco Chili, I (Ducati)	7	21.770s	28
6	Steve Martin, AUS (Ducati)	99	27.964s	28
7	Garry McCoy, AUS (Ducati)	24	43.631s	28
8	Marco Borciani, I (Ducati)	20	48.268s	28
9	Mauro Sanchini, I (Kawasaki)	6	49.327s	28
10	Ivan Clementi, I (Kawasaki)	8	54.021s	28
11	Lucio Pedercini, I (Ducati)	19	1m 09.618s	28
12	Piergiorgio Bontempi, I (Suzuki)	5	1m 24.444s	28
13	Warwick Nowland, AUS (Suzuki)	12	1 lap	27
14	Horst Saiger, A (Yamaha)	22	1 lap	27

DNF: Leon Haslam, GB (Ducati) 91, 21 laps; Troy Corser, AUS (Petronas) 4, 17 laps; Chris Walker, GB (Petronas) 9, 7 laps; Alessio Velini, I (Yamaha) 25, 6 laps; Miguel Praia, P (Ducati) 50, 2 laps; Jiri Mrkyvka, CZ (Ducati) 23, 0 laps; Gianluca Nannelli, I (Ducati) 69, 0 laps.

Fastest lap: Vermeulen, 1m 27.043s, 92.774 mph/149.306 km/h.

Superpole: Martin, 1m 26.912s, 92.914 mph/149.531 km/h.

Lap record: Noriyuki Haga, J (Aprilia), 1m 25.475s, 94.476 mph/152.044 km/h (2002).

Championship points: 1 Toseland, 201; 2 Laconi, 198; 3 Vermeulen, 187; 4 Haga, 162; 5 Chili, 160; 6 McCoy, 146; 7 Haslam, 120; 8 Martin, 119; 9 Corser, 101; 10 Borciani, 94; 11 Walker, 82; 12 Sanchini, 73; 13 Clementi, 59; 14 Bontempi, 48; 15 Nannelli, 41

Top: Toseland and Chili set the pace, Martin (99) in third. Eventual double winner Vermeulen (17) is well-placed in the pursuit.

Above right: The race-two rostrum – Toseland, Vermeulen, Laconi.

Above far right: Mauro Sanchini gently aviates the Kawasaki.

Photographs: Gold & Goose

LAGUNA SECA

It wasn't just the sun that was yellow and powerful at Laguna. The Ten Kate Honda of Vermeulen followed on its Silverstone race win with a double in the USA. A praiseworthy effort from all involved, especially as the team had never seen the track before, Vermeulen had never been there, but almost all their opponents had.

In the opener it was Vermeulen in eventual isolation, running to a four second gap over 40-year-old Chili's hybrid Duke, which was suffering from a lack of front end grip at key points, especially the Corkscrew and subsequent fast downhill curves. Martin once more ripped up the charts in qualifying to take pole position, and scored a well-deserved podium finish in the punishing conditions of race one.

The first 28-lapper contest saw both Toseland and Laconi slip down the order, their problem the opposite of Chili's... a lack of rear grip, even though all riders had opted for the softest available rear tyres. This in spite of hot 46/51-degree track temperatures.

The tactics adopted by Toseland in race one were far from soft, and way too hard for gentleman Regis and team manager Tardozzi: both riders were given ultimatums to behave by their boss, after finishing Toseland fourth, Laconi fifth. They had slid into each other, Toseland had run Laconi out to the white line on occasion, and for Toseland an air of not allowing the competition past at any price had crept in.

Toseland had led the first race, proving beyond doubt that what he sometimes lacked in other departments he could make up for in blood and iron if necessary. His chase of Vermeulen in race two, losing by only 0.465 seconds, was another sign that he was ready for a scrap.

Haga was a dumbfounded 16th in Superpole, and after his bike stalled at the start, he began race one from the pit lane. He vented his rage on the track, his pace on par with the leading bunch, better sometimes, and he worked his way to sixth.

In race two, with the top riders spread out in a rough finger formation, and with Toseland trying to make a break on revised suspension settings, fast starting Haga pulled a move on Chili, who had changed his front tyre choice after race one.

Vermeulen chased down Toseland, drawing smoke from his rear tyre as he did so, while behind, an excellent fight between Laconi and Haga, ultimately won by the former, provided some high entertainment.

With a single top ten finish for Corser and a double DNF for Walker, even on their latest revamped engine spec, it was a day of gloom in the California sunshine for Team Foggy Petronas. Saturday hadn't been too hot either, as Walker failed to qualify for Superpole.

Forced to run his second machine in race two, after his preferred steed reached its safe limit of kilometres, Martin was an uncomfortable sixth. Haslam was in outright pain, after falling and breaking his left wrist. His absence made for only fourteen finishers, in both races.

The race shuffled the title table again. Toseland regained the overall lead from Laconi, with Vermeulen's recent run of perfection putting him within 14 points.

Right: Toseland (left) lost the points lead, crashing out in race two along with Corser.

Below left: Laconi also crashed out of race two.

Below right: Wild card and local hero – James Ellison put his name on the map with a fifth and a sixth.

Bottom: Haga leads in the sunshine, Martin (99), Laconi (55), Chili (7) and Corser (4) take wider lines into Paddock Bend.

Photographs: Gold & Goose

BRANDS HATCH

New Brands Hatch owners Motor Sport Ventures had every right to be chuffed with their first taste of World Superbike, as a large crowd turned out, despite the fact that the Donington GP was held only a week beforehand.

Suitably enough, the first race of round eight featured eight riders in a fight for the spoils in the early stages, but it boiled down to a final conflict between Haga and Laconi, after long-time associate Chili fell out of contention at Surtees. With an extensively damaged bike, it was doubtful he would make race two.

The first 25-lapper was for either of the two top riders' taking until the last half lap, when Haga showed how much he wanted to win. His margin of advantage, 0.134, said it all about the closeness of this contest.

Steve Martin, a resurgent force this weekend, ran in third, a race day reward for finishing Superpole as top dog for the third time this year. Only a couple of seconds down on the leaders, he was a similar distance ahead of Vermeulen. In a triple Aussie treat Foggy Petronas rider Troy Corser was fifth, with a strong performance for the three-cylinder battler.

The real interest for the home crowd was just behind Corser. In a season when wild cards were a rarity, James Ellison ran out in an aggressive sixth and had the extraordinary pleasure of beating a plainly struggling Toseland in the process. A force at Silverstone, Ellison was an even bigger pain to the regulars at Brands. Another wild-card, Vitrans Honda rider Craig Coxhell proved that the fours were in the ascendancy, his Fireblade taking him eighth.

There were, in fact, several wild cards and one offs, as Sebastien Gimbert enjoyed a good run out on his Yamaha France R1, taking a best of ninth in race two. Giovanni Bussei, on a De Cecco Ducati 998, had rolled over from the SL Racing bunk bed in Supersport to a more fulsome quilted berth in Superbike. He was an instant hit from first qualifying.

Race two was an aggregate affair, after Italian rider Gianfranco De Matteis (PSG-1 Ducati) fell and broke his collarbone. With Chili crashing in race one also, it was a busy day in the PSG-1 garage. His bike was repaired only just in time to take part in the first section of race two. Chili had to drive out of pit lane, then, maverick that he is, he turned and headed back down the short distance to the grid, the wrong way down the track. A verbal warning later, he set off with the rest.

Haga was in the lead when the race was stopped, and the second half of the race started as it meant to go on, a close scrap between Laconi and Haga, until Laconi fell off on lap 15.

Chili crossed the line first after more superb action, but he couldn't do enough to displace Haga. Chili was distraught, albeit in second and taking cheers as though he had won. Vermeulen slipped into third place, and, not to be outdone by his more senior team-mate's fifth in race one, Chris Walker went fourth on the Petronas.

Ellison, underlining the form he had been showing in the British series on his R1, was fifth, while Bussei held off even McCoy on his old 998, recording sixth.

With the end of the season coming into view, there were now no less than four riders – Haga, Toseland, Laconi and Vermeulen – with a difference between them of only eight points.

Round 8
BRANDS HATCH, Great Britain

31 July 2004, 2.608-mile/4.197-km circuit

Race 1 25 laps, 65.200 miles/104.925 km

Pl.	Name Nat. (Machine)	No.	Time & gap	Laps
1	Noriyuki Haga, J (Ducati)	41	37m 08.172s	25
			105.338 mph/169.525 km/h	
2	Regis Laconi, F (Ducati)	55	0.134s	25
3	Steve Martin, AUS (Ducati)	99	2.273s	25
4	Chris Vermeulen, AUS (Honda)	17	4.751s	25
5	Troy Corser, AUS (Petronas)	4	8.046s	25
6	James Ellison, GB (Yamaha)	100	9.909s	25
7	James Toseland, GB (Ducati)	52	10.025s	25
8	Craig Coxhell, AUS (Honda)	35	21.797s	25
9	Chris Walker, GB (Petronas)	9	26.137s	25
10	Gianluca Nannelli, I (Ducati)	69	29.131s	25
11	Marco Borciani, I (Ducati)	20	29.769s	25
12	Giovanni Bussei, I (Ducati)	200	33.786s	25
13	Lucio Pedercini, I (Ducati)	19	35.066s	25
14	Ivan Clementi, I (Kawasaki)	8	36.419s	25
15	Piergiorgio Bontempi, I (Suzuki)	5	40.899s	25
16	Warwick Nowland, AUS (Suzuki)	12	53.857s	25
17	Alessio Velini, I (Yamaha)	25	1m 08.058s	25

DNF: Segio Fuertes, E (Suzuki) 16, 24 laps; Leon Haslam, GB (Ducati) 91, 23 laps; Pierfrancesco Chili, I (Ducati) 7, 18 laps; Sébastien Gimbert, F (Yamaha) 32, 18 laps; Garry McCoy, AUS (Ducati) 24, 11 laps; Giancarlo de Matteis, I (Ducati) 27, 11 laps; Mauro Sanchini, I (Kawasaki) 6, 7 laps; Jiri Mrkyvka, CZ (Ducati) 23, 7 laps; Miguel Praia, P (Ducati) 50, 7 laps.

Fastest lap: Chili, 1m 28.094s, 106.573 mph/171.512 km/h.

Race 2 25 laps, 65.200 miles/104.925 km

Pl.	Name Nat.(Machine)	No.	Time & gap	Laps
1	Noriyuki Haga, J (Ducati)	41	37m 05.030s	25
			105.486 mph/169.764 km/h	
2	Pierfrancesco Chili, I (Ducati)	7	0.960s	25
3	Chris Vermeulen, AUS (Honda)	17	10.639s	25
4	Chris Walker, GB (Petronas)	9	23.664s	25
5	James Ellison, GB (Yamaha)	100	24.112s	25
6	Giovanni Bussei, I (Ducati)	200	26.433s	25
7	Garry McCoy, AUS (Ducati)	24	26.852s	25
8	Craig Coxhell, AUS (Honda)	35	31.083s	25
9	Sébastien Gimbert, F (Yamaha)	32	31.221s	25
10	Mauro Sanchini, I (Kawasaki)	6	31.894s	25
11	Ivan Clementi, I (Kawasaki)	8	36.286s	25
12	Piergiorgio Bontempi, I (Suzuki)	5	54.448s	25
13	Sergio Fuertes, E (Suzuki)	16	1m 01.424s	25
14	Alessio Velini, I (Yamaha)	25	1m 20.050s	25
15	Miguel Praia, P (Ducati)	50	2 laps	23

DNF: Regis Laconi, F (Ducati) 55, 18 laps; Steve Martin, AUS (Ducati) 99, 15 laps; Warwick Nowland, AUS (Suzuki) 12, 10 laps; Marco Borciani, I (Ducati) 20, 8 laps; Lucio Pedercini, I (Ducati) 19, 7 laps; Gianluca Nannelli, I (Ducati) 69, 6 laps; Troy Corser, AUS (Petronas) 4, 3 laps; James Toseland, GB (Ducati) 52, 3 laps; Giancarlo de Matteis, I (Ducati) 27, 3 laps; Leon Haslam, GB (Ducati) 91, 3 laps.

DNS: Jiri Mrkyvka, CZ (Ducati) 23.

Fastest lap: Chili, 1m 28.201s, 106.443 mph/171.304 km/h.

Superpole: Martin, 1m 27.213s, 107.649 mph/173.245 km/h.

Lap record: Shane Byrne, GB (Ducati), 1m 26.755s, 108.217 mph/174.159 km/h (2003).

Championship points: 1 Laconi, 218; 2 Vermeulen, 216; 3 Haga, 212; 4 Toseland, 210; 5 Chili, 180; 6 McCoy, 155; 7 Martin, 135; 8 Haslam, 120; 9 Corser, 112; 10 Walker, 102; 11 Borciani, 99; 12 Sanchini, 79; 13 Clementi, 66; 14 Bontempi, 53; 15 Nannelli, 47.

Round 9

ASSEN, Holland

5 September 2004, 3.745-mile/6.027-km circuit

Race 1 16 laps, 59.920 miles/96.432 km

Pl.	Name Nat.(Machine)	No.	Time & gap	Laps
1	James Toseland, GB (Ducati)	52	33m 30.741s	16
			107.280 mph/172.650 km/h	
2	Pierfranceso Chili, I (Ducati)	7	2.138s	16
3	Regis Laconi, F (Ducati)	55	2.450s	16
4	Noriyuki Haga, J (Ducati)	41	2.566s	16
5	Chris Vermeulen, AUS (Honda)	17	9.044s	16
6	Leon Haslam, GB (Ducati)	91	15.885s	16
7	Steve Martin, AUS (Ducati)	99	16.838s	16
8	Garry McCoy, AUS (Ducati)	24	16.988s	16
9	Marco Borciani, I (Ducati)	20	18.191s	16
10	Troy Corser, AUS (Petronas)	4	19.358s	16
11	Gianluca Nannelli, I (Ducati)	69	30.934s	16
12	Chris Walker, GB (Petronas)	9	40.191s	16
13	Piergiorgio Bontempi, I (Suzuki)	5	51.079s	16
14	Warwick Nowland, AUS (Suzuki)	12	52.457s	16
15	Sergio Fuertes, E (Suzuki)	16	1m 03.638s	16
16	Robert Menzen, NL (Suzuki)	36	1m 47.636s	16

DNF: Giovanni Bussei, I (Ducati) 200, 13 laps; Jiri Mrkyvka, CZ (Ducati) 23, 8 laps; Arno Visscher, NL (Kawasaki) 38, 8 laps; Alessio Velini, I (Yamaha) 25, 5 laps; Mauro Sanchini, I (Kawasaki) 6, 4 laps; Lucio Pedercini, I (Ducati) 19, 4 laps; Ivan Clementi, I (Kawasaki) 8, 4 laps; Miguel Praia, P (Ducati) 50, 3 laps.

Fastest lap: Haga, 2m 04.360s, 108.411 mph 174.471 km/h.

Race 2 16 laps, 59.920 miles/96.432 km

Pl.	Name Nat.(Machine)	No.	Time & gap	Laps
1	Chris Vermeulen, AUS (Honda)	17	33m 31.968s	16
			107.214 mph/172.54 km/h	
2	James Toseland, GB (Ducati)	52	0.037s	16
3	Noriyuki Haga, J (Ducati)	41	0.117s	16
4	Pierfranceso Chili, I (Ducati)	7	3.905s	16
5	Regis Laconi, F (Ducati)	55	6.580s	16
6	Leon Haslam, GB (Ducati)	91	18.173s	16
7	Troy Corser, AUS (Petronas)	4	26.904s	16
8	Marco Borciani, I (Ducati)	20	33.271s	16
9	Ivan Clementi, I (Kawasaki)	8	33.516s	16
10	Chris Walker, GB (Petronas)	9	33.815s	16
11	Giovanni Bussei, I (Ducati)	200	36.358s	16
12	Piergiorgio Bontempi, I (Suzuki)	5	36.818s	16
13	Warwick Nowland, AUS (Suzuki)	12	46.401s	16
14	Sergio Fuertes, E (Suzuki)	16	im 14.282s	16
15	Robert Menzen, NL (Suzuki)	36	1m 32.984s	16
16	Miguel Praia, POR (Ducatii)	50	1m 49.752s	16

DNF: Gianluca Nannelli, I (Ducati) 69, 15 laps; Steve Martin, AUS (Ducati) 99, 15 laps; Arno Visscher, NL (Kawasaki) 38, 8 laps; Garry McCoy, AUS (Ducati) 24, 5 laps; Jiri Mrkyvka, CZ (Ducati) 23, 5 laps; Alessio Velini, I (Yamaha) 25, 1 lap.

Fastest lap: Haga, 2m 04.831s, 108.002 mph/ 173.813 km/h.

Superpole: Chili, 2m 03.103s, 109.518 mph/ 176.252 km/h.

Lap record: Colin Edwards, USA (Honda), 2m 02.395s, 110.152 mph/177.272 km/h (2002).

Championship points: 1 Toseland, 255; 2 Vermeulen, 252; 3 Laconi, 245; 4 Haga, 241; 5 Chili, 213; 6 McCoy, 163; 7 Martin, 144; 8 Haslam, 140; 9 Corser, 127; 10 Borciani, 114; 11 Walker, 112; 12 Sanchini, 79; 13 Clementi, 73; 14 Bontempi, 60; 15 Nannelli, 52.

Top: Toseland leads Laconi, Haga, Vermeulen and Chili – a win and second place regained him a narrow points lead.

Above right: Haga, Laconi and Chili have scant time to scan their pit-boards in their furious battle.

Photographs: Gold & Goose

ASSEN

Assen is a special place for Chili. He's had public punch-ups here, almost bettered Valentino Rossi's MotoGP qualifying best a couple of years ago, won races in his own right, and now added Superpole to his list of Assen highlights.

He was one of the top five riders in the championship who blasted away with both barrels all afternoon, to the point that they each took a top five finish, in both 16 lap races.

First up for a win was Toseland, a visibly changed man with a set of handlebars under his control. Having recently experienced some subterranean lows, Toseland - after a revelatory test at Mugello - had found whatever keys to the 999's often-unforgiving soul that he had obviously dropped into the bellypan at places like Brands.

Now allying an outstandingly aggressive riding style to a machine which could use rather than abuse tyres, Toseland scored a win by 2.138 seconds in race one, after a five-way fight. Not that any of the other four had a chance to lead, as Toseland headed up the order on each and every lap.

The fact that Chili, Laconi and Haga all finished within 0.4 seconds of each other shows what was going on up to that point, the first leg of a high speed dance around Assen's awe-inspiring 6.027km. Vermeulen had dropped off the leading pace at the end, thanks to a fading tyre and a recalcitrant gearchange.

In the second high-speed rodeo a three-rider group ended up with only 0.117 between them, as Vermeulen sent the roars from the yellow-clad masses at Ten Kate's home track right off the dial. Just 0.037 behind, Toseland was staking a claim right to the last yards, with Haga directly in their wake.

Chili had faded to a mere 3.9 seconds behind, with Laconi six seconds down and not happy about it.

There were a total of four different leaders in the second race, in which the lead changed eight times over the start-finish line, and many more times out on the long and demanding track. It almost made race one look pedestrian, as Vermeulen found the missing set-up from the opener, and a more co-operative gearchange. He and Toseland went through an astonishing last lap, overtaking where more experienced riders wouldn't dream of, swapping the lead like it was a white-hot coal, Haga waiting to pounce.

The high-corner-speed, big-throttle style of Leon Haslam worked well at Assen, running sixth in both races, outperforming many a bigger name with more experience. In race two he headed up a man-to-man-to-man fight with Martin and McCoy, the latter being expected to shine at Assen, until he retired with a broken oil line clamp.

Troy Corser was a tougher, faster prospect in the second race, finishing seventh and gaining in the corners what his three-cylinder machine lost in the faster sections - especially exiting slower corners.

Toseland's 45 point haul put him into the lead in the championship again, with three other riders still very much in it; Laconi, Vermeulen and Haga.

IMOLA

Expressionist art came to Imola, with this year's French action painter proving to be a master of the endlessly curving and undulating Imola landscape. The results of the second city-centre Italian track of the year delivered a double body blow to Laconi's competition, as he repossessed the championship lead in fluent style.

His approach to the races seemed clear, get away with the front-runners from his pole position, check out the pace, and then put in a push at the end, hard enough to crush the rest. Toseland was the only one to remain uncrushed, but nonetheless beaten on both occasions.

From the start Laconi's plan worked perfectly, as he pounced on Vermeulen's front-running stretch right at the terminus of the opener, winning by 1.122 seconds. Vermeulen's bike was losing front-end feel, thanks to a loose component in the steering train. Behind these two, five seconds from the lead, James Toseland brought his works Duke home third, fending off Haga in the process.

McCoy, who had actually been to the Imola circuit before, despite his lack of World Superbike mileage, went fifth, having an eventually lonely ride: eight seconds up on Martin, 18 seconds ahead of Chili.

In the second outing, it was Toseland who felt the might of Laconi, but only after another hard and fast battle of wits and wills between the two. The last laps were tense and endlessly thrilling affairs, with Laconi finally passing to win by only a sliver-like 0.041 seconds. Such was their pace that the next best rider was Steve Martin, 12 seconds away from the win.

The complete dominance also had something to do with the fact that Vermeulen was firmly out of the contest, and also that Haga had fallen out of contention for the win in spectacular fashion, as his bike let him down once more when the throttle jammed wide open. One title contender was on the skids.

Gianluca Nannelli, having started his year on the Pedercini Ducati 998, jumped ship to the Ducati SC Xerox team, to ride a spare 999. He took it to fifth at Imola, showing what could be done by a new rider with the home crowd behind him, beating McCoy on a similar bike by five seconds.

The start of race two proved to be testing for Chris Vermeulen. First his number one bike played up on the sighting lap. He switched to the spare for the warm-up lap, then following riders reported a sudden mist of oil or water from the CBR. The young Aussie was promptly high-sided, bashing his hand, hip and ankle.

Given a lift back to the pits by Giovanni Bussei (an act of charity for which the bearded Italian was punished with a pit lane ride through) Vermeulen hobbled back to his pit, climbing through a signalling gap to reach it, and started race two from pit lane, on his revived number one bike. He lapped as fast as the leaders, but too far away to hope to catch them. His title hopes were dwindling fast.

Chili was hardly in better shape at the start of each race. He had been forced to start each 21-lapper from 16th place on the grid after another Superpole mishap, making his race one seventh place an excellent result, his race two DNF more indicative of his luck this year, thanks to a broken fuel feed line.

A 12th and tenth for the Foggy Petronas team showed that Imola was not a good track for the FP-1 in race situations, and their misery was compounded as Walker was a double no-scorer, even though he finished race two – in 16th – after a gravel trap adventure.

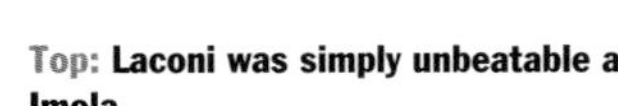

Top: Laconi was simply unbeatable at Imola.

Above centre: Chili talks tyres with Pirelli's Barbier.

Above: Vermeulen, hurt and effectively out of the championship.

Left: In race two, injury notwithstanding, Vermeulen came through from nowhere to a brave sixth.

Photographs: Gold & Goose

Round 10
IMOLA, Italy

26 September 2004, 3.065-mile/4.933-km circuit

Race 1 21 laps, 64.365 miles/103.593 km

Pl.	Name Nat.(Machine)	No.	Time & gap	Laps
1	Regis Laconi, F (Ducati)	55	38m 58.507s	21
			99.094 mph/159.476 km/h	
2	Chris Vermeulen, AUS (Honda)	17	1.122s	21
3	James Toseland, GB (Ducati)	52	5.638s	21
4	Noriyuki Haga, J (Ducati)	41	6.610s	21
5	Garry McCoy, AUS (Ducati)	24	11.974s	21
6	Steve Martin, AUS (Ducati)	99	19.998s	21
7	Pierfrancesco Chili, I (Ducati)	7	29.739s	21
8	Marco Borciani, I (Ducati)	20	30.480s	21
9	Gianluca Nannelli, I (Ducati)	69	41.211s	21
10	Leon Haslam, GB (Ducati)	91	47.972s	21
11	Ivan Clementi, I (Kawasaki)	8	50.346s	21
12	Troy Corser, AUS (Petronas)	4	53.678s	21
13	Piergiorgio Bontempi, I (Suzuki)	5	1m 14.357s	21
14	Luca Pini, I (Suzuki)	29	1m 15.707s	21
15	Doriano Romboni, I (Yamaha)	28	1m 22.993s	21
16	Andrea Mazzali, I (MV Agusta)	74	1m 41.047s	21
17	Warwick Nowland, AUS (Suzuki)	12	1m 43.993s	21
18	Giuseppe Zannini, I (Ducati)	31	1m 44.171s	21
19	Jiri Mrkyvka, CZ (Ducati)	23	1m 46.249s	21
20	Paolo Blora, I (Yamaha)	113	1m 50.276s	21
21	Giancarlo de Matteis, I (Ducati)	27	1 lap	20

DNF: Lucio Pedercini, I (Ducati) 19, 16 laps; Giovanni Bussei, I (Ducati) 200, 16 laps; Stephane Duterne, F (Kawasaki) 39, 13 laps; Sergio Fuertes, E (Suzuki) 16, 11 laps; Chris Walker, GB (Petronas) 9, 9 laps; Alessio Velini, I (Ducati) 25, 9 laps; Miguel Praia, P (Ducati) 50, 1 lap; Pawel Szkopek, POL (Suzuki) 94, 1 lap.

Fastest lap: Laconi, 1m 50.708s, 99.675 mph/160.411 km/h.

Race 2 16 laps, 59.920 miles/96.432 km

Pl.	Name Nat.(Machine)	No.	Time & gap	Laps
1	Regis Laconi, F (Ducati)	55	39m 04.926s	21
			98.822 mph/159.039 km/h	
2	James Toseland, GB (Ducati)	52	0.041s	21
3	Steve Martin, AUS (Ducati)	99	12.352s	21
4	Gianluca Nannelli, I (Ducati)	69	23.165s	21
5	Garry McCoy, AUS (Ducati)	24	28.637s	21
6	Chris Vermeulen, AUS (Honda)	17	31.718s	21
7	Lucio Pedercini, I (Ducati)	19	35.042s	21
8	Marco Borciani, I (Ducati)	20	39.077s	21
9	Ivan Clementi, I (Kawasaki)	8	39.340s	21
10	Troy Corser, AUS (Petronas)	4	39.653s	21
11	Giovanni Bussei, I (Ducati)	200	43.934s	21
12	Leon Haslam, GB (Ducati)	91	54.350s	21
13	Luca Pini, I (Suzuki)	29	1m 03.144s	21
14	Doriano Romboni, I (Yamaha)	28	1m 07.509s	21
15	Alessio Velini, I (Ducati)	25	1m 08.002s	21
16	Chris Walker, GB (Petronas)	9	1m 20.564s	21
17	Andrea Mazzali, I (MV Agusta)	74	1m 24.381s	21
18	Warwick Nowland, AUS (Suzuki)	12	1m 28.430s	21
19	Jiri Mrkyvka, CZ (Ducati)	23	1m 43.373s	21
20	Giuseppe Zannini, I (Ducati)	31	1 lap	20
21	Miguel Praia, P (Ducati)	50	1 lap	20
22	Paolo Blora, I (Yamaha)	113	1 lap	20
23	Pawel Szkopek, POL (Suzuki)	94	1 lap	20
24	Stephane Duterne, F (Kawasaki)	39	2 laps	19

DNF: Norikyuki Haga, J (Ducati) 41, 9 laps; Piergiorgio Bontempi, I (Suzuki) 5, 8 laps; Pierfrancesco Chili, I (Ducati) 7, 5 laps; Sergio Fuertes, E (Suzuki) 16, 4 laps.

DNS: Giancarlo de Matteis, I (Ducati) 27.

Fastest lap: Haga, 1m 50.914s, 99.490 mph/160.113 km/h.

Superpole: Laconi, 1m 49.818s, 100.483 mph/161.711 km/h.

Lap record: Troy Bayliss, AUS (Ducati), 1m 48.389s, 101.807 mph/163.843 km/h (2002).

Championship points: 1 Laconi, 295; 2 Toseland, 291; 3 Vermeulen, 282; 4 Haga, 254; 5 Chili, 222; 6 McCoy, 185; 7 Martin, 170; 8 Haslam, 150; 9 Corser, 137; 10 Borciani, 130; 11 Walker, 112; 12 Clementi, 85; 13 Sanchini, 79; 14 Nannelli, 72; 15 Bontempi, 63.

Round 11
MAGNY-COURS, France
26 September 2004, 3.065-mile/4.933-km circuit

Race 1 23 laps, 63.043 miles/101.453 km

Pl.	Name Nat.(Machine)	No.	Time & gap	Laps
1	James Toseland, GB (Ducati)	52	39m 29.197s	23
			95.789 mph/154.158 km/h	
2	Noriyuki Haga, J (Ducati)	41	0.492s	23
3	Regis Laconi, F (Ducati)	55	3.802s	23
4	Sébastien Gimbert, F (Yamaha)	32	7.827s	23
5	Steve Martin, AUS (Ducati)	99	13.826s	23
6	Pierfrancesco Chili, I (Ducati)	7	25.341s	23
7	Leon Haslam, GB (Ducati)	91	28.993s	23
8	Chris Walker, GB (Petronas)	9	32.456s	23
9	Garry McCoy, AUS (Ducati)	24	42.453s	23
10	Stephane Duterne, F (Kawasaki)	39	50.955s	23
11	Piergiorgio Bontempi, I (Suzuki)	5	1m 02.192s	23
12	Lucio Pedercini, I (Ducati)	19	1m 09.547s	23
13	Stefano Cruciani, I (Kawasaki)	15	1m 15.209s	23
14	Alessio Velini, I (Ducati)	25	1m 15.891s	23
15	Pawel Szkopek, POL (Suzuki)	94	1m 23.974s	23
16	Warwick Nowland, AUS (Suzuki)	12	1m 24.172s	23
17	Berto Camlek, SLO (Yamaha)	77	1m 44.433s	23
18	Miguel Praia, P (Ducati)	50	1 lap	22
19	Carl Berthelsen, N (Suzuki)	33	1 lap	22

DNF: Troy Corser, AUS (Petronas) 4, 13 laps; Chris Vermeulen, AUS (Honda) 17, 11 laps; Gianluca Nannelli, I (Ducati) 69, 11 laps; Giovanni Bussei, I (Ducati) 200, 7 laps; Jiri Mrkyvka, CZ (Ducati) 23, 7 laps; Teodor Myszkowski, POL (Yamaha) 78, 4 laps; Ivan Clementi, I (Kawasaki) 8, 1 lap; Sergio Fuertes, E (Suzuki) 16, 1 lap; Marco Borciani, I (Ducati) 20, 0 laps.

Fastest lap: Martin, 1m 42.312s, 96.442 mph/155.208 km/h.

Race 2 23 laps, 63.043 miles/101.453 km

Pl.	Name Nat.(Machine)	No.	Time & gap	Laps
1	Noriyuki Haga, J (Ducati)	41	39m 34.329s	23
			95.582 mph/153.825 km/h	
2	James Toseland, GB (Ducati)	52	3.155s	23
3	Regis Laconi, F (Ducati)	55	5.790s	23
4	Sébastien Gimbert, F (Yamaha)	32	4.753s	23
5	Pierfrancesco Chili, I (Ducati)	7	17.507s	23
6	Leon Haslam, GB (Ducati)	91	21.303s	23
7	Troy Corser, AUS (Petronas)	4	21.476s	23
8	Chris Walker, GB (Petronas)	9	37.621s	23
9	Garry McCoy, AUS (Ducati)	24	45.483s	23
10	Warwick Nowland, AUS (Suzuki)	12	53.552s	23
11	Stephane Duterne, F (Kawasaki)	39	55.496s	23
12	Sergio Fuertes, E (Suzuki)	16	59.276s	23
13	Pawel Szkopek, POL (Suzuki)	94	1m 11.724s	23
14	Miguel Praia, P (Ducati)	50	1 lap	22
15	Berto Camlek, SLO (Yamaha)	77	1 lap	22
16	Teodor Myszkowski, POL (Yamaha)	78	1 lap	22

DNF: Carl Berthelsen, N (Suzuki) 33, 19 laps; Marco Borciani, I (Ducati) 20, 18 laps; Chris Vermeulen, AUS (Honda) 17, 18 laps; Alessio Velini, I (Ducati) 25, 18 laps; Piergiorgio Bontempi, I (Suzuki) 5, 16 laps; Stefano Cruciani, I (Kawasaki) 15, 16 laps; Steve Martin, AUS (Ducati) 99, 10 laps; Gianluca Nannelli, I (Ducati) 69, 7 laps; Jiri Mrkyvka, CZ (Ducati) 23, 0 laps.

DNS: Giovanni Bussei, I (Ducati) 200; Lucio Pedercini, I (Ducati) 19.

Fastest lap: Haga, 1m 42.475s, 96.288 mph/154.961 km/h.

Superpole: Corser, 1m 41.547s, 97.168 mph/156.377 km/h.

Lap record: Neil Hodgson, GB (Ducati), 1m 41.219s, 97.483 mph/156.884 km/h (2003).

Final World Championship points: see page 171.

MAGNY COURS

With Laconi in front of Toseland in the run up to the championship finale, the last race taking place in France, and with Laconi taking in more of a blessing from the Ducati bosses than Toseland's quiet Anglo nature could muster, the Frenchman was very much in the driving seat for the title on the final weekend.

Now, with Vermeulen injured, Haga realistically out of it after his Imola mishaps, there were two battles going on within the Fila Ducati camp – one for the race wins and the other for the title itself.

Vermeulen was ruled out of a dream championship with a double no score after two technical problems. Honour aplenty for all involved in the Ten Kate Honda campaign, but no big trophy in year one.

Some said Laconi would bend under pressure, as he had done at Magny Cours the previous year, when – in third place overall – he ended his season fourth, behind one James Toseland.

Fifth in Superpole, despite his pace in regulation qualifying, gave a clue to Laconi's race-day action, after some tyre choice issues arose. With tension overflowing from the factory Ducati pit, Laconi had to chase home not just the first race winner Toseland, who rode on a full-steam setting for all 23 laps, but eventual second-place man Haga.

Toseland and Haga enjoyed a fight early on, with Vermeulen in third, Laconi breathing in his exhaust vapour and wild card Gimbert fifth. Laconi went to third at Adelaide, just as Vermeulen's bike started to misbehave for the first time.

Only Toseland and Haga led the first race over the finish line, with Toseland's unbroken run of 17 up-front laps ending with the crucial final one, giving him the win by only 0.492 seconds. Laconi languished in third, losing grip and confidence in his front tyre as the race wore on – a factor of his heavy front end riding style. To his credit, he never gave up, setting his best lap of the race on lap 15.

Local wild card Sebastien Gimbert, on his Yamaha France R1, perked up the crowd after qualifying impressively, and did it again in race one taking

fourth place, with Steve Martin running fifth, some six seconds adrift of the leaders.

In race two the hole-shot went to Superpole winner Corser again as Toseland and Vermeulen played wrestle-mania. Both wheelying a little and thus unbalanced going off the line, they were on a crash course until Toseland poked out an elbow to stop a possible bike-to-bike contact. He needn't have bothered, as Vermeulen once more ground to a halt, thanks to a faulty crank sensor.

The same front tyre problems that afflicted Laconi in race one gave Toseland no chance to beat Haga to the win, but the key was in beating Laconi into third place. Toseland had already overtaken him in the points after race one's dramas, but his pure determination to succeed seemed to be the difference between the two on the day.

Toseland's mature and belief-laden day of glory was particularly significant given the fact that at 23 years, 11 months and 29 days he was the youngest ever champion.

Behind the big three Gimbert was once more fourth, ahead of Chili and Haslam. Troy Corser ended his Foggy Petronas career with a seventh.

Rookie of the year proved to be Leon Haslam, winning US $20,000 for his trouble, and he secured a seventh in race one, sixth in race two.

Above: Wild card Gimbert was a popular double fourth on the Yamaha.

Above left: Corser was a happy Superpole winner, but the Petronas suffered in race conditions.

Top: Haga backs it in, under pressure from Toseland (52), Laconi (55) and the rest of the pack.

Left: New champion Toseland celebrates with his factory Ducati squad.

Photographs: Gold & Goose

Toseland's up and down season grew in strength and ended in triumph for the youngest ever Superbike champion. Here he crosses the line as champion at Magny Cours.
Photograph: Gold & Goose

WORLD SUPERBIKE CHAMPIONSHIP RESULTS 2004

Position	Rider	Nationality	Machine	Valencia/1	Valencia/2	Phillip Island/1	Phillip Island/2	Misano/1	Misano/2	Monza/1	Monza/2	Oschersleben/1	Oschersleben/2	Silverstone/1	Silverstone/2	Laguna Seca/1	Laguna Seca/2	Brands Hatch/1	Brands Hatch/2	Assen/1	Assen/2	Imola/1	Imola/2	Magny-Cours/1	Magny-Cours/2	Points total
1	James Toseland	GB	Ducati	25	20	16	-	6	10	20	20	20	20	-	11	13	20	9	-	25	20	16	20	25	20	336
2	Regis Laconi	F	Ducati	-	-	25	-	25	20	25	25	10	25	-	16	11	16	20	-	16	11	25	25	16	16	327
3	Noriyuki Haga	J	Ducati	-	25	8	10	13	13	-	-	25	-	25	20	10	13	25	25	13	16	13	-	20	25	299
4	Chris Vermeulen	AUS	Honda	4	11	20	20	11	4	13	-	1	8	20	25	25	25	13	16	11	25	20	10	-	-	282
5	Pierfrancesco Chili	I	Ducati	20	13	7	16	16	25	-	-	16	-	16	-	20	11	-	20	20	13	9	-	10	11	243
6	Garry McCoy	AUS	Ducati	9	10	11	25	-	-	16	16	7	13	13	8	9	9	-	9	8	-	11	11	7	7	199
7	Steve Martin	AUS	Ducati	-	16	13	-	9	16	-	8	11	-	10	10	16	10	16	-	9	-	10	16	11	-	181
8	Leon Haslam	GB	Ducati	11	7	-	6	5	11	11	13	9	16	11	13	7	-	-	-	10	10	6	4	9	10	169
9	Troy Corser	AUS	Petronas	-	5	3	11	20	9	7	11	13	-	9	7	6	-	11	-	6	9	4	6	-	9	146
10	Marco Borciani	I	Ducati	13	8	9	13	-	6	9	10	-	-	8	5	5	8	5	-	7	8	8	8	-	-	130
11	Chris Walker	GB	Petronas	16	9	6	8	10	3	8	9	-	9	-	4	-	-	7	13	4	6	-	-	8	8	128
12	Ivan Clementi	I	Kawasaki	-	2	5	7	4	-	5	6	5	7	6	6	-	6	2	5	-	7	5	7	-	-	85
13	Mauro Sanchini	I	Kawasaki	2	6	10	9	-	5	-	7	6	10	-	3	8	7	-	6	-	-	-	-	-	-	79
14	Gianluca Nannelli	I	Ducati	10	-	4	4	8	-	-	-	4	11	-	-	-	-	6	-	5	-	7	13	-	-	72
15	Piergiorgio Bontempi	I	Suzuki	1	-	-	5	7	1	6	5	2	5	7	2	3	4	1	4	3	4	3	-	5	-	68
16	Lucio Pedercini	I	Ducati	-	3	-	-	-	8	-	4	-	-	-	1	4	5	3	-	-	-	-	9	4	-	41
17	Sergio Fuertes	E	Suzuki	8	4	-	-	-	-	10	-	-	-	3	-	-	-	-	3	1	2	-	-	-	4	35
18	Sébastien Gimbert	F	Yamaha	-	-	-	-	-	-	-	-	-	-	-	-	-	-	-	7	-	-	-	-	13	13	33
19	James Ellison	GB	Yamaha	-	-	-	-	-	-	-	-	-	-	-	9	-	-	10	11	-	-	-	-	-	-	30
20	Warwick Nowland	AUS	Suzuki	5	-	1	2	-	-	-	-	-	-	5	-	-	3	-	-	2	3	-	-	-	6	27
21	Giovanni Bussei	I	Ducati	-	-	-	-	-	-	-	-	-	-	-	-	-	-	4	10	-	5	-	5	-	-	24
22	Alessio Velini	I	Ducati	-	-	2	3	3	-	-	3	-	4	-	-	-	-	-	2	-	-	-	1	2	-	20
23	Horst Saiger	A	Yamaha	7	1	-	-	-	-	3	2	-	-	-	-	2	2	-	-	-	-	-	-	-	-	17
24	Craig Coxhell	AUS	Honda	-	-	-	-	-	-	-	-	-	-	-	-	-	-	8	8	-	-	-	-	-	-	16
25	Jiri Mrkyvka	CZ	Ducati	6	-	-	-	-	-	-	-	-	3	4	-	-	-	-	-	-	-	-	-	-	-	13
26	Luca Pini	1	Suzuki	-	-	-	-	-	7	-	-	-	-	-	-	-	-	-	-	-	-	2	3	-	-	12
27	Stephane Duterne	F	Kawasaki	-	-	-	-	-	-	-	-	-	-	-	-	-	-	-	-	-	-	-	-	6	5	11
28	Andy Meklau	A	Suzuki	-	-	-	-	-	-	-	-	3	6	-	-	-	-	-	-	-	-	-	-	-	-	9
29	Jurgen Oelschläger	D	Honda	-	-	-	-	-	-	-	-	8	-	-	-	-	-	-	-	-	-	-	-	-	-	8
30	Miguel Praia	P	Ducati	3	-	-	-	-	-	-	-	-	-	2	-	-	-	-	1	-	-	-	-	-	2	8
31	Giancarlo de Matteis	I	Ducati	-	-	-	-	-	-	4	-	-	-	-	-	-	-	-	-	-	-	-	-	-	-	4
32=	Pawel Szkopek	POL	Suzuki	-	-	-	-	-	-	-	-	-	-	-	-	-	-	-	-	-	-	-	-	1	3	4
32=	Ivan Sala	I	Suzuki	-	-	-	-	2	-	2	-	-	-	-	-	-	-	-	-	-	-	-	-	-	-	4
34	Stefano Cruciani	I	Kawasaki	-	-	-	-	-	-	-	-	-	-	-	-	-	-	-	-	-	-	-	-	3	-	3
35=	Gianmaria Liverani	I	Ducati	-	-	-	-	1	2	-	-	-	-	-	-	-	-	-	-	-	-	-	-	-	-	3
35=	Doriano Romboni	I	Yamaha	-	-	-	-	-	-	-	-	-	-	-	-	-	-	-	-	-	-	1	2	-	-	3
37	Carl Berthelsen	N	Suzuki	-	-	-	-	-	-	-	-	-	2	-	-	-	-	-	-	-	-	-	-	-	-	2
38=	Berto Camlek	SLO	Yamaha	-	-	-	-	-	-	-	-	-	-	-	-	-	-	-	-	-	-	-	-	-	1	1
[illegible]	[illegible]	NL	Suzuki	-	-	-	-	-	-	-	-	-	-	-	-	-	-	-	-	-	1	-	-	-	-	1

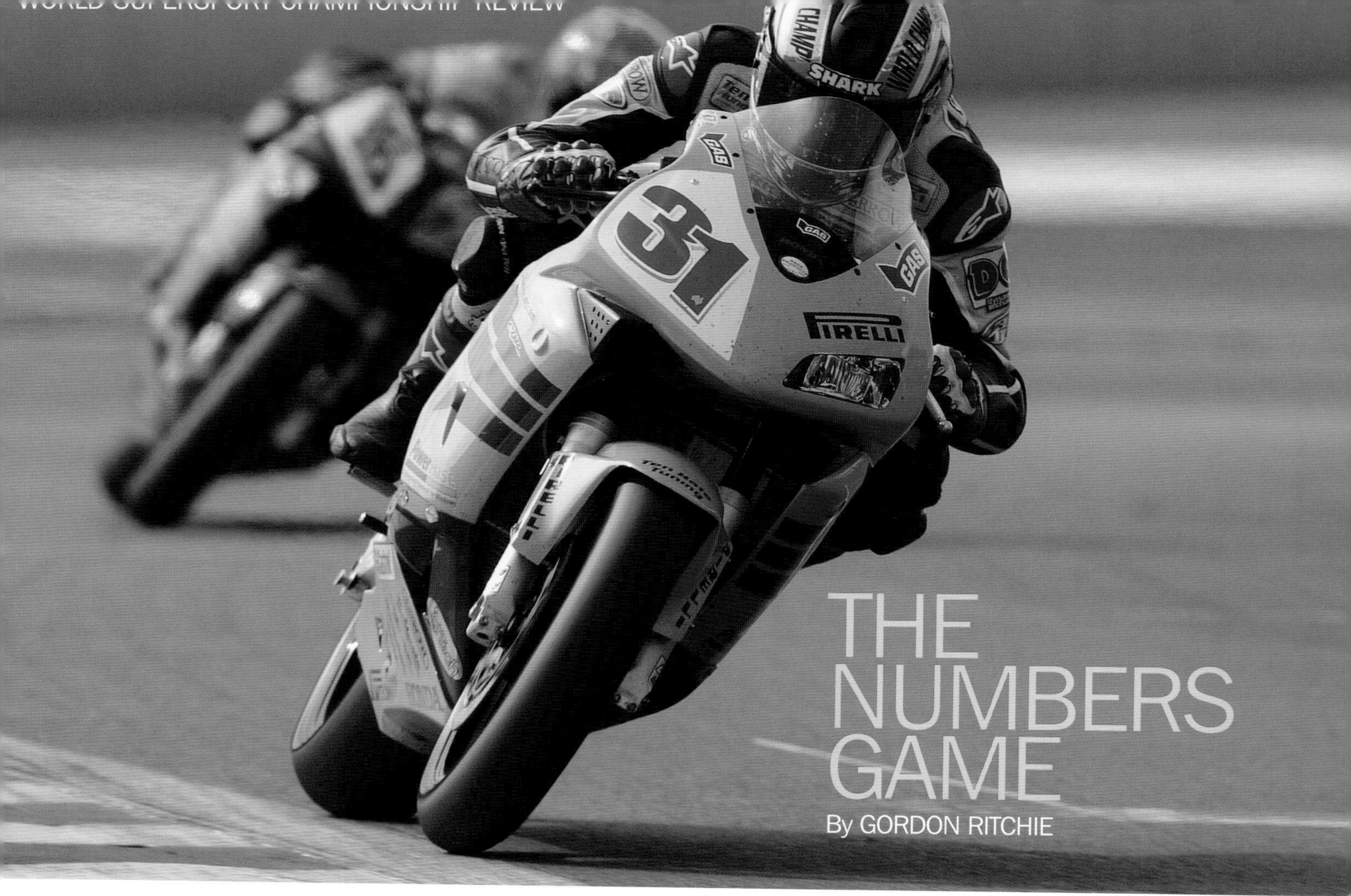

THE NUMBERS GAME

By GORDON RITCHIE

Top: Muggeridge in front – a familiar position for the Honda rider.

Above: Karl Muggeridge was a worthy successor to former Australian champions Vermeulen and Pitt.

Above centre: Ten Kate team-mate and compatriot Broc Parkes was the next best thing.

Above right: Rare Honda-free podium in Valencia: Foret, van den Goorbergh and one-time top-three Suzuki rider Fujiwara.
Photographs: Gold & Goose

THE World Championship class that best represents the products the global manufacturers actually sell once more enticed and entertained, but like any evolving organism, the latest mutations of the category caught the world with its preconceptions exposed.

After Vermeulen's impressive winning run in 2003, plus record points haul for the Ten Kate Honda Team, we all expected a more closely fought battle for outright supremacy this time round in the world of six - if only because a full factory seven, in the form of the 749cc twin-cylinder Ducati, promised more than just a different engine note.

But, for the third straight year, the Supersport planet would be painted – actually slathered – bright yellow, not just by the champion Karl Muggeridge, but with his fellow Aussie and Ten Kate team-mate Broc Parkes joining up by season's end.

It shouldn't really have been that way, but once again, in record-breaking style, it was largely a one-rider, one-manufacturer, and one-team benefit – a ten-venue Ten Kate whirlwind tour, with familiar stage direction and props but a new leading man.

There were, given the political and financial fallout from the Pirelli one-make supplier deal and the simple downturn in WSS budgets, fewer bikes which we could even loosely call 'factory.'

For Honda there were six not eight, with one new team sheltering under the wide wingspan of Honda support. The Ten Kate pairing were joined by the experienced Klaffi Honda rider Sebastien Charpentier, plus new revelation and deserved rookie of the year, Max Neukirchner, who had never even ridden a four stroke before testing here...

A swerve away from Yamaha power saw Team Italia Megabike campaign CBR600RRs, in the experienced hands of Alessio Corradi (out injured and unloved by season's end, replaced by MotoGP refugee Michel Fabrizio) and rookie Denis Sacchetti.

Yamaha shrunk their effort to four YZF-R6s (an occasional five at end of season) for the in-house Team Yamaha Italia (nee Belgarda) squad and the Yamaha Motor Germany outfit. The Italians ran the now seasoned WSS force of Jurgen van den Goorbergh and 2002 champion Fabien Foret, conveniently available after Kawasaki pulled out. 2001 champion Andrew Pitt would also join them for the last three races.

In the Yamaha Motor Germany team 2003 Sugo race winner Christian Kellner was teamed up with another proven entity, Aussie Kevin Curtain. In sheer weight of Antipodean numbers, Supersport was something of a Diggers' World Tour yet again.

Suzuki, unlike most of their rivals, had no Aussies, but they had an all-new GSX-R600 to play with, only to rue its over-stiff chassis and consequently deafening chatter. One podium all year told the story loudly enough. With the Superbike arm of the Alstare squad now chopped off, Francis Batta's boys ran to three, Stephane Chambon (1999 Champ), Katsuaki Fujiwara and Vittorio Iannuzzo.

The most exciting entry was that of Ducati, waiting a year to unleash the 749R and putting it in the hands of European Superstock Championship runner up Lorenzo Lanzi, with only moderate success. Part of their confidence in Supersport 2004-style was that with new merit – they would be at no tyre disadvantage.

Yet tyres were once more a sticky subject, not least at round one.

Winter testing had suggested hopes of a free-for-all might be in vain, and that the three-in-a-row winning streak of Muggeridge at the tail end of 2003 would probably continue at round one in Valencia. Practice times unmistakeably hollered the same thing.

Come the race and the FIM decided to exercise the right they had under the new tyre rules, and make pole man Muggeridge use one of the sets of control tyres they took possession of at every round. To the horror and rage of the Ten Kate team, Muggeridge experienced grip problems that had not arisen in previous race simulations on supposedly the same tyre choice, and he finished eighth.

Dark mutterings ensued, but arch-rival van den Goorbergh won, his team-mate Foret second, with Fujiwara's Suzuki third.

Muggeridge's season moved to another shocker in round two, on home territory at Phillip Island. Again on pole, he would run out 12th, after problems with an engine misfire.

This left local Honda/Michelin regular Josh Brookes, making a weekend swap to Pirellis, free to win the race from his near constant companion, Curtain. With van den Goorbergh third at PI it was looking bleak for Muggeridge, now in tenth place and with only eight races to claw it back.

Over the next three, however, "Muggas" would take two poles and three wins - and hop from tenth to third, to second and then take the lead in the series.

His first win at Misano, round three, was a clear one from Curtain and van den Goorbergh, while the subsequent Monza race was also a Muggeridge benefit, but only after Foret (and sixth place Iannuzzo) were disqualified due to faulty ignition cut-out switches. Parkes thus got his first podium, a second place, with van den Goorbergh third, some 13 seconds down on the leader.

Muggeridge's first hat trick was completed by a win at Oschersleben in late May, but it took a bit longer than that for him to be finally credited with it. Having just edged out Parkes, with Charpentier a rallying third, Muggeridge and all the top Hondas were subsequently excluded for something as prosaic as an out-of-spec rear wheel spindle.

In Supersport, parts have to be homologated as individual items, as well as components on a complete homologated machine. As it transpired, not even Honda has someone who weighs each item individually. Rather, because of the deadline for homologation papers to arrive with the FIM (in turn because the final production bikes are usually not even built when homologation takes place) the size, shape, and material of construction of each component are fed into a computer by the manufacturer and a homologation mass is reached by calculation, with a real-world plus-or-minus tolerance allowed by the FIM.

The rear wheel spindle on the Ten Kate and Klaffi machines, and every other Honda in the field, were the same standard parts as on the road bikes in the car park – something they also must be by regulation. Trouble was, every standard CBR600RR wheel spindle ever made also happened to be out of tolerance in the paper world of the FIM rulebook.

Ten Kate were once more apoplectic at the initial FIM decision to exclude the top three. The competition, who had allegedly tipped off the FIM to the error, were laughing so hard they cried into their pasta and beer for a while– until they realised that more than one component of their own machines was also not quite to regulation.

After much discussion in Geneva, measurement of off-the-shelf Honda parts all over Europe and embarrassed silences, common sense reigned. Honda were fined for their uncharacteristic error in homologation, the "Oschersleben Three" got their points back, no complaints were levied at the other manufacturers, and everybody marched on to the next race at Silverstone, with worn-out rulebooks firmly locked away for a while.

In England Muggeridge would be relegated to second best for the last time in 2004, as Foret secured a win in a classic race. All top four riders - Foret, Muggeridge, Parkes and Ducati rider Lanzi – were within 0.7 seconds at the flag.

The long summer break was a troubling time for some, relaxing for the other King Karl, and sure enough the magical Muggeridge mystery tour took in Brands Hatch, Assen, Imola and finally Magny Cours in almost unimpeachable winning style. Only Parkes barred the path to legend, temporarily, as he finally won pole from Muggeridge at Magny Cours.

Yamaha only scored two podiums in the last four WSS outings, as Muggeridge and Charpentier led home van den Goorbergh at Brands; returnee Pitt at Assen.

The last two races were an all Honda benefit, with the same finishing order of Muggeridge, Parkes and Charpentier. Game, very definitely, over.

Muggeridge simply transcended the class in all respects in 2004, dropping only five points in the last eight races of the year. To put his achievements into perspective, he took one round less to beat Vermeulen's previous record points total, and secured the overall win with a race in hand. In addition, he took a new record of seven race wins in a year, eight poles and, in almost every session, he comprehensively hoovered the wind out of everyone else's sails.

Three riders championships in a row for Ten Kate and Honda, each more imposing than the last.

EUROPEAN SUPERSTOCK CHAMPIONSHIP

If Hondas ruled the Supersport roost then the cock of the Superstock walk was the angular and aggressive Yamaha YZF-R1. With no Superbike effort to worry about, Yamaha ploughed some budget into Team Italia Lorenzini by Leoni, and the Yamaha Motor Germany team, which featured Turkish wonder-kid Kenan Sofuoglu and Belgian battler Didier Vankeymeulen.

The Italians, Lorenzo Alfonsi and Gianluca Vizziello, proved most efficacious in almost every case, taking all but one of the nine race wins; an eventual four each. Riccardo Chiarello had the honour of presenting Suzuki and Alstare with their lone success of the season, at Imola.

Long term leader Vizziello looked a little more suited to the champions' robes with two rounds left, but a bizarre accident in the pre-race promotional mini-Supermotard race at Imola – organised by embarrassed promoters FGSport – left Vizziello with severe radius and ulna fractures. This allowed Alfonsi an open field - but in a final bizarre twist he had to wait until the last round at Magny Cours, after his gear linkage broke in the penultimate race at Imola, leaving him out of the points.

Still 16 points adrift of Vizziello, he had to finish in the top two in France. After a moment of mid-race doubt, Alfonsi conquered his nerves, reeled in the full 25 points, scoring a final 169 to Vizziello's 160. Sofuoglu went third with 104, Vankeymeulen fourth on 90.

In other circumstances the nature of the eventual championship win would have been devastating for one rider, euphoric for another. But true tragedy had already struck the Superstock community in 2004, at Assen, when 20-year-old rider Alessio Perilli was killed after a collision with other riders on a particularly high-speed section. It made way for changes in 2005, with 15-20 year old riders limited to 600 Superstock machines, in a whole new class, while the existing series will cater for up to 24 year-olds.

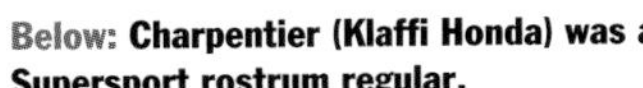

Below: Charpentier (Klaffi Honda) was a Supersport rostrum regular.

Below left: Yamaha's Kevin Curtain at Monza.

Below centre: Lorenzo Alfonsi celebrates his Yamaha championship at the final Superstock round at Magny Cours.

Bottom: Former champion Stephane Chambon was back on the Suzuki.

Photographs: Gold & Goose

SIDECAR REVIEW

WEBSTER AND WOODHEAD'S GRAND SLAM

By JOHN McKENZIE

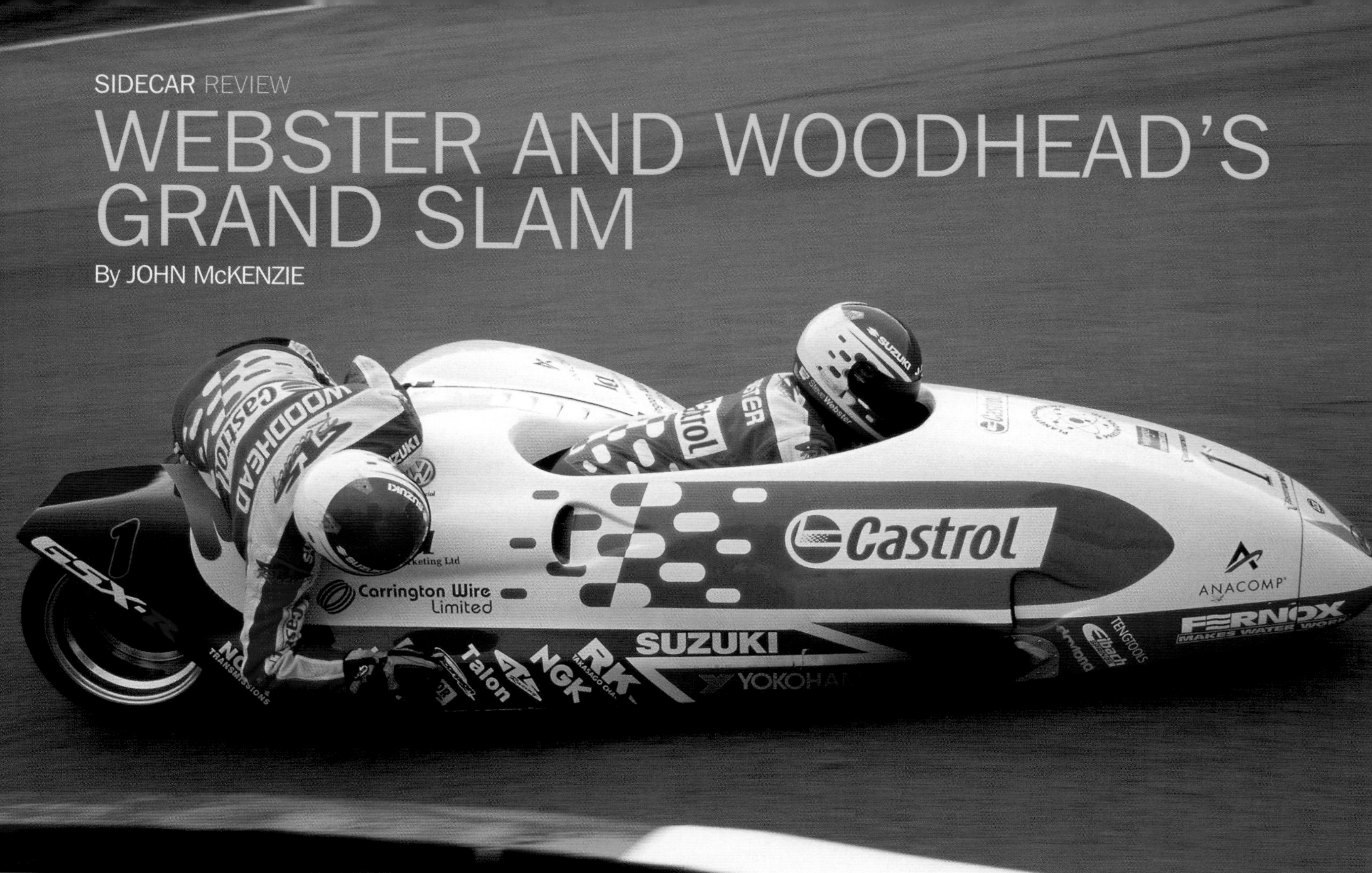

Top: Above: Steve Webster and Paul Woodhead defeated all comers.
Photograph: John McKenzie

THE sidecar class survived its worst ever season in 2004. Amid dealings of Byzantine complexity and Machiavellian insincerity, two versions of the official World Championship series collapsed. Fifty-five years of history were saved at the 11th hour, by a stop-gap one-weekend "FIM World Cup".

In 2003, WSB had hosted the three-wheelers. The plan to repeat this evaporated, then a proposed Britain-based series at BSB rounds failed at the last moment. The season had already started when the FIM instituted the World Cup, a one-day three-race event that would at least preserve the continuity of the championship for the future.

Unravelling the various manoeuvrings would only lend the oxygen of publicity, and further inflate the ballooning egos of those few avaricious self-aggrandising wheeler-dealers and petty bureaucrats who conspired and contrived to do down this most uncomplicated of racing classes.

Perhaps advantageously unencumbered by agents, fair-weather friends and (self-) promoters, the sidecars had to fend for themselves, and in 2004 they did so grandly, with three major titles to strive for in place of the World Championship.

As a result, there were many positive aspects to a season of ever-spectacular and ever-faster track action. Read the story of how one man (and his passenger) once again continued to bolster his place in history, and feel humbled by the unparalleled camaraderie that fosters the sidecar racers' ongoing willingness to turn up and race.

At the time of writing, it had been confirmed that a full eight-round 2005 World Championship had been sanctioned by the FIM, to be arranged at venues where they would be top billing. The early list of dates included a race in St.Petersburg, Russia, which will be the first ever FIM World Championship road race on Russian soil. Other events will be at more usual venues.

Despite what some might say or think, the sidecars are going to be around for a bit longer yet …

The FIM World Cup

Announced mid-season to counter the FIM's fear of losing continuity of a World Championship inaugurated in 1949, the new World Cup featured an arduous programme of three races (50 laps in total!) in one day, September 5, at the tough Schleiz circuit in Germany. The three-wheelers were more than ready for it.

The first leg, an eleven-lap dash, started at 11.00. After qualifying on pole with a margin of more than 3.5 seconds, Castrol Suzuki pair Steve Webster and current passenger Paul Woodhead got their customary bad start. From tenth on the first lap, Webster had to pick steadily through, taking the lead with four laps to go. Once at the front, a couple of fast laps got him a clear win by four seconds, to get day's first haul of 25 points in the bag. Dutchman Martin Van Gils took second, with German Mike Roscher third.

An hour later, and the second leg – this time 17 laps, with the result also counting for UEM points –was a similar story. After a tussle, Webster accelerated away to take another 4.5-second victory, and another crucial 25 points. Van Gils was second again, but Tom Hanks/Phil Biggs took the third rostrum placing.

In the third leg, a full 22 laps, after coming under pressure from Hanks, Tim and Tristan Reeves (on Webbo's 2003 outfit), Roscher and Van Gils, Webster pulled away again after only seven laps. This win was by more than 13 seconds – three out of three, and a record-breaking tenth World (Cup) Title for Webster, his third with Paul Woodhead.

The Yorkshireman now has more individual world championships in one class than anyone in the history of the FIM World Championships. Only Giacomo Agostini with 15 (7 in the 350s, and 8 in the 500s) and Angel Nieto 13 (6 in the 50/80s and 7 in the 125s) have won more World Titles.

"It hasn't sunk in yet, because I'm totally worn out," he said in Germany. "We've raced 50 laps over three races today – the most ever in one day. But it's been worth it. At the start of the season we didn't have a World title to aim for. Thanks to Superside and the FIM for sorting it out."

UEM EUROPEAN CHAMPIONSHIP

The European series started at Vallelunga in Italy on May 15, and finished on October 9 at Cartagena in Spain, taking in an assortment of eastern and northern European circuits in between.

At Vallelunga, Webster and Woodhead blasted from pole to win the 20-lap race in baking 28-degree heat by almost three seconds. Tim and Tristan Reeves had snatched the lead on lap two; three laps later Hanks relegated Webster to third. But the experienced defender waited his time, and at half distance started to move through to take the lead with eight laps to go.

A fortnight later, more baking heat and track temperatures of 42 degrees waited at the Hungaroring. After an early three-way dice, Hanks dropped back as Reeves and Webster continued to jostle for the lead. With five laps to go, Webster made his move and left a flagging Reeves, to win by seven seconds, with Hanks a lonely third.

Webster and Reeves were both away on British Championship duty at Silverstone – a chance for pole qualifier Hanks, Van Gils, and Gallros to reel in some points at Rijeka. Unfortunately, 70mph winds on race day forced cancellation. Controversially, the race was rescheduled for October at Cartegena, the only one of several cancelled UEM races to be treated thus.

July storms hit the next round too, at Most in the Czech Republic. The schedule had to be hastily rearranged around heavy downpours, and the late race cut by two laps. At least the sidecars had a dry track.

Reeves wrested the lead from fast starting Finn Pekka Paivarinta on lap two, leaving the Finn to fight off Hanks, as Webster worked through from sixth on lap one. By the start of lap four Webster was second; with five of 16 laps to go, he finally dispossessed Reeves of the lead, and went on to win by almost four and a half seconds from Hanks, whose pressure on Reeves caused him to miss a gear exiting the hairpin. There was a mere half-second between Hanks and Reeves at the flag.

Almost 17 years to the day since he won his first World Championship at Anderstorp, Webster's hopes of extending the UEM title lead were dashed at the August 7 meeting. Recently ennobled as a Freeman of York (and rewarded with archaic grazing rights!), Webster's race ended in the gravel with five laps to go when the chair wheelhub casting collapsed at high speed. Reeves, now alone out front, was gifted his first international win (and the championship lead), with Hanks 5 seconds down, Swedish veteran Gallros making up the rostrum.

The second World Cup race at Schleiz also counted for this championship, and his win gave Webster an eight-point overall lead.

Two weeks later, at the same track for the next round, Dutch pair Martien and Tonnie Van Gils's outfit suffered a major engine blow-up, showering the track with oil through the racing line at turn 2 after just four laps. Hanks and Biggs close behind skidded and flipped into the gravel trap. Two corners later Gallros, who had picked up oil on his tyres, also crashed out. Fortunately there were no injuries, but the red flags came out.

In spite of the best attempts, the track was deemed impossible to clean, and results taken from the end of lap three, with half points awarded. while debris was cleared. Reeves led from Webster at that point, with Hanks awarded fourth.

The lost Rijeka race was now scheduled for the Friday before the final round on October 9 at Cartagena. Only Rijeka qualifiers were eligible, so Webster and Reeves watched from the pit. A win for Hanks would have given him the points lead, for a last-race showdown. Unfortunately for the challenger, race-long clutch trouble consigned him for fourth, 18 seconds behind winner Galross, and just 1.5 points clear of Webster.

Now Hanks had to finish ahead of Webster for the title, a feat he had never previously achieved. For once, pole starter Webster got away fast, and after the usual opening-lap scuffles, he, Reeves and Hanks were soon pulling away.

Hanks's hopes were dashed after only four laps, when he retired with a blown engine. Now all Webster had to do was finish. He didn't resist as Reeves took off in the lead, and he won in spite of skidding off on the last lap after tangling with backmarkers.

Second was enough to give Webster and Woodhead the Championship to add to their FIM World Cup title, whilst the 25 points for victory gave Reeves second position overall in the championship, just 2.5 points ahead of the luckless Tom Hanks and Phil Biggs.

The Eastern Airways British Championship

The first race at Knockhill at the start of May was cancelled after the meeting was abandoned following an earlier solo crash. Three weeks later, the series did begin at Mondello park, with a win and a second each for Webster/Woodhead and the Reeves pair. Former British GP winner Derek Brindley was twice third, making a comeback after several years away.

Jorg Steinhausen visited the Silverstone round, but he and Reeves were early retirements from the first leg, giving Webster victory by more than four seconds over Greg Lambert, back from the TT. He had robbed Brindley of third on the final lap.

On Sunday, gremlins fixed, Steinhausen scorched away, then disputed the lead fiercely with winner Webster, who caught at half distance and set a new record. Reeves took third

Two more convincing wins and another lap record at Croft at the end of the month extended Webbo's lead over Reeves to 44 points. The first was in damp, dismal conditions; Sunday's win on aggregate time after a red flag – but ultimately in dominant style. Richard Gatt and Paul Randall were twice third.

More problems at Knockhill for round five: Saturday racing was lost to bad weather. Brindley struck lucky with intermediate tyres on a drying track for the first rescheduled ten-lapper, Webster second – like everyone else, on full wets. Heavy rain for the afternoon race meant another tyre gamble. Brian Pedder/Rod Steadman took their first national win. Webster was fourth, Brindley tenth, but Reeves a valuable second.

At Brands Hatch for the August Bank Holiday weekend, Webster had to battle back through from fourth. He got back ahead of Brindley and soon-to-retire Steinhausen for a forceful battle and narrow win over Reeves. On Sunday Webster again fought through from fourth, running a string of eight record laps to make sure of another win over Reeves and Steinhausen.

The seventh round was at Assen, minus both Webster and Reeves, at Schleiz for the World Cup. Brindley put on a masterful display to win both races, resisting early pressure from Steinhausen in race one, and dominating the second.

Castle Combe in late September saw Reeves win race eight, the ever-improving Greg Lambert six seconds behind. Brindley third, with Webster an unaccustomed fourth after picking a wrong rear tyre. No such mistake in leg two. Webster won by 17 seconds, smashing Reeves's new lap record. Reeves and Lambert were on the rostrum.

At the penultimate round, a third visit to Knockhill, Webster got the better of Reeves only in the dash to the flag on a damp track – his ninth win of the series; Andy Laidlow took his first podium. Webster was in control of the second race when he coasted to a halt with an electrical problem. Reeves pounced on the opportunity to close the points lead back to 27, to take the title to the final round, at Mallory Park on October 17. Brindley took second, with Lambert back on the rostrum in third.

Two races left. A win in the first would make Webster unassailable, to claim all three significant titles, to sign off a glorious season, his 21st at the top level. Steve and passenger Woodhead did so majestically, blasting away from the start with brutal precision. Reeves was 13 seconds back at the end; Lambert third.

Webster raced two at his leisure, Reeves second again, Gatt third. The giant of the class ended up with a 37-point margin.

"Paul and I joked about winning all three championships, but we just didn't think it was possible," said a joyful Webster. "But everything we planned has come together. It's been a team effort. The bike got better all through a very fulfilling season."

With pole position almost everywhere, lap records seemingly at will, and 20 wins in 25 finishes. Webster is almost unbeatable. And the rest know it.

Below: Brothers in arms – Tim and Tristram Reeves, here at Brands Hatch, were persistent challengers.
Photograph: John McKenzie

ISLE OF MAN TT REVIEW

NEW HERO FOR THE OLD COURSE

By MAC McDIARMID

PRECISELY 100 years after the first motorsport event on the Isle of Man, it was all change for TT '04. A major review of the races resulted, amongst numerous other measures, in the abandonment of early morning practice, the end (temporarily, as it turned out) of six lap races and the transfer of control of the event from the ACU to the Isle of Man. But above all there would be no David Jefferies. For three years until his death during practice for last year's races, the big Yorkshireman had almost single-handedly carried the mantle of the TT, winning races and trashing lap records with equal abandon. Many of us feared that in his absence the races would become as moribund as they had been with the departure of Hislop and Fogarty a decade earlier.

But cometh the hour, cometh the man. By the Wednesday of practice week it was clear that DJ's boots could be filled - and, fittingly, by one of his closest racing friends. John McGuinness began his evening's work with a record-shattering Junior lap on his R6 Yamaha, 122.92mph, five seconds inside Ryan Farquhar's official record set in last year's race.

Impressive stuff, but we hadn't seen anything yet. Barely 40 minutes later the Morecambe rider eased his Yamaha R1 Superbike around the 37.73 mile course at 127.34mph -- fractionally inside DJ's 2002 lap record.

"The bike's a projectile," McGuinness enthused of a machine which had given so many problems in British Superbike competition, yet had needed scarcely any setting up for the Mountain Course. A month earlier he'd predicted that if the Yamaha "hits the bottom of Bray and it's stable and fast, we're in with a shout. If I get to Ago's in a straight line, I'll be grinning."

He was grinning now. "It's the fastest thing ever", he said of the hastily-prepared R1, "and so, so stable. I've never known the TT to be like this. Conditions tonight were ideal - no wind, no sun, and the track is in really good condition."

These same conditions had put many of the top riders well ahead of the game. Even before his record lap, McGuinness had confided that he'd be "happy to race the Superbike now... just a bit of fine tuning to do." Some of that tuning had already been done - to McGuinness's head - by his one-off team manager, none other than eight-times TT winner, Jim Moodie. In less than a week the Scot's combination of attention to detail and ruthless preparation had helped transform his protege from the forgotten man of British racing to the man to beat.

Other top riders were equally content. Ian Lougher (Honda CBR1000R) and Bruce Anstey (TAS Suzuki GSX-R1000) pronounced themselves satisfied with the week so far, the latter with a scintillating lap at over 126mph. But Anstey's team-mate, 2003 double-winner Archibald had already suffered one engine failure and a broken steering damper, and he'd conclude practice week on his backside at Suby Bridge. Ryan Farquhar's efforts to put a Kawasaki in the frame were handicapped by a wrist broken in a quad accident, whilst fellow fancied Irishman Martin Finnegan was plagued by suspension troubles. Another slimmed-down Irishman, Richard Britton, was also content, despite outbraking himself into the Creg and headbutting the bales.

The same couldn't be said of Shaun Harris, twice a winner last year. Even half a paddock away his body language spoke of a discontented man, struggling to find the measure of his hardware.

With the loss of morning practice, losing the whole of the long Thursday afternoon session might have compromised many teams' setting up. Yet by the conclusion of what was otherwise one of the most benign practice weeks anyone could remember, McGuinness inevitably led the rankings in F1 and Junior, also topping the Production 1000cc leaderboard with a lap of 121.91 on Friday evening.

Robert Dunlop, in what would be his last TT (it was announced during the week that the Ultra Lightweight race will be scrapped from future events, and injuries render him incapable of racing anything bigger), topped the 125cc standing at 109.67mph. Britton led the 400cc class of the same event with 110.04mph on his RVF400 Honda. Meanwhile Anstey, flying in every class in which he competed, headed the Production 600s at 118.81mph.

With the retirement of 10 times winner Rob Fisher, the class of the sidecar field was Manxman Dave Molyneux, now with 22 year-old compatriot Daniel Sayle in the chair. Molly's Tuesday lap at 112.81ph was half a second inside his own lap record, set way back in '99. His closest challenger, Ian Bell, winner of last year's first sidecar race later withdrew after a high-speed crash at Hillberry.

Twenty-four hours later, as the first rain of the week fell - inevitably - as the sidecars prepared to leave, Molyneux instructed his new passenger to "Text your mum we'll be stopping by, and to have steak and chips and a cuppa ready." Dan's mum runs the Island's 'Pub of the Year', not more than two metres from the circuit. Ten minutes later spectators are startled to see the DMR outfit slew into the Sulby Glen Hotel car park. "What's the problem?" asks one. "Peckish", responds Molly.

Less cool by far was the French pairing of Claude Montagnier and Laurent Astier. In the same session in which Molyneux claimed his fastest lap, they managed to crash at Ballacraine, but carried on until black-flagged at Kirk Michael. Allowed to proceed, they clipped the wall a few miles further on at Ginger Hall before being black-flagged yet again at Ramsey. Is black, perhaps, the new black and white?

As practice week drew to a close, the organisers announced the race format for future years. Out would go the Formula One and Ultra Lightweight events, the former being replaced by a Superbike race to WSB specifications. Following the same philosophy of adopting classes similar to those raced elsewhere, the Production events would be replaced by a 1000cc Superstock TT. Both the existing Supersports (Junior) and F2 Sidecar divisions would be retained, each enjoying two races. The finale of the week, the Senior, would be open to Superbike, Supersports and Superstock machines. The Superbike and Senior events will be over six laps.

FORMULA 1 TT

The last Formula One TT in history wasn't a great race, but will be remembered for the sheer speed with which McGuinness attacked the Mountain Course. Having returned from a track inspection in Moodie's helicopter, he pronounced conditions "perfect", and proceeded to demonstrate just how ideal they were - boosted by a pep talk from his pilot.

The plan, one Moodie had refined during his own TT career, was to seize control of the race from the first yard, just as Joey and Hizzie had done in their primes. John had his instructions - the Moodie look, the wagging finger - all he had to do was carry them out. When he reached Ballacraine faster than any rider, ever, it was all slotting into place. From a standing start he lapped at 127.68mph, 3.2 seconds faster than Jefferies's record from two years earlier, to lead Anstey by 10 seconds, with the notoriously slow-starting Archibald third.

On lap two McGuinness averaged over 128mph from Ramsey to Ramsey, easing ahead of Archibald on the road and his signals confirming that he was also extending his lead over Anstey. A slick pit stop allowed Archibald to claw back a few seconds, but the result was never in doubt, as McGuinness eased the pace on the final lap to give Yamaha only their second win in the 27-year history of the event. McGuinness's winning margin was 18 seconds from Archibald, with Anstey third. McGuinness's Yamaha team-mate Jason Griffiths placed fourth, with Ian Lougher fifth on a Honda Fireblade plagued by front suspension problems. Ireland's Richard Britton completed the top six, although his fancied compatriots, Finnegan and Farquhar endured frustrating races. Farquhar was black-flagged at Kirk Michael for a machine inspection, with Finnegan retiring at half distance.

"Absolutely amazing, everything went faultlessly", declared the winner. "I tried really hard to haul in Archibald and Lougher on the first lap, and it paid off. I caught Archibald at Barregarrow... passed him on Sulby Straight - Yamaha horsepower - and knew it was in the bag barring something unlucky. From then on me and Adrian were mostly together, so I could read his signals - "second, plus 13" as well as my own. The last time over the Mountain I had the usual worries. I imagined a misfire at Brandywell, and the fuel light was on, so it was an anxious few miles to the finish."

Such was the pace of the race that Ian Armstrong averaged over 119mph to finish ninth, which didn't so much as gain him a silver replica. Instead, the Sowerby Bridge rider earned the fastest bronze replica in TT history.

The race was marred by the death of Colin Breeze, from Kibworth in Leicestershire. The popular 44 year-old, winner of the 1999 Senior MGP, crashed fatally at Quarry Bends. This brought the list of deaths to three. French newcomer Serge le Moal died less than two miles into his first practice lap when he appeared to go straight on at Braddan Bends, and four days later Lincolnshire resident, Manxman Paul Cowley died at Black Dub after being thrown from the sidecar driven by Glyn Jones.

Left: **McGuinness starts the week perfectly, taking the R1 Yamaha to a record Formula 1 win.**
Photograph: Dave Collister/www.photocycles.com

Above: **This year's new TT hero John McGuinness and son.**
Photograph: Dave Purves

Right: Molyneux and Sayle were an unbeatable sidecar pairing.
Photograph: Dave Purves

SIDECAR RACE 'A'

In becoming the first all-Manx pairing to win a TT, Molyneux and Sayle didn't quite have time to stop for a cuppa, but their 59-second winning margin was comfortable enough. Starting first on the road, the pair led by six seconds at the first commentary point at Glen Helen, and went on inexorably to extend their lead until the end of the three-lap event. Their winning average was 111.33mph, narrowly outside the race record, with a fastest lap at 112.61mph a tantalising 1.6 seconds outside the record.

But the race wasn't without anxiety. Their DMR's Honda power-plant had developed a worrying rattle on the eve of the race, and Molyneux only persevered with it when engine builder Slick Bass - Fogarty's former WSB mechanic - had insisted it was fine. Bass was clearly correct. (It later turned out to be inconsequential primary drive backlash.)

"There's no living with Molly", declared runner-up Nick Crowe, also Honda-powered. "That thing of his is a missile, even when it's not running right." Crowe, with passenger Darren Hope, was pleased to record his first 110mph TT lap on the way to second place. Third was the Yamaha of Steve Norbury and Scott Parnell. Former sidecar world champion Klaus Klaffenbock, riding in his first TT, achieved his principle ambition by lapping at over 100mph -- 101.95mph - on lap two, although his 19th place was just one outside the replicas.

Top: McGuinness again, on his way to Junior glory.

Above: Kiwi Bruce Anstey battled all the way for the 1000cc Production TT win.
Photographs: Dave Collister/www.photocycles.com

Right: Leaping into history... Manx resident Chris Palmer won the last-ever 125 TT.
Photograph: Dave Purves

ULTRA-LIGHTWEIGHT 125 cc TT

The last 125cc TT in history was marked - if in no way marred - by a subdued demonstration, as many of the leading competitors donned black armbands in mourning at their loss. A two hour delay due to cloud on the Mountain gave the protest extra air-time as the Radio TT commentators struggled to fill the gap.

The winner, many of us hoped, would be Robert Dunlop, in what would be his last TT race. Fastest in practice, yet still gravely handicapped by injuries sustained at Ballaugh a decade before, his would have been a popular win. Yet it was not to be. After one lap Lougher led by 4.4 seconds from last year's winner, Chris Palmer, with Dunlop barely a second adrift. On lap two the Welshman narrowly extended his advantage, only for Palmer to edge ahead by Glen Helen on the final lap. Palmer charged on obliviously, misreading a "+45" signal as "+4.5", recording a new lap record at 110.52mph, unaware that his closest rival had retired at Milntown when bodywork came loose, lifting the drive chain off the sprocket. Palmer's race time, 108.93mph, was also a record, almost 58 seconds ahead of his nearest rival.

Lougher's misfortune promoted Dunlop to second, whilst Nigel Beattie got the better of a race-long battle with local rider Garry Bennett to take third.

Palmer, now a Manx resident, was close to tears after making "a little bit of TT history". Dunlop was simply gutted. "You've no idea how hard it is for me to ride round here", he grimaced over a beer. "I gave it everything but it just wasn't enough."

LIGHTWEIGHT 400 cc

Run concurrently with the 125s, the last 400cc TT brought another emphatic performance from McGuinness as he repeated his win of 12 months earlier. The F1 winner already held a convincing lead by Glen Helen, just 10 miles into the race, extended to 17 seconds after a standing-start lap at 111.44mph. He went on to win by over 33 seconds, although neither his 110.28mph race average speed nor his 112.04mph fastest lap quite eclipsed the remarkable marks set by Moodie in the Superspots 400 event way back in '93.

Roy Richardson held second place until his Honda went off-song, allowing veteran Steve Linsdell to bring his Yamaha into second place. Former Manx Grand Prix winner Mark Parrett claimed third on the same Honda on which Richard Quayle had won the event two years ago, with the slowing Richardson in fourth.

"I really enjoyed that," grinned McGuinness, whose only problem was a loose boot. "It's a fun little bike to ride," he said of the V-four Honda, "a bit like a scooter."

1000 cc PRODUCTION TT

Postponed from Monday to Tuesday by a curious Manx inversion - bright sunshine on the Mountain but fog near the coast - the big Production race was won by New Zealand's Bruce Anstey, but he had to battle all the way. On the opening lap McGuinness stamped his authority on yet another race, breaking the old lap record by 6.3 seconds from a standing start. Barely a second behind the Yamaha R1 lay Anstey's TAS Suzuki, with Lougher's Honda Fireblade a mere 0.4 seconds further adrift.

Most of the leading machines' fuel ranges were marginal for two laps over the 37.73 mile course. Lougher's attempts to eke out his supply contributed to his slipping from second to fourth on lap two. On the same lap, Anstey edged ahead of McGuiness on corrected time with a blistering lap record of 125.10mph, whilst slowing for the pits.

On the final lap, the Kiwi extended his lead by 12.8 seconds from McGuinness, with Jason Griffiths third on another R1, just 5.8 seconds behind. Lougher missed the rostrum by almost the same margin, but lay comfortably ahead of Adrian Archibald, who had struggled after a steady opening lap on which he had overshot Signpost Corner. Richard Britton placed sixth on another Suzuki.

If the race had been keenly anticipated partly on account of the searing new sports bikes recently launched by Yamaha, Honda and Kawasaki, the victory was a tribute to the tried-and-tested qualities of the Suzuki GSX-R1000. The top four riders all broke both the existing race and lap records. Local rider Paul Hunt took the award for the first 750, bringing his GSX-R750 Suzuki into 11th place overall, whilst on a similar machine Maria Costello became the fastest woman ever around the TT course with a lap at 114.73mph - only to retire on lap two.

JUNIOR TT

John McGuinness's mercurial week continued in the Junior TT, whilst the miserable luck of the Irish was just as unrelenting. The Yamaha man put in the sort of blistering opening stint we'd come to expect, with Ryan Farquhar hot on his heels for half a lap until the Irishman's McAdoo Kawasaki exploded at Sulby, giving him not a single finish so far. Adding insult, McGuiness's opening lap shaved a second off Farquhar's record from last year, leaving him 12 seconds ahead of Britton after a lap, with Anstey a further second adrift in third. Lougher's threat expired when he was lucky to walk away from a high-speed crash at Union Mills. Archibald lay fifth until his Suzuki went sick at Rhencullen on the final lap.

Despite tricky conditions - several road accidents had left oil residues on the course - McGuinness continued to push on lap two, posting a new record lap of 112.87mph as he slowed for the pits. After a slick fill-up he continued to consolidate his position, leading by almost half a minute after three laps, then easing the pace as his fuel light began blinking to finish 17 seconds ahead of Anstey, with a new race record of 120.57mph for the four-lap race.

An ebullient McGuinness explained that he'd ridden "like a startled hare". For his part Anstey conceded that he hadn't pushed hard enough from the start, and had been handicapped at the pit stop by the Suzuki's narrow filler neck.

Griffiths, McGuinness's Yamaha Motors team-mate, continued an impressively consistent week with third place. Britton, handicapped by a faulty gear-change, clung on to take fourth, ahead of Parrett and the luckless Martin Finnegan. Chris Palmer brought his RS Honda into 26th place to take the 250cc two-stroke award.

SIDECAR RACE 'B'

The second sidecar race was an exact blueprint of the first - the same 1-2-3, and precisely the same imperious performance from Molyneux and Sayle.

At 111.87mph, the Manx pairing's opening lap was almost half a minute faster than their nearest contenders, a margin which doubled with a new lap record of 113.17mph second time around. Despite easing back drastically on the third and final tour - their race time was actually slower than in Saturday's event -- their winning margin was over 37 seconds.

"The perfect ending to a perfect week", was Molly's summation. With the long-standing business of overwriting his 1999 lap record out of the way, Molyneux's sights must now be on whittling away just another 0.3 seconds to post the first sub-20 minute sidecar lap.

PRODUCTION 600 cc TT

By the final race day we were speculating that we might be witnessing a repeat of 1999, the only year since 1981 when no Irishman won a TT. Or perhaps that they'd be claiming that any bloke called McGuinness must be part Irish.

In fact Friday was the day that luck returned to its proverbial home. McGuinness's golden touch deserted him, as the steering damper fell off his R6 in the morning and his R1's clutch packed up in the afternoon. He was leading both races at the time.

In the Production race, the most incident-packed of the week, Ryan Farquhar recorded a maiden TT win by just 2.3 seconds in treacherous drying conditions. Although many of his opponents suffered setbacks, it was a worthy win for the Irishman, who had led throughout until overhauled by McGuinness during their pit-stops, only to charge back to parity within ten miles. Remarkably, this was Kawasaki's first win in precisely 20 years, since the late Geoff Johnson took a 900 Ninja to honours in the '84 production race.

A hard-charging Anstey set the fastest lap of the race on the final circuit to place second, nine seconds clear of an exhausted McGuinness. Griffiths, Lougher, his Honda persistently cutting out, and Raymond Porter rounded off the top six.

Top: **Adrian Archibald salvaged a bad week to head a Suzuki 1-2-3 in the Senior.**
Photograph: Dave Purves

Above: **Anstey, TAS-Suzuki's Hector Neal and Archibald celebrate their Senior top two.**
Photograph: Dave Collister/www.photocycles.com

SENIOR TT

By Senior day Adrian Archibald had become heartily sick of seeing John McGuinness breeze by him half-way through the opening lap - and it happened again. To no-one's surprise McGuinness led after an opening lap of 127.19 mph, by 10 seconds from Lougher, with Archibald, Griffiths, Anstey and Paul Hunt completing the top six.

Then the gremlins struck. Griffiths retired with clutch trouble, then McGuinnesss followed suit - practically within walking distance of his Yamaha team-mate. Lougher's battery went flat at Ramsey. Farquhar retired at the pits. This promoted Hunt to an improbable rostrum position, only for the Manxman's R1 to wreck its clutch.

Archibald hung on to round off an otherwise wretched week to win by 30 seconds from TAS Suzuki team-mate Anstey, in what proved to be an anticlimactic race. Victory meant that he also retained the Joey Dunlop trophy for best overall performance in F1 and Senior, the third successive year the Ballymoney man has taken this lucrative award.

Gary Carswell, the first Manxman to stand on the Senior podium for 81 years, placed third for a GSX-R 1-2-3, ahead of Parrett, Finnegan and Chris Heath.

US RACING REVIEW

OLD TRICKS...

By PAUL CARRUTHERS

Above: Mladin leads Duhamel, on track and for the crown.

Right: Ben Bostrom, finally a winner at Laguna Seca.

Photographs: Tom Riles

MAT Mladin was up to his old tricks in 2004. The Australian dominated early, gave his competition some glimmer of hope mid-season, then slammed the door in their faces at the penultimate round, allowing him to cruise to a fifth AMA Superbike title one race later.

Although Mladin didn't match his win total of 10 from the season before, he did win eight of the 18 races. And his points haul was larger than in 2003, the Suzuki rider amassing 584 points in '04 to beat his nearest challenger by 33. He didn't win as often, but he didn't falter either, the tyre problem that dogged him in 2003 only rearing its ugly head once in '04, and that led to a more consistent season. By the end he had been on the podium 14 times out of the 18 races and his worst two results were a pair of sixths - once when he had to stop for the aforementioned tyre change in Colorado, the other when he cruised to the title in the first of the two races at the final round in Virginia.

Other than that, Mladin was always at, or near, the front, with the result of a fifth championship for a man who knows exactly how to go about winning titles.

As always, Mladin's Yoshimura Suzuki GSX-R1000 was immaculately prepared by his almost-all-Aussie crew, and it never hesitated. Mladin was also thankful to the team for coming up with some late-season horsepower. He used it to thwart the mighty Honda CBR1000RRs that had started to become menacing in the middle portion of the series.

Mladin won his fifth title in six years against the usual cast of characters, and on familiar racetracks. As always, the AMA season kicked off at Daytona International Speedway, with the majority of the top men still shaking in their boots after seeing at least two of their comrades suffer tyre-failure-related crashes at the Speedway during pre-season testing.

The year began with the waters muddied somewhat by a new class structure that now featured two 1000cc classes - Superbike and Superstock (formerly featuring 750cc machines). There were also two 600cc classes - Formula Xtreme (previously featuring 1000cc machines) and 600cc Supersport. Suddenly presented with choices as to where to showcase their motorcycles, the manufacturers went in different directions and the result was confusion - especially on the part of race fans.

Naturally, Suzuki opted to defend its Superbike crown with Mladin and teammate Aaron Yates. Honda would also compete in Superbike with its brand-new CBR1000RR set to make its debut in 2004 in the capable hands of veteran Miguel Duhamel, former World Superbike man Ben Bostrom, and upstart Superbiker Jake Zemke. Duhamel and Zemke would also ride tricked-out Honda CBR600RRs in the Formula Xtreme class, basically turning that into a two-bike series.

Ducati would be back with what looked to be a solid threat – Eric Bostrom on the new 999 and armed with Michelin tyres (the French company appearing ready for an all-out assault on the mostly Dunlop-shod series). The Ducati Austin team also looked strong on paper, with a full commitment from the factory in Italy.

But that was it for the Superbike class: Three factory teams... and a horde of privateers hoping to fill in behind them to make up the top 10.

Kawasaki and Yamaha opted to go to the Superstock class, with Tommy Hayden and his youngest brother Roger Lee set to ride Kawasakis in both the Superstock and Supersport classes; while Yamaha had four riders - Jamie Hacking, Damon Buckmaster, Aaron

Gobert and Jason DiSalvo - poised for Superstock and Supersport. Both manufacturers had machines capable of competing in Superbike, but both chose the alternate route. Ultimately, both would have success, but the Superbike class would suffer in their absence.

On the track at Daytona, Mladin and his merry men showed why they are the most successful in the paddock when they opted early on for a three-stop strategy in the 200 (naturally, they kept it a secret). "We were either going to win the race or lose the race," Mladin said. "And it worked out for us, and we won."

Win they did, the Aussie using his fresher tyres to perfection to beat Zemke - in his Daytona 200 debut - by over seven seconds. Duhamel finished third, and that was it for the factory stars.

Yates had a tough day at the office on his factory Suzuki, crashing in the closing stages after clashing with backmarker Anthony Fania, then opting to fight the privateer in clear view of both race fans and a television audience. Not a good idea. The Georgian would end up suspended by the AMA and fined by Suzuki. The effect the incident had on Yates was long-lasting, and his season suffered because of it. It wasn't until the end that Yates appeared to be back to where he was prior to the incident.

As is the norm at Daytona, the Ducati failed to finish, though Eric Bostrom did put the bike on pole position for the race. Ben Bostrom's Honda failed him as well and that all translated into a privateer, Jack Pfeifer, finishing fourth in the Daytona 200 - two laps behind! Not sure this is what the AMA had in mind for its new-look class structure, but if they were trying to ensure privateer success in Superbike racing, they'd done so. It was easy - simply remove half the factories from the class.

In winning both races in the first doubleheader round of the year at California Speedway in Southern California, Mladin not only jumped out to a 24-point lead in the championship, he also became the AMA's all-time Superbike win leader with 27 victories, surpassing Duhamel's 26 wins. The pair would toss that record back and forth like a Frisbee all season.

The Fontana round also showed that at least early on it was Zemke - not the Bostroms and not Duhamel - who looked to be Mladin's main threat for the title. Thus far, the rookie was showing signs of consistency, and consistency is what it takes to compete with Mladin. Zemke was fourth in race one and third in race two in Fontana, and held second in the series standings.

Eric Bostrom, his Ducati and his Michelins, also looked formidable at this point - even though they were beaten handily by Mladin in both races in California. Hey, at least he was second. If only Daytona would have gone better… but those words always ring true for Ducati.

From Southern California the series moved to Northern California and the doubleheader round at Infineon Raceway. It was there that Zemke came to the fore. But first things first: Mladin won again in race one, easily besting Duhamel and Zemke. In race two, however, Zemke looked to have things under control as he roared out to a big lead. But it went horribly wrong when his teammate Duhamel caught and passed him in the final corner. It was the French Canadian's first win of the year and it left Zemke devastated, the young rider basically snatching defeat from the jaws of victory. Many wondered just how he would respond in the next round. After all, he'd come within 0.196 of a second of a breakthrough first-time victory.

Mladin was fourth in race two and not too happy that his teammate, Yates, with absolutely zero chance of taking the title, had beaten him to the flag, taking away points that might ultimately have been costly.

Any real Ducati threat also seemingly went by the wayside at Infineon, with Eric Bostrom a distant fifth in the first race and a crasher in the second. If you non-finish a single race in the AMA Superbike Series, it's nearly impossible to make it up. Bostrom wouldn't.

Instead of being the final round of the series as it was a year ago, the immaculate Barber Motorsports Park hosted round four in 2004 and what came out of it was more heartbreak for Zemke. This time it was Mladin driving a stake in the rookie's chest. Zemke led most of the race, but on the final lap, Mladin went past, beating him to the line by just .011 of a second. Again, Zemke had led the entire race. And, again, he'd lost on the final lap. Duhamel, meanwhile, was well back in third with Eric Bostrom coming home fourth.

When it happened to Zemke again the very next day - this time at the hands of Duhamel - it was hard not to feel for him. Again, Zemke led almost the entire race. And again, he lost out. This time the stab wound was gentler with Duhamel passing him on the penultimate lap instead of the last, to beat him by 0.377 of a second.

Zemke had lost both races at Barber by a combined total of .488 of a second. But wait. Believe it or not, it was worse than that: Zemke had now lost the last three AMA Superbike Nationals by .584 of a second. Three races by just over half a second. And he was handling it all quite well, thank you.

Mladin finished third in race two at Barber and he left Alabama with five wins out of seven races and a lead of 25 points over Duhamel. It looked as though Mladin's early season work was complete.

Eric Bostrom owns Pikes Peak International Raceway in Colorado. Always has, probably always will. Bostrom came into Colorado stone cold, his championship hopes dashed as he struggled to get comfortable on the Ducati and its Michelin tyres. But Pikes seems to cure any ailment that Bostrom has, and this year was no different as he stormed off to his first (and only) win of the season, bringing some levity to the team that was in a serious funk before it arrived in the Rocky Mountains.

Bostrom beat... you guessed it – Zemke, or Mr. Second Place. Yates was third with Duhamel fourth. Mladin suffered his only tyre failure of the season and had to pit for a new one. Still, he ended up sixth, losing some points to Zemke and Duhamel but not enough to fret over. At least not yet.

With the series headed to the ultra-fast Road America in Wisconsin for round five, Mladin knew he and the Suzuki would suffer there. The Hondas were fast and getting faster by the minute. Turns out, Mladin was right. Duhamel won both races in the cheese state, beating Mladin in race one and Zemke in race two. Mladin's points lead had dwindled to only 10 over the suddenly scorching hot Duhamel. And much to Mladin's chagrin, the tracks weren't getting any slower.

With Brainerd International Speedway featuring the longest front straight and fastest turn one in the series, it figured to be Hondaville when the AMA series arrived and in a way it was. Still, Mladin hung tough.

The good news: Finally, Zemke won. The former dirt tracker and speedway racer discarded the bridesmaid dress in Minnesota, taking his first Superbike National victory at Brainerd. The Erion Honda rider had held off the advances of both Duhamel and Mladin to win by 1.1 seconds. Not only was the King Kong-sized monkey off Zemke's back, he was also slowly but surely becoming a factor in the title chase. After 11 of 18 races, only 10 points separated first (Mladin) from third (Zemke). Mladin had 358, Duhamel 352 and Zemke 348. Tight at the top. And suddenly a three-man race for the championship.

Ben Bostrom had done nothing much to speak of in 2004. In fact, he'd done nothing much to speak of in 2003 either. But that changed at the World Superbike/AMA combination event at Laguna Seca. It was there that Bostrom was reborn, a vision problem that had been hampering him all season apparently behind him. He'd picked up a new trainer as well and his program had undergone extensive change. Now he was peddling a bicycle as a warm-up before races. And it worked. Bostrom won the race, his first of the season and first in almost three years, beating Mladin and Duhamel.

Bostrom - and the rest of the top AMA men - had also proven superior in lap times to their World Superbike counterparts, on Pirelli spec tyres!

The race, however, was a disaster for Zemke, his CBR1000RR suffering electrical problems that forced him down the order after leading early. He would finish seventh and see that Mladin's lead was back to 10 points - over Duhamel.

SHOEI
HONDA
ROCKET
DUNLOP
CBR
Racing
HRC
HONDA
Renthal
17

98
SHOEI
PARTS UNLIMITED
PJ1
HONDA
ROCKET
PARTS UNLIMITED
PJ1
98
98

Mladin and Zemke split wins at the Mid-Ohio Sports Car Course, the Australian barely besting Duhamel in race one with Zemke beating Ben Bostrom and Mladin in race two. But the second race was a debacle for Duhamel. The man with the best chance of knocking Mladin off his throne crashed out of the race, putting Mladin squarely back in the catbird seat.

It was at Road Atlanta that Mladin won his fifth AMA Superbike title. Although he didn't wrap it up there, he did the hard work to put the title out of reach of his rivals. Riding at the limit for two solid days, Mladin won both races, beating Duhamel both times. Frustration boiled over after the first race, with the two nearly coming to blows. But with two crushing victories over his rival, the end was near. For all practical purposes, this one was over.

Ben Bostrom ended up third in the first race with Zemke fourth. In the second race it was more of the same, and Mladin left Road Atlanta with a 42-point lead over Zemke. Game over.

With the final in Virginia round put on hold because of Hurricane Ivan, Mladin had to wait to earn his fifth title. But when the race was ultimately held a few weeks after the scheduled date, he did what he needed to do. He finished sixth in the first race, running at the front until realizing that he was better off slowing and taking the title than risk someone crashing him out. Duhamel won, from Yates and Ben Bostrom. Then came the two European Ducati imports - Lorenzo Lanzi and Regis Laconi - who ventured to the U.S. after the completion of the World Superbike/World Supersport Series to join Eric Bostrom. But Bostrom wasn't there, his bum shoulder keeping him out of yet another race.

Mladin wanted to race for victory in race two, but he jumped the start, stalled his motor and was nearly collected by three-quarters of the field. Then he had to stop for a ride-through penalty and that was that. Except that he fought through the pack to finish an impressive fourth, ending his season in Mladin fashion with a hard ride.

Duhamel won again, setting an AMA record for winning three races on a single day (two Superbike races and the Formula Xtreme finale). Duhamel beat Yates and Ben Bostrom again. Mladin caught and passed Laconi for fourth, with Lanzi dropping out with mechanical problems early on.

Duhamel's two Superbike victories on the day also put him back into a tie with Mladin on the all-time win list. The pair will start the 2005 season with 32 wins apiece.

Mladin ended the year with a record haul of points - 584 to Duhamel's 551, the senior Honda man taking second in the title chase when Zemke was forced out of the final round after injuring himself in a practice crash. Mladin had won eight races, Duhamel six, Zemke two and the Bostroms one apiece.

"To win one is difficult," Mladin said after an unprecedented fifth title. "To win five, I mean, it just shows how strong the team is and how strong everybody is in the whole Yoshimura Suzuki crew. It's nice and we're already thinking about next year. We've got testing planned now. We've had a glimpse of the new bike, and we're looking forward to it."

Support class racing in this year's series was hot and heavy, with all but the Formula Xtreme title going to the very last round.

The 600cc Supersport class ended up being a battle between two brothers – Tommy and the younger Roger Lee Hayden. A few years back, Tommy Hayden lost a title to his younger brother, Nicky - now of the Repsol Honda MotoGP team. He wasn't prepared to let that happen again and this time the older brother came out on top, Tommy defeating Roger Lee in the final round to earn the title. Both had won four races on the season on their factory Kawasakis, but it was Tommy on top in the final point standings.

With the Superstock class being elevated in prestige by going to 1000cc, Yamaha ended up dominating the series. The man who would be king was Aaron Gobert, the middle Gobert brother. The Australian won just one race along the way, but he was consistently fast and always near the front. His teammate Jamie Hacking won more races (four), but an injury hurt his chances and he came up just short at season's end. It was a well-earned title for Gobert, the man who nearly lost his life in a horrific pileup at Daytona almost three years before.

The Formula Xtreme title went to Duhamel, the veteran's seventh AMA road racing championship. Duhamel beat out his teammate Zemke for the championship with Suzuki rider Vincent Haskovec finishing third.

Opposite page: Veteran Miguel Duhamel (top) ended as the strongest Honda rider, but fast rookie Jake Zemke (bottom) was a strong mid-season title challenger.

Below: Eric Bostrom, here heading Mladin and Duhamel, took one victory at Pikes Peak, in an otherwise disappointing Michelin debut season.

Photographs: Tom Riles

BRITISH SUPERBIKE REVIEW

GETTING BETTER ALL THE TIME

By GARY PINCHIN (Motor Cycle News)

Above: BSB gained international stature, with support from all four Japanese factories versus Ducati.
Photograph: Clive Challinor Motor Sport Photography

YOU know a championship has scaled the dizzy heights of success when the Honda Racing Corporation (HRC) sends its prized machinery and technicians to compete.

Normally direct HRC involvement is only considered appropriate at world level, but there was nothing normal about the 2004 season.

The Motorcycle Sport Manufacturers Association (MSMA) had to all intents and purposes black-balled the World Superbike Championship at the end of 2003. HRC, however, had a brand new FireBlade, to develop for the prestigious Suzuka Eight Hour race. Even if they'd had the will for WSB, the Pirellis ruled it out, as HRC run Michelins in the Eight Hour. Where to do the job?

With the domestic All Japan Superbike series at a low ebb, and their factory-backed American Honda team running AMA Superbike on Dunlops, they had one choice of top international competition left – the British Superbike Championship.

The team based itself at the old Castrol Honda WSB headquarters on the outskirts of the sleepy Lincolnshire town of Louth, and was managed by current Honda Racing boss (and former Castrol Honda boss) Neil Tuxworth, who retained many of his old staff. However, along with the four specially-prepared HRC factory FireBlades came several Japanese technicians, with former GP star Tadayuki Okada acting as link-man between Louth and Japan. Michelin and Showa also provided top-level support, flying staff in to test and race throughout the year. It was one of the biggest budget teams ever seen in BSB.

Tuxworth signed Michael Rutter, a rider with unrivalled experience on the British tracks, and one of the most technically astute competitors in BSB – experience that would prove vital in the development, not just of a brand new bike, but also of the new tyres. HRC added Ryuichi Kiyonari. He had won the 2002 All Japan Supersport title, then was thrust into MotoGP for one season, after the untimely death of Daijiro Kato at the start of 2003.

But even with two top riders, an absolutely huge budget and the best technical support possible, HRC failed to win the title.

It was a tough job. Honda Racing had competed in 2003 BSB with Colin Edwards' title-winning SP2 V-twin. They ran Dunlops (although the bike had been developed on Michelins), and it proved difficult to adapt it to tight British circuits. For 2004 they were starting at ground zero, with no data. Michelin were in a similar boat, having last raced in the British series in 1999 with Red Bull Ducati.

Rutter had to shoulder the bulk of the development work, as Kiyonari lacked not only development skills but also experience of the British tracks ... except for Donington Park, on a MotoGP bike.

To the delight of HRC director Kyoji Nakajima, who flew in for the Silverstone opening round from the Barcelona MotoGP pre-season test, Rutter won the first race in changing conditions. Starting from pole on a wet track, Rutter beat his Japanese team-mate Ryuichi Kiyonari across the line by just over two seconds. Kiyonari had crashed in practice but managed to qualify on the front row and impressed in both races.

Rutter made an appalling start in race two but battled his way back through the field to hound Suzuki's Reynolds and Kiyonari but by the time he was in touch with them he'd used the best of his tyres and had to be content with third.

For Honda, the first round of the series flattered to deceive. Despite Honda's technical support and big spend, the title went to John Reynolds and Rizla Suzuki, the well-supported Crescent Suzuki dealer team from Bournemouth. Experience gave them the edge. It was the team's third year with the GSX-R1000 and they had a wealth of data to work from.

Reynolds and the GSX-R1000 had finished 2003 by far the strongest package – stronger even than title-winners Shane Byrne and the MonsterMob Ducati 998 F02, who racked up their winning points running virtually unbeaten in the first half of the year.

Rizla Suzuki got technical support from the factory, and Yukio Kagayama's second season on the team showed just how committed to BSB the company actually was – but while they supplied some factory parts, most development was done in-house at Crescent's well-appointed workshop. They took early delivery of their 2004 GSX-R1000s and, using knowledge gained from two previous years with the model, transformed them into title-winning race bikes.

The engine now had factory pistons – which looked very similar in design and weight to those in the MotoGP GSV-R – and titanium con-rods, a much lighter package than the previous year's Carillo rods/Yoshimura pistons. BSB rules specify stock crankshafts, the teams were allowed to fit lighter flywheels to allow the engine to spin up faster. They also continued to experiment with camshafts and cam timing, and there was a new twin-outlet Yoshimura tri-oval exhaust, while the latest generation Motec engine management system allowed them to incorporate an air bleed fast-idle system like that on Honda's MotoGP RCV. This reduces engine braking to assist the slipper clutch, and make the bike smoother to ride into corners.

Rizla Suzuki also had new Ohlins gas forks and the latest remote-adjuster shocks, though Reynolds quickly ditched these after trying them in practice at Silverstone, going back to the conventional Ohlins he had used in 2003. Third in the first race, he had to work hard to win the second, after intense pressure from the two Honda riders.

Brands Hatch was next, and Reynolds won the first race. He looked set to claim the next to make it three in a row, but a tangle with backmarkers put him third, with Rutter second to Emmett in the dash to the line.

The Suzukis were rampant at the next round at Snetterton, where Kagayama scored an emotional victory in race one, just eight months after nearly losing his life at Cadwell. The Japanese rider was back to his world-class best as he held off Reynolds by four tenths.

Reynolds bounced back to win the second race and edged into a 10-point championship lead as his rival Rutter finished third and second in the two races, again hampered by bad starts.

Oulton Park, and again the Suzukis prevailed, with Kagayama on top each time – out-smarting Reynolds in race one, and then dominating race two. Even so, JR still edged into an 18-point lead as Rutter took two more thirds. His Blade had a new clutch and he got off the line better in race one, only to be beaten up by the pack in the first corner; then in race two an electrical problem forced him to start from the back of the grid on his spare bike.

After clocking over 200mph on his way to winning the North West 200 the previous weekend, Rutter looked ready to dominate around tight, bumpy Mondello Park. He took pole and won the second race, but a crash in the first gave Reynolds an even bigger points gap at the top of the championship table. Reynolds, with two second places, left the Irish circuit 33 points clear of the Honda man.

Rutter seemed to have bounced back at Thruxton, with a win and a second to MonsterMob's Sean Emmett in race two; and clawed his way back into contention for the title after Reynolds clashed with temporary team-mate Gregorio Lavilla in the second race. Reynolds sustained a fractured collar-bone, but shook off the effects of the injury to score an incredible win in the first race at Brands just two weeks later.

It was typical of the roller-coaster season that even though Reynolds could only finish seventh in the second race, Rutter failed to capitalise on his misfortune. with tyre problems in the wet first race and a misfire in the second. It was the start of a grim mid-season spell for the Honda man, with just 43 points in six races (Knockhill and Mallory followed Brands), while Reynolds racked up 108.

Now there were four rounds left, two races at each ... and Rutter was 73 points down. But he managed to lift himself again, with a brilliant double win at Croft, where Reynolds struggled to get the bike working to his liking. Rutter also won the next race, at Cadwell, after Reynolds uncharacteristically crashed out chasing him and the other Honda of Kiyonari.

Rutter had Reynolds against the ropes, but he failed to deliver the killer blow. Instead of backing it up with another win, he made a really curious tyre choice for round two at Cadwell, opting for wets in the second race. As the track dried, he was forced to quit. In true pro racer style he took the rap for the tyre call, but it seemed a little odd that Kiyonari also made the same decision – and it only became clear much later that speculation that HRC or Michelin were calling the shots rather than the riders, was actually bang on the mark.

Ironically Reynolds also struggled with tyre problems, and managed only eighth. Now he led by only 33 points. It could have been a lot less had Rutter been able to run intermediates like his Dunlop-shod rivals had available. The truth was, the Michelin intermediates took too long to come up to working temperature. Rutter would have been riding a fine line between survival and crashing had he gone for that option.

With the pressure on, Reynolds delivered a performance befitting

Below: HRC's rising son Ryuichi Kyonari was drafted into the HM Plant-backed Honda team.

Bottom: Top Honda rider Michael Rutter, heading late-season super-sub James Haydon (8), was the major rival to champion Reynolds.

Photographs: Clive Challinor Motor Sport Photography

Above: **Popular Japanese rider Yukio Kagayama celebrates an emotional victory at Cadwell Park, avenging his near-fatal 2003 crash.**

Top: **Rizla-Suzuki team-mate John Reynolds had to dig deep for both speed and courage to win his third national title.**
Photographs: Clive Challinor Motor Sport Photography

a champion to win both Oulton races to extend his title lead to 43 points going to the final round. He didn't have an easy weekend though. In the first race he had to fight off Rutter and a highly motivated Emmett in a tense elbows-out, two-part race, punctuated, as so often in 2004, by rain. Rutter initially led the second race but Reynolds took control at the chicane on the fifth lap, and Kagayama soon pushed Rutter back to third, though the Honda rider got him back on the last lap, when Yuki's rear tyre was shredded.

At the final round at Donington Park, Reynolds needed just eight points to be assured of the title, even if Michael Rutter won both races. Reynolds wasn't about to settle for that, but with the HRC FireBlades looking more competitive at Donington than they had all year, Reynolds had to be content with third place in the first race. It was enough to clinch the title.

There were heroic individual performances aplenty. Yukio Kagayama's second season of BSB will long be remembered as one of the emotional highs of the series. So near to death after his horrific crash at Cadwell the previous Bank Holiday Monday, Yukio made a miraculous recovery and was ready to race as the season began. But he was still far from fit – his smashed pelvis required further surgery, and he had suffered massive internal injuries to his lower organs, with a whole world of pain including blood poisoning. He would ride all year with a colostomy bag.

Despite the trauma, Yuki showed he'd lost none of his desire or aggression, and was competitive from the very first test in Valencia, even though he had difficulty walking and getting on and off his bike. Fourth in the first raced, he only had to wait a month before chalking up his first win at Snetterton. Even that meant more pain. Yuki highsided at Russells on Friday, landing with a mighty whack to the pelvis. Amazingly, no damage was done beyond severe bruising, that left medics wondering whether it would be physically possible for him to race two days later. But Yuki is made of stern stuff, and after a weekend of intensive physio courtesy of BSB's top grade medical team, he stunned everyone by winning the first race. Needless to say it was tears all round in the Rizla camp.

The popular Yuki backed it up with a double at Oulton Park. Teammate Reynolds had been full of encouragement at Snetterton, but he was far from chuffed now, after Yuki had shadowed him for race one, only to sucker-punch him with a last-lap pass. He sat out Thruxton on medical advice, after breaking his collarbone testing for the Eight Hour in Japan. Then he came back with a sterling end of year run, including another tear-jerking victory at Cadwell. The celebratory burnout at the site of his 2003 accident pretty much said it all.

Third in the championship, his legion of British fans will see him in 2005 only at the Silverstone and Brands WSB rounds, after the factory shifted him to the Alstare Suzuki team. It's a coup for WSB to have such a charismatic personality, but a deep loss for the British series.

The revelation of 2004 was Scott Smart – but only to those who hadn't been paying attention. Smart's talent had been smouldering for a long time. It was just lacking the right team and combination to really ignite the fire.

The son of Paul was British 250 champion in 1997, then spent two years as a GP grid filler, on outclassed machinery. Returning to Britain to rebuild his career, 2000 was soul-destroying, with an underfunded team. The next year Smart did his own thing – building his own bikes, driving himself to the tracks, being his own race mechanic as well as racing. Supersport runner-up in 2002, his incredible commitment finally earned him a Superbike ride with Hawk Kawasaki for 2003. It was tough, on an old ZX-7RR, but it was good preparation.

The comparatively low-budget team had new ZX-10s, but no one gave them a hope in hell and it looked like Smart's career might stall again. The bikes arrived late, there were no factory parts or technical help, and, if the truth be known, they didn't really have anyone with the experience to build a race bike from a production machine. But having Smartie on board helped no end.

He and team engine builder John Trigger camped at Frank Wrathall's workshop near Preston for several months to develop the engine. With a depth of electronics experience, Smart built wiring looms and developed engine management software. He produced a lot of carbon parts including airboxes, and used his F1 contacts for things like the special velocity stacks for the injection bodies.

His own pre-season training programme went out of the window, but it ensured Hawk gave everyone a real kick up the backside from the very start of the year. Others struggled with the gas forks, Hawk persevered and made them work. In any case, they didn't have a pile of '03 conventional forks lying around to call upon.

Smart immediately got to grips with the new bike, outscoring Glen Richards, the star of the 2003 season. Fast and consistent, he piled up points in the first eight races. His first race win finally came in the fifth round, with a dramatic last corner pass of John Reynolds at Mondello, after a sensational final lap. Reynolds had a comfortable 1.3s lead at the start, but as he relaxed his pace Smart got the whiff of victory. Smart was out of the saddle, he was pushing that hard, but as Reynolds cruised into Dunlop – the final hairpin, Smart stuffed his ZX10 underneath him, and then won the drag race to the line by a scant 0.002s.

He also won a rain-affected race at Knockhill and thrashed the opposition fair and square at Mallory. By year's end, Smart was the most wanted rider in the paddock. Next year he'll be John Reynolds's team-mate at Rizla Suzuki.

Sean Emmett started 2004 as a title favourite when he signed for MonsterMob Ducati. The Paul Bird-owned team had won the title the previous two years – with Steve Hislop and Shane Byrne. Emmett had been a more than capable race winner during the same period, but various team-related problems meant he saw neither season out with the team he had started with.

2004 was hardly any easier. Nobody had expected the new 999 Ducati to be such a fickle machine. When Neil Hodgson won the WSB title on it the previous year, there was talk about peculiar handling problems. Everyone thought Ducati would overcome this for 2004, but they didn't. At WSB Pierfrancesco Chili openly criticised his 999, switching back to a 998; in the USA Eric Bostrom could only win once all year. And the handling problems seemed to be accentuated on the tight and bumpy British tracks.

At tracks with fast flowing sections, like Brands Hatch, Emmett would fly, and when he's on a mission there's no faster competitor. At tighter corners and on bumpy surfaces he was desperate – as at Oulton early in the year when he did the unthinkable and pulled out of a race. He said the bike was unrideable, his team boss said he wasn't trying. It was the start of a war of words between the pair, aired quite openly in the press.

What made it worse was that instead of focusing on the machine, blame was put on Emmett's life-style, which is rather eccentric, for a professional racer. When he was off the pace his drinking and smoking habits, and general lack of fitness training, were thrown in his face – as was his alleged lack of commitment. This was conveniently overlooked when he was doing well - especially at the Brands Indy circuit. Knocked off in race one, he picked himself and won the second, despite being covered in cuts and bruises. If that wasn't commitment, then what was?

He only won one other race – at Thruxton - but even that weekend was shrouded in controversy. Sensational all weekend, he should have won the first race but for a moment of madness. In the final corner, so relieved to be back to winning form, he took his hand off the bars to wave to the crowd in the chicane grandstand and was nearly highsided. By the time he recovered, he had dropped to third. At least he made amends winning the second race.

Emmett was fifth in the championship, completing the turbulent season with a third at Donington, his ninth podium. But before the final meeting he had agreed a deal to ride for the Virgin Yamaha team in 2005. Rob McElnea's more compassionate style of management should suit the laid-back Emmett much more than the confrontational style of his 2004 employer.

Kiyonari was sixth overall. He started the season well, hit a midterm lull and then bounced back with a series of strong results at the tail end, culminating with a sensational double win at Donington that put even his own team-mate in the shade. With a season under his belt. we should see a faster and more consistent Kiyo in 2005, a championship contender at that.

Aussie Dean Thomas will be a contender in 2005 too, now that he's signed for Hawk Kawasaki. The Sendo Ducati rider finished seventh overall, and was often very fast in qualifying, narrowly missing pole several times, but never really managed to put together a convincing race. This was less his own short-coming, more that the ex-Toseland 998 F02 was way past its best.

Virgin Yamaha had a pretty appalling year, after what had seemed a promising pre-season test for Steve Plater and Gary Mason on the brand new R1s at Cartegena. They felt fast, without anybody else to measure up to, but when they started racing it was clear the bike came up well short.

When Steve Plater bust his wrist badly at Oulton, out-of-work James Haydon stepped up to help the team out … and at Knockhill gave the team their only win of the year. Everyone thought they'd sorted out the bike's handling problems but this was not the case.

Plater returned to show brief glimpses of his incredible aggression. Mason was smooth and tidy as ever, but they were put in the shade by young Tommy Hill. Winning the R6 Cup in 2003 earned him a place on the Virgin Yamaha BSB, and he often out-performed his team-mates early in the year – on sheer bravado, prepared to push the unwieldy bike harder than the more experienced riders.

As the season wore on Tommy showed he could qualify up front and was capable of running at the front of the pack with BSB star player – but only early in the race. If he can learn to sustain that pace for race distance, Hill could be Britain's brightest hope.

Hill stays with Virgin for 2005; 2004 R6 Cup winner Richard Wren joins him and Emmett on the red bikes. Plater's signed with Sendo Kawasaki, joined by privateer cup rider Jon Kirkham; Mason is off to MonsterMob Honda with Michael Laverty and an as-yet unnamed third rider.

If 2004 was good, 2005 should be better. Even as the season ended talk of new teams started, and with GSE coming back to run factory Ducatis with Haydon and Leon Haslam, Paul Bird expanding to a three-man Honda team with backing from Eddie Stobart, Hawk having an opportunity to run factory engines against Rizla Suzuki and HRC, series promoters Dorna look like having a very healthy championship, and the international stature of BSB will be maintained.

Below left: **James Haydon substituted for injured Plater … and won a race for Virgin Yamaha.**

Below: **Tommy Hill was rookie of the year, showing pace and promise on the second Yamaha.**

Photographs: Clive Challinor Motor Sport Photography

Above: **Above: Two-times winner Scott Smart worked hard to fettle the new Kawasaki and revive his career, and was the revelation of 2004.**

Left: **Sean Emmett had a difficult time on the Monster-Mob Ducati.**

Photographs: Clive Challinor Motor Sport Photography

MAJOR RESULTS

OTHER CHAMPIONSHIP RACING SERIES WORLDWIDE

Compiled by KAY EDGE

Endurance World Championship

ASSEN 500, Assen Circuit, Holland, 12 April 2004.
Endurance World Championship, round 1. 129 laps of the 2.412-mile/3.881-km circuit, 311.148 miles/500.649 km

1 Suzuki Castrol Team, F: Vincent Philippe/Olivier Four/Matthieu Lagrive (Suzuki GSXR), 3h 01m 29.671s, 102.843 mph/165.509 km/h.

2 Yamaha GMT 94, F: Sébastien Gimbert/William Costes/David Checa (Yamaha YZF), 129 laps; **3** Yamaha Endurance Moto 38, F: Gwen Giabbani/Frédéric Jond/Stephane Duterne (Yamaha YZF), 126; **4** WRT Honda Austria, A: Erwin Wilding/Karl Truchsess (Honda CBR 1000), 124; **5** Bridgestone Bikers, D: Tim Röthig/Ralf Schwickerath (Suzuki GSXR), 123; **6** Suzuki Jet Team, CH: Claude Alain Jaggi/Eric Monot/Sylvain Waldmeier (Suzuki GSXR), 122; **7** Diablo 666 Bolliger, GB: James Hutchins/Nick Pilborough/Mike Edwards (Kawasaki ZX10R), 122; **8** Ducati Team Spring, I: Lorenzo Mauri/Matteo Colombo/Bellezza (Ducati 999R), 122; **9** Suzuki Team Innodrom, D: Sandor Bitter/Lars Albrecht/Niggi Schmassmann (Suzuki GSXR), 122; **10** Suzuki No Limits Team, I: Roberto Ruozi/Andrea Giachino/Moreno Codeluppi (Suzuki GSXR), 121; **11** Burger King Lust Team, D: Gerd Peter Meyer/Stefan Meyer/Mattias Bormann (Suzuki), 121; **12** Yamaha Endurance Belgie, B: Danny Scheers/Koen Reymenants (Yamaha YZF), 120; **13** Benelli X-One, I: Andrea Perselli/Paolo Tessari/Maurizio Barghiacchi (Benelli Tornado), 119; **14** Pajic-Kawasaki, NL: Mile Pajic/Visscher (Kawasaki ZX10R), 118; **15** Kawasaki Endurance, D: Sebric/Hahn (Kawasaki ZX10), 118.

Fastest lap: Gimbert/Costes/Checa, 1m 21.925s, 105.969 mph/170.541 km/h.

Championship points: **1** Suzuki Castrol Team, 25; **2** Yamaha GMT 94, 20; **3** Yamaha Endurance Moto 38, 16; **4** WRT Honda Austria, 13; **5** Bridgestone Bikers, 11; **6** Suzuki Jet Team, 10.

ZHUHAI 6 HOURS, Zhuhai Circuit, China, 2 May 2004.
Endurance World Championship, round 2. 216 laps of the 2.672-mile/4.300-km circuit, 577.152 miles/928.800 km

1 Yamaha GMT 94, F: David Checa/William Costes/Christophe Guyot (Yamaha YZF), 6h 00m 40.470s, 95.989 mph/154.480 km/h.

2 Suzuki Zongshen Team, PRC: Stephane Mertens/Lerats Vanstaen/Bruno Bonhuil (Suzuki GSXR), 214 laps; **3** Yamaha Endurance Moto 38, F: Gwen Giabbani/Frédéric Jond/Sohier (Yamaha YZF), 213; **4** Kawasaki Bolliger Team, CH: Laurent Brian/David Morillon/Marcel Kellenberger (Kawasaki ZX10), 213; **5** Yamaha Austria Racing Team, A: Igor Jerman/Thomas Hinterreiter/Horst Saiger (Yamaha YZF), 212; **6** Suzuki Castrol Team, F: Vincent Philippe/Olivier Four/Matthieu Lagrive (Suzuki GSXR), 210; **7** Shell Endurance Academy, GB: Marko Rothlaan/Alek Dubelski (Suzuki GSXR), 210; **8** Suzuki Jet Team, CH: Eric Monot/Sylvain Waldmeier/Claude Alain Jaggi (Suzuki GSXR), 209; **9** Suzuki Fabi Corse, I: Fabio Capriotti/Patrizio Fabi (Suzuki GSXR), 206; **10** Diablo 666 Bolliger, GB: Mike Edwards/Nick Pilborough/James Hutchins (Kawasaki ZX10R), 205; **11** Yamaha Phase One Endurance, GB: Sebastien Scarnato/Dean Ellison/Steve Brogan (Yamaha ZXR), 201; **12** Suzuki Fagersjo, S: Tobias Andersson/Lars Carlberg (Suzuki GSXR), 200; **13** Suzuki No Limits Team, I: Andrea Giachino/ Moreno Codeluppi/Roberto Ruozi (Suzuki GSXR), 200; **14** Suzuki Eurosport Benelux, B: Eddy Peeters/Patrick de la Ruelle (Suzuki GSXR), 200; **15** Yamaha Maco Moto, SLO: Jiri Drazdak/Mazzoli/Martin Kuzma (Yamaha YZF), 200.

Fastest lap: Checa/Costes/Guyot, 1m 36.687s, 99.480 mph/160.100 km/h.

Championship points: **1** Yamaha GMT 94, 45; **2** Suzuki Castrol Team, 35; **3** Yamaha Endurance Moto 38, 32; **4** Suzuki Zongshen Team, 20; **5** Suzuki Jet Team, 18; **6** Diablo 666 Bolliger, 15.

12 HOURS OF ALBACETE, Albacete, Spain, 5 June 2004.
Endurance World Championship, round 3. 448 laps of the 2.299-mile/3.700-km circuit, 1029.952 miles/1657.600 km

1 Suzuki Castrol Team, F: Vincent Philippe/Olivier Four/Matthieu Lagrive (Suzuki GSXR), 12h 00m 33.336s, 82.033 mph/132.020 km/h.

2 Yamaha GMT 94, F: David Checa/Sébastien Gimbert/William Costes (Yamaha YZF), 446 laps; **3** Yamaha Endurance Moto 38, F: Gwen Giabbani/Stephane Duterne/Frédéric Jond (Yamaha YZF), 445; **4** Yamaha Austria Racing Team, A: Horst Saiger/Marc Garcia/Igor Jerman (Yamaha YZF), 438; **5** Kawasaki Bolliger Team, CH: Marcel Kellenberger/David Morillon/Frédéric Moreira (Kawasaki ZX10R), 437; **6** WRT Honda Austria, A: Erwin Wilding/Karl Truchsess/Dobe (Honda CBR 1000), 432; **7** Shell Endurance Academy, GB: Henry Fincher/Alek Dubelski/ Marko Rothlaan (Yamaha YZF), 427; **8** Suzuki Jet Team, CH: Claude Alain Jaggi/Eric Monot/Sylvain Waldmeier (Suzuki GSXR), 426; **9** Suzuki Team Innodrom, D: Sandor Bitter/Lars Albrecht/Niggi Schmassman (Suzuki GSXR), 422; **10** Suzuki No Limits Team, I: Andrea Giachino/Moreno Codeluppi/Roberto Ruozi (Suzuki GSXR), 421; **11** Kawasaki Endurance, D: Thomas Roth/Koch/Werner Döhler (Kawasaki ZX10R), 421; **12** Diablo 666 Bolliger, GB: James Hutchins/Kevin Falcke/Nick Pilborough (Kawasaki ZX10R), 420; **13** Yamaha Maco Moto, SLO: Jiri Drazdak/Vallisari/Martin Kuzma (Yamaha YZF), 417; **14** Benelli X-One, I: Andrea Perselli/Paolo Tessari/Maurizio Bargiacchi (Benelli Tornado), 416; **15** Yamaha Endurance Belgie, B: Danny Scheers/Koen Reymenants/Geudens (Yamaha 1000), 414.

Fastest lap: Giabbani/Duterne/Jond, 1m 33.610s, 83.947 mph/135.100 km/h.

Championship points: **1** Yamaha GMT 94, 75; **2** Suzuki Castrol Team, 73; **3** Yamaha Moto Endurance 38, 56; **4** Yamaha Austria Racing Team, 31; **5** Suzuki Jet Team and Kawasaki Bolliger Team, 30.

SUZUKA EIGHT HOURS, Suzuka International Circuit, Japan, 25 July 2004.
Endurance World Championship, round 4. 210 laps of the 3.617-mile/5.821-km circuit, 759.570 miles/1222.41 km

1 Seven Stars Honda, J: Tohru Ukawa/Hitoyasu Izutsu (Honda CBR 1000), 8h 01m 35.115s, 94.635 mph/152.300 km/h.

2 Yoshimura Suzuki Jomo, J: A. Watanabe/Yukio Kagayama (Suzuki GSXR), 209 laps; **3** Yamaha GMT 94, F: David Checa/Sébastien Gimbert/William Costes (Yamaha YZF), 204; **4** Yamaha Austria Racing Team, A: Horst Saiger/James Ellison/Igor Jerman (Yamaha YZF), 201; **5** Yamaha Phase One Endurance, GB: Dean Ellison/Sebastien Scarnato/Marko Rothlaan (Yamaha YZF), 200; **6** Team Surf Aoki, J: M. Hisazumi/N. Yamada (Suzuki GSXR), 195; **7** Team Little Wing, J: T. Moru/Fumihisa Asano (Honda CBR 1000), 191; **8** Suzuki Castrol Team, F: Vincent Philippe/S. Giles/Olivier Four (Suzuki GSXR), 190; **9** Honda Dream Mino DD Boys, J: Y. Takahashi/T. Shiragami (Honda CBR 1000), 189; **10** HMF Verity, J: Y. Takamiya/A. Igarashi (Honda CBR 1000), 188; **11** Z-Tech Team Garage, J: N. Mukai/S. Shimizu (Suzuki GSXR), 187; **12** Apan Club XA, J: T. Yamamoto/M. Akiya (Suzuki GSXR), 187.

Fastest lap: Ukawa/Izutsu, 2m 11.025s, 99.382 mph/159.940 km/h.

Championship points: **1** Yamaha GMT 94, 99; **2** Suzuki Castrol Team, 85; **3** Yamaha Endurance Moto 38, 56; **4** Yamaha Austria Racing Team, 51; **5** Seven Stars Honda, 38; **6** Suzuki Jet Team, Kawasaki Bolliger Team and Yoshimura Suzuki Jomo, 30.

24 STUNDEN VON OSCHERSLEBEN, Oschersleben Circuit, Germany, 14-15 August 2004.
Endurance World Championship, round 5. 883 laps of the 2.279-mile/3.667-km circuit, 2012.357 miles/3237.961 km

1 Yamaha GMT 94, F: David Checa/Sébastien Gimbert/William Costes (Yamaha YZF), 24h 00m 55.745s, 83.778 mph/134.828 km/h.

2 Yamaha Austria Racing Team, A: Horst Saiger/Thomas Hinterreiter/Igor Jerman (Yamaha YZF), 865 laps; **3** Yamaha Endurance Moto 38, F: Gwen Giabanni/Stephane Duterne/Sebastien Scarnato (Yamaha YZF), 859; **4** Suzuki Jet Team, CH: Claude-Alain Jaggi/Eric Monot/Sylvain Waldmeier (Suzuki GSXR), 851; **5** Bridgestone Bikers, D: Arne Tode/Tim Röthig/Thomas Cyzborra (Suzuki GSXR), 841; **6** Hepelmann Racing Team, D: Hans Josef Hepelmann/Reinhard Krächter/Oliver Wrede (Yamaha YZF), 833; **7** Engel-Racing-Team, GER: Ronny Linke /Robert König/Stefan Steinbach (Suzuki GSX-R1000 PRB), 833; **8** Ingenys Racing Rosenstadt,GER: Marco Apel/Jochen Moeckel/René Raub (Suzuki GSX-R750 PRB), 830; **9** Team 76 - Motorrad Klein, AUT: Gerhard Klein/Eric Raunegger/Mike Edwards (Yamaha YZF-R1 SBK) 829; **10** Kawasaki Endurance Deutschland, GER: Thomas Roth /Werner Dähler/Ronny Wehran/Mark Bruning (Kawasaki ZX10R SBK) 827; **11** JLC Moto Uteanatum, FRA Anthony Delhalle/Emmanuel Thuret/Emmanuel Cheron (Suzuki GSX-R1000 SPR);, **12** Bergmann & Söhne Racing, GER: Rüdiger Seefeldt/Heinz Platacis/Axel Reimann (Suzuki GSX-R1000 SPR); **13** Projecteam Honda Endurance, GER: Roger Maher/Rainer Kissner/Hubertus Junker, (Honda CBR1000RR SBK); **14** MSF Sauerland, GER: Claus-Peter Eckert/Peter Eickelmann/Dirk Debus/Mathias Ebert (Suzuki GSX-R1000 PRB); **15** Team Innodrom Racing, GER: Sandor Bitter/Lars Albrecht/Niggi Schmassmann (Suzuki GSX-R1000 SPR).

Fastest lap: Checa/Gimbert/Costes, 1m 30.435s, 90.704 mph/145.974 km/h.

Championship points: **1** Yamaha GMT 94, 149; **2** Yamaha Austria Racing Team, 91; **3** Yamaha Endurance Moto 38, 88; **4** Suzuki Castrol Team, 85; **5** Suzuki Jet Team, 56; **6** Seven Stars Honda, 38.

200 MIGLIA DI VALLELUNGA, Vallelunga Circuit, Italy, 3 October 2004.
Endurance World Championship, round 6. 100 laps of the 2.006-mile/3.228-km circuit, 200.600 miles/322.800 km

1 Suzuki Castrol Team, F: Vincent Philippe/Olivier Four/Christophe Cogan (Suzuki GSXR), 2h 16m 00.655s, 88.895 mph/143.062 km/h.

2 Yamaha GMT 94, F: David Checa/Christophe Guyot/William Costes (Yamaha YZF), 100 laps; **3** Yamaha Endurance Moto 38, F: Gwen Giabbani/Thierry Mulot/Frédéric Protat (Yamaha YZF), 100; **4** Yamaha Phase One Endurance, GB: Stéphane Mertens/Sebastien Scarnato (Yamaha YZF), 99; **5** WRT Honda Austria, A: Frédéric Moreira/Dean Ellison (Honda CBR 1000), 99; **6** Ducati DRE, I: Marc Garcia/Gianmaria Liverani/Dario Marchetti (Ducati 999R), 99; **7** Yamaha Austria Racing Team, A: Dean Thomas/Mike Edwards (Yamaha YZF), 99; **8** Kawasaki Bolliger Team, CH: Marcel Kellenberger/ David Morillon (Kawasaki ZX10R), 98; **9** Diablo 666 Bolliger, GB: James Hutchins/Kevin Falcke/Steve Mizera (Kawasaki ZX10R), 97; **10** Bridgestone Bikers, D: Tim Röthig/Arne Tode (Suzuki GSXR), 96; **11** Ducati Team Spring, I: Lorenzo Mauri/Matteo Colombo (Ducati 999R), 96; **12** Shell Endurance Academy, GB: Henry Fincher/Marko Rothlaan/Alek Dubelski (Suzuki GSXR), 96; **13** Suzuki No Limits Team, I: Roberto Ruozi/Andrea Giachino/Moreno Codeluppi (Suzuki GSXR), 95; **14** Fagersjo, S: Lars Carlberg/Magnus Karlsson (Yamaha YZF), 95; **15** Kawasaki Endurance, D: Thomas Roth/Mark Brüning (Kawasaki ZX10R), 95.

Fastest lap: Philippe/Four/Cogan, 1m 19.528s.

Final World Championship points

1 Yamaha GMT 94, F	169
2 Suzuki Castrol Team, F	110
3 Yamaha Endurance Moto 38, F	104
4 Yamaha Austria Racing Team, A	100
5 Suzuki Jet Team, CH	56

6=Bridgestone Bikers, D and WRT Honda Austria, A, 39; 8=Kawasaki Bolliger Team, CH and Seven Stars Honda, J, 38; **10** Yamaha Phase One Endurance, GB, 35; **11** Yoshimura Suzuki Jomo, J, 30; **12** Shell Endurance Academy, GB, 29; **13** Diablo 666 Bolliger, GB, 28; **14**=Suzuki Team Innodrom, D and Kawasaki Endurance, D, 26.

Isle of Man Tourist Trophy Races

ISLE OF MAN TOURIST TROPHY COURSE, 5-11 June 2004. 37.73-mile/60.72-km course.
Formula One TT (4 laps, 150.92 miles/242.88 km)

1 John McGuinness (Yamaha R1), 1h 12m 13.2s, 125.38 mph/201.78 km/h.

2 Adrian Archibald (Suzuki GSXR), 1h 12m 31.8s; **3** Bruce Anstey (Suzuki GSXR), 1h 12m 58.0s; **4** Jason Griffiths (Yamaha R1), 1h 13m 20.3s; **5** Ian Lougher (Honda CBR), 1h 13m 27.7s; **6** Richard Britton (Suzuki GSXR), 1h 13m 53.1s; **7** Mark Parrett (Yamaha R1), 1h 15m 26.5s; **8** Chris Heath (Honda CBR), 1h 15m 37.0s.

Fastest lap: McGuinness, 17m 43.8s, 127.68 mph/205.48 km/h.

Lightweight TT (4 laps, 150.92 miles/242.88 km)

1 John McGuinness (Honda 400), 1h 22m 06.4s, 110.28 mph/177.48 km/h.

2 Steve Linsdell (Yamaha 400), 1h 22m 39.6s; **3** Mark Parrett (Honda 400), 1h 22m 42.4s; **4** Roy Richardson (Honda 399), 1h 23m 02.0s; **5** John Barton (Yamaha 400), 1h 23m 44.8s; **6** Derran Slous (Yamaha 400), 1h 24m 04.7s; **7** Alan Bennie (Yamaha 400), 1h 24m 47.8s; **8** Jim Hodson (Yamaha 400), 1h 24m 54.7s; **9** Thomas Montano (Yamaha 400), 1h 25m 18.9s; **10** Robert J. Price (Yamaha 399), 1h 25m 24.8s; **11** Manfred Vogl (Kawasaki 398), 1h 25m 42.2s.

Fastest lap: McGuiness, 20m 12.3s, 112.04 mph/180.31 km/h.

Ultra-Lightweight TT (4 laps, 150.92 miles/242.88 km)

1 Chris Palmer (Honda 125), 1h 23m 07.6s, 108.93 mph/175.31 km/h.

2 Robert Dunlop (Honda 125), 1h 24m 05.5s; **3** Nigel Beattie (Honda 125), 1h 25m 56.4s; **4** Garry Bennett (Honda 125), 1h 26m 05.1s; **5** Matt Jackson (Honda 125), 1h 26m 20.6s; **6** Mark Tyrrell (Honda 125), 1h 26m 47.2s.

Fastest lap: Palmer, 20m 28.9s, 110.52 mph/177.86 km/h.

Production 1000 TT (3 laps, 113.19 miles/182.16 km)

1 Bruce Anstey (Suzuki GSXR), 54m 53.5s, 123.72 mph/199.11 km/h.

2 John McGuinness (Yamaha R1), 55m 11.5s; **3** Jason Griffiths (Yamaha R1), 55m 17.3s; **4** Ian Lougher (Honda CBR), 55m 22.7s; **5** Adrian Archibald (Suzuki GSXR), 55m 49.5s; **6** Richard Britton (Suzuki 1000), 56m 24.5s; **7** Mark Parrett (Yamaha R1), 56m 32.8s; **8** Gary Carswell (Yamaha 1000), 56m 57.8s; **9** Ian Armstrong (Yamaha 1000), 57m 22.2s.

Fastest lap: Anstey, 18m 05.7s, 125.10 mph/201.33 km/h.

Junior TT (4 laps, 150.92 miles/242.88 km)

1 John McGuinness (Yamaha R6), 1h 15m 06.0s, 120.57 mph/194.04 km/h.

2 Bruce Anstey (Suzuki 600), 1h 15m 23.0s; **3** Jason Griffiths (Yamaha R6), 1h 15m 45.6s; **4** Richard Britton (Honda 600), 1h 16m 10.8s; **5** Mark Parrett (Yamaha R6), 1h 16m 27.3s; **6** Martin Finnegan (Yamaha R6), 1h 16m 53.9s; **7** Gordon Blackley (Honda 600), 1h 16m 58.1s; **8** Raymond Porter (Suzuki 600), 1h 17m 02.0s; **9** Paul Hunt (Suzuki 600), 1h 17m 08.9s; **10** Chris Heath (Yamaha R6), 1h 17m 24.2s; **11** Nigel Beattie (Yamaha 600), 1h 17m 58.1s; **12** Ian Hutchinson (Suzuki 600), 1h 17m 59.1s; **13** Philip Stewart (Honda 600), 1h 18m 04.3s; **14** David Bell (Honda 600), 1h 18m 41.6s.

Fastest lap: McGuinness, 18m 25.4s, 122.87 mph/197.74 km/h.

Production 600 TT (3 laps, 113.19 miles/182.16 km)

1 Ryan Farquhar (Kawasaki ZX6), 57m 46.6s, 117.54 mph/189.16 km/h.

2 Bruce Anstey (Suzuki 600), 57m 48.9s; **3** John McGuinness (Yamaha R6), 57m 57.9s; **4** Jason Griffiths (Yamaha R6), 58m 07.9s; **5** Ian Lougher (Honda 600), 58m 21.1s; **6** Raymond Porter (Suzuki 600), 58m 44.0s; **7** Chris Heath (Yamaha 600), 58m 45.8s; **8** Gordon Blackley (Honda 600), 58m 48.0s; **9** Adrian Archibald (Suzuki 600), 58m 51.7s; **10** Mark Parrett (Honda 600), 58m 55.3s; **11** Tommy Clucas (Honda 600), 58m 59.1s; **12** Shaun Harris (Honda 600), 59m 01.8s; **13**

Richard Britton (Honda 600), 59m 08.7s; **14** Martin Finnegan (Yamaha 600), 59m 11.3s; **15** Davy Morgan (Yamaha R6), 59m 33.1s; **16** Alan Jackson (Honda 600), 59m 44.1s; **17** Chris Palmer (Suzuki 600), 59m 57.1s; **18** Dean Silvester (Yamaha R6), 1h 00m 08.2s; **19** Thomas Montano (Yamaha R6), 1h 00m 15.0s; **20** David Bell (Honda 600), 1h 00m 15.3s; **21** Guy Martin (Suzuki 600), 1h 00m 25.8s; **22** Stefano Bonetti (Suzuki 598), 1h 00m 26.02s; **23** Seamus Greene (Honda 600), 1h 00m 30.3s; 24 Ian Armstrong (Yamaha R6), 1h 00m 36.5s.
Fastest lap: Farquhar, 19m 01.9s, 118.94 mph/191.42 km/h.

Senior TT (4 laps, 150.92 miles/242/88 km)
1 Adrian Archibald (Suzuki GSXR), 1h 13m 08.1s, 123.81 mph/199.25 km/h.
2 Bruce Anstey (Suzuki GSXR), 1h 13m 38.3s; **3** Gary Carswell (Suzuki GSXR), 1h 15m 03.3s; **4** Mark Parrett (Yamaha R1), 1h 15m 09.9s; **5** Martin Finnegan (Yamaha 1000), 1h 15m 10.7s; **6** Chris Heath (Honda 1000), 1h 15m 22.1s; **7** Guy Martin (Suzuki GSXR), 1h 15m 24.9s; **8** Gordon Blackley (Honda CBR), 1h 16m 00.0s; **9** David Bell (Suzuki GSXR), 1h 16m 20.4s; **10** Ian Armstrong (Yamaha 1000), 1h 16m 32.3s; **11** Jun Maeda (Honda CBR), 1h 16m 36.1s; **12** Chris Palmer (Suzuki 1000), 1h 16m 37.8s.
Fastest lap: John McGuinness (Yamaha R1), 17m 47.9s; 127.19 mph/204.69 km/h.

Sidecar TT: Race A (3 laps, 113.19 miles/182.16 km)
1 Dave Molyneux/Daniel Sayle (Honda 600), 1h 01m 00.0s, 111.33 mph/179.17 km/h.
2 Nick Crowe/Darran Hope (Honda 600), 1h 01m 59.0s; **3** Steve Norbury/Scott Parnell (Yamaha 600), 1h 02m 51.8s; **4** Roy Hanks/Dave Wells (Yamaha 599), 1h 03m 02.5s; **5** Gregory Lambert/Ivan Murray (Honda 600), 1h 03m 23.4s; **6** Philip Dongworth/Stuart Castles (Kawasaki 600), 1h 03m 44.8s.
Fastest lap: Molyneux/Sayle, 20m 06.1s, 112.61 mph/ 181.23 km/h.

Sidecar TT: Race B (3 laps, 113.19 miles/182.16 km)
1 Dave Molyneux/Daniel Sayle (Honda 600), 1h 01 04.2s; 111.20 mph/178.96 km/h.
2 Nick Crowe/Darran Hope (Honda 600), 1h 01m 41.6s; **3** Steve Norbury/Scott Parnell (Yamaha 600), 1h 02m 22.3s; 4 Roy Hanks/Dave Wells (Yamaha 599), 1h 02m 32.7s; **5** Gary Bryan/Steven Hedison (Yamaha 600), 1h 03m 04.9s; **6** Gregory Lambert/Ivan Murray (Honda 600), 1h 03m 11.0s; **7** John Holden/Jamie Winn (Honda 600), 1h 03m 59.4s.
Fastest lap: Molyneux/Sayle, 20m 00.2s, 113.17 mph/ 182.13 km/h.

AMA Chevrolet Superbike Championship

Presented by Parts Unlimited

DAYTONA INTERNATIONAL SPEEDWAY - Daytona Beach, Florida, 3-6 March, 200.00 miles/321.869 km
1 Mat Mladin (Suzuki GSX-R1000).
2 Jake Zemke (Honda CBR1000RR); **3** Miguel Duhamel (Honda CBR1000RR); **4** Jack Pfeifer (Suzuki GSX-R1000); **5** Lee Acree (Suzuki GSX-R1000); **6** Ricky Orlando (Suzuki GSX-R1000); **7** Pascal Picotte (Yamaha YZF-R1); **8** Opie Caylor (Suzuki GSX-R1000); **9** Scott Jensen (Suzuki GSX-R1000); **10** Eric Wood (Suzuki GSX-R1000).

CALIFORNIA SPEEDWAY - Fontana, California, 2-4 April, 66.080 miles/106.345 km
Race 1
1 Mat Mladin (Suzuki GSX-R1000).
2 Eric Bostrom (Ducati 999R); **3** Miguel Duhamel (Honda CBR1000RR); **4** Jake Zemke (Honda CBR1000RR); **5** Geoff May (Suzuki GSX-R1000); **6** Steve Crevier (Suzuki GSX-R1000); **7** Larry Pegram (Yamaha YZF-R10); **8** Martin Craggill (Suzuki GSX-R1000); **9** John Haner (Suzuki GSX-R1000); **10** Opie Caylor (Suzuki GSX-R1000).

Race 2
1 Mat Mladin (Suzuki GSX-R1000).
2 Eric Bostrom (Ducati 999R); **3** Jake Zemke (Honda CBR1000RR); **4** Miguel Duhamel (Honda CBR1000RR); **5** Ben Bostrom (Honda CBR1000RR); **6** Steve Crevier (Suzuki GSX-R1000); **7** Geoff May (Suzuki GSX-R1000); **8** Larry Pegram (Yamaha YZF-R1); **9** Lee Acree (Suzuki GSX-R1000); **10** Eric Wood (Suzuki GSX-R1000).

INFINEON RACEWAY - Sonoma, California, 30 April - 2 May, 60.320 miles/97.060 km
Race 1
1 Mat Mladin (Suzuki GSX-R1000).
2 Miguel Duhamel (Honda CBR1000RR); **3** Jake Zemke (Honda CBR1000RR); **4** Ben Bostrom (Honda CBR1000RR) **5** Eric Bostrom (Ducati 999R); **6** Joshua Kurt Hayes (Kawasaki ZX-10R); **7** (Suzuki GSX-R1000); **8** Larry Pegram (Yamaha YZF-R1) **9** Geoff May (Suzuki GSX-R1000); **10** Aaron Yates (Suzuki GSX-R1000).

Race 2
1 Miguel Duhamel (Honda CBR1000RR).
2 Jake Zemke Honda (CBR1000RR); **3** Aaron Yates (Suzuki GSX-R1000); **4** Mat Mladin (Suzuki GSX-R1000); **5** Ben Bostrom (Honda CBR1000RR); **6** Steve Crevier (Suzuki GSX-R1000); **7** Joshua Kurt Hayes (Kawasaki ZX-10R); **8** Larry Pegram (Yamaha YZF-R1); **9** Geoff May (Suzuki GSX-R1000); **10** Shawn M Higbee (Suzuki GSX-R1000).

BARBER MOTORSPORTS PARK - Birmingham, Alabama, 14-16 May, 64.400 miles/103.040 km
Race 1
1 Mat Mladin (Suzuki GSX-R1000).
2 Jake Zemke (Honda CBR1000RR); **3** Miguel Duhamel (Honda CBR1000RR); **4** Eric Bostrom (Ducati 999R); **5** Joshua Hayes (Kawasaki ZX-10R); **6** John Haner (Suzuki GSX-R1000); **7** Geoff May (Suzuki GSX-R1000); **8** Jeremy Toye (Yamaha YZF-R1); **9** Eric Wood (Suzuki GSX-R1000); **10** Shawn Higbee (Suzuki GSX-R1000).

Race 2
1 Miguel Duhamel (Honda CBR1000RR).
2 Jake Zemke (Honda CBR1000RR); **3** Mat Mladin (Suzuki GSX-R1000); **4** Aaron W Yates (Suzuki GSX-R1000); **5** Ben Bostrom (Honda CBR1000RR); **6** Joshua Hayes (Kawasaki ZX-10R); **7** Eric Bostrom (Ducati 999R); **8** John Haner (Suzuki GSX-R1000); **9** Geoff May (Suzuki GSX-R1000); **10** Jeremy Toye (Yamaha YZF-R1).

PIKES PEAK INTERNATIONAL RACEWAY - Fountain, Colorado, 22-23 May, 23 May, 52.6 miles, 84.160 km
1 Eric Bostrom (Ducati 999R).
2 Jake Zemke (Honda CBR1000RR); **3** Aaron Yates (Suzuki GSX-R1000); **4** Miguel Duhamel (Honda CBR1000RR); **5** Ben Bostrom (Honda CBR1000RR); **6** Mat Mladin (Suzuki GSX-R1000); **7** Joshua Hayes (Kawasaki ZX-10R); **8** Shawn Higbee (Suzuki GSX-R1000); **9** Ricky Orlando (Kawasaki ZX-10R); 10 Geoff May (Suzuki GSX-R1000).

ROAD AMERICA - Elkhart Lake, Wisconsin, 4-6 June, 64.00 miles/102.998 km
Race 1
1 Miguel Duhamel (Honda CBR1000RR).
2 Mat Mladin (Suzuki GSX-R1000); **3** Jake Zemke (Honda CBR1000RR); **4** Ben Bostrom (Honda CBR1000RR); **5** Eric Bostrom (Ducati 999R); **6** Steve Crevier (Suzuki GSX-R1000); **7** Aaron Yates (Suzuki GSX-R1000); **8** Geoff May (Suzuki GSX-R1000); **9** Shawn Higbee (Suzuki GSX-R1000); **10** Eric Wood (Suzuki GSX-R1000).

Race 2
1 Miguel Duhamel (Honda CBR1000RR).
2 Jake Zemke (Honda CBR1000RR); **3** Mat Mladin (Suzuki GSX-R1000); **4** Aaron Yates (Suzuki GSX-R1000); **5** Ben Bostrom (Honda CBR1000RR); **6** Eric Bostrom (Ducati 999R); **7** Steve Crevier (Suzuki GSX-R1000); **8** Larry Pegram (Yamaha YZF-R1); **9** Geoff May (Suzuki GSX-R1000); **10** Eric Wood (Suzuki GSX-R1000).

BRAINERD INTERNATIONAL RACEWAY - Brainerd, Minnesota, 25-27 June, 63.00 miles/100.800 km
1 Jake Zemke (Honda CBR1000RR).
2 Miguel Duhamel (Honda CBR1000RR); **3** Mat Mladin (Suzuki GSX-R1000); **4** Eric Bostrom (Ducati 999R); **5** Ben Bostrom (Honda CBR1000RR); **6** Joshua Hayes (Kawasaki ZX-10R); **7** Aaron Yates (Suzuki GSX-R1000); **8** Pascal Picotte (Yamaha YZF-R1); 9 Jacob Holden (Suzuki GSX-R1000); **10** Geoff May (Suzuki GSX-R1000).

MAZDA RACEWAY, LAGUNA SECA - Monterey, California, 10 July, 61.600 miles/98.560 km
Race 1
1 Ben Bostrom (Honda CBR1000RR).
2 Mat Mladin (Suzuki GSX-R1000); **3** Miguel Duhamel (Honda CBR1000RR); **4** Aaron Yates (Suzuki GSX-R1000); **5** Eric Bostrom (Ducati 999R); **6** Joshua Hayes (Kawasaki ZX-10R); **7** Jake Zemke (Honda CBR1000RR); **8** Jacob Holden (Suzuki GSX-R1000); **9** Larry Pegram (Yamaha YZF-R1); **10** Geoff May (Suzuki GSX-R1000).

MID-OHIO SPORTS CAR COURSE - Lexington, Ohio, 23-25 July, 62.400 miles/99.840 km
Race 1
1 Mat Mladin (Suzuki GSX-R1000).
2 Miguel Duhamel (Honda CBR1000RR); **3** Aaron Yates (Suzuki GSX-R1000); **4** Ben Bostrom (Honda CBR1000RR); **5** Jake Zemke (Honda CBR1000RR); **6** Joshua Hayes (Kawasaki ZX-10R); **7** Eric Bostrom (Ducati 999R); **8** Jacob Holden (Suzuki GSX-R1000); **9** John Haner (Suzuki GSX-R1000); **10** Larry Pegram (Yamaha YZF-R1).

Race 2
1 Jake Zemke (Honda CBR1000RR).
2 Ben Bostrom (Honda CBR1000RR); **3** Mat Mladin (Suzuki GSX-R1000); **4** Aaron Yates (Suzuki GSX-R1000); **5** Joshua Hayes (Kawasaki ZX-10R); **6** Jacob Holden (Suzuki GSX-R1000); **7** Eric Bostrom (Ducati 999R); **8** Larry Pegram (Yamaha YZF-R1); **9** Eric Wood (Suzuki GSX-R1000); **10** John Haner (Suzuki GSX-R1000).

ROAD ATLANTA - Braselton, Georgia, 3-5 September, 63.500 miles/101.389 km
Race 1
1 Mat Mladin (Suzuki GSX-R1000).
2 Miguel Duhamel (Honda CBR1000RR); **3** Ben Bostrom (Honda CBR1000RR); **4** Jake Zemke (Honda CBR1000RR); **5** Aaron Yates (Suzuki GSX-R1000); **6** John Haner (Suzuki GSX-R1000); **7** Geoff May (Suzuki GSX-R1000); **8** Eric Wood (Suzuki GSX-R1000); **9** Shawn Higbee (Suzuki GSX-R1000); **10** Opie Caylor (Suzuki GSX-R1000).

Race 2
1 Mat Mladin (Suzuki GSX-R1000).
2 Miguel Duhamel (Honda CBR1000RR); **3** Ben Bostrom (Honda CBR1000RR); **4** Jake Zemke (Honda CBR1000RR); **5** Joshua Hayes (Kawasaki ZX-10R); **6** John Haner (Suzuki GSX-R1000); **7** Larry Pegram (Yamaha YZF-R1); **8** Martin Craggill (Suzuki GSX-R1000); **9** Eric Wood (Suzuki GSX-R1000); **10** Geoff May (Suzuki GSX-R1000).

VIRGINIA INTERNATIONAL RACEWAY - Alton, Virginia, 9-10 October, 62.300 miles/ 99.680 km.
Race 1
1 Miguel Duhamel (Honda CBR1000RR).
2 Aaron Yates (Suzuki GSX-R1000); **3** Ben Bostrom (Honda CBR1000RR); **4** Lorenzo Lanzi (Ducati 999R); **5** Regis Laconi (Ducati 999R); **6** Mat Mladin (Suzuki GSX-R1000); **7** Joshua Hayes (Kawasaki ZX-10R); **8** Jacob Holden (Suzuki GSX-R1000); **9** Geoff May (Suzuki GSX-R1000); **10** Michael Smith (Suzuki GSX-R1000).

Race 2
1 Miguel Duhamel (Honda CBR1000RR).
2 Aaron Yates (Suzuki GSX-R1000); **3** Ben Bostrom (Honda CBR1000RR); **4** Mat Mladin (Suzuki GSX-R1000); **5** Regis Laconi (Ducati 999R); **6** Joshua Hayes (Kawasaki ZX-10R); **7** Martin Craggill (Suzuki GSX-R1000); **8** Michael Smith (Suzuki GSX-R1000); **9** Geoff May (Suzuki GSX-R1000); **10** Jeremy Toye (Yamaha YZF-R1).

Final Championship Points

1	Mat Mladin	584
2	Miguel Duhamel	551
3	Jake Zemke	490
4	Ben Bostrom	422
5	Geoff May	388

6 Aaron Yates, 363; **7** Eric Bostrom, 336; **8** Joshua Hayes, 316; **9** Eric Wood, 314; **10** John Haner, 312.

Supersport World Championship

VALENCIA, Spain, 29 February 2004. 2.489-mile/4.005-km circuit.
Supersport World Championship, round 1 (23 laps, 57.247 miles/92.115 km)
1 Jurgen van den Goorbergh, NL (Yamaha), 38m 27.439s, 89.300 mph/143.715 km/h.
2 Fabien Foret, F (Yamaha); **3** Katsuaki Fujiwara, J (Suzuki); **4** Lorenzo Lanzi, I (Ducati); **5** Stéphane Chambon, F (Suzuki); **6** Vittorio Iannuzzo, I (Suzuki); **7** Werner Daemen, B (Honda); **8** Karl Muggeridge, AUS (Honda); **9** Kevin Curtain, AUS (Yamaha); **10** Stefano Cruciani, I (Kawasaki); **11** Matthieu Lagrive, F (Suzuki); **12** Arne Tode, D (Yamaha); **13** Matteo Baiocco, I (Yamaha); **14** Max Neukirchner, D (Honda); **15** Kai Borre Andersen, N (Kawasaki).
Fastest lap: Broc Parkes, AUS (Honda), 1m 39.065s, 90.435 mph/145.541 km/h.
Championship points: 1 van den Goorbergh, 25; **2** Foret, 20; **3** Fujiwara, 16; **4** Lanzi, 13; **5** Chambon, 11; **6** Iannuzzo, 10.

PHILLIP ISLAND, Australia, 28 March 2004. 2.762-mile/4.445 km circuit.
Supersport World Championship, round 2 (21 laps, 58.002 miles/93.345 km)
1 Joshua Brookes, AUS (Honda), 34m 12.301s, 101.743 mph/163.739 km/h.
2 Kevin Curtain, AUS (Yamaha); **3** Jurgen van den Goorbergh, NL (Yamaha); **4** Broc Parkes, AUS (Honda); **5** Sébastien Charpentier, F (Honda); **6** Fabien Foret, F (Yamaha); **7** Alessio Corradi, I (Honda); **8** Max Neukirchner, D (Honda); **9** Lorenzo Lanzi, I (Ducati); **10** Stéphane Chambon, F (Suzuki); **11** Katsuaki Fujiwara, J (Suzuki); **12** Karl Muggeridge, AUS (Honda); **13** Vittorio Iannuzzo, I (Suzuki); **14** Stefano Cruciani, I (Kawasaki); **15** Matthieu Lagrive, F (Suzuki).
Fastest lap: van den Goorbergh, 1m 37.084s, 102.418 mph/164.826 km/h.
Championship points: 1 van den Goorbergh, 41; **2** Foret, 30; **3** Curtain, 27; **4** Brookes, 25; **5** Fujiwara, 21; **6** Lanzi, 20.

MISANO, Italy, 18 April 2004. 2.523-mile/4.060-km circuit.
Supersport World Championship, round 3 (23 laps, 58.029 miles/93.380 km)
1 Karl Muggeridge, AUS (Honda), 42m 11.937s, 82.500 mph/132.771 km/h.
2 Kevin Curtain, AUS (Yamaha); **3** Jurgen van den Goorbergh, NL (Yamaha); **4** Katsuaki Fujiwara, J (Suzuki); **5** Alessio Corradi, I (Honda); **6** Lorenzo Lanzi, I (Ducati); **7** Stéphane Chambon, F (Suzuki); **8** Giovanni Bussei, I (Ducati); **9** Vittorio Iannuzzo, I (Suzuki); **10** Walter Tortoroglio, I (Suzuki); **11** Massimo Roccoli, I (Yamaha); **12** Antonio Carlacci, I (Yamaha); **13** Matthieu Lagrive, F (Suzuki); **14** Denis Sacchetti, I (Honda); **15** Eli Chen, ISR (Honda).

Fastest lap: Broc Parkes, AUS (Honda), 1m 47.789s, 84.257 mph/135.598 km/h.

Championship points: **1** van den Goorbergh, 57; **2** Curtain, 47; **3** Muggeridge, 37; **4** Fujiwara, 34; **5** Lanzi and Foret, 30 (

MONZA, Italy, 16 May 2004. 3.620-mile/5.793-km circuit.

Supersport World Championship, round 4 (16 laps, 57.925 miles/92.676 km)

1 Karl Muggeridge, AUS (Honda), 30m 27.772s.

2 Broc Parkes, AUS (Honda); **3** Jurgen van den Goorbergh, NL (Yamaha); **4** Sébastien Charpentier, F (Honda); **5** Christian Kellner, D (Yamaha); **6** Max Neukirchner, D (Honda); **7** Giovanni Bussei, I (Ducati); **8** Vittoriano Guareschi, I (Ducati); **9** Matthieu Lagrive, F (Suzuki); **10** Jan Hanson, S (Honda); **11** Roccolo Massimo, I (Yamaha); **12** Denis Sacchetti, I (Honda); **13** Diego Giugovaz, I (Honda); **14** Ron van Steenbergen, NL (Honda); **15** Lorenzo Lanzi, I (Ducati).

Fastest lap: Muggeridge, 1m 53.396s, 114.944 mph/183.911 km/h.

Championship points: **1** van den Goorbergh, 73; **2** Muggeridge, 62; **3** Curtain, 47; **4** Fujiwara, 34; **5** Parkes, 33; **6** Lanzi, 31.

OSCHERSLEBEN, Germany, 30 May 2004. 2.279-mile/3.667-km circuit.

Supersport World Championship, round 5 (28 laps, 63.812 miles/102.676 km)

1 Karl Muggeridge, AUS (Honda), 42m 41.262s.

2 Broc Parkes, AUS (Honda); **3** Sébastien Charpentier, F (Honda); **4** Stéphane Chambon, F (Suzuki); **5** Max Neukirchner, D (Honda); **6** Katsuaki Fujiwara, J (Suzuki); **7** Jurgen van den Goorbergh, NL (Yamaha); **8** Christian Kellner, D (Yamaha); **9** Alessio Corradi, I (Honda); **10** Lorenzo Lanzi, I (Ducati); **11** Barry Veneman, NL (Suzuki); **12** Kai Borre Andersen, N (Kawasaki); **13** Denis Sacchetti, I (Honda); **14** Werner Daemen, B (Honda); **15** Sébastien Le Grelle, B (Honda).

Fastest lap: Parkes, 1m 30.386s, 90.754 mph/146.054 km/h.

Championship points: **1** Muggeridge, 87; **2** van den Goorbergh, 82; **3** Parkes, 53; **4** Curtain, 47; **5** Fujiwara, 44; **6** Charpentier, 40.

SILVERSTONE, Great Britain, 13 June 2004. 3.129-mile/5.036-km circuit.

Supersport World Championship, round 6 (19 laps, 59.451 miles/95.684 km)

1 Fabien Foret, F (Yamaha), 37m 33.642s, 94.975 mph/152.847 km/h.

2 Karl Muggeridge, AUS (Honda); **3** Broc Parkes, AUS (Honda); **4** Lorenzo Lanzi, I (Ducati); **5** Kevin Curtain, AUS (Yamaha); **6** Jurgen van den Goorbergh, NL (Yamaha); **7** Pere Riba, E (Kawasaki); **8** Sébastien Charpentier, F (Honda); **9** Alessio Corradi, I (Honda); **10** Stéphane Chambon, F (Suzuki); **11** Max Neukirchner, D (Honda); **12** Craig Jones, GB (Triumph); **13** Matteo Baiocco, I (Yamaha); **14** Sébastien Le Grelle, B (Honda); **15** Matthieu Lagrive, F (Suzuki).

Fastest lap: Charpentier, 1m 57.261s, 96.070 mph/154.609 km/h.

Championship points: **1** Muggeridge, 107; **2** van den Goorbergh, 92; **3** Parkes, 69; **4** Curtain, 58; **5** Foret, 55; **6** Lanzi, 50.

BRANDS HATCH, Great Britain, 1 August 2004. 2.608-mile/4.197-km circuit.

Supersport World Championship, round 7 (23 laps, 59.984 miles/96.531 km)

1 Karl Muggeridge, AUS (Honda), 34m 44.195s, 103.606 mph/166.737 km/h.

2 Sébastien Charpentier, F (Honda); **3** Jurgen van den Goorbergh, NL (Yamaha); **4** Broc Parkes, AUS (Honda); **5** Kevin Curtain, AUS (Yamaha); **6** Alessio Corradi, I (Honda); **7** Katsuaki Fujiwara, J (Suzuki); **8** Stéphane Chambon, F (Suzuki); **9** Anthony West, AUS (Honda); **10** Lorenzo Lanzi, I (Ducati); **11** Max Neukirchner, D (Honda); **12** Luke Quigley, GB (Suzuki); **13** Tom Tunstall, GB (Honda); **14** Walter Tortoroglio, I (Suzuki); **15** Matthieu Lagrive, F (Suzuki).

Fastest lap: Fabien Foret, F (Yamaha), 1m 29.638s, 104.737 mph/168.558 km/h.

Championship points: **1** Muggeridge, 132; **2** van den Goorbergh, 108; **3** Parkes, 82; **4** Curtain, 69; **5** Charpentier, 68; **6** Lanzi, 56.

ASSEN, Holland, 5 September 2004. 3.745-mile/6.027 km circuit.

Supersport World Championship, round 8 (16 laps, 59.920 miles/96.432 km)

1 Karl Muggeridge, AUS (Honda), 34m 14.542s, 104.993 mph/168.970 km/h.

2 Sébastien Charpentier, F (Honda); **3** Andrew Pitt, AUS (Yamaha); **4** Broc Parkes, AUS (Honda); **5** Jurgen van den Goorbergh, NL (Yamaha); **6** Jan Hanson, S (Honda); **7** Max Neukirchner, D (Honda); **8** Arie Vos, NL (Kawasaki); **9** Christian Kellner, D (Yamaha); **10** Barry Veneman, NL (Suzuki); **11** Kai Borre Andersen, N (Kawasaki); **12** Stefano Cruciani, I (Kawasaki); **13** Stéphane Chambon, F (Suzuki); **14** Matthieu Lagrive, F (Suzuki); **15** Matteo Baiocco, I (Yamaha).

Fastest lap: Pitt, 2m 07.430s, 105.800 mph/170.268 km/h.

Championship points: **1** Muggeridge, 157; **2** van den Goorbergh, 119; **3** Parkes, 95; **4** Charpentier, 88; **5** Curtain, 69; **6** Chambon and Lanzi, 56.

IMOLA, Italy, 26 September 2004. 3.065-mile/4.933-km circuit.

Supersport World Championship, round 9 (21 laps, 64.365 miles/103.593 km)

1 Karl Muggeridge, AUS (Honda), 39m 56.749s, 96.685 mph/155.600 km/h.

2 Broc Parkes, AUS (Honda); **3** Sébastien Charpentier, F (Honda); **4** Lorenzo Lanzi, I (Ducati); **5** Fabien Foret, F (Yamaha); **6** Andrew Pitt, AUS (Yamaha); **7** Michel Fabrizio, I (Honda); **8** Stéphane Chambon, F (Suzuki); **9** Matteo Baiocco, I (Yamaha); **10** Alessandro Antonello, I (Kawasaki); **11** Max Neukirchner, D (Honda); **12** Craig Coxhell, AUS (Yamaha); **13** Denis Sacchetti, I (Honda); 14 Katsuaki Fujiwara, J (Suzuki); **15** Christian Kellner, D (Yamaha).

Fastest lap: Muggeridge, 1m 53.160s, 97.515 mph/156.935 km/h.

Championship points: **1** Muggeridge, 182; **2** van den Goorbergh, 119; **3** Parkes, 115; **4** Charpentier, 104; **5** Curtain and Lanzi, 69.

MAGNY COURS, France, 3 October 2004. 2.741-mile/4.411-km circuit.

Supersport World Championship, round 10 (22 laps, 60.302 miles/97.042 km)

1 Karl Muggeridge, AUS (Honda), 38m 34.820s, 93.777 mph/150.919 km/h.

2 Broc Parkes, AUS (Honda); **3** Sébastien Charpentier, F (Honda); **4** Lorenzo Lanzi, I (Ducati); **5** Jurgen van den Goorbergh, NL (Yamaha); **6** Andrew Pitt, AUS (Yamaha); **7** Craig Coxhell, AUS (Yamaha); **8** Max Neukirchner, D (Honda); **9** Matthieu Lagrive, F (Suzuki); **10** Matteo Baiocco, I (Yamaha); **11** Massimo Roccoli, I (Yamaha); **12** Barry Veneman, NL (Suzuki); **13** Christian Kellner, D (Yamaha); **14** Jimmy Lindstrom, S (Honda); **15** Philippe Donischal, F (Suzuki).

Fastest lap: Parkes, 1m 44.457s, 94.461 mph/152.020 km/h (record).

Final World Championship points

1 Karl Muggeridge, AUS	207
2 Broc Parkes, AUS	135
3 Jurgen van den Goorbergh, NL	130
4 Sébastien Charpentier, F	120
5 Lorenzo Lanzi, I	82

6 Kevin Curtain, AUS, 69; **7** Fabien Foret, F, 66; **8** Stéphane Chambon, F, 64; **9** Max Neukirchner, D, 63; **10** Katsuaki Fujiwara, J, 55; **11** Alessio Corradi, I, 44; **12** Andrew Pitt, AUS, 36; **13** Christian Kellner, D, 30; **14** Matthieu Lagrive, F, 27; **15** Joshua Brookes, AUS, 25.

British Championships

SILVERSTONE INTERNATIONAL CIRCUIT, 28 March 2004. 2.213-mile/3.561-km circuit.

THINK! British Superbike Championship, rounds 1 and 2 (2 x 22 laps, 48.686 miles/78.342 km)

Race 1

1 Michael Rutter (Honda), 36m 18.615s, 80.32 mph/129.26 km/h.

2 Ryuichi Kiyonari (Honda); **3** John Reynolds (Suzuki); **4** Yukio Kagayama (Suzuki); **5** Sean Emmett (Ducati); **6** Marty Nutt (Yamaha); **7** Scott Smart (Kawasaki); **8** Dean Thomas (Ducati); **9** Glen Richards (Kawasaki); **10** Craig Coxhell (Honda); 11 Stuart Easton (Ducati); **12** James Ellison (Yamaha); **13** Jon Kirkham (Suzuki); **14** Tommy Hill (Yamaha); **15** Sam Corke (Suzuki).

Fastest lap: Rutter, 1m 37.543s, 81.67 mph/131.44 km/h.

Race 2

1 John Reynolds (Suzuki), 32m 10.864s, 90.63 mph/145.85 km/h.

2 Ryuichi Kiyonari (Honda); **3** Michael Rutter (Honda); **4** Sean Emmett (Ducati); **5** Scott Smart (Kawasaki); **6** Dean Thomas (Ducati); **7** Stuart Easton (Ducati); **8** Gary Mason (Yamaha); **9** Steve Plater (Yamaha); **10** Tommy Hill (Yamaha); **11** Jon Kirkham (Suzuki); **12** Craig Coxhell (Honda); **13** Dennis Hobbs (Suzuki); **14** Dean Ellison (Ducati); **15** James Ellison (Yamaha).

Fastest lap: Rutter, 1m 26.890s, 91.68 mph/147.55 km/h (record).

Championship points: **1** Reynolds and Rutter, 41; **3** Kiyonari, 40; **4** Emmett, 24; **5** Smart, 21; **6** Thomas, 19.

British Supersport Championship, round 1 (20 laps, 44.260 miles/71.220 km)

1 Karl Harris (Honda), 30m 24.585s, 87.18 mph/140.30 km/h.

2 Craig Jones (Triumph); **3** Michael Laverty (Ducati); **4** Pere Riba (Kawasaki); **5** Leon Camier (Honda); **6** Kieran Murphy (Honda); **7** Cal Crutchlow (Honda); **8** Jay Vincent (Honda); **9** Adrian Coates (Suzuki); **10** Tommy Sykes (Suzuki); **11** Luke Quigley (Suzuki); **12** Jonathan Rea (Honda); **13** Tom Tunstall (Honda); **14** Shane Norval (Honda); **15** Lee Jackson (Honda).

Fastest lap: Jones, 1m 30.125s, 88.39 mph/142.25 km/h.

Championship points: **1** Harris, 25; **2** Jones, 20; **3** Laverty, 16; **4** Riba, 13; **5** Camier, 11; **6** Murphy, 10.

British 125GP Championship, round 1 (10 laps, 22.130 miles/35.610 km)

1 Christian Elkin (Honda), 18m 46.809s, 70.46 mph/113.39 km/h.

2 Kris Weston (Honda); **3** Eugene Laverty (Honda); **4** Steven Neate (Honda); **5** John Pearson (Honda); **6** Michael Wilcox (Honda); **7** Tom Grant (Honda); **8** Tye Kinton (Honda); **9** Daniel Cooper (Honda); **10** Ryan Saxelby (Honda); **11** Jon Vincent (Honda); **12** William Dunlop (Honda); **13** Toby Markham (Honda); **14** James Ford (Honda); **15** Dan Linfoot (Honda).

Fastest lap: Rob Guiver (Honda), 1m 47.340s, 74.22 mph/119.44 km/h.

Championship points: **1** Elkin, 25; **2** Weston, 20; **3** Laverty, 16; **4** Neate, 13; **5** Pearson, 11; **6** Wilcox, 10.

BRANDS HATCH INDY CIRCUIT, 12 April 2004. 1.226-mile/1.973-km circuit.

THINK! British Superbike Championship, rounds 3 and 4 (2 x 30 laps, 36.780 miles/59.190 km)

Race 1

1 John Reynolds (Suzuki), 24m 28.876s, 90.20 mph/145.16 km/h.

2 Michael Rutter (Honda); **3** Yukio Kagayama (Suzuki); **4** Scott Smart (Kawasaki); **5** Gary Mason (Yamaha); **6** Ryuichi Kiyonari (Honda); **7** Sam Corke (Suzuki); **8** Jon Kirkham (Suzuki); **9** Tommy Hill (Yamaha); **10** Kieran Clarke (Yamaha); **11** Steve Plater (Yamaha); **12** Dennis Hobbs (Suzuki); **13** Malcolm Ashley (Ducati); **14** James Ellison (Yamaha); **15** James Buckingham (Suzuki).

Fastest lap: Reynolds, 46.537s, 94.85 mph/152.65 km/h.

Race 2

1 Sean Emmett (Ducati), 23m 26.496s, 94.20 mph/151.60 km/h.

2 Michael Rutter (Honda); **3** John Reynolds (Suzuki); **4** Scott Smart (Kawasaki); **5** Yukio Kagayama (Suzuki); **6** Ryuichi Kiyonari (Honda); **7** Glen Richards (Kawasaki); **8** Dean Thomas (Ducati); **9** Gary Mason (Yamaha); **10** Tommy Hill (Yamaha); **11** Jon Kirkham (Suzuki); **12** Steve Plater (Yamaha); **13** Kieran Clarke (Yamaha); **14** Dennis Hobbs (Suzuki); **15** James Buckingham (Suzuki).

Fastest lap: Rutter, 46.302s, 95.33 mph/153.43 km/h.

Championship points: **1** Reynolds, 82; **2** Rutter, 81; **3** Kiyonari, 60; **4** Emmett, 49; **5** Smart, 47; **6** Kagayama, 40.

British Supersport Championship, round 2 (28 laps, 34.328 miles/55.244 km)

1 Jay Vincent (Honda), 23m 19.965s, 88.33 mph/142.15 km/h.

2 Luke Quigley (Suzuki); **3** Simon Andrews (Yamaha); **4** Pere Riba (Kawasaki); **5** Tom Tunstall (Honda); **6** Michael Laverty (Ducati); **7** Kieran Murphy (Honda); **8** Lee Jackson (Honda); **9** Jamie Robinson (Yamaha); **10** Shane Norval (Honda); **11** Hilton Hincks (Honda); **12** Craig Sproston (Honda); **13** Martin Buckles (Yamaha); **14** Lee Longden (Honda); **15** Daniel Fowler (Yamaha).

Fastest lap: Leon Camier (Honda), 47.791s, 92.36 mph/148.65 km/h.

Championship points: **1** Vincent, 33; **2** Laverty and Riba, 26; **4** Harris and Quigley, 25; 6 Jones, 20.

British 125GP Championship, round 2 (21 laps, 25.746 miles/41.433 km)

1 Michael Wilcox (Honda), 18m 01.489s, 85.77 mph/138.03 km/h.

2 Eugene Laverty (Honda); **3** Ashley Beech (Honda); **4** John Pearson (Honda); **5** Ryan Saxelby (Honda); **6** Kris Weston (Honda); **7** Steven Neate (Honda); **8** Tom Bridewell (Honda); **9** Aaron Walker (Aprilia); **10** Joe Dickinson (Honda); **11** Richard Murphy (Honda); **12** Daniel Cooper (Honda); **13** Tom Grant (Honda); **14** James Ford (Honda); **15** Nathan Pallett (Honda).

Fastest lap: Rob Guiver (Honda), 49.402s, 89.35 mph/143.80 km/h.

Championship points: **1** Laverty, 36; **2** Wilcox, 35; **3** Weston, 30; **4** Elkin, 25; **5** Pearson, 24; 6 Neate, 22

SNETTERTON CIRCUIT, 25 April 2004. 1.952-mile/3.141-km circuit.

THINK! British Superbike Championship, rounds 5 and 6

Race 1 (25 laps, 48.800 miles/78.525 km)

1 Yukio Kagayama (Suzuki), 27m 50.976s, 105.13 mph/169.19 km/h.

2 John Reynolds (Suzuki); **3** Michael Rutter (Honda); **4** Sean Emmett (Ducati); **5** Scott Smart (Kawasaki); **6** Dean Thomas (Ducati); **7** Ryuichi Kiyonari (Honda); **8** Tommy Hill (Yamaha); **9** Glen Richards (Kawasaki); **10** James Haydon (Ducati); **11** James Ellison (Yamaha); **12** Dennis Hobbs (Suzuki); **13** Sam Corke (Suzuki); **14** James Buckingham (Suzuki); **15** Chris Martin (Suzuki).

Fastest lap: Reynolds, 1m 06.070s, 106.36 mph/171.16 km/h.

Race 2 (24 laps, 46.848 miles/75.384 km)

1 John Reynolds (Suzuki), 26m 40.720s, 105.36 mph/169.56 km/h.

2 Michael Rutter (Honda); **3** Sean Emmett (Ducati); **4** Yukio Kagayama (Suzuki); **5** Dean Thomas (Ducati); **6** Scott Smart (Kawasaki); **7** Glen Richards (Kawasaki); **8** Steve Plater (Yamaha); **9** Ryuichi Kiyonari (Honda); **10** Tommy Hill (Yamaha); **11** Gary Mason (Yamaha); **12** James Ellison (Yamaha); **13** Craig Coxhell (Honda); **14** James Haydon (Ducati); **15** Kieran Clarke (Yamaha).

Fastest lap: Rutter, 1m 05.904s, 106.62 mph/171.60 km/h (record).

Championship points: **1** Reynolds, 127; **2** Rutter, 117; **3** Emmett and Kagayama, 78; **5** Kiyonari, 76; 6 Smart, 68.

British Supersport Championship, round 3 (22 laps, 42.944 miles/69.102 km)

1 Michael Laverty (Ducati), 23m 14.750s, 100.76 mph/162.16 km/h.

2 Karl Harris (Honda); **3** Pere Riba (Kawasaki); **4** Luke Quigley (Suzuki); **5** Simon Andrews (Yamaha); **6** Jay Vincent (Honda); **7** Tom Sykes (Suzuki); **8** Adrian Coates (Suzuki); **9** Craig Jones (Triumph); **10** Matt Llewellyn (Ducati); **11** Nicky Moore (Honda); **12** Shane Norval (Honda); **13** Craig Sproston (Honda); **14** Hilton Hincks (Honda); **15** Daniel Fowler (Yamaha).

Fastest lap: Harris, 1m 08.616s, 102.41 mph/164.81 km/h (record).

Championship points: **1** Laverty, 51; **2** Harris, 45; **3** Vincent, 43; **4** Riba, 42; **5** Quigley, 38; **6** Andrews and Jones, 27.

British 125GP Championship, round 3 (18 laps, 35.136 miles/56.538 km)
1 Eugene Laverty (Honda), 23m 04.147s, 91.38 mph/147.06 km/h.
2 John Pearson (Honda); 3 Christian Elkin (Honda); 4 Kris Weston (Honda); 5 Steven Neate (Honda); 6 Michael Wilcox (Honda); 7 Ryan Saxelby (Honda); 8 Brian Clark (Honda); 9 Paul Robinson (Honda); 10 Rob Guiver (Honda); 11 Tom Bridewell (Honda); 12 Daniel Cooper (Honda); 13 Jon Vincent (Honda); 14 Tom Grant (Honda); 15 Benji Dawson (Honda).
Fastest lap: Laverty, 1m 14.254s, 94.63 mph/152.30 km/h.
Championship points: 1 Laverty, 61; 2 Wilcox, 45; 3 Pearson, 44; 4 Weston, 43; 5 Elkin, 41; 6 Neate, 33.

OULTON PARK INTERNATIONAL, 3 May 2004. 2.692-mile/4.332-km circuit.
THINK! British Superbike Championship, rounds 7 and 8
Race 1 (16 laps, 43.072 miles/69.312 km)
1 Yukio Kagayama (Suzuki), 26m 14.357s, 98.49 mph/158.50 km/h.
2 John Reynolds (Suzuki); 3 Michael Rutter (Honda); 4 Dean Thomas (Ducati); 5 Scott Smart (Kawasaki); 6 Glen Richards (Kawasaki); 7 Gary Mason (Yamaha); 8 Sean Emmett (Ducati); 9 Tommy Hill (Yamaha); 10 James Ellison (Yamaha); 11 Craig Coxhell (Honda); 12 Dennis Hobbs (Suzuki); 13 Sam Corke (Suzuki); 14 Jon Kirkham (Suzuki); 15 James Buckingham (Suzuki).
Fastest lap: Kagayama, 1m 37.392s, 99.50 mph/160.14 km/h (record).

Race 2 (18 laps, 48.456 miles/77.976 km)
1 Yukio Kagayama (Suzuki), 29m 27.256s, 98.70 mph/158.84 km/h.
2 John Reynolds (Suzuki); 3 Michael Rutter (Honda); 4 Dean Thomas (Ducati); 5 Scott Smart (Kawasaki); 6 Leon Haslam (Ducati); 7 Gary Mason (Yamaha); 8 James Ellison (Yamaha); 9 Glen Richards (Kawasaki); 10 Noriyuki Haga (Ducati); 11 Craig Coxhell (Honda); 12 Jon Kirkham (Suzuki); 13 Kieran Clarke (Yamaha); 14 Tommy Hill (Yamaha); 15 James Buckingham (Suzuki).
Fastest lap: Rutter, 1m 37.272s, 99.63 mph/160.33 km/h (record).
Championship points: 1 Reynolds, 167; 2 Rutter, 149; 3 Kagayama, 128; 4 Smart, 89; 5 Emmett, 86; 6 Kiyonari, 76.

British Supersport Championship, round 4 (16 laps, 43.072 miles/69.312 km)
1 Karl Harris (Honda), 26m 59.802s, 95.72 mph/154.05 km/h.
2 Michael Laverty (Ducati); 3 Jay Vincent (Honda); 4 Simon Andrews (Yamaha); 5 Cal Crutchlow (Honda); 6 Leon Camier (Honda); 7 Pere Riba (Kawasaki); 8 Craig Jones (Triumph); 9 Luke Quigley (Suzuki); 10 Adrian Coates (Suzuki); 11 Tom Tunstall (Honda); 12 Kieran Murphy (Honda); 13 Matt Llewellyn (Ducati); 14 Tom Sykes (Suzuki); 15 Lee Jackson (Honda).
Fastest lap: Laverty, 1m 40.529s, 96.40 mph/155.14 km/h (record).
Championship points: 1 Laverty, 71; 2 Harris, 70; 3 Vincent, 59; 4 Riba, 51; 5 Quigley, 45; 6 Andrews, 40.

British 125GP Championship, round 4 (11 laps, 29.612 miles/47.652 km)
1 Michael Wilcox (Honda), 20m 55.845s, 84.88 mph/136.60 km/h.
2 Christian Elkin (Honda); 3 Steven Neate (Honda); 4 Joe Dickinson (Honda); 5 Tom Bridewell (Honda); 6 Richard Murphy (Honda); 7 Paul Robinson (Honda); 8 Jon Vincent (Honda); 9 Tye Kinton (Honda); 10 James Ford (Honda); 11 Leon Morris (Aprilia); 12 James Westmoreland (Honda); 13 Dan Linfoot (Honda); 14 Toby Markham (Honda); 15 Thomas Hayward (Honda).
Fastest lap: Neate, 1m 48.028s, 89.71 mph/144.37 km/h.
Championship points: 1 Wilcox, 70; 2 Elkin and Laverty, 61; 4 Neate, 49; 5 Pearson, 44; 6 Weston, 43.

MONDELLO PARK, 23 May 2004. 2.176-mile/3.502-km circuit.
THINK! British Superbike Championship, rounds 9 and 10 (2 x 18 laps, 39.168 miles/63.036 km)
Race 1
1 Scott Smart (Kawasaki), 30m 33.487s, 76.92 mph/123.79 km/h.
2 John Reynolds (Suzuki); 3 Glen Richards (Kawasaki); 4 Yukio Kagayama (Suzuki); 5 Dean Thomas (Ducati); 6 Sean Emmett (Ducati); 7 James Buckingham (Suzuki); 8 Craig Coxhell (Honda); 9 James Haydon (Yamaha); 10 Kieran Clarke (Yamaha); 11 Jon Kirkham (Suzuki); 12 Dennis Hobbs (Suzuki); 13 James Ellison (Yamaha); 14 Sam Corke (Suzuki); 15 Derek Shiels (Suzuki).
Fastest lap: Reynolds, 1m 40.892s, 77.66 mph/124.98 km/h (record).

Race 2
1 Michael Rutter (Honda), 30m 33.011s, 76.94 mph/123.82 km/h.
2 John Reynolds (Suzuki); 3 Scott Smart (Kawasaki); 4 Glen Richards (Kawasaki); 5 Yukio Kagayama (Suzuki); 6 Tommy Hill (Yamaha); 7 Sean Emmett (Ducati); 8 Kieran Clarke (Yamaha); 9 Craig Coxhell (Honda); 10 James Buckingham (Suzuki); 11 Dennis Hobbs (Suzuki); 12 James Haydon (Yamaha); 13 Jon Kirkham (Suzuki); 14 Stuart Easton (Ducati); 15 Cameron Donald (Suzuki).
Fastest lap: Reynolds, 1m 40.731s, 77.78 mph/125.18 km/h (record).
Championship points: 1 Reynolds, 207; 2 Rutter, 174; 3 Kagayama, 152; 4 Smart, 130; 5 Emmett, 105; 6 Thomas, 84.

British Supersport Championship, round 5 (16 laps, 34.816 miles/56.032 km)
1 Simon Andrews (Yamaha), 27m 46.729s, 75.22 mph/121.05 km/h.
2 Michael Laverty (Ducati); 3 Karl Harris (Honda); 4 Tom Sykes (Suzuki); 5 Cal Crutchlow (Honda); 6 Pere Riba (Kawasaki); 7 Jay Vincent (Honda); 8 Leon Camier (Honda); 9 Luke Quigley (Suzuki); 10 Craig Jones (Triumph); 11 Paul Young (Honda); 12 Jonathan Rea (Honda); 13 Hilton Hincks (Honda); 14 Lee Jackson (Honda); 15 Darran Lindsay (Honda).
Fastest lap: Andrews, 1m 43.121s, 75.98 mph/122.28 km/h (record).
Championship points: 1 Laverty, 91; 2 Harris, 86; 3 Vincent, 68; 4 Andrews, 65; 5 Riba, 61; 6 Quigley, 52.

British 125GP Championship, round 5 (12 laps, 26.112 miles/42.024 km)
1 Eugene Laverty (Honda), 21m 48.097s, 71.88 mph/115.68 km/h.
2 Paul Robinson (Honda); 3 Christian Elkin (Honda); 4 Tom Bridewell (Honda); 5 Rob Guiver (Honda); 6 Brian Clark (Honda); 7 Joe Dickinson (Honda); 8 Tom Grant (Honda); 9 Tim Stott (Honda); 10 Ashley Beech (Honda); 11 William Dunlop (Honda); 12 Tye Kinton (Honda); 13 Andrew Sewell (Honda); 14 Aaron Walker (Aprilia); 15 Jay Glynn (Honda).
Fastest lap: Michael Wilcox (Honda), 1m 47.795s, 72.69 mph/116.98 km/h (record).
Championship points: 1 Laverty, 86; 2 Elkin, 77; 3 Wilcox, 70; 4 Neate, 49; 5 Pearson, 44; 6 Weston, 43.

THRUXTON CIRCUIT, 6 June 2004. 2.356-mile/3.792-km circuit.
THINK! British Superbike Championship, rounds 11 and 12
Race 1 (22 laps, 51.832 miles/83.424 km)
1 Michael Rutter (Honda), 28m 24.161s, 109.49 mph/176.21 km/h.
2 John Reynolds (Suzuki); 3 Sean Emmett (Ducati); 4 Gregorio Lavilla (Suzuki); 5 Dean Thomas (Ducati); 6 Scott Smart (Kawasaki); 7 Gary Mason (Yamaha); 8 James Ellison (Yamaha); 9 Tommy Hill (Yamaha); 10 Kieran Clarke (Yamaha); 11 Craig Coxhell (Honda); 12 James Buckingham (Suzuki); 13 Ryuichi Kiyonari (Honda); 14 Jon Kirkham (Suzuki); 15 Stuart Easton (Ducati).
Fastest lap: Emmett, 1m 16.114s, 111.43 mph/179.33 km/h.

Race 2 (20 laps, 47.120 miles/75.840 km)
1 Sean Emmett (Ducati), 25m 45.597s, 109.75 mph/176.63 km/h.
2 Michael Rutter (Honda); 3 Gregorio Lavilla (Suzuki); 4 Scott Smart (Kawasaki); 5 James Ellison (Yamaha); 6 Tommy Hill (Yamaha); 7 Kieran Clarke (Yamaha); 8 Ryuichi Kiyonari (Honda); 9 Craig Coxhell (Honda); 10 James Buckingham (Suzuki); 11 Jon Kirkham (Suzuki); 12 Stuart Easton (Ducati); 13 Dennis Hobbs (Suzuki); 14 Sam Corke (Suzuki); 15 Cameron Donald (Suzuki).
Fastest lap: Rutter, 1m 16.329s, 111.11 mph/178.82 km/h.
Championship points: 1 Reynolds, 227; 2 Rutter, 219; 3 Smart, 153; 4 Kagayama, 152; 5 Emmett, 146; 6 Thomas, 95.

British Supersport Championship, round 6 (18 laps, 42.408 miles/68.256 km)
1 Karl Harris (Honda), 23m 38.851s, 107.60 mph/173.17 km/h.
2 Leon Camier (Honda); 3 Michael Laverty (Ducati); 4 Luke Quigley (Suzuki); 5 Pere Riba (Kawasaki); 6 Jonathan Rea (Honda); 7 Jay Vincent (Honda); 8 Paul Young (Honda); 9 Shane Norval (Honda); 10 Tom Sykes (Suzuki); 11 Lee Jackson (Honda); 12 Jamie Robinson (Yamaha); 13 Kieran Murphy (Honda); 14 Tom Tunstall (Honda); 15 Cal Crutchlow (Honda).
Fastest lap: Camier, 1m 18.095s, 108.60 mph/174.78 km/h.
Championship points: 1 Harris, 111; 2 Laverty, 107; 3 Vincent, 77; 4 Riba, 72; 5 Andrews and Quigley, 65.

British 125GP Championship, round 6 (14 laps, 32.984 miles/53.088 km)
1 Eugene Laverty (Honda), 19m 22.810s, 102.11 mph/164.33 km/h.
2 Michael Wilcox (Honda); 3 Christian Elkin (Honda); 4 Brian Clark (Honda); 5 John Pearson (Honda); 6 Joe Dickinson (Honda); 7 Kris Weston (Honda); 8 Tom Bridewell (Honda); 9 Ashley Beech (Honda); 10 James Webb (Honda); 11 Daniel Cooper (Honda); 12 Leon Morris (Aprilia); 13 Toby Markham (Honda); 14 Rob Guiver (Honda); 15 James Westmoreland (Honda).
Fastest lap: Laverty, 1m 21.850s, 103.62 mph/166.76 km/h.
Championship points: 1 Laverty, 111; 2 Elkin, 93; 3 Wilcox, 90; 4 Pearson, 55; 5 Weston, 52; 6 Neate, 49.

BRANDS HATCH GRAND PRIX CIRCUIT, 20 June 2004. 2.608-mile/4.197-km circuit.
THINK! British Superbike Championship, rounds 13 and 14 (2 x 20 laps, 52.160 miles/83.940 km)
Race 1
1 John Reynolds (Suzuki), 33m 42.324s, 92.89 mph/149.49 km/h.
2 Sean Emmett (Ducati); 3 John McGuinness (Kawasaki); 4 Yukio Kagayama (Suzuki); 5 Michael Rutter (Honda); 6 James Haydon (Yamaha); 7 Tommy Hill (Yamaha); 8 Leon Haslam (Ducati); 9 Sam Corke (Suzuki); 10 Dean Thomas (Ducati); 11 Dennis Hobbs (Suzuki); 12 Chris Platt (Kawasaki); 13 Jon Kirkham (Suzuki); 14 Craig Coxhell (Honda); 15 James Ellison (Yamaha).
Fastest lap: Reynolds, 1m 34.820s, 99.02 mph/159.36 km/h.

Race 2
1 Leon Haslam (Ducati), 32m 19.096s, 96.87 mph/155.90 km/h.
2 Sean Emmett (Ducati); 3 Yukio Kagayama (Suzuki); 4 James Haydon (Yamaha); 5 Scott Smart (Kawasaki); 6 John McGuinness (Kawasaki); 7 John Reynolds (Suzuki); 8 Tommy Hill (Yamaha); 9 Craig Coxhell (Honda); 10 Gary Mason (Yamaha); 11 Steve Brogan (Yamaha); 12 Sam Corke (Suzuki); 13 James Ellison (Yamaha); 14 Michael Rutter (Honda); 15 Dennis Hobbs (Suzuki).
Fastest lap: Reynolds, 1m 34.315s, 99.55 mph/160.21 km/h.
Championship points: 1 Reynolds, 261; 2 Rutter, 232; 3 Emmett, 186; 4 Kagayama, 181; 5 Smart, 164; 6 Thomas, 101.

British Supersport Championship, round 7 (17 laps, 44.336 miles/71.349 km)
1 Karl Harris (Honda), 28m 47.398s, 92.44 mph/148.77 km/h.
2 Jay Vincent (Honda); 3 Pere Riba (Kawasaki); 4 Matt Llewellyn (Ducati); 5 Simon Andrews (Yamaha); 6 Danny Beaumont (Honda); 7 Michael Laverty (Ducati); 8 Jonathan Rea (Honda); 9 Martin Buckles (Yamaha); 10 Lee Jackson (Honda); 11 Barry Venemann (Suzuki); 12 Dean Ellison (Honda); 13 Tom Tunstall (Honda); 14 Sam Owens (Honda); 15 Jarno Janssen (Suzuki).
Fastest lap: Andrews, 1m 38.196s, 95.62 mph/153.88 km/h.
Championship points: 1 Harris, 136; 2 Laverty, 116; 3 Vincent, 97; 4 Riba, 88; 5 Andrews, 76; 6 Quigley, 65.

British 125GP Championship, round 7 (13 laps, 33.904 miles/54.561 km)
1 Christian Elkin (Honda), 23m 57.107s, 84.98 mph/136.76 km/h.
2 Michael Wilcox (Honda); 3 John Pearson (Honda); 4 Rob Guiver (Honda); 5 Kris Weston (Honda); 6 Joel Morris (Honda); 7 James Webb (Honda); 8 Brian Clark (Honda); 9 Tom Bridewell (Honda); 10 Eugene Laverty (Honda); 11 Tom Grant (Honda); 12 Thomas Hayward (Honda); 13 James Ford (Honda); 14 James Westmoreland (Honda); 15 Paul Robinson (Honda).
Fastest lap: Elkin, 1m 40.374s, 93.54 mph/150.54 km/h.
Championship points: 1 Elkin, 118; 2 Laverty, 117; 3 Wilcox, 110; 4 Pearson, 71; 5 Weston, 63; 6 Bridewell, 52.

KNOCKHILL CIRCUIT, 4 July 2004. 1.299-mile/2.091-km circuit.
THINK! British Superbike Championship, rounds 15 and 16 (2 x 25 laps, 32.475 miles/52.275 km)
Race 1
1 Scott Smart (Kawasaki), 22m 53.543s, 85.08 mph/136.92 km/h.
2 James Haydon (Yamaha); 3 Yukio Kagayama (Suzuki); 4 John Reynolds (Suzuki); 5 Jon Kirkham (Suzuki); 6 Gary Mason (Yamaha); 7 James Ellison (Yamaha); 8 Iain MacPherson (Ducati); 9 Michael Rutter (Honda); 10 Ryuichi Kiyonari (Honda); 11 Chris Platt (Kawasaki); 12 Kieran Clarke (Yamaha); 13 Chris Martin (Suzuki); 14 Dennis Hobbs (Suzuki); 15 Craig Coxhell (Honda).
Fastest lap: Kagayama, 52.867s, 88.42 mph/142.31 km/h.

Race 2
1 James Haydon (Yamaha), 23m 42.685s, 82.15 mph/132.21 km/h.
2 Sean Emmett (Ducati); 3 John Reynolds (Suzuki); 4 Michael Rutter (Honda); 5 Yukio Kagayama (Suzuki); 6 Scott Smart (Kawasaki); 7 John McGuinness (Kawasaki); 8 Craig Coxhell (Honda); 9 Dean Thomas (Ducati); 10 James Ellison (Yamaha); 11 Jon Kirkham (Suzuki); 12 Kieran Clarke (Yamaha); 13 Sam Corke (Suzuki); 14 Ryuichi Kiyonari (Honda); 15 Dennis Hobbs (Suzuki).
Fastest lap: Emmett, 54.123s, 86.37 mph/139.00 km/h.
Championship points: 1 Reynolds, 290; 2 Rutter, 252; 3 Kagayama, 208; 4 Emmett, 206; 5 Smart, 199; 6 Thomas, 108.

British Supersport Championship, round 8 (23 laps, 29.877 miles/48.093 km)
1 Paul Young (Honda), 21m 56.004s, 81.70 mph/131.48 km/h.
2 Karl Harris (Honda); 3 Michael Laverty (Ducati); 4 Pere Riba (Kawasaki); 5 Tom Sykes (Suzuki); 6 Kieran Murphy (Honda); 7 Cal Crutchlow (Honda); 8 Craig Jones (Triumph); 9 Lee Jackson (Honda); 10 Bob Grant (Honda); 11 Adrian Coates (Suzuki); 12 Torquil Paterson (Honda); 13 Jason Mitchell (Kawasaki); 14 Lee Longden (Honda); 15 Shane Norval (Honda).
Fastest lap: Young, 55.976s, 83.51 mph/134.40 km/h.
Championship points: 1 Harris, 156; 2 Laverty, 132; 3 Riba, 101; 4 Vincent, 97; 5 Andrews, 76; 6 Quigley, 65.

British 125GP Championship, round 8 (19 laps, 24.681 miles/39.729 km)
1 Paul Robinson (Honda), 19m 40.917s, 75.21 mph/121.04 km/h.
2 Christian Elkin (Honda); 3 Rob Guiver (Honda); 4 Michael Wilcox (Honda); 5 Brian Clark (Honda); 6 Tom Bridewell (Honda); 7 Eugene Laverty (Honda); 8 John Pearson (Honda); 9 Ashley Beech (Honda); 10 James Ford (Honda); 11 Jon Vincent (Honda); 12 Kris Weston (Honda); 13 Ross Walter (Honda); 14 Joe Dickinson (Honda); 15 Joel Morris (Honda).
Fastest lap: Elkin, 1m 00.588s, 77.16 mph/124.17 km/h.
Championship points: 1 Elkin, 138; 2 Laverty, 126; 3 Wilcox, 123; 4 Pearson, 79; 5 Weston, 67; 6 Bridewell and Robinson, 62.

MALLORY PARK CIRCUIT, 18 July 2004. 1.390-mile/2.237-km circuit.
THINK! British Superbike Championship, rounds 17 and 18 (2 x 30 laps, 41.700 miles/67.110 km)
Race 1

1 John Reynolds (Suzuki), 26m 15.170s, 95.30 mph/ 153.37 km/h.
2 Yukio Kagayama (Suzuki); 3 Scott Smart (Kawasaki); 4 Ryuichi Kiyonari (Honda); 5 James Haydon (Yamaha); 6 Michael Rutter (Honda); 7 Sean Emmett (Ducati); 8 Dean Thomas (Ducati); 9 John McGuinness (Kawasaki); 10 Dennis Hobbs (Suzuki); 11 Steve Plater (Yamaha); 12 Kieran Clarke (Yamaha); 13 Iain MacPherson (Ducati); 14 Gary Mason (Yamaha); 15 James Ellison (Yamaha).
Fastest lap: Kagayama, 51.741s, 96.71 mph/155.64 km/h.

Race 2
1 Scott Smart (Kawasaki), 27m 40.337s, 90.41 mph/ 145.50 km/h.
2 John Reynolds (Suzuki); 3 Ryuichi Kiyonari (Honda); 4 James Haydon (Yamaha); 5 Sean Emmett (Ducati); 6 Tommy Hill (Yamaha); 7 Gary Mason (Yamaha); 8 Dean Thomas (Ducati); 9 John McGuinness (Kawasaki); 10 Steve Plater (Yamaha); 11 Craig Coxhell (Honda); 12 Dennis Hobbs (Suzuki); 13 James Ellison (Yamaha); 14 Iain MacPherson (Ducati); 15 Yukio Kagayama (Suzuki).
Fastest lap: Kiyonari, 51.931s, 96.35 mph/155.07 km/h.
Championship points: 1 Reynolds, 335; 2 Rutter, 262; 3 Smart, 240; 4 Kagayama, 229; 5 Emmett, 226; 6 Kiyonari and Thomas, 124.

British Supersport Championship, round 9 (28 laps, 38.920 miles/62.636 km)
1 Karl Harris (Honda), 25m 04.525s, 93.12 mph/149.86 km/h.
2 Jay Vincent (Honda); 3 Leon Camier (Honda); 4 Michael Laverty (Ducati); 5 Paul Young (Honda); 6 Matt Llewellyn (Ducati); 7 Cal Crutchlow (Honda); 8 Adrian Coates (Suzuki); 9 Tom Sykes (Suzuki); 10 Kieran Murphy (Honda); 11 Luke Quigley (Suzuki); 12 Lee Jackson (Honda); 13 Jamie Robinson (Yamaha); 14 Stuart Easton (Ducati); 15 Hilton Hincks (Honda).
Fastest lap: Vincent, 52.758s, 94.84 mph/152.64 km/h.
Championship points: 1 Harris, 181; 2 Laverty, 145; 3 Vincent, 117; 4 Riba, 101; 5 Andrews, 76; 6 Quigley, 70.

British 125GP Championship, round 9 (24 laps, 33.360 miles/53.688 km)
1 Christian Elkin (Honda), 22m 20.257s, 89.60 mph/ 144.20 km/h.
2 Ashley Beech (Honda); 3 Eugene Laverty (Honda); 4 Brian Clark (Honda); 5 Kris Weston (Honda); 6 Joe Dickinson (Honda); 7 Tom Bridewell (Honda); 8 Joel Morris (Honda); 9 Tom Grant (Honda); 10 Jenny Tinmouth (Honda); 11 James Webb (Honda); 12 John Pearson (Honda); 13 Thomas Hayward (Honda); 14 Steven Neate (Honda); 15 Andrew Sewell (Honda).
Fastest lap: Beech, 54.953s, 91.06 mph/146.54 km/h
Championship points: 1 Elkin, 163; 2 Laverty, 142; 3 Wilcox, 123; 4 Pearson, 83; 5 Weston, 78; 6 Bridewell, 71.

CROFT CIRCUIT, 15 August 2004. 2.127-mile/3.423-km circuit.
THINK! British Superbike Championship, rounds 19 and 20 (2 x 22 laps, 46.794 miles/75.306 km)
Race 1
1 Michael Rutter (Honda), 30m 10.136s, 93.06 mph/ 149.77 km/h.
2 Yukio Kagayama (Suzuki); 3 Scott Smart (Kawasaki); 4 Ryuichi Kiyonari (Honda); 5 John Reynolds (Suzuki); 6 James Haydon (Yamaha); 7 Sean Emmett (Ducati); 8 Dean Thomas (Ducati); 9 Tommy Hill (Yamaha); 10 John McGuinness (Kawasaki); 11 James Ellison (Yamaha); 12 Paul Brown (Ducati); 13 Craig Coxhell (Honda); 14 Dennis Hobbs (Suzuki); 15 Jon Kirkham (Suzuki).
Fastest lap: Rutter, 1m 21.487s, 93.96 mph/151.22 km/h.

Race 2
1 Michael Rutter (Honda), 30m 08.942s, 93.12 mph/ 149.86 km/h.
2 Scott Smart (Kawasaki); 3 John Reynolds (Suzuki); 4 Ryuichi Kiyonari (Honda); 5 James Haydon (Yamaha); 6 Gary Mason (Yamaha); 7 John McGuiness (Kawasaki); 8 Craig Coxhell (Honda); 9 James Ellison (Yamaha); 10 Steve Plater (Yamaha); 11 Sean Emmett (Ducati); 12 Paul Brown (Ducati); 13 Jon Kirkham (Suzuki); 14 Dennis Hobbs (Suzuki); 15 James Buckingham (Suzuki).
Fastest lap: Reynolds, 1m 21.245s, 94.24 mph/151.67 km/h.
Championship points: 1 Reynolds, 362; 2 Rutter, 312; 3 Smart, 276; 4 Kagayama, 249; 5 Emmett, 240; 6 Kiyonari, 150

British Supersport Championship, round 10 (20 laps, 42.540 miles/68.460 km)
1 Jay Vincent (Honda), 28m 17.303s, 90.22 mph/145.20 km/h.
2 Leon Camier (Honda); 3 Karl Harris (Honda); 4 Tom Sykes (Suzuki); 5 Luke Quigley (Suzuki); 6 Adrian Coates (Suzuki); 7 Matt Llewellyn (Ducati); 8 Stuart Easton (Ducati); 9 Cal Crutchlow (Honda); 10 Jamie Robinson (Yamaha); 11 Tom Tunstall (Honda); 12 Sam Owens (Honda); 13 Hilton Hincks (Honda); 14 Phil Stewart (Honda); 15 Billy McConnell (Honda).
Fastest lap: Camier, 1m 23.923s, 91.24 mph/146.83 km/h.
Championship points: 1 Harris, 197; 2 Laverty, 145; 3 Vincent, 142; 4 Riba, 101; 5 Camier, 85; 6 Quigley, 81.

British 125GP Championship, round 10 (16 laps, 34.032 miles/54.768 km)
1 Eugene Laverty (Honda), 24m 50.226s, 82.21 mph/ 132.30 km/h.
2 Kris Weston (Honda); 3 Christian Elkin (Honda); 4 Joe Dickinson (Honda); 5 Michael Wilcox (Honda); 6 James Webb (Honda); 7 Daniel Cooper (Honda); 8 Tom Bridewell (Honda); 9 Dan Linfoot (Honda); 10 Paul Robinson (Honda); 11 Jon Vincent (Honda); 12 John Pearson (Honda); 13 Thomas Hayward (Honda); 14 James Westmoreland (Honda); 15 Toby Markham (Honda).
Fastest lap: Dickinson, 1m 28.578s, 86.44 mph/139.12 km/h.
Championship points: 1 Elkin, 179; 2 Laverty, 167; 3 Wilcox, 134; 4 Weston, 98; 5 Pearson, 87; 6 Bridewell, 79.

CADWELL PARK CIRCUIT, 30 August 2004. 2.180-mile/3.508-km circuit.
THINK! British Superbike Championship, rounds 21 and 22
Race 1 (15 laps, 32.700 miles/52.620 km)
1 Michael Rutter (Honda), 22m 31.896s, 87.07 mph/ 140.13 km/h.
2 Ryuichi Kiyonari (Honda); 3 Yukio Kagayama (Suzuki); 4 James Haydon (Yamaha); 5 Tommy Hill (Yamaha); 6 Dean Thomas (Ducati); 7 Glen Richards (Kawasaki); 8 Kieran Clarke (Yamaha); 9 John McGuinness (Kawasaki); 10 Sean Emmett (Ducati); 11 Gary Mason (Yamaha); 12 Jon Kirkham (Suzuki); 13 Paul Brown (Ducati); 14 James Ellison (Yamaha); 15 Chris Martin (Suzuki).
Fastest lap: Kagayama, 1m 29.105s, 88.07 mph/141.74 km/h.

Race 2 (18 laps, 39.240 miles/63.144 km)
1 Yukio Kagayama (Suzuki), 27m 37.598s, 85.22 mph/ 137.15 km/h.
2 Scott Smart (Kawasaki); 3 Sean Emmett (Ducati); 4 Dean Thomas (Ducati); 5 Glen Richards (Kawasaki); 6 James Haydon (Yamaha); 7 Kieran Clarke (Yamaha); 8 John Reynolds (Suzuki); 9 John McGuinness (Kawasaki); 10 James Ellison (Yamaha); 11 Sam Corke (Suzuki); 12 Gus Scott (Suzuki); 13 Craig Coxhell (Honda); 14 Jon Kirkham (Suzuki); 15 Michael Pensavalle (Ducati).
Fastest lap: Kagayama, 1m 29.995s, 87.20 mph/ 140.34 km/h.
Championship points: 1 Reynolds, 370; 2 Rutter, 337; 3 Smart, 296; 4 Kagayama, 290; 5 Emmett, 262; 6 Kiyonari, 170.

British Supersport Championship, round 11 (16 laps, 34.880 miles/56.128 km)
1 Jay Vincent (Honda), 25m 40.032s, 81.53 mph/131.21 km/h.
2 Tom Sykes (Suzuki); 3 Stuart Easton (Ducati); 4 Michael Laverty (Ducati); 5 Matt Llewellyn (Ducati); 6 Luke Quigley (Suzuki); 7 Pere Riba (Kawasaki); 8 Craig Jones (Triumph); 9 Simon Andrews (Yamaha); 10 Paul Young (Honda); 11 Adrian Coates (Suzuki); 12 Tom Tunstall (Honda); 13 Jamie Robinson (Yamaha); 14 Lee Jackson (Honda); 15 Sam Owens (Honda).
Fastest lap: Vincent, 1m 31.222s, 86.03 mph/138.45 km/h.
Championship points: 1 Harris, 197; 2 Vincent, 167; 3 Laverty, 158; 4 Riba, 110; 5 Quigley, 91; 6 Sykes, 87.

British 125GP Championship, round 11 (14 laps, 30.520 miles/49.112 km)
1 Ashley Beech (Honda), 22m 17.890s, 82.12 mph/ 132.16 km/h.
2 Christian Elkin (Honda); 3 Eugene Laverty (Honda); 4 Kris Weston (Honda); 5 Joel Morris (Honda); 6 Brian Clark (Honda); 7 Michael Wilcox (Honda); 8 Joe Dickinson (Honda); 9 Rob Guiver (Honda); 10 Steven Neate (Honda); 11 Tom Bridewell (Honda); 12 Daniel Cooper (Honda); 13 Aaron Walker (Aprilia); 14 James Westmoreland (Honda); 15 Thomas Hayward (Honda).
Fastest lap: Beech, 1m 34.419s, 83.11 mph/133.76 km/h.
Championship points: 1 Elkin, 199; 2 Laverty, 183; 3 Wilcox, 143; 4 Weston, 111; 5 Pearson, 87; 6 Bridewell, 84.

OULTON PARK INTERNATIONAL, 12 September 2004. 2.692-mile/4.332-km circuit.
THINK! British Superbike Championship, rounds 23 and 24 (2 x 18 laps, 48.456 miles/77.976 km)
Race 1
1 John Reynolds (Suzuki), 29m 36.353s, 98.20 mph/ 158.04 km/h.
2 Michael Rutter (Honda); 3 Yukio Kagayama (Suzuki); 4 Sean Emmett (Ducati); 5 Steve Plater (Yamaha); 6 Glen Richards (Kawasaki); 7 Dean Thomas (Ducati); 8 Scott Smart (Kawasaki); 9 Tommy Hill (Yamaha); 10 Paul Brown (Ducati); 11 Gary Mason (Yamaha); 12 Ryuichi Kiyonari (Honda); 13 John McGuinness (Kawasaki); 14 James Haydon (Yamaha); 15 James Ellison (Yamaha).
Fastest lap: Emmett, 1m 37.200s, 99.70 mph/ 160.45 km/h (record)

Race 2
1 John Reynolds (Suzuki), 29m 33.529s, 98.35 mph/ 158.28 km/h.
2 Michael Rutter (Honda); 3 Yukio Kagayama (Suzuki); 4 Sean Emmett (Ducati); 5 Dean Thomas (Ducati); 6 Ryuichi Kiyonari (Honda); 7 Steve Plater (Yamaha); 8 James Haydon (Yamaha); 9 Glen Richards (Kawasaki); 10 Tommy Hill (Yamaha); 11 Kieran Clarke (Yamaha); 12 Craig Coxhell (Honda); 13 James Ellison (Yamaha); 14 Jon Kirkham (Suzuki); 15 James Buckingham (Suzuki).
Fastest lap: Kagayama, 1m 37.471s, 99.42 mph/160.01 km/h.
Championship points: 1 Reynolds, 420; 2 Rutter, 377; 3 Kagayama, 322; 4 Smart, 304; 5 Emmett, 288; 6 Kiyonari, 184.

British Supersport Championship, round 12 (16 laps, 43.072 miles/69.312 km)
1 Karl Harris (Honda), 27m 04.288s, 95.46 mph/153.63 km/h.
2 Tom Sykes (Suzuki); 3 Jay Vincent (Honda); 4 Leon Camier (Honda); 5 Craig Jones (Triumph); 6 Stuart Easton (Ducati); 7 Cal Crutchlow (Honda); 8 Adrian Coates (Suzuki); 9 Pere Riba (Kawasaki); 10 Kieran Murphy (Honda); 11 Tom Tunstall (Honda); 12 Luke Quigley (Suzuki); 13 Jamie Robinson (Yamaha); 14 Shane Norval (Honda); 15 Sam Owens (Honda).
Fastest lap: Camier, 1m 40.279s, 96.64 mph/ 155.53 km/h (record).
Championship points: 1 Harris, 222; 2 Vincent, 183; 3 Laverty, 158; 4 Riba, 117; 5 Sykes, 107; 6 Camier, 98.

British 125GP Championship, round 12 (14 laps, 37.688 miles/60.648 km)
1 Ashley Beech (Honda), 25m 17.339s, 89.41 mph/ 143.89 km/h.
2 Eugene Laverty (Honda); 3 Kris Weston (Honda); 4 Steven Neate (Honda); 5 Brian Clark (Honda); 6 Michael Wilcox (Honda); 7 Daniel Cooper (Honda); 8 Aaron Walker (Aprilia); 9 James Webb (Honda); 10 Dan Linfoot (Honda); 11 Joel Morris (Honda); 12 Tom Bridewell (Honda); 13 Toby Markham (Honda); 14 Tom Grant (Honda); 15 James Ford (Honda).
Fastest lap: Beech, 1m 47.292s, 90.32 mph/145.36 km/h.
Championship points: 1 Laverty, 203; 2 Elkin, 199; 3 Wilcox, 153; 4 Weston, 127; 5 Beech, 106; 6 Bridewell, 88.

DONINGTON PARK GRAND PRIX CIRCUIT, 19 September 2004. 2.500-mile/4.023-km circuit.
THINK! British Superbike Championship, rounds 25 and 26 (2 x 20 laps, 50.000 miles/80.460 km)
Race 1
1 Ryuichi Kiyonari (Honda), 32m 05.596s, 93.42 mph/ 150.35 km/h.
2 Michael Rutter (Honda); 3 John Reynolds (Suzuki); 4 Scott Smart (Kawasaki); 5 Sean Emmett (Ducati); 6 Glen Richards (Kawasaki); 7 Dean Thomas (Ducati); 8 James Haydon (Yamaha); 9 Gary Mason (Yamaha); 10 Tommy Hill (Yamaha); 11 James Ellison (Yamaha); 12 Jon Kirkham (Suzuki); 13 Chris Martin (Suzuki); 14 Yukio Kagayama (Suzuki); 15 James Buckingham (Suzuki).
Fastest lap: Kiyonari, 1m 32.386s, 97.41 mph/156.77 km/h (record).

Race 2
1 Ryuichi Kiyonari (Honda), 30m 57.801s, 96.82 mph/ 155.82 km/h.
2 Michael Rutter (Honda); 3 Sean Emmett (Ducati); 4 Scott Smart (Kawasaki); 5 Yukio Kagayama (Suzuki); 6 John Reynolds (Suzuki); 7 Dean Thomas (Ducati); 8 James Haydon (Yamaha); 9 James Ellison (Yamaha); 10 Steve Plater (Yamaha); 11 John McGuinness (Kawasaki); 12 Gary Mason (Yamaha); 13 Paul Brown (Ducati); 14 Tommy Hill (Yamaha); 15 Craig Coxhell (Honda).
Fastest lap: Rutter, 1m 32.033s, 97.79 mph/ 157.37 km/h (record).

British Supersport Championship, round 13 (18 laps, 45.000 miles/72.414 km)
1 Craig Jones (Triumph), 29m 00.659s, 93.00 mph/ 149.67 km/h.
2 Michael Laverty (Ducati); 3 Tom Sykes (Suzuki); 4 Jay Vincent (Honda); 5 Pere Riba (Kawasaki); 6 Karl Harris (Honda); 7 Cal Crutchlow (Honda); 8 Paul Young (Honda); 9 Luke Quigley (Suzuki); 10 Simon Andrews (Yamaha); 11 Adrian Coates (Suzuki); 12 Tom Tunstall (Honda); 13 Kieran Murphy (Honda); 14 Jamie Robinson (Yamaha); 15 Leon Camier (Honda).
Fastest lap: Laverty, 1m 35.733s, 94.01 mph/ 151.29 km/h (record).

British 125GP Championship, round 13 (15 laps, 37.500 miles/60.345 km)
1 Christian Elkin (Honda), 25m 39.809s, 87.60 mph/ 140.98 km/h.
2 Matthieu Gines (Honda); 3 Joel Morris (Honda); 4 Joe Dickinson (Honda); 5 John Pearson (Honda); 6 Aaron Walker (Aprilia); 7 James Webb (Honda); 8 Brian Clark (Honda); 9 Daniel Cooper (Honda); 10 Thomas Hayward (Honda); 11 James Ford (Honda); 12 Jon Vincent (Honda); 13 Steven Neate (Honda); 14 William Dunlop (Honda); 15 Nathan Pallett (Honda).
Fastest lap: Clark, 1m 41.461s, 88.70 mph/142.75 km/h.

Final British Superbike Championship points

1 John Reynolds	446
2 Michael Rutter	417
3 Yukio Kagayama	335
4 Scott Smart	330
5 Sean Emmett	315

6 Ryuichi Kiyonari, 234; 7 Dean Thomas, 193; 8 James Haydon, 181; 9 Tommy Hill, 137; 10 Glen Richards, 125; 11 Gary Mason, 116; 12 James Ellison, 111; 13 Craig Coxhell, 92; 14 John McGuiness, 86; 15 Jon Kirkham, 77.

Final British Supersport Championship points

1 Christian Elkin	224
2 Eugene Laverty	203
3 Michael Wilcox	153
4 Kris Weston	127
5 Ashley Beech	106

6 John Pearson, 98; 7 Brian Clark, 92; 8 Tom Bridewell, 88; 9 Joe Dickinson, 84; 10 Steven Neate, 73; 11 Paul Robinson, 68; 12 Rob Guiver, 55; 13 Joel Morris, 51; 14 Daniel Cooper, 49; 15 James Webb, 46.

Final British 125GP Championship points

1 Karl Harris	232
2 Jay Vincent	196
3 Michael Laverty	178
4 Pere Riba	128
5 Tom Sykes	123

6 Luke Quigley, 102; 7 Leon Camier, 99; 8 Craig Jones, 93; 9 Simon Andrews, 89; 10 Cal Crutchlow, 75; 11 Paul Young, 63; 12 Adrian Coates, 62; 13 Matt Llewellyn, 52; 14 Kieran Murphy, 51; 15 Tom Tunstall, 42.